Prospective Memory in Clinical Populations

Prospective memory has emerged as an important aspect of episodic memory. Prospective memory involves remembering to complete a previously formed intention. Successful prospective memory performance is important in daily life tasks such as taking medications or paying bills and has been related to compliance with treatment.

Prospective memory has now been studied in many clinical populations as well as across the lifespan. Although prospective memory is recognized as an important aspect of daily life, there has been only limited crossover from the research literature to clinical practice. The wealth of research findings needs to be translated to evidence-based clinical approaches that are uniquely tailored to individual populations. Each chapter of *Prospective Memory in Clinical Populations* covers current knowledge of prospective memory deficits in a population; approaches to clinical assessment; any published evidence-based approaches to treatment; and suggestions for management.

This book was originally published as a special issue of *The Clinical Neuropsychologist*.

Sarah A. Raskin is the Charles A. Dana Professor of Psychology and Neuroscience at Trinity College, Hartford Connecticut, USA. Her scholarly interests focus on investigating techniques to improve cognitive functioning after injury to the brain.

Prospective Memory in Clinical Populations

Edited by
Sarah A. Raskin

Routledge
Taylor & Francis Group
LONDON AND NEW YORK

First published 2020
by Routledge
2 Park Square, Milton Park, Abingdon, Oxon, OX14 4RN

and by Routledge
52 Vanderbilt Avenue, New York, NY 10017

Routledge is an imprint of the Taylor & Francis Group, an informa business

British Library Cataloguing-in-Publication Data
A catalogue record for this book is available from the British Library

ISBN13: 978-0-367-43752-7

Typeset in Myriad Pro
by codeMantra

Publisher's Note
The publisher accepts responsibility for any inconsistencies that may have arisen during the conversion of this book from journal articles to book chapters, namely the inclusion of journal terminology.

Contents

Citation Information

The chapters in this book were originally published in *The Clinical Neuropsychologist*, volume 32, issue 5 (June 2018). When citing this material, please use the original page numbering for each article, as follows:

Introduction

Prospective memory in clinical populations
Sarah A. Raskin
The Clinical Neuropsychologist, volume 32, issue 5 (June 2018) pp. 741–747

Chapter 1

Prospective memory in autism: theory and literature review
Daniel P. Sheppard, Jelle P. Bruineberg, Anett Kretschmer-Trendowicz and Mareike Altgassen
The Clinical Neuropsychologist, volume 32, issue 5 (June 2018) pp. 748–782

Chapter 2

Prospective memory in children with attention deficit hyperactivity disorder: a review
Karley-Dale S. Talbot, Ulrich Müller and Kimberly A. Kerns
The Clinical Neuropsychologist, volume 32, issue 5 (June 2018) pp. 783–815

Chapter 3

A review of prospective memory impairments in developmental dyslexia: evidence, explanations, and future directions
James H. Smith-Spark
The Clinical Neuropsychologist, volume 32, issue 5 (June 2018) pp. 816–835

Chapter 4

Schizophrenia and prospective memory impairments: a review
Ya Wang, Raymond C. K. Chan and David H. K. Shum
The Clinical Neuropsychologist, volume 32, issue 5 (June 2018) pp. 836–857

Chapter 5

A systematic review of prospective memory in HIV disease: from the laboratory to daily life
Gunes Avci, David P. Sheppard, Savanna M. Tierney, Victoria M. Kordovski, Kelli L. Sullivan and Steven Paul Woods
The Clinical Neuropsychologist, volume 32, issue 5 (June 2018) pp. 858–890

Chapter 6

A review of prospective memory in individuals with acquired brain injury
Sarah A. Raskin, Jasmin Williams and Emily M. Aiken
The Clinical Neuropsychologist, volume 32, issue 5 (June 2018) pp. 891–921

Chapter 7

Prospective memory impairment in multiple sclerosis: a review
Isabelle Rouleau, Emmanuelle Dagenais, Alexandra Tremblay, Mélanie Demers, Élaine Roger, Céline Jobin and Pierre Duquette
The Clinical Neuropsychologist, volume 32, issue 5 (June 2018) pp. 922–936

Chapter 8

Prospective memory functioning in individuals with Parkinson's disease: a systematic review
Alberto Costa, Carlo Caltagirone and Giovanni Augusto Carlesimo
The Clinical Neuropsychologist, volume 32, issue 5 (June 2018) pp. 937–959

Chapter 9

Mild cognitive impairment and prospective memory: translating the evidence into neuropsychological practice
Glynda J. Kinsella, Kerryn E. Pike, Marina G. Cavuoto and Stephen D. Lee
The Clinical Neuropsychologist, volume 32, issue 5 (June 2018) pp. 960–980

Chapter 10

Time-based prospective memory in children and adolescents with 22q11.2 deletion syndrome
Céline Souchay, Lydia Dubourg, Nicola Ballhausen, Maude Schneider, Charline Cerf, Katharina Schnitzspahn, Laurence Faivre, Matthias Kliegel and Stephan Eliez
The Clinical Neuropsychologist, volume 32, issue 5 (June 2018) pp. 981–992

Chapter 11

Prospective memory in first-degree relatives of patients with schizophrenia
Saima Saleem, Devvarta Kumar and Ganesan Venkatasubramanian
The Clinical Neuropsychologist, volume 32, issue 5 (June 2018) pp. 993–1001

Chapter 12

Long-term prospective memory impairment following mild traumatic brain injury with loss of consciousness: findings from the Canadian Longitudinal Study on Aging
Marc Bedard, Vanessa Taler and Jason Steffener
The Clinical Neuropsychologist, volume 32, issue 5 (June 2018) pp. 1002–1018

Chapter 13

Prospective memory impairment in idiopathic REM sleep behavior disorder
Ondrej Bezdicek, Tomáš Nikolai, Jiří Nepožitek, Pavla Peřinová, David Kemlink, Pavel Dušek, Iva Příhodová, Simona Dostálová, Veronika Ibarburu, Jiří Trnka, Karel Kupka, Zuzana Mecková, Jiří Keller, Josef Vymazal, Evžen Růžička, Karel Šonka and Petr Dušek
The Clinical Neuropsychologist, volume 32, issue 5 (June 2018) pp. 1019–1037

Contributors

Emily M. Aiken Neuroscience Program, Trinity College, Hartford, USA.

Mareike Altgassen Donders Institute for Brain, Cognition and Behaviour, Radboud University, Nijmegen, The Netherlands.

Gunes Avci Department of Psychology, University of Houston, USA.

Nicola Ballhausen Faculty of Psychology and Educational Sciences, University of Geneva, Switzerland.

Marc Bedard Bruyere Research Institute, Ottawa, Canada; School of Psychology, University of Ottawa, Canada.

Ondrej Bezdicek First Faculty of Medicine, Department of Neurology and Center of Clinical Neuroscience, Charles University and General University Hospital, Prague, Czech Republic.

Jelle P. Bruineberg Department of Philosophy, Institute for Logic, Language and Computation, University of Amsterdam, Amsterdam.

Carlo Caltagirone IRCCS Fondazione Santa Lucia, Rome, Italy; Dipartimento di Medicina dei Sistemi, Tor Vergata University, Rome, Italy.

Giovanni Augusto Carlesimo Psychology Department, Niccolo Cusano University, Rome, Italy; IRCCS Fondazione Santa Lucia, Rome, Italy; Dipartimento di Medicina dei Sistemi, Tor Vergata University, Rome, Italy.

Marina G. Cavuoto School of Psychology & Public Health, La Trobe University, Melbourne, Australia; Caulfield Hospital, Melbourne, Australia.

Charline Cerf Centre de Genetique & FHU-TRANSLAD, Hospital and University of Dijon, France.

Raymond C. K. Chan Neuropsychology and Applied Cognitive Neuroscience Laboratory, CAS Key Laboratory of Mental Health, Institute of Psychology, Beijing, China; Department of Psychology, University of Chinese Academy of Sciences, Beijing, China.

Alberto Costa Psychology Department, Niccolo Cusano University, Rome, Italy; IRCCS Fondazione Santa Lucia, Rome, Italy.

Emmanuelle Dagenais Department of Psychology, Universite du Quebec a Montreal, Canada.

Mélanie Demers Department of Psychology, Universite du Quebec a Montreal, Canada.

Simona Dostálová First Faculty of Medicine, Department of Neurology and Center of Clinical Neuroscience, Charles University and General University Hospital, Prague, Czech Republic.

Lydia Dubourg Developmental Imaging and Psychopathology Lab, Faculty of Medicine, University of Geneva, Switzerland.

Pierre Duquette Centre de recherche du Centre Hospitalier de l'Universite de Montreal (CRCHUM), Canada.

Pavel Dušek First Faculty of Medicine, Department of Neurology and Center of Clinical Neuroscience, Charles University and General University Hospital, Prague, Czech Republic.

Petr Dušek First Faculty of Medicine, Department of Neurology and Center of Clinical Neuroscience, Charles University and General University Hospital, Prague, Czech Republic. Faculty of Medicine, Institute of Nuclear Medicine, Charles University and General University Hospital, Prague, Czech Republic.

Stephan Eliez Developmental Imaging and Psychopathology Lab, Faculty of Medicine, University of Geneva, Switzerland.

Laurence Faivre Centre de Genetique & FHU-TRANSLAD, Hospital and University of Dijon, France.

Veronika Ibarburu First Faculty of Medicine, Department of Neurology and Center of Clinical Neuroscience, Charles University and General University Hospital, Prague, Czech Republic.

Céline Jobin Neurology Service, Hopital du Sacre-Coeur de Montreal, Canada.

Jiří Keller Department of Radiology, Na Homolce Hospital, Prague, Czech Republic.

David Kemlink First Faculty of Medicine, Department of Neurology and Center of Clinical Neuroscience, Charles University and General University Hospital, Prague, Czech Republic.

Kimberly A. Kerns Department of Psychology, University of Victoria, Canada.

Glynda J. Kinsella School of Psychology & Public Health, La Trobe University, Melbourne, Australia; Caulfield Hospital, Melbourne, Australia.

Matthias Kliegel Faculty of Psychology and Educational Sciences, University of Geneva, Switzerland.

Victoria M. Kordovski Department of Psychology, University of Houston, USA.

Anett Kretschmer-Trendowicz Department of Psychology, Technische Universitaet Dresden, Germany.

Devvarta Kumar Department of Clinical Psychology, National Institute of Mental Health and Neuro Sciences, India.

Karel Kupka First Faculty of Medicine, Institute of Nuclear Medicine, Charles University and General University Hospital, Prague, Czech Republic.

Stephen D. Lee School of Psychology & Public Health, La Trobe University, Melbourne, Australia; Caulfield Hospital, Melbourne, Australia.

Zuzana Mecková First Faculty of Medicine, Department of Medical Physics, Charles University and General University Hospital, Prague, Czech Republic.

Ulrich Müller Department of Psychology, University of Victoria, Canada.

Jiří Nepožitek First Faculty of Medicine, Department of Neurology and Center of Clinical Neuroscience, Charles University and General University Hospital, Prague, Czech Republic.

Tomáš Nikolai First Faculty of Medicine, Department of Neurology and Center of Clinical Neuroscience, Charles University and General University Hospital, Prague, Czech Republic.

Pavla Peřinová First Faculty of Medicine, Department of Neurology and Center of Clinical Neuroscience, Charles University and General University Hospital, Prague, Czech Republic.

Kerryn E. Pike School of Psychology & Public Health, La Trobe University, Melbourne, Australia.

Iva Příhodová First Faculty of Medicine, Department of Neurology and Center of Clinical Neuroscience, Charles University and General University Hospital, Prague, Czech Republic.

Sarah A. Raskin Neuroscience Program, Trinity College, Hartford, USA; Department of Psychology, Trinity College, Hartford, USA.

Élaine Roger Centre de recherche du Centre Hospitalier de l'Universite de Montreal (CRCHUM), Canada.

Isabelle Rouleau Department of Psychology, Universite du Quebec a Montreal, Canada.

Evžen Růžička First Faculty of Medicine, Department of Neurology and Center of Clinical Neuroscience, Charles University and General University Hospital, Prague, Czech Republic.

Saima Saleem Mind Plus Healthcare Pvt. Ltd. Ludhiana, India.

Maude Schneider Developmental Imaging and Psychopathology Lab, Faculty of Medicine, University of Geneva, Switzerland.

Katharina Schnitzspahn School of Psychology, University of Aberdeen, UK.

Daniel P. Sheppard Donders Institute for Brain, Cognition and Behaviour, Radboud University, Nijmegen, The Netherlands.

David P. Sheppard Department of Psychology, University of Houston, USA.

David H. K. Shum Neuropsychology and Applied Cognitive Neuroscience Laboratory, CAS Key Laboratory of Mental Health, Institute of Psychology, Beijing, China; School of Applied Psychology, Griffith University, Gold Coast, Australia; Menzies Health Institute Queensland, Griffith University, Gold Coast, Australia.

James H. Smith-Spark Division of Psychology, School of Applied Sciences, London South Bank University, UK.

Karel Šonka First Faculty of Medicine, Department of Neurology and Center of Clinical Neuroscience, Charles University and General University Hospital, Prague, Czech Republic.

Céline Souchay Laboratoire de Psychologie et Neurocognition, University of Grenoble, France.

Jason Steffener Interdisciplinary School of Health Sciences, University of Ottawa, Canada.

Kelli L. Sullivan Department of Psychology, University of Houston, USA.

Karley-Dale S. Talbot Department of Psychology, University of Victoria, Canada.

Vanessa Taler Bruyere Research Institute, Ottawa, Canada; School of Psychology, University of Ottawa, Canada.

Savanna M. Tierney Department of Psychology, University of Houston, USA.

Alexandra Tremblay Department of Psychology, Universite du Quebec a Montreal, Canada.

Jiří Trnka First Faculty of Medicine, Institute of Nuclear Medicine, Charles University and General University Hospital, Prague, Czech Republic.

Ganesan Venkatasubramanian Department of Psychiatry, National Institute of Mental Health and Neuro Sciences, India.

Josef Vymazal Department of Radiology, Na Homolce Hospital, Prague, Czech Republic.

Ya Wang Neuropsychology and Applied Cognitive Neuroscience Laboratory, CAS Key Laboratory of Mental Health, Institute of Psychology, Beijing, China; Department of Psychology, University of Chinese Academy of Sciences, Beijing, China.

Jasmin Williams Neuroscience Program, Trinity College, Hartford, USA.

Steven Paul Woods Department of Psychology, University of Houston, USA.

The Clinical Neuropsychologist

Editor in Chief: Yana Suchy - University of Utah, Salt Lake City, UT, USA

Print ISSN 1385–4046, Online ISSN 1744–4144

The Clinical Neuropsychologist (TCN) serves as the premier forum for (1) state-of-the-art clinically-relevant scientific research, (2) in-depth professional discussions of matters germane to evidence-based practice, and (3) clinical case studies in neuropsychology. Of particular interest are papers that can make *definitive statements* about a given topic (thereby having implications for the standards of clinical practice) and those with the potential to *expand today's clinical frontiers* (e.g., introduction of a disorder that is typically not under the purview of clinical neuropsychology, yet presents with neurocognitive sequelae; introduction of new assessment or intervention tools). Research on all age groups, and on both clinical and normal populations, is considered.

INTRODUCTION

Prospective memory in clinical populations

Sarah A. Raskin

ABSTRACT

Objective: Prospective memory (PM) has emerged as a form of episodic memory that is frequently impaired in a variety of clinical populations. Neuropsychologists who routinely evaluate these populations are often unaware of the possibility of PM deficits or the impact these deficits may have on everyday functioning. The objective of this special issue is to provide an overview of the nature of prospective deficits in a range of clinical populations, to discuss neuropsychological assessment techniques, and to critically evaluate management strategies. **Method**: We solicited papers from established researchers and issued a general call for papers for the special issue on PM in clinical populations. **Results**: We received submissions from the nine authors that we solicited. These submissions range from developmental disorders, including autism, attention deficit hyperactivity disorder, and dyslexia; to disorders of adulthood, such as schizophrenia, HIV, brain injury, and multiple sclerosis; and finally disorders that tend to occur at older ages, such as Parkinson's disease and mild cognitive impairment. In addition, we have included four original research articles that provide novel data on other populations. These are children and adolescents with 22q11.2 deletion syndrome, first-degree relatives of people with schizophrenia, individuals with mild brain injury, and individuals with idiopathic REM sleep behavioral disorder. **Conclusions**: The issue highlights the need for clinical neuropsychologists to be aware of the possible existence of deficits in PM in a variety of clinical populations and the importance of both assessment and management strategies to reduce the impact on daily life.

Prospective memory (PM), i.e. the ability to remember to execute a previously formed intention (e.g. Kvavilashvili, 1992), has emerged as an important aspect of episodic memory. The cognitive functions required for successful PM performance include attention, retrospective memory recall, and planning. Prospective remembering itself involves forming the intention, monitoring time or recognizing a cue in the environment, and acting upon the intention at the appropriate time, and performance evaluation once the task is completed. Two particular types of prospective remembering have been identified – time based and event based. Time-based intentions are those that must be completed at a particular time (e.g. please call your doctor at 2:00 pm); event-based intentions, on the other hand, require completion of the intention in response to a cue in the environment (e.g. when you see your therapist, please remind her to give you a copy of your medical records). Successful PM performance is critical in daily life tasks such as taking medications or paying bills. Deficits in PM can be mistaken for lack of initiation or poor compliance with treatment, making an accurate assessment of PM worthwhile.

With increasing recognition of the importance of PM for daily functioning, there has been an increased interest in PM research. With this growing interest, there have been special issues published on this topic in *Applied Cognitive Psychology* (2000), *The International Journal of Psychology* (2003), and the *Canadian Journal of Experimental Psychology* (2011). However, the previously published special issues have primarily focused on theoretical issues in cognitive psychology. Furthermore, seven years have passed since the publications of the most recent special issues. Thus, it has become clear that the field would benefit from an updated overview of the current state of the PM research, as well as from a review of both the theoretical perspectives on PM construct and the practical clinical information on the assessment and treatment of individuals with PM deficits. These then are the goals of the present special issue.

The issue begins with a series of review articles that all follow a similar structure: current knowledge of PM deficits in that population, including neurological etiology if known; approaches to clinical assessment of PM for individuals with that disorder; the types of errors most often seen in that population in daily life; any published evidence-based approaches to treatment; and suggestions for management of PM deficits for individuals with the disorder. Four original research articles then follow that highlight newer research questions in populations that have not been previously studied as extensively.

The first three articles cover neurodevelopmental disorders. The article by Sheppard, Bruineberg, Kretschmer-Trendowicz, and Altgassen (2018) provides an overview of PM in individual with autism. These authors provide an analysis of the deficits of PM within an embodied predictive-coding account. In other words, they postulate that people with autism have their attention drawn to stimuli in the environment that are not relevant to the PM cue. The reduction in the relevance and salience of the PM cue, in combination with poor prediction, lead to failures to complete PM tasks. This theoretical account leads the authors to suggest embodied interventions such as providing clear and consistent structures and expectations. The next article, by Talbot, Muller, and Kerns (2017), synthesizes the small number of studies that have investigated PM in children with attention deficit/hyperactivity disorder. These children have demonstrated greater deficits in time-based, as compared to event-based, PM tasks, which the authors relate to underdeveloped executive functions. They highlight the need for a clinical measure of PM for children and recommendations are made for multicomponent psychosocial strategies, including compensatory approaches, to mitigate any deficits. The review of PM in individuals with dyslexia by Smith-Spark (2017) mentions effects in children but the main focus is on adults with dyslexia. The authors report that these individuals have greater difficulty with time-based than event-based tasks; nevertheless, deficits on episodic event-based tasks and on tasks that have a longer delay have been found. The authors relate this difficulty to potential deficits in accessing episodic retrospective memories as well as executive function deficits in shifting away from the ongoing task. Specific compensatory recommendations are made, including the use of mobile reminding devices.

The special issue then turns to disorders of adulthood including schizophrenia, HIV, adults with brain injury, and multiple sclerosis. The review by Wang, Chan, and Shum (2017) focuses on individuals with schizophrenia, providing an analysis of the components of PM that have been found to be impaired in a sometimes conflicting literature. Overall, the authors find that people with schizophrenia are more likely to make errors due to a lack of awareness of the need to make a response suggesting that this is a primary deficit in prospective remembering itself. There is some evidence that time-based PM is more impaired than event-based PM, and that people with schizophrenia are more greatly affected by increases in time delays. Perhaps of greatest importance is the consistent findings that PM performance is related to negative symptoms as well as to functioning in daily life, including medication adherence. Lastly, the authors offer a number of intervention suggestions, including increasing awareness.

Individuals with HIV represent one of the more extensively studied clinical populations with respect of PM. This relatively extensive literature is reviewed by Avci et al. The authors suggest that PM deficits in this population are evident primarily when strategic, rather than automatic, cognitive processes are involved. Thus, they suggest that findings of greater time-based than event-based impairments are due to failures in strategic monitoring. With this model, the authors incorporate the findings of greater deficits with longer time delays and a relationship between both executive functions and time perception with PM performance. They also review potential biomarkers for PM and common comorbidities. Importantly, they highlight the research demonstrating the interaction of age and performance within those who have HIV. The authors provide ample evidence for the effect of PM on daily life, including medication management and medication adherence, which are critical in this population. In terms of management of deficits, the authors suggest approaches that focus on improving strategic monitoring as well as behavioral techniques for daily living skills.

In the review of the relatively large number of studies of individuals with brain injury by myself and my colleagues (Raskin, Williams, & Aiken), we also find that the current research supports the multi-process theory. That is, individuals with brain injury show greater deficits in time-based than event-based tasks and show an increased effect of longer time delays. In general, deficits are increased in conditions that require greater attention, working memory, or strategic monitoring. Within this framework, a number of other potential areas of investigation are discussed, including the effects of cue focality and the relationship between the cue and the intention. The relationships among laboratory-based tasks, clinical measures, and self-report questionnaires are discussed, with the suggestion that each of these assessment approaches may be tapping into different aspects of PM functioning. Turning to remediation suggestions, the greatest number of studies has focused on compensatory devices such as pagers, smart phones, programmable watches, and planners. However, there is some evidence for both rote repetition and visual imagery training as rehabilitation techniques may show more promise in terms of generalizability. We suggest that the heterogeneity of brain injury lends itself to the need for individualized treatment techniques that could include compensation as well as training focused on attention, time perception, recognition of the cue, reinforcement of the memory for the intention itself, enactment, etc., depending on the deficit observed in the individual. Finally, we suggest that the literature on episodic future thinking may provide insights for training techniques that generalize to daily life.

The review of PM in individuals with multiple sclerosis by Rouleau et al. (2017) also highlights the relationship between PM and functioning in daily life. In a limited number of studies, individuals with multiple sclerosis were found to have greater deficits on longer time delays and on items that required a verbal response rather than an action response. A strong relationship has been demonstrated between PM performance and executive function measures. PM deficits have also been found to be related to symptoms such as pain, and to be predictive of activities in daily life such as medication adherence. The authors suggest that high cue salience improves performance, and that psychoeducation and increasing awareness represent important interventions, combined with cognitive rehabilitation techniques in individual cases.

The final two review articles turn to disorders of aging, namely Parkinson's disease and mild cognitive impairment. In reviewing the literature on PM in Parkinson's disease, Costa, Caltagirone, and Carlesimo (2017) do not find consistent evidence for a differential effect of time-based vs. event-based cues. Like many of the other disorders reviewed, PM performance has been found to be related to executive functioning and to activities of daily living. There is some evidence to suggest that specific deficits in PM are related to an inability to shift mental set, but that there are separate deficits in the retrospective recall of the item to be remembered. Finally, the authors present some evidence to suggest that PM is not impaired in all individuals with Parkinson's disease, but only in those who are experiencing mild cognitive impairment. Similarly, the review of PM in individuals with mild cognitive impairment by Kinsella, Pike, Cavuoto, and Lee (2018) does not find evidence for a differential deficit in either time- or event-based items. In addition, there is evidence for deficits in habitual items that are routine, such as bringing in the newspaper each morning. This suggests a primary deficit in working memory in addition to PM deficits. The authors provide a description of a novel treatment approach that embeds implementation of intentions and compensatory devices within a group treatment protocol.

The remaining articles are original research articles that provide novel data on PM in clinical populations not covered by the review articles due to the relative recency of findings of deficits. The first paper demonstrates time-based PM deficits in children and adolescents with 22q11.2 deletion syndrome. Souchay et al. (2017) tested children ages 6–14 years on a video driving game that requires the child to remember to add fuel to the car when fuel levels are low. The participants with 22q11.2DS were less likely to remember to add fuel and also checked the fuel gage less often. The authors suggest that this could be due to a reduction in strategic monitoring, lower motivation to complete the task, or deficits in working memory.

The next original research article examines PM in first-degree relatives of individuals with schizophrenia. Saleem, Kumar, and Venkatasubramanian (2017) used a laboratory task modeled after those of Einstein and McDaniel (1990). They report that first-degree relatives show impairments in prospective remembering compared to healthy adults, but that these impairments are less severe than those seen among individuals who have been diagnosed with schizophrenia. The impairment was found to be greater for event-based tasks than for time-based tasks. This finding may be an artifact of the task; however, as all three groups performed better on the time-based task than the event-based task, a finding that is uncommon in the literature.

Next, as part of the Canadian Longitudinal Study on Aging, Bedard, Taler, and Steffener (2017) administered the Miami Prospective Memory Test to a large cohort of individuals with mild traumatic brain injury (TBI). The majority reported less than one minute of loss of consciousness, and all were at least one-year post injury. The Miami Prospective Memory Test contains one event-based task and two time-based tasks, although only one time-based task was used in this study. The results showed a disproportionate deficit on time-based PM performance for those who experienced a mild TBI. The findings on the event-based task were somewhat more difficult to interpret, as those participants who had experienced a mild brain injury with a loss of consciousness of less than a minute performed better on this task than healthy adults. Further analyses suggested that this finding may have been due to the fact that this group was younger than controls.

The final article by Bezdicek et al. (2017) measures PM performance in individuals with REM sleep behavior disorder. These individuals demonstrated deficits in both retrospective memory on the Rey Auditory Verbal Learning Test and PM on the Memory for Intentions Test (MIST). In addition, event-based PM was impaired but time-based was not. The event-based PM deficit is suggested to be related to the retrospective memory impairment such that the cue to the intention is not successfully retrieved and recognized. Interestingly, the time-based performance was significantly related to dopamine depletion measured by dopamine transporter imaging using SPECT.

There are several common themes that emerge across the articles in this special issues: first, studies consistently find at least some deficits of PM across a variety of disorders. This consistency highlights how important it is for clinicians to be aware of the possibility of PM deficits in individual clients. Although assessment of PM can be lengthy, clinicians should be aware that it can be a useful adjunct to their current assessment measures, especially in cases where there is a suspicion of a deficit or where there are problems in daily life that might suggest such a deficit (forgetting to take medications, go to scheduled appointments, purchase needed items, pay bills, etc.). In addition, when these deficits are detected, clinicians may want to make specific recommendations for compensatory strategies or treatment techniques to reduce the impact of these deficits. There are now two standardized clinical measures with normative data, the Cambridge Assessment of PM (CAMPROMPT) (Wilson et al., 2005) and the MIST (Raskin, Buckheit, & Sherrod, 2010). A number of the articles in this issue have utilized one of these two measures. There is no comprehensive clinical measure for children at this time, and this need is mentioned by a few of the articles on developmental disorders (Sheppard et al. 2018, Talbot et al., 2017).

Second, many of the articles in this issue conclude that clinical populations have greater deficits in time-based than event-based tasks, and that this has been related to deficits in strategic monitoring as described by the multi-process theory (Einstein, McDaniel, Richardson, Guynn, & Cunfer, 1995). This theory suggests that some PM tasks can be completed more or less automatically, such as when a cue in the environment is sufficiently salient, while others require more controlled processing resources. It is generally assumed that time-based tasks require greater processing resources in order to monitor time and self-initiate the intention with no external cuing. However, several articles in this special issue (Costa et al., 2017; Kinsella et al., 2018) have found impairments in the event-based PM, in the context of normal time-based PM performance. Interestingly, in all cases, these patterns were observed in older populations. This seems to be related to a loss of retrospective memory functioning as a part of the aging process, which differentially impacts cue encoding needed for event-based tasks.

Third, not surprisingly, past research on PM has demonstrated that PM relies on prefrontal cortical mediation, most often Brodmann's area 10 (Benoit, Gilbert, & Burgess, 2011). The Attention to Delayed Intention (AtoDI) model uses imaging data to explain the brain regions responsible for intention maintenance and retrieval (Cona, Scarpazza, Sartori, Moscovitch, & Bisiacchi, 2015). Specifically, the model proposes that the dorsal frontoparietal network is involved in maintenance and allocation of top-down attention that is used both to monitor for the occurrence of the PM cue and to maintain the intention in mind. The ventral frontoparietal network, on the other hand, mediates the bottom-up attention automatically captured by the occurrence of the prospective cues and used during retrieval. Consistent with past findings and with the AtoDI model, several of the articles in this issue (Avci et al., 2017; Costa et al., 2017; Raskin et al., 2018; Rouleau et al., 2017; Smith-Spark, 2017; Talbot et al., 2017) point out a relationship between performance on tasks of PM and tests of executive functioning, and make suggestions that it is the prefrontal dysfunction that occurs in each disorder that is mediating the PM deficits.

Fourth, rehabilitation strategies covered by the articles in this issue include compensatory strategies, such as datebooks, smartphones, and other electronic reminders. Environmental modifications are also discussed by several authors. Other strategies that may show promise include the use of visual imagery, implementation of intentions, time awareness training, and goal management training. Several authors make the point that rehabilitation is most successful when it is individually tailored and that PM training must take into consideration social and emotional factors that may impact performance (e.g. Raskin et al., 2018).

Finally, several of the articles highlight some new areas of research that strive to build bridges between related fields of study. For example, the research on episodic future thinking, the ability to imagine specific personal episodes that may occur in the future (Szpunar, 2010), is certainly related to realization of intentions in important ways and may provide a framework for future treatment strategies (Terrett et al., 2015). And the use of implementation of intentions (Gollwitzer & Sheeran, 2006) typically utilized in studies of weight loss or other long-term goal attainment has been suggested to facilitate PM (Mcdaniel, Howard, & Butler, 2008) and has been modified with mixed success as a treatment method for PM deficits in a few of the articles in this issue. These both seem to be areas of research that could be expanded in the future.

Disclosure statement

No potential conflict of interest was reported by the author.

ORCID

Sarah A. Raskin http://orcid.org/0000-0002-4310-4278

References

Avci, G., Sheppard, D., Tierney, S., Kordovski, V., Sullivan, K., & Woods, S. P. (2017). A systematic review of prospective memory in HIV disease: From the laboratory to daily life. *The Clinical Neuropsychologist, 32* (5), 858–890.

Bedard, M., Taler, V., & Steffener, J. (2017). Long-term prospective memory impairment following mild traumatic brain injury with loss of consciousness: Findings from the Canadian Longitudinal Study on Aging. *The Clinical Neuropsychologist, 32* (5), 1002–1018.

Benoit, R. G., Gilbert, S. J., & Burgess, P. W. (2011). A neural mechanism mediating the impact of episodic prospection on farsighted decisions. *The Journal of Neuroscience, 31*, 6771–6779.

Bezdicek, O., Nikolai ,T., Nepozitek, J., Perinova, P., Kemlink, D., Dusek, P., … Dusek, P. (2017). Prospective memory impairment in Idiopathic REM sleep behavior disorder. *The Clinical Neuropsychologist, 32* (5), 1019–1037.

Cona, G., Scarpazza, C., Sartori, G., Moscovitch, M., & Bisiacchi, P. (2015). Neural bases of PM: A meta-analysis and the "Attention to Delayed Intention" (AtoDI) model. *Neuroscience Biobehavioral Reviews, 52*, 21–37.

Costa ,A., Caltagirone, C., & Carlesimo ,G. (2017). Prospective memory functioning in Individuals with Parkinson's disease: A systematic review. *The Clinical Neuropsychologist, 32* (5), 937–959.

Einstein, G. O., & McDaniel, M. A. (1990). Normal aging and PM. *Journal of Experimental Psychology: Learning, Memory, and Cognition, 16*, 717–726.

Einstein, G. O., McDaniel, M. A., Richardson, S. L., Guynn, M. J., & Cunfer, A. R. (1995). Aging and PM: Examining the influences of self-initiated retrieval processes. *Journal of Experimental Psychology: Learning, Memory, and Cognition, 2*, 996–1007.

Gollwitzer, P., & Sheeran, P. (2006). Implementation intentions and goal achievement: A meta- analysis of effects and processes. *Advances in Experimental Social Psychology, 38*, 69–119.

Kinsella, G., Pike, K., Cavuoto, M., & Lee, S. (2018). Mild cognitive impairment and Prospective memory: Translating the evidence into neuropsychological practice. *The Clinical Neuropsychologist, 35* (5), 960–980.

Kvavilashvili, L. (1992). Remembering intentions: A critical review of existing experimental paradigms. *Applied Cognitive Psychology, 6*, 507–524.

Mcdaniel, M., Howard, D., & Butler, K. (2008). Implementation intentions facilitate prospective memory under high attention demands. *Memory and Cognition, 36*, 716–724.

Raskin, S., Buckheit, C., & Sherrod, C. (2010). *Memory for intentions screening test: Manual*. Lutz, FL: Psychological Assessment Resources Inc.

Raskin, S., Williams, J., & Aiken, E. (2018). A review of prospective memory in individuals with acquired brain injury. *The Clinical Neuropsychologist, 32* (5), 891–921.

Rouleau, I., Dagenais, E., Tremblay, A., Demers, M., Roger, E., Jobin, C., & Duquette, P. (2017). Prospective memory impairment in multiple sclerosis: A review. *The Clinical Neuropsychologist, 32* (5), 922–936.

Saleem, S., Kumar, D., & Venkatasubramanian, G. (2017). Prospective memory in first- degree relatives of patients with schizophrenia. *The Clinical Neuropsychologist, 32* (5), 993–1001.

Sheppard, D., Bruineberg, J., Kretschmer-Trendowicz, A., & Altgassen, M. (2018). Prospective memory in autism: Theory and literature review. *The Clinical Neuropsychologist, 32* (5), 748–782.

Smith-Spark, J. (2017). A review of prospective memory impairments in developmental dyslexia: Evidence, explanations, and future directions. *The Clinical Neuropsychologist, 32* (5), 816–835.

Souchay C., Dubourg, L., Ballhausen, N., Schneider, M., Cerf, C., Schnitzspahn, K., … Eliez, S. (2017). Time-based prospective memory in children and adolescents with 22q11.2 deletion syndrome . *The Clinical Neuropsychologist, 32* (5), 981–992.

Szpunar, K. (2010). Episodic future thought: An emerging concept. *Perspectives in Psychological Science, 5*, 142–162.

Talbot, K., Muller, U., & Kerns, K. (2017). Prospective memory in children with attention deficit hyperactivity disorder: A review. *The Clinical Neuropsychologist, 32* (5), 783–815.

Terrett, G., Rose, N., Henry, J., Bailey, P., Altgassen, M., Phillips, L., … Rendell, P. G. (2015). The relationship between PM and episodic future thinking in younger and older adulthood. *The Quarterly Journal of Experimental Psychology, 69*, 310–323.

Wang, Y., Chan, R., & Shum, D. (2017). Schizophrenia and prospective memory impairments: A review. *The Clinical Neuropsychologist, 32* (5), 836–857.

Wilson, B. A., Emslie, H., Foley, J., Shiel, A., Watson, P., Hawkins, K., Groot, Y. (2005). *The Cambridge PM Test*. London: Harcourt Assessment.

OPEN ACCESS

Prospective memory in autism: theory and literature review

Daniel P. Sheppard, Jelle P. Bruineberg, Anett Kretschmer-Trendowicz and Mareike Altgassen

ABSTRACT

Objective: The current article set out to review all research conducted to date investigating prospective memory (PM) in autism. **Method**: All studies on PM in autism are first described, followed by a critical review and discussion of experimental findings within the multiprocess framework. PM in autism is then considered through an embodied predictive-coding account of autism. **Results**: Overall, despite somewhat inconsistent methodologies, a general deficit in PM in autism is observed, with evidence mostly in line with the multiprocess framework. That is, for tasks that are high in cognitive and attentional demand (e.g. time-based tasks; event-based cues of non-focality or low salience) PM performance of autistic participants is impaired. Building upon previous work in predictive-coding, and the way in which expected precision modulates attention, we postulate mechanisms that underpin PM and the potential deficits seen in autism. Furthermore, a unifying predictive-coding account of autism is extended under embodied predictive-coding models, to show how a predictive-coding impairment accounts not only for characteristic autistic difficulties, but also for commonly found differences in autistic movement. **Conclusions**: We show how differences in perception and action, core to the development of autism, lead directly to problems seen in PM. Using this link between movement and PM, we then put forward a number of holistic, embodied interventions to support PM in autism.

General introduction

Autism spectrum conditions (ASC; henceforth, autism) are characterized by impairments in social communication, restricted interests, and activities and, most recently, atypical reactivity to sensory input (American Psychiatric Publishing [APA], 2013). The clinical picture and cognitive skills of autistic[1] people may differ in severity (Hill, 2004). However, even autistic adults of average or above average cognitive ability find everyday life problematic (e.g. housekeeping, financial matters). They have, for example, difficulties obtaining and maintaining employment that corresponds to their intellectual ability (Howlin, 1998) and coordinating social activities, e.g. organizing appointments with peers (Häußler, 2003) and living independently (Anderson, Shattuck, Cooper, Roux, & Wagner, 2014). Autistic children often have problems in school due to poor time management and organization, e.g. homework is often left at school (Mackinlay, Charman, & Karmiloff-Smith, 2006). These apparent organizational difficulties in autism are supported by empirical work revealing problems with prioritizing, coordinating and sequencing activities and hence, with planning ahead (Mackinlay et al., 2006; Ozonoff et al., 2004); such difficulties have been related to deficits in prospective memory (Altgassen, Koban, & Kliegel, 2012; Mackinlay et al., 2006). PM describes the ability to remember to execute intentions after a delay at a certain time (time-based tasks; TBPM) or event (event-based PM tasks, EBPM, Einstein & McDaniel, 1996), such as remembering to go to the hairdresser at 3 pm, or to buy batteries in the corner shop on the way home. Many occupational and social demands require PM, and PM is essential for the development and maintenance of autonomy and independence. Frequent failures to remember to complete planned activities may endanger professional careers, social relationships or even impose serious risks on physical well-being (Kliegel, Jäger, Altgassen, & Shum, 2008).

Prospective remembering is complex, and comprises multiple processes and phases, across varying time-spans. First, the individual has to form the intention, and store it in (retrospective) memory while being engaged in other ongoing tasks (OT). This (filled) delay between encoding and retrieval of the intended action may range from seconds over minutes to several hours or days (Ellis & Kvavilashvili, 2000). When the appropriate moment for intention initiation arises, other ongoing activities have to be inhibited and the individual has to switch to the prospective action and execute it as planned (Kliegel, Martin, McDaniel, & Einstein, 2002). Research differentiates between a prospective (remembering 'that' you have to do something) and a retrospective component (remembering 'what' and 'when'). The prospective component is supported by attention demanding processes that are closely aligned with executive functioning which serve to monitor the environment for prospective cues (e.g. Smith & Bayen, 2004), inhibit performing the ongoing activity, and to switch to the prospective intention at the appropriate moment (Marsh, Hicks, & Watson, 2002; West, 2011). The retrospective component supports the encoding and subsequent retrieval of the intention when a target stimulus is encountered and shares many processes with explicit episodic memory in recognition and cued-recall tasks (Einstein & McDaniel, 1996; Smith & Bayen, 2004; West & Krompinger, 2005). Recently, episodic future thinking, the ability to mentally simulate and thus pre-experience future events (Atance & O'Neill, 2001), has been linked to the intention formation phase (Altgassen et al., 2014). In line with these behavioral data, imaging studies indicate an involvement of frontal and medial-temporal structures in prospective remembering (for a recent review see Burgess, Gonen-Yaacovi, & Volle, 2011). Frontally mediated (executive control) processes seem to influence PM performance more strongly than temporally mediated (retrospective memory) processes (Brunfaut, Vanoverberghe, & d'Ydewalle, 2000; Kliegel, Eschen, & Thöne-Otto, 2004). Most recently, Cona, Bisiacchi, Sartori, and Scarpazza (2016; Cona, Scarpazza, Sartori, Moscovitch, & Bisiacchi, 2015) further specified the underlying neural networks and involved cognitive processes in their 'Attention to Delayed Intention' model. Specifically, they state that a dorsal frontoparietal network supports top-down attentional and memory processes that are needed to monitor for the PM cue and to keep the intention in mind, whereas a ventral frontoparietal network (in addition to the insula and posterior cingulate cortex) is mainly involved in the retrieval phase and supports bottom-up attentional processes (externally by the PM cue and internally by the mental representation of the PM cue and the intended action).

Importantly, different PM tasks vary in the extent to which they require these cognitive resources. TBPM tasks have been assumed to put higher demands on individuals' executive control resources than event-based tasks; there is no external cue that may prompt retrieval of the intended action, and the individual has to actively keep track of the elapsing time (Einstein & McDaniel, 1996). However, depending on the specific task features, EBPM tasks may also put high demands on executive control processes. Specifically, with regard to EBPM, two prominent conceptual models have been developed that allow for theory-based predictions on factors that determine the involvement of executive control in PM; namely the *multiprocess framework*[2] (McDaniel & Einstein, 2000) and the *preparatory attention and memory processes theory* (PAM, Smith, 2003; Smith & Bayen, 2004). For the multiprocess framework, McDaniel and Einstein (2000) suggested a range of factors and contexts that can determine the extent to which an EBPM task invokes relatively effortful or automatic retrieval processes: task importance, the type of PM cue (e.g. salient vs. non-salient cues or cues that are more or less focal to the OT), the OT (e.g. more vs. less demanding), and individual differences (e.g. in cognitive resources, personality). Given that PM tasks are dual task situations consisting of an ongoing activity and the embedded PM task, both tasks compete for (limited) attentional and executive control resources (Einstein & McDaniel, 1996). Hence, characteristics of both task levels will affect the more or less controlled allocation of those resources (please see McDaniel, Umanath, Einstein, & Waldum, 2015, for a recent discussion of the multiprocess framework). In contrast, the PAM model posits that that *all* PM tasks require executive control resources for the PM cue to be detected, but that the extent to which these resources are needed depends on task characteristics.

Thus, there is good evidence that strong executive control, episodic memory, and future thinking abilities are critical for successful PM, particularly so when PM tasks involve, for example, cues of low salience or low focality (EBPM) that are difficult to detect, or no environmental cues at all (TBPM). It is therefore of concern that problems with executive control and memory are well known in autism. Executive difficulties are typically seen in planning (Mackinlay et al., 2006; Ozonoff et al., 2004) and switching flexibly between different tasks or foci of attention (Corbett, Constantine, Hendren, Rocke, & Ozonoff, 2009; Kenworthy, Yerys, Anthony, & Wallace, 2008; Leung & Zakzanis, 2014; Ozonoff et al., 2004; but see Geurts, Corbett, & Solomon, 2009 for a critical review). Tasks assessing the inhibition of prepotent responses have resulted in more ambiguous findings (Corbett et al., 2009; Geurts, Verte, Oosterlaan, Roeyers, & Sergeant, 2004; Lopez, Lincoln, Ozonoff, & Lai, 2005; Pellicano et al., 2017). Evidence from retrospective (episodic) memory studies indicate impairments in free recall tasks that provide little memory support (Bowler, Gardiner, Grice, & Saavalainen, 2000), whereas more structured tasks that put lower demands on self-initiated processing, such as cued recall and recognition tasks (Barth, Fein, & Waterhouse, 1995; Bowler, Gardiner, & Grice, 2000), seem to be spared. In line with the well-documented deficits of autistic individuals in episodic memory and theory of mind (e.g. Baron-Cohen, Leslie, & Frith, 1985; Leekam & Perner, 1991; Perner, Frith, Leslie, & Leekam, 1989; see Baron-Cohen, 2000 for a review), reduced episodic future thinking has been reported in autism (e.g. Lind & Bowler, 2010; Lind, Bowler, & Raber, 2014; Lind, Williams, Bowler, & Peel, 2014; Terrett et al., 2013). It may be that these memory deficits are in some way related to impaired executive functioning, given the correlations found in other clinical populations between executive functions and episodic memory (Baudic et al., 2006; Greene, Hodges, & Baddeley, 1995) as well as future thinking (de Vito et al., 2012)

Furthermore, it is possible that these executive functions, seen as important to PM, are driven by attentional processes (Garon, Bryson, & Smith, 2008; Posner & Rothbart, 2000), processes which have also been shown as impaired in autism (e.g. problems with disengagement, Landry & Bryson, 2004) visual attention (Mann & Walker, 2003), joint attention (e.g. looking at or listening to people, Klin, Jones, Schultz, & Volkmar, 2003; Schultz, 2005), and reduced divided attention (Althaus, De Sonneville, Minderaa, Hensen, & Til, 1996; Ciesielski, Knight, Prince, Harris, & Handmaker, 1995) (cf. a review, Allen & Courchesne, 2001). Indeed, problems with attending to relevant sensory information have even been situated as core to autism (Lawson, Rees, & Friston, 2014; Pellicano & Burr, 2012; Van de Cruys, Van der Hallen, & Wagemans, 2017; Van de Cruys et al., 2014). Such problems would thus have a profound impact on PM performance in autism.

In summary, PM represents a ubiquitous daily process, critical to independent living. Successful execution of PM tasks requires the recruitment and coordination of several (socio) cognitive processes, processes that may rely fundamentally on effective attentional and executive control processes. Given the weight of evidence demonstrating autistic impairment in such processes, and the potentially debilitating PM failures this may lead to, it is vital to better understand prospective remembering in autism, its underlying mechanisms and the environmental conditions that best support it.

Therefore, the first section of the current review will summarize all literature directly investigating PM in autism to date, arriving at the conclusion that, relative to the non-autistic population, PM in autism appears to be impaired. Then, in an attempt to better understand why autistic individuals in particular may demonstrate such difficulties, we will consider the complex dynamic nature of PM, the environment in which it is situated, and the demands this puts on individuals to coordinate and act under such an environment. With this in mind, we will build upon the cognitive explanations of the PM process offered by the multiprocess framework (McDaniel & Einstein, 2000) by considering PM as embedded within a complex dynamic environment, and, as such, apply and further develop an existing account of autism, namely the Bayesian predictive-coding account of Van de Cruys et al. (2014, 2017). Finally, we will describe how this account, and the multiprocess framework, leads to useful, embodied interventions, many of which are already widely implemented in practice.

PM in autism – literature review

A literature search was conducted on the Web of Science for all papers including the terms 'autism' and 'prospective memory', in the title, published up until December 2016. The search returned 36 studies. After the inclusion of 2 of the current authors' unpublished works, and subsequent screening, 13 studies were available for review (see Figure 1). The following section will review each of the studies, beginning with three studies demonstrating spared PM ability, followed by five studies demonstrating a PM deficit, and ending with five studies revealing mixed results (e.g. preserved EBPM but diminished TBPM). For brevity, the studies will only be summarized, with key points highlighted. A full description of the methods and results is presented in Table 1, but for an in-depth description and critique of all studies, including further statistical data (such as effect sizes), we refer to the recently published meta-analysis of Landsiedel, Williams, and Abbot-Smith (2017) on PM in autism. Finally, an

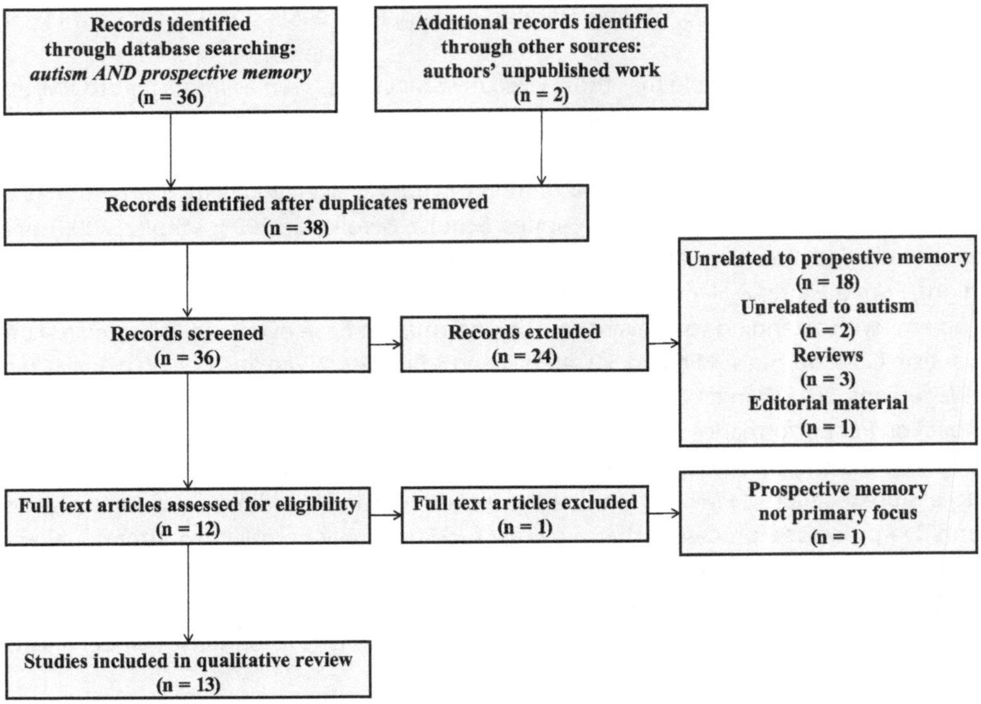

Figure 1. PRISMA flow-chart (Moher, Liberati, Tetzlaff, Altman, & Group, 2009) illustrating literature search process.

overall summary will be presented, describing patterns or commonalities evident between the studies to help elucidate variations in performance, and to discern possible cognitive functions that may contribute to the variation in PM performance.

Intact PM in autism

The three papers to find intact PM in autism investigated EBPM in children of around 10 years old (Altgassen, Schmitz-Hübsch, & Kliegel, 2010; Sheppard, Terrett, Rendell, & Altgassen, 2017) and young adults (Altgassen & Koch, 2014). All three studies employed a typical Einstein–McDaniel computer-based EBPM paradigm in which participants first completed a single, computer-based task (OT). They were then informed they would work on the task again in the near future, but it would contain an additional task (PM), which they completed after a short, filled delay,

No main group effects for EBPM emerged, a result in support of intact EBPM in autism. With the exception of the 'low salience' condition in Sheppard et al. (2017), all PM cues were rather salient (distinctive, as compared to the OT) being either a change of target word color to blue (Altgassen & Koch, 2014), a change of border color from black to red (Sheppard et al., 2017) or a whole screen color change to yellow (Altgassen, Schmitz-Hübsch, & Kliegel, 2010b). PM cues were focal for the Altgassen and Koch (2014) study non-focal for the other two studies.

No group effects were found in OT performance (differences in Altgassen & Koch, 2014; were limited by ceiling effects). Two studies showed adverse effects of the additional PM

Table 1. Overview of all studies on prospective memory in autism.

	Participant information					PM				OT				
Intact PM	Sample size (mean age)	Gender	Intellectual ability measures	Severity of ASC symptoms	Diagnostic and exclusion criteria	Task description	(Filled) delay length	Main effects	Interactions	Task description	Number of trials	Main effects	Interactions	Control variables
Altgassen, Schmitz-Hubsch, and Kliegel (2010)	19 ASC children ($M = 10.6$) 19 controls ($M = 10.6$)	ASC: 18 m, 1 f Controls: 16 m, 3 f	WISC-III vocabulary test: ASC $M = 9.6$ Controls $M = 11.8$ Block design: ASC $M = 10.1$ Controls $M = 11.0$	High-functioning ASC (IQ > 85)	Diagnoses established with ADI-R* and ADOS** No exclusion criteria mentioned	Non-focal EBPM: • press specific key when background turns yellow (5 PM trials)	~10min filled delay (other cognitive tests)	No effects for accuracy and reaction times	–	Computerized visuo-spatial working memory task	• single task block: 10 • dual-task block: 100	Accuracy • no group effect • effect of task block: single OT > dual-task No effects for reaction times	No significant interaction	DEX: ASC < controls ASC: DEX correlates negatively with PM hits
Altgassen and Koch (2014)	22 ASC adults ($M = 25.8$) 22 controls ($M = 25.6$)	ASC: 20 m, 2 f Controls: 20 m, 2 f	WASI matrices: ASC $M = 10.5$ Controls $M = 10.2$	9 high-functioning ASC (IQ > 85) 13 Asperger's syndrome	Expert clinical evaluation according to DSM-IV criteria Exclusion criteria: other psychiatric or neurological disorders, drug or alcohol abuse	Non-focal EBPM: • press specific key when color of words turns blue (4 PM trials per inhibitory load block)	~10min filled delay (other cognitive tests)	No effects for accuracy	No significant interaction	Computerized word categorization task Within-subject manipulation of inhibitory load (high, low)	• single OT: 20 • single inhibition task (high or low): 20 • dual-task: OT plus inhibiton task (high or low): 46 • triple task: OT plus inhibition task (high or low) plus PM: 96	Accuracy OT • group effect: controls > ASC • task block effect: single OT > dual-task low inhibitory load > dual-task high inhibitory load > both triple task blocks Accuracy inhibition • no group effect • inhibitory load effect: single task conditions > dual- and triple-tasks low inhibitory load > dual- and triple-tasks high inhibitory load	No significant interactions	–

Sheppard et al. (2017)	24 ASC ($M = 11.3$) 23 controls ($M = 11.1$)	ASC: 24 m, 0 f Controls: 7 m, 16 f	WISC-III & WNV vocabulary test: ASC $M = 11.7$ Controls $M = 10.4$ Matrices: ASC $M = 61.6$ Controls $M = 53.8$	High-functioning ASC (IQ > 85) SRS T score: ASC > Ctrl $M_{ASC} = 72.86$ $M_{ctrl} = 43.95$ SSP – visual: ASC > Ctrl $M_{ASC} = 18.19$ $M_{ctrl} = 23.85$ SSP – auditory: ASC > Ctrl $M_{ASC} = 14.29$ $M_{ctrl} = 25.35$	Expert clinical evaluation according to DSM-IV criteria Exclusion criteria: other psychiatric or neurological disorders	Focal EBPM: • press specific key on presentation of PM targets 3 conditions, within-subjects, each with 4 different PM cues • low salience • high Visual • high auditory	~8 min (vocabu-lary, matrices, digit span tests)	No effects for accuracy Reaction times: • no group effect • salience effect: low salience > high salience	Reaction times: • for both groups low salience > high visual salience, but only ASC: low salience > high auditory salience	Computerized picture-based categorization task	• single task block: 20 • dual-task block: 70	No effects for accuracy Reaction times • no group effect • task block effect: single OT < dual-task blocks; low salience > high salience (visual and auditory)	No significant interactions	–
Altgassen et al. (2009)	11 ASC children ($M = 9.6$) 11 controls ($M = 10.6$)	ASC: 9 m, 2 f Controls: 6 m, 5 f	WISC-III vocabulary test: ASC $M = 9.4$ Controls $M = 11.6$ Block design: ASC $M = 12.9$ Controls $M = 11.0$	High-functioning ASC (IQ > 85)	Diagnoses established with ADOS and 3di Exclusion criteria: other psychiatric or neurological disorders	TBPM: Press specific key every 2min (5 PM trials) Press other specific key for clock check	~10 min (other cognitive tests)	Correct PM responses: ASC < controls Clock checks: • group effect: ASC < controls • interval effect: increased time monitoring when target times approached	Interaction ($p < .06$): controls checked time more frequently as target time approached	Computerized visuo-spatial working memory task	• single task block: 10 • dual-task block: 85	Accuracy • group effect: ASC< controls in the dual task No effects for reaction times but: cost to OT by adding PM task: controls > ASC	No significant interactions	–

(*Continued*)

Table 1. (*Continued*).

	Participant information					PM					OT				
Intact PM	Sample size (mean age)	Gender	Intellectual ability measures	Severity of ASC symptoms	Diagnostic and exclusion criteria	Task description	(Filled) delay length	Main effects	Interactions	Task description	Number of trials	Main effects	Interactions	Control variables
Brandimonte et al. (2011)	Study 1: 30 ASC ($M = 8.3$) 30 controls ($M = 8.3$) Study 2 focuses on ADHD instead of ASC and will not be discussed here	ASC: 21 m, 9 f Controls: 21 m, 9 f	WISC-III Full Scale IQ: ASC $M = 87.0$ Controls $M = 89.0$	CARS: $M_{ASC} = 35.5 \rightarrow$ mild to moderate ASC	Diagnoses according to DSM-IV criteria Exclusion criteria: other behavioral disorders, learning deficits, chromosomal or neurological conditions	Focal EBPM: press specific key on presentation of PM target Go/NoGo: press nothing on presentation of target EBPM + Go/NoGo 2 cues; each 4× Single OT: no additional task	No filled delay	Accuracy • group effect for PM hits: ASC < controls • no group difference in the Go/NoGo condition Reaction times for the PM task: ASC> controls	–	Computerized categorization task; between-subjects	• single OT: 80 • dual-task block: 80 • OT plus Go/NoGo task: 80	Accuracy • group effect: ASC < controls • no category effect • costs to OT by adding PM task only for controls: single OT > dual-task Reaction times • group effect: ASC> controls • no category effect	No significant interactions	–
Yi et al. (2014)	25 ASC ($M = 7.7$) 25 age-matched controls ($M = 7.7$) 28 ability-matched controls ($M = 5.8$)	ASC: 19 m, 6 f Age-matched controls: 19 m, 6 f Ability-matched controls: 19 m, 6 f	PPVT-R: ASC $M = 4.56$ Age-matched controls N/A Ability-matched controls $M = 4.75$ Raven test: ASC $M = 21.1$ Age-matched controls $M = 31.8$ Ability-matched controls $M = 21.4$	No information	Expert clinical evaluation, diagnoses according to DSM-IV criteria Exclusion criteria: other developmental or psychiatric disorders, intellectual disability, congenital deafness	Non-focal EBPM: • hand card with heart shape to experimenter (5 PM trials)	No filled delay	Accuracy ASC < controls (age- and ability-matched); age-matched controls > ability-matched controls	–	Card naming game	5 sets of 10 cards	–	–	ASC: PM predicted by Raven Test and Block Span Ability-matched controls: PM predicted by Day–Night Stroop Age-matched controls: no correlations

Altgassen et al. (2012)	25 ASC ($M = 21.8$) 25 controls ($M = 21.8$)	ASC: 20 m, 5 f Controls: 19 m, 6 f	WASI Vocabulary test: ASC $M = 9.2$ Controls $M = 10.2$ Matrices: ASC $M = 11.0$ Controls $M = 11.4$	High-functioning ASC (IQ > 85) or Asperger's syndrome	Expert clinical evaluation, diagnoses according to DSM-IV criteria Diagnoses established with ADI-R and ADOS	EBPM: prepare tea when water is boiling and kettle changing color; switch off egg cooker when it is beeping TBPM: remove tea bag after 3min; put butter on table 6min prior to guests' arrival Red Pencil: repeat 'red pencil' after experimenter	~10 min (digit ordering, trail making test, Tower of Hanoi)	EBPM accuracy: ASC < controls TBPM accuracy: ASC < controls Red pencil: ASC < controls	–	Real-life breakfast task: participants had to prepare breakfast for 4 people following certain rules and time constraints	–	ASC < controls on all measures (rule adherence; planning; plan adherence; efficiency) except switching	–	EBPM and TBPM correlates with planning, task completion, rule adherence, switching, efficiency TBPM (but not EBPM) correlates with Red Pencil, DEX, trail making test, digit ordering, and marginally Tower of Hanoi
Kretschmer et al. (2014)	17 ASC ($M = 35.6$) 17 controls ($M = 39.9$)	ASC: 14 m, 19 f Controls: 4 m, 31 f	PPVT-4: ASC $M = 212.1$ Controls $M = 210.1$ Raven: ASC $M = 40.8$ Controls $M = 40.6$	High-functioning ASC (IQ > 80)	Expert clinical evaluation Diagnoses established with ADI-R and ADOS Exclusion criteria: neurological or psychiatric disorders, present or past drug or alcohol abuse	EBPM: e.g. take medication at dinner TBPM: e.g. use inhaler at 11 am EBPM & TBPM each day 4 tasks (2 regular, 2 irregular); total PM=24 2 conditions, between-subject: • implementation intentions • standard instructions	No filled delay	Accuracy • group effect: ASC < controls • PM cue effect: EBPM > TBPM • regularity effect: regular > irregular • no effect of encoding	• regularity: group x irregular ASC < controls; ASC regular > ASC irregular; no effect controls • regularity x PM cue: both conditions EBPM > TBPM; TBPM regular > TBPM irregular; EBPM no difference • Encoding x PM cue: both conditions EBPM > TBPM • no other interaction	Virtual week (computerized; 3 days)	–	–	–	–

(*Continued*)

Table 1. (*Continued*).

	Participant information					PM				OT				
Intact PM	Sample size (mean age)	Gender	Intellectual ability measures	Severity of ASC symptoms	Diagnostic and exclusion criteria	Task description	(Filled) delay length	Main effects	Interactions	Task description	Number of trials	Main effects	Interactions	Control variables
Henry et al. (2014)	30 ASC (M = 10.1) 30 controls (M = 10.0)	ASC: 24 m, 6 f Controls: 19 m, 11 f	WASI Full Scale IQ: ASC M = 112.9 Controls M = 115.3 Verbal IQ: ASC M = 110.3 controls M = 114.9 Performance IQ: ASC M = 114.5 controls M = 118.3	Highfunctioning ASC or Asperger's syndrome	Expert clinical evaluation, diagnoses according to DSM-IV criteria Exclusion criteria: other psychiatric or neurological disorders	EBPM: e.g., take medication at dinner TBPM: e.g., use asthma inhaler at 11 am EBPM & TBPM each 4 tasks per day (2 regular, 2 irregular); total PM=24	No filled delay	Accuracy - group effect: ASC < control - PM cue effect: EBPM > TBPM - absorption: Low > High - no effect of regularity	- group x PM cue: TBPM: ASC < controls; EBPM: ASC = controls - regularity x PM cue: EBPM: regular = irregular; TBPM: regular > irregular - no other interaction	Virtual week (computerized; children's version, 3 days) within-subjects: high absorption: specific die rolls before moving on, manual movement low absorption: any die roll, auto movement	–	–	–	ASC: TBPM correlates with Full Scale IQ, ABAS, Stroop switching; no correlations for EBPM Controls: TBPM with semantic switching, ABAS; EBPM with semantic switching Williams,
Williams et al. (2013)	21 ASC (*M* = 10.6) 21 controls (*M* = 10.6)	Not reported	WASI Verbal IQ: ASC *M* = 103.6 Controls *M* = 106.5 Performance IQ: ASC *M* = 110.2 Controls *M* = 107.5	13 autistic disorder, 8 Asperger's syndrome	Diagnoses established according to conventional criteria	Focal EBPM: press specific key when passing a lorry (max 6) TBPM: refuel car by pressing key (6 trials), check fuel by pressing other specific key	No filled delay	PM accuracy • EBPM: no group effects • TBPM: ASC< controls Fuel checks • linear increase per interval • no group effect	ASC: TBPM< EBPM, controls: TBPM=EBPM	Video game of driving car (collecting tokens and avoid hitting hazards)	–	Accuracy • no group effect • effect of condition: TBPM block < EBPM	No significant interactions	ASC: TBPM failures with mentalizing Controls: TBPM failures with Wisconsin Card Sorting test (approaching significance)

Williams et al. (2014)	17 ASC ($M = 31.1$) 17 controls ($M = 31.9$)	ASC: 14 m, 3 f Controls: 14 m, 3 f	WASI Full Scale IQ: ASC $M = 114.1$ Controls $M = 117.7$ Verbal IQ: ASC $M = 111.4$ Controls $M = 114.6$ Performance IQ: ASC $M = 113.5$ Controls $M = 116.9$	4 autistic disorder, 13 Asperger's syndrome	Diagnoses established according to conventional criteria (13 with ADOS) Exclusion criteria: psychotropic medication, illegal drugs. neurological or psychiatric disorders-	Non-focal EBPM: press 'm' every time a musical instrument appeared in list TBPM: press 'P' every 2mins; spacebar for clock	No filled delay	PM accuracy • no group effect • effect of cue: TBPM < EBPM PM RT/precision • group effect: ASC > controls • no effect of cue Clock checks • linear increase per interval • no group effect	PM accuracy ASC < controls in TBPM, but not EBPM PM RT/precision • no interaction Clock checks • no interaction	Computerized presentation of single words (N=7) for 1s followed by all 7 words for 4s: final list same or different?	40 lists for EBPM and 40 for TBPM	Accuracy • no main effects no response times reported	No significant interactions	ASC: EBPM correlates with verbal storage span, verbal processing No correlations for TBPM Controls: EBPM correlates with visual storage span No correlations for TBPM
Sheppard et al. (2016)	14 severe ASC ($M = 9.3$) 14 mild ASC ($M = 10.1$) 26 controls ($M = 5.1$)	ASC: 27 m, 1 f Controls: 14 m, 3 f	No information; measures of reading, writing and number skills	CARS: Severe ASC $M = 42.3$ mild ASC $M = 30.9$	Diagnoses according to DSM-IV criteria	EBPM: 1) clap when hear music (2 trials); 2) don't feed puppet grapes (2 trials); 3) get reward at end (1 trial) memory: name of puppet	Distractor game (60s)	Accuracy • Total PM: Severe ASC < Mild ASC = controls (same for clapping & feeding tasks) • Reward: no group effect • Name recall: no group effect	–	Feed puppet food	–	–	–	Correlation between PM and CARS scores approaching significance

Notes: ABAS = Adaptive Behavior Assessment Scale; ADI-R = Autism Diagnostic Interview – Revised; ADOS = Autism Diagnostic Observation Scale; ASC = Autism Spectrum Condition; CARS = Childhood Autism Rating Scale; DEX = Dysexecutive Questionnaire; 3di = Developmental, Dimensional and Diagnostic Interview; EBPM = Event-Based Prospective Memory; PM = Prospective Memory; PPVT = Peabody Picture Vocabulary Test; OT = Ongoing Task; SRS = Social Responsiveness Scale; SSP = Short Sensory Profile; TBPM = Time-Based Prospective Memory; WASI = Wechsler Abbreviated Scale of Intelligence; WISC-III = Wechsler Intelligence Scale for Children – Third Edition; WNV = Wechsler Non-Verbal scale of ability.

task on OT performance, which is in line with the premised central role of the allocation of limited attentional resources in the PM process, as posited by the multiprocess framework. This notion was particularly supported by Sheppard et al. (2017) in that the costs to OT performance were significantly reduced when the additional PM task involved cues of high salience, and thus, facilitated more automatic (less attentionally demanding) retrieval processes.

A further result of note from the Sheppard et al. (2017) study involved their novel addition of an auditory cue (beep) condition. The PM hits were higher in this condition, for both groups, compared to the control condition, as they were for the visual salience condition. However, perhaps more interestingly, while both groups were also faster to respond in the visual salience condition, compared to the control condition, only the autistic group were also faster in the auditory condition. This was particularly interesting given that the autistic group, but not the control group, were reported to exhibit atypical and hypersensitive reactivity to visual and auditory sensory information, as measured by the Short Sensory Profile (SSP; McIntosh, Miller, Shyu, & Dunn, 1999), a behavioral characteristic commonly seen in autism (Ashburner, Ziviani, & Rodger, 2008; Tomchek & Dunn, 2007).

Taken together, these three studies suggest that EBPM is intact in autism, while also identifying certain characteristics of the process, particularly cue salience, that may be of particular importance and benefit to the PM ability of autistic individuals. All studies employed simple and/or calibrated OTs, and focal and/or rather salient cues, which arguably resulted in a net reduction of cognitive load. In contrast to these papers, the studies discussed in the next section found impaired PM in autism, and employed EBPM and/or TBPM tasks.

Impaired PM in autism

Two of the studies to find impaired PM in autism investigated only TBPM (Altgassen, Sheppard, & Hendriks, 2017; Altgassen, Williams, Bölte, & Kliegel, 2009). Both studies employed a standard Einstein–McDaniel computer-based TBPM paradigm, the primary difference between versions being that participants press a button at given target times, rather than on presentation of a cue. Participants' time-monitoring behavior is recorded as the frequency with which they check the clock (via key press), thought to be a measure of strategic, attention switching processes.

Overall, both studies saw TBPM deficits in autistic children and adolescents, compared to non-autistic controls. Furthermore, while all participants in both studies increased their time monitoring as the target time approached, the autistic participants in Altgassen et al. (2009) checked the time less frequently overall. While this time-monitoring behavior was spared in the autistic participants in Altgassen et al. (2017), the autistic participants of both studies appeared to check the time less frequently in the critical time interval closest to the target time, although this difference was only close to significance in the study of Altgassen et al. (2009, $p = .06$).

Altgassen et al. (2017) went further by investigating the role of motivation, manipulated via the PM instructions. Results revealed that performance was better for all participants of both groups in the 'personal motivation' condition ('If you also manage to press this button every minute, you will receive 5 euros'), compared to the social ('It would really help me out if you could remember to press this button every minute') and the low (standard instruction) motivation conditions; the performance within the latter two groups did not differ. Planned comparisons, however, revealed this effect to be driven by the control group only.

Regarding OT performance, controls in the Altgassen et al. (2009) study were more accurate than autistic participants, while groups did not differ in response times. In contrast, there were no group differences in terms of accuracy in the Altgassen et al. (2017) study and autistic participants responded faster to OT stimuli than controls. Moreover, the cost to OT of the additional PM task, seen in both groups in Altgassen et al. (2017) was only evident in the control group in Altgassen et al. (2009).

Taken together, these results demonstrate that when PM tasks rely primarily on strategic retrieval processes (as is the case with TBPM), and comprise OTs with high demands on attentional control resources (visuo-spatial working memory task and two-back task, respectively), autistic individuals perform less well than non-autistic controls. The lack of any motivation effect on PM in the autistic participants could be a result of a general lower level of motivation for the tasks, possibly linked to a less-developed sense of self (discussed in more detail later in the current paper). However, given that OT performance was also impacted, and time monitoring was less frequent and/or less strategic, it may be that attentional resources were at capacity, rendering the ability of the manipulation to influence attention less effective.

However, reduced PM performance is also possible from EBPM paradigms, as demonstrated by the studies of Brandimonte, Filippello, Coluccia, Altgassen, and Kliegel (2011) and Yi et al. (2014). While both studies saw impaired EBPM in the autistic group, they varied considerably in methodology. Brandimonte et al. (2011) employed a standard EBPM computer-based paradigm and found the autistic children to respond slower, and with less success, to the black and white PM target pictures than non-autistic controls. Yi et al. (2014), on the other hand, applied the same card-naming paradigm as employed in the landmark study of Kvavilashvili, Messer, and Ebdon (2001) in which young children named a stack of cards (OT), passing any cards that had a heart in one corner to the experimenter (PM). Yi and colleagues compared the performance of the autistic children to that of age-matched controls and to ability-matched controls, with the latter group being significantly younger than the two other groups. Results showed that the autistic children remembered to pass significantly less PM target cards to the experimenter than both control groups, an indication that EBPM is difficult for young autistic children, even in the face of a very simple OT.

In contrast to the previously described EBPM studies that saw preserved PM in autistic participants, these studies included PM cues of arguably low salience (line drawings in same format as OT picture trials and a small red heart in the corner of a card, in the Brandimonte et al. (2011) and Yi et al. (2014) studies, respectively. Thus, the task of controlling attention, identifying the relevant cue and retrieving the intention was, according to the multiprocess framework, necessarily more strategic, placing higher demands on attentional control resources, likely compounded by the younger age of the participants (around eight-years-old).

The study described henceforth examined both TBPM and EBPM within one sample by way of the Dresden Breakfast Task (Altgassen et al., 2012), a task designed to assess PM ability under naturalistic conditions. Participants were required to prepare the table for breakfast for their three friends' arrival. This was to be completed in a particular way, as per a given set of rules and a photograph, within seven minutes; participants were encouraged to plan their actions beforehand. Four PM tasks were embedded within the main task: two EBPM, and two TBPM (also see Table 2 for a description of the main assessment techniques).

Analysis of the video-recorded performance of the participants revealed that controls outperformed the autistic participants in *every* measure of the Dresden Breakfast Task, other than switching. That is to say, controls were better at forming plans and adhering to them, adhering to rules, executing plans fully and effectively, and performing all TBPM and EBPM tasks. Furthermore, controls outperformed autistic participants on a standard laboratory PM task, and scored better at self-report and computer-based executive function measures. This study therefore provides evidence that, under complex and naturalistic conditions, which require participants to coordinate themselves and their execution of several tasks, either sequentially or in parallel, PM performance is severely impaired in autistic individuals, even for EBPM. However, this was the first study to investigate both TBPM and EBPM in the same sample under such conditions, and so it is useful to compare the results with a study with similarly complex and multitask demands, namely with one employing the Virtual Week (Kretschmer, Altgassen, Rendell, & Bölte, 2014).

Kretschmer et al. (2014) employed a computerized version of Virtual Week (also see Table 2 for a description of the main assessment techniques), a board game that imitates daily PM task demands, originally devised by Rendell and Craik (2000). In brief, players roll virtual dice and move their tokens around the board a total of three times (three virtual days). When passing an event square, players must pick up a card and choose an activity from one of three options (e.g. have toast for breakfast), and are only permitted to move on once they roll the number corresponding to their chosen option (OT). EBPM and TBPM tasks are embedded within the game, equally split into either 'regular' tasks (e.g. take medication at breakfast – EBPM), or 'irregular' tasks (e.g. call plumber at 5 pm – TBPM). To perform the task, players press the 'perform task' button, which presents the task within a list of (distractor) tasks. The virtual time, which is linked to the movement of the tokens on the board, can be seen on a digital clock produced on-screen via key press.

Half of all participants were assigned to an 'implementation intention' condition in which they repeated 'if-then' statements on presentation of the PM task, such as 'when it is 5 pm I will press the "perform task" button and select "phone the number."' Implementation intentions have been posited to strengthen the task-cue association, thereby increasing the probability that the retrieval of the task would be more automatically triggered by presentation of the cue (Gollwitzer, 1999). Indeed, much of the previous work on implementation intentions in populations with reduced planning ability (e.g. older adults; Kliegel, Martin, McDaniel, Einstein, & Moor, 2007) has shown that this particular encoding strategy can be effective in improving PM performance (Chasteen, Park, & Schwarz, 2001), and so the authors hypothesized that this may also be important for their autistic participants.

The autistic participants performed less well than non-autistic controls across all PM tasks, replicating the PM difficulties experienced by autistic participants in multitask conditions, as seen in (Altgassen et al., 2012). Both groups performed better on the regular tasks than the irregular tasks, and a group x regularity interaction revealed the autistic participants to have performed worse than controls on the irregular tasks. Surprisingly, the implementation-intentions did not benefit either group.

PM in autism – mixed results

Thus far, studies reviewed have demonstrated either intact or impaired PM in autism, across both EBPM *and* TBPM paradigms. Three of the four following studies also included both event- and time-based cues, but, rather than showing a complete deficit, reveal only TBPM, but not EBPM deficits. The final study to be reviewed employed only a EBPM paradigm, but the results were mixed in that differences emerged between participants grouped according to a measure of autism severity. The first study discussed will be that of Henry et al. (2014) as it, like that of Kretschmer et al. (2014), employed the Virtual Week, but with children, rather than adults.

Other than participant age, the methodology employed by Henry et al. (2014) was much the same as Kretschmer et al. (2014), but was adapted to include tasks relevant to children. Also, rather than an implementation condition in this study, the authors included a 'low OT absorption' condition, which allowed children to move on from an event card with any dice roll, rather than the standard specific number; furthermore, participants were not required to move the token manually around the board as this was done automatically, further reducing overall cognitive demand.

In contrast to Kretschmer et al. (2014) the main group effect, whereby controls outperformed autistic participants, was qualified by a group by cue-type interaction, revealing that, while both groups performed better on EBPM than TBPM tasks, autistic participants only performed worse than controls on the TBPM tasks. This pattern was somewhat mirrored by a cue-type x regularity interaction, in that varying the regularity of the tasks did not result in differences in EBPM performance, but performance in irregular TBPM tasks was worse than that of the regular TBPM tasks.

This pattern again emerged in the studies by Williams, Boucher, Lind, and Jarrold (2013) and Williams, Jarrold, Grainger, and Lind (2014) which investigated both EBPM and TBPM in autistic children and autistic adults, respectively. In Williams et al. (2013) the PM of autistic children was investigated by way of an engaging computer game in which the children had to drive a car down a road, taking care to avoid obstacles and other vehicles (OT) while collecting gold coins (also see Table 2 for a description of the main assessment techniques). Using a within-subjects design, children's PM was assessed across two separate sessions in which they either had to remember to press a certain key when passing a lorry (EBPM), or to refuel after 80s (TBPM). Performance in the TBPM condition was further supported by the fuel gage turning red with 20s to go. Upon a fail, the car would stop, the OT score would be reset to zero, and a reminder presented on screen of 'Don't forget to refuel!'. In a fashion similar to that of previous TBPM studies, participants could press a certain key to check the fuel level.

No differences emerged between groups in OT performance, with both groups performing similarly on the car driving game. The PM results, however, revealed a TBPM deficit, but not an EBPM deficit, in the autistic children, compared to non-autistic children. Furthermore, only the autistic children fared better in their EBPM performance compared to their TBPM performance, although some caution is needed with interpretation as the autistic children were at ceiling in the EBPM task. Fuel-monitoring behavior showed the expected linear increase toward the TBPM target time, for both groups, indicating that strategic monitoring was intact in this autism group. Interestingly, measures of cognitive flexibility and mentalizing did show impairments in the autistic group, but only autistic mentalizing was associated with TBPM performance. The results of this study again confirmed that EBPM success is possible even for autistic children if PM cues are focal and salient; when external cues are absent, and strategic processes are necessary, as in TBPM tasks, performance may be impaired.

The study by Williams et al. (2014) found very similar results in autistic adults, though this was achieved using a more common computer-based paradigm. Specifically, participants had to remember to press a different key whenever a musical instrument appeared (EBPM) or every two minutes (TBPM), while judging whether the list presented on-screen was the same as the words previously presented one by one (OT). Again, participants could press a certain key at any moment to bring up a display of a digital clock.

With regard to OT performance, no group or cue differences emerged. With regard to PM accuracy, overall TBPM performance was worse than EBPM. Further, as in the previously described study, EBPM performance between the two groups was similar, whereas autistic TBPM performance was worse than that of controls. Analysis of the response precision of TBPM (i.e. the temporal distance to the target time) and the reaction time of the EBPM revealed no overall differences between TBPM and EBPM performance. However, the analysis did reveal that autistic participants were less precise in the TBPM task, but no slower in the EBPM task. The monitoring of the time did not differ between groups, showing the expected linear increase as the target time approached.

The final study to be summarized is that conducted by Sheppard, Kvavilashvili, and Ryder (2016), which investigated the relationship between autism symptom severity and PM performance. To accomplish this, the study included a group severely autistic children (as categorized by the Childhood Autism Rating Scale – CARS; Schopler, Reichler, DeVellis, & Daly, 1980), and adapted the methods (e.g. participant matching, task design) in novel ways accordingly. Children were engaged in three simple games, played with a hand puppet, which measured their EBPM. Recalling the puppet's name provided a measure of RM.

The inclusion of severely autistic children proved an important aspect, as, overall, only the severe, and not the mild autism group demonstrated poorer PM than the non-autistic controls. A group × task interaction revealed, however, that, remarkably, the severely autistic children performed as well as the non-autistic children on the task that involved picking up a spring toy when leaving the room.

This study, therefore, suggests that variation in autistic symptoms, a common occurrence in a population well known for its heterogeneity (Jeste & Geschwind, 2014), plays an important role PM performance. Furthermore, EBPM success is possible for severely autistic individuals if they are sufficiently motivated.

Literature summary and critique

At first glance, it is clear that very few of the reviewed investigations employed common methodologies. If, for instance, studies employed comparable age groups and OTs, they varied on cue-types and control variables, and yielded contrasting OT results (Altgassen et al., 2009 vs. Altgassen et al., 2010); if studies shared very similar paradigms, they varied on age group and yielded contrasting PM results (Kretschmer et al., 2014 vs. Henry et al., 2014). The current literature could, therefore, be considered inconsistent and unreliable and, to an extent, this is true. Thus, to provide clarity and reliability, future research must endeavor to consistently replicate findings. Importantly, the recent meta-analysis and review by

Landsiedel et al. (2017) came to a similar conclusion as the current paper, finding a reliable TBPM impairment, and a small (although less reliable), EBPM impairment. With this in mind, the apparent methodological inconsistency could also be viewed as a strength in that, across a broad range of ages and methodologies, patterns have emerged that provide important insight into PM in autism.

Firstly, of the 19 experiments conducted across the 13 studies, which included participants ranging in age from 8 to 41, 14 (73.7%) revealed a PM deficit, compared to controls. More specifically, all 7 TBPM experiments, and 6 of the 12 EBPM experiments, were suggestive of PM impairment. Considering the consistent TBPM results, it seems clear that when autistic individuals cannot depend on any external cue, but must instead rely on internal signals and self-generated and initiated strategies, such as regularly switching attention and inhibiting action without prompt, PM tasks are particularly difficult. This notion is further supported by those studies (e.g. Brandimonte et al., 2011) that did not find any cost to the OT of adding the PM task, suggesting that attention was not successfully diverted from the OT in order to monitor for and execute the PM task. Difficulty with strategically allocating attentional resources would also explain the poorer performance found in half of the EBPM studies; when cues were low in salience (e.g. Kretschmer et al., 2014) or non-focal (e.g. Yi et al., 2014), or the attention competing OT was high in cognitive demand (e.g. Altgassen et al., 2012, 2017), then autistic performance suffered, compared to non-autistic controls. In contrast, however, when these factors were reversed, and so dependence on self-initiated strategy was reduced, and automatic retrieval facilitated, then PM performance was spared. This pattern of results thus supports the multiprocess framework (McDaniel & Einstein, 2000).

When looking at the different phases of prospective remembering and keeping in mind the well-documented deficits of people with autism in attention, executive functioning, retrospective memory, and episodic future thinking, we expect to find reduced performance in virtually all phases of prospective remembering (namely, intention formation, intention retention, intention initiation and execution). So far, only one study on PM in autism has included a measure of intention formation (i.e. planning; Altgassen et al., 2012), and reported reduced autistic performance, and only one study tried to manipulate intention formation (i.e. implementation intentions; Kretschmer et al., 2014). All other studies have focused on the phases of intention initiation and execution (as has the vast majority of PM research in general), and have found the discussed mixed results (e.g. Henry et al., 2014; Sheppard et al., 2017) that are generally in line with the multiprocess framework. Intention retention has not been directly investigated, but first evidence points to retrospective memory load affecting PM in autism. Specifically, Kretschmer et al.'s study reported reduced autistic deficits with regular PM tasks that put less demands on retrospective memory as compared to irregular tasks. Similarly, Henry et al. (2014) found larger autistic PM deficits for irregular TBPM tasks.

However, an important limitation of the reviewed PM studies is that all but one (Sheppard et al., 2016) include only mildly to moderately autistic participants, of average to above average IQ. The PM evidence does not therefore fully represent the autistic population, a population known for its heterogeneity (Masi, DeMayo, Glozier, & Guastella, 2017), which is, indeed, an issue across the autism literature. The study by Sheppard et al. (2016) does highlight the importance of considering symptomatic variation in autism and how it relates to PM performance, revealing a difference in PM performance between 'severely' and 'mildly' autistic children. However, in this case, severity classification was made on the basis of a composite CARS score (Schopler et al., 1980), disguising the variation of behaviors that contributed to the total score. Thus, while the Sheppard et al. (2016) paper was an important step in the (PM) autism literature, much more needs to be done to more accurately represent the population. Therefore, while symptom severity and other aspects of the heterogeneous condition may have contributed to the PM performances seen in the literature, caution is needed when generalizing the conclusions to the entire autism population.

Taken together, despite the heterogeneous methodology of the conducted studies, and the relative homogeneity of the participants, a pattern emerges that suggests autistic individuals will likely find PM tasks that demand a high level of attentional control and strategic processing, such as those involving multiple sub-tasks and/or cues of low salience, very difficult. These findings are in line with the everyday difficulties of people with autism with planning ahead, and the organization and coordination of (complex) activities.

In terms of improving PM performance and reducing everyday difficulties, reducing the cognitive/strategic demand of PM tasks by increasing the automaticity of retrieval processes, would almost certainly be of benefit to autistic individuals, indeed, to all populations. However, all PM and autism studies conducted so far, with exception of the Dresden Breakfast Task, employed typical laboratory-based tasks that provide high experimental control, but low ecological validity, and which may not be able to reflect the complexity of real-life tasks.

The dynamic characteristics of PM

In reality, daily tasks are significantly more complex than the scenarios presented in typical laboratory-based dual-task PM paradigms. For instance, some tasks will only involve a short delay, with few competing tasks and no social interaction, such as remembering to check out with an electronic travel card when alighting the bus after a short journey. In contrast, others will involve long delays and human interaction, in the face of several other tasks and social and cultural expectations, such as passing on a message to a friend at the end of a busy academic conference. Importantly, therefore, PM is a variable, multitask process which demands the fluid and dynamic control of attentional control resources to facilitate the integration and execution of all aforementioned PM-critical cognitive mechanisms, the exact calibration of which depends heavily on context. This between- and within-PM task variability is to some extent recognized by the recent dynamic multiprocess framework proposed by Scullin, McDaniel, and Shelton (2013), which argues for the need for dynamic utilization of automatic and strategic retrieval processes over time, given the temporal variability of PM demands. Therefore, in practice, while investigating discrete cognitive mechanisms, such as executive function (e.g. reducing switching and inhibition demands by increasing cue salience) provides some indication as to the role of that specific mechanism, it ignores the interrelated, systemic and social characteristics of the PM process. One further critical factor in the dynamic PM process is individual difference, that is, how individuals are variably equipped to function in such a complex environment, a factor particularly important to consider for the autistic population who are known for their cognitive and behavioral heterogeneity (Georgiades, Szatmari, & Boyle, 2013; Jeste & Geschwind, 2014).

Thus, to properly understand PM, and so devise the most effective interventions, it is important to consider any processes that may be fundamental to the development of the cognitive and behavioral functions needed for prospective remembering and their dynamic integration and utilization, while also recognizing the dynamic and contextual requirements of PM as demanded from an ever changing physical and social environment. With this in mind, the following section will briefly examine the potentially fundamental role of predictive coding in the PM process. Furthermore, via the predictive-coding account of account by Van de Cruys et al. (2014), we will show how these predictive-coding deficits that may be primary to autism would result in the cognitive and PM deficits seen in the literature.

In recognition of the dynamic agent–environment interactions inherent to PM, we extend the role of predictive coding in PM, and the account of autism, to not just include perception, but also movement and affect, as is the case in predictive models formulated under active inference (Clark, 2015; Joffily & Coricelli, 2013; Kiverstein & Miller, 2015; Pezzulo, Rigoli, & Friston, 2015). In this way, the notions put forward in the current paper will shed light not only on processes fundamental to PM, but also on the underlying causes of autism. In addition, by better understanding fundamental atypicalities in perception, action and movement, the development of better targeted interventions is supported that not only improve daily PM performance, but also inform clinical practice and help target specific learning to improve autistic individuals' lives as a whole.

A unifying predictive-coding account of autism

Simply described, predictive coding is an account of perception in which the main task of the perceptual system is to minimize the prediction-error between predicted and actual sensory input (Clark, 2013; Rao & Ballard, 1999). Under this account, the brain continuously generates predictions about future incoming sensory information (top-down), based on the current context and associated prior experiences, which are subsequently compared with input received (bottom-up). While predictions serve to minimize prediction-error, a resulting prediction-error can be used to optimize the prediction, which in turn minimizes prediction-error, a process that cycles in perpetuity. Through prediction-errors and their minimization, the brain gradually comes to learn the statistical structure of the environment, i.e. how distal structures in the environment give rise to proximal sensory input (for more detailed introductory accounts to predictive coding, see Clark, 2013, 2015; Hohwy, 2013).

However, as Van de Cruys et al. (2014) note, due to the 'fluctuating nature of regularities in the world, and the stochastic and noisy biological system through which we experience it [...]' (p.1) there is a limit to what can be predicted and hence there will always be some residual prediction-error. Therefore, a critical ability is to learn which prediction-errors are behaviorally relevant, and so should be attended to and used to update predictions, and which can be ignored.

For instance, upon entering a café, one may be surprised by the weight of the door when opening. This is a useful prediction-error, and should update the future prediction of *that particular door*. Once inside, one would expect, and so predict, to hear the sound of the milk steaming machine. If a familiar café, one would even be able to predict well the location of the sound, and have some idea of the sound's particular characteristics. However, it would be practically impossible to predict the exact time, and the exact volume and clarity as experienced by the perceiver (influenced, for example, by talking, head cold, a particularly loud/busy moment). Therefore, the sound of the steam machine would almost always generate an error. However, this error could never be reduced and should thus receive minimal attention, and should not update the model of what to expect in a café; that is, nothing further could be learnt from this experience (irreducible uncertainty, Van de Cruys et al. (2014), so the error should be assigned low confidence (*precision*) that it is attention worthy.

Thus, within an optimal prediction model of a steam machine in a café, the occurrence of the sound at any given moment will essentially be surprising, but not unexpected.

Clearly, then, being able to flexibly and context-sensitively vary the precision of prediction-errors is critical for optimal learning and attention allocation (Feldman & Friston, 2010). An understanding of the errors that still offer reducible uncertainty facilitates the efficient direction of attention toward errors that can be further reduced, i.e. real learning opportunities. Conversely, assigning equal and high weight to each and every error would result in attention being drawn to errors which will always occur and cannot be reduced, thus depleting valuable and limited cognitive processing power, and needlessly updating prediction models. Precision, therefore, is seen as the fundamental mechanism of learning and attention (Van de Cruys et al., 2014) and has a clear and important role in PM.

If, as posited by the multiprocess framework (McDaniel & Einstein, 2000) the allocation of attentional resources is central to the PM process, then an optimum precision weighting mechanism is essential to successful PM performance. Selectively attending to relevant information and ignoring the high volume of other information would facilitate time monitoring, or the monitoring for and identification of PM cues (particularly for those of low salience and non-focality), or the switching of attention from one task to another. Furthermore, attenuating the relentless barrage of irrelevant sensory information is important for the development and application of other, higher level cognitive processes critical to PM, such as planning, retrospective memory, episodic future thinking and critical thinking and reasoning (regarding, say, the context and environment within which the PM is likely to be situated).

Using the previous example of a café, it is easy to see the importance of precision to PM. One would rely on the high-level concept of a café to form a 'café-prediction', from which one would expect, and thus assign low precision to, the tumultuous stream of relatively lower level errors (e.g. sudden bursts of laughter, or cups being dropped to the floor) allowing them to be ignored within (and thus not update) my 'café-prediction' model. This would free up attentional resources, which would be particularly important for demanding PM tasks within the café, such as monitoring the time in order to call your boss at a certain time, or to monitor for a cue indicating your coffee is ready, after which you might stop your conversation (OT) and pick up the coffee which has been placed at the end of the counter.

Pertinently for the current review, Van de Cruys et al. (2014), in their unifying account of autism, put forward the selective and contextual weighting of precision, a mechanism essential to attentional control and so to PM, as the core deficit of the condition. Specifically, they situate the core deficit in the High, Inflexible Precision of Prediction-Errors in Autism (HIPPEA). This means that impaired precision allocation results in attention often being drawn to what is effectively noise, thus demanding valuable and limited cognitive resources, drawing attention away from real and important learning opportunities, and needlessly updating prediction models. The authors posit that this uniformly high precision, irrespective of context, accounts for the characteristic impairments and difficulties commonly seen in autism, such as atypical sensory processing (Ashburner et al., 2008; Ben-Sasson et al., 2009; Robertson & Baron-Cohen, 2017; Tomchek & Dunn, 2007), social communication difficulties, and insistence on sameness and repetitive behaviors, as efforts to reduce confusing and unpleasant environmental uncertainty (American Psychiatric Publishing, 2013). Specifically, high sensory precision may result in a constant barrage of seemingly unfamiliar, attention grabbing signals, each of which would arguably be at best surprising and distracting; at worst, shocking and frightening. Importantly, prediction itself is not impaired in autism, as is evidenced by superior performance in situations with high consistency and predictability, for example in structured visual search tasks (O'Riordan, Plaisted, Driver, & Baron-Cohen, 2001).

Assuming the validity of the Van de Cruys et al. (2014) account, the deficit of HIPPEA leads directly to the PM impairments seen in the population. It would explain, for example, poor PM performance, relative to non-autistic participants, when PM cues were low in salience (e.g. high precision attributed to each and every error would result in all sensory input being 'salient' and deserving of attention). This would load heavily on limited cognitive resources, and would also diffuse the relevance and contextual salience of the PM cue, making it much harder to discern. Thus, the predictive-coding account of Van de Cruys arguably contributes much to the understanding of autism, and to PM. An important potential criticism of the account, however, may be that, so far, much of the literature has been mainly theoretical and conceptual in nature, dealing with autism using the tools and concepts derived from predictive coding and provides therefore nothing more than stories (Bowers & Davis, 2012). Although the unification of a disparate range of impairments under one theory is progress in its own right, we agree that much further work is needed. In particular, the development of quantitative computational models that are able to make predictions about updating, learning, and the adjustment of precision on a trial-by-trial basis (Van de Cruys et al., 2017), would greatly advance the field. For example, the aim of the rapidly emerging field of *computational psychiatry* is to infer the hidden causes (such as the structure of the parameters of an internal model) of measurable quantities (such as actions, reaction times and symptoms; Friston, Stephan, Montague, & Dolan, 2014; Schwartenbeck & Friston, 2016; Stephan & Mathys, 2014). Furthermore, in their recent paper, Van de Cruys et al. (2017) put forward substantial empirical data in support of their account.

So far, we have only focused on the perceptual aspect of prediction-error minimization. However, PM does not simply involve the perception and processing of external sensory signals. Rather, it is a complex process that depends critically on perception *and* action. Specifically, it requires the effective coordination of the mind (perception, desires, intentions), the body (bodily sensations, action) and the environment (PM cues and/or target times; social or occupational expectations; competing sensory and social demands for attention) to ensure successful action at the appropriate moment. Consequently, to fully relate predictive coding to PM and to autism, we need to extend HIPPEA to more embodied predictive-coding models derived from *active inference* (Bruineberg, Kiverstein, & Rietveld, 2016; Pezzulo et al., 2015; Seth, 2013).

According to active inference, action, as well as perception, is integral to the predictive-coding and error minimization process. That is, agents do not only try to predict the current state of the environment, but also cause their environment to be in an optimal state (i.e. a state of physical, social and cultural well-being/safety) *through action*. For example, according to active inference, 'intending to post an important letter in a post box' works like determining the need of posting a letter, expecting oneself (with high precision) to post the letter and then selecting an action (reaching into a bag, grasping the letter, then posting it through the slit in the post box) that fulfils that expectation. Only if an agent has the right predictions (both about what will be an optimal state, and about how it can reach that state), it can cause the environment to confirm to those expectations and consequently lead to an actually optimal state beneficial to the agent (Bruineberg et al., 2016).

Put in more concrete terms, for individuals to flourish in their environment, they must understand their needs in terms of their physical and mental well-being (expected states), and meet them by perceiving and acting upon the environment in an as efficient and beneficial way as possible. This includes among others the congruency of the sensory weighting of prediction-error (precision) with the volatility of the environment and the trade-off between action and perception (Palmer, Lawson, & Hohwy, 2017). Therefore, the role of prediction-error minimization, and the impact of any impairment such as HIPPEA, becomes much more significant, as it mediates all interactions between the brain, the body, and the environment within and between all hierarchical levels (i.e. low-level stimulus to high level concepts/abstractions), facilitating understanding of the self and the world in which it is situated. Active inference and error minimization is therefore deeply interwoven into everyday processes, not least the PM process.

Given then, the essential role of prediction and error precision in mediating the relationships between the brain, the body, and the environment, the adverse consequence of HIPPEA, the precision-weighting deficit put forward as core to autism (Van de Cruys et al., 2014, 2017) already deemed significant to PM, becomes much more problematic. It means that autism is not solely a problem of perceptual evidence accumulation, but involves deficits in the interactions between all levels and modalities (e.g. between simple, sensory signals and higher level conceptual/constructed beliefs), between the brain and body, and the ways they coordinate to respond and act upon the environment. Thus, HIPPEA makes a whole range of other autism phenomena intelligible such as their difficulties with understanding internal states, evidenced by a high prevalence of alexithymia (Milosavljevic et al., 2016), difficulties with interoception (Shah, Hall, Catmur, & Bird, 2016), differences in rhythm and timing (Isenhower et al., 2012; Sheridan & McAuley, 1997), movement and associated social difficulties (Cook, 2016; Cook, Blakemore, & Press, 2013), and diminished sense of agency (Grynszpan et al., 2012; Sperduti, Pieron, Leboyer, & Zalla, 2014; Zalla, Miele, Leboyer, & Metcalfe, 2015), linked to deficits in episodic memory and episodic future thinking (Lind, 2010). We think that extending the unifying account of autism of Van de Cruys et al. (2014) in such an embodied way, brings the account closer to more embodied unifying accounts of autism such as the one offered by De Jaegher (2015) which places differences in movement, rhythm and coordination, between the self, others and environment as responsible for the emergence of autism. Thus, the embodied HIPPEA and enactive accounts of autism both describe systematic differences in movement and perception that ultimately blend with a different conceptual and social understanding of the environment; indeed, a different way of making sense of the world. We feel that together, both accounts offer a more encompassing account of autism. Furthermore, the difficulties caused by such as account would greatly impact upon PM performance.

PM tasks reflect one aspect of the fundamental real-world demand of navigating a complex physical, social and cultural environment, and so require the efficient coordination of the brain, body, and environment to remain in a state of well-being. For example, the environment will create PM demands (work supervisor asks you to pass on important information to a work colleague), generating intentions within the individual (pass message on to colleague). This intention is internalized in terms of relative value (need to please supervisor; consequence for colleague of not receiving message; likely personal emotional state – personal, physical and social consequences of success/failure) which would interact with chances of success (beliefs about own ability to successfully execute task, given likely future

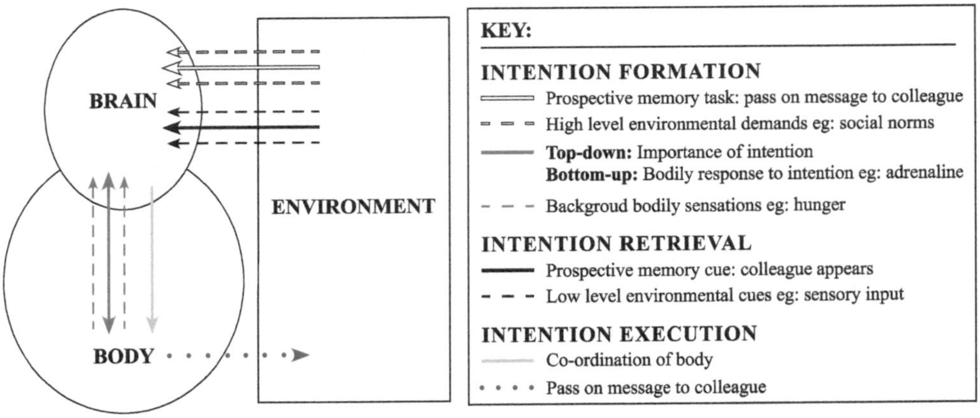

Figure 2. Diagram depicting the role of predictive processing in mediating between the brain, body, and environment throughout the prospective memory process. Illustrates importance of attending to relevant cues (solid arrows), via effective precision-weighting, against a barrage of competing, often task-irrelevant, information (dashed arrows).

context in which task/cue is situated, and predicted ability to employ appropriate action within it; see Figure 2). These states are accompanied by physiological responses (increased heart rate, adrenaline/cortisol) and associated affective responses (arousal, worry, stress) that would need to be understood in the context of their situatedness in a socio-cultural setting. In addition, successfully realizing the PM task requires understanding how attentional resources are employed to perceive relevant cues (recalling my supervisor's request upon seeing my colleague). What is crucial then, is for the agent to be selectively perturbed by aspects of the environment (change your behavior when seeing your colleague, but try to not get distracted by your phone) in a way that is in line with longer term plans and goals and the demands of the situation (such as your supervisor's request). Such selective openness to aspects of the environment (or 'affordances') and coordinating with them in an adequate way represents a process fundamental to life and mind (Bruineberg & Rietveld, 2014).

Seeing PM as reflecting this fundamental life processes means that interventions aimed at addressing issues that may be affecting such life processes (e.g. HIPPEA in embodied predictive coding) would also benefit PM performance.

Clinical application

According to HIPPEA (Van de Cruys et al., 2014, 2017), autism emerges primarily from an impaired prediction-error precision weighting process, resulting in and manifesting as sub-optimal learning and attentional mechanisms. When considered in the context of active inference and the brain–body–environment system, HIPPEA would disrupt the critical continuous and reciprocal learning between all three states of the system, resulting in impaired communication and understanding between the brain and the body, and their perception and action in and with the environment. Given these assumptions, autistic individuals would benefit from holistic and embodied interventions that would support them in attending to and engaging with themselves and the world, which would in turn support their PM performance.

As posited by the above assumptions, autistic people experience difficulty in perceiving and acting in the often *irreducibly* uncertain world. One obvious way in which to support such a difficulty is to reduce the irreducible uncertainty as much as possible, and provide predictable clear expectations and a safe physical, social, and cultural environment. This provision of clear, consistent structure, and expectation in the environment is the core principal of the Treatment and Education of Autistic and related Communication-handicapped Children approach (TEACCH; Mesibov, Shea, & Schopler, 2004) which is widely implemented within charities and schools and has good levels of reported effectiveness (Mesibov & Shea, 2010; Panerai, Ferrante, & Zingale, 2002). According to TEACCH, schools/environments should provide autistic individuals with as predictable and 'low arousal' physical environments as possible, for example, low sensory input and similar classroom configuration across all classes (e.g. same furniture, consistently arranged and decorated display boards, neutral colors). Reducing the uncertainty in the environment would not only reduce anxiety but would provide a safe, predictable platform from which to learn. These TEACCH principles could also be directly applied to the PM environment: reducing the physical and social uncertainty in the environment parallels the reduction in cognitive load inferred to be beneficial in empirical PM work (e.g. use of salient cues, simple OT). Providing clear PM instructions that are additionally supported by visual cues, could enhance encoding and increase the physical/perceptual salience of the cue, thus decreasing executive control demands by increasing automaticity of intention retrieval. To increase effectiveness, this approach could easily be incorporated into a person's existing communication strategy. For instance, an autistic child's tailored Picture Exchange Communication System (PECS; Bondy & Frost, 1994) could be employed to provide need-appropriate verbal and visual task instructions when supporting them in bringing their sports kit to school the following day. The relevant symbols could be placed on the appropriate day on the child's daily visual timetable, with copies taken home on the day to act as salient PM cues.

Furthermore, if autism is indeed associated with sub-optimal attentional processes, which may result in difficulties attending to relevant and important cues (internal and external), autistic individuals may benefit from interventions that focus on practicing and training attention. For example, the program Attention Autism (Dawson et al., 2004), originally developed to support the development of joint attention, has been found to improve attention by providing engaging sensory objects. This intervention would thus support the general development of the understanding to engage with relevant cues in the environment, cues which afford personal and social benefits. The benefit to PM of improving attention by way of interventions such as Attention Autism (Dawson et al., 2004) is thus clear: the ability to identify, and allocate attention toward, appropriate event-based cues in a complex environment would be developed, facilitating more frequent automatic retrieval.

A further method of improving self and internal understanding and the relationship with the environment – or the brain–body–environment system – would be to facilitate impaired learning through interventions that involve the use and coordination of all three of these states. Moving, acting and perceiving to achieve internal (fun, pleasure) and external (social interaction, PM tasks) goals, and post-action perception and reflection on the internal (emotions, feelings, bodily responses) and external (effective communication, understanding others' behavior, successfully executing a PM task) physical and social results, would support the understanding of one's own function in one's physical and social environment, and improve PM performance at every phase. One would slowly become more attuned to one's own body and its responses and actions within its environment. Examples for such embodied/enactive approaches are movement (for a review, see Lee, Lambert, Wittich, Kehayia, & Park, 2016), drama (Corbett et al., 2011), music (Whipple, 2004), and art therapies (Koch, Mehl, Sobanski, Sieber, & Fuchs, 2014) that are currently already employed to support autistic people.

The approaches described above can be incorporated to generate more concrete, PM-specific support and learning strategies. One approach would be to augment the largely non-conscious, impaired embodied predictive coding and error weighting processes that are involved at every PM phase, with explicit, metacognitive processes. Metacognition has been shown to be important in PM, suggesting, for example, that attention-allocation strategies depend somewhat on metacognitive expectations of the PM task demands (Rummel & Meiser, 2013), and an awareness of one's cognitive difficulties may encourage the use of reminders to make sure one does not forget the implementation of the delayed intention (Gilbert, 2015; Phillips, Henry, & Martin, 2008). Although, interestingly, a recent study by Cherkaoui and Gilbert (2017) found that autistic participants gave good metacognitive judgments of their (poorer) PM abilities and predictions of performance, but did not compensate with an increased use of reminders. It may be that the autistic participants differed only in their metacognitive control, but not awareness, in line with the, albeit scarce, literature pointing to difficulties autism in metacognitive control, and to deficits in using monitoring processes to influence cognitive control (for similar results see Grainger, Williams, & Lind, 2016; Wilkinson, Best, Minshew, & Strauss, 2010; but see Wojcik, Allen, Brown, & Souchay, 2011 for contrasting findings).

Given the benefit of metacognitive strategies to the learning of those who experience learning difficulties (Chevalier, Parrila, Ritchie, & Deacon, 2017) it may be that autistic individuals, indeed any individuals that experience PM difficulties, would benefit from training and support in the use of direct PM metacognitive strategies. Such training could be designed by drawing on the principles of TEACCH (Mesibov et al., 2004) to provide a highly structured, cyclical PM predict-perform-evaluate processes, scaffolded appropriately according to individual cognitive and communication needs (e.g. the use of PECS symbols as mentioned above). Figure 3 provides an example of how this could be implemented in, for example, schools, to be completed by children with an appropriate level of adult support. Through this sheet, children would be encouraged to consciously consider a particular PM task, such as remembering their swimming kit, and why it is important to them. Children would also predict the likely environment in which the intention will be executed, how difficult it will be, what reminders or cues they will use and, ultimately, their likely chances of success. The children could then evaluate their predictions and performance, once the task was over, comparing them with what was experienced, informing future strategy and predictions for the same or similar tasks in the future. This cyclical process would augment the predictive processing problems we posit to adversely affect PM in autism, while also developing PM-specific, and more general, metacognitive ability. It would also have the added benefit of directly supporting the factors posited by the multiprocess framework (McDaniel & Einstein, 2000) to influence attention allocation and intention retrieval during the PM process (such as deeper intention encoding, stronger cue-action association, as well as highlighting cue salience and task importance).

To summarize, the findings of the PM and autism literature shows that making small changes to the PM environment, such as clearly demonstrating the value of completing the

Table 2. Description of assessment techniques.

Task name	Task description	Time to complete	PM cue type	Cue delay length	Psychometric properties	Appropriate age range	Appropriate severity range	References
Dresden Breakfast task	Preparation of breakfast following certain rules and time restrictions	15 min (including planning; excluding delay)	2 EBPM tasks (each 1×) and 2 TBPM tasks (each 1×)	5 min	Inter-rater reliability was high in the Altgassen et al. (2012) study (plan performance $r = .95$; plan adherence $r = .93$); validity shown by detrimental effects of various disorders and aging	Starting from about 12 years	Mild to moderate	Real-life version; used in autism and older adults: Altgassen et al. (2012); Hering, Cortez, Kliegel, and Altgassen (2014) virtual version; used in ADHD and older adults: Altgassen, Kretschmer, and Kliegel (2014); Altgassen et al. (2015)
Driving game	Computer-based driving game	8 min per condition	2 conditions: (a)1 EBPM task (6×) (b)1 TBPM task (6×)	No delay	–	7–14 years	Mild to moderate	Williams et al. (2013)
Virtual Week	Computer-based board game that imitates daily PM task demands	About 45 min	EBPM & TBPM each day 4 tasks (2 regular, 2 irregular); total of 3 days, thus 24 PM tasks	No delay	Good reliability (Cronbach's Alpha) ranging between .57 and .84 for Henry et al. (2014) and .62 and .86 for Kretschmer et al. (2014); validity indicated by detrimental effects of various forms of pathology and aging (see review Rendell & Henry, 2009)	Children version: 8–12 years adult version: starting from around 13 years	Mild to moderate	Children's version: Henry et al. (2014) adult version: used, e.g. in autism, older adults, multiple sclerosis, Parkinson's disease, traumatic brain injury: Kretschmer et al. (2014); Altgassen et al., 2015; Rendell, Henry, Phillips, de la Piedad Garcia, Booth, Phillips, and Kliegel (2012); Foster, Rose, McDaniel, and Rendell (2013); Mioni, Rendell, Henry, Cantagallo, and Stablum (2013)

Note: EBPM = Event-Based Prospective Memory; PM = Prospective Memory; TBPM = Time-Based Prospective Memory.

I have to remember to	--
I am good at remembering tasks like this	very true 1 2 3 4 5 not true at all
This task is important to me because	-- --
I forget to do this task	rarely sometimes often every time

PREDICTION		EVALUATION	
I think this task will be	very easy 1 2 3 4 5 very difficult	Did I remember?	Yes No
It might be difficult to remember because	------------------------------ ------------------------------ ------------------------------	This task was	very easy 1 2 3 4 5 very difficult
I can try and make it easier by	------------------------------ ------------------------------ ------------------------------	I remembered / forgot this task because	------------------------------ ------------------------------ ------------------------------
To remind me to do this I will use:	smart watch alarm Google Calendar alert iPad alarm swimming symbol in bag	My reminders were	very helpful 1 2 3 4 5 unhelpful
Other reminder	------------------------------	Because	------------------------------ ------------------------------
I will remember my swimming kit	definately 1 2 3 4 5 unlikely	Next time I will	------------------------------ ------------------------------ ------------------------------

Figure 3. PM metacognition worksheet to support individuals with specific PM tasks. Metacognitive awareness and control would be developed by encouraging individuals to regularly predict and evaluate their PM performance, based on their understanding of self-PM ability, task importance, past performance, self-chosen reminders/cues, and the likely environment in which it will occur. Levels of support, formatting, could be adapted to an individual need-appropriate level, e.g. full adult support, the use of symbols in place of words.

task may improve PM performance. Such a demonstration might increase motivation, offset an impaired understanding of self and may improve PM performance by supporting intention encoding, shielding of the intention from PM-irrelevant stimuli, encouraging monitoring for the PM cue and enabling switching to the intended action. Furthermore, the salience of the cue, both in terms of the sensory distinctiveness as historically described by the PM literature, and in terms of its relevance to the task, may influence the extent to which retrieval of the intention relies on automatic vs. strategic, executive control processes.

Conclusion

The evidence from studies conducted to date strongly suggests that autistic individuals experience difficulty with PM. However, the few studies in which autistic PM performance was spared, even for severely autistic children, demonstrated that PM success is possible under very structured conditions, with simple OTs, highly salient, focal PM cues and motivating rewards. According to the multiprocess framework, these conditions more automatically encourage the allocation of attention toward PM cues, supporting intention retrieval and execution, and rely less on cognitive functions that are impaired in autism (e.g. executive functions, retrospective memory, episodic future thinking).

According to our proposed account of autism, the commonly found cognitive, social and motor deficits in autism are deeply underpinned by an impaired prediction-error weighting ability. This impairment disrupts the development and understanding of the brain–body–environment relationships and interactions, culminating in differences in the way that autistic people perceive, move, and make sense of the world. Thus, these differences fundamental to autism may lead to their problems with functioning successfully in the world, a critical aspect of which is successfully performing the frequent and challenging PM tasks. Therefore, while treating the 'symptoms' of poor PM performance by increasing, for example, cue salience and focality, is easily implemented and almost certain to result in better performance, we propose to directly address problems of prediction and action through embodied autism and PM research paradigms and interventions.

Notes

1. We have used identity-first, rather than person-first, language throughout the paper in line with the preferences of the autism community (Kenny et al., 2015; Sinclair, 2013).
2. The current paper will focus on the multiprocess framework as it is the theory most used by the reviewed studies.

Disclosure statement

No potential conflict of interest was reported by the authors.

ORCID

Mareike Altgassen http://orcid.org/0000-0002-2644-8298

References

Allen, G., & Courchesne, E. (2001). Attention function and dysfunction in autism. *Frontiers in Bioscience, 6*, D105–D119.

Altgassen, M., Koban, N., & Kliegel, M. (2012). Do adults with autism spectrum disorders compensate in naturalistic prospective memory tasks? *Journal of Autism and Developmental Disorders, 42*, 2141–2151. doi:10.1007/s10803-012-1466-3. Retrieved from http://www.ncbi.nlm.nih.gov/pubmed/22350339

Altgassen, M., & Koch, A. (2014). Impact of inhibitory load on remembering delayed intentions in autism. *International Journal of Developmental Disabilities, 60*(3), 198–204.

Altgassen, M., Kretschmer, A., & Kliegel, M. (2014). Task dissociation in prospective memory performance in individuals with ADHD. *Journal of Attention Disorders, 18*(7), 617–624.

Altgassen, M., Rendell, P. G., Bernhard, A., Henry, J. D., Bailey, P. E., Phillips, L. H., & Kliegel, M. (2015). Future thinking improves prospective memory performance and plan enactment in older adults. *Quarterly Journal of Experimental Psychology, 68*(1), 192–204.

Altgassen, M., Rendell, P. G., Bernhard, A., Henry, J. D., Bailey, P. E., Phillips, L. H., & Kliegel, M. (2014). Future thinking improves prospective memory performance and plan enactment in older adults. *Quarterly Journal of Experimental Psychology*, 1–13. doi:10.1080/17470218.2014.956127. Retrieved from http://www.ncbi.nlm.nih.gov/pubmed/25191929

Altgassen, M., Schmitz-Hübsch, M., & Kliegel, M. (2010). Event-based prospective memory performance in autism spectrum disorder. *Journal of Neurodevelopmental Disorders, 2*(1), 2–8. doi:10.1007/s11689-009-9030-y. Retrieved from http://www.ncbi.nlm.nih.gov/pubmed/22127837

Altgassen, M., Sheppard, D. P., & Hendriks, M. (2017). Do importance instructions improve time-based prospective remembering in autism specturm conditions. Manuscript in preparation.

Altgassen, M., Williams, T. I., Bölte, S., & Kliegel, M. (2009). Time-based prospective memory in children with autism spectrum disorder. *Brain Impairment, 10*(1), 52–58.

Althaus, M., De Sonneville, L. M. J., Minderaa, R. B., Hensen, L. G. N., & Til, R. B. (1996). Information processing and aspects of visual attention in children with the DSM-III-R diagnosis "pervasive developmental disorder not otherwise specified" (PDDNOS): I. Focused and divided attention. *Child Neuropsychology, 2*(1), 17–29. Retrieved from <Go to ISI>://WOS:A1996UR97600003

American Psychiatric Publishing. (2013). *Diagnostic and statistical manual of mental disorders* (5th ed.). Washington, DC: Author.

Anderson, K. A., Shattuck, P. T., Cooper, B. P., Roux, A. M., & Wagner, M. (2014). Prevalence and correlates of postsecondary residential status among young adults with an autism spectrum disorder. *Autism, 18*(5), 562–570.

Ashburner, J., Ziviani, J., & Rodger, S. (2008). Sensory processing and classroom emotional, behavioral, and educational outcomes in children with autism spectrum disorder. *American Journal of Occupational Therapy, 62*(5), 564–573.

Atance, C. M. & O'Neill, D. K. (2001). Episodic future thinking. *Trends in Cognitive Sciences, 5*, 533–539.

Baron-Cohen, S. (2000). Theory of mind and autism: A review. *International Review of Research in Mental Retardation, 23*, 169–204.

Baron-Cohen, S., Leslie, A. M., & Frith, U. (1985). Does the autistic child have a "theory of mind"? *Cognition, 21*(1), 37–46.

Barth, C., Fein, D., & Waterhouse, L. (1995). Delayed match-to-sample performance in autistic-children. *Developmental Neuropsychology, 11*(1), 53–69. Retrieved from <Go to ISI>://A1995RD00200004

Baudic, S., Barba, G., Thibaudet, M. C., Smagghe, A., Remy, P., & Traykov, L. (2006). Executive function deficits in early Alzheimer's disease and their relations with episodic memory. *Archives of Clinical Neuropsychology, 21*(1), 15–21.

Ben-Sasson, A., Hen, L., Fluss, R., Cermak, S. A., Engel-Yeger, B., & Gal, E. (2009). A meta-analysis of sensory modulation symptoms in individuals with autism spectrum disorders. *Journal of Autism and Developmental Disorders, 39*(1), 1–11.

Bondy, A. S., & Frost, L. A. (1994). The picture exchange communication system. *Focus on Autism and Other Developmental Disabilities, 9*(3), 1–19.

Bowers, J. S., & Davis, C. J. (2012). Bayesian just-so stories in psychology and neuroscience. *Psychological Bulletin, 138*(3), 389.

Bowler, D. M., Gardiner, J. M., & Grice, S. J. (2000). Episodic memory and remembering in adults with Asperger syndrome. *Journal of Autism and Developmental Disorders, 30*(4), 295–304. Retrieved from http://www.ncbi.nlm.nih.gov/entrez/query.fcgi?cmd=Retrieve&db=PubMed&dopt=Citation&list_uids=11039856

Bowler, D. M., Gardiner, J. M., Grice, S., & Saavalainen, P. (2000). Memory illusions: False recall and recognition in adults with Asperger's syndrome. *Journal of Abnormal Psychology, 109*(4), 663–672. Retrieved from http://www.ncbi.nlm.nih.gov/entrez/query.fcgi?cmd=Retrieve&db=PubMed&dopt=Citation&list_uids=11195990

Brandimonte, M. A., Filippello, P., Coluccia, E., Altgassen, M., & Kliegel, M. (2011). To do or not to do? Prospective memory versus response inhibition in autism spectrum disorder and attention-deficit/hyperactivity disorder. *Memory, 19*(1), 56–66. 932274272 [pii]. doi:10.1080/09658211.2010.535657. Retrieved from http://www.ncbi.nlm.nih.gov/entrez/query.fcgi?cmd=Retrieve&db=PubMed&dopt=Citation&list_uids=21240748

Bruineberg, J., Kiverstein, J., & Rietveld, E. (2016). The anticipating brain is not a scientist: The free-energy principle from an ecological-enactive perspective. *Synthese*, 1–28.

Bruineberg, J., & Rietveld, E. (2014). Self-organization, free energy minimization, and optimal grip on a field of affordances. *Frontiers in Human Neuroscience, 8*, 599.

Brunfaut, E., Vanoverberghe, V., & d'Ydewalle, G. (2000). Prospective remembering of Korsakoffs and alcoholics as a function of the prospective-memory and on-going tasks. *Neuropsychologia, 38*(7), 975–984. Retrieved from <Go to ISI>://000087160700008

Burgess, P. W., Gonen-Yaacovi, G., & Volle, E. (2011). Functional neuroimaging studies of prospective memory: What have we learnt so far? *Neuropsychologia, 49*(8), 2246–2257. doi:10.1016/j.neuropsychologia.2011.02.014. Retrieved from <Go to ISI>://000292805700012

Chasteen, A. L., Park, D. C., & Schwarz, N. (2001). Implementation intentions and facilitation of prospective memory. *Psychological Science, 12*(6), 457–461.

Cherkaoui, M., & Gilbert, S. J. (2017). Strategic use of reminders in an 'intention offloading'task: Do individuals with autism spectrum conditions compensate for memory difficulties? *Neuropsychologia, 97*, 140–151.

Chevalier, T. M., Parrila, R., Ritchie, K. C., & Deacon, S. H. (2017). The role of metacognitive reading strategies, metacognitive study and learning strategies, and behavioral study and learning strategies in predicting academic success in students with and without a history of reading difficulties. *Journal of Learning Disabilities, 50*(1), 34–48.

Ciesielski, K. T., Knight, J. E., Prince, R. J., Harris, R. J., & Handmaker, S. D. (1995). Event-related potentials in cross-modal divided attention in autism. *Neuropsychologia, 33*(2), 225–246. Retrieved from https://www.ncbi.nlm.nih.gov/pubmed/7746366

Clark, A. (2013). Whatever next? Predictive brains, situated agents, and the future of cognitive science. *Behavioral and Brain Sciences, 36*(3), 181–204.

Clark, A. (2015). *Surfing uncertainty: Prediction, action, and the embodied mind*. Oxford: Oxford University Press.

Cona, G., Bisiacchi, P. S., Sartori, G., & Scarpazza, C. (2016). Effects of cue focality on the neural mechanisms of prospective memory: A meta-analysis of neuroimaging studies. *Scientific Reports, 6*, 25983. Retrieved from <Go to ISI>://WOS:000375905300001

Cona, G., Scarpazza, C., Sartori, G., Moscovitch, M., & Bisiacchi, P. S. (2015). Neural bases of prospective memory: A meta-analysis and the "Attention to Delayed Intention" (AtoDI) model. *Neuroscience & Biobehavioral Reviews, 52*, 21–37. doi:10.1016/j.neubiorev.2015.02.007. Retrieved from http://www.ncbi.nlm.nih.gov/pubmed/25704073

Cook, J. (2016). From movement kinematics to social cognition: The case of autism. *Philosophical Transactions of the Royal Society B: Biological Sciences, 371*(1693), 20150372.

Cook, J. L., Blakemore, S.-J., & Press, C. (2013). Atypical basic movement kinematics in autism spectrum conditions. *Brain, 136*(9), 2816–2824.

Corbett, B. A., Constantine, L. J., Hendren, R., Rocke, D., & Ozonoff, S. (2009). Examining executive functioning in children with autism spectrum disorder, attention deficit hyperactivity disorder and typical development. *Psychiatry Research, 166*(2–3), 210–222. doi:10.1016/j.psychres.2008.02.005. Retrieved from <Go to ISI>://000265344500014

Corbett, B. A., Gunther, J. R., Comins, D., Price, J., Ryan, N., Simon, D., … Rios, T. (2011). Brief report: Theatre as therapy for children with autism spectrum disorder. *Journal of Autism and Developmental Disorders, 41*(4), 505–511.

Dawson, G., Toth, K., Abbott, R., Osterling, J., Munson, J., Estes, A., & Liaw, J. (2004). Early social attention impairments in autism: Social orienting, joint attention, and attention to distress. *Developmental Psychology, 40*(2), 271.

De Jaegher, H. (2015). Embodiment and sense-making in autism. *Frontiers in Integrative Neuroscience, 7*, 15.

de Vito, S., Gamboz, N., Brandimonte, M. A., Barone, P., Amboni, M., & Della Sala, S. (2012). Future thinking in Parkinson's disease: An executive function? *Neuropsychologia, 50*(7), 1494–1501.

Einstein, G. O., & McDaniel, M. A. (1996). Retrieval processes in prospective memory: Theoretical approaches and some new findings. In M. A. Brandimonte, G. O. Einstein, & M. A. McDaniel (Eds.), *Prospective memory: Theory and applications* (pp. 115–142). Mahwah, NJ: Lawrence Erlbaum.

Ellis, J., & Kvavilashvili, L. (2000). Prospective memory in 2000: Past, present, and future directions. *Applied Cognitive Psychology, 14*, S1–S9. Retrieved from <Go to ISI>://000168094200001

Feldman, H., & Friston, K. (2010). Attention, uncertainty, and free-energy. *Frontiers in Human Neuroscience, 4*, 215.

Foster, E. R., Rose, N. S., McDaniel, M. A., & Rendell, P. G. (2013). Prospective memory in Parkinson disease during a virtual week: Effects of both prospective and retrospective demands. *Neuropsychology, 27*(2), 170–181.

Friston, K. J., Stephan, K. E., Montague, R., & Dolan, R. J. (2014). Computational psychiatry: The brain as a phantastic organ. *The Lancet Psychiatry, 1*(2), 148–158.

Garon, N., Bryson, S. E., & Smith, I. M. (2008). Executive function in preschoolers: A review using an integrative framework. *Psychological Bulletin, 134*(1), 31.

Georgiades, S., Szatmari, P., & Boyle, M. (2013). Importance of studying heterogeneity in autism. *Neuropsychiatry, 3*(2), 123–125.

Geurts, H. M., Corbett, B., & Solomon, M. (2009). The paradox of cognitive flexibility in autism. *Trends in Cognitive Sciences, 13*(2), 74–82. doi:10.1016/j.tics.2008.11.006. Retrieved from <Go to ISI>://000263635900005

Geurts, H. M., Verte, S., Oosterlaan, J., Roeyers, H., & Sergeant, J. A. (2004). How specific are executive functioning deficits in attention deficit hyperactivity disorder and autism? *Journal of Child Psychology and Psychiatry, 45*(4), 836–854. Retrieved from <Go to ISI>://000221805400017

Gilbert, S. J. (2015). Strategic use of reminders: Influence of both domain-general and task-specific metacognitive confidence, independent of objective memory ability. *Consciousness and Cognition, 33*, 245–260.

Gollwitzer, P. M. (1999). Implementation intentions: Strong effects of simple plans. *American Psychologist, 54*(7), 493.

Grainger, C., Williams, D. M., & Lind, S. E. (2016). Metacognitive monitoring and control processes in children with autism spectrum disorder: Diminished judgement of confidence accuracy. *Consciousness and Cognition, 42*, 65–74.

Greene, J. D., Hodges, J. R., & Baddeley, A. D. (1995). Autobiographical memory and executive function in early dementia of Alzheimer type. *Neuropsychologia, 33*(12), 1647–1670.

Grynszpan, O., Nadel, J., Martin, J.-C., Simonin, J., Bailleul, P., Wang, Y., … Constant, J. (2012). Self-monitoring of gaze in high functioning autism. *Journal of Autism and Developmental Disorders, 42*(8), 1642–1650.

Häußler, A., Happel, C., Tuckermann, A., Altgassen, M. & Adl-Amini, K. (2003). *SOKO Autismus. Gruppenangebote zur Förderung SOzialer KOmpetenzen bei Menschen mit Autismus* [SOKO autism: A group setting to teach social skills in people with autism]. Dortmund: Verlag Modernes Lernen.

Henry, J. D., Terrett, G., Altgassen, M., Raponi-Saunders, S., Ballhausen, N., Schnitzspahn, K. M., & Rendell, P. G. (2014). A Virtual Week study of prospective memory function in autism spectrum disorders. *Journal of Experimental Child Psychology, 127*, 110–125. doi:10.1016/j.jecp.2014.01.011 Retrieved from <Go to ISI>://WOS:000341554200009.

Hering, A., Cortez, S. A., Kliegel, M., & Altgassen, M. (2014). Revisiting the age-prospective memory-paradox: The role of planning and task experience. *European Journal of Ageing, 11*(1), 99–106.

Hill, E. L. (2004). Evaluating the theory of executive dysfunction in autism. *Developmental Review, 24*(2), 189–233.

Hohwy, J. (2013). *The predictive mind*. Oxford: Oxford University Press.

Howlin, P. (1998). Psychological and educational treatments for autism. *Journal of Child Psychology and Psychiatry, 39*(3), 307–322.

Isenhower, R. W., Marsh, K. L., Richardson, M. J., Helt, M., Schmidt, R., & Fein, D. (2012). Rhythmic bimanual coordination is impaired in young children with autism spectrum disorder. *Research in Autism Spectrum Disorders, 6*(1), 25–31.

Jeste, S. S., & Geschwind, D. H. (2014). Disentangling the heterogeneity of autism spectrum disorder through genetic findings. *Nature Reviews Neurology, 10*(2), 74–81.

Joffily, M., & Coricelli, G. (2013). Emotional valence and the free-energy principle. *PLoS Computational Biology, 9*(6), e1003094.

Kenny, L., Hattersley, C., Molins, B., Buckley, C., Povey, C., & Pellicano, E. (2015). Which terms should be used to describe autism? Perspectives from the UK autism community. *Autism*, 1362361315588200.

Kenworthy, L., Yerys, B. E., Anthony, L. G., & Wallace, G. L. (2008). Understanding executive control in autism spectrum disorders in the lab and in the real world. *Neuropsychology Review, 18*(4), 320–338.

Kiverstein, J., & Miller, M. (2015). The embodied brain: Towards a radical embodied cognitive neuroscience. *Frontiers in Human Neuroscience, 9*, 237.

Kliegel, M., Eschen, A., & Thöne-Otto, A. I. T. (2004). Planning and realization of complex intentions in traumatic brain injury and normal aging. *Brain and Cognition, 56*(1), 43–54. doi:10.1016/j.bandc.2004.05.005. Retrieved from <Go to ISI>://000224313600007

Kliegel, M., Jäger, T., Altgassen, M., & Shum, D. (2008). Clinical neuropsychology of prospective memory. In M. Kliegel, M. A. McDaniel, & G. O. Einstein (Eds.), *Prospective memory: Cognitive, neuroscience, developmental, and applied perspectives* (pp. 283–308). Mahwah, NJ: Lawrence Erlbaum.

Kliegel, M., Martin, M., McDaniel, M. A., & Einstein, G. O. (2002). Complex prospective memory and executive control of working memory: A process model. *Psychological Test and Assessment Modeling, 44*(2), 303.

Kliegel, M., Martin, M., McDaniel, M. A., Einstein, G. O., & Moor, C. (2007). Realizing complex delayed intentions in young and old adults: The role of planning aids. *Memory & Cognition, 35*(7), 1735–1746.

Klin, A., Jones, W., Schultz, R., & Volkmar, F. (2003). The enactive mind, or from actions to cognition: Lessons from autism. *Philosophical Transactions of the Royal Society B: Biological Sciences, 358*(1430), 345–360. Retrieved from <Go to ISI>://WOS:000181286200008

Koch, S. C., Mehl, L., Sobanski, E., Sieber, M., & Fuchs, T. (2014). Fixing the mirrors: A feasibility study of the effects of dance movement therapy on young adults with autism spectrum disorder. *Autism*, 1362361314522353.

Kretschmer, A., Altgassen, M., Rendell, P. G., & Bölte, S. (2014). Prospective memory in adults with high-functioning autism spectrum disorders: Exploring effects of implementation intentions and retrospective memory load. *Research in Developmental Disabilities, 35*(11), 3108–3118.

Kvavilashvili, L., Messer, D. J., & Ebdon, P. (2001). Prospective memory in children: The effects of age and task interruption. *Developmental Psychology, 37*(3), 418.

Landry, R., & Bryson, S. E. (2004). Impaired disengagement of attention in young children with autism. *Journal of Child Psychology and Psychiatry, 45*(6), 1115–1122.

Landsiedel, J., Williams, D. M., & Abbot-Smith, K. (2017). A meta-analysis and critical review of prospective memory in autism spectrum disorder. *Journal of Autism and Developmental Disorders, 47*(3), 646–666.

Lawson, R. P., Rees, G., & Friston, K. J. (2014). An aberrant precision account of autism. *Frontiers in Human Neuroscience, 8*, 302.

Lee, K., Lambert, H., Wittich, W., Kehayia, E., & Park, M. (2016). The use of movement-based interventions with children diagnosed with autism for psychosocial outcomes – A scoping review. *Research in Autism Spectrum Disorders, 24*, 52–67.

Leekam, S. R., & Perner, J. (1991). Does the autistic child have a metarepresentational deficit? *Cognition, 40*(3), 203–218.

Leung, R. C., & Zakzanis, K. K. (2014). Brief report: Cognitive flexibility in autism spectrum disorders: A quantitative review. *Journal of Autism and Developmental Disorders, 44*(10), 2628–2645.

Lind, S. E. (2010). Memory and the self in autism. *Autism, 14*(5), 430–456.

Lind, S. E., & Bowler, D. M. (2010). Episodic memory and episodic future thinking in adults with autism. *Journal of Abnormal Psychology, 119*(4), 896–905.

Lind, S. E., Bowler, D. M., & Raber, J. (2014). Spatial navigation, episodic memory, episodic future thinking, and theory of mind in children with autism spectrum disorder: Evidence for impairments in mental simulation? *Frontiers in Psychology, 5*, 1411.

Lind, S. E., Williams, D. M., Bowler, D. M., & Peel, A. (2014). Episodic memory and episodic future thinking impairments in high-functioning autism spectrum disorder: an underlying difficulty with scene construction or self-projection? *Neuropsychology, 28*(1), 55–67.

Lopez, B. R., Lincoln, A. J., Ozonoff, S., & Lai, Z. (2005). Examining the relationship between executive functions and restricted, repetitive symptoms of autistic disorder. *Journal of Autism and Developmental Disorders, 35*(4), 445–460. Retrieved from <Go to ISI>://000231601200005

Mackinlay, R. J., Charman, T., & Karmiloff-Smith, A. (2006). High-functioning children with autism spectrum disorder: A novel test of multitasking. *Brain and Cognition, 61*(1), 14–24. Retrieved from <Go to ISI>://000238382600003

Mann, T. A., & Walker, P. (2003). Autism and a deficit in broadening the spread of visual attention. *Journal of Child Psychology and Psychiatry, 44*(2), 274–284.

Marsh, R. L., Hicks, J. L., & Watson, V. (2002). The dynamics of intention retrieval and coordination of action in event-based prospective memory. *Journal of Experimental Psychology-Learning Memory and Cognition, 28*(4), 652–659. doi:10.1037//0278-7393.28.4.652. Retrieved from <Go to ISI>://000176490400004

Masi, A., DeMayo, M. M., Glozier, N., & Guastella, A. J. (2017). An overview of autism spectrum disorder, heterogeneity and treatment options. *Neuroscience Bulletin*, 1–11.

McDaniel, M. A., & Einstein, G. O. (2000). Strategic and automatic processes in prospective memory retrieval: A multiprocess framework. *Applied Cognitive Psychology, 14*, S127–S144. doi:10.1002/acp.775. Retrieved from <Go to ISI>://000168094200009

McDaniel, M. A., Umanath, S., Einstein, G. O., & Waldum, E. R. (2015). Dual pathways to prospective remembering. *Frontiers in Human Neuroscience, 9*, 392.

McIntosh, D., Miller, L., Shyu, V., & Dunn, W. (1999). Development and validation of the short sensory profile. *Sensory profile manual*, 59–73.

Mesibov, G. B., & Shea, V. (2010). The TEACCH program in the era of evidence-based practice. *Journal of Autism and Developmental Disorders, 40*(5), 570–579.

Mesibov, G. B., Shea, V., & Schopler, E. (2004). *The TEACCH approach to autism spectrum disorders*. New York, NY: Springer Science & Business Media.

Milosavljevic, B., Carter Leno, V. C., Simonoff, E., Baird, G., Pickles, A., Jones, C. R., … Happé, F. (2016). Alexithymia in adolescents with autism spectrum disorder: Its relationship to internalising difficulties, sensory modulation and social cognition. *Journal of Autism and Developmental Disorders, 46*(4), 1354–1367.

Mioni, G., Rendell, P. G., Henry, J. D., Cantagallo, A., & Stablum, F. (2013). An investigation of prospective memory functions in people with traumatic brain injury using Virtual Week. *Journal of Clinical and Experimental Neuropsychology, 35*(6), 617–630.

Moher, D., Liberati, A., Tetzlaff, J., Altman, D. G., & Group, P. (2009). Preferred reporting items for systematic reviews and meta-analyses: The PRISMA statement. *PLoS Medicine, 6*(7), e1000097.

O'Riordan, M. A., Plaisted, K. C., Driver, J., & Baron-Cohen, S. (2001). Superior visual search in autism. *Journal of Experimental Psychology: Human Perception and Performance, 27*(3), 719.

Ozonoff, S., Cook, I., Coon, H., Dawson, G., Joseph, R. M., Klin, A., … Wrathall, D. (2004). Performance on Cambridge Neuropsychological Test Automated Battery subtests sensitive to frontal lobe function in people with autistic disorder: Evidence from the collaborative programs of excellence in autism network. *Journal of Autism and Developmental Disorders, 34*(2), 139–150. Retrieved from http://www.ncbi.nlm.nih.gov/entrez/query.fcgi?cmd=Retrieve&db=PubMed&dopt=Citation&list_uids=15162933

Palmer, C. J., Lawson, R. P., & Hohwy, J. (2017). Bayesian approaches to autism: Towards volatility, action, and behavior. *Psychological Bulletin, 143*(5), 521.

Panerai, S., Ferrante, L., & Zingale, M. (2002). Benefits of the Treatment and Education of Autistic and Communication Handicapped Children (TEACCH) programme as compared with a non-specific approach. *Journal of Intellectual Disability Research, 46*(4), 318–327.

Pellicano, E., & Burr, D. (2012). When the world becomes 'too real': A Bayesian explanation of autistic perception. *Trends in Cognitive Sciences, 16*(10), 504–510.

Pellicano, E., Kenny, L., Brede, J., Klaric, E., Lichwa, H., & McMillin, R. (2017). Executive function predicts school readiness in autistic andtypical preschool children. *Cognitive Development, 43*, 1–13.

Perner, J., Frith, U., Leslie, A. M., & Leekam, S. R. (1989). Exploration of the autistic child's theory of mind: knowledge, belief, and communication. *Child Development, 60*(3), 688–700.

Pezzulo, G., Rigoli, F., & Friston, K. (2015). Active inference, homeostatic regulation and adaptive behavioural control. *Progress in Neurobiology, 134*, 17–35.

Phillips, L. H., Henry, J. D., & Martin, M. (2008). Adult aging and prospective memory: The importance of ecological validity. In M. Kliegel, M. A. McDaniel, & G. O. Einstein (Eds.), *Prospective memory: Cognitive, neuroscience, developmental, and applied perspectives* (pp. 161–185). Mahwah, NJ: Lawrence Erlbaum.

Posner, M. I., & Rothbart, M. K. (2000). Developing mechanisms of self-regulation. *Development and Psychopathology, 12*(3), 427–441.

Rao, R. P., & Ballard, D. H. (1999). Predictive coding in the visual cortex: A functional interpretation of some extra-classical receptive-field effects. *Nature Neuroscience, 2*(1), 79–87.

Rendell, P. G., & Craik, F. I. (2000). Virtual week and actual week: Age-related differences in prospective memory. *Applied Cognitive Psychology, 14*(7), S43–S62.

Rendell, P. G., & Henry, J. D. (2009). A Review of Virtual Week for Prospective Memory Assessment: Clinical Implications. *Brain Impairment, 10*, 14–22.

Rendell, P. G., Henry, J. D., Phillips, L. H., de la Piedad Garcia, X., Booth, P., Phillips, P., & Kliegel, M. (2012). Prospective memory, emotional valence, and multiple sclerosis. *Journal of Clinical and Experimental Neuropsychology, 34*(7), 738–749.

Robertson, C. E., & Baron-Cohen, S. (2017). Sensory perception in autism. *Nature Reviews. Neuroscience, 18*(11), 671.

Rummel, J., & Meiser, T. (2013). The role of metacognition in prospective memory: Anticipated task demands influence attention allocation strategies. *Consciousness and Cognition, 22*(3), 931–943.

Schopler, E., Reichler, R. J., DeVellis, R. F., & Daly, K. (1980). Toward objective classification of childhood autism: Childhood Autism Rating Scale (CARS). *Journal of Autism and Developmental Disorders, 10*(1), 91–103.

Schultz, R. T. (2005). Developmental deficits in social perception in autism: The role of the amygdala and fusiform face area. *International Journal of Developmental Neuroscience, 23*(2–3), 125–141. Retrieved from <Go to ISI>://WOS:000227943900002

Schwartenbeck, P., & Friston, K. (2016). Computational phenotyping in psychiatry: A worked example. *eneuro, 3*(4), ENEURO. 0049–0016.

Scullin, M. K., McDaniel, M. A., & Shelton, J. T. (2013). The Dynamic Multiprocess Framework: Evidence from prospective memory with contextual variability. *Cognitive Psychology, 67*(1–2), 55–71.

Seth, A. K. (2013). Interoceptive inference, emotion, and the embodied self. *Trends in Cognitive Sciences, 17*(11), 565–573.

Shah, P., Hall, R., Catmur, C., & Bird, G. (2016). Alexithymia, not autism, is associated with impaired interoception. *Cortex, 81*, 215–220.

Sheppard, D. P., Kvavilashvili, L., & Ryder, N. (2016). Event-based prospective memory in mildly and severely autistic children. *Research in Developmental Disabilities, 49–50*, 22–33.

Sheppard, D. P., Terrett, G., Rendell, P. G., & Altgassen, M. (2017). Did you hear? Auditory prospective memory cues benefit autistic children more than non-autistic children. Manuscript submitted for publication.

Sheridan, J., & McAuley, J. D. (1997). Rhythm as a cognitive skill: Temporal processing deficits in autism. *Proceedings of the Fourth Australiasian Cognitive Science Conference*, Newcastle, NSW.

Sinclair, J. (2013). Why I dislike "person first" Language. *Autonomy, The Critical Journal Of Interdisciplinary Autism Studies, 1*(2). Retrieved from http://www.larry-arnold.net/Autonomy/index.php/autonomy/article/view/OP1

Smith, R. E. (2003). The cost of remembering to remember in event-based prospective memory: Investigating the capacity demands of delayed intention performance. *Journal of Experimental Psychology: Learning, Memory, and Cognition, 29*(3), 347–361. Retrieved from http://www.ncbi.nlm.nih.gov/entrez/query.fcgi?cmd=Retrieve&db=PubMed&dopt=Citation&list_uids=12776746

Smith, R. E., & Bayen, U. J. (2004). A multinomial model of event-based prospective memory. *Journal of Experimental Psychology: Learning, Memory, and Cognition, 30*(4), 756–777. Retrieved from http://www.ncbi.nlm.nih.gov/entrez/query.fcgi?cmd=Retrieve&db=PubMed&dopt=Citation&list_uids=15238021

Sperduti, M., Pieron, M., Leboyer, M., & Zalla, T. (2014). Altered pre-reflective sense of agency in autism spectrum disorders as revealed by reduced intentional binding. *Journal of Autism and Developmental Disorders, 44*(2), 343–352.

Stephan, K. E., & Mathys, C. (2014). Computational approaches to psychiatry. *Current Opinion in Neurobiology, 25*, 85–92.

Terrett, G., Rendell, P. G., Raponi-Saunders, S., Henry, J. D., Bailey, P. E., & Altgassen, M. (2013). Episodic future thinking in children with autism spectrum disorder. *Journal of Autism and Develepmental Disorders, 43*(11), 2558–2568.

Tomchek, S. D., & Dunn, W. (2007). Sensory processing in children with and without autism: A comparative study using the short sensory profile. *American Journal of Occupational Therapy, 61*(2), 190–200.

Van de Cruys, S., Evers, K., Van der Hallen, R., Van Eylen, L., Boets, B., de-Wit, L., & Wagemans, J. (2014). Precise minds in uncertain worlds: Predictive coding in autism. *Psychological Review, 121*(4), 649.

Van de Cruys, S., Van der Hallen, R., & Wagemans, J. (2017). Disentangling signal and noise in autism spectrum disorder. *Brain and Cognition, 112*, 78–83.

West, R. (2011). The temporal dynamics of prospective memory: A review of the ERP and prospective memory literature. *Neuropsychologia, 49*(8), 2233–2245. doi:10.1016/j.neuropsychologia.2010.12.028. Retrieved from http://www.ncbi.nlm.nih.gov/pubmed/21187107

West, R., & Krompinger, J. (2005). Neural correlates of prospective and retrospective memory. *Neuropsychologia, 43*(3), 418–433. doi:10.1016/j.neuropsychologia.2004.06.012. Retrieved from <Go to ISI>://000227313700010

Whipple, J. (2004). Music in intervention for children and adolescents with autism: A meta-analysis. *Journal of Music Therapy, 41*(2), 90–106.

Wilkinson, D. A., Best, C. A., Minshew, N. J., & Strauss, M. S. (2010). Memory awareness for faces in individuals with autism. *Journal of Autism and Developmental Disorders, 40*(11), 1371–1377.

Williams, D., Boucher, J., Lind, S., & Jarrold, C. (2013). Time-based and event-based prospective memory in autism spectrum disorder: The roles of executive function and theory of mind, and time-estimation. *Journal of Autism and Developmental Disorders, 43*, 1555–1567. doi:10.1007/s10803-012-1703-9. Retrieved from http://www.ncbi.nlm.nih.gov/pubmed/23179340

Williams, D., Jarrold, C., Grainger, C., & Lind, S. (2014). Diminished time-based, but undiminished event-based, prospective memory among intellectually high-functioning adults with autism spectrum disorder: Relation to working memory ability. *Neuropsychology, 28*(1), 30.

Wojcik, D. Z., Allen, R. J., Brown, C., & Souchay, C. (2011). Memory for actions in autism spectrum disorder. *Memory, 19*(6), 549–558.

Yi, L., Fan, Y., Joseph, L., Huang, D., Wang, X., Li, J., & Zou, X. (2014). Event-based prospective memory in children with autism spectrum disorder: The role of executive function. *Research in Autism Spectrum Disorders, 8*(6), 654–660.

Zalla, T., Miele, D., Leboyer, M., & Metcalfe, J. (2015). Metacognition of agency and theory of mind in adults with high functioning autism. *Consciousness and Cognition, 31*, 126–138.

Prospective memory in children with attention deficit hyperactivity disorder: a review

Karley-Dale S. Talbot, Ulrich Müller and Kimberly A. Kerns

ABSTRACT

Objective: The objective of the paper is to synthesize the research on prospective memory (PM) in children with attention-deficit/hyperactivity disorder (ADHD). **Method:** Research on PM and ADHD in youth was synthesized according to the PRISMA guidelines and a summary of the types of PM deficits typically seen in these children, as well as the methods currently available to assess and treat these deficits is provided. Suggestions on ways to better manage PM deficits in children's everyday lives are also discussed. **Results:** Six studies have investigated PM in children with ADHD. The majority of these studies found a deficit in time-based PM, but not event-based PM. The mechanisms underlying this deficit, however, are still unknown. There are currently no specific measures available to clinically assess PM in children and there are no specific evidence-based interventions available that specifically target PM deficits in children with ADHD. **Conclusion:** Remediation strategies aimed at compensating for these PM deficits in daily life may be most useful. Nevertheless, more research is necessary to better understand PM in children with ADHD.

Introduction

Prospective memory (PM) refers to one's ability to remember to do something at some point in the future. In adults, intact PM abilities are required to remember to pay bills on time or take blood pressure medication after breakfast. Similarly, intact PM abilities in children enable them to remember to hand in their homework on time or to bring their soccer cleats to practice. Across the lifespan humans rely on PM to carry out both mundane and essential daily tasks. As such, any disruptions in this ability can have severe consequences for a person's capacity to adaptively function in his or her everyday life (Shum, Cross, Ford, & Ownsworth, 2008). In fact, errors in PM have been found to account for 50–80% of all everyday memory failures in typically developing adults and are associated with initial doctor consults in those experiencing Subjective Cognitive Decline (Camp, Foss, Stevens, & O'Hanlan, 1996; Kvavilashvili, Messer, & Ebdon, 2001; Terry, 1988). Given the importance of PM for everyday functioning, researchers have become interested in uncovering its underlying mechanisms.

Current research suggests that successful PM performance is partially dependent on intact executive functions (EFs). EFs are cognitive processes that are required for the conscious, top-down control of action, thought, and emotions, and are associated with neural systems involving the prefrontal cortex (PFC; see Zelazo & Müller, 2010). A population of individuals that have consistently been found to exhibit difficulties with EFs are those with a diagnosis of Attention-Deficit/Hyperactivity Disorder (ADHD; Bahçivan, Ayvaşik, & Alyanak, 2015; Nigg, Blaskey, Huang-Pollock, & Rappley, 2002; Willcutt, Doyle, Nigg, Farone, & Pennington, 2005). Given the relationships between (a) PM and EFs, and (b) EFs and ADHD, it is reasonable to expect that individuals with ADHD might also demonstrate deficits in PM. PM and EF deficits have both been associated with academic, occupational, and interpersonal difficulties as well as an overall decreased quality of life (Biederman et al., 2004; Cuttler, Relkov, & Taylor, 2014; Graf, 2012; Nigg et al., 2002; Shum et al., 2008; Uekermann et al., 2010). Therefore, it is important to obtain a better understanding of the PM deficits in children with ADHD to inform intervention efforts and, in so doing, help to improve overall functioning earlier on in development. Thus, the purpose of this paper is to review the literature available on PM in children with ADHD, outline the specific PM deficits associated with this disorder, and explain how they might manifest in everyday life. Clinical assessment measures and evidence-based treatments and interventions to evaluate and improve PM abilities in children with ADHD will also be summarized. Finally, suggestions on how best to manage PM deficits in individuals with ADHD will be provided.

Models of prospective memory

Memory is not a unitary system. Rather, different memory types and processes have been distinguished (Schacter, Gilbert, & Wegner, 2010). For the purposes of the present paper, the distinction between PM and retrospective memory (RM) is relevant. PM in general differs from RM in that it is a memory for (1) something which must be done in the future and (2) *when* it must be completed, vs. a memory for an event or information about something that has already occurred (e.g. often incorporated in terms such as semantic, episodic, or procedural memory). Experimental PM tasks share the following three components: (1) a delay between the formation of an intention and its performance, (2) a lack of an explicit reminder to perform the intention, and (3) a need to disrupt an ongoing task in order to perform the intended action (Ellis, 1996; Rendell, Vella, Kliegel, & Terrett, 2009). These components of a PM task are thought to ensure ecological validity of the task as it is argued they mimic demands of ongoing activities in daily life (Einstein & McDaniel, 1990; Mahy, Moses, & Kliegel, 2014).

According to Ellis (1996), there are five general phases in the successful execution of PM: (1) formation and encoding, (2) a retention interval, (3) a performance interval, (4) initiation and execution of the intended action, and (5) evaluation of the outcome. Phase 1 is acknowledged as the RM component of a PM task as it involves long-term storage of an intention that requires the use of encoding. Consequently, phases 2–5 constitute the prospective component. In the first phase, the focus is on forming an intention, retaining the action, and encoding the retrieval context. Put more simply, the first phase involves deciding what one wants to do and in what context one wants to do it. The second and third phases refer to the delay between encoding and retrieval and the point when the intended action should be retrieved, respectively. It is important to note that the retention and performance interval durations may vary considerably and that an associated memory for action can be retrieved at any point during these two phases. That being said, for one to successfully perform PM, one must remember the intention (which was encoded in phase 1) at the appropriate time (appropriate retrieval context). At this point, phases 4 and 5 can take place, completing the action. According to Einstein and McDaniel (2005), the successful execution of a PM task relies variably on three distinct, yet concurrent cognitive processes: PM, RM, and EF. According to Ellis (1996), the PM component of the model includes remembering the memory for action at the appropriate moment without the explicit external prompt (e.g. being told). In contrast, the retrospective component encompasses the recollection of the specific action to be performed once the prospective intention to act has been retrieved.

To date, behavioral, electrophysiological, and neuroimaging studies have provided evidence for a moderate association between EFs and PM in children and adults, suggesting that EF plays an important role in PM execution across the lifespan (Burgess, Gonen-Yaacovi, & Volle, 2010; Deouell & Knight, 2009; Mahy et al., 2014; West, 2010). These findings, in addition to evidence demonstrating age-related improvements in children's PM functioning analogous to, as well as correlated with, those observed in EFs (Kerns, 2000; Kerns & Price, 2001; Mackinlay, Kliegel, & Mäntylä, 2009; Rendell et al., 2009; Shum et al., 2008; Talbot & Kerns, 2014; Wang, Kliegel, Liu, & Yang, 2008; Zinke et al., 2010), led Mahy and colleagues (2014) to propose a model of PM development grounded in the development of EFs. Based on a review of the literature on PM in children, these researchers conceptualized PM as relying on associative processes involved in RM for the intentions (e.g. memory for the content of the intention), but also on executive processes involved in carrying out the prospective intention at the appropriate time while engaged in a distracting ongoing task. The aim of their executive framework model was to delineate specific EFs as important for specific phases of PM. For example, Mahy and colleagues (2014) proposed that working memory, inhibition, set-shifting, and monitoring were the specific EFs involved in PM execution. Specifically, they suggested that working memory is responsible for keeping the intention activated, inhibition is involved in interrupting the ongoing task, set-shifting is required to switch back and forth between the ongoing task and the PM task, and monitoring – both internal (mind-monitoring; e.g. refreshing the prospective intention) and external (e.g. detecting the prospective cue) – is involved in the identification of the appropriate time to respond.

In addition to identifying the EFs involved in PM, Mahy and colleagues (2014) made three key predictions about when such EFs would be especially important to PM development. Firstly, their model predicts that a certain level of EF is necessary (beyond RM) for the successful execution of a PM task. This suggests that individuals who have underdeveloped EF abilities will be more likely to display deficits in PM irrespective of intact RM abilities. As individuals with ADHD demonstrate underdeveloped EF abilities, it can be hypothesized that they, too, would be more likely to display such PM deficits. Secondly, their model predicts that the development of PM lags behind that of EF development, suggesting that improvements in PM should follow improvements in EF. Thirdly, the model predicts that errors in PM relate to the developmental trajectories of specific EFs, suggesting that older children's PM errors are more likely to be attributed to later developing EFs, like set-shifting, rather than to earlier developing EFs such as working memory.

Subtypes of prospective memory

Although alternate forms of PM have been defined in the literature, developmental researchers have predominately focused on two subtypes – event-based and time-based. These are differentiated based on the context in which the memory for action is initiated (Ellis, 1996). Event-based PM refers to a memory for action in response to a physical external cue (e.g. remembering to relay a message after seeing a friend), whereas time-based PM refers to a memory for action that occurs at a specific time or after a specific time period has elapsed (e.g. calling a friend back after lunch or at 2 pm). Whereas event-based PM is triggered by an observable cue (e.g. the friend), time-based PM arguably relies more heavily on the higher-order EFs and requires self-initiated monitoring or retrieval processes as well as self-initiated interruption (of a potentially more appealing ongoing activity) for its successful execution. Consequently, time-based PM is believed to be more difficult to successfully execute than event-based PM (Einstein & McDaniel, 1996; Kliegel, Ropeter, & Mackinlay, 2006; Yang, Chan, & Shum, 2011). For example, if the time-based PM task is to call a friend back at 2 pm, in order for the task to be successfully executed, the individual would have to maintain the intention in memory, monitor the time (either externally via a clock or internally using time estimation processes) to ensure that he does not miss the appropriate time at which to respond (e.g. 2 pm), and successfully disengage from the ongoing activity to perform the intended action (e.g. call the friend). However, if the event-based task is to relay a message to a colleague in person, an individual need not continuously monitor the time, he need only be minimally aware of his environment. Upon identifying the friend, the memory would be automatically triggered, and then he must only execute the task to ensure successful completion of the PM process.

Consistent with theories proposing that event- and time-based PM differ in terms of the extent to which they rely on EFs, a neuroimaging study conducted by Gonneaud and colleagues (Gonneaud, Rauchs, Groussard, Landeau, et al., 2014) found differential activation across PM subtypes, suggesting underlying differences in strategic monitoring. In particular, the authors found the occipital areas to be more activated during event-based PM. In contrast, they found a network comprising of the dorsolateral prefrontal cortex (PFC), the cuneus/precuneus, and, to a lesser extent, the inferior parietal lobule, superior temporal gyrus, and the cerebellum to be more activated in time-based PM. According to Gonneaud and colleagues, these findings demonstrate that individuals allocate their attentional resources differently depending on the PM subtype being investigated. In particular, the activation of the occipital areas is argued to facilitate external target monitoring of an event-based cue. In contrast, the dorsolateral PFC network activation may reflect the involvement of time estimation processes required for successful execution of time-based PM. Taken together, the findings suggest that event- and time-based PM engage different mechanisms likely reflecting monitoring strategies and brain systems specific to each subtype, providing support for the notion of distinct PM subtypes.

ADHD symptoms relating to PM deficits

Attention-Deficit/Hyperactivity Disorder (ADHD) is a neurodevelopmental disorder characterized by persistent and pervasive difficulties with attention and/or hyperactivity-impulsivity (DSM-5, American Psychiatric Association, 2013). According to the fifth edition of the

Diagnostic and Statistical Manual, a diagnosis of ADHD can be subdivided into three presentations – primarily inattentive, primarily hyperactive-impulsive, or combined – depending on the prevalence of the core symptoms in the individual's presentation (American Psychiatric Association, 2013). It is estimated that approximately 5% of children in the United States of America are diagnosed with some form of ADHD (American Psychiatric Association, 2013). Although it is usually diagnosed in childhood, it may persist through adolescence and continue into adulthood in up to 65% of all cases diagnosed (Kessler, Adler, Barkley, et al., 2005). Children with ADHD are also likely to experience symptoms associated with a variety of comorbid disorders (i.e. anxiety, oppositional defiant, or learning) (American Psychiatric Association, 2013; Biederman, 2005; Tarver, Daley, & Sayal, 2014).

In addition to the primary symptoms of inattention and/or hyperactivity-impulsivity, children with ADHD experience impairment in a range of developmental, cognitive, emotional, social, and academic domains (Diamantopoulou, Rydell, Thorell, & Bohlin, 2007; Uekermann et al., 2010; Sjöwall, Roth, Lindqvist, & Thorell, 2013; Tarver et al., 2014; Wehmeier, Schacht, & Barkley, 2010). For example, children with ADHD have been found to have difficulties with many cognitive abilities reliant upon frontal brain systems such as: EFs, emotion regulation, motivation, social cognition, and prospective memory (Bahçivan et al., 2015; Barkley, 2006; Forslund, Brocki, Bohlin, Granqvist, & Eninger, 2016; Sjöwall, Backman, & Thorell, 2015; Talbot & Kerns, 2014; Tarver et al., 2014; Tomasi & Volkov, 2012). Consequently, children with ADHD often experience a range of social, interpersonal, and academic problems (Barkley, 2006; Diamantopoulou et al., 2007; Nijmeijer et al., 2008; Peasgood, Bhardwaj, Biggs, & Sonuga-Barke, 2016; Sibley, Evans, & Serpell, 2010).

Consistent with prominent theories of ADHD put forth by Barkley (1997) and Sonuga-Barke (2002), children with ADHD have consistently been shown to display deficits in various aspects of EFs, as well as processes closely related to EFs. Specifically, they have been found to exhibit impairments in working memory, inhibition, time estimation, planning, organization, self-monitoring, self-regulation, and task-switching relative to their age- and IQ-matched typically developing peers (Bahçivan et al., 2015; Brocki, Eninger, Thorell, & Bohlin, 2010; Holmes et al., 2014; McInerney & Kerns, 2003; Shaw, Stringaris, Nigg, & Leibenluft, 2014; Sjöwall et al., 2013; Talbot & Kerns, 2014; Walg, Oepen, & Prior, 2012). As a consequence, children with ADHD often:

(1) Have difficulty attending to, and keeping in mind information that they need to manipulate in some way (e.g. mental arithmetic, task instructions).
(2) Struggle to inhibit their responses, often acting before thinking (e.g. call out in class or interrupt others).
(3) Lose track of time and/or misperceive how much time they have left to complete tasks (e.g. have difficulty completing tasks quickly).
(4) Plan impulsively, resulting in poorly organized work (e.g. disjointed sentences in a hand-written composition).
(5) Get upset easily and have difficulty re-regulating afterwards.
(6) Struggle to quickly switch their attention between tasks, making multi-tasking quite difficult. This is especially difficult if they are required to switch from a highly motivating task to another, less interesting one (e.g. free time to reading).

Consequently, the EF deficits observed in children with ADHD put them at a high risk for significant impairments in academic and interpersonal functioning (Biederman et al., 2004; Nigg et al., 2002; Sjöwall et al., 2013).

Another prominent feature of ADHD is a disruption of the reward-motivational pathways in the brain (Tarver et al., 2014; Ma, van Duijvenvoorde, & Scheres, 2016; van Hulst et al., 2017). According to Luman, Ooosterlaan, and Sergeant (2005), this disruption has been found to be associated with an aberrant sensitivity to reinforcement, including reward, punishment, and reinforcement schedules (e.g. alterations in reinforcement frequency and/or delay in administration). This means that relative to their typically developing peers, children with ADHD require more powerful and frequent reinforcement to optimally perform especially mundane or difficult tasks (e.g. chores or homework), reflective of an elevated reward threshold (Haenlein & Caul, 1987). Additionally, these children will more often choose an immediate reward irrespective of (a) previous feedback or (b) whether the delayed reward is larger/better (Luman et al., 2005; Sonuga-Barke, Sergeant, Nigg, & Willcutt, 2008). It has also been proposed that children with ADHD have a diminished sensitivity to punishment, suggesting that they are less likely to alter their behavior based on an increased likelihood of punishment (Luman et al., 2005; Quay, 1997). Taken together, it seems plausible that disrupted motivational-reward systems may contribute to the pathophysiology of ADHD.

Neuropathology of ADHD

Delayed development of EFs and disrupted reward-motivational networks are hypothesized to play a significant role in the pathophysiology of ADHD (Barkley, 1997; El Sayed, Larsson, Persson, Santosh, & Rydelius, 2003; Keune, Wiedemann, Schneidt, & Schönenberg, 2015; Ma et al., 2016; Rubia, 2007; Sonuga-Barke, 2002; Sjöwall et al., 2013; Tomasi & Volkov, 2012). This hypothesis has been supported by several neuroimaging studies using functional magnetic resonance imaging (*f*MRI) and diffusion tensor imaging (DTI) (Cortese et al., 2012; van Ewijk, Heslenfeld, Zwiers, Buitelaar, & Oosterlaan, 2012). Recent research suggests that abnormal interactions between large-scale brain networks play a major role in the pathophysiology of ADHD. For example, studies involving individuals with ADHD have found evidence of atypical functional connections within the Default Mode Network (DMN) and between the DMN and other networks, independent of developmental stage (Fair et al., 2009, 2010; Posner, Park, & Wang, 2014; Tomasi & Volkov, 2012). The DMN consists of a set of brain regions (i.e. precuneus/posterior cingulate cortex, the medial prefrontal cortex, and the lateral and inferior parietal cortex; Fox et al., 2005) associated with wakeful rest and internal activities such as daydreaming (Buckner, Andrews-Hanna, & Schacter, 2008). When a person shifts attention from internal activities to external events, the DMN becomes deactivated, with stronger deactivation correlated with heavier attentional demands (Buckner et al., 2008). Failure to deactivate the DMN results in poorer performance on measures of inhibition (Li, Yan, Bergquisdt, & Sinha, 2007), suggesting that 'inappropriate persistence of DMN activity may interfere with sustained attention, particularly on attentionally demanding tasks' (Posner et al., 2014, p. 7). Studies investigating the role of the DMN in ADHD generally show reduced functional connectivity within DMN and weaker or absent negative correlations between the DMN and the cognitive control network (i.e. dorsal anterior cingulate cortex, supplementary motor area, dorsolateral prefrontal cortex, inferior frontal junction, anterior insular cortex, and posterior parietal cortex (Posner et al., 2014). This decreased correlation is consistent with the failure to suppress DMN activity during cognitive control, which has been hypothesized to account for several of the EF deficits typically observed in this population (Posner et al., 2014).

Consistent with structural and functional imaging findings, several DTI studies have found alterations in white matter microstructure integrity in widespread areas in the brain including the fronto-striatal-cerebellar neurocircuit (Hong et al., 2014). However, a systematic review of ADHD using DTI found the microstructural connection disturbances to be most consistently demonstrated in the right anterior corona radiata, right forceps minor, bilateral internal capsule, and left cerebellum – structures previously implicated in the pathophysiology of ADHD (van Ewijk et al., 2012). While disruptions in microstructural connectivity, especially in the DMN, may play a role in the pathophysiology of ADHD, it is unlikely that this accounts for all the observed differences between individuals with and without ADHD (van Ewijk et al., 2012). It is more likely these differences are due to a complex interaction between the underlying neural substrates and the brain networks (Fair et al., 2009).

Other resting state functional connectivity MRI have implicated cognitive (involving dorsolateral prefrontal cortex) and limbic (involving orbitofrontal and anterior cingulate) cortico-striato-thalamo-cortical (CSTC) loops in ADHD (for a review, see Posner et al., 2014).

Given the delays in EFs that have been documented for children with ADHD, it would be expected, following the framework by Mahy and colleagues (2014), that children with ADHD will also exhibit PM difficulties. Like their EF difficulties, problems with PM can also lead to academic and social difficulties. Indeed, at school, children with ADHD appear to exhibit difficulties with PM such as forgetting to complete their assignments on time and/or to hand them in altogether. They may also forget to attend after/before school meetings/events for extracurricular activities (e.g. choir or track and field). At home, these children may forget to do their chores or to pass on phone messages/notes to their parents. In the social domain, PM deficits of children with ADHD may manifest as forgetting to call a friend back as they had promised or forgetting to return an item they borrowed. Thus, individuals with PM difficulties may be characterized as 'unreliable' and 'unmotivated', further highlighting the negative impact on academics and interpersonal relationships these difficulties can have for children (Graf, 2012).

Deficits in EFs in children with ADHD would explain a number of EF- and PM- related symptoms such as inattention, hyperactivity-impulsivity, and impairments in working memory, inhibition, time estimation, and time- and event-based PM. This makes it extremely difficult to determine whether children with ADHD exhibit a true deficit in PM or if the deficit is a further manifestation of dysfunction of core EF components. Likewise, the role of motivation, the predominant symptom presentation of the disorder, and/or the presence of comorbid disorders may make it difficult to ascertain the real source of the deficit. Nevertheless, PM difficulties are associated with negative outcomes and reduced quality of life for the child and should be addressed with intervention as soon as possible.

Current knowledge of prospective memory deficits in children with ADHD

In this section, PM difficulties in children with ADHD will be reviewed. The review will be organized by PM subtype (event-based, time-based) as previous research has found that children with ADHD show differential impairments on these subtypes.

Methods

Search strategy

A systematic review was conducted, following the recommendations outlined in the PRISMA guidelines (Moher, Liberati, Tetzlaff, & Altman, 2009). A literature search was done using the PsycINFO database to identify the relevant studies (January 1987 to July 2017) investigating prospective memory (event- or time-based) in children with ADHD using the Boolean/Phrase search (see automated search protocol below). Literature was selected from the past 30 years as comprehensive reviews have not yet been done with this population.

The initial search strategy aimed to identify all the empirical literature exploring event or time-based prospective memory performance in children with ADHD. Prospective memory performance in children with a diagnosis of ADHD were identified and then summarized.

Inclusion criteria

Given the scarcity of papers investigating the domain of prospective memory in children with ADHD, a liberal approach to the inclusion of relevant articles in these domains was adopted. Studies included in the systematic review were selected from the initial pool if they met the following criteria: (a) included either an event-based or time-based PM outcome measure, (b) included a non-ADHD control or comparison group, (c) provided adequate information in terms of results and description of study (i.e. means, standard deviations[*SD*s], *t*-test or *F*-test, and *n*-values), and (d) provided separate data on participants with ADHD if the study sample was a mixed population. Studies from all countries of origin were considered, but non-English publications were excluded in this review. Only studies published in peer-reviewed journals were selected. The following data were extracted: study population characteristics, prospective memory subtype, operationalization and assessment of theory constructs, and study outcomes.

Participants included in the systematic review were children, aged 6–13 years, with a primary diagnosis of ADHD-C, ADHD-PI, or ADHD-PH and studies that used recognized diagnostic criteria. Only studies that included some type of event-based or time-based PM measure were included. A total of nine studies were initially yielded from the search protocol. Three of these studies were excluded (one study [Lewis, Thomas, Molteno, Kliegel, et al., 2016] was excluded because it focused on children with Fetal Alcohol Syndrome and not on children with ADHD, the other two studies [Alexander, Noyes, MacBrayer, et al., 1998; Chapieski, Evankovich, Hiscock, & Collins, 2011] were excluded because they did not target prospective memory). Upon removal of all articles that did not meet inclusion criteria, a final sample of six studies was tabulated (See Figure. 1).

Automated search protocol

(('prospective memory' OR 'event-based prospective memory' OR 'time-based prospective memory').

AND ('Attention-Deficit/Hyperactivity Disorder*' OR 'Attention Deficit Hyperactivity Disorder*' OR 'ADHD*' OR 'AD/HD*' OR 'ADD' OR 'Attention Deficit Disorder*' OR 'ADHD-*' OR 'predominantly inattenti*' OR 'predominantly hyperacti*' OR 'combined*').

AND ('child' OR 'child*' OR 'adolescen*' OR 'school-age*' OR 'youth' OR 'minor*'))

PsycINFO search limits

- Population Group: Human;
- Language: English;
- Age Groups: Childhood (birth – 12 yrs); Adolescence (13–17 yrs).

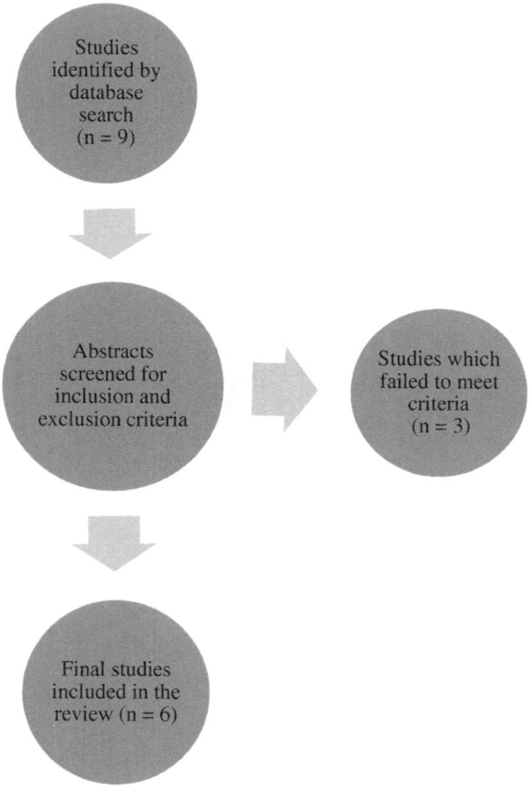

Figure 1. Flow chart of the review process.

Results

A total of six out of the nine studies found met inclusion criteria. A list of these studies and their characteristics are detailed in Table 1. The included studies were diverse in their methodologies and included both event- and/or time-based PM outcome measures. Four studies evaluated event-based PM and four studies evaluated time-based PM. Additionally, three studies evaluated only event-based PM, three studies only time-based PM, two studies both time- and event-based PM, but not in the same paradigm, and one study time- and event-based in the same paradigm.

Table 1. Study characteristics and main results of the studies on prospective memory in.

Authors	ADHD presentation type (*N*)	ADHD sample size (% Male)	ADHD mean age (*SD*)	Control sample size (% Male)	Control mean age (*SD*)	PM[a] test	PM sub-type	Ongoing task	Results
Kerns and Price (2001)	Mixed, not specified	Exp.[b] 1: *N* = 10 (70)	Exp. 1: 10.5 (2.0)	Exp. 1: *N* = 10 (70)	Exp. 1: 10.5 (1.8)	Experimental	Event-based and time-based	Other measures (EB)	TBPM[c] deficit only compared to controls independent of attention difficulties
		Exp. 2: *N* = 21 (76)	Exp. 2: 9.4 (1.8)	Exp. 2: *N* = 21 (76)	Exp. 2: 9.3 (1.8)			*CyberCruiser* (TB)	
Kliegel et al. (2006)	ADHD-C	*N* = 20 (100)	8.8 (.48)	*N* = 20 (100)	8.9 (.48)	Experimental	Event-based and activity-based	HEXE[d]	No EBPM[e] deficits, but was at the expense of ongoing task performance
Zinke et al. (2010)	ADHD-PI (10) ADHD-C (12)	*N* = 22 (82)	9.8 (.89)	*N* = 39 (64)	9.73 (.74)	Experimental	Time-based	1-back picture task	TBPM deficit independent of ongoing task difficulty or frequency or accuracy of time monitoring
Brandimonte et al. (2011)	Mixed, not specified	*N* = 30 (93)	8.34 (1.62)	*N* = 30 (93)	8.17 (1.39)	Experimental	Event-based	Categorization task	No EBPM deficits despite difficulties with inhibition
Talbot and Kerns (2014)	ADHD-C	*N* = 36 (75)	10.86 (1.52)	*N* = 33 (49)	10.89 (1.76)	Experimental PRMQC[f]	Event-based and time-based	*Super Little Fisherman* (EB)	EB and TBPM deficits.
								CyberCruiser-II (TB)	TBPM deficit independent of time reproduction ability. ADHD symptom severity and PRMQC scores related to TB, but not EBPM
Mioni et al. (2017)	Mixed, not specified	*N* = 23 (79)	10.89 (1.04)	*N* = 23 (70)	10.89 (.91)	Experimental	Time-based	Cartoon watching	TBPM deficit. TBPM related to time perception in controls only

[a]Prospective Memory.
[b]Experiment.
[c]Time-based Prospective Memory.
[d]'Heidelberger Exekutivfunktionsdiagnostikum' a diagnostic test of executive function (Kliegel & Martin, 2002).
[e]Event-based Prospective Memory.
[f]Prospective Retrospective Memory Questionnaire for Children.

Event-based PM in ADHD

An early study of PM in children (8 to 13 years old) with ADHD investigated both event-based and time-based PM (Kerns & Price, 2001) and found that performance across PM subtypes differed such that the children with ADHD performed similarly to age-, gender-, and IQ-matched controls on the event-based PM task, but differed from controls on the time-based PM task. On the event-based tasks, children were given a simple set of instructions of what to do when a cue was given. For example, for one event-based task children were required to remember to stand up, walk to the door, and turn the doorknob whenever the experimenter snapped his/her fingers. Four event-based tasks were used in total (with a 40-min lag between the instructions and the cue, while the other two had a 20-min lag), consistent with the lab-based PM task paradigm proposed by Einstein and McDaniel (1990). Each event-based PM task was scored out of 2, with a score of 1 being awarded if the participant remembered that s/he was to perform an action, yet could not remember what the action was (e.g. loss of content).

Similar to the findings of Kerns and Price (2001), Brandimonte and colleagues (2011) found that 6- to 13-year-old children with ADHD performed similarly to controls on their event-based PM task. Brandimonte and colleagues (2011) asked children with and without ADHD to complete a computerized categorization task (ongoing task) which required them to identify to which category a simple line drawing belonged (e.g. animal/food or clothing/furniture). Participants made category choices by pressing a specific colored key (red/green) on the keyboard. While completing the ongoing task, children were also asked to remember to press a different key whenever they saw a target picture (e.g. a specific animal). The target picture was presented four times over the course of the ongoing task and performance was measured by the number of correctly completed PM tasks (out of 4). Unlike Kerns and Price (2001), Brandimonte and colleagues (2011) could compare the two groups based on their performance on the ongoing task. They found that children with ADHD performed the categorization task equally as fast as controls; however, they made more errors when responding.

The third and final study investigating event-based PM in children with ADHD was conducted by Talbot and Kerns (2014) using the *Super Little Fisherman* task. In this event-based PM paradigm, children between the ages of 8 and 13 years were asked to catch as many fish as possible by extending their fishing line by pressing and holding the mouse button. When a fish swam by, the child would release the mouse button to draw the fishing line up and catch the fish. Before beginning the ongoing task, participants were provided with the event-based PM task instructions. They were told to remember to click on the cat (who was in the boat with the fisherman) whenever they saw a specific target fish on the screen (angel fish; event-based PM cue). Unlike previous studies, Talbot and Kerns (2014) found that relative to controls, children in the ADHD group performed significantly worse on the event-based PM task irrespective of their ongoing task performance.

Time-based PM in ADHD

Time-based PM performance in children with ADHD has been measured using a variety of different task paradigms, yet all the studies to-date have found similar results. E.g. Kerns and Price (2001) found that children with ADHD performed significantly worse on a time-based

PM task than controls. To measure time-based PM performance, Kerns and Price (2001) used a novel measure of time-based PM called the CyberCruiser (Kerns, 2000). The CyberCruiser task was designed to be both naturalistic and engaging by mimicking a video game in which children (8 to 13 year olds) were required to drive their car along a road and maneuver around other traffic and occasional hazards to gain points (ongoing task) using a joystick. In addition to the ongoing task, children were required to remember to monitor the amount of fuel in their car and refuel (PM task) only when the gas gage was within the red area (indicating it was less than one fourth full). The children could check their fuel level by pressing an additional button at any time during the task, but could only fill the tank in the interval between 50 and 60 s after each fill.

In addition, they found that the severity of ADHD symptoms (e.g. hyperactivity) on a parent-report measure of ADHD symptomatology (Conner's) was significantly related to time-based PM difficulties. Specifically, children with higher parent-reported levels of hyperactivity were also more likely to make time-based PM errors. Performance on a measure of sustained attention (Continuous Performance Test) was also related to difficulties with time-based PM. However, difficulties with sustained attention were not sufficient to fully account for the time-based PM deficits in the children with ADHD.

Although the CyberCruiser appears to be a more ecologically valid measure of time-based PM that children enjoyed and engaged in, the task is not without its limitations. The paradigm was criticized by Zinke and colleagues (2010) for not considering the participants' performance on the ongoing task (e.g. driving the car and avoiding obstacles). Zinke and colleagues (2010) argued that the time-based PM deficits in children with ADHD relative to controls observed in the Kerns and Price (2001) study might be better explained by difficulties with the ongoing task.

To address these concerns, Zinke and colleagues (2010) investigated the role of ongoing task difficulty and time-monitoring in time-based PM performance in 8- to 10-year-olds with and without ADHD. Unlike Kerns and Price (2001), Zinke and colleagues (2010) used a more traditional paradigm to measure time-based PM. They embedded their PM task into a computerized, 10-min, one-back visual working memory test (ongoing task). During the ongoing task, children were asked to remember to press a key on the keyboard every two minutes (±1 s; time-based PM task). Similar to previous studies, participants could monitor the passage of time via digital clock timer by pressing the spacebar on the keyboard. Consistent with other research, Zinke and colleagues (2010) found their ADHD group to perform worse than controls on the time-based PM task. In addition, they also found that neither ongoing task difficulty (as measured by accuracy and reaction time) nor overall frequency of clock checks (time-monitoring) differed between the two groups.

Similar to Zinke and colleagues (2010), Talbot and Kerns (2014) also investigated the role of ongoing task difficulty on time-based PM performance in children aged 7–13 years old. Talbot and Kerns (2014) developed an adapted version of the original CyberCruiser, the CyberCruiser-II. In this task, children were asked to fly a spaceship through space and avoid obstacles to earn points. Similar to the CyberCruiser, the CyberCruiser-II required children to monitor their fuel gage (by pressing a button) and fill their tank when the needle on the gage was in the red area (providing a 10-s response window). The main difference between the two tasks, however, was that the CyberCruiser-II paradigm included an ongoing task-only phase of game play which allowed the researchers to investigate the relationship between ongoing task performance and PM difficulties across the groups. Consistent with Zinke and colleagues' (2010) findings, Talbot and Kerns (2014) found that time-based PM deficits in children with ADHD remained even after controlling for ongoing task performance.

The most recent, study of time-based PM in children with ADHD was conducted by Mioni and colleagues (2017). Like Mioni and colleagues (2017), Talbot and Kerns (2014) investigated the role of time perception on time-based PM functioning in children (mean age 10.89 years) with and without ADHD. In the time-based PM task, children were asked to closely watch an 11-min cartoon (ongoing task) while also remembering to press a button every 2-min (PM task). Like Talbot and Kerns (2014) and Zinke and colleagues (2010), Mioni and colleagues' task required children to monitor the timer which was observable for two-second increments by clicking another button on the keyboard. Consistent with all other time-based studies, Mioni and colleagues found time-based PM deficits in children with ADHD relative to controls irrespective of ongoing task difficulty. However, unlike Talbot and Kerns (2014), Mioni and colleagues found a relationship between time perception and PM performance, though this was only observed in the control group. Based on their findings, the researchers suggested that children with ADHD are less able to use their cognitive resources in an efficient manner when performing complex tasks (i.e. a PM dual-task paradigm).

Combined event- and time-based PM in ADHD

To-date there has only been one study investigating both event- and time-based PM performance in children with ADHD within the same task paradigm. This study, conducted by Kliegel and colleagues (2006), was aimed at investigating PM performance in a more ecologically valid way by having participants complete both event- and time-based PM tasks during a multi-tasking task and within a limited time frame. Kliegel and colleagues (2006) developed a modified version of the Six Elements Test, which they called the 'HEXE' (ongoing task). In this computerized task, children were asked to remember to engage in four different sub-tasks within a 2-min time frame (represented by a visual timer that was constantly in view on the top of the computer screen; time-based PM task) according to a set of rules. In addition, the participants were required to remember to initiate playing the HEXE game after they completed a prior task (event-based PM task). Successful performance of each PM task was recorded as well as whether the participants engaged in an optimal sequence (i.e. starting the task with only one item of each subtask), violated any rules, and followed their initial plan. Ongoing task performance was also evaluated (number and accuracy of attempted items in the HEXE sub-tasks).

Findings from the HEXE study showed that children with ADHD were able to perform as well as controls at self-initiated switching (time and event-based PM tasks) and optimal sequence performance. However, similar to findings obtained by Brandimonte and colleagues (2011), children with ADHD tended to make more errors on the sub-task items than controls, further suggesting that better PM performance comes at the expense of ongoing task performance. Additionally, findings indicated that the formation and delayed execution of complex PM is somewhat affected by ADHD. For example, children with ADHD were found to react more impulsively in explicit pre-planning and were less able to retain and implement their plans on how they would complete the HEXE task.

Discussion of ADHD research findings on PM

Overall, the research to-date suggests that children with ADHD demonstrate a deficit in time-based PM, whereas performance on event-based PM is relatively preserved (Kerns & Price, 2001; Kliegel et al., 2006; Mioni et al., 2017; Zinke et al., 2010). In fact, overall, children with ADHD were found to perform equally as well as controls on various event-based PM tasks, despite some evidence suggesting that this may be at the cost of ongoing task performance (see Brandimonte et al., 2011 and Kliegel et al., 2006).

The deficit in time-based PM, and relative preservation of event-based PM in children with ADHD is consistent with cognitive theories of PM. According to Kliegel and colleagues (2001), time-based PM is more difficult to perform as it requires the use of higher-order EFs in order to internally cue an individual to carry out an intended action and inhibit the performance of the ongoing task to successfully enact it. In contrast, event-based PM is thought to be easier to carry out as it relies more heavily on retrospective memory abilities and less on functions dependent on the frontal brain systems (Groot, Wilson, Evans, & Watson, 2001; Kliegel et al., 2001; Mackinlay et al., 2009; Shum, Cahill, Hohaus, O`Gorman, & Chan, 2012). As ADHD is characterized as a neurodevelopmental disorder that preferentially affects these systems by, among others, disrupting various EFs, it is anticipated that errors in time-based PM would also be observed in individuals with this disorder. By contrast, errors pertaining to cued retrospective memory are rarely found in children with ADHD which would explain why children with this disorder have not shown difficulties with event-based PM.

Another explanation for differential impairment in PM types in children with ADHD is that these children typically perform better on cued memory tasks when the cue is distinct and/or salient (Altgassen, Kliegel, & Martin, 2009; Altgassen, Kretschmer, & Kliegel, 2014; Brandimonte et al., 2011; Brewer, Knight, Marsh, & Unsworth, 2010; Mahy et al., 2014; Kerns & Price, 2001; Kliegel et al., 2006; Smith, Hunt, McVay, & McConnell, 2007). Additionally, they have also been found to benefit from structure – both in their environment and within a task (see below; Kewley, 2005). Therefore, children with ADHD are likely to perform better during lab-based event-based PM tasks given the structured environment, nature of typical lab-based PM tasks, and the tendency for event-based cues to be both distinct and salient (e.g. snapping of fingers; Altgassen et al., 2014; Brandimonte et al., 2011; Kerns & Price, 2001; Kliegel et al., 2006; McDaniel & Einstein, 2000). It is, therefore, unsurprising that children with ADHD have consistently been found to perform similarly to controls on event-based PM tasks in controlled research settings. Their ability to successfully execute event-based PM tasks in their everyday, less-structured environments has yet to be determined.

Much less is known about the mechanisms associated with the time-based PM deficit observed in children with ADHD. It has been hypothesized that executive dysfunction in this population best accounts for the time-based PM difficulties. In particular, difficulties with time estimation, time-monitoring, working memory, inhibitory control, impulsive planning, sustained attention, and task-switching have all been hypothesized to account for the observed deficit in time-based PM (Kerns & Price, 2001; Kliegel et al., 2006; Mioni et al., 2017; Talbot & Kerns, 2014; Zinke et al., 2010). However, to-date, there appears to be little consensus as to the ADHD-specific EF deficit accounting for the most variability within time-based PM performance. That said, researchers appear to agree that the time-based PM deficits cannot be explained by age, IQ, or ongoing task difficulty (Altgassen et al., 2014; Brandimonte et al., 2011; Mioni et al., 2017; Talbot & Kerns, 2014; Zinke et al., 2010).

Kerns and Price (2001) and Mioni and colleagues (2017) noted that children with ADHD exhibited a less-efficient checking strategy compared to controls. Specifically, the children with ADHD checked the gas gage more frequently right after they had forgotten to fill their tank whereas the control participants checked the gas gage more frequently just before a fill was required. They suggested that the differences in fuel checking may be accounted for by differences in time perception abilities as children with ADHD have also been found to have difficulties with time estimation relative to controls (Barkley, Murphy, & Bush, 2001; Barkley et al., 2001; González-Garrido et al., 2008; Hwang, Gau, Hsu, & Wu, 2010; Kerns, McInerney, & Wilde, 2001; Kerns & Price, 2001; Luman et al., 2005; McInerney & Kerns, 2003; Talbot & Kerns, 2014). While time estimation has been suggested as possible reason for difference in time-based PM abilities in children with ADHD, findings have been mixed. Although Mioni and colleagues found time estimation, as measured using a time reproduction paradigm, to be a significant predictor of time-based PM performance in typically developing children, neither Talbot and Kerns (2014) nor Mioni and colleagues (2017) found this to be the case in children with ADHD. In addition, although Mioni and colleagues (2017) were able to replicate the differences in time-monitoring strategy observed by Kerns and Price (2001), neither Altgassen et al. (2014), nor Talbot and Kerns (2014), nor Zinke et al. (2010) could. This suggests that further research is required to elucidate the relationship between time-monitoring or time estimation and time-based PM in this population. Zinke and colleagues (2010), however, did find some evidence to suggest that the clock-checking behavior in the interval preceding the time-based PM target time (frequency of checks and accuracy) may contribute to the observed group differences in time-based PM performance. Specifically, they found that the control group checked the clock in the 30-s interval preceding the PM target time more frequently than the ADHD group. They also found differences between the groups in the computed mean time deviations between participants' last clock check and the PM target time (accuracy). Taken together, Zinke and colleagues (2010) hypothesized that these differences might better account for the observed differences in PM performance between the groups. Additionally, Talbot and Kerns (2014) hypothesized that the relation between time estimation and PM may depend on the measure of time estimation, as children's time reproduction abilities differ based on interval length. Mullins, Bellgrove, Gill, and Robertson (2005), for example, found the greatest discrepancies in time reproduction performance of children with ADHD and controls for the longer time durations (e.g. 45–60 s), and tasks requiring briefer durations may be less-sensitive measures.

Children with ADHD have also been found to exhibit working memory deficits relative to same-aged controls (Kliegel et al., 2006). As working memory has been argued to be one of the four core components involved in the successful execution of PM (see Mahy et al., 2014), it is no surprise that differences in working memory abilities have been hypothesized to account for the difficulties in PM observed in children with ADHD (Altgassen et al., 2014; Kerns & Price, 2001; Talbot & Kerns, 2014; Zinke et al., 2010). Consistent with the executive framework of PM development proposed by Mahy et al. (2014) and other theories of PM (see Einstein & McDaniel, 1996), working memory difficulties have been found to relate specifically to difficulties with the retention stage of the PM model (Kliegel et al., 2006; Mahy et al., 2014). Accordingly, both event- and time-based PM would require intact working memory abilities for successful PM execution. That said, it has been argued that the working memory load is higher in time-based PM tasks as they require the individual to frequently remember to check the time to ensure that the appropriate moment to execute the planned intention has not been missed (Einstein & McDaniel, 1996). Consistent with this hypothesis, studies have found working memory to relate to time-based PM performance. Interestingly, however, none have found working memory to account for a significant proportion of the variability in time-based PM scores after controlling for other variables (i.e. demographic and IQ; Kerns & Price, 2001; Kliegel et al., 2006; Mioni et al., 2017), suggesting that the deficits in working memory observed in children with ADHD are insufficient to account for their difficulties with time-based PM.

Difficulty with response inhibition has also been hypothesized to account for the time-based PM deficit found in children with ADHD (Altgassen et al., 2014; Brandimonte et al., 2011; Kerns & Price, 2001). Response inhibition refers to the ability to overcome a prepotent response (e.g. to stop oneself from interrupting a conversation) and impairments in this ability are frequently reported in individuals with ADHD (e.g. calling out answers without putting up one's hand or engaging in risky behavior before thinking [Barkley, 1997; Boonstra, Kooji, Oosterlan, Sergeant, & Buitelaar, 2010]). According to Mahy and colleagues (2014), intact inhibitory control mechanisms are essential for successful PM execution because they are required for interrupting the ongoing task at the correct target time. Inhibitory control has been argued to be even more important for time-based PM tasks relative to event-based PM tasks as individuals need to frequently interrupt the ongoing task to monitor the time (e.g. clock, timer, or gas gage) via internally-mediated clock-checking (Altgassen et al., 2014). Accordingly, it would be expected that inhibitory control is significantly related to time-based PM performance, and indeed, this has consistently been found in typically developing children (Ślusarczyk & Niedźwieńska, 2013; Wang, Kliegel, Liu, & Yang, 2008) and children with ADHD (Cuttler et al., 2014; Kerns & Price, 2001; Kliegel et al., 2006). However, this relationship does not fully account for the time-based PM deficits observed in individuals with ADHD either. Based on their findings, Brandimonte and colleagues (2011) argue that response inhibition and PM rely on different cognitive mechanisms for successful execution. In contrast, Altgassen and colleagues (2014) believe that future studies aimed at directly manipulating the inhibitory load of the time-based PM task at specific task phases would prove fruitful in assessing the impact of this ability in PM execution in ADHD.

Impulsivity is a complex personality trait that is characterized by a tendency to perform rapid, unplanned actions without having thought ahead about the potential consequences (Dickman, 1990). It is one of the cardinal symptoms associated with a diagnosis of ADHD (American Psychiatric Association, 2013) and is often related to decreased performance on tasks that measure sustained attention and EFs (Brandimonte et al., 2011; Cuttler et al., 2014). According to Patton, Stanford, and Barratt (1995), impulsivity encompasses the following three inter-related dimensions: attentional impulsiveness, motor impulsiveness, and non-planning impulsiveness. Both attentional and non-planning impulsiveness have been found to relate to deficits in PM (Cuttler et al., 2014; Kliegel et al., 2006). Attentional impulsiveness refers to difficulties sustaining attention and experiencing racing thoughts and thought insertions whereas non-planning impulsiveness is defined by Barratt (1985) as involving a lack of forethought, planning, and careful thinking as well as a dislike for challenging mental tasks.

In a study comparing groups of children with ADHD to controls, Kliegel and colleagues (2006) found that the children with ADHD had more difficulties in forming intentions to complete an action as a result of more impulsive and less efficient planning. For example, children with ADHD were less likely to voice their plans on how to complete a task to researchers and they were less likely to develop a plan that ensured that they did not violate any rules of the task. Kliegel and colleagues concluded that impulsive planning, characteristic of children with ADHD (see Clark, Prior, & Kinsella, 2000; Oosterlan, Scheres, & Sergeant, 2005; and Sonuga-Barke, Williams, Hall, & Saxton, 1996), leads to problems with the retention and implementation stages of PM.

A number of studies have similarly shown that impulsivity is related to PM performance. For instance, Cuttler and colleagues (2014) investigated the role of impulsivity in successful PM performance, using a non-clinical sample of undergraduate students. Consistent with earlier results, they found higher levels of impulsivity to relate to poorer PM performance. In particular, they found attentional impulsiveness to relate most strongly to time-based PM and argued that this is because time-based PM tasks occur in the absence of a salient cue and demand more attentional resources for their successful completion. This finding is consistent with that of Talbot and Kerns (2014) who also found higher levels of parent-reported inattention to relate specifically to time-based PM performance. Similarly, Kerns and Price (2001) found time-based PM difficulties to relate to sustained attention on both objective neuropsychological tests and parent-report measures. That said, though related to time-based PM, the severity of parent-reported symptoms of inattention was not found to be a significant predictor of time-based PM deficits in children with ADHD after controlling for other variables (i.e. age and IQ).

While these studies provide consistent evidence to suggest that various EFs are important for the successful execution of time-based PM in children with ADHD, no single EF has been found to uniquely predict time-based PM deficits. Other processes may provide better accounts for their time-based PM difficulties. According to Mahy and colleagues (2014), there are a number of factors that may directly or indirectly (via EF) affect PM that have yet to be investigated in children with ADHD. For example, motivation has been found to significantly influence PM performance in typically developing children (Causey & Bjorklund, 2014; Ceci & Bronfenbrenner, 1985; Kliegel, Brandenberger, & Aberle, 2010). Specifically, greater levels of intrinsic motivation to perform a PM intention has been found to improve PM in children (Mahy et al., 2014) as well as on tasks of time estimation (McInerney & Kerns, 2003) and behavioral inhibition (Michel, Kerns, & Mateer, 2005). As there is increasing evidence to suggest that children with ADHD experience deficits in motivation such that they require stronger incentives to modify their behavior than typically-developing peers (Kollins, Lane, & Shipiro, 1997), and a failure to delay gratification, and prefer small immediate rewards over large delayed rewards (Sonuga-Barke, 2003; Tripp & Wickens, 2008), an investigation of the effect of motivation in this population on time-based PM performance could shed light on this issue.

Clinical assessment of prospective memory

Although research has contributed to our understanding of PM, clinical assessment of PM is also important, where individuals with deficits in PM, like those with ADHD, can be identified for remediation/interventions. Currently, there are no specific assessment measures for identifying PM deficits in children or adults with an ADHD diagnosis. In fact, there are few clinical assessment measures available to identify PM deficits in adults, and even fewer for children, and for those available there are several issues that strongly limit their interpretability. For these reasons, PM abilities in children presenting with ADHD symptoms are rarely formally assessed, instead, they are more indirectly addressed via self- or parent-report measures of ADHD symptomatology or executive dysfunction.

Currently, there are only four clinical PM assessment tools for adults (>16 years) including the Rivermead Behavioral Memory Test (RBMT; Wilson, Cockburn, & Baddeley, 1985), the Cambridge Prospective Memory Test (CAMPROMT; Wilson et al., 2005), the Test Écologique de Mémoire Prospective (TEMP; Potvin, Rouleau, Audy, Charbonneau, & Giguère, 2011) and the Memory for Intentions Screening Test (MIST™). The most popular of these measures is the Memory for Intentions Screening Test (MIST™). The MIST was designed to be a relatively brief clinical measure of PM to be used with adult populations who frequently experience deficits in PM (e.g. dementia, traumatic brain injury; Raskin, 2009). This measure includes both event- and time-based PM cues and has items with varying delay periods and response types. Unlike the other adult PM measures, the MIST has also been found to be a sensitive and specific measure in clinical groups, with adequate psychometric properties (Woods, Moran, Dawson, et al., 2008).

For children, there are very few clinical assessment tools for PM. Wilson and colleagues (1993) modified the RBMT for use with children aged 5–11 years (RBMT-C). This test was developed to be an ecologically valid measure of a wide range of memory functions to be used with children with brain injury to gage their memory deficits (Wilson, Cockburn, Baddeley, & Hiorns, 1989). It has four parallel versions, includes long- and short-term memory tasks within visual, verbal, episodic, and visual-spatial tasks. The specific prospective tests include remembering names, times, messages, and belongings. For example, on the Remembering Belongings task, the examiner shows and hides a package of stickers while the child watches. S/he then tells the child to remind him/her about the stickers and show him/her where they were hidden at the end of the session. It is a standardized measure and normative data is available for six age bands.

Major limitations of the RBMT-C include lack of revisions for over 20 years, with some of the tasks (i.e. remembering to mail a postcard to the clinician) not being consistent with current typical everyday prospective tasks. Likewise, available normative data are also in need of revision and expansion as the original sample sizes were relatively small (336 typically developing; 36 patient). Finally, the RBMT-C was developed to measure a wide-range of everyday memory functions, with relatively few probes or specific indices of PM.

In 2010, Mills and colleagues developed the Memory for Intentions Screening Test for Youth (MISTY) to measure PM deficits in children aged 4–12, by modifying the MIST™ protocol. The MISTY contains eight different tasks that vary in response type, delay period, and cue type, but has shorter time delays and more child-appropriate PM tasks (e.g. 'When I hand you a blue marker, draw a house on your paper'). It also allows the clinician to analyze the types of PM errors (i.e. loss of time, task substitution, loss of content, and other). Preliminary evidence suggests that the MISTY measures PM in children effectively (Mills, Garbarino, & Raskin, 2010). Still, there are a number of limitations that hamper the utility of the MISTY in clinical settings, including an insufficient number of trials (four each for event- and time-based; Potvin et al., 2011) and uncertain ecological validity. Finally, normative data is currently unavailable, making objective comparison between clinical groups and typically developing children impossible. Consequently, it is difficult to accurately interpret and predict future PM functioning outside of the assessment context with any confidence (Goldstein, 1996; Potvin et al., 2011; Sbordone, 1996). As the main goals of neuropsychological assessment are to identify areas of strength and weakness and to predict future functioning, it can be argued that the MISTY is not suitable for clinical purposes. Finally, the reliability, sensitivity, and validity of the MISTY is still unknown, which is a further reason for why it is not currently used in clinical settings.

Given the significance of intact PM abilities in successful everyday functioning, it is important to use up-to-date ecologically valid clinical assessment measures. However, current clinical measures of PM are primarily based on research or lab-based PM tasks. This is problematic because such tasks are generally unrepresentative of typical daily PM tasks (e.g. after two minutes, press a key, when in real life very few PM demands would have a 2-min time window). In addition, these clinical assessments are typically conducted in a controlled environment, have short duration intervals before performance of the PM task (usually 20 min or less), and thus provide for short delays between task introduction and execution. They consist of few tasks, and do not allow for compensatory strategy use. Indeed, in a naturalistic PM study, Talbot (2015) found that MISTY PM scores did not relate to parent ratings of everyday PM difficulties, while there was a relationship between parent ratings on PM performance on the naturalistic PM tasks children were asked to perform. Therefore, performance on current clinical PM measures may only loosely reflect children's everyday PM abilities and should be interpreted with caution, highlighting the importance of developing more ecologically valid clinical measures of PM.

Another approach to the naturalistic measurement of PM in children is to obtain data on PM functioning via report from others who may have experience with the child's ability to complete future intentions. With this goal in mind, Talbot and Kerns (2014) modified an adult-report Prospective Retrospective Memory Questionnaire, designed by Smith and colleagues (2000), to develop the Prospective Retrospective Memory Questionnaire for Children (PRMQC). The PRMQC is a brief (16-item) parent-report questionnaire that asks parents to respond to simple statements about the frequency of their child's RM and PM failures. For example, one question asks: 'Does your child fail to do something he/she was supposed to do a few minutes later even though it's there in front of him/her, like turning off the TV or Gameboy or picking up his/her backpack before heading to school?' (PM question). The PRMQC was used in a study with children with ADHD and was found to relate to laboratory-based measures of PM and parent reports of ADHD symptom severity (Talbot & Kerns, 2014). Likewise, Kliegel and JÄger (2006) developed a different modified version of the PRMQ to be used with preschoolers and found that parents and caregivers could adequately rate their children's RM and PM difficulties. Taken together, both child versions of the PRMQ appear to be valid and sensitive measures of everyday PM errors in children, despite their reliance on parent-report, which can be unduly influenced by parents' worries about their child's behaviors. However, one limitation of the PRMQC is that scores are not broken down by event-based or time-based PM items and, thus, provide only a generalized measure of PM difficulties. Additionally, as the PRMQC has primarily been used as an experimental measure of PM abilities, normative data is not yet available. Furthermore, even though PRMQC scores have been found to be related to ADHD symptom severity (Talbot & Kerns, 2014), the PRMQC in itself does not provide any information on the basis of which it could be determined whether PM errors reflect a specific PM deficit or if they are due to working memory and/or executive function deficits. Consequently, the PRMQC may be useful primarily as a supplemental measure of everyday PM abilities in children with ADHD.

Alternatively, existing self- and other-report behavior measures of ADHD symptoms and/or EFs might also be useful in ascertaining whether a PM difficulty is also present in a child. For example, the Conners Third Edition™ rating scales (parent, teacher, and self-report) and the Behavior Rating Inventory of Executive Function (BRIEF®; Gioia, Isquith, Guy, & Kenworthy, 2000) are instrumental in both the screening of ADHD as well as with the evaluation of everyday EF deficits (Packiam Alloway et al., 2009; Toplak, Bucciarelli, Jain, & Tannock, 2009). In fact, the BRIEF-parent report includes two items in its Planning/Organization subscale that address PM difficulties specifically (i.e. forgetting to complete one of two intended actions and forgetting to complete a task that was asked of him/her). Though two items on an EF measure are insufficient to draw meaningful conclusions about PM functioning, the administration of such scales, together with parent/child reports of PM, can help clarify whether EF deficits and attention contribute to the parent/child's reports of everyday PM errors. This could also inform the decision of whether to separately evaluate a child's PM ability using available clinical or experimental tasks. Taken together, parent-report measures like the PRMQ and PRMQC can also potentially provide an objective measure of PM ability that can then be used to ascertain the ecological validity of clinical assessment measures of PM. Measures such as these have the potential to aid in the diagnosis of specific PM deficits and the provision of specific intervention recommendations.

Evidence-based prospective memory intervention and treatment approaches

Given the limited knowledge about PM in children with ADHD, no studies to-date have reported on the development of specific cognitive interventions or treatment strategies to remediate time-based PM deficits in this population. That said, there have been a few studies investigating the effectiveness of rehabilitation strategies aimed at ameliorating PM in children with other neurologic conditions (e.g. pediatric traumatic brain injury). Additionally, numerous intervention and treatment approaches have been developed to use with children with ADHD. As the PM errors typically made by children with ADHD are hypothesized to relate most significantly to difficulties with inattention, motivation, and specific executive functions, it is likely that intervention approaches aimed at remediating these difficulties could also generalize to time-based PM.

Cognitive rehabilitation broadly refers to a systematic intervention developed to improve cognitive and/or behavioral difficulties after a pathological process to try to enhance daily functioning (Axelrod et al., 2002). According to Sohlberg and Mateer (2001), cognitive rehabilitation typically involves both restoration and compensation. Restoration aims to restore functions that have been lost and includes strategies like rehearsal techniques chunking/mnemonic methods, and/or computerized brain training activities aimed at improving sustained attention and reducing distractibility (Schaffer & Geva, 2016). Compensation, however, is based on the idea that planning abilities and external cues can be recruited to moderate the primary deficit by offering effective means to circumvent the deficit (e.g. time-based PM) using external devices (Cicerone et al., 2011). Behavior management has also been argued to support the learning and generalization of acquired skills across contexts (van't Hooft & Norberg, 2009). Behavior management uses operant conditioning techniques, social learning principles, emotion-focused coping, and mediation to achieve behavior change (Schaffer & Geva, 2016).

Interventions intended to compensate for PM deficits have consistently been shown to circumvent PM difficulties in children and adolescents with traumatic brain injury (DePompei et al., 2008; Schaffer & Geva, 2016). For example, a series of studies by van't Hooft and colleagues (van't Hooft, Andersson, Sejersen, Bartfai, & von Wendt, 2003, van't Hooft et al., 2005, 2007) demonstrated a significant improvement in PM ability when children, aged 9–16 years, used daily diaries. Similarly, the use of electronic devices, like NeuroPage and other personal digital assistance systems, has been found to be effective in enhancing children's PM performance (Schaffer & Geva, 2016). Unfortunately, however, the authors did not specify whether the observed gains in PM performance were presentation type specific. Nonetheless, it can be argued that compensatory strategies aimed at reducing the need for self-initiated monitoring would effectively alter time-based PM tasks into event-based PM tasks. In doing so, children with ADHD would be likely to benefit immensely as their event-based PM abilities remain relatively intact.

Research also demonstrates that behavior management techniques are effective in enhancing PM (Schaffer & Geva, 2016). Specifically, reinforcement learning using monetary incentives has increased PM performance in children following traumatic brain injury (DePompei et al., 2008). Given that children with ADHD are more responsive to external motivation, it is possible that the employment of sufficiently tangible reinforcement for the appropriate and consistent use of compensatory strategies/devices may lead to significant improvements in time-based PM performance. There is also evidence to suggest that consistent use of such compensatory devices will foster long-term spontaneous use and would require less salient and frequent reinforcements over time (Wilson et al., 2009).

As difficulties with working memory, inhibitory control, inattention, planning, and set-shifting have all been found to relate to time-based PM deficits in children with ADHD, it is possible that specific interventions that restore these skills in this population might also restore time-based PM functioning. Although a review of the ADHD intervention research is beyond the scope of this paper, a few specific interventions that might be effective will be outlined. In particular, evidence-based interventions aimed at improving attention, working memory, and organizational skills are good candidates for enhancing time-based PM functioning.

Difficulties with working memory are related to difficulties with sustained attention (Engle, 2002) and inhibitory control (Conway, Cowan, & Bunting, 2001; Markovitch, Boseovski, & Knapp, 2007). Similarly, deficits in working memory, attention, and inhibitory control are associated with difficulties with time-based PM in children with ADHD (see above). Since there is some evidence to suggest that benefits from working memory training (WMT) programs also generalize to response inhibition and reduce inattention in children with ADHD (Green et al., 2012), perhaps these programs would also increase time-based PM performance.

WMT programs typically involve short periods of fairly intensive training on computerized tasks designed to tax working memory capacity (Melby-Lervåg & Hulme, 2016). Currently, there are a variety of computerized WMT programs available commercially that are marketed for the treatment of ADHD in children. A recent meta-analysis of computerized WMT programs pointed to a lack of convincing evidence of generalization to other skills including inhibitory control and inattention in individuals with or without ADHD (Melby-Lervåg & Hulme, 2013, 2016). Despite the lack of evidence to-date supporting the generalization of WMT programs, advocates of direct training approaches have argued that comprehensive

WMT programs that factor in motivation, metacognition, and strategy training may result in more generalizable skills to natural settings (Butler & Copeland, 2002; Kerns, MacSween, Vander Weeken, & Grupposo, 2010; Sohlberg & Mateer, 2001). In addition, a study conducted by Richter, Mödden, Eling, and Hildebrandt (2015) found WMT to improve both working memory and PM (event- and time-based) in non-amnestic adults with an acquired brain lesion. Future research should examine whether comprehensive WMT programs affect time-based PM.

In contrast to specific EF training programs, there is some evidence to support the use of more generalized psychosocial interventions to indirectly affect some EFs in children with ADHD (Diamond, 2012; Diamond & Lee, 2011; Miranda, Presentación, Siegenthaler, & Jara, 2011). Miranda and colleagues (2011) used an intensive multicontextual psychosocial intervention that integrated three different programs (cognitive behavioral and behavior modification for home and school), implemented with children, parents, and teachers during a 10-week period. Following the intervention, gains in visuospatial memory and planning and in parent and teacher behavioral ratings of hyperactivity or impulsivity and inattention in children with ADHD were found. Given the relationship between time-based PM, planning, and inattention, it is possible that such an intervention would also restore time-based PM.

While sole pharmacological interventions using psychostimulants are often the first line of treatment for children with ADHD (Purdie, Hattie, & Carroll, 2002), multimodal treatments combining the use of psychostimulants and psychosocial/behavioral interventions have found better short-term gains (3- and 9-months of intervention) for domains of functional impairment including academic achievement, social skills, and parenting practices (Hinshaw, Arnold, & For the MTA Cooperative Group, 2015). It is therefore possible that improvements may also generalize to time-based PM.

In summary, there are currently no specific evidence-based interventions available to improve time-based PM in children with ADHD. Behavioral strategies using external motivation have been found to be helpful in increasing the likelihood that a child with ADHD will use specific strategies (e.g. diaries) to compensate for PM difficulties. Interventions designed to directly target specific EF skills (e.g. WMT programs) have been found to produce short-term, non-generalizable improvements and should therefore be used with caution if the goal is to ameliorate PM difficulties. That said, it is possible that specific EF training programs can produce generalized effects on time-based PM if they are sufficiently motivating, promote metacognitive awareness, and teach strategies. Finally, treatment approaches that combine psychostimulants with multicomponent, multicontextual psychosocial interventions appear to hold the most promise in reducing PM deficits in children with ADHD. This is because they directly target the core symptoms of the disorder (e.g. inattention, hyperactivity-impulsivity, and motivation) while also indirectly enhancing some EF skills associated with time-based PM deficits (e.g. planning and working memory). Clearly, much more research is needed to determine the most efficacious intervention strategy to employ to restore/compensate for time-based PM deficits in children with ADHD.

Suggestions for prospective memory deficit management in daily life

Irrespective of the efficacy of interventions targeted at improving PM, it is important to identify additional methods that can be used to manage time-based PM difficulties in everyday life. As there is no literature available on specific PM management strategies for children with ADHD, the authors suggest that many strategies typically recommended by psychologists and behavior consultants to manage the EF deficits in children with ADHD (see Dawson & Guare, 2009) are likely to also help compensate for time-based PM deficits as well. Similarly, strategies targeted at helping to compensate for retrospective memory difficulties will likely be helpful as well. Importantly, however, the strategies provided in this section are not an exhaustive list and some strategies may not work for every child or for every situation (e.g. home vs. school). It will, therefore, be important to implement new strategies on a trial-by-trial basis with a lot of direct input from the child to help ensure maximum benefit. Finally, we do not expect that *all* the suggested strategies be implemented, but that relevant strategies will be trialed based on the individual needs of the child.

In general, strategies that target time-based PM deficits in children with ADHD are aimed at improving time perception and awareness. For instance, calendars and planners should be introduced early and used regularly (Barkley, 1998; Dawson & Guare, 2009). This will not only help children better understand the concept of time (i.e. the relation between days, months, and years), it will also help them to learn to organize and plan their free time accordingly (Dawson & Guare, 2009). Calendars and planners can also serve as a visual reminder of upcoming events (Barkley, 1998). Color coding activities that are relevant for the child (i.e. on a family calendar) may also be helpful to highlight the most pertinent information for the child as this makes the information more likely to be seen and remembered (i.e. makes the cue more salient).

Because children with ADHD exhibit relatively intact event-based PM abilities, we suggest strategies aimed at turning traditional time-based PM tasks into event-based tasks, which should increase the likelihood the child will successfully remember to carry out the PM task. This means that attaching external cues (e.g. visuals or timers) to trigger their memories should improve their PM performance (see also Barkley, 1998; Dawson & Guare, 2009). For example, using phone notifications and reminders should help trigger children's memories (see also van't Hooft et al., 2003, 2005, 2007). In addition, having timers and clocks consistently within view may also be beneficial. However, if the clock is not in plain view and/or sufficiently salient, the child is less likely to benefit from this strategy (Barkley, 1998; see also Altgassen et al., 2009, 2014; Brandimonte et al., 2011; Brewer et al., 2010; Mahy et al., 2014; Kerns & Price, 2001; Kliegel et al., 2006) because the cue to prospectively remember needs to be salient (Smith et al., 2007). Making particular tasks (e.g. before/after school, bedtime) habitual may also help increase the likelihood that the child will remember to complete them. By completing a series of tasks in the same way every day, children will be less reliant on their working memories to remember what they are supposed to do and are less likely to forget to complete the task (Ellis, 1996). In addition, it may be helpful to teach/encourage children to plan for the activities of the next day as part of their evening/bed-time routine. This might entail ensuring that everything that is needed for the next day is in the child's backpack and/or placed beside the door so that it is not forgotten. Similarly, providing a visual checklist of the tasks to be completed before leaving the house and posting it in front of the door will serve as a visual reminder and help children remember, while also acting as a reinforcer that keeps the child accountable for his intentions (Barkley, 1998; Dawson & Guare, 2009).

Overall, strategies aimed at (a) increasing time perception and awareness and (b) decreasing EF demands are likely to help compensate for the time-based PM deficit typically observed in children with ADHD. It is possible that by transforming time-based PM tasks into event-based tasks using external cues in the form of visual and/or verbal reminders, children with ADHD will be able to perform PM tasks similarly to their typically developing peers. However, it will be important to employ these strategies in early development so that they become habitual at a younger age and are, therefore, more likely to be used efficiently in the long-term (Dawson & Guare, 2009). As children with ADHD also exhibit motivational differences relative to their peers, they may be more receptive to the inclusion of above-mentioned strategies if they are reinforced using external rewards and/or token economies (Dawson & Guare, 2009; see also DePompei et al., 2008).

Conclusion

Intact PM is essential for daily functioning across the lifespan. It is what enables us to remember to pay bills on time or to buy milk on the way home from the store. When PM is not functioning properly, there can be serious consequences (your power is turned off, or your kids will not have milk for their cereal in the morning, or worse, you will not have milk for your coffee). Unfortunately for some populations, like those with a diagnosis of ADHD, difficulties with PM are common and are associated with a variety of interpersonal, academic, and/or occupational difficulties.

Children with ADHD will present with one or more core symptoms of either inattention and/or hyperactivity-impulsivity. Associated with the disorder is a delay in EF development and a disruption of the motivational system. Because these children show difficulties with attention and EF, it is not surprising that these children also exhibit difficulties in PM relative to their typically developing peers (as successful PM performance is argued to rely on intact EFs). What is surprising, however, is the lack of research on PM in this population.

In this paper, PM in children with ADHD was examined. Surprisingly, very little research has been conducted on PM in children with ADHD, despite theoretical models that suggest that PM should be impaired in these children. Of the six studies that have directly investigated the relationship between PM and ADHD, there is a consensus that the PM deficit in this population is subtype specific, with time-based PM being negatively affected and event-based PM remaining relatively intact. It has been hypothesized that the subtype-specific deficit observed in children with ADHD can be attributed to the increased EF involvement required for the successful execution of time-based PM as compared to event-based PM. However, research on the specific EFs involved in successful time-based PM performance have yielded contradictory results, which may differ depending on the population being studied (e.g. typically developing or those with ADHD; see Mioni et al., 2017). Additionally, the impact of the disrupted motivational system has been virtually unexplored.

Given the state of the research, it is also not surprising that no specific assessment measures of PM ability have been developed for use in this population. The assessment measures that are currently available to measure PM in children have not yet been validated, and normative data are still not available. There are research questionnaires, like the modified PRMQ-C, that show promise as a potential parent-report measure of everyday PM difficulties in children, but they are also not without limitations. Current symptom-based questionnaire measures, like the BRIEF or Conners, may also be used to tap into PM performance in children with ADHD when followed up with specific questions by a trained examiner.

Currently, there are no specific evidence-based interventions available to improve PM in children with ADHD. Interventions aimed at compensating for PM deficits have been found to be helpful in other neurological populations (children with traumatic brain injury). Behavior modification methods (e.g. reward systems) may also be helpful in increasing the likelihood that compensatory strategies will be adopted by children in the long term. In addition, intervention programs designed to improve specific EFs (e.g. WMT programs) may also lead to generalized improvement in time-based PM, if they contain motivational rewards, consider the impact of metacognitive abilities, and teach strategies use. That said, there are many strategies that can be employed on a daily basis to limit the potential negative impact time-based PM deficits may cause for children with ADHD.

Clearly, the research on PM in children with ADHD is in its infancy and would benefit from much more directed attention. Specifically, it would be important to look more closely at the role of motivation in PM performance and whether this may differ amongst subtypes of PM. As particular EFs have so far been insufficient in accounting for the time-based PM deficit in this population, perhaps focusing on the PM component of the PM task might prove more fruitful. It may also be helpful to use neuroimaging techniques to determine whether differences in connectivity/activity in certain brain regions may account for their difficulties. Additionally, as was briefly touched upon in the intervention section, the impact of metacognitive awareness and/or metamemory may also help to explain some of the observed differences in performance compared to their typically developing peers. Finally, it will be important to determine whether differences in PM remain the same depending on the ADHD symptom presentation being researched as there is some evidence to suggest that there are other differences between ADHD presentation types apart from the prevalence of the core symptoms (see Diamantopoulou et al., 2007). Similarly, it might be informative to determine the effect of gender and/or the presence of a comorbid disorder on PM functioning in children with ADHD. Once these issues have been addressed, we will be in a better position to understand PM functioning in children with ADHD and then use this knowledge to develop more appropriate assessment measures and intervention methods.

As our review has shown, the research on PM in children with ADHD has yielded contradictory findings suggesting something other than EF deficits in time perception, working memory, or inhibitory control are driving the observed deficit in time-based PM in this population. As such, the complex roles of disrupted motivational systems, neurobiology, and genes offer a promising avenue for future research into clarifying the basis of this deficit. Similarly, systematic research comparing different methodologies of measuring PM in children with ADHD would make a valuable contribution to answering this question.

Limitations of this review

Because this is a relatively new area of research, there is a small corpus of studies to draw on. Furthermore, the extant studies investigating PM in children with and without ADHD typically have small sample sizes and most fail to differentiate between different types of ADHD, both factors that limit the interpretability of the findings. A further limitation of these studies is that research in this area has relied predominately on experimental paradigms. Though methodologically rigorous, it has been argued that performance-based (experimental) PM paradigms may lack ecological validity (Rose, Rendell, McDaniel, Aberle, & Kliegel, 2010; Talbot, Müller, & Kerns, 2015). Only one study has used a second method (parent-report) to assess the cross-validity of PM measures. Systematically comparing PM performance on lab-based tasks, naturalistic tasks, and parent- and teacher-report measures will be an important avenue for future investigation.

Finally, research into ADHD has skyrocketed in the past 30 years resulting in more advanced understanding of the disorder across multiple domains of study (i.e. neurobiology, neurophysiology, neuropsychology, and genetics); Specifically, a variety of different pathways for ADHD have been suggested (e.g. cognitive control, reward processing, and temporal processing – see de Zeeuw et al., 2012; Sonuga-Barke, Sergeant, Nigg, & Willcutt, 2008). A systematic evaluation of the relations between different ADHD endophenotype candidates and different subtypes of PM (e.g. time-based vs. event-based) using a multi-trait multi-method approach would contribute to our understanding of PM functioning in this population and inform the design of interventions.

Disclosure statement

The authors reported no conflict of interest.

Funding

This work was supported by the Canadian Network for Research and Innovation in Machining Technology, Natural Sciences and Engineering Research Council of Canada [grant Canada Graduate Scholorships – Doctoral].

References

Alexander, J. M., Noyes, C. R., MacBrayer, E. K., Schwanenflugel, P. J., & Fabricius, W. V. (1998). Concepts of mental activities and verbs in children of high and average intelligence. *Gifted Child Quarterly, 42*(1), 16–28.

Altgassen, M., Kliegel, M., & Martin, M. (2009). Event-based prospective memory in depression: The impact of cue focality. *Cognition and Emotion, 23*(6), 1041–1055.

Altgassen, M., Kretschmer, A., & Kliegel, M. (2014). Task dissociation in prospective memory performance in individuals with ADHD. *Journal of Attention Disorders, 18*(7), 617–624.

American Psychiatric Association. (2013). *Diagnostic and statistical manual of mental disorders* (5th ed.). Arlington, VA: American Psychiatric Publishing.

Axelrod, B., Heilbronner, R., Barth, J., Larrabee, G., Faust, D., Pliskin, N., … Silver, C. (2002). *Cognitive rehabilitation: Official statement of the national academy of neuropsychology*. Denver, CO: National Academy of Neuropsychology.

Bahçivan, S. R., Ayvaşik, H. B., & Alyanak, B. (2015). Executive functioning in subtypes of attention deficit hyperactivity disorder. *Archives of Neuropsychiatry, 52*, 386–392.

Barkley, R. A. (1997). Behavioral inhibition, sustained attention, and executive functions: Constructing a unifying theory of ADHD. *Psychological Bulletin, 121*(1), 65–94.

Barkley, R. A. (1998). Attention-deficit/hyperactivity disorder. *Scientific American*, 66–71.

Barkley, R. A. (2006). *Attention-deficit/hyperactivity disorder: A Handbook for diagnosis and treatment* (3rd ed.). New York, NY: Guilford Press.

Barkley, R. A., Murphy, K. R., & Bush, T. (2001). Time perception and reproduction in young adults with attention deficit hyperactivity disorder. *Neuropsychology, 15*(3), 351–360.

Barratt, E. S. (1985). Impulsiveness subtraits: Arousal and information processing. In J. T. Spence & C. E. Izard (Eds.), *Motivation, emotion and personality* (pp. 137–146). North Holland: Elsevier Science Publishers.

Biederman, J. (2005). Attention-deficit/hyperactivity disorder: A selective overview. *Biological Psychiatry, 57*, 1215–1220.

Biederman, J., Monuteaux, M. C., Doyle, A. E., Seidman, L. J., Wilens, T. E., Ferrero, F., ... Faraone, S. V. (2004). The impact of executive function deficits and attention-deficit/hyperactivity disorder (ADHD) on academic outcomes in children. *Journal of Consulting and Clinical Psychology, 72*(5), 757–766.

Boonstra, A. M., Kooji, J. J., Oosterlan, J., Sergeant, J. A., & Buitelaar, J. K. (2010). To act or not to act, that's the problem: Primarily inhibition difficulties in adult ADHD. *Neuropsychology, 24*, 209–221.

Brandimonte, M. A., Filippello, P., Coluccia, E., Altgassen, M., & Kliegel, M. (2011). To do or not to do? Prospective memory versus response inhibition in autism spectrum disorder and attention-deficit/hyperactivity disorder. *Memory, 19*(1), 56–66.

Brewer, G., Knight, J., Marsh, R. L., & Unsworth, N. (2010). Individual differences in event-based prospective memory: Evidence for multiple processes supporting cue detection. *Memory and Cognition, 38*(3), 304–311.

Brocki, K. C., Eninger, L., Thorell, L., & Bohlin, G. (2010). Interrelations between executive function and symptoms of hyperactivity/impulsivity and inattention in preschoolers: A two year longitudinal study. *Journal of Abnormal Child Psychology, 38*, 163–171.

Buckner, R., Andrews-Hanna, J., & Schacter, D. (2008). The brain's default network. *Proceedings of the National Academy of Sciences, 107*, 4734–4739.

Burgess, P. W., Gonen-Yaacovi, G., & Volle, E. (2010). Functional neuroimaging studies of prospective memory: What have we learnt so far? *Neuropsychologia, 49*, 2246–2257.

Butler, R. W., & Copeland, D. W. (2002). Attentional processes and their remediation in children treated for cancer: A literature review and the development of a therapeutic approach. *Journal of the International Neuropsychological Society, 8*, 115–124.

Camp, C. J., Foss, J. W., Stevens, A. B., & O'Hanlan, A. M. (1996). Improving prospective memory task performance in persons with Alzheimer's disease. In M. Bradimonte, G. O. Einstein, & M. A. McDaniel (Eds.), *Prospective memory: Theory and applications* (pp. 351–367). Mahwah: Erlbaum.

Causey, K. B., & Bjorklund, D. F. (2014). Prospective memory in preschool children: Influences of agency, incentive, and underlying cognitive mechanisms. *Journal of Experimental Child Psychology, 127*, 36–51.

Ceci, S. J., & Bronfenbrenner, U. (1985). 'Don't forget to take the cupcakes out of the oven': Prospective memory, strategic time-monitoring, and context. *Child Development, 56*, 152–164.

Chapieski, L., Evankovich, K., Hiscock, M., & Collins, R. (2011). Everyday verbal memory and pediatric epilepsy. *Epilepsy and Behavior, 21*(3), 285–290.

Cicerone, K., Langenbahn, D., Braden, C., Malec, J., Kalmar, K., Fraas, M., ... Ashman, T. (2011). Evidence-based cognitive rehabilitation: Updated review of the literature from 2003 through 2008. *Archives of Physical Medicine and Rehabilitation, 92*, 519–530.

Clark, C., Prior, M., & Kinsella, G. J. (2000). Do executive function deficits differentiate between adolescents with ADHD and oppositional defiant/conduct disorder? A neuropsychological study using the six elements test and hayling sentence completion test. *Journal of Abnormal Child Psychology, 28*, 403–414.

Conway, A. R., Cowan, N., & Bunting, M. F. (2001). The cocktail party phenomenon revisited: The importance of working memory capacity. *Psychonomic Bulletin & Review, 8*(2), 331–335.

Cortese, S., Kelly, C., Chabernaud, C., Proal, E., Di Martino, A., Nilham, M. P., & Castellanos, F. X. (2012). Toward systems neuroscience of ADHD: As meta-analysis of 55 fMRI studies. *American Journal of Psychiatry, 169*, 1038–1055.

Cuttler, C., Relkov, T., & Taylor, S. (2014). Quick to act, quick to forget: The link between impulsiveness and prospective memory. *European Journal of Personality, 28*, 560–568.

Dawson, P., & Guare, R. (2009). *Smart but scattered*. New York, NY: Guilford Press.

Deouell, L. Y., & Knight, R. T. (2009). Executive function and higher order cognition: EEG studies. *Encyclopedia of Neuroscience, 4*, 105–109.

DePompei, R., Gillette, Y., Goetz, E., Xenopoulos-Oddsson, A., Bryen, D., & Dowds, M. (2008). Practical applications for use of PDAs and smartphones with children and adolescents who have traumatic brain injury. *Neurorehabilitation, 23*, 487–499.

de Zeeuw, P., Weusten, J., van Dijk, S., van Belle, J., & Durston, S. (2012). Deficits in cognitive control, timing and reward sensitivity appear to be dissociable in ADHD. *Public Library of Science, 7*, e51416.

Diamantopoulou, S., Rydell, A.-M., Thorell, L. B., & Bohlin, G. (2007). Impact of executive functioning and symptoms of attention deficit hyperactivity disorder on children's peer relations and school performance. *Developmental Neuropsychology, 32*(1), 521–542.

Diamond, A. (2012). Activities and programs that improve children's executive functions. *Current Directions in Psychological Science, 21*, 335–341.

Diamond, A., & Lee, K. (2011). Interventions shown to aid executive function development in children 4 to 12 years old. *Science, 333*(6045), 959–964.

Dickman, S. J. (1990). Functional and dysfunctional impulsivity: Personality and cognitive correlates. *Journal of Personality and Social Psychology, 58*(1), 95–102.

Einstein, G. O., & McDaniel, M. A. (1990). Normal aging and prospective memory. *Journal of Experimental Psychology. Learning, Memory, and Cognition, 16*(4), 717–726.

Einstein, G. O. & McDaniel, M. A. (1996). Retrieval processes in prospective memory: Theoretical approaches and some new empirical findings. In M. Brandimonte, G. O. Einstein, & M. A. McDaniel (Eds.), *Prospective memory: Theory and applications* (pp. 115–141). Mahwah, NJ: Lawrence Erlbaum Associates.

Einstein, G. O., & McDaniel, M. A. (2005). Prospective memory: Multiple retrieval processes. *Current Directions in Psychological Science, 14*, 286–290.

El Sayed, E., Larsson, J. O., Persson, H. E., Santosh, P. J., & Rydelius, P. A. (2003). 'Maturational lag' hypothesis of attention deficit hyperactivity disorder: An update. *Acta Paediatrica, 92*(7), 776–784.

Ellis, J. (1996). Prospective memory or the realization of delayed intentions: A conceptual framework for research. In M. Brandimonte, G. O. Einstein, & M. A. McDaniel (Eds.), *Prospective memory: Theory and applications* (pp. 1–22). Mahwah, NJ: Lawrence Erlbaum Associates.

Engle, R. W. (2002). Working memory capacity as executive attention. *Current Directions in Psychological Science, 11*, 19–23.

van Ewijk, H., Heslenfeld, D. J., Zwiers, M. P., Buitelaar, J. K., & Oosterlaan, J. (2012). Diffusion tensor imaging in attention deficit/hyperactivity disorder: A systematic review and meta-analysis. *Neuroscience & Biobehavioral Reviews, 36*, 1093–1106.

Fair, D. A., Cohen, A. L., Power, J. D., Dosenbach, N. U., Church, J. A., Miezen, F. M., … Petersen, S. (2009). Functional brain networks develop from a 'local to distributed' organization. *PLoS Computational Biology, 5*, e1000381.

Fair, D., Posner, J., Nagel, B., Bathula, D., Dias, T., Mills, K., … Nigg, J. T. (2010). Atypical default network connectivity in youth with attention-deficit/hyperactivity disorder. *Biological Psychiatry, 68*, 1084–1091.

Forslund, T., Brocki, K. C., Bohlin, G., Granqvist, P., & Eninger, L. (2016). The heterogeneity of attention-deficit/hyperactivity disorder symptoms and conduct problems: Cognitive inhibition, emotion regulation, emotionality, and disorganized attachment. *British Journal of Developmental Psychology, 34*, 371–387.

Fox, M. D., Snyder, A. Z., Vincent, J. L., Corbetta, M., Van Essen, D. C., & Raichle, M. E. (2005). The human brain is intrinsically organized into dynamic, anticorrelated functional network. *Proceedings of the National Academy of Sciences, 102*, 9673–9678.

Gioia, G. A., Isquith, P. K., Guy, S., & Kenworthy, L. (2000). *Behaviour rating inventory of executive function professional manual*. Lutz, FL: Psychological Assessment Resources.

Goldstein, G. (1996). Functional considerations in neuropsychology. In R. J. Sbordone & C. J. Long (Eds.), *Ecological validity of neuropsychological testing* (pp. 91–112). Delray Beach, FL: GR Press/St. Lucie Press.

Gonneaud, J., Rauchs, G., Groussard, M., Landeau, B., Mézenge, F., de La Sayette, V., … Desgranges, B. (2014). How do we process event-based and time-based intentions in the brain? An fMRI study of prospective memory in healthy individuals. *Human Brain Mapping, 35*, 3066–3082.

González-Garrido, A. A., Gómez-Velázquez, F. R., Zarabozo, D., López-Elizalde, R., Ontiveros, A., Madera-Carrillo, H., & Vega, O. L. (2008). Time reproduction disturbances in adhd children: An ERP study. *International Journal of Neuroscience, 118*, 119–135.

Graf, P. (2012). Prospective memory: Faulty brain, flaky person. *Canadian Psychology, 53*, 7–13.

Green, C. T., Long, D. L., Green, D., Iosif, A. M., Dixon, J. F., Miller, M. R., … Schweitzer, J. B. (2012). Will working memory training generalize to improve off-task behaviour in children with attention-deficit/hyperactivity disorder? *Neurotherapeutics, 9*(3), 639–648.

Groot, Y. C. T., Wilson, B. A., Evans, J., & Watson, P. (2001). Prospective memory functioning in people with and without brain injury. *Journal of the International Neuropsychological Society, 8*, 645–654.

Haenlein, M., & Caul, W. F. (1987). Attention deficit disorder with hyperactivity: A specific hypothesis of reward dysfunction. *Journal of American Academy of Child and Adolescent Psychiatry, 26*, 356–262.

Hinshaw, S. P. & Arnold, L. E., For the MTA Cooperative Group. (2015). Attention-deficit hyperactivity disorder, multimodal treatment, and longitudinal outcome: Evidence, paradox, and challenge. *WIREs Cognitive Science, 6*, 39–52.

Holmes, J., Hilton, K. A., Place, M., Alloway, T. P., Elliott, J. G., & Gathercole, S. E. (2014). Children with low working memory and children with ADHD: Same or different? *Frontiers of Human Neuroscience, 8*(976), 1–13.

Hong, S.-B., Zalesky, A., Fornito, A., Park, S., Yang, Y. H., Park, M. H., … Kim, J. W. (2014). Connectomic disturbances in attention-deficit hyperactivity disorder: A whole-brain tractography analysis. *Biological Psychiatry, 76*, 656–663.

van't Hooft, I., & Norberg, A. (2009). SMART cognitive training combined with a parental coaching programme for three children treated for medulloblastoma. *Neurorehabilitation, 25*, 1–9.

van't Hooft, I., Andersson, K., Sejersen, T., Bartfai, A., & von Wendt, L. (2003). Attention and memory training in children with acquired brain injuries. *Acta Pediatrica, 92*, 935–940.

van't Hooft, I., Andersson, K., Bergman, B., Sejersen, T., von Wendt, L., & Bartfai, A. (2005). Beneficial effect from a cognitive training programme on children with acquired brain injuries demonstrated in a controlled study. *Brain Injury, 19*, 511–518.

van't Hooft, I., Andersson, K., Bergman, B., Sejersena, T., von Wendt, L., & Bartfai, A. (2007). Sustained favorable effects of cognitive training in children with acquired brain injuries. *Neurorehabilitation, 22*, 109–116.

van Hulst, B. M., de Zeeuw, P., Bos, D. J., Rijks, Y., Neggers, S. F. W., & Durston, S. (2017). Children with ADHD symptoms show decreased activity in ventral striatum during the anticipation of reward, irrespective of ADHD diagnosis. *Journal of Child Psychology and Psychiatry, 58*(2), 206–214.

Hwang, S., Gau, S. S., Hsu, W., & Wu, Y. (2010). Deficits in interval timing measured by the dual-task paradigm among children and adolescents with attention-deficit/hyperactivity disorder. *Journal of Child Psychology and Psychiatry, 51*(3), 223–232.

Kerns, K. A. (2000). The CyberCruiser: An investigation of development of prospective memory in children. *Journal of the International Neuropsychological Society, 6*, 62–70.

Kerns, K. A., & Price, K. J. (2001). An investigation of prospective memory in children with ADHD. *Child Neuropsychology, 7*(3), 162–171.

Kerns, K. A., McInerney, R. J., & Wilde, N. J. (2001). Time reproduction, working memory, and behavioral inhibition in children with ADHD. *Child Neuropsychology, 7*(1), 21–31.

Kerns, K. A., MacSween, J., Vander Weeken, S., & Grupposo, V. (2010). Investigating the efficacy of an attention training programme in children with foetal alcohol spectrum disorder. *Developmental Neurorehabilitation, 13*, 413–422.

Kessler, R. C., Adler, L. A., Barkley, R. A., Biederman, J., Conners, C. K., Faraone, S. V., … Zaslavsky, A. M. (2005). Patterns and predictors of attention-deficit/hyperactivity disorder persistence into adulthood: Results from the national comorbidity survey replication. *Biological Psychiatry, 57*, 1442–1451.

Keune, P. M., Wiedemann, E., Schneidt, A., & Schönenberg, M. (2015). Frontal brain asymmetry in adult attention-deficit/hyperactivity disorder (ADHD): Extending the motivational dysfunction hypothesis. *Clinical Neurophysiology, 126*, 711–730.

Kewley, G. D. (2005). *Attention deficit hyperactivity disorder: What can teachers do?*. London, GB: David Fulton.

Kliegel, M., & Jäger, T. (2006). Can the prospective and retrospective memory questionnaire (PRMQ) predict actual prospective memory performance? *Current Psychology: Developmental, Personality, Social, 25*(3), 182–191.

Kliegel, M., & Martin, M. (2002). *Heidelberger Exekutivfunktionsdiagnostikum (HEXE 3.01)*. Tannustein: Scholaware.

Kliegel, M., Martin, M., McDaniel, M. A., & Einstein, G. O. (2001). Varying the importance of a prospective memory task: Differential effects across time- and event-based prospective memory. *Memory, 9*(1), 1–11.

Kliegel, M., Ropeter, A., & Mackinlay, R. (2006). Complex prospective memory in children with ADHD. *Child Neuropsychology, 12*, 407–419.

Kliegel, M., Brandenberger, M., & Aberle, I. (2010). Effect of motivational incentives on prospective memory performance in preschoolers. *European Journal of Developmental Psychology, 7*(2), 223–232.

Kollins, S. H., Lane, S. D., & Shipiro, S. K. (1997). The experimental analysis of childhood psychopathology: A laboratory matching analysis of the behaviour of children diagnosed with attention deficit hyperactivity disorder. *Psychological Record, 47*(1), 25–44.

Kvavilashvili, L., Messer, D. J., & Ebdon, P. (2001). Prospective memory in children: The effects of age and task interruption. *Developmental Psychology, 37*, 418–430.

Lewis, C. E., Thomas, K. G. F., Molteno, C. D., Kliegel, M., Meintjes, E. M., Jacobson, J. L., & Jacobson, S. W. (2016). Prospective memory impairment in children with prenatal alcohol exposure. *Alcoholism: Clinical and Experimental Research, 40*(5), 969–978.

Li, C.-S. R., Yan, P., Bergquisdt, K. L., & Sinha, R. (2007). Greater activation of the 'default' brain regions predicts stop signal errors. *NeuroImage, 38*, 640–648.

Luman, M., Ooosterlaan, J., & Sergeant, J. A. (2005). The impact of reinforcement contingencies on AD/HD: A review and theoretical appraisal. *Clinical Psychology Review, 25*, 183–213.

Ma, I., van Duijvenvoorde, A., & Scheres, A. (2016). The interaction between reinforcement and inhibitory control in ADHD: A review and research guidelines. *Clinical Psychology Review, 44*, 94–111.

Mackinlay, R. J., Kliegel, M., & Mäntylä, T. (2009). Predictors of time-based prospective memory in children. *Journal of Experimental Child Psychology, 102*, 251–264.

Mahy, C. E. V., Moses, L. J., & Kliegel, M. (2014). The development of prospective memory in children: An executive framework. *Developmental Review, 34*, 305–326.

Markovitch, S., Boseovski, J. J., & Knapp, R. J. (2007). Use it or lose it: Examining preschoolers' difficulty maintaining and executing a goal. *Developmental Science, 10*(5), 559–564.

McDaniel, M. A. & Einstein, G. O. (2000). Strategic and automatic processes in prospective memory retrieval: A multiprocess framework. *Applied Cognitive Psychology, 14*, 127–144.

McDaniel, M. A., & Einstein, G. O. (2007). *Prospective memory: An overview and synthesis of an emerging field.* Los Angeles, CA: Sage Publications.

McInerney, R. J., & Kerns, K. A. (2003). Time reproduction in children with ADHD: Motivation matters. *Child Neuropsychology, 9*(2), 91–108.

Melby-Lervåg, M., & Hulme, C. (2013). Is working memory training effective? A metanalytic review *Developmental Psychology, 49*(2), 270–291.

Melby-Lervåg, M. & Hulme, C. (2016). There is no convincing evidence that working memory training is effective: A reply to Au et al. (2014) and Karbach and Verhaeghen (2014). *Psychonomic Bulletin & Review, 23*(1), 324–330.

Michel, J. A., Kerns, K. A., & Mateer, C. A. (2005). The effect of reinforcement variables on inhibition in children with ADHD. *Child Neuropsychology, 11*(3), 295–302.

Mills, G., Garbarino, J., & Raskin, S. (personal communication) (2010). Measurement of prospective memory in children: The memory for intentions screening test for youth (MISTY).

Mioni, G., Santon, S., Stablum, F., & Cornoldi, C. (2017). Time-based prospective memory difficulties in children with ADHD and the role of time perception and working memory. *Child Neuropsychology, 23*(5), 588–608.

Miranda, A., Presentación, J., Siegenthaler, R., & Jara, P. (2011). Effects of psychosocial intervention on the executive functioning in children with ADHD. *Journal of Learning Disabilities, 46*(4), 363–376.

Moher, D., Liberati, A., Tetzlaff, J., & Altman, D. (2009). Preferred reporting items for systematic reviews and meta-analyses: The PRISMA statement. *Annals of Internal Medicine, 151*, 264–269.

Mullins, C., Bellgrove, M. A., Gill, M., & Robertson, I. H. (2005). Variability in time reproduction: Difference in ADHD combined and inattentive subtypes. *Journal of the American Academy of Child & Adolescent Psychiatry, 44*(2), 169–176.

Nigg, J. T., Blaskey, L. G., Huang-Pollock, C. L., & Rappley, M. D. (2002). Neuropsychological executive functions and DSM-IV ADHD subtypes. *Journal of American Academy of Child & Adolescent Psychiatry, 41*(1), 59–66.

Nijmeijer, J. S., Minderaa, R. B., Buitelaar, J. K., Mulligan, A., Hartman, C. A., & Hoekstra, P. J. (2008). Attention-deficit/hyperactivity disorder and social dysfunctioning. *Clinical Psychology Review, 28*(4), 692–708.

Oosterlan, J., Scheres, A., & Sergeant, J. A. (2005). Which executive functioning deficits are associated with AD/HD, ODD/CD and comorbid AD/HD+ODD/CD? *Journal of Abnormal Child Psychology, 33*(1), 69–85.

Packiam Alloway, T., Gathercole, S. E., Holmes, J., Place, M., Elliott, J. G., & Hilton, K. (2009). The diagnostic utility of behavioural checklists in identifying children with ADHD and children with working memory deficits. *Child Psychiatry and Human Development, 40*, 353–366.

Patton, J. H., Stanford, M. S., & Barratt, E. S. (1995). Factor structure of the barratt impulsiveness scale. *Journal of Clinical Psychology, 6*, 768–774.

Peasgood, T., Bhardwaj, A., Biggs, K., & Sonuga-Barke, E. J. S. (2016). The impact of ADHD on the health and well-being of ADHD children and their siblings. *European Child and Adolescent Psychiatry, 25*(11), 1217–1231.

Posner, J., Park, C., & Wang, Z. (2014). Connecting the dots: A review of resting connectivity MRI studies in attention-deficit/hyperactivity disorder. *Neuropsychology Review, 24*, 3–15.

Potvin, M.-J., Rouleau, I., Audy, J., Charbonneau, S., & Giguère, J.-F. (2011). Ecological prospective memory assessment in patients with traumatic brain injury. *Brain Injury, 25*(2), 192–205.

Purdie, N., Hattie, J., & Carroll, A. (2002). A review of the research on interventions for attention deficit hyperactivity disorder: What works best? *Review of Educational Research, 72*(1), 61–99.

Quay, H. C. (1997). Inhibition and attention deficit hyperactivity disorder. *Journal of Abnormal Child Psychology, 2*, 7–13.

Raskin, S. A. (2009). Memory for intentions screening test: Psychometric Properties and clinical evidence. *Brain Impairment, 10*(1), 23–33.

Rendell, P. G., Vella, M. J., Kliegel, M., & Terrett, G. (2009). Effect of delay on children's delay-execute perspective memory performance. *Cognitive Development, 24*, 156–168.

Richter, K. M., Mödden, C., Eling, P., & Hildebrandt, H. (2015). Working memory training and semantic structuring improves remembering future events, not past events. *Neurorehabilitation and Neural Repair, 29*(1), 33–40.

Rose, N. S., Rendell, P. G., McDaniel, M. A., Aberle, I., & Kliegel, M. (2010). Age and individual differences in prospective memory during a 'Virtual Week': The roles of working memory, vigilance, task regularity, and cue focality. *Psychology and Aging, 25*(3), 595–605.

Rubia, K. (2007). Neuro-anatomic evidence for the maturational delay hypothesis of ADHD. *Proceedings from the National Academy of Sciences of the United States of America, 104*, 19663–19664.

Sbordone, R. J. (1996). Ecological validity: Some critical issues for the neuropsychologist. In R. J. Sbordone & C. J. Long (Eds.), *Ecological validity of neuropsychological testing* (pp. 15–42). Delray Beach, FL: GR Press/St. Lucie Press.

Schacter, D. L., Gilbert, D. T., & Wegner, D. I. M. (2010). *Implicit memory and explicit memory. Psychology*. New York, NY: Worth Publishers.

Schaffer, Y., & Geva, R. (2016). Memory outcomes following cognitive interventions in children with neurological deficits: A review with a focus on under-studied populations. *Neuropsychological Rehabilitation: An International Journal, 26*(2), 286–317.

Shaw, P., Stringaris, A., Nigg, J., & Leibenluft, E. (2014). Emotion dysregulation in attention deficit hyperactivity disorder. *American Journal of Psychiatry, 171*(3), 276–293.

Shum, D. H., Cross, B., Ford, R., & Ownsworth, T. (2008). A developmental investigation of prospective memory: The effects of interruption. *Child Neuropsychology, 14*(6), 547–561.

Shum, D. H., Cahill, A., Hohaus, L. C., O`Gorman, J. G., & Chan, R. C. K. (2012). Effects of aging, planning, and interruption on complex prospective memory. *Neuropsychological Rehabilitation: An International Journal, 23*(1), 45–63.

Sibley, M. H., Evans, S. W., & Serpell, Z. N. (2010). Social cognition and interpersonal impairment in young adolescents with ADHD. *Journal of Psychopathology and Behavioral Assessment, 32*(2), 193–202.

Sjöwall, D., Roth, L., Lindqvist, S., & Thorell, L. B. (2013). Multiple deficits in ADHD: Executive dysfunction, delay aversion, reaction time variability, and emotional deficits. *Journal of Child Psychology and Psychiatry, 54*(6), 619–627.

Sjöwall, D., Backman, A., & Thorell, L. B. (2015). Neuropsychological heterogeneity in preschool ADHD: Investigating the interplay between cognitive, affective and motivation-based forms of regulation. *Journal of Abnormal Psychology, 43*, 669–680.

Ślusarczyk, E., & Niedźwieńska, A. (2013). A naturalistic study of prospective memory in pre-schoolers: The role of task interruption and motivation. *Cognitive Development, 28*(3), 179–192.

Smith, G. V., Della Sala, S., Logie, R. H., & Maylor, E. A. M. (2000). Prospective and retrospective memory in normal aging and dementia: A questionnaire study. *Memory, 8*, 311–321.

Smith, R. E., Hunt, R. R., McVay, J. C., & McConnell, M. D. (2007). The cost of event-based prospective memory: Salient target events. *Journal of Experimental Psychology: Learning, Memory, and Cognition, 33*(4), 734–746.

Sohlberg, M., & Mateer, C. (2001). *Cognitive rehabilitation: An integrative neuropsychological approach*. New York, NY: Guilford Press.

Sonuga-Barke, E. J. (2002). Psychological heterogeneity in AD/HD – a dual pathway model of behaviour and cognition. *Behavioural Brain Research, 130*, 29–36.

Sonuga-Barke, E. J. (2003). The dual pathway model of AD/HD: An elaboration of neurodevelopmental characteristics. *Neuroscience and Biobehavioral Reviews, 27*(7), 593–604.

Sonuga-Barke, E. J., Williams, E., Hall, M., & Saxton, T. (1996). Hyperactivity and delay aversion: The effect on cognitive style of imposing delay after errors. *Journal of Child Psychology and Psychiatry, 45*, 912–926.

Sonuga-Barke, E. J., Sergeant, J. A., Nigg, J., & Willcutt, E. (2008). Executive function and delay aversion in attention-deficit hyperactivity disorder: Nosologic and diagnostic implications. *Child and Adolescent Psychiatric Clinics of North America, 17*, 367–384.

Talbot, K.-D. S. (2015). *Investigating general time-based prospective memory in school- aged children using a novel naturalistic paradigm* (unpublished master's thesis). Victoria, BC, Canada: University of Victoria.

Talbot, K.-D. S., & Kerns, K. A. (2014). Event and time triggered remembering: The impact of ADHD on prospective memory performance in children. *Journal of Experimental Child Psychology, 127*, 126–143. doi:10.1016/j.jecp.2014.02.011

Tarver, J., Daley, D., & Sayal, K. (2014). Attention-deficit hyperactivity disorder (ADHD): An updated review of the essential facts. *Child: Care, Health, and Development, 40*(6), 762–774.

Terry, W. S. (1988). Everyday forgetting: Data from a diary study. *Psychological Reports, 62*, 299–303.

Tomasi, D., & Volkov, N. D. (2012). Abnormal functional connectivity in children with attention-deficit/hyperactivity disorder. *Biological Psychiatry, 71*, 443–450.

Toplak, M. E., Bucciarelli, S. M., Jain, U., & Tannock, R. (2009). Executive functions: Performance-based measures and the behaviour rating inventor of executive function (BRIEF) in adolescents with attention deficit/hyperactivity disorder (ADHD). *Child Neuropsychology, 15*, 53–72.

Tripp, G., & Wickens, J. R. (2008). Research review: Dopamine transfer deficit: A neurobiological theory of altered reinforcement mechanisms in ADHD. *Journal of Child Psychology and Psychiatry, 49*, 691–704.

Uekermann, J., Kraemer, M., Abdel-Hamid, M., Schimmelmann, B. G., Hebebrand, J., Daum, I., … Kis, B. (2010). Review: Social cognition in attention-deficit hyperactivity disorder (ADHD). *Neuroscience and Biobehavioral Reviews*, 734–743.

Walg, M., Oepen, J., & Prior, H. (2012). Adjustment of time perception in the range of seconds to milliseconds. *Journal of Attention Disorders, 19*(9), 755–763.

Wang, L., Kliegel, M., Liu, W., & Yang, Z. (2008). Prospective memory performance in preschoolers: Inhibitory control matters. *European Journal of Developmental Psychology, 5*(3), 289–302.

Wehmeier, P. M., Schacht, A., & Barkley, R. A. (2010). Social and emotional impairment in children and adolescents with ADHD and the impact on quality of life. *Journal of Adolescent Health, 46*, 209–217.

West, R. (2010). The temporal dynamics of prospective memory: A review of the ERP and prospective memory literature. *Neuropsychologia, 49*, 2233–2245.

Willcutt, E. G., Doyle, A. E., Nigg, J. T., Farone, S. V., & Pennington, B. F. (2005). Validity of the executive function theory of attention-deficit/hyperactivity disorder: A meta-analytic review. *Biological Psychiatry, 57*(11), 1336–1346.

Wilson, B. A., Cockburn, J., & Baddeley, A. (1985). *Rivermead behavioural memory test (RBMT)*. Bury St. Edmunds: Thames Valley Test Company.

Wilson, B., Cockburn, J., Baddeley, A., & Hiorns, R. (1989). The development and validation of a test battery for detecting and monitoring everyday memory. *Journal of Clinical and Experimental Neuropsychology, 11*, 855–870.

Wilson, B. A., Ivani-chalian, R., Besag, F. M. C., & Bryant, T. (1993). Adapting the rivermead behavioural memory test for use with children aged 5–10 years. *Journal of Clinical and Experimental Neuropsychology, 15*, 474–486.

Wilson, B. A., Emslie, H., Foley, J., Shiel, A., Watson, P., Hawkins, K., …Evans, J. J. (2005). *Cambridge prospective memory tests (CAMPROMT)*. London: Harcourt Assessment.

Wilson, B., Emslie, H., Evans, J., Quirk, K., Watson, P., & Fish, J. (2009). The neuropage system for children and adolescents with neurological deficits. *Developmental Neurorehabilitation, 12*, 421–426.

Woods, S. P., Moran, L. M., Dawson, M. S., Carey, C. L., Grant, I., & HIV Neurobehavioral Research Center (HNRC) Group (2008). Psychometric characteristics of the memory for intentions screening test. *The Clinical Neuropsychologist, 22*, 864–878.

Yang, T., Chan, R. C. K., & Shum, D. (2011). The development of prospective memory in typically developing children. *Neuropsychology, 25*(3), 342–352.

Zelazo, P. D., & Müller, U. (2010). Executive function in typical and a typical children. In U. Goswami (Ed.), *The Blackwell-Wiley handbook of childhood cognitive development* (2nd rev ed., pp. 574–603). Oxford: Blackwell.

Zinke, K., Altgassen, M., Mackinlay, R. J., Rizzo, P., Drechsler, R., & Kliegel, M. (2010). Time-based prospective memory performance and time-monitoring in children with ADHD. *Child Neuropsychology, 16*, 338–349.

A review of prospective memory impairments in developmental dyslexia: evidence, explanations, and future directions

James H. Smith-Spark

ABSTRACT

Objective: The effects of developmental dyslexia are not restricted solely to the processes involved in reading and spelling. Despite this broader impact on cognition, there has been very little dyslexia-related research on prospective memory (PM; memory for delayed intentions) until very recently. This paper focuses on reviewing a recent program of research which sought to explore this memory system in adults with dyslexia. **Method:** The review focuses mainly on studies of adults with dyslexia in which PM was compared with that of IQ-matched adults without dyslexia across clinical measures, computerized tests, self-report questionnaire, and more naturalistic tasks. **Results:** Across the reviewed studies, the adults with dyslexia showed a range of impairments in both laboratory and everyday settings. Dyslexia-related PM impairments occurred predominantly when cues to remembering were time-based rather than being cued by events in the environment, when delays to act upon the intention were prolonged, and when tasks were one-off events rather than being habitual. As well as being less accurate in their PM, the participants with dyslexia were also less likely to remember PM instructions over longer delay periods. **Conclusions:** PM deficits in dyslexia are considered in terms of the retrospective and prospective components of PM function. Less efficient access to verbal information in long-term memory, problems with time perception, and poorer executive functions are all considered as potential explanations for less accurate PM in dyslexia. The findings from the research program are linked to broader dyslexia theory and research. Some potential means for supporting individuals with dyslexia are considered.

Developmental dyslexia

Developmental dyslexia (henceforth, dyslexia) is characterized by core deficits in phonological processing (for reviews, see Castles & Friedmann, 2014; Vellutino, Fletcher, Snowling, & Scanlon, 2004). Alongside its well-documented effects on the processes involved in reading and spelling, dyslexia has also been found to be associated with broader impairments in cognition (e.g. Bogaerts et al., 2015; Booth, Boyle, & Kelly, 2010; Menghini, Finzi, Carlesimo, & Vicari, 2011; Smith-Spark, Fisk, Fawcett, & Nicolson, 2003; Smith-Spark, Henry, Messer,

Edvardsdottir, & Zięcik, 2016). Given the potentially wide-ranging consequences of such problems, it is important to gain a more detailed understanding of how the impact of dyslexia may extend beyond tasks involving literacy skills. To this end, the current paper reviews research on prospective memory (PM), an area of cognition which has been more-or-less ignored in the developmental dyslexia literature until very recently, despite this memory system being called upon on a daily basis across a range of different situations (e.g. McDaniel & Einstein, 2007). A better understanding of the impact of dyslexia on PM can then be used to support individuals with dyslexia across personal, educational, and employment settings.

Prospective memory

Prospective memory is memory for delayed intentions (Winograd, 1988) or 'remembering to remember' (Mäntylä, 1994). All PM tasks share two common components. A prospective (or planning) component serves to remind the individual at the appropriate moment that an intention needs to be acted upon, while a retrospective component is responsible for providing the individual with the detail of what the intended behavior actually was that needed to be performed (e.g. Einstein & McDaniel, 1996; Ellis, 1996). The uses of PM can either be habitual or one-off (or episodic) events. Intentions may need to be remembered over either the shorter-term (seconds, minutes or hours) or the longer-term (days, weeks or even months). Furthermore, the cues to prompt PM can be either event-based, where objects in the individual's surrounding environment serve as reminders that an intention needs to be acted upon (e.g. seeing a friend should remind the individual to pass on a message to him or her from another friend as intended), or time-based, where an intended action needs to be performed at some point in time in the future (e.g. needing to arrange travel insurance prior to leaving for a holiday the following week or to return a telephone call to a friend later the same day). Prospective memory can thus be divided broadly into two types depending upon the type of cue to support remembering to remember, namely event-based PM (EBPM) and time-based PM (TBPM).

Dyslexia and PM

The following subsections review the evidence for PM deficits in dyslexia. Firstly, the focus of the current review on PM in adults is explained. After that, initial work in areas of cognition related to PM which informed the research program are considered. The review then addresses the evidence obtained from self-report studies, laboratory-based work, and tasks with more naturalistic demands.

Focus of the review: PM in adults

While much of the research literature on dyslexia has focused on children and adolescents, there is also a considerable body of evidence to document its continued impact into adulthood in a range of cognitive domains, including executive functions (e.g. Brosnan et al., 2002; Smith-Spark, Henry et al., 2016), working memory (e.g. Nergård-Nilssen & Hulme, 2014; Smith-Spark & Fisk, 2007; Smith-Spark et al., 2003), and rapid naming (Nergård-Nilssen & Hulme, 2014). Broader cognitive difficulties have also been perceived by adults with dyslexia as occurring more frequently in their everyday lives (Leather, Hogh, Seiss, & Everatt, 2011; Smith-Spark, Fawcett, Nicolson, & Fisk, 2004; Smith-Spark, Henry et al., 2016). Unlike most areas of research on the effects of dyslexia, the majority of work on PM has been carried out on adults with dyslexia. This subsection will explain the reasons for this focus and give key information on the background characteristics of the samples used in the studies of PM in adults which are reviewed subsequently.

McLoughlin, Fitzgibbon, and Young (1994) have highlighted the differing demands on the cognition of an adult with dyslexia compared with that of a child. As a consequence, they argued that adults with dyslexia should not be treated simply as children with dyslexia who have 'grown up' (p. 1). Instead, the authors identified the need for more research on the cognition of adults with dyslexia in its own right. With particular respect to PM, the demands and responsibilities placed on an adult to remember are likely to be far greater. In childhood, parents, teachers, and caregivers will often provide 'external' PM support (c.f., Clark & Chalmers, 1998), reminding children of delayed intentions and ensuring that tasks are completed successfully at the appropriate point. Even when dyslexia is officially recognized in an adult and appropriate support provisions are in place, PM failure is still likely to be looked upon in an unfavorable light, especially when there are negative consequences attached to failing to meet deadlines or attend meetings (Smith-Spark, 2017).

These arguments provided the rationale for a recent program of research into PM in adults with dyslexia. Full details of the background characteristics of the samples tested are reported in Smith-Spark, Zięcik, and Sterling (2016a, 2016b, 2017a, 2017b). In all four studies, the participant groups were matched for general intelligence and differed on measures of reading and spelling. Educational psychologists' reports were checked for all participants presenting with dyslexia. Comorbidity with attention deficit (hyperactivity) disorder (ADHD) was not identified in the educational psychologists' reports. Moreover, an overlapping sample of adults with dyslexia tested by Smith-Spark, Henry et al. (2016) showed no evidence of attentional problems on the Test of Everyday Attention (Ward & Ridgeway, 1994).

Early, indirect evidence suggestive of PM problems

While the effects of dyslexia on PM have only been explored directly very recently (Khan, 2014; Smith-Spark et al., 2016a, 2016b, 2017a, 2017b), earlier research has identified dyslexia-related difficulties in areas of cognition which could be argued to draw on similar cognitive abilities to those involved in PM. Problems in the areas of organization, time-keeping, and planning have been reported in dyslexia and the relevance of these abilities to PM has recently been highlighted by Waldum and McDaniel (2016) in relation to performing complex everyday PM tasks. In children with dyslexia, difficulties with organization (Torgeson, 1977) and planning (Condor, Anderson, & Saling, 1998; Klicpera, 1983; Levin, 1990) have been found under laboratory conditions. In adult university students with dyslexia, organization and time-keeping have been self-reported as being worse (Mortimore & Crozier, 2006). Similar problems in adults with dyslexia have also been identified by their family and close friends (Smith-Spark et al., 2004).

Subjective evidence provided by self and others

Stanovich (2009) has argued that it is important to understand cognition at different levels, making a distinction between performance when carrying out a task optimally under laboratory conditions and when acting under typical, everyday conditions. He named these levels of cognition algorithmic and reflective, respectively. Investigating the reflective level of cognition requires the researcher to tap into the day-to-day experiences and perceptions of individuals relating to their own typical levels of performance and, sometimes, these self-perceptions are corroborated by reports from close associates of these individuals. Two commonly used approaches to collecting self-report data are by means of diary studies and questionnaires. Both approaches have provided insights into everyday PM in dyslexia.

A diary study conducted by Smith-Spark (2000) required adults with and without dyslexia to record errors in their everyday cognition over a two-week period, writing down the nature of each slip that they committed and the circumstances prevailing at the time that it was made. While the focus of the research was on slips of action (e.g. Reason, 1979; where habitual or routine actions go awry), the respondents also reported broader cognitive failures. Chief among these, a greater frequency of memory-related slips were reported by adults with dyslexia compared with adults without dyslexia. Many of these memory errors were retrospective (e.g. relating to forgetting previous actions or telling the same story to someone on more than one occasion) but there were also many memory failures involving PM (e.g. forgetting to post letters or to return library books as intended).

Self-report questionnaires can also be helpful in identifying patterns of PM performance over the longer-term (such as in the past month or six months). The Prospective and Retrospective Memory Questionnaire (PRMQ; Smith, Della Sala, Logie, & Maylor, 2000) is a 16-item self-report questionnaire measuring the relative frequency with which memory errors are perceived to be experienced by the respondent. The PRMQ probes both PM and retrospective memory (with the latter being episodic memory or memory for personally experienced past events). The questions on the PRMQ can be subdivided into different scales relating to the type of memory assessed (PM or retrospective memory), whether the memory was short- or longer-term, and whether the recall cue was environmental or internal to the self. The PRMQ has been used in two different studies to uncover higher frequencies of memory error in dyslexia (Khan, 2014; Smith-Spark et al., 2016a).

Khan (2014) administered the PRMQ (Smith et al., 2000) to children with and without dyslexia. The children with dyslexia self-reported more memory problems. In particular, self-cued memory was more prone to the effects of dyslexia than environmentally-cued memory. However, while this study identified increased PM problems in children with dyslexia, it should be noted that the PRMQ is aimed at adult respondents rather than children (indeed, Talbot & Kerns, 2014, have produced an adapted version of the questionnaire specifically designed for children, in which parental ratings are taken). Furthermore, there was a wide range of ages in the sample, meaning that some individuals had more opportunity to exercise their PM, having a greater degree of independence as a result of their greater maturity. The comparative ages of the children with and without dyslexia were not reported, making it difficult to determine their relative opportunity for independent PM. Moreover, details of the two group's relative scores on the screening measures were not reported and the criteria for inclusion in the group with dyslexia were not fully defined.

Smith-Spark et al. (2016a) administered the PRMQ (Smith et al., 2000) to a sample of adults with and without dyslexia. Higher frequencies of both PM and retrospective memory difficulties were reported by the respondents with dyslexia, with these problems affecting memory over both the shorter- and longer-term and when memories were environmentally- or internally-cued.

The proxy-rating PRMQ (Crawford, Henry, Ward, & Blake, 2006) employs exactly the same questions as the PRMQ but is completed by a family member or close friend of the PRMQ respondent. Smith-Spark et al. (2016a) administered it to close associates of their PRMQ respondents. These proxy-ratings also indicated a heightened frequency of PM (and, again, retrospective memory) difficulty in adults with dyslexia. The proxy-rating results are important in validating the self-reports of the adults with dyslexia and ruling out the negative self-image and self-esteem associated with the condition in adulthood (e.g. Riddick, Sterling, Farmer, & Morgan, 1999) as an explanation of the reported increased frequency of memory failure.

Unlike the PRMQ (Smith et al., 2000), the Prospective Memory Questionnaire (PMQ; Hannon, Adams, Harrington, Fries-Dias, & Gibson, 1995) is a self-report questionnaire devoted entirely to the assessment of PM performance. The PMQ's 52 questions are divided between four subscales tapping different aspects of PM performance. Three of the subscales asked respondents to estimate how frequently in the past week, month or year they had experienced particular types of PM failure. The Long-term Episodic subscale assessed self-rated PM performance where there were extended durations between forming a PM intention and being able to act upon it. The Short-term Habitual subscale, on the other hand, probed the performance of PM tasks carried out regularly over short intervals. The Internally-cued subscale measured the frequency of PM failure when there were no external cues to facilitate remembering and performance was, thus, self-initiated. A further subscale, Techniques Used to Assist Recall, assessed the frequency with which respondents used a range of strategies and tools to support their PM.

Given the PMQ's dedicated focus on PM, Smith-Spark et al. (2017a) administered it to adults with and without dyslexia in order to explore PM at a finer-grained level than that permitted by Smith et al.'s (2000) PRMQ. On the Techniques Used to Assist Recall subscale, the adults with dyslexia self-reported more frequent use of tools and technology to aid their PM than the adults without dyslexia. The group difference on this subscale was then entered as a covariate when analyzing the responses to the scales designed to measure the frequency of PM failure (see Heffernan et al., 2006, for a similar approach with teenage excessive drinkers). Overall, the group with dyslexia reported more frequent problems with their PM. More specifically, they identified problems with long-term episodic and self-initiated PM. However, the groups did not differ in the frequency of PM failure when tasks were habitual and short-term.

Laboratory-based evidence

The first direct empirical observation of PM deficits in dyslexia was reported by Smith-Spark et al. (2016b). Three computerized TBPM tasks were administered to adults with and without dyslexia. These tasks varied in the load that ongoing behavior placed on working memory resources. The adults with dyslexia were found to have less accurate PM responses than the adults without dyslexia. They also made fewer clock checks during testing, although the overall pattern of the checks over the three-minute lead-up to a PM response being due was similar to that of the adults without dyslexia. A reduced frequency of clock checking suggests either a misplaced metacognitive confidence in their timing abilities or a greater degree of attentional resources being channeled toward the ongoing task to the detriment of clock checking. However, the latter explanation does not sit well with the accuracy of PM performance, where there was no interaction between participant group and the presence or absence of additional concurrent working memory load.

The Memory for Intentions Test (MIST; Raskin, Buckheit, & Sherrod, 2010) is a well-established clinical measure of PM. It was used by Smith-Spark et al. (2017a) to explore PM in adults with dyslexia over a range of different types of task, cue, and response. Over the course of the MIST's 30-min administration, eight PM tasks were set for the participant who was engaged in an ongoing activity (completing a word search puzzle) from which they had to break out to perform the PM tasks. The PM tasks varied in the type of cue to prompt a response (time or event), the delay between receiving a PM task instruction and the task needing to be performed (two minutes or 15 min), and the type of response required (verbal or action). The adults with dyslexia displayed poorer PM overall on the MIST. At a finer-grained level, there was an interaction between dyslexia status and cue type. Compared with adults without dyslexia, the participants with dyslexia showed reduced levels of performance when TBPM was required but performed at an equivalent level when EBPM was needed. The two groups did not differ in their ability to recognize the PM instructions correctly when given a retrospective recognition test on completion of the MIST, suggesting that the PM instructions were successfully encoded and retained over the course of the test administration.

The nature of the MIST cue type interaction, in which no differences were found when event-based cues were presented, is consistent with the null findings obtained from two computerized EBPM tasks which compared adults with and without dyslexia (Zięcik, 2015). No group differences were found either when the processing of PM cues was consistent with task demands (such that both involved semantic processing; a high cue focality task) or when the ongoing task required semantic processing but event cues required featural processing (a low cue focality task). While it is inadvisable to draw any conclusions from null results, the pattern of these findings is in general agreement with those arising from the MIST and suggest that TBPM, in particular, is prone to error in dyslexia.

Naturalistic evidence

The performance of adults with dyslexia has also been explored under more everyday task demands and conditions. While findings from controlled laboratory experiments are very much the gold standard in terms of ensuring the validity of findings, it is important also to gain an understanding of how any problems so identified might actually play out in the day-to-day lives of individuals with dyslexia (cf., Stanovich, 2009). Such work can then be used to demonstrate that dyslexia-related deficits in PM are not limited to often rather contrived tasks carried out in artificial settings but actually have a negative impact on the everyday PM of those with the condition. They, thus, provide an additional source of evidence to feed into supporting adults with dyslexia appropriately in education and the workplace, highlighting areas where reasonable adjustments to practices and procedures should be made.

Smith-Spark et al. (2016b) embedded a semi-naturalistic task within their computerized TBPM testing session. The participants were instructed to remind the experimenter to save a file 40 min later as, if they did not, the data would be lost. In the meantime, they were engaged in performing other PM tasks and received no further explicit reminders about this particular task. Compared with the adults without dyslexia, those with dyslexia were found to be much less likely to remind the experimenter to save the file, thus exhibiting a TBPM deficit in response to a more ecologically valid task.

The optional naturalistic task from Raskin et al.'s (2010) MIST was also employed by Smith-Spark et al. (2017a). The participants were asked to leave a telephone message for the experimenter exactly 24 h after they had attended a laboratory-based session. This measure allowed an exploration of TBPM performance when a longer delay was imposed between intention formation. Furthermore, it placed the opportunity to act upon that intention outside the laboratory (since the laboratory setting itself provides some physical contextual cues to remember to perform a PM task). Responses were thus required under naturalistic conditions in the ongoing day-to-day life of the participant. The adults with dyslexia were found to be less likely to perform the task successfully and more likely to fail to complete it, while the adults in the group without dyslexia were more likely to complete the task successfully and less likely to fail to perform it.

As stated previously, under laboratory conditions, dyslexia-related deficits have been found to center on TBPM with EBPM performance being unaffected (Smith-Spark et al., 2017a; Zięcik, 2015). There is, however, some evidence of EBPM difficulties over extended delay intervals and in everyday conditions. Smith-Spark et al. (2017b) found evidence of less accurate EBPM in adults with dyslexia when the delay between intention formation and intention execution was of a much longer duration, with the cue being presented one week after attending a laboratory-based testing session. The participants were requested to place a missed call to the experimenter when they received a text message. The PM task required the participant to ring the experimenter on the number from which the text message had been sent but to ring off before the telephone call was received. A mobile telephone was dedicated exclusively to the experiment and, in fact, the experimenter never answered calls to its number; instead, it was used simply to log participants' responses. While making a missed call to a friend's number in order to exchange numbers is quite a common strategy in the United Kingdom, the task demands could be argued to be episodic, and to present some degree of novelty, in that leaving a missed call in response to a text message received while not in the company of the sender is not a usual or typical activity. The adults with dyslexia were less likely to respond successfully to the PM task and more likely to fail to respond. The reverse pattern of performance was found in the adults without dyslexia. Despite showing no difference in the initial encoding of the verbal instructions relating to the PM task and also reporting equivalent levels of motivation to perform the task successfully, the group with dyslexia were more likely to report having forgotten the task instructions over the course of the week between forming the intention and having the opportunity to act upon it. However, the two groups did not differ in the number of times they reported thinking about the task over the week's interval. Overall, these findings suggest that dyslexia-related deficits can be found in EBPM over extended delay intervals and when task conditions are episodic.

How can dyslexia-related PM deficits be explained?

There is, thus, a small body of literature investigating the effects of dyslexia on PM directly (Khan, 2014; Smith-Spark, 2000; Smith-Spark et al., 2016a, 2016b, 2017a, 2017b), while a number of other papers have provided indirect evidence that problems might exist in this area of cognition (Condor et al., 1998; Klicpera, 1983; Levin, 1990; Mortimore & Crozier, 2006; Smith-Spark et al., 2004; Torgeson, 1977). While the latter studies are useful in identifying where dyslexia-related problems might lie, this section will focus on the studies which have addressed PM explicitly. The results of the direct studies suggest that PM is most likely to be affected by dyslexia when TBPM rather than EBPM is needed (although see Smith-Spark et al., 2017b), when task demands are episodic rather than repeated or habitual, when delays are longer between intention formation and intention execution, and when performance has to be self-initiated rather than being offloaded to external objects.

Estimates of the likely prevalence rate of PM problems in dyslexia calculated from Smith-Spark et al. (2017a) suggest that around half of adults with dyslexia are likely to experience difficulties in this area of cognition. On the MIST, 40% of the adults with dyslexia had an overall PM accuracy score at least one *SD* lower than the control mean. On the PMQ, 50% of adults with dyslexia had total PM scores more than one *SD* greater than the control mean, indicating more frequent difficulties with PM. Similarly, 61% of the respondents with dyslexia on Smith et al.'s (2000) PRMQ produced total PM scores which were more than 1 *SD* higher than the mean of the control group, again identifying more frequent problems.

These estimated prevalence rates (albeit gained from a small number of studies) indicate the importance of understanding the effects of dyslexia on PM. It is necessary, therefore, to consider how such deficits can be explained by the dyslexia literature. Two broad theoretical approaches to dyslexia can be identified, those that consider dyslexia in terms of a core phonological processing deficit (Vellutino et al., 2004; Vellutino, 1979; for a review, see Castles & Friedmann, 2014) and those that consider broader cognitive difficulties within their frameworks (e.g. Nicolson & Fawcett, 1990; Nicolson, Fawcett, & Dean, 1995). By linking different theoretical approaches and findings from the research literature to specific PM components or task demands, it is possible to make some conjectures about the pattern of PM deficits in dyslexia. As stated previously, all PM tasks share two components (Einstein & McDaniel, 1996; Ellis, 1996), a prospective component and a retrospective component. Possible explanations of dyslexia-related PM problems will now be considered in terms of these two components and, where appropriate, will be linked to dyslexia theory.

Difficulties with the retrospective component of PM

Prospective memory deficits in dyslexia might be explained by problems with the retrospective component of PM and, more specifically, in the encoding and retrieval of verbal information in memory.

Gonneaud et al. (2011) found that in a sample of typically aging older adults, episodic retrospective memory abilities and the binding of associations between cue and action were found to be the strongest predictors of EBPM. There is some evidence to indicate that weaker binding of associations exists in dyslexia (Albano, Basso Garcia, & Cornoldi, 2016; Jones, Branigan, Parra, & Logie, 2013; Jones, Kuipers, & Thierry, 2016). For example, university students with dyslexia have been reported to have problems in binding associations between pairs of phonological and visual features (Jones et al., 2013). Cross-modal association problems may play out in PM task performance, since forming an association between task and cue is a one-off event and a (usually) verbal instruction needs to prompt a non-verbal action after a delay. The role of binding as a predictor of PM performance in dyslexia needs to be explored in future research.

Dyslexia-related problems with PM may thus arise from effective access to information in retrospective (or episodic) memory. In support of this argument, there is a small literature identifying long-term memory problems in children with dyslexia (McNamara & Wong, 2003;

Menghini, Carlesimo, Marotta, Finzi, & Vicari, 2010; Nelson & Warrington, 1980). Similarly, dyslexia-related differences have been found in adults in long-term memory representations (Smith-Spark & Moore, 2009), together with self-reported problems in remembering both facts (Mortimore & Crozier, 2006) and episodically-experienced events (Smith-Spark et al., 2016a). However, as far as the author is aware, no studies have investigated whether phonological processing abilities (measured by basic tasks such as spoonerisms or phoneme deletion; e.g. Fawcett & Nicolson, 1998) predict successful access to information held in verbal long-term memory in dyslexia, either in general or, more specifically, when PM is required. This should be investigated in future research.

With regard to the ability to remember PM instructions (i.e. the retrospective component of PM), different patterns of performance were found depending upon the delay interval and the method used to test the participants' memory. Poorer recall was reported by the participants with dyslexia in the naturalistic EBPM study reported by Smith-Spark et al. (2017b). However, no group difference was found when recognition of instructions was required by the Retrospective Recognition Questionnaire on the MIST (Raskin et al., 2010) under laboratory conditions (Smith-Spark et al., 2017a). As well as highlighting the difference between recall and recognition of verbal material, testing for memory of the EBPM instructions took place after a week's interval compared with an interval of only 30 min in the case of the MIST. There was, thus, a much longer interval over which the instructions needed to be retained in memory, increasing the chances of decay. The results might, thus, suggest quicker decay of the PM task information from memory in the adults with dyslexia. However, it should be noted that no group differences were found in the self-reported frequency with which the participants thought about the task in the week between forming the intention and receiving the text message to cue enactment of the intention. In addition, since receiving text messages is generally a daily occurrence (at the very least), there is an argument in favor of reduced cue salience being present on the naturalistic task compared with a much higher cue salience when MIST event cues are presented in a laboratory setting by an unfamiliar experimenter sitting in front of the participant. From this perspective, a greater degree of self-initiated PM would be required by the naturalistic task. Self-initiated PM will be considered in more depth when the prospective component is considered in a later section.

Ramus and Szenkovits (2008) have argued that individuals with dyslexia may have greater difficulty accessing phonological representations under specific task demands (such as when short-term memory is required, when time constraints are in place, or when conscious awareness is needed). Less effective access to verbal information relating to PM task instructions might, therefore, result in lowered PM performance in individuals with dyslexia.

Reduced effective access to phonological representations could explain, on two fronts, why poorer memory for PM instructions was found when recall was required (Smith-Spark et al., 2017b) than when recognition was tested (Smith-Spark et al., 2017a). Firstly, and most directly, the use of the MIST's Retrospective Recognition Questionnaire (Raskin et al., 2010) could support access to weaker memory representations for the participants with dyslexia by cuing recall and, thereby, reducing or eliminating the difference between the groups in the accessibility of task instructions in memory. Secondly, participants were asked whether they recalled the PM instructions one week after having been given them. This extended delay interval meant that there was a greater opportunity for memory of the instructions to decay over the intervening period than when participants were tested on the MIST instructions immediately after the end of the test administration.

There is, thus, some evidence to suggest that problems with remembering PM task instructions and accessing them reliably at the time that they are needed may explain dyslexia-related problems with PM. In summary, based on the findings of Smith-Spark et al. (2016b, 2017a), the initial encoding of PM instructions seems not to present difficulties to adults with dyslexia (based on verbal checks by the experimenter that instructions had been understood and on the results of the MIST's Retrospective Recognition Questionnaire; Raskin et al., 2010). In terms of the maintenance of instructions over the intervening period, a more equivocal pattern is demonstrated. Individuals with dyslexia reported that they thought about instructions a similar number of times as adults without dyslexia, yet were more likely to report not remembering them (Smith-Spark et al., 2017b). Poorer access to representations of the PM task in memory could be argued to be shown in the reduced levels of accuracy produced by the adults with dyslexia across different studies (Smith-Spark et al., 2016b, 2017a, 2017b). However, further research is needed to determine whether the problems experienced by adults with dyslexia in the retrospective component of PM occur at the point of encoding instructions, their representation and maintenance in memory, or effective access to them at the point at which they are required. Comparing recognition of task instructions with recall over equivalent delay periods would also be informative in understanding where differences arise.

More broadly, evidence of difficulties with the retrospective component of PM can be linked quite plausibly to explanations of dyslexia which place phonological processing problems at the core of the condition. However, the Phonological Deficit Hypothesis (e.g. Vellutino, 1979) does not seem to provide so ready an explanation of the discrepancies found between TBPM and EBPM performance nor between habitual and episodic PM responses. However, it could be argued that self-initiated performance is likely to be based on internal, language-based strategies, while visual cues will be drawn upon to a greater extent when PM is environmentally supported. To explain these findings, an appeal to broader explanations of dyslexia is needed, together with a shift in focus to considering the prospective (or planning) component of PM.

Difficulties with the prospective component of PM

Executive functions constitute a range of higher-order cognitive functions such as planning, organizing behavior, dual-task management, inhibition, set shifting, maintaining task-relevant information in memory over the period for which it is required, and controlled access to information in long-term memory (e.g. Fisk & Sharp, 2004; Miyake et al., 2000; Pennington & Ozonoff, 1996). With regard to PM, the executive functions have been argued to be engaged at the stages of forming an intention to act in the future and executing that intention at the appropriate time-point in the future, while they are not considered to be so involved in intention retention over the intervening period (Martin, Kliegel, & McDaniel, 2003). Executive functions are argued to be engaged in PM especially when self-initiated or TBPM is required (e.g. Martin et al., 2003; McDaniel & Einstein, 2000; although see Gonneaud et al., 2011; for an argument that executive functions are more engaged in EBPM tasks). As noted previously, more problems with self-initiated PM have been reported in both children and adults with dyslexia (Khan, 2014; Smith-Spark et al., 2017a), while dyslexia-related TBPM difficulties have been observed in adults with dyslexia (Smith-Spark et al., 2016b, 2017a). This section will consider how dyslexia-related problems with the prospective component of PM might be explained in terms of the executive function difficulties also documented in adults with dyslexia (e.g. Brosnan et al., 2002; Smith-Spark, Henry et al., 2016).

Several specific executive functions have been implicated in PM in other populations. Inhibition is the ability to prevent a pre-potent or habitual response in favor of more novel task-appropriate behavior (e.g. Miyake et al., 2000). Set shifting, also known as task switching, reflects the ability to shift between cognitive operations or representational sets (e.g. Miyake et al., 2000). Both inhibition and set shifting have been found to predict the PM performance of adults (Bisiacchi, Schiff, Ciccola, & Kliegel, 2009; Gonneaud et al., 2011; Schnitzspahn, Stahl, Zeintl, Kaller, & Kliegel, 2013; although see Altgassen, Vetter, Phillips, Akgün, & Kliegel, 2014, who found a predictive relationship only in children and not adults). However, while these studies are useful in indicating how executive function difficulties might have a negative impact on PM, dyslexia itself was not under investigation. Research to explore the relative roles of a range of different executive functions in contributing to PM function in dyslexia is thus still required.

Working memory (or 'updating' within Miyake et al., 2000; tripartite framework of executive functions), involves the temporary storage and processing of information in memory (e.g. Cowan, 2008). Like the executive functions already mentioned, working memory has also been found to be a positive predictor of PM (e.g. Marsh & Hicks, 1998), especially under taxing cognitive conditions (Basso, Ferrari, & Palladino, 2010). It was identified as the only executive function found to influence developmental changes in TBPM abilities by Kretschmer, Voigt, Friedrich, Pfeiffer, and Kliegel (2014).

The well-documented persistence of dyslexia-related working memory impairments into adulthood (e.g. Smith-Spark & Fisk, 2007; Smith-Spark et al., 2003) might thus suggest themselves as a potential explanation for the poorer PM found in dyslexia. However, set against this, Smith-Spark et al. (2016b) found no group by cognitive load interaction when they added a further ongoing task which loaded on working memory resources. Deficits in TBPM were shown by the group with dyslexia regardless of working memory load, seemingly ruling out an explanation of dyslexia-related TBPM problems couched in terms of working memory difficulties. However, as Smith-Spark et al. identified, the working memory load generated by the secondary ongoing task may not have been sufficiently taxing to affect TBPM performance.

The executive function of phonemic fluency requires the flexible access of information in long-term memory (Fisk & Sharp, 2004). Phonemic fluency tasks require individuals to generate as many words as possible beginning with a certain letter in a specified time (usually 60 s). Using a within-subjects design, Smith-Spark, Moss, and Dyer (2016) found that phonemic fluency predicted the extent to which PM performance declined in adult non-problem drinkers when under the influence of alcohol compared with their performance when a placebo was administered. Individuals with better phonemic fluency abilities showed a smaller decline in PM performance under alcohol than those with weaker phonemic fluency abilities.

Given that phonemic fluency is an area in which adults with dyslexia have been found to have difficulties (e.g. Brosnan et al., 2002; Smith-Spark, Henry, Messer, & Zięcik, 2017), it may well be that at least some of the PM difficulties experienced by people with dyslexia are related to this area of executive functioning and, more particularly, the efficient and flexible access of information in verbal long-term memory (Fisk & Sharp, 2004). Although the argument is more than a little tenuous at present, verbal fluency may provide a link between the contributions of executive functioning deficits and the retrospective memory difficulties considered previously in this section (see also Smith-Spark, Moss et al., 2016). However, more research to explore the relationship between verbal fluency, access to information in episodic memory, and PM is required, both in the general population and with respect to dyslexia in particular.

Therefore, given the links between executive functions and PM performance (e.g. Bisiacchi et al., 2009; Gonneaud et al., 2011; Martin et al., 2003; McDaniel & Einstein, 2000; Schnitzspahn et al., 2013), it is possible that the executive functioning deficits shown by adults with dyslexia (e.g. Brosnan et al., 2002; Smith-Spark, Henry et al., 2016) may underlie their poorer PM performance, at least where task conditions are likely to draw upon EFs for effective PM.

It has been argued that individuals draw on their executive functions in order to break out from their ongoing behavior to perform the intended PM action at the point at which it is appropriate to respond (e.g. van den Berg, Aarts, Midden, & Verplanken, 2004; Cockburn, 1995). Cockburn (1995) has argued that the Supervisory Attentional System (SAS) within Norman and Shallice's (1986) model of the control of action is involved in cue-monitoring and that this monitoring process draws on executive resources. The SAS coordinates, integrates, and controls information, drawing on attentional resources to modulate behavior. It is called upon when task novelty is high or poorly learnt action sequences are required. Cockburn also proposed that the SAS is required to act in order to allow the individual to break out from unrelated ongoing activity and carry out the PM task, suggesting that inhibition of ongoing responses (i.e. those controlled by contention scheduling processes within Norman and Shallice's model) is required for PM to proceed effectively.

Dyslexia-related PM deficits might thus result from the problems with SAS function proposed by Smith-Spark and Fisk (2007; see also Varvara, Varuzza, Sorrentino, Vicari, & Menghini, 2014), with a greater call upon the SAS being made when tasks are higher in novelty or, more generally, when they are more episodic in nature. Smith-Spark and Fisk (2007) have argued that adults with dyslexia may struggle with task novelty relative to adults without dyslexia. Their argument was based on evidence from a visuospatial working memory task, where students with dyslexia performed more poorly over the first half of the task but improved to achieve an equivalent level of recall accuracy to a group of age- and IQ-matched controls for the second half. Smith-Spark and Fisk argued that this pattern of performance might indicate a problem with setting up cognitive schemata to deal effectively with novel task demands, thereby implicating SAS dysfunction.

An explanation for PM deficits in dyslexia couched in terms of SAS deficits fits well with the nature of the problems uncovered by objective performance measures and also subjective reports, both of which have highlighted problems with episodic and/or novel tasks and self-initiated performance (Smith-Spark et al., 2016b, 2017a, 2017b). The argument that dyslexia-related PM deficits are more likely to be found when task demands are more novel is further supported by the absence of a self-reported group difference in short-term habitual PM on Hannon et al.'s (1995) PMQ (Smith-Spark et al., 2017a). Some PM theorists have argued that an individual must monitor the environment consciously for EBPM cues (as proposed by monitoring theory; e.g. Smith, 2003), while others have argued either that retrieval of intentions is more automatic (see spontaneous retrieval theory, e.g. Einstein & McDaniel, 1996) or that it is a mixture of conscious and automatic processes depending on task demands (see the multiprocess theory, McDaniel & Einstein, 2000). In dyslexia, the evidence to date (Smith-Spark et al., 2016a, 2016b, 2017a, 2017b) would seem to indicate that it is generally when conscious processes (c.f., Ramus & Szenkovits, 2008) are needed that problems with PM emerge.

Differences in time perception as an explanation

A different explanation of the TBPM deficits reported by Smith-Spark, et al. (2016b) may lie in the time perception deficits which have been reported in dyslexia (e.g. Bruno & Maguire, 1993; Khan, Abdal-hay, Qazi, Calle, & Castillo, 2014; Klein, 2002; Nicolson et al., 1995; Tallal, 1980; Wolff, 2002).

In the general PM literature, there has only been limited exploration of the role of time perception as a predictor of TBPM performance and the findings are rather equivocal. McFarland and Glisky (2009) found no relationship between time perception abilities and PM accuracy. Similarly, more accurate time perception abilities have been found to predict monitoring (or clock-checking) behavior but not PM accuracy directly (Labelle, Graf, Grondin, & Gagné-Roy, 2009; Mioni & Stablum, 2013; Vanneste, Baudouin, Bouazzaoui, & Taconnat, 2016). In contrast, Mackinlay, Kliegel, and Mäntylä (2009) and Mioni, Santon, Stablum, and Cornoldi (2016) have reported a positive relationship between time perception and the accuracy of PM performance.

However, the time perception tasks used to predict TBPM performance have generally tended to be in the seconds range (e.g. McFarland & Glisky, 2009; Mioni & Stablum, 2013; Mioni et al., 2016; Talbot & Kerns, 2014). While the weight of the evidence to date suggests a predictive relationship between time perception and PM performance (either directly, in terms of accuracy, or indirectly, through time monitoring behavior), the choice of durations over which time perception is measured does not sit comfortably with the extended range of durations typically associated with TBPM tasks (where, at the very least, delays are frequently in the order of minutes). General PM research, therefore, needs to be extended to explore durations in the range of minutes as predictors of TBPM; such durations fall in the cognitive range of time perception and temporal judgments in this range are linked to the attentional processes distributed between cognitive task performance and temporal perception (e.g. Block, George, & Reed, 1980; Glicksohn, 2001; Thomas & Weaver, 1975; Zakay & Block, 1996). Such extended durations would map on to the timings of PM tasks more directly and might show stronger predictive relationships to PM accuracy rather than time monitoring. A similar gap exists in the dyslexia literature, where time perception studies have focused on the millisecond to second range and the relationship between timing abilities and TBPM accuracy has not yet been explored. More research is thus required to explore the extent to which time perception abilities predict the TBPM performance of adults with dyslexia.

Finally, it should be noted that time perception and executive functioning abilities have been found to be related (e.g. Carelli, Forman, & Mäntylä, 2008; Mäntylä, Carelli, & Forman, 2007; Ogden, Wearden, & Montgomery, 2014), so explanations of PM deficits in dyslexia based on either construct should not be treated necessarily as entirely separate.

Supporting the PM of people with dyslexia

Prospective memory deficits have been found under controlled laboratory conditions and in tasks with more naturalistic demands and environmental contexts for recall (Smith-Spark et al., 2016b, 2017a, 2017b). The poorer PM performance observed in adults with dyslexia is also apparent in their self-perceived frequency of PM failure in everyday life (Smith-Spark et al., 2016a, 2017a). Indeed, Smith-Spark et al. (2017a) found PM difficulties at both the algorithmic and reflective levels of cognition (Stanovich, 2009) in the same sample of participants. Adults with dyslexia showed worse performance on the MIST (Raskin et al., 2010) and also self-reported more frequent problems in everyday life on the PMQ (Hannon et al., 1995). Prospective memory deficits observed under laboratory conditions would, therefore, also seem to play out in the day-to-day lives of adults with dyslexia. This body of evidence, coming both from the laboratory setting and everyday life c.f., Stanovich, 2009), should be used to support the case for reasonable adjustments to be made to the educational and employment conditions of individuals with dyslexia.

At the most general level, it is recommended that people with dyslexia try wherever possible to (i) avoid prolonged delays between formulating a delayed intention and having the opportunity to act upon it, (ii) take accurate recordings of PM task instructions for later playback, (iii) strengthen associations between PM cues and actions, and (iv) convert TBPM to EBPM tasks. The latter two recommendations could be addressed jointly through the use of intention implementations (e.g. Gollwitzer, 1999; Gollwitzer & Sheeran, 2006) in which if-then plans specify the how, when, and where of an intention being acted upon (for a meta-analytic review of the effectiveness of intention implementation in improving PM, see Chen et al., 2015). However, in older adults, Burkard, Rochat, Van der Linden, Gold, and Van der Linden (2014) have found that the success of implementation intentions in improving PM was restricted to individuals with higher working memory spans. The effectiveness of intention implementation in facilitating PM may thus be moderated by the working memory problems found in adults with dyslexia (e.g. Smith-Spark & Fisk, 2007; Smith-Spark et al., 2003, 2016). As mentioned previously, further research is needed to explore the contribution of working memory deficits to PM in dyslexia under higher cognitive load.

Altgassen, Kretschmer, and Schnitzspahn (2016) have investigated how PM can be improved through the use of repeated-encoding techniques to strengthen memory traces or through episodic future thinking (in which individuals are encouraged to project themselves into their personally experienced future, envisaging themselves performing the PM action). The latter technique proved best for adolescents, while the former was more effective in young adults. Research to explore the relative effectiveness of these different techniques should be explored in dyslexia.

Reid, Strnadová, and Cumming (2013) have highlighted the range of mobile technological supports available to adults with dyslexia, including help with organizing and remembering tasks (for a broader perspective on distributed PM and sociotechnical systems, see Grundgeiger, Sanderson, & Dismukes, 2014). However, it should be noted that it may not be sufficient simply to provide people with dyslexia with good access to technological support through educational or employee support arrangements. The responses of Smith-Spark, Zięcik et al.'s (2017a) adults with dyslexia indicated that, despite more frequent self-reported use of tools and technology to facilitate PM, they still experienced more frequent problems with PM than adults without dyslexia. This finding would suggest that providing adults with dyslexia with technological support for their PM is unlikely to be successful in the absence of explicit training and guidance in their optimal use. This concern fits with a wider literature on dyslexia-related problems with metacognition and the self-initiated identification, and adoption, of effective strategies to bring to bear on cognitive tasks (Bacon, Parmentier, & Barr, 2013; Meltzer, 1991; Torgeson & Goldman, 1977).

Conclusions

This review paper has indicated how a range of different methodological approaches have been used to uncover poorer PM in dyslexia. These data triangulate to highlight problems mainly with TBPM, episodic tasks, PM over longer delay intervals, and self-initiated performance. Some of these difficulties would appear to relate to impairments in accessing task-relevant information in long-term memory at the time at which it is required. It remains an open question as to whether executive functioning and time perception may also contribute to the PM difficulties experienced by adults with dyslexia across a range of settings. Further research in these areas has been suggested. Documenting the nature of PM failure in dyslexia is an important step toward ensuring that a greater error-proneness in day-to-day life tasks is recognized and, as a consequence, people with dyslexia are appropriately supported in educational and employment settings so that they can achieve their full potential.

Acknowledgments

The author would like to thank Dr Adam Zięcik and Dr Christopher Sterling for useful discussions concerning the ideas expressed in this paper. He is grateful also to Prof John Fisk for initial talks about PM and dyslexia and to Prof Angela Fawcett for useful recent discussions and encouragement.

Disclosure statement

No potential conflict of interest was reported by the author.

References

Albano, D., Basso Garcia, R., & Cornoldi, C. (2016). Deficits in working memory visual-phonological binding in children with dyslexia. *Psychology & Neuroscience, 9*, 411–419. doi:10.1037/pne0000066

Altgassen, M., Kretschmer, A., & Schnitzspahn, K. M. (2016). Future thinking instructions improve prospective memory performance in adolescents. *Child Neuropsychology, 28*, 1–18. doi:10.1080/09297049.2016.1158247

Altgassen, M., Vetter, N. C., Phillips, L. H., Akgün, C., & Kliegel, M. (2014). Theory of mind and switching predict perspective memory performance in adolescents. *Journal of Experimental Child Psychology, 127*, 163–175. doi:10.1016/j.jecp.2014.03.009

Bacon, A. M., Parmentier, F. B. R., & Barr, P. (2013). Visuospatial memory in dyslexia: Evidence for strategic deficits. *Memory, 21*, 189–209. doi:10.1080/09658211.2012.718789

Basso, D., Ferrari, M., & Palladino, P. (2010). Prospective memory and working memory: Asymmetrical effects during frontal lobe TMS stimulation. *Neuropsychologia, 48*, 3282–3290. doi:10.1016/j.neuropsychologia.2010.07.011

van den Berg, S. M., Aarts, H., Midden, C., & Verplanken, B. (2004). The role of executive processes in prospective memory tasks. *European Journal of Cognitive Psychology, 16*, 511–533.

Bisiacchi, P. S., Schiff, S., Ciccola, A., & Kliegel, M. (2009). The role of dual-task and task-switch in prospective memory: Behavioural data and neural correlates. *Neuropsychologia, 47*, 1362–1373. doi:10.1016/j.neuropsychologia.2009.01.034

Block, R. A., George, E. J., & Reed, M. A. (1980). A watched pot sometimes boils: A study of duration experience. *Acta Psychologica, 46*, 81–94.

Bogaerts, L., Szmalec, A., Hachmann, W. M., Page, M. P. A., Woumans, E., & Duyck, W. (2015). Increased susceptibility to proactive interference in adults with dyslexia? *Memory, 23*, 268–277.

Booth, J. N., Boyle, J. M. E., & Kelly, S. W. (2010). Do tasks make a difference? Accounting for heterogeneity of performance of children with reading difficulties on tasks of executive function: Findings from a meta-analysis. *British Journal of Developmental Psychology, 28*, 133–176. doi:10.1348/026151009X485432

Brosnan, M., Demetre, J., Hamill, S., Robson, K., Shepherd, H., & Cody, G. (2002). Executive functioning in adults and children with developmental dyslexia. *Neuropsychologia, 40*, 2144–2155. Retrieved from https://www.journals.elsevier.com/neuropsychologia

Bruno, J. E., & Maguire, S. R. (1993). Perception and allocation of time by dyslexic children. *Perceptual and Motor Skills, 77*, 419–432.

Burkard, C., Rochat, L. Juillerat, Van der Linden, A.-C., Gold, G., & Van der Linden, M. (2014). Is working memory necessary for implementation intentions to enhance prospective memory in older adults with cognitive problems? *Journal of Applied Research in Memory and Cognition, 3*, 37–43. doi:10.1016/j.jarmac.2014.01.004

Carelli, M. G., Forman, H., & Mäntylä, T. (2008). Sense of time and executive functioning in children and adults. *Child Neuropsychology, 14*, 372–386. doi:10.1080/09297040701441411

Castles, A., & Friedmann, N. (2014). Developmental dyslexia and the phonological deficit hypothesis. *Mind and Language, 29*, 270–285. doi:10.1111/mila.12050

Chen, X.-J., Wang, Y., Liu, L.-L., Cui, J.-F., Gan, M.-Y., Shum, D. H. K., & Chan, R. C. K. (2015). The effect of implementation intention on prospective memory: A systematic and meta-analytic review. *Psychiatry Research, 226*, 14–22. doi:10.1016/j.psychres.2015.01.011

Clark, A., & Chalmers, D. J. (1998). The extended mind. *Analysis, 58*, 10–23.

Cockburn, J. (1995). Task interruption in prospective memory: A frontal lobe function? *Cortex, 31*, 87–97.

Condor, A., Anderson, V., & Saling, M. (1998). Do reading disabled children have planning problems? *Developmental Neuropsychology, 11*, 485–502.

Cowan, N. (2008). What are the differences between long-term, short-term, and working memory? *Progress in Brain Research, 169*, 323–338. doi:10.1016/S0079-6123(07)00020-9

Crawford, J. R., Henry, J. D., Ward, L. A., & Blake, J. (2006). The Prospective and Retrospective Memory Questionnaire (PRMQ): Latent structure, normative data and discrepancy analysis for proxy-ratings. *British Journal of Clinical Psychology, 45*, 83–104. doi:10.1348/014466505X28748

Einstein, G. O., & McDaniel, M. A. (1996). Retrieval processes in prospective memory: Theoretical approaches and some new empirical findings. In M. Brandimonte, G. O. Einstein, & M. A. McDaniel (Eds.), *Prospective memory: Theory and application* (pp. 115–141). Mahwah, NJ: Erlbaum.

Ellis, J. (1996). Prospective memory or realization of delayed intentions: A conceptual framework for research. In M. Brandimonte, G. O. Einstein, & M. A. McDaniel (Eds.), *Prospective memory: Theory and applications* (pp. l–23). Mahwah, NJ: Lawrence Erlbaum Associates.

Fawcett, A. J., & Nicolson, R. I. (1998). *The Dyslexia Adult Screening Test (DAST)*. London: The Psychological Corporation.

Fisk, J. E., & Sharp, C. A. (2004). Age-related impairment in executive functioning: Updating, inhibition, shifting, and access. *Journal of Clinical and Experimental Neuropsychology, 26*, 874–890. doi:10.1080/13803390490510680

Glicksohn, J. (2001). Temporal cognition and the phenomenology of time: A multiplicative function for apparent duration. *Consciousness and Cognition, 10*, 1–25. doi:10.1006/ccog.2000.0468

Gollwitzer, P. M. (1999). Implementation intentions: Strong effects of simple plans. *American Psychologist, 54*, 493–503. doi:10.1037/0003-066X.54.7.493

Gollwitzer, P. M., & Sheeran, P. (2006). Implementation intentions and goal achievement: A meta-analysis of effects and processes. *Advances in Experimental Social Psychology, 38*, 69–119. doi:10.1016/S0065-2601(06)38002-1

Gonneaud, J., Kalpouzos, G., Bon, L., Viader, F., Eustache, F., & Desgranges, B. (2011). Distinct and shared cognitive functions mediate event- and time-based prospective memory impairment in normal ageing. *Memory, 19*, 360–377. doi:10.1080/09658211.2011.570765

Grundgeiger, T., Sanderson, P. M., & Dismukes, R. K. (2014). Prospective memory in complex sociotechnical systems. *Zeitschrift für Psychologie, 222*, 100–109. doi:10.1027/2151-2604/a000171

Hannon, R., Adams, P., Harrington, S., Fries-Dias, C., & Gibson, M. (1995). Effects of brain injury and age on prospective memory self-rating and performance. *Rehabilitation Psychology, 40*, 289–298.

Heffernan, T., O'Neill, T., Ling, J., Holroyd, S., Bartholomew, J., & Betney, G. (2006). Does excessive alcohol use in teenagers affect their everyday prospective memory? *Clinical Effectiveness in Nursing, 9S3*, e302–e307.

Jones, M. W., Branigan, H. P., Parra, M. A., & Logie, R. H. (2013). Cross modal binding in developmental dyslexia. *Journal of Experimental Psychology: Learning, Memory and Cognition, 39*, 1807–1822. doi:10.1037/a0033334

Jones, M. W., Kuipers, J.-R., & Thierry, G. (2016). ERPs reveal the time-course of aberrant visual-phonological binding in developmental dyslexia. *Frontiers in Human Neuroscience, 10*, 71. doi:10.3389/fnhum.2016.00071

Khan, A. (2014). An investigation into prospective memory in children with developmental dyslexia. *Frontiers in Psychology, 5*, 1308. doi:10.3389/fpsyg.2014.01308

Khan, A., Abdal-hay, A., Qazi, T., Calle, C. L., & Castillo, R. C. (2014). Time estimation in developmental dyslexia: An experimental investigation. *Open Journal of Medical Psychology, 3*, 373–381. doi:10.4236/ojmp.2014.35039

Klein, R. M. (2002). Observations on the temporal correlates of reading failure. *Reading and Writing, 15*, 207–231.

Klicpera, C. (1983). Poor planning as a characteristic of problem behavior in children with dyslexia. *Acta Paedopsychiatrica, 49*, 73–82.

Kretschmer, A., Voigt, B., Friedrich, S., Pfeiffer, K., & Kliegel, M. (2014). Time-based prospective memory in young children – Exploring executive functions as a developmental mechanism. *Child Neuropsychology, 20*, 662–676. doi:10.1080/09297049.2016.1172561

Labelle, A. A., Graf, P., Grondin, S., & Gagné-Roy, L. (2009). Time-related processes in time-based prospective memory and in time-interval production. *European Journal of Cognitive Psychology, 21*, 501–521.

Leather, C., Hogh, H., Seiss, E., & Everatt, J. (2011). Cognitive functioning and work success in adults with dyslexia. *Dyslexia, 17*, 327–338. doi:10.1002/dys.441

Levin, B. E. (1990). Organisational deficits in dyslexia: Possible frontal lobe dysfunction. *Developmental Neuropsychology, 6*, 95–110.

Mackinlay, R. J., Kliegel, M., & Mäntylä, T. (2009). Predictors of time-based prospective memory in children. *Journal of Experimental Child Psychology, 102*, 251–264. doi:10.1016/j.jecp.2008.08.006

Mäntylä, T., Carelli, M. G., & Forman, H. (2007). Time monitoring and executive functioning in children and adults. *Journal of Experimental Child Psychology, 96*, 1–19. doi:10.1016/j.jecp.2006.08.003

Mäntylä, T. (1994). Remembering to remember: Adult age differences in prospective memory. *Journal of Gerontology, 49*, P276–P282.

Marsh, R. L., & Hicks, J. L. (1998). Event-based prospective memory and executive control of working memory. *Journal of Experimental Psychology: Learning, Memory, and Cognition, 24*, 336–349.

Martin, M., Kliegel, M., & McDaniel, M. A. (2003). The involvement of executive functions in prospective memory performance of adults. *International Journal of Psychology, 38*, 195–206.

McDaniel, M. A., & Einstein, G. O. (2000). Strategic and automatic processes in prospective memory retrieval: A multiprocess perspective. *Applied Cognitive Psychology, 14*, S127–S144.

McDaniel, M. A., & Einstein, G. O. (2007). *Prospective memory: An overview and synthesis of an emerging field*. London: Sage.

McFarland, C. P., & Glisky, E. L. (2009). Frontal lobe involvement in a task of time-based prospective memory. *Neuropsychologia, 47*, 1660–1669. doi:10.1016/j.neuropsychologia.2009.02.023

McLoughlin, D., Fitzgibbon, G., & Young, V. (1994). *Adult dyslexia: Assessment, counselling and training*. London: Whurr.

McNamara, J. K., & Wong, B. (2003). Memory for everyday information in students with learning disabilities. *Journal of Learning Disabilities, 36*, 394–406.

Meltzer, L. (1991). Problem-solving strategies and academic performance in learning disabled students: Do subtypes exist? In L. V. Feagans, E. J. Short, & L. J. Meltzer (Eds.), *Subtypes of learning disabilities: Theoretical perspectives and research* (pp. 163–188). Hillsdale, NJ: Lawrence Erlbaum Associates.

Menghini, D., Carlesimo, G. A., Marotta, L., Finzi, A., & Vicari, S. (2010). Developmental dyslexia and explicit long-term memory. *Dyslexia, 16*, 213–225. doi:10.1002/dys.410

Menghini, D., Finzi, A., Carlesimo, G. A., & Vicari, S. (2011). Working memory impairment in children with developmental dyslexia: Is it just a phonological deficity? *Developmental Neuropsychology, 36*, 199–213. doi:10.1080/87565641.2010.549868

Mioni, G., Santon, S., Stablum, F., & Cornoldi, C. (2016). Time-based prospective memory difficulties in children with ADHD and the role of time perception and working memory. *Child Neuropsychology, 19*, 1–21. doi:10.1080/09297049.2016.1172561

Mioni, G., & Stablum, F. (2013). Monitoring behaviour in a time-based prospective memory task: The involvement of executive functions and time perception. *Memory, 22*, 536–552. doi:10.1080/09658211.2013.801987

Miyake, A., Friedman, N. P., Emerson, M. J., Witzki, A. H., Howerter, A., & Wager, T. D. (2000). The unity and diversity of executive functions and their contributions to complex "frontal lobe" tasks: A latent variable analysis. *Cognitive Psychology, 41*, 49–100.

Mortimore, T., & Crozier, W. R. (2006). Dyslexia and difficulties with study skills in higher education. *Studies in Higher Education, 31*, 235–251. doi:10.1080/03075070600572173

Nelson, H. E., & Warrington, E. K. (1980). An investigation of memory functions in dyslexic children. *British Journal of Psychology, 71*, 487–503.

Nergård-Nilssen, T., & Hulme, C. (2014). Developmental dyslexia in adults: Behavioural manifestations and cognitive correlates. *Dyslexia, 20*, 191–207. doi:10.1002/dys.1477

Nicolson, R. I., & Fawcett, A. J. (1990). Automaticity: A new framework for dyslexia research. *Cognition, 35*, 159–182.

Nicolson, R. I., Fawcett, A. J., & Dean, P. (1995). Time estimation deficits in developmental dyslexia: Evidence of cerebellar involvement. *Proceedings of the Royal Society of London, Series B: Biological Sciences, 259*, 43–47.

Norman, D. A., & Shallice, T. (1986). Attention to action: Willed and automatic control of behaviour. In R. J. Davidson, G. E. Schwartz, & D. Shapiro (Eds.), *Consciousness and self-regulation: Advances in research and theory*, Vol. 4 (pp. 1–18). New York, NY: Plenum Press.

Ogden, R., Wearden, J., & Montgomery, C. (2014). The differential contribution of executive functions to temporal generalisation, reproduction and verbal estimation. *Acta Psychologica, 152*, 84–94. doi:10.1016/j.actpsy.2014.07.014

Pennington, B. F., & Ozonoff, S. (1996). Executive functions and developmental psychopathology. *Journal of Child Psychology and Psychiatry, 37*, 51–87.

Ramus, F., & Szenkovits, G. (2008). What phonological deficit? *Quarterly Journal of Experimental Psychology, 61*, 129–141. doi:10.1080/17470210701508822

Raskin, S., Buckheit, C., & Sherrod, C. (2010). *Memory for intentions test*. Lutz, FL: PAR.

Reason, J. T. (1979). Actions not as planned: The price of automatization. In G. Underwood, & R. Stevens (Eds.), *Aspects of consciousness, volume 1: Psychological issues* (pp. 67–89). London: Academic Press.

Reid, G., Strnadová, I., & Cumming, T. (2013). Expanding horizons for students with dyslexia in the 21st century: Universal design and mobile technology. *Journal of Research in Special Educational Needs, 13*, 175–181. doi:10.1111/1471-3802.12013

Riddick, B., Sterling, C., Farmer, M., & Morgan, S. (1999). Self-esteem and anxiety in the educational histories of adult dyslexic students. *Dyslexia, 5*, 227–248.

Schnitzspahn, K. M., Stahl, C., Zeintl, M., Kaller, C. P., & Kliegel, M. (2013). The role of shifting, updating and inhibition in prospective memory performance in young and older adults. *Developmental Psychology, 49*, 1544–1553. doi:10.1037/a0030579

Smith, R. E. (2003). The cost of remembering to remember in event-based prospective memory: Investigating the capacity demands of delayed intention performance. *Journal of Experimental Psychology: Learning, Memory, and Cognition, 29*, 347–361.

Smith, G., Della Sala, S., Logie, R. H., & Maylor, E. A. (2000). Prospective and retrospective memory in normal ageing and dementia: A questionnaire study. *Memory, 8*, 311–321.

Smith-Spark, J. H. (2000). *Memory in adult dyslexics: An exploration of the working memory system* (Unpublished PhD thesis). Sheffield: University of Sheffield.

Smith-Spark, J. H. (2017). Everyday memory in adults with dyslexia. In A. Fawcett (Ed.), *DAS Handbook 2017* (pp. 267–280). Singapore: Dyslexia Association of Singapore.

Smith-Spark, J. H., Fawcett, A. J., Nicolson, R. I., & Fisk, J. E. (2004). Dyslexic students have more everyday cognitive lapses. *Memory, 12*, 174–182.

Smith-Spark, J. H., & Fisk, J. E. (2007). Working memory functioning in developmental dyslexia. *Memory, 15*, 34–56. doi:10.1080/09658210601043384

Smith-Spark, J. H., Fisk, J. E., Fawcett, A. J., & Nicolson, R. I. (2003). Central executive impairments in adult dyslexics: Evidence from phonological and visuospatial working memory performance. *European Journal of Cognitive Psychology, 15*, 567–587.

Smith-Spark, J. H., Henry, L. A., Messer, D. J., Edvardsdottir, E., & Zięcik, A. P. (2016). Executive functions in adults with developmental dyslexia. *Research in Developmental Disabilities, 53–54*, 323–341. doi:10.1016/j.ridd.2016.03.001

Smith-Spark, J. H., Henry, L. A., Messer, D. J., & Zięcik, A. P. (2017). Verbal and non-verbal fluency in adults with developmental dyslexia: Phonological processing or executive control problems? *Dyslexia, 23*, 234–250. doi:10.1002/dys.1558

Smith-Spark, J. H., & Moore, V. (2009). The representation and processing of familiar faces in dyslexia: Differences in age of acquisition effects. *Dyslexia, 15*, 129–146. doi:10.1002/dys.365

Smith-Spark, J. H., Moss, A. C., & Dyer, K. (2016). Do baseline executive functions mediate prospective memory performance under a moderate dose of alcohol? *Frontiers in Psychology, 7*. Article 1325. doi:10.3389/fpsyg.2016.01325

Smith-Spark, J. H., Zięcik, A. P., & Sterling, C. (2016a). Self-reports of increased prospective and retrospective memory problems in adults with developmental dyslexia. *Dyslexia, 22*, 245–262. doi:10.1002/dys.1528

Smith-Spark, J. H., Zięcik, A. P., & Sterling, C. (2016b). Time-based prospective memory in adults with developmental dyslexia. *Research in Developmental Disabilities, 49–50*, 34–46. doi:10.1016/j.ridd.2015.11.006

Smith-Spark, J. H., Zięcik, A. P., & Sterling, C. (2017a). Adults with developmental dyslexia show selective impairments in time-based and self-initiated prospective memory: Self-report and clinical evidence. *Research in Developmental Disabilities, 62*, 247–258. doi:10.1016/j.ridd.2016.12.011

Smith-Spark, J. H., Zięcik, A. P., & Sterling, C. (2017b). The event-based prospective memory of adults with developmental dyslexia under naturalistic conditions. *Asia Pacific Journal of Developmental Differences, 4*, 17–33.

Stanovich, K. E. (2009). Distinguishing the reflective, algorithmic, and autonomous minds: Is it time for a tri-process theory? In J. St. B. T. Evans, & K. Frankish (Eds.), *In two minds: Dual processes and beyond* (pp. 55–88). New York, NY: Oxford University Press.

Talbot, K. D., & Kerns, K. A. (2014). Event- and time-triggered remembering: The impact of attention deficit hyperactivity disorder on prospective memory performance in children. *Journal of Experimental Child Psychology, 127*, 126–143. doi:10.1016/j.jecp.2014.02.011

Tallal, P. (1980). Auditory temporal perception, phonics and reading disabilities in children. *Brain and Language, 9*, 182–198.

Thomas, E. A. C., & Weaver, W. B. (1975). Cognitive processing and time perception. *Perception & Psychophysics, 17*, 363–367.

Torgeson, J. K. (1977). The role of nonspecific factors in the task performance of learning disabled children: A theoretical assessment. *Journal of Learning Disabilities, 10*, 27–34.

Torgeson, J. K., & Goldman, T. (1977). Verbal rehearsal and short-term memory in reading-disabled children. *Child Development, 48*, 56–60.

Vanneste, S., Baudouin, A., Bouazzaoui, B., & Taconnat, L. (2016). Age-related differences in time-based prospective memory: The role of time estimation in the clock monitoring strategy. *Memory, 24*, 812–825. doi:10.1080/09658211.2015.1054837

Varvara, P., Varuzza, C., Sorrentino, A. C. P., Vicari, S., & Menghini, D. (2014). Executive functions in developmental dyslexia. *Frontiers in Human Neuroscience, 8*, 120. doi:10.3389/fnhum.2014.00120

Vellutino, F. R. (1979). *Dyslexia: Theory and research*. Cambridge, MA: MIT Press.

Vellutino, F. R., Fletcher, J. M., Snowling, M. J., & Scanlon, D. M. (2004). Specific reading disability (dyslexia): What have we learned in the past four decades? *Journal of Child Psychology and Psychiatry, 45*, 2–40.

Waldum, E. R., & McDaniel, M. A. (2016). Why are you late? Investigating the role of time management in time-based prospective memory. *Journal of Experimental Psychology: General, 145*, 1049–1061. doi:10.1037/xge0000183

Ward, T., & Ridgeway, V. (1994). *Test of Everyday Attention*. Harlow: Pearson Assessment.

Winograd, E. (1988). Some observations on prospective remembering. In M. M. Gruneberg, P. E. Morris, & R. N. Sykes (Eds.), *Practical aspects of memory: Current research and issues*, Vol. 1 (pp. 348–353). Chichester: Wiley.

Wolff, P. H. (2002). Timing precision and rhythm in developmental dyslexia. *Reading and Writing, 15*, 179–206.

Zakay, D., & Block, R. A. (1996). The role of attention in time estimation processes. In M. A. Pastor, & J. Artieda (Eds.), *Time, internal clocks and movement* (pp. 143–164). Amsterdam: Elsevier Science.

Zięcik, A. P. (2015). *Prospective memory in adults with developmental dyslexia* (Unpublished PhD thesis). London: London South Bank University.

Schizophrenia and prospective memory impairments: a review

Ya Wang , Raymond C. K. Chan and David H. K. Shum

ABSTRACT

Objective: Prospective memory (PM) is the ability to remember to carry out intended actions in the future. Prospective forgetting has been shown to be one of the key cognitive impairments that contribute to medication non-adherence, reduced independence, and social dysfunction in individuals with schizophrenia. This review aimed to provide an up to date appraisal of the nature and extent of PM impairments in individuals with schizophrenia and those who are at risk and to discuss clinical applications in this area. **Method:** We searched and reviewed relevant studies in this area between 2013 and August 2017. **Results:** Findings of studies conducted so far indicate that PM is severely impaired in schizophrenia. The most frequent type of PM errors in individuals with schizophrenia is no response, or failure to carry out the intended action. PM impairments in schizophrenia have been found to be related to everyday functioning. For individuals with schizophrenia, a number of assessment techniques have been developed to assess PM. These include: self-report questionnaires, computerized tasks, psychometric test batteries, and virtual reality tasks. So far, a few studies have used the compensatory approach to improve PM performance in individuals with schizophrenia and those who are at risk, and the results reported are promising. Based on findings of these studies, suggestions for the development of interventions for PM impairments in individuals with schizophrenia are provided. **Conclusions:** PM dysfunction is an important impairment in individuals with schizophrenia, and more rehabilitation studies to improve PM performance in these individuals are needed.

Introduction

Prospective memory (PM) refers to the ability to remember to do something at a particular point in the future (Einstein & McDaniel, 1990), for example, to remember to attend a doctor's appointment to review medication management on Wednesday at 10 am. PM is important because many daily activities are dependent on it. In a typical PM task, an intention needs to be formed first (e.g. what needs to be done and under what conditions), then the individual engages in something else called the ongoing task. While performing the ongoing task, the individual needs to maintain the intention and monitor the PM cue. When a PM cue appears and is detected, the individual needs to retrieve the intention and make a PM response.

According to the nature of the cue, PM can be divided into time-, event-, and activity-based (Kvavilashvili & Ellis, 1996). Time-based PM requires an individual to remember to execute an intention at a particular time, or after a period of time (e.g. attend a wedding next Sunday). Event-based PM requires someone to execute an intention at the appearance of a cue (e.g. buy bread when one passes by a supermarket). Activity-based PM requires someone to execute an intention at the end of an activity (e.g. send an email after dinner). It is generally accepted that there are two components of PM: prospective and retrospective (Ellis, 1996). The prospective component involves the retrieval of and carry out the intended action at the appropriate point in the future, and the retrospective component involves recalling the content of the intended action (Ellis, 1996). In the literature, the most widely cited theories of PM are the Preparatory Attention and Memory (PAM) (Smith, 2003) theory and the Multi-Process Theory (Einstein & McDaniel, 2005). While the former proposes that all PM processing requires cognitive resources, the latter hypothesizes that PM can be executed with or without effort or cognitive resources, depending on a number of factors (e.g. the cognitive demands of the ongoing task, the saliency of the PM cue, the association between the ongoing and PM task, etc.).

Schizophrenia is a world-wide severe psychiatric disease and is associated with a wide range of cognitive impairments (Green & Harvey, 2014; Heinrichs, 2005; Schulz & Murray, 2016). Compared to retrospective memory (RM) impairments, PM impairments have not been studies as systematically and extensively in individuals with schizophrenia. To date, a meta-analytic review (viz., Wang et al., 2009) and a systematic review (viź., Ordemann, Opper, & Davalos, 2014) have been undertaken. Wang et al.'s (2009) meta-analysis showed that schizophrenia patients were impaired in all types of PM, with time-based PM more impaired than event-based PM. In addition, it was found that PM was inversely correlated with negative symptoms and education. Ordemann et al.'s (2014) review showed that schizophrenia patients lacked awareness of their PM impairments. Furthermore, they found that PM impairments were not related to chronicity and medications, but were related to independent living skills in schizophrenia. The present study aimed to include updated findings in this area, and to include aspects not covered in Wang et al. (2009) and Ordemann et al. (2014). These include components of PM impairments and types of PM errors, longitudinal studies, approaches to clinical assessment of PM, evidence-based approaches to treatment, and suggestions for development of interventions for PM impairments. Since schizophrenia has been considered to be part of a spectrum, we also included studies with non-psychotic first-degree of relatives and individuals with schizotypal personality features in our review.

Method

The selection of papers was based on the PRISMA guideline (Hutton et al., 2015). We searched the *Web of Science* from 2013 [Ordemann et al. (2014) searched for papers up to 2013] to 2 August 2017 using the keywords: schizophrenia and prospective memory. We restricted the studies to peer-reviewed papers written in English. A total of 117 entries were retrieved. After excluding studies not on PM or not in schizophrenia-related samples, 23 studies remained. After further excluding 1 review, 1 meta-analysis, and 3 papers covered by

Ordemann et al. (2014), 18 studies remained for the final review (Figure 1 shows the flowchart of paper selection). A summary of these studies is presented in Table 1. For some parts of the review (e.g. studies related to participants with schizotypal personality features, non-psychotic first-degree relatives of schizophrenia), papers published before 2013 were also reviewed if the content was not discussed in detail in Wang et al. (2009) and Ordemann et al. (2014).

Results and discussion

Current knowledge of PM impairments in individuals with schizophrenia

PM impairments in individuals with schizophrenia and related populations

Results of Wang et al.'s (2009) meta-analytic study showed that individuals with chronic schizophrenia were impaired on PM with a large effect size, with time-based PM more impaired than event-based PM. Moreover, they reported that PM impairments were correlated with a number of factors such as severity of negative symptoms and education. In their systematic review, Ordemann et al. (2014) showed that PM impairments were not related to chronicity in schizophrenia, specifically, that individuals with first-episode schizophrenia also showed PM impairments. They also suggested that PM impairments in individuals with schizophrenia are considered a primary impairment. Since these two reviews, a number of studies that examined PM impairments in individuals with schizophrenia have been published. Three studies (Au, Man, Shum, et al., 2014, 2016; Au et al. 2016; Demeter et al., 2016)

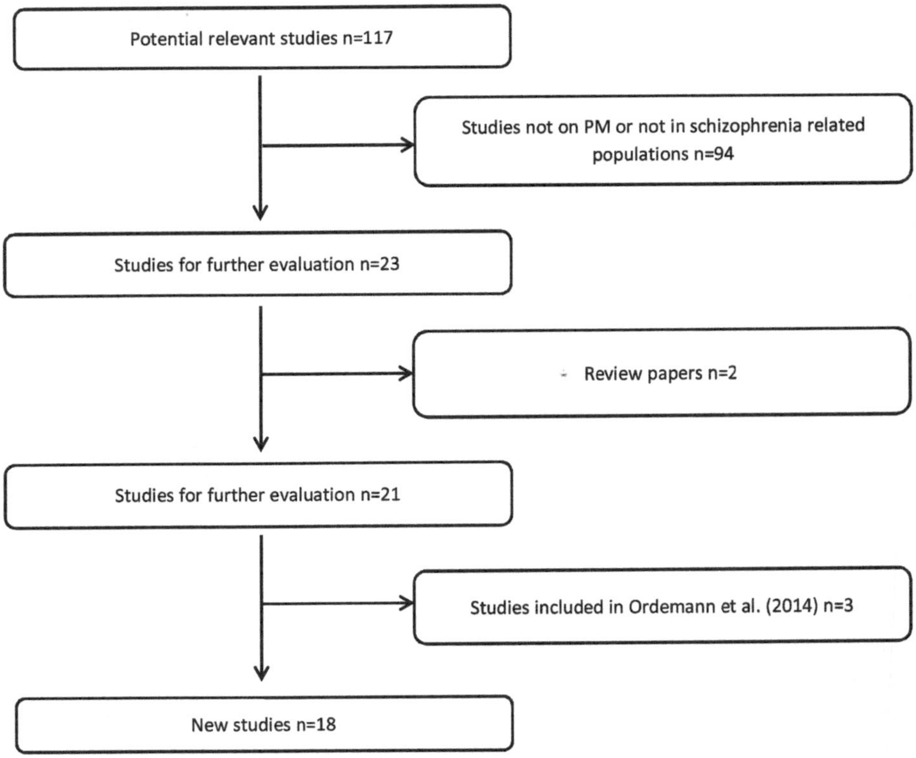

Figure 1. Flowchart of paper selection.

Table 1. Summary of studies.

Study	Participants	PM type	Measure	Results
Behavioral studies				
Au, Man, Shum et al., 2014	Chronic schizophrenia patients ($n = 44$) and matched controls ($n = 44$)	Event, time	CAMPROMPT-C	Patients were impaired on total and subscale of the CAMPROMPT-C. Patients showed comparable deficits in PM subtypes. Education, IQ, and retrospective memory were correlated with PM. The clinical utility of the CAMPROMPT-C was supported.
Au, Man, Xiang et al., 2014	Chronic schizophrenia patients ($n = 44$)	Event, time	CAMPROMPT-C	In bivariate analyses, overall community living skills correlated with PM total and subscales scores. In multivariate analyses, event-based PM was more predictive of community living skills than time-based PM.
Au et al., 2016	Chronic schizophrenia patients ($n = 44$), bipolar disorder ($n = 76$), and healthy controls ($n = 44$)	Event, time	CAMPROMPT-C	Both patient groups showed similar level of PM impairments.
Cheung et al., 2015	First-episode schizophrenia ($n = 58$) and matched healthy controls ($n = 37$)	Event, time	Computer test	Both event- and time-based PM were impaired at baseline in schizophrenia patients, only time-based PM was impaired at 1 year follow-up. Schizophrenia patients showed a gradual improvement in both time- and event-based PM 12 months after illness onset. Compared to event-based PM, deficit in time-based PM persisted.
Demeter et al., 2016	Chronic schizophrenia patients ($n = 20$) and matched healthy controls ($n = 20$)	Event	Computer test	Patients showed impairments in the execution condition but not maintenance condition. PM performance in execution condition was correlated with impaired executive function in schizophrenia.
Lam et al., 2013	Chronic schizophrenia patients ($n = 82$)	Event, time, activity	Computer test, CAPM	Time- and event-based PM predicted medication management at baseline. At three-month follow-up, medication non-adherent group performed poorer in time- and event-based PM. Insight and PANSS general score significantly predicted medication non-adherence in the community. Time- and event-based PM moderated the predictive power of insight and PANSS general score.

Liu et al., 2017	First-episode schizophrenia patients ($n = 30$), healthy controls ($n = 30$)	Event	Computer test	Both cue identification and intention retrieval were impaired in schizophrenia compared with healthy controls, with a large effect size for cue identification and a medium effect size for intention retrieval. After controlling for working memory and retrospective memory, the patients were still impaired in cue identification. However, the difference in intention retrieval between the two groups was no longer significant.
Lui et al., 2015	First-episode schizophrenia patients ($n = 91$), healthy controls ($n = 83$)	Event, time	Computer test, PRMQ	Patients were impaired in time- and event-based PM. Cognitive flexibility predicted time- and event-based PM, working memory predicted event-based PM. 'Cognitive-preserved' patients tended to perform poorer in time-based PM than controls matched in IQ and other neuropsychological functions.
Man et al., 2016	First-episode schizophrenia patients ($n = 44$), healthy controls ($n = 42$)	Event, time	VRPMT-CV, CAMPROMPT-C	VRPMT-CV showed good construct validity, test-retest reliability, sensitivity and specificity in first-episode schizophrenia.
Zhou, Hou et al., 2014	First-episode schizophrenia ($n = 47$), first-degree non-psychotic relatives ($n = 50$), healthy controls ($n = 51$)	Event, time	CAMPROMPT-C	First-degree relatives were impaired in both time- and event-based PM. Time-based PM was related to verbal learning and inhibition, event-based PM was related to flexibility in first-degree relatives of schizophrenia.
Zhou, Xiang et al., 2014	First-episode schizophrenia ($n = 55$)	Event, time	CAMPROMPT-C	Higher scores on time-based PM at baseline predicted remission at 8-week follow-up.
Zhou et al., 2017	First-episode schizophrenia patients ($n = 32$), healthy controls ($n = 17$)	Event, time	CAMPROMPT-C	Event-based PM showed significant improvement in patients at 1-year follow-up. Remitters performed better on event-based PM than non-remitters.
Neural basis studies				
Chen et al., 2015	Symptom remitted chronic schizophrenia ($n = 20$) and healthy controls ($n = 20$)	Event	ERP	Patients with schizophrenia performed poorly on the PM task compared with healthy controls. On the neural level, the N300 (related to PM cue detection) was reliable across these 2 groups, and did not show significant group difference. However, the amplitude of the prospective positivity (related to PM intention retrieval) was significantly attenuated in symptomatically remitted schizophrenia patients relative to healthy controls.

(Continued)

Table 1. *(Continued).*

Study	Participants	PM type	Measure	Results
Chen, Wang et al., 2016	Chronic schizophrenia patients ($n = 22$) and healthy controls ($n = 25$)	Event	fMRI	Patients performed significantly worse on the PM task. Furthermore, they exhibited decreased brain activation in frontal cortex including the right superior frontal gyri (Brodmann area 10), and other related brain areas like the anterior cingulate gyrus, parietal and temporal cortex, including precuneus, parahippocampal gyrus and putamen.
Wang et al., 2014	Individuals with schizotypal features ($n = 19$) and without schizotypal features ($n = 22$)	Event	fMRI	Schizotypal and control groups did not differ in behavioral PM performance. However, participants with schizotypal features showed decreased activations in the inferior and medial frontal cortex (BA 45, and 8) compared to those without schizotypal features.
Intervention studies				
Chen et al., 2014	Individuals with schizotypal features ($n = 51$) and without schizotypal features ($n = 51$)	Event	Computer test	Implementation intentions improved PM performances in both schizotypal and control groups. In the low cognitive load condition, both the schizotypal and non-schizotypal groups in the implementation intention condition showed improvement on PM task without ongoing task cost, suggesting automatic processing. In the high cognitive load condition, the non-schizotypal group did not show improvement on PM performance with implementation intention; the schizotypal group showed improvement on PM performance with ongoing task cost.
Chen, Liu et al., 2016	Chronic schizophrenia patients ($n = 50$) and healthy controls ($n = 50$)	Event	Computer test	Patients were impaired in PM. Implementation intentions improved PM performances for both patients and controls. Implementation intentions improved PM performance in patients in both the low and high cognitive load conditions without ongoing task cost, suggesting that implementation intentions improved PM remembering in an automatic way.

Khoratty et al., 2015	Participants with early psychosis ($n = 30$) and healthy controls ($n = 33$)	Event, time	Computer test, BAPM, CAMPROMPT	Participants with early psychosis showed PM deficits, implementation intentions improved PM performance in individuals with early psychosis.

Notes: BAPM – Brief Assessment of Prospective Memory; CAMPROMPT – Cambridge Prospective Memory Test; CAMPROMPT-C – Chinese version of the Cambridge Prospective Memory Test; CAPM – Comprehensive Assessment of Prospective Memory; ERP – Event-Related Potential; fMRI, functional Magnetic Resonance Imaging; PRMQ – Prospective and Retrospective Memory Questionnaire; VRPMT-CV – Virtual Reality Prospective Memory Test—Chinese version.

found severe PM impairments in individuals with chronic schizophrenia. Three studies (Cheung et al., 2015; Liu et al., 2017; Lui et al., 2015) showed that first-episode and even first-episode medication-naïve individuals with schizophrenia demonstrated PM impairments. Overall, results of these subsequent studies are generally consistent with the findings of previous studies reviewed by Wang et al. (2009) and Ordemann et al. (2014).

Among the recent research, two studies examined the neural basis of PM impairments in schizophrenia. Adopting a functional magnetic resonance imaging (fMRI) paradigm, Chen et al. (Chen, Wang et al., 2016) indicated that individuals with schizophrenia showed lower accuracy on an event-based PM task than healthy controls, and these clinical individuals presented decreased activations in the prefrontal cortex, including Brodmann Area 10, and other brain areas such as the anterior cingulate gyrus, precuneus, parahippocampal gyrus, and putamen. These results suggest that PM impairments in schizophrenia are related to brain areas that mediate neurocognitive processes such as attentional control, intention encoding, and maintenance. In another study, Chen et al. (2015) used event-related potentials (ERP), and showed that compared to healthy controls, remitted individuals with schizophrenia did not show significant difference on N300, but they showed significantly reduced prospective positivity amplitude. While N300 is a component related to PM cue detection, prospective positivity is a component related to intention retrieval. These results, therefore, suggested that remitted individuals with schizophrenia were impaired in the retrieval of intention but not in the detection of PM cues. In addition, the amplitude of prospective positivity was significantly correlated with PM performance in individuals with remitted schizophrenia but not in healthy controls.

First-degree relatives of individuals with schizophrenia have a higher rate of developing schizophrenia than general population (Gottesman, 1991), and they have been found to show cognitive impairments compared to healthy controls (Trandafir, Méary, Schürhoff, Leboyer, & Szöke, 2006). Several studies (Lui et al., 2011; Wang et al., 2010; Zhou et al., 2014) have examined PM performance in non-psychotic first-degree relatives of individuals with schizophrenia. The results of these studies are not consistent. Wang et al. (2010) found that non-psychotic first-degree relatives (consisting of both parents and siblings) of individuals with schizophrenia showed impairments in both time- and event-based PM but not activity-based PM. However, in that study, they did not present the results of parents and siblings separately. Zhou et al. (2014) recruited the offspring and siblings of individuals with schizophrenia, and found that compared to healthy controls, these non-psychotic relatives were impaired in both time- and event-based PM. In addition, offspring and siblings did not show significant difference on PM performance. However, in that study, the relatives were less educated than the healthy controls, and statistical control were used to address this difference. In their study, Lui et al. (2011) specifically compared PM performance among non-psychotic siblings of schizophrenia patients, schizophrenia patients, and healthy controls, and found that compared to healthy controls, non-psychotic siblings did not show impairments in any types of PM. To date, no studies have been conducted to examine the neural correlates of PM in relatives of schizophrenia patients. Future studies should separate parents, siblings, and offspring into participant subgroups and to recruit healthy controls that are better matched to them, and to explore the neural basis of PM in these subgroups.

Individuals with schizotypal personality features are considered to fall into the lower end of the schizophrenia spectrum and are at high risk for developing schizophrenia (Cadenhead, Perry, Shafer, & Braff, 1999). Individuals with schizotypal personality features have also been shown to exhibit cognitive impairments (Bergida & Lenzenweger, 2006; Kopp, 2007). A number of studies (Chan et al., 2008; Chen et al., 2014; Henry, Rendell, Rogers, Altgassen, & Kliegel, 2012; Wang, Chan, Yu, et al., 2008; Wang et al., 2011, 2014) have examined PM performance in individuals with schizotypal personality features. Wang, Chan, Yu et al. (2008) found that these individuals (screened using the Schizotypal Personality Questionnaire) showed significantly poorer performance on perceptual time-based and semantic event-based PM tasks than healthy controls. In another study, Chan et al. (2008) showed that individuals with schizotypal personality features were impaired in event-based PM. However, the demographic variables of the two groups of participants in these two studies were not well matched with their respective controls, and these differences had to be statistically controlled for. Using a computerized PM task that included both focal and nonfocal PM cues and the Virtual Week, Henry et al. (2012), did not find any PM impairments in individuals with schizotypal personality features. Therefore, whether PM is impaired in these individuals, requires further study.

One study has explored the neural correlates of PM in individuals with schizotypal personality features. Wang et al. (2014) conducted an fMRI study using an event-based PM task in these individuals. Results showed that participants with schizotypal personality features showed reduced activations in the inferior and medial frontal lobes (Brodmann Areas 45 and 8) compared to the controls, even though the two groups did not show significant differences in their behavioral PM performance.

Impairment of different types of PM in schizophrenia

Regarding performance on different types of PM tasks in individuals with schizophrenia, results are consistent in that all types of PM were impaired. To determine if one type of PM task is significantly more impaired in individuals with schizophrenia, we compared their performance on time- and event-based PM tasks because these are most commonly used in research studies. As mentioned in Ordemann et al. (2014), some studies found that time-based PM were significantly more impaired than event-based PM (e.g. Shum, Ungvari, Tang, & Leung, 2004; Wang, Chan, Hong, et al., 2008), while other studies did not find this difference (e.g. Au, Man, Shum, et al., 2014; Henry, Rendell, Kliegel, & Altgassen, 2007; Lui et al., 2011; Woods, Twamley, Dawson, Narvaez, & Jeste, 2007). In their meta-analytic study, Wang et al. (2009) confirmed that time-based PM was significantly more impaired than event-based PM in individuals with schizophrenia. However, in looking at the results of studies that were published since 2009 (e.g. Au, Man, Shum, et al., 2014; Lui et al., 2011, 2015; Raskin et al., 2014; Zhou et al., 2012; Zhuo et al., 2013), most of them did not show that individuals with schizophrenia were disproportionally more impaired in time-based PM than event-based PM (Au, Man, Shum, et al., 2014; Lui et al., 2011, 2015; Raskin et al., 2014). Several studies (Zhou et al., 2012; Zhuo et al., 2013) did not analyze whether schizophrenia patients showed differential impairments in time- and event-based PM, but reported similar effect sizes for these two types of PM impairment in individuals with schizophrenia.

Regarding the original finding in the Wang et al. (2009) meta-analytic review that time-based PM was more severely impaired than event-based PM in schizophrenia, it was suggested that time-based PM need more self-initiation than event-based PM because time-based PM does not have an external cue to trigger retrieval of the planned intention (Shum et al., 2004; Wang et al., 2009). However, one cannot simply say that time-based PM is more difficult than event-based PM because there are other factors which also influenced

PM performance. For example, how often the participants were required to perform PM actions (every minute, every two minutes or every 15 min) could also affect performance. This delay was found to have an effect on PM performance (Raskin et al., 2014). In addition, for event-based PM, the focality (focal or nonfocal) of PM cue has also been found to have an effect on performance (Kliegel, Jäger, & Phillips, 2008). Although Henry et al. (2012) did not find an effect of cue saliency on the degree of PM impairments in individuals with schizophrenia, cue focality has been found to affect PM performance (Kliegel et al., 2008) and focal and nonfocal cues are considered to involve different neural mechanisms (Cona, Bisiacchi, Sartori, & Scarpazza, 2016; McDaniel, LaMontagne, Beck, Scullin, & Braver, 2013). Thus, when comparing whether one type of PM is significantly more impaired than the other type, one needs to take these factors into consideration and to ensure that the tasks used are comparable.

Components of PM impairment and types of PM errors in schizophrenia

The questions of which component(s) of PM is impaired and what types of PM errors are commonly found in individuals with schizophrenia were not covered or discussed in the reviews by Wang et al. (2009) or Ordemann et al. (2014). Several studies have been conducted to examine which component(s) of PM was impaired in schizophrenia. Woods et al. (2007) used the Memory for Intention Screening Test (MIST) to assess PM in individuals with schizophrenia. Results of their study showed that these individuals were impaired on PM. However, the schizophrenia and control groups did not differ on a recognition task after test, suggesting that intention formation and maintenance were relatively intact, with cue detection and intention retrieval likely being responsible for the overall PM failure. Wang, Chan, Hong, et al. (2008) further examined this issue. In their study, participants were asked to recall task requirements after they have finished the PM task. Results indicated that individuals with schizophrenia showed impairment on free recall of task requirements. Furthermore, even including only those individuals with schizophrenia who could recall task requirements, the schizophrenia group was still found to perform significantly poorer than the control group. These results suggested that intention maintenance, cue detection, and intention retrieval all contributed to the overall PM impairments. In another study that examined this issue, Liu et al. (2017) manipulated the load in cue detection and intention retrieval. Results of their study showed that both cue detection and intention retrieval components of PM were impaired in schizophrenia. After controlling for working memory and retrospective memory, cue detection PM was still impaired in individuals with schizophrenia. Altgassen, Kliegel, Rendell, Henry, and Zöllig (2008) found that PM was impaired even when the retrospective memory load was minimal. In addition, both prospective and retrospective components of PM were found to contribute to PM impairment in individuals with schizophrenia. Taken together, these results suggested that cue detection, intention retrieval, prospective, and retrospective components of PM are all impaired in individuals with schizophrenia.

Several studies have been conducted to examine what were the common types of PM errors in individuals with schizophrenia. In studies that use the MIST and the Virtual Week, types of errors were recorded and reported. Henry et al. (2007) explored the pattern of errors on the Virtual Week in schizophrenia, and five types of errors were recorded for this task: Late (PM response was made after the correct time period but before the virtual day), Miss (participants totally forget the PM cue), No Content (participants remembered something should be done at the right time, but did not know what to do), Wrong Content (participants remembered a wrong thing to do at a correct time), and Other Wrong (participants remembered to do something at a wrong time). Results demonstrated that individuals with schizophrenia showed more Misses on all types of PM tasks and took longer time to respond on the time-check task. No significant difference was found on other types of errors.

Woods et al. (2007) examined types of PM errors in individuals with schizophrenia using the MIST. Results of their study indicated that these individuals showed more No Response (participant did not make any responses to a PM cue), Loss of Time (participants make a correct response but at an incorrect time), and Task Substitution (participants make a wrong response on a PM cue) errors than healthy controls. In another study, Raskin et al. (2014) showed that individuals with schizophrenia only showed more No Response errors than healthy controls, and the differences in other error types did not reach statistical significance. Overall, results of the studies reviewed suggest that Miss or No Response errors were consistently found to be more frequent in individuals with schizophrenia than in healthy controls, suggesting the primacy of problems with the prospective component of PM.

Relationship between PM and other cognitive functions

PM is a complex construct that involves multiple cognitive functions, such as attention, retrospective memory, switching, inhibition, and executive function. Therefore, it has been found to correlate significantly with these cognitive functions (Lui et al., 2015; Twamley et al., 2008; Wang, Chan, Hong, et al., 2008). A question has been raised regarding whether individuals with schizophrenia will still be impaired on PM if these cognitive processes have been controlled for. According to Ordemann et al. (2014), several studies (Altgassen et al., 2008; Henry et al., 2007; Wang, Chan, Hong, et al., 2008) have found that PM impairment still remained in individuals with schizophrenia after controlling for other cognitive processes. Thus, they suggested that PM impairment is a primary rather than secondary impairment of schizophrenia. The same conclusion was drawn by Lui et al. (2015) based on the results of their study. Nevertheless, Liu et al. (2017) found that after controlling for working memory and retrospective memory, only the cue identification but not intention retrieval component of PM remained significantly different between individuals with schizophrenia and controls. These results suggest that further studies are needed to clarify this issue, albeit that at least PM cue identification could be considered a primary impairment of schizophrenia.

Relationship between PM with medication adherence and functional outcome

PM has been reported to correlate significantly with medication adherence and functional outcome. This issue was not mentioned in Wang et al. (2009), and not discussed in detail in Ordemann et al.'s (2014) review. Zogg, Woods, Sauceda, Wiebe, and Simoni (2012) reviewed the literature and found that PM impairment was a risk factor for medication non-adherence in general. Lam, Lui, Wang, Chan, and Cheung (2013) found that in individuals with schizophrenia all three types of PM correlated significantly with medication management ability as measured by the Medication Management Ability Assessment. In addition, at three-month follow-up, the medication adherent and non-adherent groups showed significant difference in time- and event-based PM performance. The relationship between PM and medication management ability was also found by Raskin et al. (2014) in their study.

Twamley et al. (2008) explored the relationship between PM and functional capacity and found that better PM was predictive of higher functional capacity, better than that provided by demographic and disease factors. Au, Man, Xiang, et al. (2014) found that community living skills were correlated with event- and time-based PM performance, and event-based PM performance was found to be predictive of the level of community living skills after controlling for demographic and clinical variables. Although Xiang, Shum, Chiu, Tang, and Ungvari (2010) did not find a significant relationship between PM and social functioning, most previous studies have shown that PM plays an important role in medication adherence and functional outcome in schizophrenia patients.

Longitudinal studies of PM in schizophrenia

The topic of longitudinal study of PM in individuals with schizophrenia was not included in the reviews by Wang et al. (2009) and Ordemann et al. (2014). Longitudinal studies allow us to determine whether PM impairments in these individuals are stable over time. There are three longitudinal studies on PM performance in individuals with schizophrenia and those who are at risk. Wang et al. (2011) explored the 6-month test–retest reliability of PM performance in participants with schizotypal personality features, and found that PM performance was stable in these participants. Cheung et al. (2015) conducted a one-year follow-up study in individuals with first-episode schizophrenia and found that these individuals showed gradual improvement in time- and event-based PM in 12 months after the onset of disease. While time-based PM impairment was found to be stable and persisted over the 12 months, event-based PM seemed to have improved and did not remain impaired. In their study, Zhou, Xiang, et al. (2014) found that higher scores on time-based PM at baseline predicted remission at 8-week follow-up. However, they did not measure PM at follow-up. Zhou et al. (2017) conducted a 1-year follow-up study in first-episode schizophrenia and found that event-based PM improved over time, and this improvement was associated with clinical remission. Clinically remitted patients showed significantly better performance in event-based PM than non-remitted patients. More longitudinal studies that involve longer follow up are needed to clarify the stability of PM impairment in these individuals and those who are at risk.

Approaches to clinical assessment of PM for individuals with schizophrenia

A number of assessment instruments have been developed to assess PM. In this section, we review the instruments that have been applied in the schizophrenia population. Table 2 presents a brief summary of these instruments.

Self-report questionnaires

Two of the most commonly used self-report PM questionnaires are the Prospective and Retrospective Memory Questionnaire (PRMQ; Smith, Sala, Logie, & Maylor, 2000) and the Comprehensive Assessment of Prospective Memory (CAPM; Roche, Fleming, & Shum, 2002). The PRMQ was originally developed to measure memory problems in older adults and dementia. Several studies have used this questionnaire in individuals with schizophrenia (Chan et al., 2008, 2013; Lui et al., 2015). They found that schizophrenia did not report

Table 2. Summary of PM assessments.

PM assessment	Definition and/or example item	Studies reported psychometric properties	Studies in Schizophrenia
Self-report questionnaires			
PRMQ	It is a 16-item questionnaire and included prospective and retrospective factors. An example item on PM: 'Do you forget to buy something you planned to buy, like a birthday card, even when you see the shop?'	Crawford, Smith, Maylor, Della Sala, and Logie (2003)	Chan et al. (2008), Lui et al. (2015)
CAPM	It originally includes 36 items and includes 33 items in the Chinese version. It includes 2 factors: instrumental activities of daily living (e.g. Forgetting an appointment with your doctor or therapist) and basic activities of daily living (e.g. Forgetting to eat a meal)	Chan et al. (2010), Chau, Lee, Fleming, Roche, and Shum (2007)	Lam et al. (2013)
BAPM	Short version of CAPM. It includes 16 items and the same two factors as CAPM	Man et al. (2011)	Khoratty et al. (2015)
Computerized tasks			
Computerized tasks	PM is embedded in computerized ongoing task (e.g. answering general knowledge questions, doing word categorization, or making lexical/idiom decision). The PM task usually involves pressing a specified key under different conditions, depending on whether one wants to assess time-, event-, or activity PM		Altgassen et al. (2008), Wang, Chan, Hong et al. (2008), Wang, Chan, Yu et al. (2008), Cheung et al. (2015), Henry et al. (2012), Liu et al. (2017), Lui et al. (2015)
Psychometric test batteries			
MIST	It measures event- and time-based PM with short (2 min) or long (15 min) delays, participants need to make verbal or action responses when a PM cue is detected. An example task is 'In exactly 15 min please tell me it is time to take a break'	Raskin (2009), Woods et al. (2008)	Woods et al. (2007), Twamley et al. (2008), Raskin et al. (2014)
Virtual Week	It is a test battery that simulates daily life activities using a board game. In each virtual day, there are 10 PM tasks: 4 regular, 4 irregular and 2 time check. An example of a regular event-based task is 'take antibiotics at breakfast and dinner'	Henry et al. (2007), Rendell and Henry (2009)	Henry et al. (2007, 2012)

(Continued)

Table 2. (*Continued*).

PM assessment	Definition and/or example item	Studies reported psychometric properties	Studies in Schizophrenia
CAMPROMPT(-C)	It consists of 3 event-based and 3 time-based PM tasks. They are embedded in a general knowledge quiz and word finding puzzles. An example task is to give a map to the examiner when he/she comes across a question containing the words 'great wall'	Man, Chan, and Yip (2015)	Au, Man, Shum et al. (2014), Au, Man, Xiang et al. (2014), Au et al. (2016), Khoratty et al. (2015), Zhou, Hou et al. (2014), Zhou, Xiang et al. (2014), Zhou et al. (2017)
Virtual reality assessment			
VRPMT	It is a non-immersive virtual reality test of PM. In the test, the participant is required to navigate different shops in a virtual shopping center to buy things from the shopping list. Three event-based (e.g. press the 'T' key in response to sales announcements) and 3 time-based (e.g. send a text message 4 min after the start of the test) PM tasks are embedded in the shopping task	Man et al. (2016)	Man et al. (2016)

Notes: BAPM – Brief Assessment of Prospective Memory; CAMPROMPT – Cambridge Prospective Memory Test; CAPM – Comprehensive Assessment of Prospective Memory; MIST – Memory for Intentions Screening Test; PRMQ – Prospective and Retrospective Memory Questionnaire; VRPMT – Virtual Reality Prospective Memory Test.

significantly poorer PM problems than controls, and the self-reported PM problems did not correlate with objective PM performance.

The CAPM was originally developed to examine PM failure in patients with brain injuries. Lam et al. (2013) used this questionnaire in their study and found that individuals with schizophrenia did not report more PM problems than healthy controls. A short version of the CAPM, Brief Assessment of Prospective Memory (BAPM) has also been developed (Man, Fleming, Hohaus, & Shum, 2011).

Computerized tasks

For objective assessment of PM, many studies used computerized PM tasks pioneered by Einstein and McDaniel (1990). In this kind of task, the person is usually asked to undertake two tasks, an ongoing and a PM task. The strength of this task is that the reaction time of PM task and ongoing task can be recorded, and the PM task can be easily controlled and manipulated. For example, RM load (Altgassen et al., 2008), PM cue focality (focal/nonfocal; Henry et al., 2012), and component of processing (cue detection/intention retrieval) have been introduced as task manipulations (Liu et al., 2017). The limitation of these tasks is they are different from daily PM activities that individuals might normally be required to perform.

Psychometric test batteries

There are several commonly used psychometric PM test batteries, namely, the Memory for Intentions Screening Test (MIST) (Raskin, 2009), the Virtual Week (Rendell & Henry, 2009), and the Cambridge Prospective Memory Test (CAMPROMPT) (Groot, Wilson, Evans, & Watson, 2002). The MIST takes about 30 min to administer and complete. In designing the battery, the authors took several variables related to PM into consideration: type of cue (event-based, time-based), type of response (verbal, action), length of delay period (short, long). It has eight PM measures. Details of the test can be found in Raskin (2009). The ongoing task in this test includes word search puzzles. Woods et al. (2007), Twamley et al. (2008), and Raskin et al. (2014) have used the MIST with individuals with schizophrenia in their study.

The Virtual Week (Rendell & Craik, 2000) is a test battery that simulates daily life activities using a board game. In undertaking the battery, the test taker move around the board with the roll of a dice. The hours of a day are marked on the board and each circuit of the board represents a virtual day. When participants move around the board, they are required to make choices on the daily activities and remember to carry out everyday activities (PM tasks). The regular and irregular tasks all include the same numbers of time- and event-based tasks. Details of the test can be found in Rendell and Henry (2009).The original version has seven virtual days, however, five virtual days and three virtual days versions have also been developed. Henry et al. (2007, 2012) have used this test in their study of individuals with schizophrenia and at-risk individuals.

The CAMPROMPT (Groot et al., 2002) consists of three event-based and three time-based PM tasks and its administration takes about 30 min. During the ongoing task, the test taker is required to make PM responses. Six studies (Au, Man, Shum, et al., 2014; Au, Man, Xiang, et al., 2014; Au et al., 2016; Zhou et al., 2017; Zhou, Hou, et al., 2014, Zhou, Xiang, et al., 2014) have used this test in their study of individuals with schizophrenia.

The strength of these psychometric PM test batteries is that they are similar to daily PM activities, but their weaknesses are the time and effort required to administer and score the tests, while observing the test takers. One of these batteries, namely, the Virtual Week has been computerized to overcome some of these limitations.

Virtual reality assessment

The Virtual Reality Prospective Memory Test (VRPMT) (Man et al., 2016) is a non-immersive virtual reality test of PM. It is the Chinese version of the Virtual Reality Shopping Test (VRST) (Canty et al., 2014), which was developed to measure PM in patients with traumatic brain injury. In their study, Man et al. (2016) showed that the VRPMT is a valid and reliable test, and had good sensitivity and specificity in discriminating individuals with first episode schizophrenia from healthy controls. The test takes approximately 14 min to administer. The strength of this test is its similarity with daily PM activities, with the primary drawback being that some clinical participants found it difficult to understand and follow the instructions even after tutorial sessions (Man et al., 2016).

Evidence-based approaches to treatment of PM impairment in schizophrenia

There are two primary approaches of cognitive training: restorative and compensatory. The restorative approach aims to augment or repair the underlying impaired functions, whereas the compensatory approach attempts to develop strategies to overcome the impaired underlying function to reach a good level of performance (Twamley, Jeste, & Bellack, 2003). Both approaches have been shown to improve PM performance in older adults (Hering, Rendell, Rose, Schnitzspahn, & Kliegel, 2014).

For individuals with schizophrenia and those who are at risk, four studies have been conducted to improve PM. All of them adopted the compensatory approach. Twamley, Vella, Burton, Heaton, and Jeste (2012) conducted a randomized controlled trial that included 69 patients with primary psychotic disorders. These individuals were assigned to the standard pharmacotherapy alone (control group) and standard pharmacotherapy and compensatory cognitive training (training group) groups. The training group received a two-hour training session once a week for 12 weeks. The training included intervention targets for PM, attention, learning/memory, and executive functioning. The strategies targeting PM included activities such as calendar use, to-do-lists, and prioritizing tasks. Results showed that compared to the control group, the training group showed improvement on PM as measured by the MIST ($p = 0.05$) at three-month follow-up.

Three other studies used implementation intentions as the strategy to improve PM. This is a brief encoding strategy in the form of 'if I meet X, then I will do Y' (Gollwitzer, 1999). When applied to PM, participants received the PM instructions in the 'if … then …' format, and read the instructions aloud for a few times (most studies used three times). Sometimes it was used in combination with a self-imagery strategy. Chen et al. (2014) applied implementation intentions to individuals with schizotypal personality features and their results showed that event-based PM performance can be improved in both high and low cognitive load conditions. In another study, Khoratty et al. (2015) applied this strategy to individuals with early psychosis and their results showed that event-based PM benefited from implementation intentions in these participants. In the standard instruction condition, PM performance in the early psychosis group was significantly lower than the matched controls. However, in the implementation intentions condition, PM performance in individuals with early psychosis and healthy controls did not show significant differences. Furthermore, PM improvement was not found to be at the cost of ongoing task performance. Finally, Chen, Liu et al. (2016) applied implementation intentions to individuals with schizophrenia and their results showed that this technique improved event-based PM in both low and high cognitive load conditions without ongoing task cost. However, evidence of improvement is lacking for time-based PM. These results showed that compensatory strategies were effective in improving PM performance in individuals with schizophrenia and those who are at risk. However, most of these studies are not randomized control trials. Moreover, most of the reviewed studies instructed participants to use the strategy once. Therefore, the effects of longer and more frequent intervention are not known. Finally, it is unclear if the effects of these interventions will last very long or if they can be generalized to other everyday PM tasks.

Suggestions for the development of interventions for PM in schizophrenia

For the development of interventions for PM impairments in schizophrenia, an important consideration is to make them aware of the PM impairments. Educating patients with schizophrenia about the prevalence of PM deficits may increase their willingness to adopt compensatory strategies. Given that some previous studies have shown that self-reported PM problems in schizophrenia were not significantly different from those of healthy controls (Chan et al., 2008; Lui et al., 2011, 2015), this means that individuals with schizophrenia may lack self-awareness of PM impairments and some training may be carried out to improve their self-awareness before PM treatment.

After patients have developed awareness of their PM impairments, clinicians or rehabilitation workers can teach them how to use some strategies to avoid PM failures, and ask them to use compensatory strategies both consciously and automatically. Although there are only a few studies on PM rehabilitation in schizophrenia, some suggestions can be developed based on results of studies conducted using other populations. For example, in the encoding phase, implementation intentions can be used to increase PM performance (Chen, Liu et al., 2016). Enactment in encoding can also improve PM performance (Pereira et al., 2015). In addition, encoding the intention in multiple modality (e.g. verbal, visual) may also help (Potvin, Rouleau, Sénéchal, & Giguère, 2011). For example, to give a message to a friend, one can rehearse the friend's name and visualize the face of the friend at the same time.

During the maintenance phase, one possible technique is to reduce the delay. This is because as the delay between intention formation and execution increases, the performance on PM tasks would decrease (McBride, Beckner, & Abney, 2011). For instance, individuals with schizophrenia can be taught to carry out intended actions immediately when he/she thinks about it, and not to wait until later. Another technique is to use the 'stop' strategy (Fish et al., 2007), during which an individual can occasionally stop the things he/she is doing and thinks about his/her goal and see what needs to be done.

A number of strategies can be used during the retrieval phase. These include making the PM cue more salient (e.g. to place the garbage bin near the door to remind one to empty it); associating the PM task with a routine activity (e.g. taking medicine after dinner); writing notes and using calendar (write down things that need to be done in the diary and to develop a habit of checking the diary regularly). Other related strategies are to use external aids such as alarm clock, cell phone text message, and to-do-list, etc. It is also possible that playing some computer games can increase working memory and/or executive functions (Hayden, 2012), which subsequently may improve PM (Smith & Bayen, 2005; West & Bowry, 2005).

Conclusion

This study aimed to provide an update review of studies on PM in individuals with schizophrenia and related populations, and highlight findings that were not covered by the previous two reviews/meta-analysis. We found that individuals with schizophrenia showed severe PM impairments, and this finding mainly reinforces the conclusions of the previous reviews. Moreover, time-based PM impairments tended to be more stable over time, and the type of PM errors (no response, miss) suggested that prospective component seem to be an important impairment in PM. These findings extended the conclusions reported in previous reviews. Importantly, PM impairments in schizophrenia have been found to be related to medication adherence and functional outcomes in schizophrenia, and again these findings extended the conclusions of previous reviews. Another finding that extends the conclusion of previous reviews is that PM impairments were related to dysfunctions in prefrontal cortex and other related regions in schizophrenia. Two parts of our paper were not covered by previous reviews. First, there are several approaches to assess PM in schizophrenia and each has its own strengths and weaknesses. Second, only a small number of rehabilitation studies (<5) have been conducted to improve PM in this population. While there is some encouraging evidence of improvement in PM, more randomized controlled trials that examine dosage, retention, and generalization of treatment effects are needed. The present review concluded with some suggestions for the development of interventions for PM impairments in individuals with schizophrenia.

Disclosure statement

No potential conflict of interest was reported by the authors.

Funding

This work was supported by the National Science Foundation of China [grant number 31571130], [grant number 81571317]; the Beijing Training Project for the Leading Talents in S & T [grant number Z151100000315020]; the Beijing Brain Cognition and Brain Medicine Project [grant number Z161100000216138].

ORCID

Ya Wang http://orcid.org/0000-0001-5764-6740
David H. K. Shum http://orcid.org/0000-0002-4810-9262

References

Altgassen, M., Kliegel, M., Rendell, P., Henry, J. D., & Zöllig, J. (2008). Prospective memory in schizophrenia: The impact of varing retrospective-memory load. *Journal of Clinical & Experimental Neuropsychology, 30*(7), 777–788.

Au, R. W. C., Man, D., Shum, D., Lee, E., Xiang, Y.-T., Ungvari, G. S., & Tang, W.-K. (2014). Assessment of prospective memory in schizophrenia using the Chinese version of the Cambridge Prospective Memory Test: A controlled study. *Asia-Pacific Psychiatry, 6*(1), 54–61. doi:10.1111/j.1758-5872.2012.00217.x

Au, R. W. C., Man, D., Xiang, Y.-T., Shum, D., Lee, E., Ungvari, G. S., & Tang, W.-K. (2014). Prospective memory predicts the level of community living skills in schizophrenia. *Psychiatry Research, 219*(1), 86–91. doi:10.1016/j.psychres.2014.04.055

Au, R. W. C., Xiang, Y.-T., Ungvari, G. S., Lee, E., Shum, D. H. K., Man, D., & Tang, W.-K. (2016). Prospective memory performance in persons with schizophrenia and bipolar disorder and healthy persons. *Perspectives in Psychiatric Care*. doi:10.1111/ppc.12172

Bergida, H., & Lenzenweger, M. F. (2006). Schizotypy and sustained attention: Confirming evidence from an adult community sample. *Journal of Abnormal Psychology, 115*, 545–551.

Cadenhead, K. S., Perry, W., Shafer, K., & Braff, D. L. (1999). Cognitive functions in schizotypal personality disorder. *Schizophrenia Research, 37*, 123–132. doi:10.1016/S0920-9964(98)00147-9

Canty, A. L., Fleming, J., Patterson, F., Green, H. J., Man, D., & Shum, D. H. K. (2014). Evaluation of a virtual reality prospective memory task for use with individuals with severe traumatic brain injury. *Neuropsychological Rehabilitation, 24*(2), 238–265. doi:10.1080/09602011.2014.881746

Chan, R. C. K., Wang, Y., Ma, Z., Hong, X., Yuan, Y., Yu, X., … Gong, Q. (2008). Objective measures of prospective memory do not correlate with subjective complaints in schizophrenia. *Schizophrenia Research, 103*(1–3), 229–239. doi:10.1016/j.schres.2008.02.019

Chan, R. C. K., Qing, Y.-H., Wu, Q.-P., & Shum, D. (2010). Prospective memory in healthy Chinese people: The latent structure of the comprehensive assessment of prospective memory questionnaire. *Neuropsychological Rehabilitation, 20*(3), 459–470.

Chan, R. C. K., Lui, S. S. Y., Wang, Y., Liu, A. C. Y., Chui, W. W. H., Shum, D. H. K., & Cheung, E. F. C. (2013). Patients with bipolar disorders share similar but attenuated prospective memory impairments with patients with schizophrenia. *Psychological Medicine, 43*(8), 1639–1649.

Chau, L. T., Lee, J. B., Fleming, J., Roche, N., & Shum, D. (2007). Reliability and normative data for the Comprehensive Assessment of Prospective Memory (CAPM). *Neuropsychological Rehabilitation, 17*(6), 707–722. doi:10.1080/09602010600923926

Chen, X. J., Wang, Y., Liu, L. L., Shi, H. S., Wang, J., Cui, J. F., … Chan, R. C. K. (2014). The effect and mechanisms of implementation intention on prospective memory in individuals with and without schizotypal personality features. *Memory, 22*(4), 349–359. doi:10.1080/09658211.2013.792841

Chen, G., Zhang, L., Ding, W., Zhou, R., Xu, P., Lu, S., & Cui, H. (2015). Event-related brain potential correlates of prospective memory in symptomatically remitted male patients with schizophrenia. *Frontiers in Behavioral Neuroscience, 9*, 262. doi:10.3389/fnbeh.2015.00262

Chen, X. J., Liu, L. L., Cui, J. F., Gan, M. Y., Li, C. Q., Neumann, D. L., … Chan, R. C. K. (2016). The effect and mechanisms of implementation intention in improving prospective memory performance in schizophrenia patients. *Psychiatry Research, 244*, 86–93. doi:10.1016/j.psychres.2016.07.035

Chen, X. J., Wang, Y., Wang, Y., Yang, T. X., Zou, L. Q., Huang, J., … Chan, R. C. K. (2016). Neural correlates of prospective memory impairments in schizophrenia. *Neuropsychology, 30*(2), 169–180. doi:10.1037/neu0000225

Cheung, E. F. C., Lui, S. S. Y., Wang, Y., Yang, T.-X., Shum, D. H. K., & Chan, R. C. K. (2015). Time-based but not event-based prospective memory remains impaired one year after the onset of schizophrenia: A prospective study. *Schizophrenia Research, 169*(1–3), 147–152. doi:10.1016/j.schres.2015.09.015

Cona, G., Bisiacchi, P. S., Sartori, G., & Scarpazza, C. (2016). Effects of cue focality on the neural mechanisms of prospective memory: A meta-analysis of neuroimaging studies. *Scientific Reports, 6*, 193. doi:10.1038/srep25983

Crawford, J. R., Smith, G., Maylor, E. A., Della Sala, S., & Logie, R. H. (2003). The prospective and retrospective memory questionnaire (PRMQ): Normative data and latent structure in a large non-clinical sample. *Memory, 11*(3), 261–275.

Demeter, G., Szendi, I., Domján, N., Juhász, M., Greminger, N., Szollosi, A., & Racsmány, M. (2016). Preserved intention maintenance and impaired execution of prospective memory responses in Schizophrenia: Evidence from an event-based prospective memory study. *Frontiers in Psychology, 7*, 593. doi:10.3389/fpsyg.2016.00593

Einstein, G. O., & McDaniel, M. A. (1990). Normal aging and prospective memory. *Journal of Experimental Psychology: Learning, Memory, and Cognition, 16*, 717–726.

Einstein, G. O., & McDaniel, M. A. (2005). Prospective memory: Multiple retrieval processes. *Current Directions in Psychological Science, 14*, 286–290.

Ellis, J. A. (1996). Prospective memory or the realization of delayed intentions: A conceptual framework for research. In M. Brandimonte, G. O. Einstein, & M. A. McDaniel (Eds.), *Prospective memory: Theory and Applications* (pp. 1–22). Mahwah, NJ: Erlbaum.

Fish, J., Evans, J. J., Nimmo, M., Martin, E., Kersel, D., Bateman, A., … Manly, T. (2007). Rehablitation of executive dysfunction following brain injury: "Content-free" cueing improves everyday prospective memory performance. *Neuropsychologia, 45*, 1318–1330.

Gollwitzer, P. M. (1999). Implementation intentions: Strong effects of simple plans. *American Psychologist, 54*(7), 493–503.

Gottesman, I. I. (1991). *Schizophrenia genesis: The oringin of madness*. New York, NY: Freeman.

Green, M. F., & Harvey, P. D. (2014). Cognition in schizophrenia: Past, present, and future. *Schizophrenia Research: Cognition, 1*(1), e1–e9. doi:10.1016/j.scog.2014.02.001

Groot, Y. C., Wilson, B. A., Evans, J., & Watson, P. (2002). Prospective memory functioning in people with and without brain injury. *Journal of International Neuropsychological Society, 8*(5), 645–654.

Hayden, E. C. (2012). Game on. *Nature, 483*, 24–26.

Heinrichs, D. W. (2005). The primacy of cognition in Schizophrenia. *American Psychologist, 60*(3), 229–242.

Henry, J. D., Rendell, P. G., Kliegel, M., & Altgassen, M. (2007). Prospective memory in schizophrenia: Primary or secondary impairment? *Schizophrenia Research, 95*, 179–185. doi:10.1016/j.schres.2007.06.003

Henry, J. D., Rendell, P. G., Rogers, P., Altgassen, M., & Kliegel, M. (2012). Prospective memory in schizophrenia and schizotypy. *Cognitive Neuropsychiatry, 17*(2), 133–150.

Hering, A., Rendell, P. G., Rose, R. S., Schnitzspahn, K. M., & Kliegel, M. (2014). Prospective memory training in older adults and its relevance for successful aging. *Psychological Research, 78*(6), 892–904. doi:10.1007/s00426-014-0566-4

Hutton, B., Salanti, G., Caldwell, D. M., Chaimani, A., Schmid, C. H., Cameron, C., … Moher, D. (2015). The PRISMA extension statement for reporting of systematic reviews incorporating network meta-analyses of health care interventions: Checklist and explanations. *Annals of Internal Medicine, 162*, 777–784. doi:10.7326/M14-2385

Khoratty, N., Wang, Y., Lloyd, C., Williams, P. L., Chan, R. C. K., & Shum, D. H. K. (2015). Forming implementation intentions improves prospective memory in early psychosis. *Psychiatry Research, 228*(3), 265–271. doi:10.1016/j.psychres.2015.05.101

Kliegel, M., Jäger, T., & Phillips, L. H. (2008). Adult age differences in event-based prospective memory: A meta-analysis on the role of focal versus nonfocal cues. *Psychology and Aging, 23*(1), 203–208.

Kopp, B. (2007). Mnemonic intrusions into working memory in psychometrically identified schizotypal individuals. *Journal of Behavior Therapy and Experimental Psychiatry, 38*(1), 56–74.

Kvavilashvili, L., & Ellis, J. (1996). Varieties of intention: Some distinctions and classifications. In M. E. Brandimonte, G. O. Einstein, M. A. McDaniel (Eds.), *Prospective memory: Theory and applications* (pp. 23–51). Mahwah, NJ: Lawrence Erlbaum Associates.

Lam, J. W. S., Lui, S. S. Y., Wang, Y., Chan, R. C. K., & Cheung, E. F. C. (2013). Prospective memory predicts medication management ability and correlates with non-adherence to medications in individuals with clinically stable schizophrenia. *Schizophrenia Research, 147*(2–3), 293–300. doi:10.1016/j.schres.2013.04.010

Liu, D., Ji, C., Zhuo, K., Song, Z., Wang, Y., Mei, L., … Jiang, K. D. (2017). Impaired cue identification and intention retrieval underlie prospective memory deficits in patients with first-episode schizophrenia. *Australian and New Zealand Journal of Psychiatry, 51*(3), 270–277. doi:10.1177/0004867416640097

Lui, S. S. Y., Wang, Y., Liu, A. C. Y., Chui, W. W. H., Gong, Q-y, Shum, D., … Chan, R. C. K. (2011). Prospective memory in patients with first-onset schizophrenia and their non-psychotic siblings. *Neuropsychologia, 49*(8), 2217–2224. doi:10.1016/j.neuropsychologia.2011.04.002

Lui, S. S. Y., Wang, Y., Yang, T.-X., Liu, A. C. Y., Chui, W. W. H., Yeung, H. K. H., … Chan, R. C. K. (2015). Problems in remembering to carry out future actions in first-episode schizophrenia: Primary or secondary impairment? *Journal of Psychiatric Research, 61*, 141–149. doi:10.1016/j.jpsychires.2014.11.007

Man, D. W. K., Fleming, J., Hohaus, L., & Shum, D. (2011). Development of the brief assessment of prospective memory (BAPM) for use with traumatic brain injury populations. *Neuropsychological Rehabilitation, 21*(6), 884–898. doi:10.1080/09602011.2011.627270

Man, D. W. K., Chan, M. K. L., & Yip, C. C. K. (2015). Validation of the Cambridge Prospective Memory Test (Hong Kong Chinese version) for people with stroke. *Neuropsychological Rehabilitation, 25*(6), 895–912. doi:10.1080/09602011.2014.997253

Man, D. W. K., Ganesan, B., Yip, C. C. K., Lee, C. O. P., Tsang, S. Y. L., Yu, P. W. P., ... Shum, D. H. K. (2016). Validation of the virtual-reality prospective memory test (Hong Kong Chinese version) for individuals with first-episode schizophrenia. *Neuropsychological Rehabilitation,*. doi:10.1080/09602011.2016.1251949

McBride, D. M., Beckner, J. K., & Abney, D. H. (2011). Effects of delay of prospective memory cues in an ongoing task on prospective memory task performance. *Memory and Cognition, 39*(7), 1222–1231. doi:10.3758/s13421-011-0105-0

McDaniel, M. A., LaMontagne, P., Beck, S. M., Scullin, M. K., & Braver, T. S. (2013). Dissociable neural routes to successful prospective memory. *Psychological Science, 24*(9), 1791–1800.

Ordemann, G. J., Opper, J., & Davalos, D. (2014). Prospective memory in schizophrenia: A review. *Schizophrenia Research, 155*, 77–89. doi:10.1016/j.schres.2014.03.008

Pereira, A., de Mendonça, A., Silva, D., Guerreiro, M., Freeman, J., & Ellis, J. (2015). Enhancing prospective memory in mild cognitive impairment: The role of enactment. *Journal of Clinical and Experimental Neuropsychology, 37*(8), 863–877. doi:10.1080/13803395.2015.1072499

Potvin, M.-J., Rouleau, I., Sénéchal, G., & Giguère, J.-F. (2011). Prospective memory rehabilitation based on visual imagery techniques. *Neuropsychological Rehabilitation, 21*(6), 899–924. doi:10.1080/09602011.2011.630882

Raskin, S. A. (2009). Memory for intentions screening test: Psychometric properties and clinical evidence. *Brain Impairment, 10*(1), 23–33. doi:10.1375/brim.10.1.23

Raskin, S. A., Maye, J., Rogers, A., Correll, D., Zamroziewicz, M., & Kurtz, M. (2014). Prospective memory in schizophrenia: Relationship to medication management skills, neurocognition, and symptoms in individuals with schizophrenia. *Neuropsychology, 28*(3), 359–365. doi:10.1037/neu0000040

Rendell, P. G., & Craik, F. I. M. (2000). Virtual week and actual week: Age-related differences in prospective memory. *Applied Cognitive Psychology, 14*(7), S43–S62.

Rendell, P. G., & Henry, J. (2009). A review of virtual week for prospective memory assessment: Clinical implications. *Brain Impairment, 10*(1), 14–22.

Roche, N. L., Fleming, J. M., & Shum, D. H. K. (2002). Self-awareness of prospective memory failure in adults with traumatic brain injury. *Brain Injury, 16*(11), 931–945. doi:10.1080/02699050210138581

Schulz, S. C., & Murray, A. (2016). Assessing cognitive impairment in patients with Schizophrenia. *The Journal of Clinical Psychiatry, 77*(Suppl 2), 3–7. doi:10.4088/jcp.14074su1c.01

Shum, D., Ungvari, G. S., Tang, W. K., & Leung, J. P. (2004). Performance of Schizophrenia patients on time-, event-, and activity-based prospective memory tasks. *Schizophrenia Bulletin, 30*, 693–702.

Smith, R. E. (2003). The cost of remembering to remember in event-based prospective memory: Investigating the capacity demands of delayed intention performance. *Journal of Experimental Psychology: Learning, Memory, and Cognition, 29*, 347–361. doi:10.1037/0278-7393.29.3.347

Smith, R. E., & Bayen, U. J. (2005). The effects of working memory resource availability on prospective memory: A formal modeling approach. *Experimental Psychology, 52*(4), 243–256.

Smith, G., Sala, S. D., Logie, R. H., & Maylor, E. A. (2000). Prospective and retrospective memory in normal ageing and dementia: A questionnaire study. *Memory, 8*(5), 311–321.

Trandafir, A., Méary, A., Schürhoff, F., Leboyer, M., & Szöke, A. (2006). Memory tests in first-degree adult relatives of schizophrenic patients: A meta-analysis. *Schizophrenia Research, 81*, 217–226.

Twamley, E. W., Jeste, D. V., & Bellack, A. S. (2003). A review of cognitive training in Schizophrenia. *Schizophrenia Bulletin, 29*(2), 359–382.

Twamley, E. W., Woods, S. P., Zurhellen, C. H., Vertinski, M., Narvaez, J. M., Mausbach, B. T., ... Jeste, D. V. (2008). Neuropsychological substrates and everyday functioning implications of prospective memory impairment in schizophrenia. *Schizophrenia Research, 106*, 42–49. doi:10.1016/j.schres.2007.10.030

Twamley, E. W., Vella, L., Burton, C. Z., Heaton, R. K., & Jeste, D. V. (2012). Compensatory cognitive training for psychosis: Effects in a randomized controlled trial. *The Journal of Clinical Psychiatry, 73*(09), 1212–1219. doi:10.4088/JCP.12m07686

Wang, Y., Chan, R. C. K., Hong, X., Ma, Z., Yang, T., Guo, L., … Shum, D. (2008). Prospective memory in Schizophreia: Further clarification of nature of impairment. *Schizophrenia Research, 105*, 114–124. doi:10.1016/j.schres.2008.07.002

Wang, Y., Chan, R. C. K., Yu, X., Shi, C., Cui, J., & Deng, Y. (2008). Prospective memory deficits in subjects with schizophrenia spectrum disorders: A comparison study with schizophrenic subjects, psychometrically defined schizotypal subjects, and healthy controls. *Schizophrenia Research, 106*(1), 70–80. doi:10.1016/j.schres.2007.07.020

Wang, Y., Cui, J., Chan, R. C. K., Deng, Y., Shi, H., Hong, X., & Li, Zhanjiang (2009). Meta-analysis of prospective memory in schizophrenia: Nature, extent, and correlates. *Schizophrenia Research, 114*, 64–70. doi:10.1016/j.schres.2009.07.009

Wang, Y., Chan, R. C. K., Cui, J., Deng, Y., Huang, J., Li, H., … Shum, D. (2010). Prospective memory in non-psychotic first-degree relatives of patients with schizophrenia. *Psychiatry Research, 179*, 285–290. doi:10.1016/j.psychres.2009.07.011

Wang, Y., Chan, R. C. K., Cui, J. F., Yang, T. X., Deng, Y. Y., Gong, Q. Y., & Shum, D. (2011). Stability of prospective memory deficits in individuals with schizotypal personality traits. *Psychiatry Research, 189*(1), 156–157. doi:10.1016/j.psychres.2011.01.002

Wang, Y., Yang, T.-X., Su, L., Yan, C., Wang, Y., Huang, J., … Zeng, Y.-W. (2014). Neural correlates of prospective memory in individuals with schizotypal personality features. *Neuropsychology, 28*(3), 373–381. doi:10.1037/neu0000035

West, R., & Bowry, R. (2005). Effects of aging and working memory demands on prospective memory. *Psychophysiology, 42*, 698–712.

Woods, S. P., Twamley, E. W., Dawson, M. S., Narvaez, J. M., & Jeste, D. V. (2007). Deficits in cue detection and intention retrieval underlie prospective memory impairment in schizophrenia. *Schizophrenia Research, 90*, 344–350. doi:10.1016/j.schres.2006.11.005

Woods, S. P., Moran, L. M., Carey, C. L., Dawson, M. S., Iudicello, J. E., Gibson, S., … Atkinson, J. H. (2008). Prospective memory in HIV infection: Is "remembering to remember" a unique predictor of self-reported medication management? *Archives of Clinical Neuropsychology, 23*, 257–270.

Xiang, Y.-T., Shum, D., Chiu, H. F. K., Tang, W.-K., & Ungvari, G. S. (2010). Association of demographic characteristics, symptomatology, retrospective and prospective memory, executive functioning and intelligence with social functioning in Schizophrenia. *Australian and New Zealand Journal of Psychiatry, 44*(12), 1112–1117.

Zhou, F.-C., Xiang, Y.-T., Wang, C.-Y., Dickerson, F., Au, R. W. C., Zhou, J.-J., … Ungvari, G. S. (2012). Characteristics and clinical correlates of prospective memory performance in first-episode schizophrenia. *Schizophrenia Research, 135*(1-3), 34–39.

Zhou, F.-C., Hou, W.-M., Wang, C.-Y., Ungvari, G. S., Chiu, H. F. K., Correll, C. U., … Xiang, Y.-T. (2014). Prospective memory performance in non-psychotic first-degree relatives of patients with Schizophrenia: A controlled study. *PLoS One, 9*(11), e111562. doi:10.1371/journal.pone.0111562

Zhou, F.-C., Xiang, Y.-T., Wang, C.-Y., Dickerson, F., Kreyenbuhl, J., Ungvari, G. S., … Chiu, H. F. K. (2014). Predictive value of prospective memory for remission in first-episode Schizophrenia. *Perspectives in Psychiatric Care, 50*, 102–110. doi:10.1111/ppc.12027

Zhou, F.-C., Wang, C.-Y., Ungvari, G. S., Ng, C. H., Zhou, Y., Zhang, L., … Xiang, Y.-T. (2017). Longitudinal changes in prospective memory and their clinical correlates at 1-year follow-up in first-episode schizophrenia. *PLoS One, 12*(2), e0172114. doi:10.1371/journal.pone.0172114

Zhuo, K., Lu, Y., Yang, Z., Fan, X., Song, Z., Liao, L., … Liu, D. (2013). Prospective memory performance in patients with drug-naïve, first-episode psychosis. *Schizophrenia Research, 143*(2–3), 285–290.

Zogg, J. B., Woods, S. P., Sauceda, J. A., Wiebe, J. S., & Simoni, J. M. (2012). The role of prospective memory in medication adherence: A review of an emerging literature. *Journal of Behavioral Medicine, 35*(1), 47–62. doi:10.1007/s10865-011-9341-9

A systematic review of prospective memory in HIV disease: from the laboratory to daily life

Gunes Avci, David P. Sheppard, Savanna M. Tierney, Victoria M. Kordovski, Kelli L. Sullivan and Steven Paul Woods

ABSTRACT

Objective: Prospective memory (PM) is described as the capacity to form and maintain an intention that is executed in response to a specific cue. Neural injury and associated neurocognitive disorders are common among persons living with HIV disease, who might therefore be susceptible to impairment in PM. **Method:** This literature review utilized a structured qualitative approach to summarize and evaluate our current understanding of PM functioning in people living with HIV disease. 33 studies of PM in HIV+ persons met criteria for inclusion. **Results:** Findings showed that HIV is associated with moderate deficits in PM, which appear to be largely independent of commonly observed comorbid factors. The pattern of PM deficits reveals dysregulation of strategic processes that is consistent with the frontal systems pathology and associated executive dysfunction that characterizes HIV-associated neural injury. The literature also suggests that HIV-associated PM deficits present a strong risk of concurrent problems in a wide range of health behaviors (e.g. medication non-adherence) and activities of daily living (e.g. employment). Early attempts to improve PM in HIV disease have revealed that supporting strategic processes might be effective for some individuals. **Conclusions:** HIV-associated PM deficits are common and exert a significant adverse effect on the daily lives and health of infected persons. Much work remains to be done to understand the cognitive architecture of HIV-associated PM deficits and the most efficient means to enhance PM functioning and improve health outcomes in persons living with HIV.

Introduction

Prospective memory (PM) is a form of episodic memory that entails the capacity to form and maintain an intention that is ultimately executed in response to a specific cue, such as the occurrence of an event or a specific time. In simpler terms, PM is defined as our ability to 'remember to remember.' Everyday examples of PM range from common household tasks, such as remembering to switch off the lights upon leaving a room, to vitally important health-related tasks, such as remembering to take a prescribed medication after a meal or attend a health care appointment at 2 pm. This review focuses on PM functioning in persons living with HIV disease, including: (1) the frequency, severity, and cognitive architecture of HIV-associated PM deficits; (2) HIV disease correlates of PM deficits; (3) the impact of common clinicodemographic comorbidities (e.g. older age and depression) on the expression of HIV-associated PM deficits; (4) the unique contribution of PM deficits to everyday functioning in HIV and (5) ways to enhance PM functioning in HIV. To orient the reader, we begin with a brief overview of the central nervous system complications of HIV infection and summarize our theoretical framework for the review, which adopts the Multiprocess Model (McDaniel & Einstein, 2000)

NeuroAIDS and HIV-associated Neurocognitive Disorders

HIV-1 enters the central nervous system quickly, sometimes within days of infection (Davis et al., 1992). While the virus does not directly infect neurons, it can nevertheless cause neural and glial injury by both direct (i.e. viral proteins, such as gp120 and tat) and indirect (e.g. inflammatory and vascular) mechanisms (Saylor et al., 2016). The adverse effects of HIV are apparent throughout the neocortex and various white matter tracts, but neuropathological changes are most commonly observed in frontostriatal circuits (Ellis, Langford, & Masliah, 2007). HIV-associated neurocognitive disorders (HAND) are evident in approximately one-third to one-half of persons infected with HIV, with the characteristic pattern of impairment reflecting a preferential disruption of prefrontostriatal circuits (Heaton et al., 2014; Reger, Welsh, Razani, Martin, & Boone, 2002). Deficits in motor coordination, information processing speed, working memory, and executive functions are frequently observed in people with HIV (e.g. Heaton et al., 2010), whereas deficits in neurocognitive functions associated with the posterior neocortex, such as visuoperception, are less frequently seen (e.g. Reger et al., 2002).

Episodic retrospective memory impairment is quite common among HIV+ persons, with most prevalence estimates ranging between 40 and 60% (e.g. Rippeth et al., 2004). The etiology of the retrospective memory impairment in HIV is likely multifactorial, primarily reflecting the adverse effects of the virus on frontostriatal circuits (e.g. Ellis et al., 2007), as well as mediotemporal structures (e.g. Maki et al., 2009). The profile of HIV-associated retrospective memory deficits is characterized as a mixed encoding and retrieval problem; that is, diminished free recall and limited use of higher-order organizational strategies in the setting of relatively spared retention and recognition (e.g. Delis et al., 1995; Gongvatana et al., 2009; Woods et al., 2006). Although there is heterogeneity in the expression of HIV-associated retrospective memory deficits (e.g. Murji et al., 2003; Obermeit et al., 2015), most research portrays it as one of dysfunction in the strategic (i.e. executive) aspects of encoding and retrieval. Of clinical relevance, HIV-associated retrospective memory deficits are reliably associated with poorer everyday functioning outcomes, including medication non-adherence (for a review see Casaletto, Weber, Iudicello, & Woods, 2017). Drawing from this literature, our laboratory has taken a theoretical approach to understanding the nature, extent, functional impact, and remediability of PM deficits in HIV disease.

Multiprocess model of prospective memory

There are a few viable conceptual models of PM in the literature (for a review see Kliegel, McDaniel, & Einstein, 2008), all of which tend to agree on some cognitive processes involved in successful execution of a future intention, which include: (1) forming an intention, (2) associating the intention with a retrieval cue (e.g. a certain time or the occurrence of a specific event), (3) retaining this association over a delay interval during which PM cue monitoring may occur when one is engaged in an ongoing task, (4) detecting the PM retrieval cue, (5) disengaging from the ongoing task and retrieving the appropriate intention from retrospective memory, and (6) executing the planned PM action (for a review see Kliegel, McDaniel, & Einstein, 2008). The Multiprocess Model (McDaniel & Einstein, 2000) of PM was chosen to guide this critical review since it is among the most influential theories across the literature, and in HIV specifically. In brief, the Multiprocess Model suggests that PM is a complex, multidimensional cognitive faculty with varying degrees of automatic and strategic processes. The strategic component of PM is guided by a resource-demanding executive system served by frontostriatal circuits whereby individuals voluntarily and effortfully engage in prospective remembering. The automatic component of PM is a more spontaneous process served by mediotemporal and posterior regions that explains why sometimes an intended action simply 'pops into mind' on its own (Einstein & McDaniel, 1990) or reflexively when encountering a strong cue (Ellis & Nimmo-smith, 1993). The neuroimaging studies with nonclinical populations have consistently demonstrated the involvement of rostral prefrontal cortex in PM (e.g. Burgess, Quayle, & Frith, 2001), although there is also evidence for the broader role of the frontoparietal network (e.g. Cona, Scarpazza, Sartori, Moscovitch, & Bisiacchi, 2015), medial temporal cortex (e.g. Gordon, Shelton, Bugg, McDaniel, & Head, 2011), and insula (Cona et al., 2015).

One of the most widely investigated aspects of PM is whether the retrieval cue is time-based or event-based. That is, PM cues may take the form of an event, such as remembering to buy milk when driving by a grocery store (i.e. event-based), or the passage of time, such as taking a medication at 8 pm (i.e. time-based). Whereas successful event-based PM performance is believed to be relatively automatic because cue detection is more reflexive given the salience of environmental cues, time-based PM is hypothesized to be more strategic because it is dependent on cognitive control processes involved in time monitoring. In other words, time-based tasks tend to require greater voluntary, strategic monitoring processes that are self-initiated than do event-based tasks (McDaniel & Einstein, 2000). It is important to recognize however, that there is considerable variability in the automatic versus strategic demands of event-based tasks. For example, highly salient event-based cues (e.g. a loud alarm) rely on more automatic processes and result in better PM performance whereas less salient cues (e.g. a subtle, non-focal visual cue) require more strategic monitoring processes and result in lower PM success (Einstein, McDaniel, Manzi, Cochran, & Baker, 2000; McDaniel & Einstein, 2000).

Viewed through the Multiprocess framework, one therefore might predict that: (1) persons living with HIV disease would evidence greater impairment the strategic as compared to the automatic aspects of PM; (2) such strategic PM deficits would confer an increased risk of poorer everyday functioning outcomes; and (3) supporting strategic processing would improve PM performance in HIV disease. Below we review the available published evidence that has examined these hypotheses.

Methods

Due to the relatively circumscribed number of studies on the topic of PM in HIV disease, we were able to include all the published papers and take a hybrid approach to reviewing and summarizing the literature. Specifically, we: (1) conducted a structured qualitative review; (2) report effect sizes when possible and relevant; and (3) provide PM data from a large, well-characterized HIV+ cohort. It was our view that this hybrid approach to reviewing the literature provided a more rigorous, comprehensive, and informative view on the topic than would be provided by any individual approach alone.

Study identification

To identify articles for inclusion in this review, we adhered to PRISMA guidelines (Liberati, 2009). Specifically, we reviewed PubMed/ MEDLINE, Web of Science, and SCOPUS. Each published database was searched separately across the years 2000–2016 using the following key words: prospective memory, memory for intentions, HIV, and AIDS. To be included, an article must have used a self-report or performance-based measure of prospective memory in human participants with verified HIV seropositivity. Full text was retrieved for any articles with inclusion potential. Upon inspection of the content, we included all of the published studies in this review. This approach minimizes our risk of bias. We also reviewed each article identified for additional published articles that met inclusion criteria. The search strategy generated a total of 33 published articles on the topic of PM in HIV disease (see Table 1).

Effect size extraction

Although this review primarily adopts a structured, qualitative method to summarizing the extant literature, we also made an effort to adhere to longstanding recommendations in neuropsychology to consider effect sizes to supplement the findings of null hypothesis significance testing (Bezeau & Graves, 2001). Thus, we extracted, report, and summarize effect size data wherever possible throughout this review to supplement our simple tallying of 'significant' findings per standard null hypothesis testing (i.e. *p* values). If a given study did not include an effect size estimate, we calculated effect sizes by drawing the relevant data (e.g. *M* and *SD*) from the paper or by contacting the study authors. For summary purposes, all effect sizes were converted to Cohen's d values using standard methods. Note that this approach was not intended to serve the same function as a rigorous meta-analysis; rather we strove to incorporate effect sizes in a systematic way in an effort to better understand and summarize the magnitude of the null hypothesis significance testing findings across this literature.

Cohort data

Finally, we also drew from a cohort study of 427 HIV+ persons and 203 HIV− participants with PM measures in an effort to provide empirical data to illustrate specific points in this review and/or address controversial issues (e.g. HIV disease severity) that may have been underpowered across the individual studies reviewed. All participants in this cohort provided informed, written consent and were assessed under IRB-approved protocols at the UCSD

Table 1. Study details and key findings from manuscripts included in the systematic review.

Authors	Title	Sample(s)	PM Task(s)	Key findings
Carey et al. (2006)	Prospective memory in HIV-1 infection	42 HIV+ 29 HIV−	MIST, MIST 24-h	The HIV+ participants demonstrated deficits in time-and event-based PM, as well as more frequent 24-h delay PM failures
Woods et al. (2006)	Markers of macrophage activation and axonal injury are associated with prospective memory in HIV-1	35 HIV+	MIST	Higher levels of MCP-1 in plasma, and soluble receptor for tumor necrosis factor type II and tau in cerebrospinal fluid were associated with lower PM but not with retrospective memory.
Martin et al. (2007)	Characteristics of prospective memory deficits in HIV-seropositive substance-dependent individuals: Preliminary observations	31 HIV+ 35 HIV− (all substance-dependent individuals)	Habitual event- and time-based tasks with the clinical neuropsychological battery as the ongoing task	HIV+ participants showed deficits in time- but not event-based PM. Time-based PM performance was a significant predictor of risky sexual practices in entire sample.
Woods et al. (2007)	Frequency and predictors of self-reported prospective memory complaints in individuals infected with HIV	75 HIV+ 60 HIV−	MIST, PRMQ	Self reported PM symptoms were elevated in HIV+ persons, but did not correspond to actual PM abilities.
Woods, Iudicello, et al. (2008)	HIV-associated prospective memory impairment increases risk of dependence in everyday functioning	66 HIV+	MIST, PRMQ	HIV-associated PM impairment and elevated PM symptoms were each independently associated with greater dependence in instrumental activities of daily living.
Woods, Moran, et al. (2008)	Prospective memory in HIV infection: Is "remembering to remember" a unique predictor of self-reported medication management?	87 HIV+ on ART	MIST, MIST 24-h, PRMQ	PM was associated with self-reported medication management, independent of other cognitive functions, psychiatric, psychosocial, and environmental factors.
Woods et al. (2009)	Timing is everything: Antiretroviral non-adherence is associated with impairment in time-based prospective memory	79 HIV+ on ART	MIST, MIST 24-h, PRMQ	Individuals classified as non-adherent to ARTs using electronic medication monitoring had significantly lower PM performance, particularly on time-based PM, but did not differ on PRMQ or MIST 24-h.
Contardo et al. (2009)	Relationship of prospective memory to neuropsychological function and antiretroviral adherence	97 HIV+ on ART (all substance-dependent individuals)	MIST	PM loaded separately from retrospective memory and executive functions and was the only correlate of ART adherence.
Gupta et al. (2010)	Is prospective memory a dissociable cognitive function in HIV infection?	162 HIV+	MIST, AAIM	PM loaded on a unique factor, apart from tests of retrospective memory, executive functions, and motor skills.
Woods et al. (2010)	The semantic relatedness of cue-intention pairings influences event-based prospective memory failures in older adults with HIV infection	35 HIV+ (≤40 years) 48 HIV+ (≥50 years) 20 HIV− (≤40 years) 15 HIV− (≥50 years)	MIST, AAIM	Significant additive effects of aging and HIV on event-based PM, especially when PM cue was not semantically related to intention

(Continued)

Table 1. *(Continued).*

Authors	Title	Sample(s)	PM Task(s)	Key findings
Zogg et al. (2010)	HIV-associated prospective memory impairment in the laboratory predicts failures on a semi-naturalistic measure of health care compliance	139 HIV+	MIST, MIST 24-h, PRMQ	MIST, but not PRMQ, was a significant predictor of MIST 24-h after controlling for demographics, retrospective memory and executive functions, and psychiatric factors.
Iudicello et al. (2011)	Misremembering future intentions in methamphetamine dependent individuals	20 HIV + 19 HIV− (all methamphetamine-dependent individuals)	MIST, MIST 24-h	No effect of HIV on time- or event-based PM in persons with methamphetamine dependence.
Weber et al. (2011)	An examination of the age-prospective memory paradox in HIV-infected adults	53 HIV+ (≤40 years) 88 HIV+ (≥50 years) 59 HIV− (≤40 years) 54 HIV− (≥50 years)	MIST time-based scale, MIST 24-h, PRMQ	Older HIV+ adults performed worse than their younger HIV+ counterparts on laboratory tasks of PM but performed comparably on a naturalistic PM task.
Woods et al. (2011)	Prospective memory deficits are associated with unemployment in persons living with HIV infection	59 HIV+ Unemployed 49 HIV+ Employed	MIST, MIST 24-h, PRMQ	MIST, but not PRMQ or MIST 24-h, was independently associated with employment status.
Zogg et al. (2011)	Are time- and event-based prospective memory comparably affected in HIV infection?	143 HIV+ 43 HIV−	MIST	HIV+ individuals demonstrated deficits in time-based PM compared to HIV− adults, as well as a trend-level difference on event-based PM, which was driven by the participants with HAND.
Doyle et al. (2012)	Aging, prospective memory, and health-related quality of life in HIV infection	41 HIV+ (≤40 years) 72 HIV+ (≥50 years)	MIST, MIST 24-h, PRMQ	Self-reported PM was an independent predictor of health-related QoL in the overall sample; however, time-based PM was only associated with health-related QoL in the younger group.
Hoare et al. (2012)	A diffusion tensor imaging and neuropsychological study of prospective memory impairment in South African HIV positive individuals	128 HIV+ (40 DTI) 32 HIV− (10 DTI)	MIST, PRMQ	PM associated with fractional anisotropy values in all regions. HIV effect for time-, but not event-based, PM.
Morgan, Weber, et al. (2012)	Longer ongoing task delay interval exacerbate prospective memory deficits in HIV-associated Neurocognitive Disorders (HAND)	49 HAND 78 HIV−	MIST, PRMQ	HAND group performed worse on long-delay time-based PM tasks and reported more long-delay PM symptoms but there was no group effect on short-delay PM performance or symptoms.
Poquette et al. (2012)	Prospective memory and antiretroviral medication non-adherence in HIV: An analysis of ongoing task delay length using the memory for intentions screening test	74 HIV+ on ART	MIST	Poor long-delay time-based PM was uniquely predictive of poor ART adherence as measured by electronic monitoring.
Blackstone, Woods et al. (2013)	Memory-Based Strategies for Antiretroviral Medication Management: An Evaluation of Clinical Predictors, Adherence Behavior Awareness, and Effectiveness	223 HIV+ on ART	MIST	Poor event-based PM performance was associated more frequent use of ART adherence strategies.

Doyle et al. (2013)	Prospective memory in HIV-associated Neurocognitive Disorders (HAND): The neuropsychological dynamics of time monitoring	55 HAND 108 HIV–	MIST, MIST 24-h	HAND group demonstrated poorer strategic time monitoring, which was related to lower time-based PM.
Casaletto et al. (2014)	Self-predictions of prospective memory in HIV-Associated Neurocognitive Disorders: Evidence of a metamemory deficit	72 HAND+ 131 HAND- 150 HIV–	MIST, PRMQ	HAND+ group reported more everyday PM symptoms but were inaccurately overconfident in their PM task predictions compared to HAND- and HIV–. PM overconfidence was associated with executive dysfunction and ART nonadherence.
Coulehan et al. (2014)	The role of decision-making ability in HIV/AIDS: impact on prospective memory	89 HIV+	MIST, MIST 24-h	Risky decision-making performance predicted PM independent of executive functions.
Loft et al. (2014)	Allowing brief delays in responding improves event-based prospective memory for young adults living with HIV disease	57 HIV+ young adults	Ongoing lexical decision-making task with an embedded focal and non-focal task with varying onset PM response time	Delaying the execution of PM responses increased PM performance accuracy, particularly for non-focal targets.
Woods et al. (2014)	Task importance affects event-based prospective memory performance in adults with HIV-associated neurocognitive disorders and HIV-infected young adults with problematic substance use	Study 1: 15 HAND+, 35 HAND-, 31 HIV– Study 2: 58 HIV+ youth (33 with SUD)	Ongoing lexical decision-making task with a non-focal event-based PM paradigm	Emphasizing PM task importance vs. the ongoing task normalized PM accuracy in HAND and SUD.
Doyle, Morgan, et al. (2015)	Time estimation and production in HIV-associated neurocognitive disorders (HAND)	53 HAND+ 120 HAND- 113 HIV–	MIST	Time estimation and production correlated with time-, but not event-based PM in HIV.
Doyle, Weber, et al. (2015)	Habitual prospective memory in HIV disease	36 HAND+ 70 HAND- 115 HIV–	Computerized habitual time-based PM task with an ongoing cognitive and emotional Stroop task	HAND+ individuals had elevated PM repetition errors. Worse habitual PM was associated with poorer learning and dependence in real-world outcomes, including ART nonadherence.
Sheppard et al. (2015)	Does older age confer an increased risk of incident neurocognitive disorders among persons living with HIV disease?	56 HIV+ (≥50 years)	MIST	PM performance at baseline was associated with incident neurocognitive disorder at one-year follow-up.

(Continued)

Table 1. *(Continued).*

Authors	Title	Sample(s)	PM Task(s)	Key findings
Avci et al. (2016)	The effects of HIV disease and older age on laboratory-based, naturalistic, and self-perceived symptoms of prospective memory: Does retrieval cue type and delay interval matter?	48 HIV+ (≤40 years) 112 HIV+(≥50 years) 77 HIV− (≤40 years) 77 HIV− (≥50 years)	MIST, MIST 24-h, PRMQ	Older age and HIV had independent effects on long-delay time-based PM in the laboratory, whereas on a naturalistic PM task older HIV− adults performed better than older HIV+ adults and younger persons. Older age, but not HIV, was associated with a relative sparing of self-perceived PM failures in daily life across longer delay self-cued intervals.
Sheppard et al. (2016)	Pill burden influences the association between time-based prospective memory and antiretroviral therapy adherence in younger but not older HIV-infected adults	117 HIV+(≥50 years) 82 HIV+ (≤40 years)	MIST	In the older group, better time-based PM performance was associated with higher likelihood of ART adherence, irrespective of pill burden. Within the younger sample, time-based PM was positively related to adherence only in participants with lower pill burden.
Sirois et al. (2016)	Associations of memory and executive functioning with academic and adaptive functioning among youth with perinatal HIV exposure and/or infection	258 HIV+ youth	PROMACY	PM was uniquely predictive of verbal and mathematical academic achievement.
Faytell, Doyle, Naar-King, Outlaw, Nichols, Casaletto, et al. (in press)	Visualization of future task performance improves naturalistic prospective memory for some younger adults living with HIV disease	60 HIV+ youth	MIST	Visualization at encoding improved naturalistic event-based PM for HIV+ youth with low time-based PM and normal learning.
Faytell, Doyle, Naar-King, Outlaw, Nichols, Twamley, et al. (in press)	Calendaring and alarms can improve naturalistic time-based prospective memory for youth infected with HIV	47 HIV+ youth	MIST	Calendaring and alarms improved naturalistic time-based PM performance, which was not associated with the MIST.

Notes: AAIM = Abbreviated Assessment of Intentional Memory; ART = Antiretroviral Therapy; DTI = Diffusion Tensor Imaging; HAND = HIV-associated Neurocognitive Disorders; MCP-1 = Monocyte Chemoattractant Protein-1; MIST = Memory for Intentions Screening Test; MIST 24-h = 24-h delay trial of Memory for Intentions Screening Test; PRMQ = Prospective and Retrospective Memory Questionnaire; PROMACY = Prospective Memory Assessment for Children and Youth; PM = Prospective Memory; QoL = quality of life; SUD = Substance Use Disorder.

HIV Neurobehavioral Research Program in between 2005 and 2013. Participants with histories of serious neurological (e.g. seizure disorders, stroke) or psychiatric (e.g. psychosis) conditions, estimated verbal IQ scores <70, and active substance use disorders (SUD) were excluded. All participants completed the research version (Woods, Moran, Dawson et al., 2008) of the Memory for Intentions Screening Test (Raskin, Buckheit, & Sherrod, 2010) as part of a comprehensive neurocognitive and medical evaluation (see Woods et al., 2009 for details). Basic descriptive data on this cohort is provided in Table 2.

Measurement of PM

The laboratory-based PM measures in the studies included in this review always included an ongoing task and prospective tasks. As the participant worked on the ongoing task, s/he was required to remember to execute certain behavior (i.e. PM) as a response to a cue (i.e. event-based) or after the passage of time (i.e. time-based). The majority of the studies reviewed utilized the research version (Woods et al., 2008) of the Memory for Intentions Screening Test (MIST; Raskin et al., 2010) to study PM in HIV. The MIST is a standardized measure where participants are asked to perform eight different PM tasks over a 30-min period, during which time they are engaged in a word-search puzzle (i.e. ongoing task). The eight PM tasks are balanced in terms of delay interval (i.e. 2-min or 15-min delay), cue (i.e. time-based or event-based cue), and response modality (i.e. verbal or a physical response). Incorrect responses are coded in terms of errors of omission (e.g. lack of response) and commission (e.g. task substitution errors).

Table 2. Participant demographic and disease characteristics.

	Total Sample (n = 630)	HIV+ (n = 427)	HIV– (n = 203)	p	Group differences
Age (years)	42.5 (13.9)	42.3 (13.4)	42.9 (15)	–	–
Education (years)	13.6 (2.6)	13.3 (2.5)	14.2 (2.7)	<.0001	H+ <HIV–
Ethnicity/race					
African-American	26%	27.6%	22.7%	–	–
Asian	1.6%	1.4%	2%	–	–
Hispanic	18.1%	18.3%	17.7%	–	–
White	53.3%	52%	56.2%	–	–
Gender (% men)	79.5%	86.2%	65.5%	<.0001	H+ >HIV–
Major depression	49.6%	57.8%	34.7%	<.0001	H+ >HIV–
Generalized anxiety	10.6%	14%	4.5%	.0002	H+ >HIV–
Substance dependence	49.3%	54.5%	39.9%	.0008	H+ >HIV–
Hepatitis C virus	–	17.9%	9.5%	.005	H+ >HIV–
Estimated duration of infection (months)	–	140.3 (100.2)	–	–	–
AIDS (%)	–	50.9%	–	–	–
CD4 count (cells/μl)	–	566.6 (284.9)	–	–	–
Nadir CD4 (cells/μl)	–	231.1 (190.6)	–	–	–
cART status (% rx)	–	84.1%	–	–	–
Plasma RNA (detectable)	–	30.5%	–	–	–
On cART	–	19.8%	–	–	–

Notes: AIDS = Acquired immune deficiency syndrome; CD4 = Cluster of differentiation 4; cART = combination antiretroviral therapy; HIV = Human Immunodeficiency Virus; Parenthetical values are SD; Major depression, generalized anxiety, and substance dependence include lifetime diagnoses.

The MIST also has a naturalistic PM component (i.e. MIST 24-h task) that was used by several studies reviewed in this paper. Participants are instructed to leave a telephone message for the researcher the following day specifying the number of hours slept the night after the assessment. The use of mnemonic strategies such as electronic calendars is permitted on this naturalistic component, but is not explicitly encouraged.

Finally, the Prospective and Retrospective Memory Questionnaire (PRMQ; Smith, Della Sala, Logie, & Maylor, 2000) is another commonly used measure of PM, which appeared in several studies reviewed here. The PRMQ consists of 16 questions about everyday memory errors including eight PM complaints, which are separated into further subscales: four short-term items, half of which are self-cued (e.g. 'Do you decide to do something in a few minutes' time and then forget to do it?') and half environmentally cued (e.g. 'Do you intend to take something with you before leaving a room or going out, but minutes later leave it behind, even though it's there in front of you?'). There also are four long-term PM items, half of which are self-cued (e.g. 'Do you forget appointments if you are not prompted by someone else or by a reminder such as a calendar or diary?') and the other half of which are environmentally cued (e.g. 'Do you forget to buy something you planned to buy, like a birthday card, even when you see the shop?'). Participants are asked to rate how often each type of memory failure has occurred on a 5-point scale.

Cognitive neuropsychology of PM in HIV

Studies consistently show that HIV is associated with mild-to-moderate deficits in PM, including elevations in self-reported PM symptoms (e.g. Woods et al., 2007), diminished PM performance in the laboratory (e.g. Carey et al., 2006), and PM failures in daily life (e.g. Avci, Loft, Sheppard, Woods, & HIV Neurobehavioral Research Program (HNRP) Group, 2016; Carey et al., 2006). A total of 12 studies examined group differences on PM performance by serostatus, with all 12 reporting significant effects. The average effect size was .47 (*d* ranged between −.35 and .96). Importantly, across these studies, the observed PM deficits in HIV disease are not better explained by demographics (e.g. age, education), various medical and psychiatric comorbidities (e.g. depression), or general cognitive impairment (e.g. Avci et al., 2016). As detailed below, some of these clinicodemographic factors can modulate the expression of HIV-associated PM deficits, but they do not appear to be interpretive confounds per se.

Consistent with the predictions of the Multiprocess theory, HIV-associated PM deficits are primarily driven by strategic rather than automatic processes. We tend to observe larger deficits on time-based PM tasks as compared to event-based tasks (Carey et al., 2006; Martin et al., 2007; Morgan, Weber, et al., 2012; Zogg et al., 2011). This observation is supported by the examination of effect sizes reported by studies investigating time- and event-based PM in HIV+ and HIV− persons ($K = 12$; HIV+ $n = 787$, HIV− $n = 763$). The average effect size for time-based PM was .61 and for event-based was .37 (Figure 1). Even when we restricted the sample of studies to those that included both time- and event-based PM ($K = 6$; HIV+ $n = 484$, HIV− $n = 443$), as opposed to just one or the other, the effect size differences persisted ($d = .63$ for time-based PM and $d = .31$ for event-based PM). There are several possible reasons why time-based PM may be more sensitive to HAND than event-based PM, including psychometric factors such as differential task difficulty (see Chapman & Chapman, 1973). For example, ceiling effects are not uncommon on event-based PM tasks involving more automatic processes, especially in healthy adults (see Raskin et al., 2011). Another potential explanation

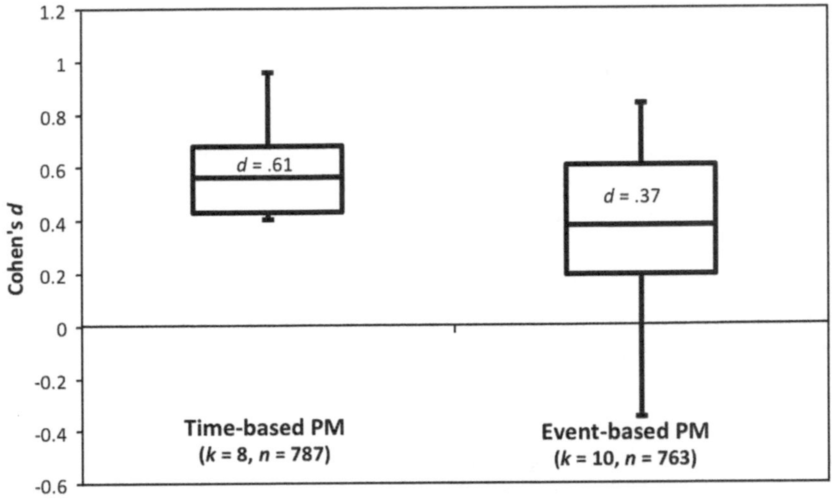

Figure 1. Box-and-whisker plot of effect sizes (Cohen's *d*) for time- and event-based prospective memory (PM) in HIV+ vs. HIV− samples.
Note: *k* = number of effect sizes, *n* = total sample size.

is that by disrupting frontostriatal systems, HIV is more likely to affect strategic PM processes, which are more closely linked to time- vs. event-based PM. This more theoretical explanation of the pattern of findings is explored in detailed below.

HIV-associated deficits on time-based PM appear to be driven by failures in strategic monitoring, as supported by findings of increased omission errors in the setting of normal performance on the ongoing task and post-test recognition trials. Further evidence concerning the strategic resource demands of HIV-associated deficits in time-based PM was reported by Doyle et al. (2013) who demonstrated that individuals with HAND checked the clock (i.e. time monitoring) significantly less often than the comparison group during a time-based PM task. Subsequent analyses revealed that the frequency of clocking checking was positively related to overall time-based (but not event-based) PM performance, as well as executive functions (i.e. verbal fluency). It was also reported that time perception was associated with the time-based PM but not event-based PM in another study of HIV disease (Doyle, Morgan, Weber, & Woods, 2015). The third line of evidence supporting a primary strategic time-based PM deficit in HIV is provided by studies on the delay effect: namely the notion from the Multiprocess theory that longer delays place greater demands on limited executive resources supporting cue detection and monitoring (McDaniel & Einstein, 2000). In 2012, Morgan, Weber et al. reported that persons with HAND performed more poorly than seronegatives on longer (i.e. 15-min) but not shorter (i.e. 2-min) PM delay tasks, particularly for time-based cues. In this study, long-delay time-based PM was associated with executive functions (e.g. cognitive flexibility and planning), thus further supporting the strategic hypothesis of HIV-associated PM deficits.

It is also important to recognize that event-based PM deficits can also be observed in HIV disease and, when present, tend to reflect impairment in both strategic and automatic processes. As reviewed above, while time-based tasks are almost invariably strategically demanding, event-based PM tasks can vary in their strategic vs. automatic processing demands. Although event-based PM deficits are evident (Carey et al., 2006), especially in persons with HAND (Zogg et al., 2011), these deficits tend to show up as intrusion errors (e.g. responding to the PM cue with the incorrect intent content) and correlate more strongly with retrospective memory (Zogg et al., 2011). However, Woods et al. (2014) and Loft et al. (2014) suggest that event-based PM deficits are a function of poor allocation of attention during monitoring. Moreover, Woods, Dawson, Weber, Grant, and HIV Neurobehavioral Research Center (HNRC) Group (2010) showed that event-based PM deficits are exacerbated by semantically unrelated cue-intention pairings, again suggesting that strategic processes are also affected.

Although these findings add support to the growing body of research elucidating strategic monitoring processes in the event-based PM functioning of HIV+ adults, fewer studies have specifically looked at the role of highly automatic processes. Examining HIV effects using classic paradigms from the experimental literature, such as focal (i.e. spontaneous/automatic) versus non-focal cues (Kliegel, Jäger, & Phillips, 2008) informed by the Multiprocess theory, ongoing task load as informed by the multinomial model (Smith & Bayen, 2006), contextual factors (e.g. emotional salience), or PM deactivation/aftereffects (e.g. Walser, Goschke, Möschl, & Fischer, 2016) may be useful in elucidating underlying mechanisms.

Disease factors and PM in HIV

HIV disease (e.g. nadir CD4 counts) and treatment (e.g. the CNS penetrance of combination antiretroviral therapy [cART]) factors can moderate the expression of HIV-associated neurocognitive disorders (Ellis et al., 2007). However, our review of the PM literature in HIV suggests that clinical disease severity does not play a strong role in the nature or extent of HIV-associated PM deficits. Indeed, such associations, if present, are usually derived from simple univariate analyses that do not consider confounds and tend to be both quite small and elusive. Specifically, we identified a total of 31 analyses in 9 studies with 827 HIV+ participants that examined the relationship between clinical HIV disease variables and PM. Effect sizes were not reliably available across these analyses, which were exclusively secondary or tertiary subanalyses. With regard to HIV treatment factors, five studies have reported null associations between cART status and PM (e.g. Doyle, Weber, et al. 2015; Martin et al., 2007; Weber et al., 2011; Woods et al., 2010; Zogg et al., 2010), which was consistent with analyses from our own cohort (see Figure 2). Of course, such findings are quite limited in the cART era given that most participants in research are prescribed therapy. We did not identify any prospective studies of the benefits of cART initiation on PM nor the possible association between CNS penetrance of cART regimens (e.g. Letendre el al., 2008) and PM in HIV. Similarly, none of the five studies that have evaluated the association between plasma or CSF viral load have reported significant associations, which aligns with findings from our cohort (see Figure 2). Investigations of the relationship of current CD4 cell counts to PM revealed a similar null pattern that parallels our cohort findings (see Figure 2), with only 1 of the 7 analyses in extant literature reporting a significant association.

With regard to historical disease indicators (viz., infection duration, nadir CD4 count, and AIDS status), we see slightly more mixed, but still largely null findings reported across the literature. Specifically, only 3 of three out of 10 analyses showed significant associations between PM and AIDS status or nadir CD4 count, while zero of four studies found relationships between PM and estimated duration of infection. In our cohort, we see moderate effect size associations between PM and longer duration of infection and having a historical AIDS

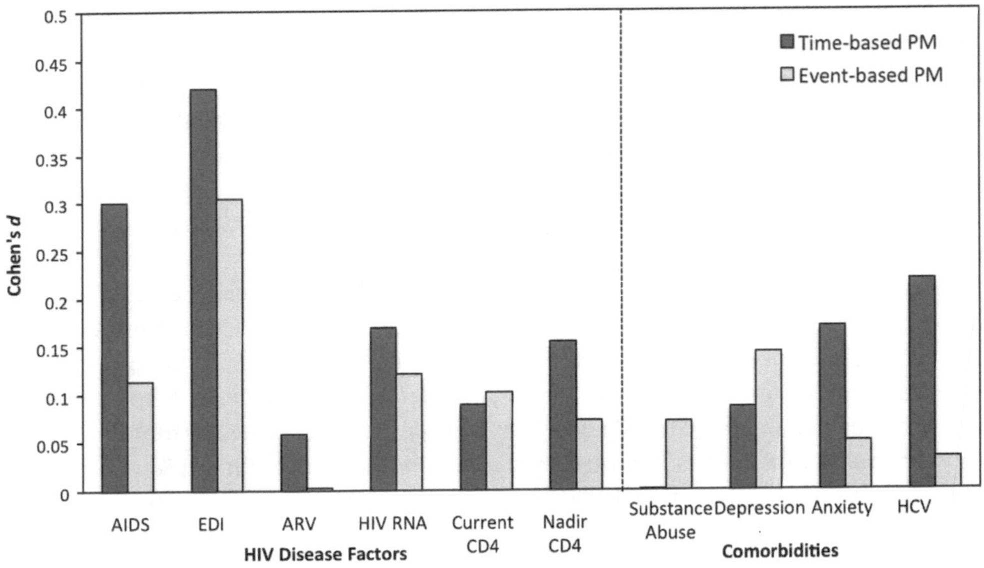

Figure 2. Effect size estimates (Cohen's *d*) of the association between prospective memory (PM) and HIV disease characteristics and common comorbidities (*n* = 416).
Notes: AIDS = Acquired Immune Deficiency Syndrome; EDI = Estimated Duration of Infection; CD4 = Cluster of Differentiation 4; ARV = Antiretroviral therapy; HCV = Hepatitis C Virus.

diagnosis (see Figure 2); however, both of these associations are confounded by older age. That is, persons with longer durations of infection and AIDS diagnoses are older, which – as noted below in this review – is a major contributor to HIV-associated PM deficits. In fact, when infection duration, AIDS, and age were entered simultaneously as predictors of PM in our cohort, only age emerges as an independent contributor ($p < .05$).

Only two studies to date have directly examined potential neurobiological underpinnings of PM impairment in HIV using more sophisticated biomarkers rather than standard clinical indicators. In 2006, Woods and colleagues reported that poorer PM performance was associated with higher levels of monocyte chemoattractant protein-1 (MCP-1) in plasma ($d = 1.1$), and soluble receptor for tumor necrosis factor type II ($d = 1.5$) and tau in cerebrospinal fluid ($d = 1.3$), which in turn were not associated with retrospective memory scores (mean $d = .2$). PM was not associated with immunological variables, viral RNA, astrocytosis, or growth factors (mean $d = .3$). Taken together, such findings were interpreted to suggest that PM impairment in HIV may reflect specific neuropathogenic mechanisms of macrophage activation and neuroaxonal injury. More recently, Hoare et al. (2012) investigated the relationship of white matter integrity to PM among 40 HIV+ individuals using diffusion tensor imaging (DTI). Results revealed that PM functioning was associated with decreased fractional anisotropy in the white matter tracts that relay through the anterior prefrontal cortical regions, including the genu of the corpus callosum, the cingulum and the superior corona radiata.

Taken together, these findings seem to suggesting that peripheral immunovirological factors may not play a primary role in the neuropathogenesis of HIV-associated PM deficits. Biomarkers of neuroaxonal integrity (e.g. tau, DTI) show stronger associations with PM in HIV-infected persons, but such findings should still be considered preliminary and await replication and extension with other methods, including volumetric MRI indices and functional MRI (task-based and resting state), in order to better understand the neural architecture of HIV-associated PM deficits. Such studies might include seronegative participants and/or other neuropsychological populations (e.g. traumatic brain injury) in order to determine whether the associations between neuroaxonal injury and PM are unique in HIV. In terms of neuroimaging, much work remains to be done in order to determine the brain structural and functional underpinnings of HIV-associated PM deficits, with studies needed to map the neuropathophysiology of performance-based PM impairments onto brain volumes, white matter pathways, metabolism, neurochemical abnormalities (e.g. spectroscopy), as well as functional studies to understand the relevant networks of neuronal activity associated with PM in HIV disease. Investigators might also examine the possible role of host (e.g. APOE) and viral genetics, proteomics, and other novel biomarker approaches in the expression of PM deficits in HIV.

Clinicodemographic comorbidities and PM in HIV

Aging

Age is an important factor in understanding the effects of HIV on PM for two reasons: (1) The prevalence and incidence of older adults living with HIV is on the rise (Smit et al., 2015; Smith, Delpech, Brown, & Rice, 2010); and (2) Among seronegative populations, older age is strongly associated with declines in PM (Henry, MacLeod, Phillips, & Crawford, 2004). The last two decades have witnessed significant advances in the effectiveness of cART, which has resulted in a tremendous rise in the number of older adults (aged ≥50) living with HIV disease (Smit et al., 2015). As HIV-infected individuals age, they are at increased risk for acquiring HIV-associated, Non-AIDS (HANA) conditions (e.g. cardiovascular disease), including HAND (Valcour et al., 2004). The downstream effects of HAND are particularly important for older HIV+ adults, who are more vulnerable to the adverse impact of HAND on retention in HIV care (Jacks et al., 2015) and everyday functioning (e.g. Morgan, Iudicello, et al., 2012), including and medication management capacity (Thames et al., 2011). Importantly, lower baseline PM in the laboratory is strongly predictive of incident HAND at one-year follow-up among older HIV+ adults ($d = .96$; Sheppard et al., 2015). Independent of HIV, aging processes have significant adverse impacts on PM functioning (Henry et al., 2004). Consistent with Multiprocess theory, aging in the absence of HIV carries mild-to-moderate effects on PM tasks with high strategic demands (for review, see McDaniel & Einstein, 2011), such as time-based cues and semantically unrelated cue-intention pairings on event-based tasks (Henry et al., 2004). PM deficits are also uniquely predictive of poorer everyday functioning in older adults (e.g. Woods, Weinborn, Velnoweth, Rooney, & Bucks, 2012; Woods et al., 2011). Thus, there is overlap in the severity, profile, and functional impact of PM deficits in aging and HIV disease that raises questions regarding the possible additive or synergistic effects of these risk factors in combination.

Laboratory findings of PM and age in HIV

Previous investigations of PM among middle-aged HIV+ individuals show that older age is associated with poorer overall PM performance (Poquette et al., 2012) and time monitoring (i.e. clock checking) during PM tasks (Doyle et al., 2013). Three studies to date have shown independent effects of aging (cohen's d values range .52–.86) and HIV (d range .40–.79) on

PM, which appear to be more prominent among strategically demanding tasks (Avci et al., 2016; Weber et al., 2011; Woods et al., 2010). For example, Weber et al. (2011) reported evidence of additive effects of HIV (*d* = .40) and aging (*d* = .86) on time-based PM (see also Figure 3). Using an event-based PM paradigm, Woods et al. (2010) showed additive effects of HIV (*d* = .79) and aging (*d* = .52) when the retrieval cue and intention were semantically unrelated (e.g. 'When I show you a picture of a cow, snap your fingers.'), suggesting that older HIV+ adults may be particularly impaired on the strategic aspects of PM. Indeed, lower semantically unrelated event-based PM performance was associated with executive dysfunction (i.e. cognitive flexibility and planning; *d* = .67) in older HIV+ adults (Woods et al., 2010). A more recent study by Avci et al. (2016) manipulated PM cue type (event- vs. time-based) and delay interval (i.e. time between cue intention and execution of the PM action) to show that older age (*d* = .75) and HIV (*d* = .67) have additive adverse effects on strategically demanding PM (e.g. time-based PM, longer delay intervals). In each of these studies the independent effects of aging (*d* range .52–.86) and HIV (*d* range .40–.79) were independent from global neurocognitive functioning and HIV disease characteristics. While these three studies provide support for additive independent effects of both HIV and aging on PM – particularly for strategically demanding PM – there does not appear to be an interaction between HIV and aging on PM. In other words, as shown in Figure 3 using data from our cohort, while HIV infection and older age each appear to confer increased risk for poorer PM performances, there is no evidence showing a disproportionate risk for PM problems due to the combined effects of HIV and aging compared to that of HIV or older age infection alone.

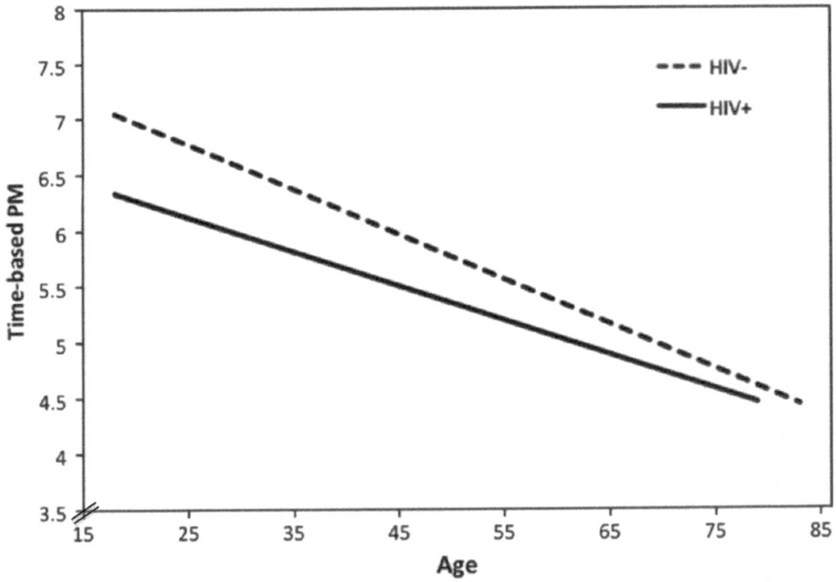

Figure 3. Relationship between age and strategically demanding time-based prospective memory (PM) in HIV+ (*n* = 427) and HIV– (*n* = 203) adults.

Naturalistic findings of PM and age in HIV

While studies in the laboratory provide insights into the mechanisms underlying PM performance in a well-controlled environment, there remain important external demands and modulating variables (e.g. compensatory strategies) that can affect how PM is expressed in the real world. A representative example of such a phenomena is the 'age-PM' paradox first described in seronegative adults (Rendell & Thomson, 1999), wherein older adults perform more poorly on PM tasks in the laboratory but perform the better than their younger counterparts when it comes to PM tasks in the real world (e.g. medication adherence). However, in HIV disease it appears that there is no strong evidence for such an age advantage in naturalistic tasks. For example, older HIV+ adults often demonstrate largely comparable adherence to their cART regimes as compared to younger adults (e.g. Hinkin et al., 2004). Similarly, Weber et al. (2011) showed that older HIV+ adults performed comparably to their younger counterparts on a naturalistic PM task in which they were asked to call the examiner 24hrs after their study visit and report how many hours they slept the previous night ($d = .08$). In a more recent study using the same naturalistic paradigm, Avci et al. (2016), showed that older seronegative individuals performed better than older HIV+ s and younger persons irrespective of HIV status (odds ratios range = 1.9 [1.1, 3.7] to 2.4 [1.3, 4.5]). There was a similar lack of an age effect on self-reported PM symptoms in daily life among the HIV+ persons in this study ($d = .11$). One possible explanation for lack of an aging benefit for naturalistic PM tasks vis-à-vis a clear age-related advantage in the laboratory in HIV is insufficient use of compensatory strategies. For example, Weber et al. (2011) reported that older, but not younger, HIV+ adults showed a relationship between naturalistic PM performance and self-reported use of PM-based ($d = .77$) and external compensatory strategies (e.g. using salient reminders; $d = .64$). Future studies should investigate the possible moderating and mediating effects of compensatory strategy use in older adults to better understand how the aging HIV+ population will perform on PM tasks in the laboratory and in the real world. We also know little about the effects of HIV on PM in children, which represents an important area for further investigation. In the one study to date, PM was uniquely predictive of verbal and mathematical academic achievement (Sirois et al., 2016).

Other demographic factors

Little is known about the role of non-age-related demographic factors, such as sex, education, and ethnicity, on the expression of HIV-associated PM deficits. No prospective studies have expressly evaluated these potentially important questions and only a handful of studies examined here reported incidental associations (e.g. Zogg et al., 2010). Data from our HIV+ cohort suggest that these three factors are not strongly related to laboratory-based, self-reported, and naturalistic PM at the univariate level ($ps > .05$), with a few exceptions: (1) Higher education is weakly related to laboratory-based PM ($d = .2$); (2) Women tend to report more PM symptoms than men in daily life ($d = .39$); and (3) Caucasians are slightly more likely than non-Caucasians to complete the MIST 24hr naturalistic trial ($d = .37$; see also Zogg et al., 2010). It remains to be determined whether these other demographic factors mediate or moderate the expression of HIV-associated neurocognitive deficits (or their relationships with everyday functioning outcomes).

Psychiatric and medical comorbidities

Co-occurring conditions are common in HIV infection, which can take the form of longstanding risk factors for acquisition of the virus (e.g. mood disorders), shared risk factors for infectious disease (e.g. substance abuse, hepatitis C virus [HCV]), and possible consequences of chronic HIV disease itself (e.g. vascular disease). To fully understand PM functioning in HIV, it may be important to not only examine the neurocognitive and disease factors that contribute to performance decline, but to also explore relevant comorbidities which may influence PM abilities. Our review of the literature revealed 32 analyses in 10 studies with 958 HIV+ participants that examined the relationship of specific comorbidities (i.e. substance use, HCV, and neuropsychiatric symptoms) to PM in HIV.

Neuropsychiatric comorbidities

The lifetime prevalence estimates of neuropsychiatric comorbidities such as anxiety, apathy, fatigue, and depression are as high as 50% among the HIV-infected population (e.g. Ciesla & Roberts, 2001). Findings are largely null with regard to the role of such neuropsychiatric comorbidities in the expression of HAND (e.g. Cysique et al., 2007), with a few larger studies reporting significant effects that are accompanied by small effect sizes (e.g. Castellon et al., 2006). To date, formal examination of these neuropsychiatric conditions in relation to PM in HIV has been similarly null in the literature and in our cohort (see Figure 2). For example, none of the nine analyses investigating the effects of comorbid anxiety ($k = 7$; Mean Cohen's $d = .35$) or fatigue ($k = 2$; Mean Cohen's $d = -.32$) on laboratory-based PM function have reported significant associations per standard null hypothesis testing. Ten analyses have been published regarding the relationship of depression to PM, with only one reporting significant findings: Zogg et al. (2010) found that HIV+ individuals with greater levels of self-reported depression (but not those with diagnoses of major depressive disorder) were more likely to fail a semi-naturalistic PM task ($d = -1.52$). However, formal prospective studies are needed to more definitively answer these questions, using rigorous diagnostic methods for these complex neuropsychiatric syndromes and careful consideration of potentially confounding factors (e.g. syndrome overlap, comorbidities). Moreover, we do not yet know the influence of apathy on PM in HIV. Apathy is observed in approximately 40% of HIV-infected persons, is an independent predictor of poorer health and everyday functioning outcomes in HIV, and is associated with the integrity of the same frontal-subcortical networks (for a review see Lanctôt et al., 2017 and Kamat, Woods, Marcotte, Ellis, & Grant, 2012) that support PM. Not surprisingly, mood symptoms are positively related to self-reported PM symptoms in daily life in HIV (e.g. Avci et al., 2016; Woods et al., 2007). Thus, it is possible that apathy may influence the expression of PM complaints, performance deficits, and/or symptoms in daily life.

Substance use disorders

The estimated lifetime prevalence rate of SUD in HIV disease is nearly 70% (Heaton et al., 2010) and as many as 20% of HIV-infected adults meet recent criteria for SUD (U.S.; Pence, Miller, Whetten, Eron, & Gaynes, 2006). SUDs confer additive risk of neurocognitive disorders (e.g. Rippeth et al., 2004) and adverse functional outcomes (e.g. Blackstone, Iudicello et al., 2013) in the setting of HIV disease. Moreover, there is growing evidence that SUD are independently associated with elevated PM symptoms and laboratory-based PM deficits (e.g. Weinborn, Woods, Nulsen, & Park, 2011), which can increase engagement in HIV transmission risk behaviors (e.g. Weinborn, Bucks, Stritzke, Leighton, & Woods, 2013). However, our review of the literature yielded only nine analyses examining the relationship of substance use to PM in HIV, eight of which reported null findings (Coulehan et al., 2014; Doyle, Weber, et al., 2015; Iudicello et al., 2011; Weber et al., 2011; Woods et al., 2007, 2014; Zogg et al., 2010). Only results of Woods and colleagues (2014) showed that PM accuracy improved significantly among individuals with SUD when the importance of the PM study task was emphasized, suggesting that SUD may increase the amount of cognitive attentional resources needed to support PM performance in young adults with HIV infection ($d = .91$). Indeed the Woods et al. (2014) investigation is unique in its inclusion of participants with current substance dependence. Interestingly, the exclusion criteria regarding substance use for the analyses that reported null effects of SUD on PM ranged from reports of dependence within 1 month to 5 years, which may increase risk of Type II error. Further limitations of this literature include absence of factorial designs and the lack of consideration of different substances of abuse, which may vary in their neurotoxicity and subsequent effects on PM (Verdejo-García, López-Torrecillas, Aguilar de Arcos, & Pérez-García, 2005).

Hepatitis C

It is estimated that one-third of individuals living with HIV are also infected with HCV (Mohsen, Murad, & Easterbrook, 2005). Akin to HIV, HCV is neurovirulent (e.g. Forton et al., 2005) and is associated with increased prevalence (e.g. Hilsabeck, Hassanein, Carlson, Zegler, & Perry, 2003) and incidence (Sheppard et al., 2015) of neurocognitive impairment reflecting the traditional pattern of frontosubcortical involvement. In the setting of HIV, HCV co-infection can have additive effects on the prevalence and severity of neurocognitive dysfunction (e.g. Miller et al., 2016), although the literature on this topic is mixed (see Clifford et al., 2014). With regard to PM specifically, we discovered four analyses that evaluated whether HCV co-infection worsens HIV-associated PM deficits. Three of the four studies reported null results. Only Avci et al. (2016) reported a significant association between HCV and PM, but this was in a mixed sample of persons with and without HIV disease. In our HIV+ cohort, co-infection with HCV was associated with significantly worse PM (see Figure 2); however, as with the historical HIV disease analyses reported above, the HCV co-infected group was markedly older ($p < .0001$) and the inclusion of age in a multivariable regression eradicated the apparent HCV effects on PM ($p > .10$). Thus, there is currently no strong evidence that co-infection with HCV exacerbates HIV-associated PM deficits. However, prospective factorial studies that include persons with and without HCV and HIV are needed to more definitively answer this question. Indeed, we currently do not know if HCV alone has an impact on PM and, if so, what is the profile and everyday functioning implications of such deficits? Such studies may also wish to examine the possible associations between PM and HCV RNA, as well as biomarkers of liver disease severity (e.g. fibrosis).

Everyday functioning and PM

One of the more compelling reasons to study PM in HIV is that this construct is held to be ecologically relevant. In fact, everyday examples are commonly used to drive home the clinical importance of PM, such as remembering to take one's medication as prescribed. In this way, PM is purported to capture unique aspects of daily life that are not measured by traditional neurocognitive tasks of retrospective memory or executive functions and thus may be of tremendous clinical value. Our review of the literature uncovered 12 published studies ($n = 1185$) that used PM to predict an everyday functioning outcome in HIV-positive participants. All of these studies used performance-based measures of PM, and the majority of them ($k = 10$) used the MIST. The everyday functioning outcomes measured in these studies included activities of daily living (ADL) ($k = 2$), medical compliance ($k = 8$), employment ($k = 1$), health-related quality of life (HRQoL) ($k = 1$), and risk taking ($k = 1$). We derived effect size estimates from all of these studies, which showed an average Cohen's d value of .45 ($SD = .22$), suggesting generally small-to-medium effect size associations between PM and everyday functioning outcomes. As shown in Figure 4, the associations were somewhat stronger for time-based PM (mean $d = .56$) than for event-based PM (mean $d = .36$), which was more comparable to effect size estimates for measures of retrospective memory (mean $d = .36$, typically measured with tasks of list and story recall) and executive functions (mean $d = .36$, typically measured with tasks of cognitive flexibility and planning). In the following section, we review each of the study findings in greater detail.

Activities of daily living

Everyday functioning deficits are highly prevalent among individuals infected with HIV, and a recent study found that 61% of HIV-positive participants were functionally dependent (Blackstone, Iudicello, et al., 2013). The association between ADLs and PM in HIV has been investigated in two studies thus far (Doyle, Weber, et al., 2015; Woods, Iudicello, et al., 2008). Both studies reported a significant (and independent) association between PM and functional status. In one study ($n = 106$), Doyle, Weber, et al. (2015) found an association ($d = .28$) between laboratory performance on an experimental habitual PM task (i.e. repetitions) and a global functioning composite score that incorporated employment status, self-reported declines in basic and instrumental ADLs, clinician-rated functional impairment, and

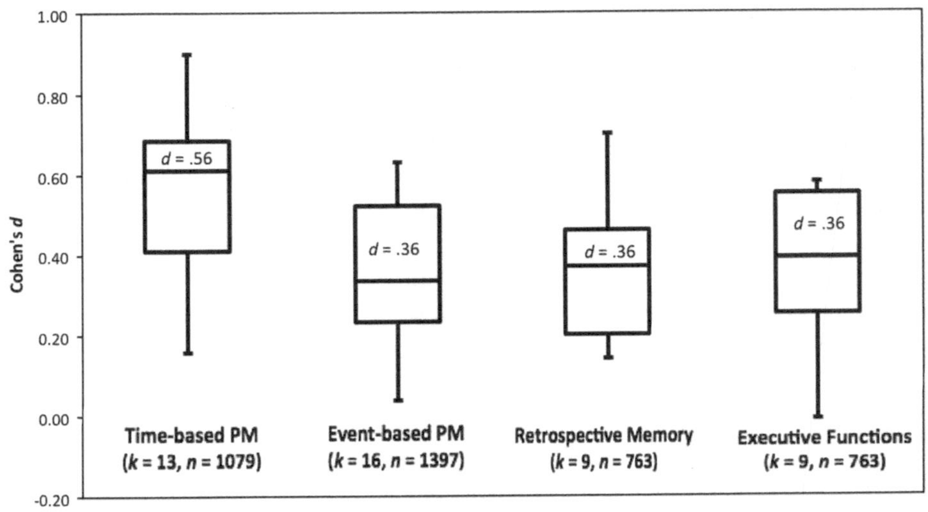

Figure 4. Box-and-whisker plot of effect sizes (Cohen's *d*) for the associations between everyday functioning outcomes and neurocognitive domains of time-based PM, event-based PM, retrospective memory, and executive functions.

Note: k = number of effect sizes, n = total sample size, PM = prospective memory.

self-reported cognitive symptoms. This association was independent of demographic, psychiatric, and HIV disease characteristics. Another study ($n = 66$) found that declines in instrumental ADLs were moderately associated with performance on both time-based ($d = .61$) and event-based ($d = .49$) PM tasks, even after controlling for retrospective memory and affective distress (Woods, Iudicello, et al., 2008). This literature provides preliminary evidence for a moderate independent association between PM and self-reported declines in ADLs in HIV disease. These findings await extension to a longitudinal design to determine whether baseline PM predicts incident dependence in ADLs and/or whether fluctuations in PM and ADLs travel together. Furthermore, future studies may wish to take advantage of performance-based ADL measures rather than exclusively relying on self-report. For example, skills-based measures of household tasks (e.g. cooking) and/or virtual reality simulators may be fruitful approaches to determine the extent to which PM is associated with functional capacity.

Medical compliance

Medication adherence

Adherence to cART regimens is crucial to disease management in HIV, and non-adherence can lead to increased viral loads, greater risk of HIV transmission, and faster disease progression (e.g. Bangsberg et al., 2001). Unfortunately, estimates from a recent meta-analysis suggest that over 40% of adults with HIV disease are non-adherent with their medication (Ortego, Huedo-Medina, Vejo, & Llorca, 2011). Our review yielded five published studies on the topic of PM and HIV medication adherence, all of which reported some significant associations independent of demographic, psychiatric, and disease factors. These studies measured adherence with the Medication Event Monitoring System (MEMS; Aprex Corporation, Union City, CA), which uses pill bottles with microchips to collect data anytime a participant opens or closes a pill bottle. Participants are considered adherent if they take at least 90% of their prescribed doses over four weeks. One study ($n = 79$) reported that adherent participants performed better than the non-adherent group on overall ($d = .54$) and time-based ($d = .60$) measures of PM in the laboratory; however, they did not significantly differ on event-based PM tasks ($d = .28$; Woods et al., 2009). Another study ($n = 74$) found that adherent and non-adherent groups differed on a time-based PM task with a 15-min delay ($d = .77$), which was mostly driven by errors of omission (Poquette et al., 2012). However, the groups did not differ on the event-based task with a 15-min delay ($d = .23$) or the PM tasks with a 2-min delay ($d = .18$). Additionally, one study ($n = 106$) found that performance on a habitual laboratory-based PM task was significantly correlated with adherence above and beyond relevant clinicodemographic factors ($d = .39$) (Doyle, Weber, et al., 2015). A recent study ($n = 199$) also found that time-based PM was associated with medication adherence in older adults (age $\geq$ 50 years) irrespective of pill burden ($d = .55$; Sheppard et al., 2016). However, in younger participants, the association between time-based PM and adherence ($d = .65$) was only significant among those with a low pill burden. A final study ($n = 97$) used a neuropsychological testing battery to determine which cognitive domains were most strongly associated with adherence in HIV-positive participants with a history of substance abuse (Contardo, Black, Beauvais, Dieckhaus, & Rosen, 2009). An exploratory factor analysis of these domains found that only one factor, comprised of performance-based PM scores, was significantly correlated with adherence ($d = .47$). Overall, the literature provides consistent evidence for a significant relationship between performance-based PM (and in particular, time-based PM) and medication adherence in HIV as measured by MEMS.

Medication management

Instead of measuring adherence with the MEMS, one research study investigated the association between PM and responses to a medication management questionnaire. While the questionnaire measures participants' perceptions of their medication-taking behaviors rather than their objective performance, self-reported adherence has been shown to be reliably associated with other measures of adherence, including electronic drug monitoring (e.g. MEMS) and HIV RNA viral load (Simoni et al., 2006). In this study of HIV-positive participants who were prescribed cART ($n = 87$), both time-based ($d = .72$) and event-based ($d = .63$) measures of laboratory PM performance were independently associated with self-reported medication management (Woods, Moran, et al., 2008). Even when accounting for other medical, psychosocial, environmental, and cognitive factors, performance-based PM remained a significant predictor of medication management, thus supporting the incremental ecological relevance of PM in HIV disease.

Medical instructions

Besides medication adherence, general health care compliance (e.g. following instructions after a medical appointment) is also important for HIV disease management. Two research studies have looked at PM and health care compliance using a semi-naturalistic task in which participants were asked to make a telephone call 24 h after their laboratory session. In the first study ($n = 139$), researchers found that compliance with the semi-naturalistic task was associated with both time-based ($d = .41$) and event-based ($d = .55$) PM performance in the laboratory (Zogg et al., 2010). After controlling for demographic (e.g. education) and neurocognitive (e.g. working memory) factors, overall performance-based PM was an independent predictor of task compliance. Similarly, the second study ($n = 106$) found that performance on a habitual PM task was an independent predictor of compliance with the semi-naturalistic health care task ($d = .63$; Doyle, Weber, et al., 2015). Such findings may be particularly relevant considering recent efforts to examine the role of HAND across the treatment spectrum in HIV disease, from initial engagement to retention in healthcare (e.g. Jacks et al., 2015).

Employment

Recent research from the Centers for Disease Control and Prevention (2016) estimates that 47% of HIV+ adults in the United States are unemployed. Unemployment may be associated with PM deficits in several ways. For example, PM may be important for job performance (e.g. remembering to complete a task) and may also impact the job search process (e.g. meeting application deadlines and attending interviews). One study has examined this question in 108 HIV+ (Woods et al., 2011), finding that lower scores on overall ($d = .58$) and event-based ($d = .53$) PM were associated with a higher rate of unemployment, while time-based PM performance was associated with unemployment at the trend level ($d = .41$). Overall PM performance remained an independent predictor of unemployment even after controlling for demographic, neurocognitive, psychiatric, and HIV disease factors. Thus, PM abilities may independently impact individuals' ability to engage in gainful employment, although these relationships were cross-sectional and thus await further rigorous longitudinal studies to determine whether baseline PM predicts incident unemployment or return-to-work (e.g. Van Gorp, Baerwald, Ferrando, Mcelhiney, & Rabkin, 1999). Furthermore, studies are needed to examine the role of PM in work-related function in currently employed individuals, for example on-the-job performance and productivity, with consideration of potential mediating and moderating factors (e.g. level of functioning, compensatory strategies, oversight).

Health-related quality of life

Individuals with HIV disease tend to report lower HRQoL than the general population (e.g. Hays et al., 2000). We are aware of only one study (n = 113) that has investigated the role of PM in HRQoL among younger (age ≤40 years) and older (age ≥50 years) individuals with HIV (Doyle et al., 2012). In this study, time-based PM performance was a significant predictor of HRQoL in younger (d = .90) but not older (d = .16) adults. Among the younger group, the association between PM and mental HRQoL was independent of other related factors (i.e. neurocognitive disorders, current major depressive disorder, lifetime substance dependence, and CD4 count); however, the association between PM and physical HRQoL was reduced to the level of a trend (p = .05) after controlling for these factors. Event-based PM was not significantly associated with HRQoL in either the younger (d = .41) or older (d = .04) group. Doyle et al. (2012) proposed that the age discrepancy in the relationship between PM and HRQoL may be a result of older adults using more compensatory strategies than younger adults. Thus, further research is needed to examine the role of PM in HRQoL and health perceptions across the lifespan in HIV disease, including a careful examination of possible mediating and moderating factors. For example, it is possible that PM deficits adversely affect HRQoL through their association with everyday functioning outcomes such as medical compliance and employment, as has been shown in healthy older adults (see Woods et al., 2015).

Risk-taking

PM may also relate to risk-taking, since individuals with impaired PM may not remember their intentions to abstain from risky behavior, as has been shown in seronegative youth and substance abusers (Weinborn et al., 2013). Risk-taking is particularly relevant to HIV disease because the virus can be contracted through risky sexual and drug use practices. Participants in a preliminary study of risk behaviors (n = 66) included HIV+ and seronegative substance-dependent individuals (Martin et al., 2007). Performance on a time-based PM task (d = .80), but not an event-based PM task (d = .20), was significantly associated with a self-report questionnaire of high-risk sexual and drug injection behaviors (Martin et al., 2007). Unfortunately, this is the only study that has investigated risk-taking and PM in HIV, and future research is needed to replicate these findings and determine potential mediating and moderating factors.

PM symptoms

Although this review focuses on performance-based PM measures as predictors of everyday functioning in HIV, we would be remiss to omit the literature on self-reported PM symptoms.

HIV is associated with elevations in self-reported PM symptoms, which relate more strongly to affective distress than to actual PM performance (e.g. Woods et al., 2007). However, the potential relevance of self-reported PM complaints should not necessarily be dismissed out of hand, as they are independently associated with some functional outcomes in HIV disease. Indeed, what we measure in the lab does not always translate easily to daily life. To our knowledge, six HIV studies have looked at the association between everyday functioning and self-reported PM complaints on the PRMQ (Smith et al., 2000). Three of these studies found significant correlations between PM complaints and functional outcomes, and importantly, these associations were independent of affective distress (Doyle et al., 2012; Woods, Moran, et al., 2008; Woods, Iudicello, et al., 2008). However, the remaining three studies failed to find significant associations between PM complaints and functioning (Woods et al., 2009, 2011; Zogg et al., 2010). Although the six studies looking at self-reported PM and everyday functioning reported a high effect size on average (mean $d = .85$), the results were highly variable (interquartile range = .22, 1.38). Interestingly, the association between PM complaints and everyday functioning was unrelated to cue type, with studies reporting the same overall effect sizes for both strategic ($d = .85$) and more automatic ($d = .85$) PM complaints. In general, there seems to be a strong, yet inconsistent, relationship between PM complaints and everyday functioning. Therefore, although PM complaints do not necessarily reflect performance-based PM ability, both measures are affected in HIV disease and may be relevant to real-world outcomes.

Meta-PM

Given the discrepancy between self-reported complaints and performance on laboratory tasks, one study investigated metacognitive awareness of PM abilities, or meta-PM, in individuals with HIV disease. In this study, participants with HAND demonstrated worse meta-PM for time-based, but not event-based, PM, compared to participants without HAND (Casaletto, Doyle, Weber, Woods, & The HIV Neurobehavioral Research Program (HNRP) Group, 2014). This study also found that overconfidence in time-based PM abilities among participants with HAND ($n = 51$) was a significant predictor of medication non-adherence. Therefore, in addition to the clinical relevance of performance-based and self-reported PM abilities, the discrepancy between these measures may also be a significant predictor of functional outcomes in individuals with HIV.

Future directions for PM and everyday functioning research in HIV

Overall, the literature provides evidence that PM deficits are associated with poorer everyday functioning among individuals with HIV disease, and time-based PM performance may be a more consistent predictor of functional ability than event-based PM. Since performance-based PM tasks and self-reported PM complaints reflect two different but clinically relevant constructs, future studies of PM should include both performance-based and self-report measures. The research regarding PM and medication adherence is relatively robust, but investigations into other domains of everyday functioning are still in their infancy. Indeed, there is still much to learn about the association between PM and performance-based functional outcomes (e.g. medication management skills). For example, we do not know whether improvements in PM translate into improvements in daily life, which would have important implications for the treatment of individuals with HIV. The literature on PM and everyday functioning would also benefit from a wider variety of studies addressing the complex relationship between these variables in HIV. In particular, analysis of critical mediating and moderating factors is needed, including consideration of such variables as motivation, insight, real-world task demands, and use of compensatory strategies. Additionally, longitudinal studies could shed light on the progression of PM deficits and functional dependence over time. Interestingly, two studies (Doyle et al., 2012; Sheppard et al., 2016) have reported different associations between PM and everyday outcomes in younger vs. older adults. Given the continued growth of the older HIV+ population, longitudinal studies in this area would be highly relevant.

Enhancing PM in HIV

Although much of the present literature has been focused on the mechanisms and functional impact of HIV-associated PM deficits, an emerging body of work is examining techniques and strategies to bolster PM performance in HIV disease. A review of the PM mechanisms literature in HIV with an eye toward remediation lends some empirical support to prospective hypothesis testing for remediation. Namely, HIV is associated with impairment in more strategically demanding PM processes, but spares relatively automatic PM functions. Therefore, one might expect that supporting strategic processes and/or automatizing the demands of PM at encoding, monitoring, or cue detection phases could enhance PM performance for persons with HIV disease. The four studies that have taken a prospective approach to improving PM in HIV+ persons are reviewed below (Faytell, Doyle, Naar-King, Outlaw, Nichols, Twamley, et al., in press; Faytell, Doyle, Naar-King, Outlaw, Nichols, Casaletto, et al., in press; Loft et al., 2014; Woods et al., 2014) and are summarized in Figure 5.

Two studies have focused on enhancing monitoring to event-based cues as a means of improving PM in HIV disease. One avenue for improving PM performance is by increasing the salience of cues to one's attention, thereby reducing attentional constraints and triggering spontaneous automatic processes. Using an experimental paradigm in a sample of

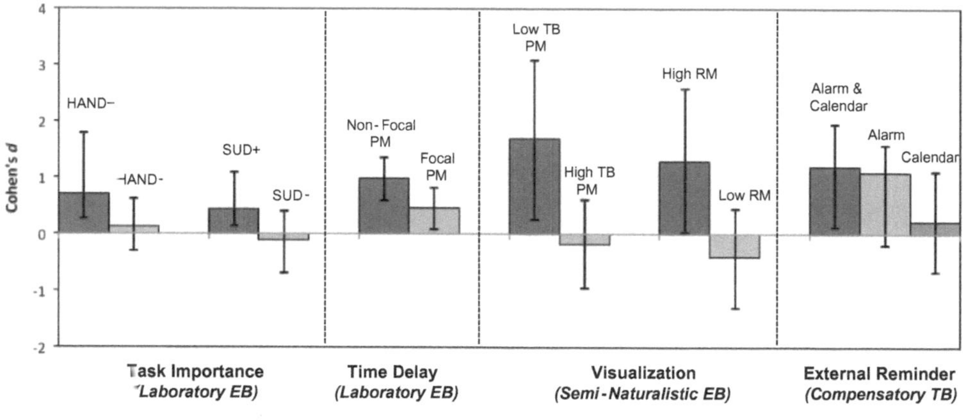

Figure 5. Effect size estimates (Cohen's *d*) and moderators of approaches to improve prospective memory (PM) across 6 samples of HIV+ adults.

Note: HAND = HIV-Associated Neurocognitive Disorders; SUD = Substance Use Disorders; TB = time-based; EB = event-based; RM = retrospective memory.

HIV+ young adults, Loft et al. (2014) tested the hypothesis that imposing a mandatory time delay between the cue onset and the response of a task can improve accuracy in an event-based PM task. The authors found that a delay as short as 600 ms between cue onset and response time significantly improved accuracy in the PM task, particularly when the PM cue was non-focal to the task (see Figure 5). This delay arguably allowed participants to sufficiently assess the ongoing task stimuli for PM-related features. Results from the study have implications for everyday life, for example, by suggesting that by slowing down the surrounding environment, HIV+ young adults allow themselves to fully process stimuli and engage in appropriate behaviors to complete PM goals. In a second study, Woods et al. (2014) tested the hypothesis that drawing attention to the importance of a PM task relative to a concurrent ongoing task would enhance strategic allocation of cognitive resources to the PM cue and thus improve PM task performance. In 2 parallel experiments, the authors demonstrated that individuals with HAND (Experiment 1) or SUD (Experiment 2) showed significantly lower event-based PM accuracy when the importance of the ongoing task was emphasized (i.e. a high strategic demand condition), but improved significantly and no longer evidenced impairment when the importance of the PM task was emphasized (see Figure 5). Such findings suggest that increasing attentional allocation to PM cues may mitigate HIV-associated event-based PM deficits.

Faytell, Doyle, Naar-King, Outlaw, Nichols, Twamley, et al. (in press) focused on improving HIV-associated PM deficits in the encoding phase by drawing upon visualization literature. They hypothesized that enhancing the strength of the cue-intention pairing by way of a brief visualization exercise would provide support for impaired strategic PM processes and thus improve performance. In this study, young HIV+ adults were randomized to either visualize themselves completing semi-naturalistic event-based PM task (i.e. manage their medications upon seeing the grooved pegboard test that was administered as part of a standard neuropsychological battery) or to more simply repeat the PM task instructions (i.e. an active control condition). The visualization intervention resulted in improved semi-naturalistic PM performance relative to the control condition, but only in individuals who demonstrated poor initial time-based PM and those who had intact retrospective learning ability (see Figure 5). Interestingly, individuals with good initial time-based performance had an 80% accuracy rate on the semi-naturalistic task and did not show substantial benefit of the visualization exercise. Thus, individual differences in neurocognitive ability moderate the response to visualization (and perhaps other interventions) in HIV+ young adults.

To our knowledge, only one study has examined the effectiveness of behavioral strategies to improve naturalistic time-based PM. Faytell, Doyle, Naar-King, Outlaw, Nichols, Casaletto, et al. (in press) investigated two simple methods for improving time-based PM performance in a sample of young adults with HIV: (1) programming a mobile telephone alarm; and (2) using a calendar function on a mobile device. Participants were randomly assigned to use one, both, or neither of these approaches, which were thought to provide behavioral support to impaired strategic processes. The naturalistic PM task outcome was to contact the examiner daily for a week and report the number of hours the participant had slept the night prior. Results showed large effect sizes on the naturalistic PM task for the groups of participants who employed the alarm (with or without calendaring) as compared to those who used only the calendar or neither strategy (see Figure 5). This study demonstrated the effectiveness of supportive behavioral (i.e. compensatory) strategies to improve naturalistic time-based PM in HIV+ young adults.

Collectively, the reviewed work has shown promising evidence for the efficacy of PM remediation strategies in HIV. The present findings suggest that both time-based and event-based PM deficits seen in HIV are amenable to remediation. However, as illustrated in Figure 5, moderating factors are seen in each of the reviewed studies and predominate the effects in an inconsistent manner. That is, effects are variable across disease factors (e.g. HAND, substance use), aspects of the PM task (e.g. presence of a delay, aspects of the cue), and individual differences (e.g. baseline retrospective learning and PM). Additionally, three of the four studies examined behavioral strategies almost exclusively in HIV+ young adults. Future work may wish to examine the effectiveness of such strategies in older adults, as this population is more susceptible to deficits in PM (Avci et al., 2016). In fact, some research suggests that older adults with HIV may respond differently to PM cues (Woods et al., 2010), thus a thorough investigation of strategies in this susceptible population is warranted.

Some PM-enhancing methods that have been examined outside of the HIV literature may speak to future research directions. In line with the aforementioned effects of visualization on PM, the actual physical enactment of a task has similarly been shown to improve PM in healthy adults (Schult & Steffens, 2016) as well as individuals with mild cognitive impairment (Pereira et al., 2015). Errorless learning is an encoding-enhancing method during which participants are prevented from making any mistakes when learning a task. Errorless learning has been shown to improve retrospective learning by way of encouraging implicit learning and lessening the potential of cognitive interference of incorrect responses, thereby reducing demands of the memory retrieval process. Recently, errorless learning has been shown to be more effective than traditional errorful learning in improving event-based, but not time-based, prospective memory in neurologically compromised individuals (Fish, Manly, Kopelman, & Morris, 2014). Others have taken cognitive training approaches to improving PM in various populations. Sweeney et al. (2016) tested the effectiveness of a novel brief fifty minute combined PM and working memory training program in improving PM in an out-patient substance use treatment sample. The authors found that their single session training was associated with validated measures of PM and working memory, and once again, the effect of training was more robust for event-based compared to time-based PM. Similarly, Richter, Mödden, Eling, and Hildebrandt (2015) found that, among participants with compromised memory, training in working memory and practice in semantic structuring resulted in transferred effects to improved PM performance. Further, future research may also wish to examine in effectiveness of such PM remediation strategies, in eliciting change in health behaviors (e.g. adherence) and downstream effects on clinical outcomes (e.g. CD4 count) and other indicators of everyday functioning.

Concluding remarks

This structured literature review aimed to summarize and critique our current understanding of PM functioning in people living with HIV. Overall findings from this review suggest that HIV disease is associated with moderate deficits in PM, which appear to be largely independent of commonly observed comorbid factors (e.g. depression, hepatitis C co-infection) and do not vary strongly with traditional clinical markers of HIV disease severity. The pattern of PM deficits reveals dysregulation of strategic processes (e.g. resource-demanding monitoring for the cue) that is consistent with the frontal systems pathology and associated executive dysfunction that characterizes HIV-associated neural injury. In turn, there is a relative sparing of more spontaneous/automatic PM processes that are reliant on more posterior brain regions that are typically less affected in HIV disease. Older age exacerbates the effects of HIV on PM, particularly for strategic tasks as measured in the laboratory; however, age does not appear to influence more naturalistic PM performance, which may be partly due to the relative increase in compensatory strategy use that commonly accompanies older age. Of great clinical relevance, HIV-associated PM deficits confer a strong risk of concurrent problems in a wide range of health behaviors (e.g. medication non-adherence) and ADLs (e.g. employment). The clinical predictive value of PM in HIV disease is independent of sociodemographics, psychiatric comorbidity, HIV disease severity, and global neurocognitive decline, thus suggesting that the construct has some incremental ecological validity. Early attempts to improve PM in HIV disease have revealed that supporting strategic processes at encoding (e.g. visualization), monitoring (e.g. attention allocation), and cue detection (e.g. salient cues) can be effective for some individuals. Indeed, this literature highlights the importance of considering moderating factors (e.g. comorbidities, interindividual variability in neurocognitive functions) when attempting to improve PM in clinical samples. Much work remains to be done, however, in understanding the cognitive architecture of HIV-associated PM deficits, the ways in which they express themselves in daily life, and the most effective and impactful means by which clinicians can manage and improve PM functioning in persons living with HIV disease.

Acknowledgement

The views expressed in this article are those of the authors and do not reflect the official policy or position of the Department of the Navy, Department of Defense, nor the United States Government.

Disclosure statement

The authors have no financial conflicts of interest related to this work.

Funding

This work was partially supported by National Institutes of Health [grant numbers R01-MH073419 and R01-DA034497].

ORCID

Gunes Avci http://orcid.org/0000-0001-7645-0268

References

Avci, G., Loft, S., Sheppard, D., Woods, S. P., & HIV Neurobehavioral Research Program (HNRP) Group (2016). The effects of HIV disease and older age on laboratory-based, naturalistic, and self-perceived symptoms of prospective memory: Does retrieval cue type and delay interval matter? *Aging, Neuropsychology & Cognition, 23*, 716–743.

Bangsberg, D. R., Perry, S., Charlebois, E. D., Clark, R. A., Roberston, M., Zolopa, A. R., & Moss, A. (2001). Non-adherence to highly active antiretroviral therapy predicts progression to AIDS. *AIDS, 15*, 1181–1183. doi:10.1097/00002030-200106150-00015

Bezeau, S., & Graves, R. (2001). Statistical power and effect sizes of clinical neuropsychology research. *Journal of Clinical and Experimental Neuropsychology (Neuropsychology, Development and Cognition: Section A), 23*, 399–406. doi:10.1076/jcen.23.3.399.1181

Blackstone, K., Iudicello, J. E., Morgan, E. E., Weber, E., Moore, D. J., Franklin, D. R., … Woods, S. P., Translational Methamphetamine AIDS Research Center Group (2013). Human immunodeficiency virus infection heightens concurrent risk of functional dependence in persons with long-term methamphetamine use. *Journal of Addiction Medicine, 7*, 255–263.

Blackstone, K., Woods, S. P., Weber, E., Grant, I., & Moore, D. J. (2013). Memory-based strategies for antiretroviral medication management: An evaluation of clinical predictors, adherence behavior awareness, and effectiveness. *AIDS and Behavior, 17*, 74–85. doi:10.1007/s10461-012-0308-9

Burgess, P. W., Quayle, A., & Frith, C. D. (2001). Brain regions involved in prospective memory as determined by positron emission tomography. *Neuropsychologia, 39*, 545–555. doi:10.1016/s0028-3932(00)00149-4

Carey, C. L., Woods, S. P., Rippeth, J. D., Heaton, R. K., Grant, I., & HIV Neurobehavioral Research Center (HNRC) Group (2006). Prospective memory in HIV-1 infection. *Journal of Clinical and Experimental Neuropsychology, 28*, 536–548. doi:10.1080/13803390590949494

Casaletto, K. B., Doyle, K. L., Weber, E., Woods, S. P., & The HIV Neurobehavioral Research Program (HNRP) Group (2014). Self-predictions of prospective memory in HIV-associated neurocognitive disorders: Evidence of a metamemory deficit. *Archives of Clinical Neuropsychology, 29*, 818–827. doi:10.1093/arclin/acu061

Casaletto, K. B., Weber, E., Iudicello, J. E., & Woods, S. P. (2017). Real-world impact of HIV-associated neurocognitive impairment. In N. Chiaravalloti, & Y. Goverover (Eds.), *Changes in the Brain, Impact Daily Life* (pp. 211–245). New York, NY: Springer.

Castellon, S. A., Hardy, D. J., Hinkin, C. H., Satz, P., Stenquist, P. K., van Gorp, W. G., … Moore, L. (2006). Components of depression in HIV-1 infection: Their differential relationship to neurocognitive performance. *Journal of Clinical and Experimental Neuropsychology, 28*, 420–437. doi:10.1080/13803390590935444

Centers for Disease Control and Prevention. (2016). *Behavioral and clinical characteristics of persons receiving medical care for HIV infection*—Medical Monitoring Project, United States, 2014 Cycle (June 2014–May 2015) (HIV Surveillance Special Report 17). Retrieved from http://www.cdc.gov/hiv/library/reports/hiv-surveillance.html

Chapman, L. J., & Chapman, J. P. (1973). The measurement of differential deficit. *Journal of Psychiatric Research, 14*, 303–311.

Ciesla, J. A. & Roberts, J. E. (2001). Meta-Analysis of the Relationship Between HIV Infection and Risk for Depressive Disorders. *American Journal of Psychiatry, 158*, 725–730.

Clifford, D. B., Vaida, F., Kao, Y. T., Franklin, D. R., Letendre, S. L., … Collier, A. C. (2014). Absence of neurocognitive effect of hepatitis C infection in HIV-coinfected people. *Neurology, 84*, 241–250. doi:10.1212/wnl.0000000000001156

Cona, G., Scarpazza, C., Sartori, G., Moscovitch, M., & Bisiacchi, P. S. (2015). Neural bases of prospective memory: A meta-analysis and the "Attention to Delayed Intention" (AtoDI) model. *Neuroscience and Biobehavioral Reviews, 52*, 21–37. doi:10.1016/j.neubiorev.2015.02.007

Contardo, C., Black, A. C., Beauvais, J., Dieckhaus, K., & Rosen, M. (2009). Relationship of prospective memory to neuropsychological function and antiretroviral adherence. *Archives of Clinical Neuropsychology, 24*, 547–554. doi:10.1093/arclin/acp046

Coulehan, K., Byrd, D., Arentoft, A., Monzones, J., Fuentes, A., Fraser, F., … Mindt, M. R. (2014). The role of decision-making ability in HIV/AIDS: Impact on prospective memory. *Journal of Clinical and Experimental Neuropsychology, 36*, 730–741.

Cysique, L. A., Deutsch, R., Atkinson, J. H., Young, C., Marcotte, T. D., Dawson, L., … Heaton, R. K. (2007). Incident major depression does not affect neuropsychological functioning in HIV-infected men. *Journal of the International Neuropsychological Society, 13*(01), 1–11.

Davis, L. E., Hjelle, B. L., Miller, V. E., Palmer, D. L., Llewellyn, A. L., Merlin, T. L., … Wiley, C. A. (1992). Early viral brain invasion in iatrogenic human immunodeficiency virus infection. *Neurology, 42*, 1736–1736. doi:10.1212/wnl.42.9.1736

Delis, C. D., Peavy, G., Heaton, R., Butters, N., Salmon, D. P., Taylor, M., … Atkinson, J. H. (1995). Do patients with HIV-associated minor cognitive/motor disorder exhibit a "subcortical" memory profile? Evidence using the California verbal learning test. *Assessment, 2*, 151–165. doi:10.1177/107319119500200205

Doyle, K., Weber, E., Atkinson, J. H., Grant, I., Woods, S. P., & The HIV Neurobehavioral Research Program (HNRP) Group (2012). Aging, prospective memory, and health-related quality of life in HIV infection. *AIDS & Behavior, 16*, 2306–2318. doi:10.1007/s10461-011-0121-x

Doyle, K. L., Loft, S., Morgan, E. E., Weber, E., Cushman, C., Johnston, E., … The HIV Neurobehavioral Research Program (HNRP) Group (2013). Prospective memory in HIV-associated neurocognitive disorders (HAND): The neuropsychological dynamics of time monitoring. *Journal of Clinical and Experimental Neuropsychology, 35*, 359–372. doi:10.1080/13803395.2013.776010

Doyle, K. L., Morgan, E. E., Weber, E., & Woods, S. P. (2015). Time estimation and production in HIV-associated neurocognitive disorders (HAND). *Journal of the International Neuropsychological Society, 21*, 175–181. doi:10.1017/s1355617715000089

Doyle, K. L., Weber, E., Morgan, E. E., Loft, S., Cushman, C., Villalobos, J., … The HIV Neurobehavioral Research Program (HNRP) Group (2015). Habitual prospective memory in HIV disease. *Neuropsychology, 29*, 909–918. doi:10.1037/neu0000180

Einstein, G. O., & McDaniel, M. A. (1990). Normal aging and prospective memory. *Journal of Experimental Psychology: Learning, Memory, and Cognition, 16*, 717–726. doi:10.1037/0278-7393.16.4.717

Einstein, G. O., McDaniel, M. A., Manzi, M., Cochran, B., & Baker, M. (2000). Prospective memory and aging: Forgetting intentions over short delays. *Psychology and Aging, 15*, 671–683. doi:10.1037/0882-7974.15.4.671

Ellis, J. A., & Nimmo-smith, I. (1993). Recollecting naturally-occurring intentions: A study of cognitive and affective factors. *Memory, 1*, 107–126. doi:10.1080/09658219308258227

Ellis, R., Langford, D., & Masliah, E. (2007). HIV and antiretroviral therapy in the brain: Neuronal injury and repair. *Nature Reviews Neuroscience, 8*, 33–44.

Faytell, M. P., Doyle, K., Naar-King, S., Outlaw, A., Nichols, S., Twamley, E., & Woods, S. P. (in press). Calendaring and alarms can improve naturalistic time-based prospective memory for youth infected with HIV. *Neuropsychological Rehabilitation*, 1–14, doi:10.1080/09602011.2016.1236733

Faytell, M. P., Doyle, K. L., Naar-King, S., Outlaw, A. Y., Nichols, S. L., Casaletto, K. B., & Woods, S. P. (2017). Visualisation of future task performance improves naturalistic prospective memory for some younger adults living with HIV disease. *Neuropsychological Rehabilitation, 27*, 1142–1155. doi:10.1080/09602011.2015.1122636

Fish, J. E., Manly, T., Kopelman, M. D., & Morris, R. G. (2014). Errorless learning of prospective memory tasks: An experimental investigation in people with memory disorders. *Neuropsychological Rehabilitation, 25*, 159–188. doi:10.1080/09602011.2014.921204

Forton, D. M., Allsop, J. M., Cox, I. J., Hamilton, G., Wesnes, K., Thomas, H. C., & Taylor-Robinson, S. D. (2005). A review of cognitive impairment and cerebral metabolite abnormalities in patients with hepatitis C infection. *AIDS, 19*(Suppl 3), S53–S63.

Gongvatana, A., Schweinsburg, B. C., Taylor, M. J., Theilmann, R. J., Letendre, S. L., Alhassoon, O. M., … The CHARTER Group (2009). White matter tract injury and cognitive impairment in human immunodeficiency virus–infected individuals. *Journal of Neurovirology, 15*(2), 187–195. doi:10.1080/13550280902769756

Gordon, B. A., Shelton, J. T., Bugg, J. M., McDaniel, M. A., & Head, D. (2011). Structural correlates of prospective memory. *Neuropsychologia, 49*(14), 3795–3800. doi:10.1016/j.neuropsychologia.2011.09.035

Gupta, S., Paul Woods, S., Weber, E., Dawson, M. S., Grant, I., & The HIV Neurobehavioral Research Ce (2010). Is prospective memory a dissociable cognitive function in HIV infection? *Journal of Clinical and Experimental Neuropsychology, 32*, 898–908. doi:10.1080/13803391003596470

Hays, R. D., Cunningham, W. E., Sherbourne, C. D., Wilson, I. B., Wu, A. W., Cleary, P. D., … Bozzette, S. A. (2000). Health-related quality of life in patients with human immunodeficiency virus infection in the United States: Results from the HIV cost and services utilization study. *The American Journal of Medicine, 108*, 714–722. doi:10.1016/s0002-9343(00)00387-9

Heaton, R. K., Clifford, D. B., Franklin, D. R., Jr, Woods, S. P., Ake, C., Vaida, F., … Grant, I. (2010). HIV-associated neurocognitive disorders persist in the era of potent antiretroviral therapy. *Neurology, 75*, 2087–2096.

Heaton, M. P., Leymaster, K. A., Kalbfleisch, T. S., Kijas, J. W., Clarke, S. M., … McEwan, J. (2014). SNPs for parentage testing and traceability in globally diverse breeds of sheep. *PLoS One, 9*, e94851. doi:10.1371/journal.pone.0094851

Henry, J. D., MacLeod, M. S., Phillips, L. H., & Crawford, J. R. (2004). A meta-analytic review of prospective memory and aging. *Psychology and Aging, 19*, 27–39. doi:10.1037/0882-7974.19.1.27

Hilsabeck, R. C., Hassanein, T. I., Carlson, M. D., Zegler, E. A., & Perry, W. (2003). Cognitive functioning and psychiatric symptomatology in patients with chronic Hepatitis C. *Journal of the International Neuropsychological Society, 9*, 847–854.

Hinkin, C. H., Hardy, D. J., Mason, K. I., Castellon, S. A., Durvasula, R. S., Lam, M. N., & Stefaniak, M. (2004). Medication adherence in HIV-infected adults. *AIDS, 18*(Suppl 1), 19–25. doi:10.1097/00002030-200401001-00004

Hoare, J., Westgarth-Taylor, J., Fouche, J. P., Spottiswoode, B., Paul, R., Thomas, K., … Joska, J. (2012). A diffusion tensor imaging and neuropsychological study of prospective memory impairment in South African HIV positive individuals. *Metabolic Brain Disease, 27*, 289–297.

Iudicello, J.E., Weber, E., Grant, I., Weinborn, M., Woods, S.P., & The HIV Neurobehavioral Research Center (HNRC) Group (2011). Misremembering future intentions in methamphetamine-dependent individuals. *The Clinical Neuropsychologist, 25*, 269–286.

Jacks, A., Wainwright, D. A., Salazar, L., Grimes, R., York, M., Strutt, A. M., … Hasbun, R. (2015). Neurocognitive deficits increase risk of poor retention in care among older adults with newly diagnosed HIV infection. *AIDS, 29*, 1711–1714. doi:10.1097/qad.0000000000000700

Kamat, R., Woods, S. P., Marcotte, T. D., Ellis, R. J., & Grant, I. (2012). Implications of apathy for everyday functioning outcomes in persons living with HIV infection. *Archives of Clinical Neuropsychology, 27*, 520–531. doi:10.1093/arclin/acs055

Kliegel, M., Jäger, T., & Phillips, L. H. (2008). Adult age differences in event-based prospective memory: A meta-analysis on the role of focal versus nonfocal cues. *Psychology and Aging, 23*(1), 203–208. doi:10.1037/0882-7974.23.1.203

Kliegel, M., McDaniel, M. A., & Einstein, G. O. (Eds.). (2008). *Prospective memory: Cognitive, neuroscience, developmental, and applied perspectives*. Mahwah, NJ: Erlbaum.

Lanctôt, K. L., Agüera-Ortiz, L., Brodaty, H., Francis, P. T., Geda, Y. E., Ismail, Z., … Abraham, E. H. (2017). Apathy associated with neurocognitive disorders: Recent progress and future directions. *Alzheimer's & Dementia, 13*, 84–100. doi:10.1016/j.jalz.2016.05.008

Letendre, S., Marquie-Beck, J., Capparell, E., Best, B., Clifford, D., Collier, A. C., …, CHARTER Group. (2008). Validation of the CNS penetration-effectiveness rank for quantifying antiretroviral penetration into the central nervous system. *Archives of Neurology, 65*, 65. doi:10.1001/archneurol.2007.31

Liberati, A. (2009). The PRISMA statement for reporting systematic reviews and meta-analyses of studies that evaluate health care interventions: Explanation and elaboration. *Annals of Internal Medicine, 151*(4), W. doi:10.7326/0003-4819-151-4-200908180-00136

Loft, S., Doyle, K. L., Naar-King, S., Outlaw, A. Y., Nichols, S. L., Weber, E., … Woods, S. P. (2014). Allowing brief delays in responding improves event-based prospective memory for young adults living with HIV disease. *Journal of Clinical and Experimental Neuropsychology, 36*, 761–772.

Maki, P. M., Cohen, M. H., Weber, K., Little, D. M., Fornelli, D., Rubin, L. H., … Martin, E. (2009). Impairments in memory and hippocampal function in HIV-positive vs HIV-negative women: A preliminary study. *Neurology, 72*, 1661–1668. doi:10.1212/WNL.0b013e3181a55f65

Martin, E. M., Nixon, H., Pitrak, D. L., Weddington, W., Rains, N. A., Nunnally, G., … Bechara, A. (2007). Characteristics of prospective memory deficits in HIV-seropositive substance-dependent individuals: Preliminary observations. *Journal of Clinical and Experimental Neuropsychology, 29*, 496–504. doi:10.1080/13803390600800970

McDaniel, M. A., & Einstein, G. O. (2000). Strategic and automatic processes in prospective memory retrieval: A multiprocess framework. *Applied Cognitive Psychology, 14*, S127–S144. doi:10.1002/acp.775

McDaniel, M. A., & Einstein, G. O. (2011). The neuropsychology of prospective memory in normal aging: A componential approach. *Neuropsychologia, 49*, 2147–2155. doi:10.1016/j.neuropsychologia.2010.12.029

Miller, T. R., Weiss, J. J., Bräu, N., Dieterich, D. T., Stivala, A., & Rivera-Mindt, M. (2016). Greater decline in memory and global neurocognitive function in HIV/hepatitis C co-infected than in hepatitis C mono-infected patients treated with pegylated interferon and ribavirin. *Journal of NeuroVirology, 23*, 260–272. doi:10.1007/s13365-016-0494-8

Mohsen, A., Murad, S., & Easterbrook, P. (2005). Prevalence of hepatitis C in an ethnically diverse HIV-1-infected cohort in south London. *HIV Medicine, 6*, 206–215.

Morgan, E. E., Iudicello, J. E., Weber, E., Duarte, N. A., Riggs, P. K., Delano-Wood, L., … HIV Neurobehavioral Research Program (HNRP) Group. (2012). Synergistic effects of HIV infection and older age on daily functioning. *Journal of Acquired Immune Deficiency Syndromes (1999), 61*, 341–348. doi:10.1097/QAI.0b013e31826bfc53

Morgan, E. E., Weber, E., Rooney, A., Grant, I., Woods, S. P., & HIV Neurobehavioral Research Program (HNRP) Group (2012). Longer ongoing task delay intervals exacerbate prospective memory deficits in HIV-associated neurocognitive disorders (HAND). *Journal of Clinical and Experimental Neuropsychology, 34*, 416–427. doi:10.1080/13803395.2012.654764

Murji, S., Rourke, S. B., Donders, J., Carter, S. L., Shore, D., & Rourke, B. P. (2003). Theoretically derived CVLT subtypes in HIV-1 infection: Internal and external validation. *Journal of the International Neuropsychological Society, 9*, 1–16. doi:10.1017/s1355617703910010

Obermeit, L. C., Morgan, E. E., Casaletto, K. B., Grant, I., Woods, S. P., & HIV Neurobehavioral Research Program Group (2015). Antiretroviral non-adherence is associated with a retrieval profile of deficits in verbal episodic memory. *The Clinical Neuropsychologist, 29*, 197–213. doi:10.1080/13854046.2015.1018950

Ortego, C., Huedo-Medina, T. B., Vejo, J., & Llorca, F. J. (2011). Adherence to highly active antiretroviral therapy in Spain. A meta-analysis. *Gaceta Sanitaria, 25*, 282–289. doi:10.1016/j.gaceta.2010.10.016

Pence, B. W., Miller, W. C., Whetten, K., Eron, J. J., & Gaynes, B. N. (2006). Prevalence of DSM-IV-defined mood, anxiety, and substance use disorders in an HIV clinic in the southeastern United States. *Journal of Acquired Immune Deficiency Syndromes, 42*, 298–306.

Pereira, A., de Mendonça, A., Silva, D., Guerreiro, M., Freeman, J., & Ellis, J. (2015). Enhancing prospective memory in mild cognitive impairment: The role of enactment. *Journal of Clinical and Experimental Neuropsychology, 37*, 863–877. doi:10.1080/13803395.2015.1072499

Poquette, A. J., Moore, D. J., Gouaux, B., Morgan, E. E., Grant, I., & Woods, S. P. (2012). Prospective memory and antiretroviral medication non-adherence in HIV: An analysis of ongoing task delay length using the memory for intentions screening test. *Journal of the International Neuropsychological Society, 19*, 155–161. doi:10.1017/s1355617712001051

Raskin, S., Woods, S. P., Poquette, A., McTaggart, A. B., Sethna, J., Williams, R. C., & Tröster, A. I. (2011). A differential deficit in time- versus event-based prospective memory in Parkinson's disease. *Neuropsychology, 25*, 201–209.

Raskin, S., Buckheit, C., & Sherrod, C. (2010). *Memory for intentions test (MIST)*. Lutz: Psychological Assessment Resources.

Reger, M., Welsh, R., Razani, J., Martin, D. J., & Boone, K. B. (2002). A meta-analysis of the neuropsychological sequelae of HIV infection. *Journal of the International Neuropsychological Society, 8*, 410–424. doi:10.1017/s1355617702813212

Rendell, P. G., & Thomson, D. M. (1999). Aging and prospective memory: Differences between naturalistic and laboratory tasks. *The Journals of Gerontology. Series B, Psychological Sciences and Social Sciences, 54B*, P256–P269.

Richter, K. M., Mödden, C., Eling, P., & Hildebrandt, H. (2015). Working memory training and semantic structuring improves remembering future events, not past events. *Neurorehabilitation and Neural Repair, 29*, 33–40. doi:10.1177/1545968314527352

Rippeth, J. D., Heaton, R. K., Carey, C. L., Marcotte, T. D., Moore, D. J., Gonzalez, R., … Grant, I. (2004). Methamphetamine dependence increases risk of neuropsychological impairment in HIV infected persons. *Journal of the International Neuropsychological Society, 10*(01), 1–14.

Saylor, D., Dickens, A. M., Sacktor, N., Haughey, N., Slusher, B., Pletnikov, M., … McArthur, J. C. (2016). HIV-associated neurocognitive disorder – Pathogenesis and prospects for treatment. *Nature Reviews Neurology, 12*, 234–248. doi:10.1038/nrneurol.2016.27

Schult, J. C., & Steffens, M. C. (2016). The effects of enactment and intention accessibility on prospective memory performance. *Memory & Cognition, 45*, 625–638. doi:10.3758/s13421-016-0677-9

Sheppard, D. P., Woods, S. P., Bondi, M. W., Gilbert, P. E., Massman, P. J., Doyle, K. L., & HIV Neurobehavioral Research Program Group (2015). Does older age confer an increased risk of incident neurocognitive disorders among persons living with HIV disease? *The Clinical Neuropsychologist, 29*, 656–677. doi: 10.1080/13854046.2015.1077995

Sheppard, D. P., Weber, E., Casaletto, K. B., Avci, G., Woods, S. P., & The HIV Neurobehavioral Research Program (HNRP) Group (2016). Pill burden influences the association between time-based prospective memory and antiretroviral adherence in younger but not older HIV-infected adults. *Journal of the Association of Nurses in AIDS Care, 27*, 595–607. doi:10.1016/j.jana.2016.03.006

Simoni, J. M., Kurth, A. E., Pearson, C. R., Pantalone, D. W., Merrill, J. O., & Frick, P. A. (2006). Self-report measures of antiretroviral therapy adherence: A review with recommendations for HIV research and clinical management. *AIDS and Behavior, 10*, 227–245. doi:10.1007/s10461-006-9078-6

Sirois, P. A., Chernoff, M. C., Malee, K. M., Garvie, P. A., Harris, L. L., Williams, P. L., … Memory and Executive Functioning Study of the Pediatric HIV/AIDS Cohort Study (2016). Associations of memory and executive functioning with academic and adaptive functioning among youth with perinatal HIV exposure and/or infection. *Journal of the Pediatric Infectious Diseases Society, 5*(Suppl 1), S24–S32. doi:10.1093/jpids/piw046

Smit, M., Brinkman, K., Geerlings, S., Smit, C., Thyagarajan, K., van Sighem, A., … Hallett, T. B. (2015). Future challenges for clinical care of an ageing population infected with HIV: A modeling study. *The Lancet Infectious Diseases, 15*, 810–818. doi:10.1016/s1473-3099(15)00056-0

Smith, R. E., & Bayen, U. J. (2006). The source of adult age differences in event-based prospective memory: A multinomial modeling approach. *Journal of Experimental Psychology: Learning, Memory, and Cognition, 32*, 623–635. doi:10.1037/0278-7393.32.3.623

Smith, G., Della Sala, S., Logie, R. H., & Maylor, E. A. (2000). Prospective and retrospective memory in normal ageing and dementia: A questionnaire study. *Memory, 8*, 311–321.

Smith, R. D., Delpech, V. C., Brown, A. E., & Rice, B. D. (2010). HIV transmission and high rates of late diagnoses among adults aged 50 years and over. *AIDS, 24*, 2109–2115. doi:10.1097/qad.0b013e32833c7b9c

Sweeney, M. M., Rass, O., Johnson, P. S., Strain, E. C., Berry, M. S., Vo, H. T., … Johnson, M. W. (2016). Initial feasibility and validity of a prospective memory training program in a substance use treatment population. *Experimental and Clinical Psychopharmacology, 24*, 390–399. doi:10.1037/pha0000091

Thames, A. D., Kim, M. S., Becker, B. W., Foley, J. M., Hines, L. J., Singer, E. J., … Hinkin, C. H. (2011). Medication and finance management among HIV-infected adults: The impact of age and cognition. *Journal of Clinical and Experimental Neuropsychology, 33*, 200–209. doi:10.1080/13803395.2010.499357

Valcour, V., Shikuma, C., Shiramizu, B., Watters, M., Poff, P., Selnes, O., … Sacktor, N. (2004). Higher frequency of dementia in older HIV-1 individuals: The Hawaii aging with HIV-1 cohort. *Neurology, 63*, 822–827. doi:10.1212/01.wnl.0000134665.58343.8d

Van Gorp, W. G., Baerwald, J. P., Ferrando, S. J., Mcelhiney, M. C., & Rabkin, J. G. (1999). The relationship between employment and neuropsychological impairment in HIV infection. *Journal of the International Neuropsychological Society, 5*, 534–539. doi:10.1017/s1355617799566071

Verdejo-García, A. J., López-Torrecillas, F., Aguilar de Arcos, F., & Pérez-García, M. (2005). Differential effects of MDMA, cocaine, and cannabis use severity on distinctive components of the executive functions in polysubstance users: A multiple regression analysis. *Addictive Behaviors, 30*, 89–101. doi:10.1016/j.addbeh.2004.04.015

Walser, M., Goschke, T., Möschl, M., & Fischer, R. (2016). Intention deactivation: Effects of prospective memory task similarity on aftereffects of completed intentions. *Psychological Research, 81*, 961–981. doi:10.1007/s00426-016-0795-9

Weber, E., Woods, S. P., Delano-Wood, L., Bondi, M. W., Gilbert, P. E., Grant, I., & HIV Neurobehavioral Research Program (HNRP) Group (2011). An examination of the age-prospective memory paradox in HIV-infected adults. *Journal of Clinical and Experimental Neuropsychology, 33*, 1108–1118. doi:10.1080/13803395.2011.604027

Weinborn, M., Paul Woods, S., Nulsen, C., & Park, K. (2011). Prospective memory deficits in Ecstasy users: Effects of longer ongoing task delay interval. *Journal of Clinical and Experimental Neuropsychology, 33*, 1119–1128. doi:10.1080/13803395.2011.614595

Weinborn, M., Bucks, R., Stritzke, W., Leighton, A., & Woods, S. P. (2013). Time-based prospective memory predicts engagement in risk behaviors amongst substance users: Results from clinical and nonclinical samples. *Journal of the International Neuropsychological Society, 19*, 284–294.

Woods, S. P., Morgan, E. E., Marquie-Beck, J., Carey, C. L. Grant, I., Letendre, S. L., & The HIV Neurobehavioral Research Programs (HNRP) Group (2006). Markers of macrophage activation and axonal injury are associated with prospective memory in HIV-1 disease. *Cognitive and Behavioral Neurology, 19*, 217–221. doi:10.1097/01.wnn.0000213916.10514.57

Woods, S. P., Carey, C. L., Moran, L. M., Dawson, M. S., Letendre, S. L., Grant, I., & The HIV Neurobehavioral Research Center (HNRC) Group (2007). Frequency and predictors of self-reported prospective memory complaints in individuals infected with HIV. *Archives of Clinical Neuropsychology, 22*, 187–195. doi:10.1016/j.acn.2006.12.006

Woods, S. P., Iudicello, J. E., Moran, L. M., Carey, C. L., Dawson, M. S., Grant, I., & The HIV Neurobehavioral Research Center (HNRC) Group (2008). HIV-associated prospective memory impairment increases risk of dependence in everyday functioning. *Neuropsychology, 22*, 110–117. doi:10.1037/0894-4105.22.1.110

Woods, S. P., Moran, L. M., Carey, C. L., Dawson, M. S., Iudicello, J. E., Gibson, S., & The HIV Neurobehavioral Research Center (HNRC) Group (2008). Prospective memory in HIV infection: Is "remembering to remember" a unique predictor of self-reported medication management? *Archives of Clinical Neuropsychology, 23*, 257–270. doi:10.1016/j.acn.2007.12.006

Woods, S. P., Moran, L. M., Dawson, M. S., Carey, C. L., Grant, I., & HIV Neurobehavioral Research Center (HNRC) Group (2008). Psychometric characteristics of the memory for intentions screening test. *The Clinical Neuropsychologist, 22*, 864–878. doi:10.1080/13854040701595999

Woods, S. P., Dawson, M. S., Weber, E., Gibson, S., Grant, I., Atkinson, J. H., & The HIV Neurobehavioral Research Center (HNRC) Group (2009). Timing is everything: Antiretroviral non-adherence is associated with impairment in time-based prospective memory. *Journal of the International Neuropsychological Society, 15*, 42–52. doi:10.1017/S1355617708090012

Woods, S. P., Dawson, M. S., Weber, E., Grant, I., & HIV Neurobehavioral Research Center (HNRC) Group (2010). The semantic relatedness of cue-intention pairings influences event-based prospective memory failures in older adults with HIV infection. *Journal of Clinical and Experimental Neuropsychology, 32*, 398–407. doi:10.1080/13803390903130737

Woods, S. P., Weber, E., Weisz, B., Twamley, E. W., Grant, I., & The HIV Neurobehavioral Research Programs (HNRP) Group (2011). Prospective memory deficits are associated with unemployment in persons living with HIV infection. *Rehabilitation Psychology, 56*, 77–84. doi:10.1037/a0022753

Woods, S. P., Weinborn, M., Velnoweth, A., Rooney, A., & Bucks, R. S. (2012). Memory for intentions is uniquely associated with instrumental activities of daily living in healthy older adults. *Journal of the International Neuropsychological Society: JINS, 18*, 134–138. doi:10.1017/S1355617711001263

Woods, S. P., Doyle, K. L., Morgan, E. E., Naar-King, S., Outlaw, A. Y., Nichols, S. L., & Loft, S. (2014). Task importance affects event-based prospective memory performance in adults with HIV-associated neurocognitive disorders and HIV-infected young adults with problematic substance use. *Journal of the International Neuropsychological Society, 20*, 652–662. doi:10.1017/s1355617714000435

Woods, S. P., Weinborn, M., Li, Y. R., Hodgson, E., Ng, A. R. J., & Bucks, R. S. (2015). Does prospective memory influence quality of life in community-dwelling older adults? *Aging, Neuropsychology, and Cognition, 22*, 679–692. doi:10.1080/13825585.2015.1027651

Zogg, J. B., Woods, S. P., Weber, E., Iudicello, J. E., Dawson, M. S., & Grant, I. (2010). HIV-associated prospective memory impairment in the laboratory predicts failures on a semi-naturalistic measure of health care compliance. *The Clinical Neuropsychologist, 24*, 945–962. doi:10.1080/13854046.2010.501343

Zogg, J. B., Woods, S. P., Weber, E., Doyle, K., Grant, I., & The HNRP Group. (2011). Are time- and event-based prospective memory comparably affected in HIV infection? *Archives of Clinical Neuropsychology, 26*, 250–259.

A review of prospective memory in individuals with acquired brain injury

Sarah A. Raskin, Jasmin Williams and Emily M. Aiken

ABSTRACT

Objective: Prospective memory (PM) deficits have emerged as an important predictor of difficulty in daily life for individuals with acquired brain injury (BI). This review examines the variables that have been found to influence PM performance in this population. In addition, current methods of assessment are reviewed with a focus on clinical measures. Finally, cognitive rehabilitation therapies are reviewed including compensatory, restorative and metacognitive approaches. **Method:** Preferred reporting items for systematic reviews and meta-analyses guidelines were used to identify studies. Studies were added that were identified from the reference lists of these. **Results:** Research has begun to elucidate the contributing variables to PM deficits after BI, such as attention, executive function and retrospective memory components. Imaging studies have identified prefrontal deficits, especially in the region of BA10 as contributing to these deficits. There are now several clinical measures available with good psychometric properties. Rehabilitation techniques have mostly focused on compensatory strategies, but, in addition, some restorative and metacognitive approaches have shown preliminary promise. **Conclusions:** PM deficits are a common and important deficit after BI. Clinical evaluation is recommended and further understanding of rehabilitation techniques is needed.

Introduction

The ability to complete intended actions, prospective memory (PM), is critical for independent functioning. Successful performance is required for managing in vocational, home and community settings in healthy adults as well as those with neurological illnesses (e.g. Hannon, Adams, Harrington, Fries-Dias, & Gipson, 1995). Many activities of daily living (e.g. taking medications, attending appointments, purchasing food) depend upon intact PM (e.g. Raskin et al., 2014). Survivors of acquired brain injury (BI) report failures relating to PM (e.g. I forget to take my medicine) as their most frequent memory problem (Kliegel, Jager, Altgassen, & Shum, 2008; Mateer, Sohlberg, & Crinean, 1987). In fact, they perceive PM deficits as more important to their daily lives than their significant others do (Huang et al., 2014). Not surprisingly, then, there has been a large increase in interest in PM after BI in recent years, including advances in understanding the clinical manifestations, underlying neural processes, assessment and management (e.g. Knight, Harnett, & Titov, 2005; Raskin & Sohlberg, 2009).

In everyday life, successful PM performance depends on many factors, including the ability to pay attention, to maintain the intention in working memory, to call the intention to mind at the appropriate time and to recall the content of the intention (Groot, Wilson, Evans, & Watson, 2002). In addition, metacognitive abilities such as monitoring ongoing performance, evaluation of outcome, and awareness of PM limitations are required (Guynn, 2003). In any one individual, more than one of these underlying abilities may be affected. This is compounded by the heterogeneity of BI in terms of underlying damage and expressed symptoms. Thus, comprehensive assessment and rehabilitation efforts may need to be multifaceted, considering the different underlying reasons for failure at PM tasks in each individual, in what has been referred to as precision medicine (National Institutes of Health Consensus Development Panel on Rehabilitation of Persons with Traumatic Brain Injury, 1998).

Definition of prospective memory

PM is defined as the ability to remember at a particular moment that one had previously decided to carry out a particular action at that moment (Kvavilashvili, 1992). PM may require self-cued remembering from a time-based cue, (e.g. remembering to return a phone call at 3:00 pm), or may follow an event-based cue (e.g. remembering to take a roast out of the oven in response to the oven timer) (Einstein & McDaniel, 1990; Kvavilashvili, 1992). Event-based tasks are typically easier to perform, most likely because time-based tasks rely on self-initiated monitoring and retrieval (Glisky, 1996).

PM has been conceptualized using three current theories, primarily derived from studies of healthy participants and then applied to those with conditions such as BI. The Multiprocess Theory of PM suggests that PM performance can be either spontaneous or rely on strategic monitoring, depending on the nature of the task. Differences can occur due to disparities in type of task, type of cue, the nature of the ongoing task, and the individual. Thus, as mentioned, tasks that must be remembered at a particular time may require more strategic monitoring than those that occur in response to an external cue (e.g. Einstein, McDaniel, Richardson, Guynn, & Cunfer, 1995). More recently Scullin, McDaniel, and Shelton (2013) expanded this model to suggest there is a dynamic interplay between the spontaneous retrieval and the strategic monitoring, such that individuals will monitor in a context where cues are expected but then disengage from monitoring when cues are not expected. They refer to this as the Dynamic Mulitprocess Framework. The preparatory attentional and memory processes theory, on the other hand, asserts that PM always requires attentional processes that are resource demanding due to explicit monitoring or the need to maintain the intention (Smith, 2003). This is assumed to be the PM aspect of the task whereas the recall of what one was supposed to do is based on retrospective memory (RM). The Attention to Delayed Intention (AtoDI) model uses imaging data to explain the brain regions responsible for intention maintenance and retrieval (Cona, Scarpazza, Sartori, Moscovitch, & Bisiacchi, 2015). The suggestion is that the dorsal frontoparietal network is involved in maintenance and allocation of top-down attention that is used both to monitor for the occurrence of the PM cue and to maintain the intention in mind. The ventral frontoparietal network, on the other hand, mediates the bottom-up attention automatically captured by the occurrence of the PM cues and used during retrieval. Given the prevalence of attention deficits in populations such as those with BI, and the importance of PM performance to everyday life, investigating whether some aspects of PM might be spared could lead to important directions in management post BI. This review will summarize the work that has been done to identify the types of PM deficits are prevalent in people with BI, assess whether these data are suggestive of a particular pattern of difficulty, and discuss cognitive treatment strategies that have been effective.

Identification of articles for inclusion

Preferred reporting items for systematic reviews and meta-analyses (PRISMA) guidelines (Liberati et al., 2009) were used to identify studies. We reviewed PubMed/NCBI, and SCOPUS from 1990 to the year 2017. The following key words were used: prospective memory, memory for intentions, future thinking, and brain injury. To be included, an article must have used adult human participants who had experienced some form of acquired brain injury including trauma, stroke, tumor, infection, hypoxia, and encephalopathy. Controlled trials, cohort and case studies were included. There also have been three previous review articles, which were not included in this review (Fish, Wilson, & Manly, 2011; Shum, Fleming, & Neulinger, 2002; Vakil, 2005). All identified articles were subject to title and abstract screening by two independent reviewers (SR, JW). Full-text screening was applied to all abstracts considered eligible by at least one reviewer. Discrepancies in selection status and reasons for exclusion were settled between the two reviewers by discussion and adjunction of a third reviewer (EA) if needed. This yielded 84 articles. There were no articles excluded due to methodological limitations or small sample size.

In terms of the samples studied, the majority of studies involved moderate to severe injury, with only two papers reporting on mild BI specifically. All studies were on adults (over the age of 18) and the majority (82) were on individuals under 65 years of age. There were five studies specific to individuals with stroke, one with individuals post-encephalitis, 36 studies identified the sample as entirely traumatic BI, and the rest (42) were of mixed etiology. See Figure 1.

Prospective memory and brain injury

As would be expected, many of the early studies of PM after BI were largely descriptive in nature and focused on demonstrating that PM deficits exist in this group (Cockburn, 1996; Groot et al., 2002; Kinsella et al., 1996; Shum, Valentine, & Cutmore, 1999; Sohlberg, White, Evans, & Mateer, 1992a, 1992b). More recently there has been an increase in interest in this area of research with a greater focus on testing theoretical constructs (Kliegel, Eschen, & Thöne-Otto, 2004; Mathias & Mansfield, 2005; Maujean, Shum, & McQueen, 2003; Raskin, 2009; Roche, Moody, Szabo, Fleming, & Shum, 2007; Schmitter-Edgecombe & Wright, 2004).

Relationship to brain substrates

Imaging studies have suggested that PM depends on rostral prefrontal cortex (rPFC) functioning, and, in particular, Brodmann area 10 (Benoit, Gilbert, & Burgess, 2011). rPFC has been shown to be engaged during the delay period that occurs between the intention formation and the execution of the intention (Burgess, Gonen-Yaacovi, & Volle, 2011). Brain

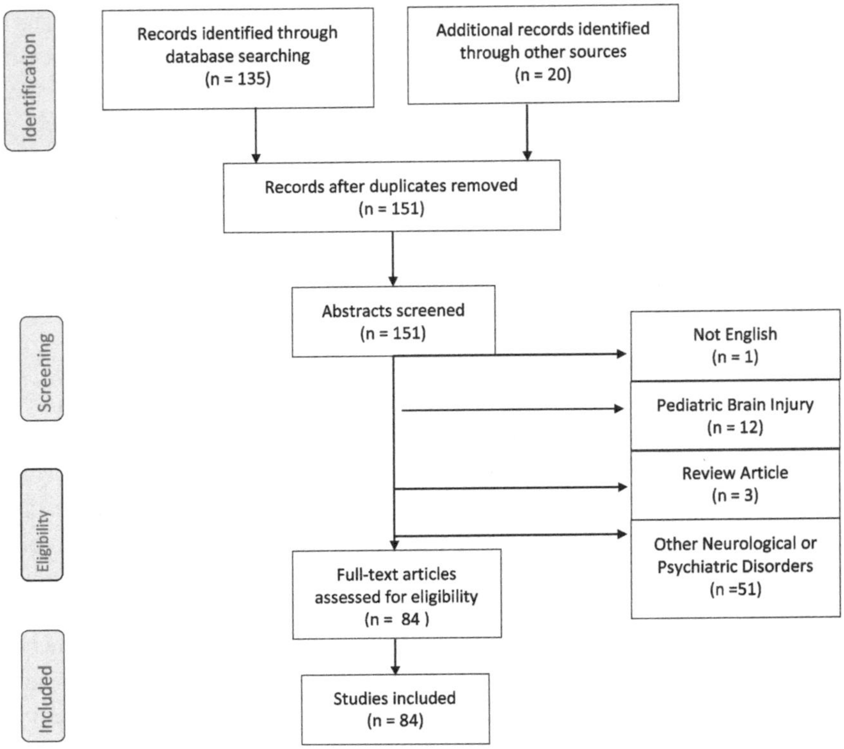

Figure 1. PRISMA flow diagram of literature search for prospective memory and brain injury. The PRISMA flow diagram depicts the flow of information throughout the different phases of this systematic review. It includes the number of records identified, included and excluded and the reasons for exclusions.

activation during PM tasks has been distinguished from activation in areas associated with vigilance, dual task performance, and working memory (West, 2008). A number of studies have documented impairment in PM functioning following injuries in prefrontal regions (e.g. Burgess, Alderman, Volle, Benoit, & Gilbert, 2009; Neulinger, Oram, Tinson, O'Gorman, & Shum, 2016; Umeda, Kurosaki, Terasawa, Kato, & Miyahara, 2011), and PM impairments have been measured in neurological disorders that are presumed to include dysfunction of prefrontal structures (Raskin, Buckheit, & Waxman, 2012; Raskin et al., 2011, 2014). Although it is acknowledged that individuals with BI have damage to large cortical regions, most demonstrate prefrontal cortical dysfunction (e.g. McAllister, 2011), and individuals with poor executive function performance (such as on the Stroop Color-Word Interference Test, Letter-Number Sequencing, Tower of London, and Controlled Oral Word Association Test) show greater PM impairment (Kliegel et al., 2004; Maujean et al., 2003; Raskin et al., 2012).

Retrospective memory contribution

A few studies of BI have tried to tease out the retrospective vs. prospective components of performance. While people with BI frequently have retrospective memory deficits, these are not always comparable to the deficits in PM. On the one hand, Carlesimo, Casadio, and Caltagirone (2004) reported that individuals with BI were less accurate in spontaneous initiation of the task but also significantly impaired compared to healthy participants at recalling the content of the information to-be-recalled. In contrast, Kliegel et al. (2004) reported that individuals with severe BI were impaired in intention formation, initiation and execution of the intention but not in retention of the intention. Henry et al. (2007) and Raskin et al. (2011) used a post-test recall to demonstrate that deficits were due to the prospective component of the task and that the participants with BI were able to successfully recall the content of the task to be performed. Finally, using a multinomial modeling approach, Pavawalla, Schmitter-Edgecombe, and Smith (2012) supported the finding that individuals with BI were significantly impaired in the prospective component of the task, and allocated fewer preparatory attentional resources to the PM task than healthy participants.

Even in studies that document retrospective memory deficits (Clune-Ryberg et al., 2011), these deficits generally do not explain the PM deficits (Mioni, Rendell, Henry, Cantagallo, & Stablum, 2013; Raskin et al., 2012). Mioni et al. (2013) used Virtual Week and compared regular (daily) to irregular (occasional) tasks. They reported that the magnitude of the PM impairment was the same for both types of tasks in people with BI, suggesting that retrospective memory failures cannot explain PM deficits since it was assumed that daily tasks place less demands on retrospective memory. Overall, retrospective memory loss is a common sequelae of BI and is likely to be a contributing factor to PM failures in daily life. However, the evidence to date suggests that PM deficits are both independent of retrospective memory loss and have a greater impact on daily functioning (Raskin et al., 2011).

Time delay

Although only a few studies have included varying time delays, individuals with BI have been shown to be able to successfully complete instructions for short time delays but not for longer ones (Raskin, 2009; Raskin & Sohlberg, 1996). The effect of time has not been investigated as a continuous variable, however, but only as a comparison of short time delays (e.g. 2 min) vs. longer time delays (e.g. 15 min).

Time-based vs. event-based cues

The relationship between time-based and event-based cues was one of the first areas of interest in PM functioning after BI. Cockburn (1996) used a single time-based activity (described in Baddeley, 1981) and a single event-based activity. She found that healthy adults performed better than a group of people with BI on both. Mathias and Mansfield (2005) used event-based tasks from the Rivermead Behavioral Memory Test and time-based tasks adapted from Einstein et al. (1995). Individuals with BI in this study performed poorly compared to healthy adults on time-based tasks but also performed poorly when compared to healthy adults on event-based tasks judged to have low personal saliency.

Time-based tasks have consistently been found to be more difficult for this population than event-based tasks. Groot et al. (2002) used the Cambridge Behavioral Prospective Memory Test and reported that individuals with BI were superior at event-based tasks compared to time-based tasks. Using the Memory for Intentions Test (MIST; Raskin, Buckheit, & Sherrod, 2010), we also found individuals with BI showed superiority for event-based vs. time-based cues (Raskin, 2009). Using a laboratory task that separated time-based, event-based, and activity-based items, once again time-based items were shown to be more difficult for a small study of 12 individuals with BI (Shum et al., 1999).

Interestingly, individuals with mild BI demonstrated deficits compared to healthy adults on the overall event-based score of the MIST but only on the longer delay (15 min) for the time-based items (Tay, Ang, Lau, Meyyappan, & Collinson, 2010). These deficits were measured both acutely after the injury and three months later.

The majority of studies have thus suggested that individuals with BI show greater impairment with time-based tasks than with event-based tasks. This is consistent with the Multi-Process Theory which suggests that time-based tasks, that require greater cognitive control and self-initiated action, will be more likely to be impaired in those with executive function deficits. The interaction of this effect with factors such as length of time and personal saliency warrant further study.

Effect of ongoing task

There has also been interest in the effect of BI on controlled attentional processes required for successful PM. Maujean et al. (2003) directly measured the effect of the cognitive demand of the ongoing task. Participants with severe BI performed more poorly than participants in the healthy adult group in the condition of high cognitive demand but not in the condition of low demand. This suggests that PM performance is differentially affected by the cognitive demand of the ongoing task in individuals with BI. It is not known from this study whether this is due to reduced attentional capacity or reduced ability to allocate cognitive resources to the PM task. Further research on ongoing task response thresholds and capacity models are also needed in this population (see Heathcote, Loft, & Remington, 2015).

Effect of type of response

To our knowledge, this has only been studied in people with BI in one study (Raskin et al., 2011). If the enactment effect (e.g. Schult & Steffens, 2016) is due to subcortical contributions, these functions may be intact in a BI population. It would be interesting to determine if individuals with BI show superiority for action intentions, as this might point to rehabilitation strategies. In the one study to look at the effect of enaction, individuals with BI did not exhibit any action superiority effect (Raskin et al., 2011), however, it is not clear from this study whether this is because the effect is eliminated, perhaps due to deficits in attention, or whether the task items were not sufficient to produce the effect (e.g. Steffens, Stulpnagel, & Schult, 2015).

Cue focality

It has been suggested that different PM tasks could very well challenge different cognitive systems depending on the task (McDaniel & Einstein, 2011). For example, tasks with focal cues may require little strategic monitoring and thus rely on the medial temporal structures while those with non-focal cues may require activity of the prefrontal cortex (e.g. McDaniel & Einstein, 2011). Focal cues are ones where the task to be completed is related to the ongoing task, whereas nonfocal cues are not related to the ongoing task. Schmitter-Edgecombe and Wright (2004) compared a high focal condition and a low focal condition in a group of individuals with severe BI. The ongoing task was to monitor words presented on a computer screen. If the word 'recall' appeared they were to state the last three words presented. All words were surrounded by different backgrounds. In the high focal condition, participants were to press a key if a particular target word appeared. In the low focal condition, participants were to press a key if a particular background pattern appeared. There were no differences between the two conditions reported for either the people with BI or the healthy participants. Thus, it is not clear if individuals with BI are unaffected by varying cue focality or if this task failed to create that effect.

Effect of task complexity

Henry et al. (2007) looked at BI performance for a computerized PM task and varied the number of target events (in essence, the load on prospective remembering). Individuals with BI were impaired on both the one target task and the four-target task compared to controls. The authors concluded that increasing the number of targets does not, therefore, increase demands on controlled attentional processes.

Predictors of prospective memory performance

Fleming et al. (2008) demonstrated that length of time in post-traumatic amnesia (PTA) and verbal fluency predicted both time and event-based scores on the Cambridge Prospective Memory Test (CAMPROMPT). Rule monitoring on executive function tasks was also found to predict PM performance, but only in individuals with TBI who also had retrospective memory deficits (Paxton & Chiaravalloti, 2014). It seems likely that other measures of severity of injury are also likely to lead to more severe PM deficits either due to medial temporal contributions to the recall of the item to be remembered or prefrontal contributions to prospective remembering itself. Given other studies that have demonstrated that PM performance is highly correlated with executive function tasks that require future planning, such as the Tower of Hanoi (Raskin & Sohlberg, 2009), we would imagine that this could be a fruitful line of future research. A measure of executive control, intraindividual variability, may also have predictive value (Stuss, Murphy, Binns, & Alexander, 2003). In addition, time estimation may also be a worthwhile area to examine as a potential predictor of successful PM performance.

Severity of injury

Individuals with mild TBI have been shown to demonstrate deficits on the MIST (Tay et al., 2010) immediately after injury and three months later, and on the Cambridge Prospective Memory Test (CAMPROMPT) three months post injury (Kinsella, Olver, Ong, Gruen, & Hammersley, 2014). However, interestingly, these were no different from the deficits observed in a trauma control group when compared to a healthy population (Kinsella et al., 2014). We are not aware of a study that has compared a group with mild BI to a group with severe BI, although the finding that PTA predicted performance (Fleming et al., 2008) suggests that there would likely be a difference.

In general, individuals with BI demonstrate poor performance in conditions when greater cognitive resources, especially those involving attention, working memory, and monitoring, are required. The one consistent finding over multiple studies is that time-based tasks are more difficult than event-based tasks (e.g. Raskin et al., 2012). This is likely explained by the greater cognitive resources required to monitor time, be aware that time has passed, and bring forward the intention. Similarly, the extra cognitive resources required to complete the ongoing task lead to greater impairments of PM as the difficulty of the ongoing task is increased (Maujean et al., 2003). For the same reason, it would be predicted that non-focal cues would be more difficult than focal cues, but this is yet to be demonstrated. This was not found to be the case in one study measuring the effect of cognitive load (Henry et al.,

2007) however this was a small sample size and the authors interpreted the finding to suggest that this aspect of PM performance was relying on automatic processes.

One area that has had a striking lack of research is whether or not individuals with BI show an action superiority effect. Given that subcortical motor structures are intact in these individuals and likely responsible for the effect, this warrants further investigation.

Similarly, there has been little research to date on issues such as severity of injury, location of lesion (e.g. medial temporal vs. prefrontal), and primary cognitive deficits, all of which could help explain not only individual differences in PM in those with BI but might also provide important data on neural and cognitive substrates of PM.

Measurement of prospective memory

Measures of PM all have some common elements. These include the encoding and formation of an intention to be performed in the future, an ongoing task during the delay period, and a cue to signal it is time to perform the intention. Research on this topic has been performed using laboratory, self-report and clinical measures. It is thought that laboratory measures provide greater ability to manipulate specific variables to answer theoretical questions (e.g. Einstein & McDaniel, 2005). Self-report measures provide data on the subjective experience of PM (Roche et al., 2007) whereas clinical measures have been used in attempts to approximate more real-world applications of PM, such as calling the experimenter at a specified time (Rendell & Thomson, 1999). Each of these measures provides valuable data on PM performance, but clear and consistent relationships between them have yet to be defined (e.g. Raskin & Sohlberg, 2009; Rendell & Thomson, 1999; Uttl & Kibreab, 2011). Given the possibility that these measures are all capturing unique and not entirely overlapping aspects of PM, it may be important to compare the findings from each.

Laboratory measures

Einstein and McDaniel (1990) introduced a dual-task laboratory paradigm that has been widely used in the literature. Like all PM tasks, there is a prospective remembering task embedded in an ongoing task, followed by a delay period. After this period, the ongoing task is reintroduced without a reminder of the PM task. The PM task, embedded in the ongoing task, is presented and the response of the participant is measured (Einstein & McDaniel, 2005). There are many different versions of this task, but, for example, the participant might be shown a series of noun–verb pairings and asked to remember them. Following this learning trial, the participant is shown a long series of nouns one at a time on the computer screen. The participant is required to press one key (e.g. 'm') if the noun represents a manmade object and a different key (e.g. 'n') if the noun represents a natural object. However, if the noun is one of the words from previous the noun-verb pairing task, the participant must instead press the 'p' key. This laboratory paradigm has proven invaluable in testing specific theoretical questions about PM performance. However, these paradigms tend to involve only one type of PM response performed repeatedly, and, compared to other measures reviewed, the ecological validity is considered low (Delprado et al., 2012). In addition, because different studies use slightly different task items, it has been shown that the sensitivity of these paradigms to neurological disorders can vary with the characteristics of the PM and ongoing tasks (e.g. Foster, McDaniel, Repovš, & Hershey, 2009). In a study done by Shum et al. (1999) using time-, event-, and activity-based PM tasks, the results revealed differences in all three types of tasks, with the individuals with TBI performing significantly worse on all tasks. In a recent study, individuals with BI performed more poorly than healthy participants in terms of false positives but not omission errors, suggesting a particular difficulty with impulsive responding and cue-detection (Raskin, Shum, Ellis, Pereira, & Mills 2017).

Self-report questionnaires

There are also several currently used self-report PM measures, including the Comprehensive Assessment of Prospective Memory (CAPM; Chau, Lee, Fleming, Roche, & Shum, 2007), the Prospective and Retrospective Memory Questionnaire (PRMQ; Crawford, Smith, Maylor, Della Sala, & Logie, 2003), and the Prospective Memory Questionnaire (Hannon et al., 1995). Essentially, these self-report measures all quantify common PM tasks that are undertaken in daily life (such as remembering to take medications or remember to return library books), and as such may have a higher personal significance then laboratory measures, such as those requiring a key press at a certain time. Questionnaires have arguably high ecological validity and allow for a greater understanding of the experience of PM failures in daily life. They are generally brief, easy to use and understand, and time-efficient (Man, Fleming, Hohaus, & Shum, 2011). However, they have not been well-correlated with other measures of PM, perhaps due to limited insight or awareness in individuals with BI (Fleming, Kennedy, Fisher, & Gill, 2009; Roche, Fleming, & Shum, 2002).

The CAPM is one questionnaire that was designed to measure PM failures. It has been demonstrated to have good reliability (Chau et al., 2007). The internal consistency of the items within the instrumental activities of daily living (IADL) subscale was .92, the basic activities of daily living (BADL) subscale was .74, and the total CAPM was .94.

The full CAPM contains three sections, one that measures frequency of PM failure, one that measures the perceived importance of these failures and the third that measures the perceived reasons for forgetting (Roche et al., 2007). It can be completed by an individual or by a family member. A principal components analysis of the first part, Section A, revealed that there were two components, one that related to BADL, such as daily self-care (e.g. accidentally forgetting to brush your teeth), and one that related to IADL, such as household management activities (e.g. forgetting an appointment with a doctor or therapist) (Chau et al., 2007). The CAPM has been used in previous studies with individuals who have BI and has demonstrated sensitivity to perceived failures in this population (Huang et al., 2014) and has been analyzed per Ellis's (1996) five phases of PM to demonstrate that those with TBI had difficulty with encoding and formation and initiation of prospective memories (Roche et al., 2007). More recently a short form has been developed, the Brief Assessment of Prospective Memory (Man et al., 2011). Using the BAPM, Man, Yip, Lee, Fleming, and Shum (2015) demonstrated a relationship between self-report on this measure and functional measures of BADL and IADL.

The Prospective and Retrospective Questionnaire was created to provide a self-report measure of both prospective and retrospective memory slips in everyday life (Smith, Del Sala, Logie, & Maylor, 2000). It consists of 16 items, eight about PM and eight about retrospective memory. It has been demonstrated to have good reliability (internal consistency). Cronbach's α was .89 for the Total, .84 for Prospective, and .80 for Retrospective scales (Crawford et al., 2003). The PRMQ has been used to measure treatment efficacy in rehabilitation studies of individuals with BI (e.g. Huckans et al., 2010; Jamieson, Cullen, McGee-Lennon, Brewster, & Evans, 2015). It has been translated into Spanish (González-Ramírez &

Mendoza-González, 2011) and several other languages including Chinese, Dutch, Finnish, French, Italian, Portuguese and Tamil.

The Prospective Memory Questionnaire has demonstrated good test-retest reliability and internal consistency as well as sensitivity to PM deficits after BI (Hannon et al., 1995). It asks about the frequency of PM failures. There are four subscales: Long-Term Episodic (e.g. 'I forgot to return books to the library by the due date'), Short-Term Habitual ('I forgot to lock my door when leaving my apartment or house'), Internally Cued ('I forgot what I was going to say in the middle of a sentence'), and Techniques to Remember, which measures the use of strategies. Reliability of the Prospective Memory Questionnaire was reported to be high, with coefficient alpha ranging from .78 to .90 for the subscales, and .92 for the total score, and test-retest reliability ranging from .64 to .88. In terms of validity, short-term prospective tasks significantly correlated with the questionnaire total score, but long-term tasks were not (Hannon et al., 1995).

Studies using questionnaires, however, have yielded mixed results. Hannon et al. (1995) found that individuals with BI reported difficulty with short-term habitual tasks but not with more long-term remembering. Roche et al. (2002) reported that individuals with BI did not report more PM problems than healthy adults, although observers did report that the individuals with BI had more problems than healthy adults. On the CAPM Section A, responses by individuals with BI were correlated with psychosocial integration but not with clinical measures of PM, demonstrating low concurrent validity (Spearman's ρ correlations with total CAMPROMPT = −.03 and with total MIST = −.14) (Fleming et al., 2009). However, relative's reports on the CAPM demonstrated better concurrent validity (Spearman's ρ correlation with total CAMPROMPT = −.33 and with total MIST = −.41). This suggests that self-report questionnaires are useful in understanding the person's own view of their prospective memory abilities, but that they may be effected by difficulties with insight and awareness that can be common in people with BI (e.g. Cockburn, 1996). Using section C of the CAPM, Roche et al. (2007) reported that persons with BI encounter difficulty specifically with encoding, formation and initiation of prospective memories. A summary is presented in Table 1.

Clinical-based measures

To our knowledge, there are currently four standardized psychometric measures of PM and these are considered more naturalistic than laboratory measures. These are the MIST (Raskin et al., 2010), the CAMPROMPT (Wilson et al., 2005), Virtual Week (Rendell & Henry, 2009) and the Royal Prince Alfred Memory Test (Radford, Lah, Say, & Miller, 2011). These tests have all shown good psychometric properties and sensitivity to PM deficits, which will be reviewed below. However, only the MIST and the CAMPROMPT are published clinical measures with established normative data. The Virtual Week and Royal Prince Alfred Memory Test, on the other hand, can be described as laboratory measures that are naturalistic and clinically-relevant.

Published clinical tests

Some of the earliest studies to clinically assess PM used the two PM items from the Rivermead Behavioral Memory Test (Wilson, Cockburn, & Baddeley, 1985). This was then expanded to form the CAMPROMPT (Wilson et al., 2005). The CAMPROMPT has three time- and three event-based PM tasks and requires 30 min. The ongoing task is a series of items including a general knowledge quiz, word-finding puzzles, mazes, etc. The person being examined is

Table 1. Self-report measures.

Name of measure	Number of items	Scales	Languages available	Publication with ABI
Prospective Memory Questionnaire	52	Long-term episodic Short-term habitual Internally cued Techniques to assist memory scale	English	Hannon et al. (1995) Raskin et al. (2011)
Prospective and Retrospective Memory Questionnaire	16	Prospective Memory Retrospective Memory	English, Chinese, Dutch, Finnish, French, German, Greek, Hindi, Italian, Japanese, Korean, Malay, Portuguese, Romanian, Spanish, Swedish, Tamil, Turkish	Huckans et al. (2010) Jamieson et al. (2015)
Comprehensive Assessment of Prospective Memory	54	Frequency of Forgetting Perceived Importance of Lapses Perceived Reasons for Forgetting	English, Chinese	Raskin, Shum et al. (2017) Roche et al. (2002) Roche et al. (2007) Fleming et al. (2008) Huang et al. (2014)

Note: ABI-acquired brain injury.

permitted to write down notes to aid in recall. People with BI show impairments on the CAMPROMPT, with the impairment being greater for time-based tasks than for event-based tasks and deficits were related to both retrospective memory performance and executive function performance (Groot et al., 2002).

The MIST can separate out different aspects of performance, such as type of cue and time delay. The MIST includes both time-based and event-based cues that are either two minutes or fifteen minutes in duration between encoding and performance. The time-based cues allow for self-initiated retrieval ('In fifteen minutes, tell me that it is time to take a break') and, unlike most laboratory tasks, the event-based cues are related to the events that need to be performed (i.e. 'When I hand you a red pen, sign your name on the paper'). The response of participants can either be an action or verbal response. The ongoing task is a word search puzzle. Due to the MIST's ability to measure different attributes of PM, it also allows for six types of errors to be analyzed if failure of a PM task were to occur (Raskin, 2009). There is a multiple choice retrospective memory questionnaire administered at the end of the test and an optional 24-h delay item. The MIST has been demonstrated to be sensitive to PM deficits in individuals with BI (Raskin, 2009) and mild TBI (Tay et al., 2010) and has been shown to have good psychometric properties (Raskin, 2009; Woods, Moran, Dawson, Carey, & Grant, 2008). The MIST was validated against the two items of the Rivermead Behavioral Memory Scale that deal with PM because at the time there was no other clinical measure of PM. The correlation of the MIST with the two items of the Rivermead in healthy individuals was .80. The test–retest reliability of the MIST was demonstrated in a group of 20 healthy participants who were given the MIST on two occasions two weeks apart. Inter-form reliability, comparing Form A and Form B in the same group of 20 participants, was found to be .89. Split half reliability was measured by Woods et al. (2008) in a healthy sample of participants as .70 using the Spearman–Brown coefficient. While the inter-item reliability of the individual trials was reported to be poor (Cronbach's $\alpha = .48$) the reliability of the six subscales was judged to be better (Cronbach's $\alpha = .89$). Several studies have also reported finding that the MIST measures a cognitive construct that is separable from retrospective memory performance (e.g. Woods et al., 2008). There are four alternate forms and it has been translated into several languages including Spanish, Portuguese, Italian and Chinese.

Clinically oriented laboratory tasks

Virtual Week is a laboratory task with items similar to tasks required in everyday life. It was originally designed as a board game and is now computerized (Mioni et al., 2013). Individuals roll dice and move along on the board where they are required to perform real-world tasks some of which are based on events, 'Buy a bus ticket when shopping,' and some of which must be performed by the time indicated on the center of the board. The time on the board automatically moves forward as the person moves to a new space. Some items are regular (performed daily) and some are irregular (performed occasionally). As stated, at the center of the board game is a virtual clock which changes as the person moves around the board. The ongoing tasks are naturalistic items such as eating meals, going to the library, or having a visit from a neighbor. The reliability of Virtual Week was investigated by Rose, Rendell, and McDaniel (2007) in a study involving healthy younger adults and older adults. Across the entire sample, reliability estimates ranged from .84 to .94 for the regular, irregular and time-check tasks. Test–retest reliability was measured in healthy adults by using an alternate form and no effect of test–retest was found (Mioni, Rendell, Stablum, Gamberini, & Bisiacchi, 2014).

Individuals with BI were shown to have difficulties with both event-based ('Buy a bus ticket when shopping') and time-based ('Take your medication at 2:00 pm') compared to healthy participants, but with greater impairment on the time-based tasks.

The Royal Prince Alfred (RPA) Prospective Memory Test is also a laboratory task with real-life items that are very similar to the MIST. It contains time- and event-based tasks and both short and long time delay intervals (Radford et al., 2011). The ongoing tasks are chosen by the examiner and can include questionnaires or other measures that themselves are part of a clinical battery. There are three alternate versions with good alternate-form reliability and it has been used in one study with a mixed group of neurological patients, including BI ($n = 2$), stroke ($n = 7$), tumor ($n = 2$) epilepsy ($n = 5$), arteriovenous malformation removal ($n = 2$) systemic lupus erythematosus ($n = 1$) and encephalitis ($n = 1$). Items performed in the session are tasks such as 'In 155 minutes time, I would like you to tell me it's time for a coffee break' and 'When my mobile phone rings, tell me you would like a drink.' The longer delay naturalistic items are returning a postcard and making a phone call. Interrater reliability was measured between two independent raters and found to be high for the control group, ICC (3, 1) .90, $p < .001$, and in the patient group, ICC (3, 1) .97, $p < .001$. Alternate form reliability was also satisfactory; Spearman correlation between Form 1 ($M = 10.3$, $SD = 1.2$) and Form 2 ($M = 10.9$, $SD = 2.1$) scores was significant in the control group, $r = .71$, $p < .05$, as was the correlation between Form 1 and Form 3 ($M = 10.9$, $SD = 1.0$) scores, $r = .71$, $p < .01$. Patients demonstrated significantly poorer RPA PM performance in terms of total score. As a measure of validity the test was compared to the MIST and a questionnaire. Surprisingly, given that the items are very similar, RPA PM scores were not significantly correlated with MIST Summary scores, $r = .18$. However, RPA PM scores were negatively correlated with subjective ratings on all three questionnaires: CAPM-Self, $r = .67$, $p < .01$; EMQ, $r = .62$, $p < .01$; and CAPM Other ratings, $r = .50$, $p < .05$. That is, better RPA PM performance was associated with fewer reported memory problems in everyday life. Information on these measures is presented in Table 2.

Naturalistic, video and virtual reality measures

Using naturalistic measures of activities of daily living, Fortin, Godbout, and Braun (2003) reported that individuals with BI had difficulty due to trouble with organizing and planning intended activities, such as preparing a meal. These authors concluded that deficits in strategic planning and event-based PM are responsible for difficulties completing activities of daily living in these patients. Knight et al. (2005) created a novel videotape task of a person driving and walking through an unfamiliar city. Participants were given a list of tasks to be completed in the city and were required to recall them when the appropriate cue appeared on the videotape. In this study, the group with BI was impaired compared to healthy adults, but demonstrated low awareness. In a subsequent study they also demonstrated that individuals with TBI were more sensitive to distraction in this environment (Knight, Titov, & Crawford, 2006).

Several virtual reality tasks have also been created to assess PM in BI. The Virtual Reality Shopping Task (Canty et al., 2014) was sensitive to BI and predicted performance on everyday activities such as independent living skills demonstrating good ecological validity. In the ongoing task, participants had to purchase 12 items in a pre-specified order from a selection of 20 shops in the virtual environment. For time-based PM tasks, text messages had to be

Table 2. Clinical measures of prospective memory.

Measure	Type of cues	Time delay	Time to administer	Alternate forms	Languages available	Psychometric properties	Publications with ABI
CAMPROMPT	Time and Event	7, 13, and 20 min	30 min	1	English, Chinese	Wilson et al. (2005)	Groot et al. (2002) Fish et al. (2007) Man, Chan et al. (2015) Fleming et al. (2008)
MIST	Time and Event; Action and Verbal	2 and 15 min; 24 h	30 min	4	English, Spanish, Chinese, Czech, Italian	Woods et al. (2008) Raskin (2009)	Raskin, Shum et al. (2017) Raskin et al. (2012) Tay et al. (2010)
Virtual Week	Time and Event; Regular and Irregular	Varies but includes 2 min 30 s and 4 min 15 s	20 min	2	English, Italian, Farsi	Rendell and Craik (2000) Rendell and Henry (2009)	Mioni et al. (2013) Mioni et al. (2015) Mioni et al. (2017)
Royal Prince Alfred Prospective Memory Test	Time and Event	15 min and 1 week	10 min	3	English	Radford et al. (2011)	Radford et al. (2011)

Note: ABI-acquired brain injury.

sent at specified times. For the event-based PM task a key had to be pressed if an announcement came over the loudspeaker for a sale.

A study utilizing a virtual reality setting of working in a furniture store did not find good sensitivity of the task to BI, although overall people with BI scored significantly more poorly than a matched control group (Sweeney, Kersel, Morris, Manly, & Evans, 2010). Individuals who had had a stroke were impaired on event- and activity-based tasks and marginally on time-based tasks (Brooks, Rose, Potter, Jayawardena, & Morling, 2004).

In addition, there are several comprehensive measures that include PM items, including the Rivermead Behavioral Memory Test, the Brain Injury Cognitive Screen (Vaughan, Neal, Mulla, Edwards, & Coetzer, 2017) and TEM-PRO (Mühl et al., 2016).

Relationship between types of measures

There have been some preliminary studies that have sought to compare the relationship between different types of measures (e.g. laboratory, clinical, self-report) (e.g. Raskin, Shum et al., 2017). Previous studies comparing questionnaires and clinical measures, for example, have yielded mixed results. Previous studies found no correlation between the CAPM and total score on the MIST, suggesting that either the two measures are measuring separate functions or that subjective experience and objective performance are not the same (Fleming et al., 2009; Raskin, Shum et al., 2017). Relatives' report on frequency of PM failure did correlate with the MIST total score as well as both the time-based cue and event-based cue scales, which suggest that the difference may be due to poor subjective awareness (Fleming et al.,

2009). No data were provided on the relationship between the CAPM and the 24 h delay item on the MIST. Another study used the PRMQ and found that while the MIST did not correlate with responses on the self-report questionnaire, the MIST did correlate with performance in daily life on 10 items over a week as reported by a significant other (Raskin & Sohlberg, 2009). Thus, this again suggests that the questionnaires are tapping into an aspect of the individual's perception of his/her performance that may not be related to the individual's actual performance.

In a study that compared the MIST to a laboratory measure, there was little relationship between these two forms of PM measurement for healthy participants but that there was a strong relationship for those with BI (Raskin, Shum, Ellis, Pereira, & Mills, 2017). For those with BI, the greatest relationship was with the event-based items on the clinical measure. This highlights the problem with using laboratory measures that include only event-based items if one is interested in a comprehensive picture of PM performance. The clinical measure was also related to false positive performance on the laboratory measure, in this case the number of PM errors. This may suggest that time-based remembering is related to self-monitoring more than event-based PM in this population.

These tasks may also require different levels of attentional resources. The laboratory measures tend to use only event-based cues; thus, they may be less attention demanding than the time-based tasks in the MIST. Furthermore, unlike the MIST, the event-based cue in the laboratory measure is usually embedded within the ongoing task, which may further serve to focus attention on the cue. On the other hand, in the laboratory paradigm the embedded PM task (i.e. press a key when you see a specific word) does not explicitly put the participant in a 'retrieval mode' and instead requires participants to enter this mode on their own. In contrast, the event cues of the MIST put participants in a retrieval mode, (i.e. by handing the participants a form requesting medical records) in which they may be aware something should happen because of the high association between the intended action and the cue. On the other hand, the CAPM queries performance on both event-based (e.g. forgetting to lock the door when leaving home) and time-based (e.g. forgetting to take tablets at a prescribed time) everyday tasks. It can be argued that the CAPM is the only one that measures tasks in which the individual must form his/her own intention and create his/her own plan for execution (e.g. Dobbs & Reeves, 1996). For the other tasks this is provided for the participants by the experimenter. However, because the CAPM relies on retrospective subjective report, it is not known if it is an accurate reflection of performance.

There are, arguably, three types of measures at this time: laboratory, psychometric and self-report. Each of these measures is useful in specific contexts. Laboratory measures are essential for their ability to control specific variables thus test hypotheses about the different aspects of cognition used in PM. Thus, laboratory measures are all constructed in a similar manner but with specific paradigms designed to answer specific questions. Because these have been primarily brought over from the cognitive psychology literature on healthy individuals, research is needed to determine the effects of these variables on people with BI and care must be taken to avoid floor effects.

Psychometric measures are useful clinically and to understand more naturalistic aspects of PM. Of these, the MIST, CAMPROMPT, and Virtual Week have the largest normative databases and psychometric properties. However, they are quite time-consuming to administer in a standard neuropsychological evaluation. Thus, a shorter measure, such as the RPA might be worth pursuing.

Self-report questionnaires are useful for understanding the individual's personal experience. It is important to note again, however, that it is likely these three types of measures are measuring aspects of PM that are overlapping but not completely overlapping. Thus, the information gleaned from one of these measures will be different from that gathered from a different measure. In particular, self-report measures do not typically correlate with standardized psychometric measures and thus, they cannot be used interchangeably. More research is needed to understand if this is due to poor insight into deficits or whether the types of PM problems queried on self-report measures are different from the types measured in psychometric tests.

In terms of clinical neuropsychological evaluations of PM performance in this population, to date only the CAMPROMPT and MIST are practical alternatives with adequate psychometric properties and well balanced normative data. A clinician could choose between the two based on a preference for a more behavioral real-world measure (CAMPROMPT) versus a measure that allows for a more fine-grained analysis of the source of any deficit (MIST). Both are time-consuming within a standard evaluation and short-forms would be useful. Of course, the limitation is that PM, by its very nature, requires a significant amount of time to pass. Thus, any short form would need to embed other measures in the delay period (see Raskin & Race, 2017) rather than just have a shorter time delay for the PM items.

Rehabilitation

Cognitive rehabilitation approaches traditionally group cognitive rehabilitation therapy (CRT) into interventions that are considered compensatory and those that are considered restorative approaches (Sohlberg, 2006). It could be argued that metacognition or self-regulation interventions constitute a third category (Kennedy et al., 2007). An example of a metacognitive approach would be training people in the use of strategies or systems that facilitate self-monitoring during PM task completion (Levine et al., 1998). All three of these rehabilitation approaches have been evaluated for their potential to address deficits in PM functioning.

Compensatory approaches to rehabilitation

Compensatory approaches can be external (such as notebooks or pagers) or internal (such as visual imagery, first letter mnemonics, or elaborative encoding). One of the oldest rehabilitation techniques for PM deficits after BI is written diaries or memory notebooks (Sohlberg, 2005). Compared to more complex electronic systems, memory notebooks are more familiar to many people with BI and facilitate recall of a diverse range of functional tasks (Sohlberg & Mateer, 1989). There are two memory notebooks formats, the standard format, Sohlberg and Mateer (1989) and the modified format, Donaghy and Williams (1998). The standard memory journal follows the format of most standard personal organizers. The four section of this diary are as follows, weekly timetable, 'to do' section, memory log, and transport notes. The modified diary has a timetable and a 'to do' column for each day, with an adjacent page for the memory log. Additionally, it contains a full year calendar for appointments to be recorded.

McKerracher, Powell, and Oyebode (2005) conducted a single case experimental design comparing these two notebook formats for a man with memory problems caused by a mild traumatic BI. The patient was given five PM tasks per week. He used both the standard and modified journal for four weeks. McKerracher et al. found that the patient managed to carry out only one of 20 PM tasks while using the standard diary, but 15 of the tasks while using the modified journal (McKerracher et al., 2005). But it is difficult to reach broad conclusions based on a single case.

There is considerable evidence that giving a notebook alone without sufficient training is not effective (Raskin & Sohlberg, 2009). Moreover, self-instructional training, emphasizing self-awareness and self-regulation was found to be more effective than a diary alone in a group of 20 participants with acquired brain injury (Ownsworth & McFarland, 1999).

Thus, there are several difficulties with the use of notebooks. These include the need for extensive training in their use, the need to have a system to keep them from becoming misplaced, and the need to have a PM span of at least five minutes to use them effectively (Raskin & Sohlberg, 2009). For comprehensive discussions of the use of memory notebooks and the importance of training individuals to use them effectively, see Sohlberg and Mateer (200‘) as well as McKerracher et al. (2005).

Electronic aids

Several electronic aids have also been evaluated to assist with PM deficits. The strongest evidence supporting the use of PM task prompting comes from a randomized, controlled trial evaluating the use of alphanumeric pagers to prompt certain simple routing behaviors (Wilson, Emslie, Quirk, & Evans, 2001). When prompted with these pagers, individuals increased completion of daily tasks from approximately 47–75% follow through (Emslie, Wilson, Quirk, Evans, & Watson, 2007; Wilson et al., 2001; Wilson, Scott, Evans, & Emslie, 2003). Moreover, some patients could remember daily activities even after the pager was removed, suggesting an internalization of the external prompt.

Similar electronic systems have been employed to call individuals' mobile phones, such as Postie (Kirsch et al., 2004) the Yahoo-Calendar System (O'Connell, Mateer, & Kerns, 2003) and Mobile Extensible Memory and Orientation System (MEMOS; Thöne-Otto & Walther, 2003) and this prompting technology has shown its utility in improving PM functioning (Van den Broek, Downes, Johnson, Dayus, & Hilton, 2000; Wade & Troy, 2001; Yasuda et al., 2002). However, these studies have been single case studies with no experimental control, so it is difficult to generalize from the results.

Like SMS text messages, the use of a smartphone has been shown to hold promise for memory rehabilitation. Multiple studies have investigated how smartphone calendar reminders have been used as a compensatory memory strategy. Calendar reminders can be accessed via smartphone calendar function, email calendar, or google calendar (Baldwin & Powell, 2015; McDonald et al., 2011). Ferguson, Friedland, and Woodberry (2015) conducted a study to determine if smartphone reminders help people complete pre-identified tasks and found a significant increase in task completion rates when smartphone prompts were present as compared with when they were absent. However, some drawbacks were the feeling of dependency and the additional stress for the participant receiving the reminders. For this reason, Evald (2015) conducted a study to investigate subjective satisfaction with and experiences of benefits and obstacles of using smartphones as a primary memory aid. Ten out of the thirteen participants (77%) stated that the reminder alarm sound and the visual pop-up messages helped them remember daily appointments and tasks (Evald, 2015). Having the capability to combine all personal communication and information into one assistive device, has shown to be effective in rehabilitation of PM. However, the risk of becoming dependent on the smartphone was reported by five participants (38%) (Evald, 2015). In addition to feelings of dependency, participants reported disadvantages such as risk of losing access to the information due to battery loss, or the loss of the device itself. Therefore, the advantages and disadvantages must be considered when smartphones are used by patients with BI as a compensatory memory strategy.

An alternative to carrying a handheld smartphone is receiving audiovisual reminders on the home television. Lemoncello, Sohlberg, Fickas, and Prideaux (2011) conducted a study that evaluated the Television Assisted Prompting (TAP) system as a novel assistive technology for cognition device. The TAP system attaches to a person's home television and allows for automated delivery of customized prompts such as reminders to complete daily activities. In this study, 23 participants experienced both the TAP condition and the typical practice (TYP) condition which instructs participants to carry out tasks using their typical methods, for two-week periods each. Lemoncello et al. (2011) found that the task completion was higher (72%) with TAP prompting than for TYP practice (43%). This suggests that when attention, memory, and executive function reminders are delivered through a familiar medium, the television, individuals with ABI will complete a greater number of tasks (Lemoncello et al., 2011).

The Voice Organizer, manufactured by Voice Powered Technology International, is a handheld device that can be trained to recognize an individual's speech patterns, store messages, and replay messages dictated by its user. A study conducted by Van den Broek et al. (2000) examined the Voice Organizer's utility in the rehabilitation of PM impairment. Through a five-participant study, it was found that substantial improvements in PM functioning while using the Voice Organizer, as compared to the absence of any one. Additionally, it was found that the removal of the Voice Organizer resulted in a decline in performance for all subjects on both the Message-Passing task which required the subject to repeat four messages to their relatives after a 9-h delay, and except for one subject for the Domestic task which required the subject to recall for tasks at prescribed times. Unfortunately, some limitations that the Voice Organizer obtains are that it cannot be used by those with significant expressive speech impairments, poor manual dexterity, or visual deficits (Van den Broek et al., 2000).

Current research demonstrates the promise of assistive technologies to help people with PM impairments (Baldwin & Powell, 2015; Gillette & Depompei, 2008; Kim, Burke, Dowds, Boone, & Park, 2000; Kirsch et al., 2004; Tam et al., 2003; Wong, Sinclair, Seabrook, McKay, & Ponsford, 2016). However, high tech devices are still not widely used by many people with brain injuries who demonstrate deficits in PM (Evald, 2015; Evans, Wilson, Needham, & Brentnall, 2003). Identified barriers for long term use include problems with a range of device characteristics, such as being overly complex or having inaccessible interfaces (LoPresti, Mihailidis, & Kirsch, 2004; Stock, Davies, & Gillespie, 2013), lack of training in their use (Wong et al., 2016) and especially cost, and fears of losing the device (Evald, 2015). This digital divide between those with access to mobile devices and those without (Gonzales, 2016) is seen in the BI community (e.g. Bryen, Carey, & Friedman, 2007; Newman, Browne-Yung, Raghavendra, Wood, & Grace, 2016). For a discussion of why technologies are used or not used see Scherer and Federici (2015). Thus, non-technological approaches are still needed.

Cognitive Symptom Management and Rehabilitation Therapy (CogSMART), developed by Twamley, Jak, Delis, Bondi, and Lohr (2014), is a 12-week compensatory cognitive training intervention that was shown to improve post-concussive symptoms, including sleep disturbance, fatigue, headaches, and tension. CogSMART includes modules with compensatory techniques for PM, attention, learning and memory, and executive functioning. The PM training included the use of to-do lists, a daily calendar, and learning to link 'can't miss reminders' to tasks to be performed. Twamley et al. (2014) evaluated the CogSMART intervention through a study consisting of fifty veterans with mild to moderate TBI. Not only did the veterans who received CogSMART rated it highly with regard to helpfulness for post-concussive symptoms and PM strategies but researchers also found that there were significant reductions in self-reported post-concussive symptoms and improvements in real-world PM tasks (Twamley et al., 2014). In addition, the gains made in PM performance on CogSMART were maintained through the one-year follow-up (Twamley et al., 2015).

Stringer developed the Ecological-oriented Neurorehabilitation of Memory (EON-Mem) which uses a treatment manual approach, standardized across patients and therapists, to train patients to compensate for memory impairment (Stringer, 2007). The EON-Mem program consists of a 4-step compensatory method, 'Word, Organize, Picture, and Rehearse' (Stringer & Small, 2011). Various modules were used to teach patients to apply this compensatory method to specific memory content. Stringer and Small (2011) designed a study to investigate the differential responses to EON-Mem from patients with all levels of memory impairment severity and diagnosis. It was found that the EON-Mem produced statistically significant improvements in everyday memory content regardless of the impairment severity (Stringer & Small, 2011).

The most commonly used internal compensation technique for prospective memory deficits in people with acquired brain injury is visual imagery. Studies using visual imagery to improve PM have been designed not to learn to create images, per se, but to use image generation to increase awareness of when a cue arrives and a response is required. Kaschel et al. (2002) trained nine patients to use visual imagery to imagine themselves fulfilling the PM task at the correct time or to the correct cue. Individuals who received 20 sessions of the imagery training showed higher rates of keeping appointments than the control group of memory impaired patients who received standard memory rehabilitation strategies. Similarly, Potvin, Rouleau, Sénéchal, and Giguère (2011) used a five-stage training program to train individuals with BI to visualize cues in a PM task. They also reported that individuals with BI demonstrated improvements in PM in daily life. On a self-report measure of PM failures, a significant reduction in failures was reported following three months for the treatment group but not for the control group. Both Grilli and McFarland (2011) and Grilli and Glisky (2010) used a technique previously found to be effective in retrospective episodic memory recall to train individuals with neurological impairment in visual imagery techniques. They reported that self-imaging resulted in better PM performance and postulated that this is due to a superiority based on mnemonic mechanisms specifically related to the self. Mioni et al. (2017) used a technique they named future event simulation that appears to be similar to these visual imagery studies (i.e. using as many sensorial details as possible to imagine the sequence of events required to complete the PM task). This future event simulation strategy was demonstrated to improve PM in individuals with BI. Raskin, Smith, et al. (2017) used a similar technique in a crossover controlled design and demonstrated improvement in PM in individuals with BI using visual imagery. Moreover, treatment gains generalized to daily life and were maintained for one year after treatment was concluded.

The modified Story Memory Technique (mSMT) teaches the participants to utilize imagery by reading stories for which they are to remember target words and form mental imagery.

Furthermore, participants are instructed to apply the mSMT to real-life memory tasks (Chiaravalloti, Dobryakova, Wylie, & DeLuca, 2015; Chiaravalloti, Sandry, Moore, & DeLuca, 2016). Individuals in the treatment group demonstrated significant improvement on the memory task, objective measures of PM, and family report of disinhibition in daily life relative to the control group. These studies show that visual imagery has excellent promise. However, the studies have been of brief duration (only 10 sessions over 5 weeks), despite evidence from cortical plasticity that repetition over time is necessary for successful long-term change in brain organization (e.g. Kolb, Cioe, & Williams, 2011), and have not measured generalization to daily life.

Restorative approaches

A restorative approach has the potential of improving functions in all aspects of a person's life, not just those directly trained. The theoretical basis of restorative approaches derives from studies of repetitive activity, which appear to facilitate neuroplasticity. That is, repeated use of a particular cognitive process should strengthen connections in the underlying neural circuitry and lead to an increase in the ability to perform that task (Kolb et al., 2011).

Sohlberg, White, Evans, and Mateer (1992a, 1992b) reported on a case study of PM restoration with a person with BI. Using a within-participant repeated measures design they implemented repetitive practice, carrying out target tasks at increasingly longer time intervals. Measurement using probes to evaluate generalization revealed a steady increase in the person's PM span. However, the training and generalization data were somewhat ambiguous, as improvement occurred in both the experimental and control conditions. In a study by Raskin and Sohlberg (1996), participants with traumatic BI were required to execute actions at future designated times. This prospective memory training involves giving a participant tasks to perform at specified times in the future, in which the length of time between task administration and task execution is systematically lengthened (Sohlberg & Raskin, 1996). Once the participant successfully completes five consecutive tasks in a row, the time interval is increased by one minute. Results supported the ability to increase participants' PM span. Participants improved on both naturalistic probes (e.g. laboratory tasks that simulated real-world tasks, such as 'When this session is over, please remind me to call your physician') and performance in daily life by use of a diary study.

Metacognitive strategies

Metacognitive strategies are designed to improve self-awareness or self-regulation. In a comprehensive review of the literature on executive function treatment, Kennedy et al. (2007) found substantial evidence from 11 intervention studies that training individuals with BI to use metacognitive regulation strategies improved problem solving, planning, and organization necessary for carrying out goal directed activity. An example of a metacognitive intervention pertinent to managing PM impairment is to provide individuals with reminders to self-regulate that can later be faded. Manly, Hawkins, Evans, Woldt, and Robertson (2001) presented participants with BI audible tones to cue them *to do the next task* in a series of 6 'hotel' tasks that were multifaceted and complex. A study conducted by Gracey et al. (2016) examined the efficacy of brief goal-directed rehabilitation paired with periodic SMS text messages to enhance executive monitoring of everyday intentions. While completing the Goal Management Training (Levine et al., 2011) program, each participant received SMS text messages containing the acronym 'STOP,' indicating one to check the status of their intentions

(Gracey et al., 2016). The authors suggested that the random occurrence of cues, SMS texts, prompted mental review of intentions that contribute to improved performance on tasks requiring attentive control of goal-directed behavior. In a similar study, Fish et al. (2007) and Fish, Manly, Kopelman, and Morris (2015) also performed a study evaluating an alerting strategy. The retrospective component of learning the task to be performed that was encoded under conditions of errorless learning with vanishing cues. Training in the PM task used a modified brief version of Goal Management Training (Levine et al., 2011). Twenty individuals with BI were sent a text message of 'stop' at varying points during the day. The message carried no content information and was not sent at the time that the activity (calling a voicemail service) needed to be performed. Nevertheless, the authors reported improvement in PM performance on the days that the message was sent, with a medium to large effect size. This suggests that nonspecific cuing can lead to enhanced goal monitoring in these individuals.

Forming implementation intentions is described as a self-regulatory strategy (Gollwitzer & Brandstätter, 1997). Unfortunately, this strategy was not shown to improve PM performance in individuals with BI (Mioni, Rendell, Terrett, & Stablum, 2015). In this study, the outcome measure was the Virtual Week task. For the implementation intentions condition, participants were instructed to form an implementation intentions statement relating to the PM task presented. This involved reforming intention into the format of, when I (cue) I will (action) (e.g. 'when I eat lunch, I will take my medication') and were required to repeat the statement 3 times aloud.

Computerized approaches

Virtual reality computerized formats have also been utilized in studies of CRT. Mathews, Mitrovic, Ohlsson, Holland, and McKinley (2016) and Mitrovic, Mathews, Ohlsson, Holland, and McKinlay (2016) used a combination of visualization and a virtual reality program with small numbers of participants who had had stroke over 10 sessions. They reported that individuals showed improvement on PM skills measured on the CAMPROMPT. Two studies used virtual reality training in individuals with stroke and measured performance in real-life settings. A 12-session virtual reality-based PM program was developed using a non-immersive form of virtual reality (VR), in which a virtual environment was generated and displayed through computers and LCD monitors (Yip & Man, 2013). People with BI demonstrated improvements in behavioral assessments of performance in both the virtual environment and a real-life setting (Yip & Man, 2013). In a similar study 20 participants with stroke were given 10 training sessions in how to use the local Mass Transit Railway stations. Participants were able to learn the transit system and showed transfer of training and increased scores on a measure of self-efficacy (Lam, Man, Tam, & Weiss, 2006).

Combination approaches

Clinically, practitioners often combine the use of external compensatory aids and metacognitive strategies to address PM deficits in patients. Fleming, Shum, Strong, and Lightbody (2005) evaluated a multi-component intervention in three individuals with BI. These interventions included self-awareness training, teaching organizational strategies, and selection of a compensatory device (e.g. notebook, electronic diary). The authors reported an improvement in PM performance based on objective memory assessments. In a follow-up randomized controlled trial, with four groups of participants, the groups with compensatory PM training demonstrated greater improvement than those given self-awareness training alone (Shum, Fleming, Gill, Gullo, & Strong, 2011).

Rehabilitation strategies that have received the most attention are compensatory strategies, especially external explicit ones such as datebooks, calendars, and reminders. It seems appropriate to include these within any treatment regimen. There is some preliminary evidence that external, implicit strategies may also be effective, such as making tasks habitual or pairing intentions like taking medication to routine tasks such as meals. Of the internal strategies, visual imagery and rote rehearsal have shown the most promise and are each likely to be an effective tool with this population. Rote rehearsal has shown the greatest gains, although it also requires the longest treatment duration. Implementation intentions, which has shown promise in other populations, was not shown to be effective, perhaps because it requires intact executive monitoring.

Thus, a recommended treatment plan might include several sessions in identifying an appropriate compensation tool and training in its use. Then the inclusion of visual imagery with rote repetition could serve to increase overall PM performance. The final sessions would then focus on generalization of treatment to daily life using something like a diary study and perhaps some training in episodic future thinking.

The literature is difficult to interpret because many of the studies reviewed are single case studies or very small sample sizes. Only three could be considered randomized controlled trials. On the other hand, there is evidence that BI is so heterogeneous that randomized controlled trials may not be the best study design and that carefully controlled multiple case study designs might be more appropriate (Wilson, 1987). Future studies would be important that attempt, at least, to create individualized treatment programs based on the underlying nature of the PM deficit (i.e. a deficit in attention vs. a deficit in time monitoring). Further, many studies reviewed used only a short duration of treatment or a low intensity of training (e.g. one hour per week). Research in cortical plasticity suggests that high intensity over a longer period is essential if restorative effects are to be achieved (Kolb et al., 2011).

Conclusions

PM is an important area of research in individuals with BI (e.g. Kliegel et al., 2008). PM has been shown to be related to activities of daily living, such as taking medications, attending appointments, and performing daily household duties (e.g. Raskin & Sohlberg, 2009), in addition to being needed in virtually all places of employment (e.g. Mateer et al., 1987). Considerable research to date has helped to clarify the nature of PM deficits (e.g. Knight et al., 2005), the underlying neural substrates (e.g. Neulinger et al., 2016), and the component cognitive processes that predict PM performance (e.g. Kliegel et al., 2004). Attention, retrospective memory and executive functioning have been shown to be important components, although they do not necessarily predict accuracy (Pavawalla et al., 2012). More research is needed to understand their individual contributions.

Individuals with BI have been consistently demonstrated to have superior event-based performance as compared to time-based performance (e.g. Raskin et al., 2011). However, more research is needed to better understand the relationship of variables such as time sense, future thinking and PM.

For example, although it has been documented that individuals with BI have dysfunction in time estimation (e.g. Schmitter-Edgecombe & Rueda, 2008), time sense in people with BI has not been systematically investigated for its role in successful PM performance to our knowledge, although preliminary data suggest that it plays a role (Raskin, 2003).

Similarly, episodic and semantic future thinking have not been systematically examined in individuals with BI (however see Rasmussen & Berntsen, 2012) and the relationship between future thinking and PM in this population could lead to interesting approaches to rehabilitation. For example, findings suggesting a relationship between them could suggest visual imagery techniques based on episodic future thinking.

It is also possible that the relationship between the cue and the intention to be performed will have a differential effect on PM performance in people with BI, given findings of an effect with aging and mild cognitive impairment (e.g. Pereira, Ellis, & Freeman, 2012a, 2012b; Pereira et al., 2015). For example, on the MIST all items are intentionally highly related (e.g. when I hand you an envelope, please self-address it). This contrasts with items that are not related (e.g. when I show you a picture of an elephant, please touch your nose). Thus, Cue-Intention Relation is another area of research that could lead to a greater understanding of the attentional processes underlying PM deficits in people with BI as well as rehabilitation strategies.

There are currently several available measures of PM. Between them most clinicians should be able to find a measure that is appropriate for their individual setting. Findings of deficits in individuals with BI and the relationship to activities of daily living and quality of life suggest that this is an area that should be assessed more consistently in clinical neuropsychological evaluations.

CRT that focuses on compensatory devices have been found to be effective and the format can be easily tailored to an individual's needs, abilities and resources. Various electronic pagers and smartphones are becoming increasingly available. More research would be helpful in elucidating the best ways to train individuals in their use, similar to techniques designed for training the use of notebooks.

More careful research is needed on restorative techniques that show promise both in improving PM in the laboratory but also in daily life. Computerized programs, like Virtual Week, may show promise for individuals with BI, as it has been shown to be helpful as a training technique in people with in older adults (Rose et al., 2015). Other computerized approaches could be created that would allow participants to augment treatment sessions with at home sessions and can be programmed to be responsive to systematically increase difficulty as the participant improves. Computer programs can also take advantage of virtual reality environments to approximate everyday scenarios.

It will be important to evaluate subgroups of people with BI to determine if certain treatments are more effective depending on level of severity or on the constellation of symptoms (e.g. attention deficits vs. executive function deficits). For example, for those with attention deficits, Attention Process Training (Palmese & Raskin, 2000; Sohlberg, McLaughlin, Pavese, Heidrich, & Posner, 2000) might be the first treatment applied. For those with primary executive function deficits Goal Management Training (Levine et al., 2011) might be more effective. Some potential approaches that have not been investigated include time estimation training, training using systematically reduced cue-intention pairing, training using systematically reduced cue focality, use of enactment, or systematically increasing the cognitive load or items to be held in memory (Raskin, Race, & Aiken, 2017). The optimum duration and intensity of treatment also needs to be determined.

Disclosure statement

No potential conflict of interest was reported by the authors.

ORCID

Sarah A. Raskin http://orcid.org/0000-0002-4310-4278

References

Baddeley, A. (1981). The cognitive psychology of everyday life. *British Journal of Psychology, 72*, 257–269.

*Baldwin, V., & Powell, T. (2015). Google calendar: A single case experimental design study of a man with severe memory problems. *Neuropsychological Rehabilitation, 25*, 617–636.

Benoit, R. G., Gilbert, S. J., & Burgess, P. W. (2011). A neural mechanism mediating the impact of episodic prospection on farsighted decisions. *Journal of Neuroscience, 31*, 6771–6779.

*Brooks, B., Rose, F., Potter, J., Jayawardena, S., & Morling, A. (2004). Assessing stroke patients' prospective memory using virtual reality. *Brain Injury, 18*, 391–401.

Bryen, D. N., Carey, A., & Friedman, M. (2007). Cell phone use by adults with intellectual disabilities. *Intellectual and Developmental Disabilities, 45*, 1–2.

Burgess, P. W., Alderman, N., Volle, E., Benoit, R. G., & Gilbert, S. J. (2009). Mesulam's frontal lobe mystery re-examined. *Restorative Neurology and Neuroscience, 27*, 493–506.

Burgess, P. W., Gonen-Yaacovi, G., & Volle, E. (2011). Functional neuroimaging studies of prospective memory: What have we learnt so far? *Neuropsychologia, 49*, 2246–2257.

*Canty, A., Fleming, J., Patterson, F., Green, H., Man, D., & Shum, D. (2014). Evaluation of a virtual reality prospective memory task for use with individuals with severe traumatic brain injury. *Neuropsychological Rehabilitation, 24*, 238–265.

Carlesimo, G., Casadio, P., & Caltagirone, C. (2004). Prospective and retrospective components in the memory for actions to be performed in patients with severe closed-head injury. *Journal of the International Neuropsychological Society, 10*, 670–688.

*Chau, L., Lee, J., Fleming, J., Roche, N., & Shum, D. (2007). Reliability and normative data for the Comprehensive Assessment of Prospective Memory (CAPM). *Neuropsychological Rehabilitation, 17*, 707–722.

*Chiaravalloti, N., Dobryakova, E., Wylie, G., & DeLuca, J. (2015). Examining the efficacy of the modified story memory technique (mSMT) in persons with TBI using functional magnetic imaging (fMRI): The TBI-MEM Trial. *Journal of Head Trauma Rehabilitation, 4*, 262–269.

*Chiaravalloti, N. D., Sandry, J., Moore, N. B., & DeLuca, J. (2016). An RCT to treat learning impairment in traumatic brain injury. *Neurorehabilitation and Neural Repair, 30*(6), 539–550.

*Clune-Ryberg, M., Blanco-Campal, A., Carton, S., Pender, N., O'Brien, D., Phillips, J., … Burke, T. (2011). The contribution of retrospective memory, attention, and executive functions to the prospective and retrospective components of prospective memory following TBI. *Brain Injury, 25*, 819–831.

Cockburn, J. (1996). Failure of prospective memory after acquired brain damage: Preliminary investigation and suggestions for future directions. *Journal of Clinical and Experimental Neuropsychology, 18*, 304–309.

Cona, G., Scarpazza, C., Sartori, G., Moscovitch, M., & Bisiacchi, P. (2015). Neural bases of prospective memory: A meta-analysis and the 'Attention to Delayed Intention' (AtoDI) model. *Neuroscience Biobehavioral Reviews, 52*, 21–37.

Crawford, J., Smith, G., Maylor, E., Della Sala, S., & Logie, R. (2003). The Prospective and Retrospective Memory Questionnaire (PRMQ): Normative data and latent structure in a large non-clinical sample. *Memory, 11*, 261–275.

Delprado, J., Kinsella, G., Ong, B., Pike, K., Ames, D., Storey, E., … Rand, E. (2012). Clinical measures of prospective memory in amnestic mild cognitive impairment. *Journal of the International Neuropsychological Society, 18*(2), 295–304.

Dobbs, A. R., & Reeves, M. B. (1996). *Prospective memory: More than memory*. Mahwah, NJ: Erlbaum.

Donaghy, S., & Williams, W. (1998). A new protocol for training severely impaired patients in the usage of memory journals. *Brain Injury, 12*, 1061–1076.

Einstein, G. O., & McDaniel, M. A. (1990). Normal aging and prospective memory. *Journal of Experimental Psychology: Learning, Memory, and Cognition, 16*, 717–726.

Einstein, G. O., & McDaniel, M. A. (2005). Prospective memory. *Current Directions in Psychological Science, 14*(6), 286–290.

Einstein, G. O., McDaniel, M. A., Richardson, S. L., Guynn, M. J., & Cunfer, A. R. (1995). Aging and prospective memory: Examining the influences of self-initiated retrieval processes. *Journal of Experimental Psychology: Learning, Memory, and Cognition, 2*, 996–1007.

Ellis, J. A. (1996). Prospective memory or the realisation of delayed intentions: A conceptual framework for research. In M. Brandimonte, G. O. Einstein, & M. A. McDaniel (Eds.), *Prospective memory: Theory and applications* (pp. 1–22). Hillsdale, NJ: Erlbaum.

Emslie, H., Wilson, B., Quirk, K., Evans, J., & Watson, P. (2007). Using a paging system in the rehabilitation of encephalitic patients. *Neuropsychological Rehabilitation, 17*, 567–581.

*Evald, L. (2015). Prospective memory rehabilitation using smartphones in patients with TBI: What do participants report? *Neuropsychological Rehabilitation, 25*(2), 283–297.

*Evans, J. J., Wilson, B. A., Needham, P., & Brentnall, S. (2003). Who makes good use of memory aids? Results of a survey of people with acquired brain injury. *Journal of the International Neuropsychological Society, 9*, 925–935.

*Ferguson, S., Friedland, D., & Woodberry, E. (2015). Smartphone technology: Gentle reminders of everyday tasks for those with prospective memory difficulties post-brain injury. *Brain Injury, 29*(5), 583–591.

*Fish, J., Evans, J. J., Nimmo, M., Martin, E., Kersel, D., Bateman, A., ... Manly, T. (2007). Rehabilitation of executive dysfunction following brain injury: 'Content-free' cueing improves everyday prospective memory performance. *Neuropsychologia, 45*(6), 1318–1330.

*Fish, J., Manly, T., Kopelman, M., & Morris, R. (2015). Errorless learning of prospective memory tasks: An experimental investigation in people with memory disorders. *Neuropsychological Rehabilitation, 25*, 159–188.

*Fish, J., Wilson, B., & Manly, T. (2011). The assessment and rehabilitation of prospective memory problems in people with neurological disorders: A review. *Neuropsychological Rehabilitation, 20*, 161–179.

*Fleming, J., Kennedy, S., Fisher, R., & Gill, H. (2009). Validity of the Comprehensive Assessment of Prospective Memory (CAPM) for use with adults with traumatic brain injury. *Brain Impairment, 10*, 34–44.

*Fleming, J., Riley, L., Gill, H., Gullo, M., Strong, J., & Shum, D. (2008). Predictors of prospective memory in adults with traumatic brain injury. *Journal of the International Neuropsychological Society, 14*, 823–831.

*Fleming, J., Shum, D., Strong, J., & Lightbody, S. (2005). Prospective memory rehabilitation for adults with traumatic brain injury: A compensatory training programme. *Brain Injury, 19*, 1–10.

Fortin, S., Godbout, L., & Braun, C. M. (2003). Cognitive structure of executive deficits in frontally lesioned head trauma patients performing activities of daily living. *Cortex, 39*, 273–291.

Foster, E., McDaniel, M., Repovš, G., & Hershey, T. (2009). Prospective memory in Parkinson disease across laboratory and self-reported everyday performance. *Neuropsychology, 23*, 347–358.

LoPresti, E. F., Mihailidis, A., & Kirsch, N. (2004). Assistive technology for cognitive rehabilitation: State of the art. *Neuropsychological Rehabilitation, 14*(1–2), 5–39.

Gillette, Y., & Depompei, R. (2008). Do PDAs enhance the organization and memory skills of students with cognitive disabilities? *Psychology in the Schools, 45*, 665–677.

Glisky, E. L. (1996). Prospective memory and the frontal lobes. In M. Brandimonte, G. O. Einstein, & M. A. McDaniel (Eds.), *Prospective memory: Theory and applications* (pp. 249–266). Mahwah, NJ: Erlbaum.

Gollwitzer, P. M., & Brandstätter, V. (1997). Implementation intentions and effective goal pursuit. *Journal of Personality and Social Psychology, 73*(1), 186–199.

Gonzales, A. (2016). The contemporary US digital divide: From initial access to technology maintenance. *Journal of Information, Communication and Society, 19*(2), 234–248.

González-Ramírez, M., & Mendoza-González, M. (2011). Spanish version of the Prospective and Retrospective Memory Questionnaire (PRMQ-S). *The Spanish Journal of Psychology, 14*, 385–391.

* Gracey, F., Fish, J. E., Greenfield, E., Bateman, A., Malley, D., Hardy, G., ... Manly, T. (2016). A randomized controlled trial of assisted intention monitoring for the rehabilitation of executive impairments following acquired brain injury. *Neurorehabil Neural Repair, 31,* 323–333.

*Grilli, M., & Glisky, E. (2010). Self-imagining enhances recognition memory in memory-impaired individuals with neurological damage. *Neuropsychology, 24,* 698–710.

*Grilli, M., & McFarland, C. (2011). Imagine that: Self-imagination improves prospective memory in memory-impaired individuals with neurological damage. *Neuropsychological Rehabilitation, 21,* 847–859.

*Groot, Y., Wilson, B., Evans, J., & Watson, P. (2002). Prospective memory functioning in people with and without brain injury. *Journal of the International Neuropsychological Society, 8,* 645–654.

Guynn, M. (2003). A two-process model of strategic monitoring in event-based prospective memory: Activation/retrieval mode and checking. *International Journal of Psychology, 38,* 245–256.

*Hannon, R., Adams, P., Harrington, S., Fries-Dias, C., & Gipson, M. (1995). Effects of brain injury and age on prospective memory self-rating and performance. *Rehabilitation Psychology, 40,* 289–298.

Heathcote, A., Loft, S., & Remington, R. (2015). Slow down and remember to remember! A delay theory of prospective memory costs *Psychological Review, 122,* 376–410.

*Henry, J., Phillips, L., Crawford, J., Kliegel, M., Theodorou, G., & Summers, F. (2007). Traumatic brain injury and prospective memory: Influence of task complexity. *Journal of Clinical and Experimental Neuropsychology, 29,* 457–466.

*Huang, J., Fleming, J., Pomery, N., O'Gorman, J. G., Chan, R., & Shum, D. (2014). Perceived importance of prospective memory failures in adults with traumatic brain injury. *Neuropsychological Rehabilitation, 24,* 61–70.

*Huckans, M., Pavawalla, S., Demadura, T., Kolessar, M., Seelye, A., Roost, N., ... Storzbach, D. (2010). A pilot study examining effects of group-based cognitive strategy training treatment on self-reported cognitive problems, psychiatric symptoms, functioning, and compensatory strategy use in OIF/OEF combat veterans with persistent mild cognitive disorder and history of traumatic brain injury. *The Journal of Rehabilitation Research and Development, 47*(1), 43–60.

*Jamieson, M., Cullen, B., McGee-Lennon, M., Brewster, S., & Evans, J. (2015). Technological memory aid use by people with acquired brain injury. *Neuropsychological Rehabilitation,* 1–18.

*Kaschel, R., Sala, S., Cantagallo, A., Fahlböck, A., Laaksonen, R., & Kazen, M. (2002). Imagery mnemonics for the rehabilitation of memory: A randomised group controlled trial. *Neuropsychological Rehabilitation, 12,* 127–153.

*Kennedy, M., Coelho, C., Turkstra, L., Ylvisaker, M., Sohlberg, M. M., Yorkston, K., ... Kahn, P. F. (2007). Intervention for executive functions after traumatic brain injury: A systematic review and meta-analysis. *Neuropsychological Rehabilitation,* iFirst, 1–43.

*Kim, H., Burke, D., Dowds, M., Boone, K., & Park, G. (2000). Electronic memory aids for outpatient brain injury: Follow-up findings. *Brain Injury, 14,* 187–196.

*Kinsella, G., Murtagh, D., Landry, A., Homfray, K., Hammond, M., O'Beirne, L., ... Ponsford, J. (1996). Everyday memory following traumatic brain injury. *Brain Injury, 10,* 499–508.

*Kinsella, G., Olver, J., Ong, B., Gruen, R., & Hammersley, E. (2014). Mild traumatic brain injury in older adults: Early cognitive outcome. *Journal of the International Neuropsychological Society, 20,* 663–671.

*Kirsch, N., Shenton, M., Spirl, E., Rowan, J., Simpson, R., Schreckenghost, D., & LoPresti, E. F. (2004). Web-based assistive technology interventions for cognitive impairments after traumatic brain injury: A selective review and two case studies. *Rehabilitation Psychology, 49,* 200–212.

*Kliegel, M., Eschen, A., & Thöne-Otto, A. (2004). Planning and realization of complex intentions in traumatic brain injury and normal aging. *Brain and Cognition, 56,* 43–54.

Kliegel, M., Jager, T., Altgassen, M., & Shum, D. (2008). Clinical neuropsychology of prospective memory. In M. Kliegel, M. A. McDaniel, & G. O. Einstein (Eds.), *Prospective memory: Cognitive, neuroscience, developmental, and applied perspectives* (pp. 283–308). Mahwah, NJ: Lawrence Erlbaum Associates.

*Knight, R., Harnett, M., & Titov, N. (2005). The effects of traumatic brain injury on the predicted and actual performance of a test of prospective remembering. *Brain Injury, 19,* 19–27.

*Knight, R., Titov, N., & Crawford, M. (2006). The effects of distraction on prospective remembering following traumatic brain injury assessed in a simulated naturalistic environment. *Journal of the International Neuropsychological Society, 12,* 8–15.

Kolb, B., Cioe, J., & Williams, P. (2011). Neuronal organization and change after brain injury. In S. Raskin (Ed.), *Neuroplasticity and neurorehabilitation* (pp. 13–37). New York, NY: Guilford Press.

Kvavilashvili, L. (1992). Remembering intentions: A critical review of existing experimental paradigms. *Applied Cognitive Psychology, 6*, 507–524.

*Lam, Y., Man, D., Tam, S., & Weiss, P. (2006). Virtual reality training for stroke rehabilitation. *NeuroRehabilitation, 21*, 245–253.

*Lemoncello, R., Sohlberg, M. M., Fickas, S., & Prideaux, J. (2011). A randomised controlled crossover trial evaluating Television Assisted Prompting (TAP) for adults with acquired brain injury. *Neuropsychological Rehabilitation, 21*(6), 825–846.

Levine, B., Schweizer, T. A., O'Connor, C., Turner, G. R., Gillingham, S., Stuss, D. T., … Robertson, I. H. (2011). Rehabilitation of executive functioning in patients with frontal lobe brain damage with goal management training. *Frontiers in Human Neuroscience, 5*, 9.

*Levine, B., Stuss, D., Milberg, W., Alexander, M., Schwartz, M., & Macdonald, R. (1998). The effects of focal and diffuse brain damage on strategy application: Evidence from focal lesions, traumatic brain injury and normal aging. *Journal of the International Neuropsychological Society, 4*, 247–264.

Liberati, A., Altman, D., Tetzlaff, J., Mulrow, C., Gotzsche, P., Ioannidis, J. P. A., … Moher, D. (2009). The PRISMA statement for reporting systematic reviews and meta-analyses of studies that evaluated health care interventions: Explanation and elaboration. *PloS Med, 6*(7): e1000100.

Man, D., Chan, M., & Yip, C. (2015). Validation of the Cambridge Prospective Memory Test (Hong Kong Chinese version) for people with stroke. *Neuropsychological Rehabilitation, 25*, 895–912.

*Man, D., Fleming, J., Hohaus, L., & Shum, D. (2011). Development of the Brief Assessment of Prospective Memory (BAPM) for use with traumatic brain injury populations. *Neuropsychological Rehabilitation, 21*, 884–898.

*Man, D., Yip, C., Lee, G., Fleming, J., & Shum, D. (2015). Self-report prospective memory problems in people with stroke. *Brain Injury, 29*, 329–335.

*Manly, T., Hawkins, K., Evans, J., Woldt, K., & Robertson, I. H. (2001). Rehabilitation of executive function: Facilitation of effective goal management on complex tasks using periodic auditory alerts. *Neuropsychologia, 40*, 271–281.

Mateer, C., Sohlberg, M., & Crinean, J. (1987). Focus on clinical research: Perceptions of memory function in individuals with closed-head injury. *Journal of Head Trauma Rehabilitation, 2*, 74–84.

*Mathews, M., Mitrovic, A., Ohlsson, S., Holland, J., & McKinley, A. (2016). A virtual reality environment for rehabilitation of prospective memory in stroke patients. *Procedia Computer Science, 96*, 7–15.

*Mathias, J., & Mansfield, K. (2005). Prospective and declarative memory problems following moderate and severe traumatic brain injury. *Brain Injury, 19*, 271–282.

Maujean, A., Shum, D., & McQueen, R. (2003). Effect of cognitive demand on prospective memory in individuals with traumatic brain injury. *Brain Impairment, 4*(2), 135–145.

McAllister, T. (2011). Neurobiological consequences of traumatic brain injury. *Diaglogues in Clinical Neuroscience, 13*, 287–300.

McDaniel, M., & Einstein, G. (2011). The neuropsychology of prospective memory in normal aging: A componential approach. *Neuropsychologia, 49*, 2147–2155.

*McDonald, A., Haslam, C., Yates, P., Gurr, B., Leeder, G., & Sayers, A. (2011). Google calendar: A new memory aid to compensate for prospective memory deficits following acquired brain injury. *Neuropsychological Rehabilitation, 21*, 784–807.

*McKerracher, G., Powell, T., & Oyebode, J. (2005). A single case experimental design comparing two memory notebook formats for a man with memory problems caused by traumatic brain injury. *Neuropsychological Rehabilitation, 15*, 115–128.

* Mioni, G., Bertucci, E., Rosato, A., Terrett, G., Rendell, P., Zamuner, M., & Stablum, F. (2017). Improving prospective memory performance with future event simulation in traumatic brain injury patients. *British Journal of Clinical Psychology, 56*, 130–148.

*Mioni, G., Rendell, P., Henry, J., Cantagallo, A., & Stablum, F. (2013). An investigation of prospective memory functions in people with traumatic brain injury using Virtual Week. *Journal of Clinical and Experimental Neuropsychology, 35*, 617–630.

*Mioni, G., Rendell, P., Stablum, F., Gamberini, L., & Bisiacchi, P. (2014). Test-retest consistency of Virtual Week: A task to investigate prospective memory. *Neuropsychological Rehabilitation, 25*, 419–447.

*Mioni, G., Rendell, P., Terrett, G., & Stablum, F. (2015). Prospective memory performance in traumatic brain injury patients: A study of implementation intentions. *Journal of the International Neuropsychological Society, 21*, 305–313.

*Mitrovic, A., Mathews, M., Ohlsson, S., Holland, J., & McKinlay, A. (2016). Computer-based post-stroke rehabilitation of prospective memory. *Journal of Applied Research in Memory and Cognition, 5*, 204–214.

Sohlberg, M., McLaughlin, K., Pavese, A., Heidrich, A., & Posner, M. (2000). Evaluation of attention process training and brain injury education in persons with acquired brain injury. *Journal of Clinical and Experimental Neuropsychology (Neuropsychology, Development and Cognition: Section A), 22*, 656–676.

*Mühl, A., Aubert, C., Wicky, G., Fédou, M., Devanthéry, F., Jungo, S., … Anne, B. (2016). Normalization of an ecologic organization and problem-solving test in a vocational rehabilitation setting: TEM-PRO. *Annals of Physical Rehabilitation and Medicine., 59*, e131–e132.

National Institutes of Health Consensus Development Panel on Rehabilitation of Persons with Traumatic Brain Injury. (1998). *Consensus conference: Rehabilitation of persons with traumatic brain injury.* Retrieved from http://www.odp.od.nih.gov/consensus/

Neulinger, K., Oram, J., Tinson, H., O'Gorman, J., & Shum, D. (2016). Prospective memory and frontal lobe function. *Aging, Neuropsychology, and Cognition, 23*, 171–183.

Newman, L., Browne-Yung, K., Raghavendra, P., Wood, D., & Grace, E. (2017). Applying a critical approach to investigate barriers to digital inclusion and online social networking among young people with disabilities. *Information Systems Journal, 27*, 559–588.

*O'Connell, M., Mateer, C., & Kerns, K. (2003). Prosthetic systems for addressing problems with initiation: Guidelines for selection, training, and measuring efficacy. *Neurorehabilitation, 18*, 9–20.

Ownsworth, T., & McFarland, K. (1999). Memory remediation in long-term acquired brain injury: Two approaches in diary training. *Brain Injury, 13*, 605–626.

Palmese, C., & Raskin, S. (2000). The rehabilitation of attention in individuals with mild traumatic brain injury, using the APT-II programme. *Brain Injury, 14*, 535–548.

*Pavawalla, S., Schmitter-Edgecombe, M., & Smith, R. (2012). Prospective memory after moderate-to-severe traumatic brain injury: A multinomial modeling approach. *Neuropsychology, 26*, 91–101.

*Paxton, J., & Chiaravalloti, N. (2014). Rule monitoring ability predicts event-based prospective memory performance in individuals with TBI. *Journal of the International Neuropsychological Society, 20*, 673–683.

Pereira, A., de Mendonca, A., Silva, D., Guerreiro, M., Freeman, J., & Ellis, J. (2015). Enhancing prospective memory in mild cognitive impairment: The role of enactment. *Journal of Clinical and Experimental Neuropsychology, 37*, 863–877.

Pereira, A., Ellis, J., & Freeman, J. (2012a). Is prospective memory enhanced by cue-action semantic relatedness and enactment at encoding? *Consciousness and Cognition, 21*, 1257–1266.

Pereira, A., Ellis, J., & Freeman, J. (2012b). The effects of age, enactment, and cue-action relatedness on memory for intentions in the Virtual Week task. *Aging, Neuropsychology, and Cognition, 19*, 549–565.

*Potvin, M. J., Rouleau, I., Sénéchal, G., & Giguère, J. F. (2011). Prospective memory rehabilitation based on visual imagery techniques. *Neuropsychological Rehabilitation, 21*(6), 899–924.

*Radford, K., Lah, S., Say, M., & Miller, L. (2011). Validation of a new measure of prospective memory: The Royal Prince Alfred Prospective Memory Test. *The Clinical Neuropsychologist, 25*, 127–140.

Raskin, S. (2003). *Time estimation and memory for intentions*. Honolulu, HI: International Neuropsychological Society.

*Raskin, S. (2009). Memory for Intentions Screening Test: Psychometric properties and clinical evidence. *Brain Impairment, 10*, 23–33.

Raskin, S., Buckheit, C., & Sherrod, C. (2010). *Memory for Intentions Screening Test: Manual*. Lutz, FL: Psychological Assessment Resources.

*Raskin, S., Buckheit, C., & Waxman, A. (2012). Effect of type of cue, type of response, time delay and two different ongoing tasks on prospective memory functioning after acquired brain injury. *Rehabilitation Psychology, 22*(1), 42–64.

Raskin, S., Maye, J., Rogers, A., Correll, D., Zamroziewicz, M., & Kurtz, M. (2014). Prospective memory in schizophrenia: Relationship to medication management skills, neurocognition, and symptoms in individuals with schizophrenia. *Neuropsychology, 28*(3), 359–365.

Raskin, S., & Race, M.* (2017). *Development of a short form of the Memory for Intentions Test*. Poster presented at the International Neuropsychological Society meeting, Cape Town, South Africa.
Raskin, S., Race, M., & Aiken, E. (2017). *A modular approach to personalized prospective memory training*. Paper presented at the International Neuropsychological Society meeting, Cape Town, South Africa.
*Raskin, S., Shum, D., Ellis, J., Pereira, A., & Mills, G. (2017). A comparison of laboratory, clinical, and self-report measures of prospective memory in healthy adults and individuals with brain injury. *Journal of Clinical and Experimental Neuropsychology*, 1–14.
*Raskin, S., Smith, M., Mills, G., Pedro, C., & Zamroziewicz, M. (2017, March 12). Prospective memory intervention using visual imagery in individuals with brain injury. *Neuropsychological Rehabilitation*, 1–16.
*Raskin, S. A., & Sohlberg, M. M. (1996). The efficacy of prospective memory training in two adults with brain injury. *Journal of Head Trauma Rehabilitation, 11*, 32–51.
*Raskin, S., & Sohlberg, M. (2009). Prospective memory intervention: A review and evaluation of a pilot restorative intervention. *Brain Impairment, 10*, 76–86.
Raskin, S., Woods, S. A., Poquette, A., J., McTaggart, A. B., Sethna, J.*, Williams, R., & Troster. A. (2011). A differential deficit in time versus event-based prospective memory in Parkinson's disease. *Neuropsychology, 25*(2), 201–209.
*Rasmussen, K., & Berntsen, D. (2012). Autobiographical future thinking after moderate to severe traumatic brain injury. *Journal of Neuropsychology, 8*, 34–52.
Rendell, P., & Craik, F. (2000). Virtual and actual week: Age-related differences in prospective memory. *Applied Cognitive Psychology*. Special Issue: New Perspectives in Prospective Memory, *14*, S43–S62.
Rendell, P., & Henry, J. (2009). A review of Virtual Week for prospective memory assessment: Clinical implications. *Brain Impairment, 10*, 14–22.
Rendell, P. G., & Thomson, D. M. (1999). Aging and prospective memory: Differences between naturalistic and laboratory tasks. *The Journals of Gerontology: Series B: Psychological Sciences and Social Sciences, 54B*(4), P256–P269.
*Roche, N., Fleming, J., & Shum, D. (2002). Self-awareness of prospective memory failure in adults with traumatic brain injury. *Brain Injury, 16*, 931–945.
Roche, N., Moody, A., Szabo, K., Fleming, J., & Shum, D. (2007). Prospective memory in adults with traumatic brain injury: An analysis of perceived reasons for remembering and forgetting. *Neuropsychological Rehabilitation, 17*, 314–334.
*Rose, N., Rendell, P., Hering, A., Kliegel, M., Bidelman, G., & Craik, F. (2015). Cognitive and neural plasticity in older adults' prospective memory following training with the Virtual Week computer game. *Frontiers in Human Neuroscience, 9*, 592.
Rose, N., Rendell, P., & McDaniel, M. (2007). *Prospective memory in a Virtual Week*. Paper presented at the Cognitive Aging Conference Down Under, Adelaide, Australia.
Scherer, M., & Federici, S. (2015). Why people use and don't use technologies: Introduction to the special issue on assistive technologies for cognition/cognitive support technologies. *NeuroRehabilitation, 37*, 315–319.
Schmitter-Edgecombe, M., & Rueda, A. (2008). Time estimation and episodic memory following traumatic brain injury. *Journal of Clinical and Experimental Neuropsychology, 30*, 212–223.
*Schmitter-Edgecombe, M., & Wright, M. (2004). Event-based prospective memory following severe closed-head injury. *Neuropsychology, 18*, 353–361.
Schult, J., & Steffens, M. (2016). The effects of enactment and intention accessibility on prospective memory performance. *Memory and Cognition*, 1–14.
Scullin, M. K., McDaniel, M. A., & Shelton, J. T. (2013). The dynamic multiprocess framework: Evidence from prospective memory with contextual variability. *Cognitive Psychology, 67*(1–2), 55–71.
*Shum, D., Fleming, J., Gill, H., Gullo, M., & Strong, J. (2011). A randomized controlled trial of prospective memory rehabilitation in adults with traumatic brain injury. *Journal of Rehabilitation Medicine, 43*, 216–223.
Shum, D., Fleming, J., & Neulinger, K. (2002). Prospective memory and traumatic brain injury: A review. *Brain Impairment, 3*, 1–16.
*Shum, D., Valentine, M., & Cutmore, T. (1999). Performance of individuals with severe long-term traumatic brain injury on time-, event-, and activity-based prospective memory tasks. *Journal of*

Clinical and Experimental Neuropsychology (Neuropsychology, Development and Cognition: Section A), 21, 49–58.
Smith, R. (2003). The cost of remembering to remember in event-based prospective memory: Investigating the capacity demands of delayed intention performance. *Journal of Experimental Psychology: Learning, Memory and Cognition, 29*, 347–361.
Smith, G., Del Sala, S., Logie, R. H., & Maylor, E. A. (2000). Prospective and retrospective memory in normal ageing and dementia: A questionnaire study. *Memory., 8*(5), 311–321.
Sohlberg, M. M. (2005). External aids: Expanding our understanding of the most widely used memory rehabilitation technique. In W. High, A. M. Sander, M. A. Struchen, & K. A. Hart (Eds.), *Rehabilitation for traumatic brain injury* (pp. 47–70). New York, NY: Oxford Press.
Sohlberg, M. M. (2006). Review article: Evidence-based instructional techniques for training procedures and knowledge in persons with severe memory impairment. *Revisita de Neuropsicologia, 1*(1), 14–19.
Sohlberg, M. M., & Mateer, C. A. (1989). Training use of compensatory memory books: A three stage behavioral approach. *Journal of Clinical and Experimental Neuropsychology, 11*, 871–891.
Sohlberg, M. M., & Mateer, C. A. (2001). *Cognitive rehabilitation: An integrative neuropsychological approach*. Andover: Taylor and Francis Books.
Sohlberg, M., & Raskin, S. (1996). Principles of generalization applied to attention and memory interventions. *Journal of Head Trauma Rehabilitation, 11*(2), 65–78.
*Sohlberg, M., White, O., Evans, E., & Mateer, C. (1992a). Background and initial case studies into the effects of prospective memory training. *Brain Injury, 6*, 129–138.
*Sohlberg, M. M., White, O., Evans, E., & Mateer, C. (1992b). An investigation of the effects of prospective memory training. *Brain Injury, 6*(2), 139–154.
Steffens, M., Stulpnagel, R., & Schult, J. (2015). Memory recall after 'learning by doing' and 'learning by viewing': Boundary conditions of an enactment benefit. *Frontiers in Psychology, 6*, 1907.
Stock, S., Davies, D., & Gillespie, T. (2013). The state of the field in applied cognitive technologies. *Inclusion, 1*, 103–120.
Stringer, A. Y. (2007). *Ecological Oriented Neurorehabilitation of Memory (EON-MEM) therapist guide*. Los Angeles, CA: Western Psychological Services.
*Stringer, A. Y., & Small, S. K. (2011). Ecologically-oriented Neurorehabilitation of Memory: Robustness of outcome across diagnosis and severity. *Brain Injury, 25*(2), 169–178.
Stuss, D., Murphy, K., Binns, M., & Alexander, M. (2003). Staying on the job: The frontal lobes control individual performance variability. *Brain, 126*, 2363–2380.
*Sweeney, S., Kersel, D., Morris, R., Manly, T., & Evans, J. (2010). The sensitivity of a virtual reality task to planning and prospective memory impairments: Group differences and the efficacy of periodic alerts on performance. *Neuropsychological Rehabilitation, 20*, 239–263.
*Tam, S., Man, W., Hui-Chan, C., Lau, A., Yip, B., & Cheung, W. (2003). Evaluating the efficacy of tele-cognitive rehabilitation for functional performance in three case studies. *Occupational Therapy International, 10*, 20–38.
*Tay, S., Ang, B., Lau, X., Meyyappan, A., & Collinson, S. (2010). Chronic impairment of prospective memory after mild traumatic brain injury. *Journal of Neurotrauma, 27*, 77–83.
*Thöne-Otto, A., & Walther, K. (2003). How to design an electronic memory aid for brain-injured patients: Considerations on the basis of a model of prospective memory. *International Journal of Psychology, 38*, 236–244.
*Twamley, E. W., Jak, A. J., Delis, D. C., Bondi, M. W., & Lohr, J. B. (2014). Cognitive Symptom Management and Rehabilitation Therapy (CogSMART) for veterans with traumatic brain injury: Pilot randomized controlled trial. *Journal of Rehabilitation Research and Development, 51*(1), 59–70.
*Twamley, E., Thomas, K., Gregory, A., Jak, A., Bondi, M., Delis, D., & Lohr, J. (2015). CogSMART compensatory cognitive training for traumatic brain injury. *Journal of Head Trauma Rehabilitation, 30*, 391–401.
*Umeda, S., Kurosaki, Y., Terasawa, Y., Kato, M., & Miyahara, Y. (2011). Deficits in prospective memory following damage to the prefrontal cortex. *Neuropsychologia, 49*, 2178–2184.
Uttl, B., & Kibreab, M. (2011). Self-report measures of prospective memory are reliable but not valid. *Canadian Journal of Experimental Psychology/Revue canadienne de psychologie expérimentale, 65*(1), 57–68.

Vakil, E. (2005). The Effect of moderate to severe traumatic brain injury on different aspects of memory: A selective review. *Journal of Clinical and Experimental Neuropsychology, 27*(8), 977–1021.

*Van den Broek, M. D., Downes, J., Johnson, Z., Dayus, B., & Hilton, N. (2000). Evaluation of an electronic memory aid in the neuropsychological rehabilitation of prospective memory deficits. *Brain Injury, 14*(5), 455–462.

Vaughan, F., Neal, J., Mulla, F., Edwards, B., & Coetzer, R. (2017). The validity of the Brain Injury Cognitive Screen (BICS) as a neuropsychological screening assessment for traumatic and non-traumatic brain injury. *The Clinical Neuropsychologist, 31*, 544–568.

*Wade, T., & Troy, J. (2001). Mobile phones as a new memory aid: A preliminary investigation using case studies. *Brain Injury, 15*, 305–320.

West, R. (2008). The cognitive neuroscience of prospective memory. In M. Kliegel, M. McDaniel, & G. Einstein (Eds.), *Prospective memory: Cognitive, neuroscience, developmental, and applied perspectives* (pp. 261–282). New York, NY: Tayler and Frances.

Wilson, B. (1987). *The Rehabilitation of Memory*. New York, NY: Guilford Press.

Wilson, B., Cockburn, J., & Baddeley, A. (1985). *Manual for the Rivermead Behavioural Memory Test*. Cambridge, UK: Thames Valley Test.

Wilson, B. A., Emslie, H., Foley, J., Shiel, A., Watson, P., Hawkins, K., … Evans, J. J. (2005). *The Cambridge Prospective Memory Test*. London: Harcourt Assessment.

*Wilson, B. A., Emslie, H. C., Quirk, K., & Evans, J. J. (2001). Reducing everyday memory and planning problems by means of a paging system: A randomised control crossover study. *Journal of Neurology, Neurosurgery, & Psychiatry, 70*, 477–482.

Wilson, B. A., Scott, H., Evans, J., & Emslie, H. (2003). Preliminary report of a NeuroPage service within a health care system. *Neurorehabilitation, 18*, 3–9.

*Wong, D., Sinclair, K., Seabrook, E., McKay, A., & Ponsford, J. (2016, October). Smartphones as assistive technology following traumatic brain injury: A preliminary study of what helps and what hinders. *Disability Rehabilitation, 17*, 1–8.

*Woods, S. P., Moran, L. M., Dawson, M. S., Carey, C. L., & Grant, I. (2008). Psychometric characteristics of the Memory for Intentions Screening Test. *The Clinical Neuropsychologist, 22*, 864–878.

*Yasuda, K., Misu, T., Beckman, B., Watanabe, O., Ozawa, Y., & Nakamura, T. (2002). Use of an IC recorder as a voice output memory aid for patients with prospective memory impairment. *Neuropsychological Rehabilitation, 12*, 155–166.

*Yip, B. C., & Man, D. W. (2013). Virtual reality-based prospective memory training program for people with acquired brain injury. *Neuro Rehabilitation., 32*(1), 103–115.

*Indicates article obtained through systematic screening

Prospective memory impairment in multiple sclerosis: a review

Isabelle Rouleau, Emmanuelle Dagenais, Alexandra Tremblay, Mélanie Demers, Élaine Roger, Céline Jobin and Pierre Duquette

ABSTRACT

Objective: Multiple sclerosis (MS) is a progressive disease of the central nervous system affecting information processing speed, episodic memory, attention, and executive functions. MS patients also often report prospective memory (PM) failures that directly impact their functional autonomy, including professional and social life. The purpose of this paper was to review the literature concerning the assessment and remediation of PM deficits in MS. **Method:** The literature pertaining to PM impairment in MS was carefully reviewed using PubMed, PsyINFO, and Google Scholar, as well as cross-references from the articles published on this topic. Since PM rehabilitation in MS patients is still in its infancy, this review mainly focuses on studies that have directly assessed PM through various measures including questionnaires, standardized clinical tests, and experimental procedures. **Conclusion:** This literature review confirms the presence of PM deficits in MS patients, even in the early stages of the disease. A further need for controlled studies on PM assessment and PM interventions in patients with MS is stressed.

Multiple sclerosis (MS) is a progressive autoimmune disease of the central nervous system (CNS) characterized by the production of widespread lesions (or plaques) in the brain and spinal cord due to an inflammatory demyelinating process (Chiaravalloti & DeLuca, 2008). It affects young people while they are actively involved in familial, social, and professional life. The disease generally begins between the ages of 20 and 40 years, although children and elderly can be affected. According to the Multiple Sclerosis International Federation (2016), MS is present in all regions of the world, but most prevalent in North American and European countries (140 and 108 per 100,000, respectively). It is also three times as likely to occur in women as in men (Jobin, Larochelle, Parpal, Coyle, & Duquette, 2010).

Although the resulting sensorimotor symptoms may significantly interfere with daily functioning, cognitive impairment is often considered as the most critical factor to affect functional adaptation (Goverover, Genova, Hillary, & DeLuca, 2007; Kalmar, Gaudino, Moore, Halper, & DeLuca, 2008), especially in regard to working status (Amato, Ponziani, Siracusa,

& Sorbi, 2001; Morrow et al., 2010; Rao, Leo, Ellington, et al., 1991). This is a major problem as cognitive disorders are commonly observed in MS, with a prevalence varying between 43 and 70% depending on the studies (Amato, Zipoli, & Portaccio, 2006; Chiaravalloti & DeLuca, 2008; DeSousa, Albert, & Kalman, 2002; Rao, Leo, Bernardin, & Unverzagt, 1991). While an isolated cognitive impairment is rarely the first manifestation of MS (Goverover, Johnston, Toglia, & DeLuca, 2007), cognitive deficits may appear in the earliest stages of the disease and worsen as it evolves (Amato et al., 2006; Bobholz & Rao, 2003).

Previous reports have indicated that the degree of cognitive impairment varies according to the MS subtype, with the secondary progressive form displaying greater cognitive deficits in comparison to the relapsing-remitting form (Brochet, Bonnet, Deloire, Hamel, & Salort-Campana, 2007; Chiaravalloti & DeLuca, 2008; Ferreira, 2010; Gaudino, Chiaravalloti, DeLuca, & Diamond, 2001; Huijbregts, Kalkers, de Sonneville, de Groot, & Polman, 2006). It does also vary from one patient to another, consistent with the heterogeneity observed in the location and number of white matter and gray matter CNS lesions (Calabrese et al., 2015) as well as other factors, including genetic background, neuropsychiatric comorbidities, and premorbid intellectual level. (Benedict & Zivadinov, 2011). Nonetheless, certain cognitive domains seem to be most commonly affected than others (Chiaravalloti & DeLuca, 2008; Goverover, Johnston, et al., 2007), namely episodic memory, working memory, information processing speed, attention (especially sustained and divided), executive functions (problem solving, planning, strategy application, etc.), and visuospatial skills (Edgar et al., 2011; Thornton & Raz, 1997; Winkelmann, Engel, Apel, & Zettl, 2007). Difficulties in social cognition have also been recently reported (Chalah & Ayache, 2017; Henry et al., 2011; Ouellet et al., 2010).

Episodic memory is one of the most frequently and consistently impaired cognitive functions in MS. A majority of the early literature has focused on retrospective episodic memory (RM), namely the ability to acquire new information and to recall it on demand, either immediately, or after a delay. While, for some authors, the primary deficit in MS is in the initial acquisition of information (DeLuca, Barbieri-Berger, & Johnson, 1994; DeLuca, Gaudino, Diamond, Christodoulou, & Engel, 1998), some consider that retrieval is also defective (Brochet et al., 2007; Ferreira, 2010; Sicotte et al., 2008), which is consistent with the significant advantage of recognition over free recall reported in a number of studies in MS (Muller et al., 2013). Along with an altered ability to learn new information, MS patients often complain of lapses in prospective memory (PM), defined as a difficulty remembering to do what they intended to do, such as forgetting to return a phone call or missing an appointment. PM impairment is known to have a detrimental impact on functional autonomy (Pirogovsky, Woods, Filoteo, & Gilbert, 2012; Woods, Weinborn, Velnoweth, Rooney, & Bucks, 2012). Indeed, in everyday life, failure to execute a planned action (or intention) at the right moment may have dramatic consequences on security (e.g. forgetting to turn off the oven) and health (e.g. forgetting to take medication) as well as it may compromise professional and social activities (e.g. forgetting to call back a friend). PM deficits are perceived by caregivers to be of greater burden than RM deficits (Smith, Del Sala, Logie, & Maylor, 2000).

This paper presents a review of the literature concerning the assessment and remediation of PM deficits in MS. For this purpose, the literature pertaining to PM impairment in MS was carefully reviewed using PubMed, PsyINFO, and Google Scholar, as well as cross-references from the articles published on this topic.

An isolated PM deficit has been reported in only one MS patient (West, McNerney, & Krauss, 2007). PM is a complex function that may be compromised by attention, working memory, retrospective memory, and executive dysfunctions, all commonly observed in MS. Despite the fact that PM and RM both involve encoding, storing, and retrieving information (i.e. an intention in the case of PM), PM differs from RM on several aspects: it involves a delay between the formation of the intention and the realization of the PM action, during which an ongoing task must be interrupted at the right moment to allow the completion of the prospective action. This moment can be expressed in terms of time (time-based [TB]: to go to the office in one hour or at 4 pm, for example) or in terms of a cue (or an event) occurring in the environment (event-based [EB]: get a bread when passing by the bakery, for example). TB tasks are generally considered as more difficult than EB tasks due to the level of self-monitoring required. However, it is possible to modulate the level of difficulty of EB tasks in many ways, such as varying the salience of the cue (highly salient cues are easier to detect than less salient cues), the strength of association between the cue and the action (strong cue–action associations lead to better performances than weak associations), or how the cue is processed (focal cues, which are processed as part of the ongoing task, are better detected that peripheral cues). Once the correct moment is identified (which corresponds to the *prospective component* [PC] of the PM task), the intended prospective action must be recalled and performed (which corresponds to the *retrospective component* [RC] of the PM task). According to the Multiprocess Theory (McDaniel & Einstein, 2000), two distinct processes, operating in parallel, may be involved in the recovery of an intention, depending on the conditions in which cue detection (EB or TB) and intention retrieval take place: (1) a strategic process, more cognitively demanding, albeit more efficient in detecting low salient cues and during engaging ongoing tasks (high absorption) or (2) an automatic process, less cognitively demanding, and particularly solicited during salient and focal cue detection and when cue and action are highly associated. Finally, a PM task may be performed only once, such as picking up a friend at the airport, or habitually (i.e. the same task must be performed repeatedly, such as taking medication). According to McDaniel, Bugg, Ramuschkat, Kliegel, and Einstein (2009), output monitoring (recognition that the action has been executed) is crucial in habitual PM tasks. Repetition errors are frequent in this type of task, probably because repeated actions are not as distinctive as are single-occurrence PM tasks. To our knowledge, no MRI or fMRI studies on PM have been performed with MS patients. According to a recent meta-analysis on the neural substrate of PM (Cona, Scarpazza, Sartori, Moscovitch, & Bisiacchi, 2015), encoding and retrieval of the intention were associated with recruitment of regions involved in retrospective memory (i.e. temporal cortex, insula, anterior and posterior cingulate cortex), whereas cue detection and intention retrieval were associated with regions involved in executive functioning (i.e. anterior prefrontal cortex, frontoparietal networks).

Despite frequent complaints from individuals failing to execute delayed intentions in everyday life, PM is not, or at the very least, rarely included in traditional neuropsychological assessments. Until recently, this was presumably due to the absence of standardized and commercially available tests aimed at specifically evaluating PM in clinical practice, such as the Memory for Intentions Test (MIST) (Raskin, 2009; Woods et al., 2008), the Cambridge Prospective Memory Test (CAMPROMPT) (Wilson, 2005), or the Rivermead Behavioral Memory Test (RBMT) (Wilson & Baddeley, 1985), which contains three PM items (i.e. the belonging, the delayed message delivery, and the appointment). In spite of their availability, clinicians remain reluctant to include new standardized PM tests in their routine evaluation due to the additional testing time required and, more importantly, to the lack of reference data from patients with diverse neuropsychological conditions needed for the clinical

Table 1. Main findings of clinical and experimental studies of prospective memory in multiple sclerosis.

Reference	Demographic data	PM measure	Findings
McIntosh-Michaelis et al. (1991)	147 MS 48y (21–80y) 34 Controls with rheumatoid arthritis 55y (33–79)	*RBMT*: 'belonging' test item only	• No significant difference found in failure rate between MS patients (57%) and patients with rheumatoid arthritis (44%)
Haupts et al. (1994)	35 MS 35.9y (21–61y) 13M/22F 30 NC 35.3y (24–55y) 11M/19F	*RBMT*: complete test including PM items (belonging, appointment and message)	• In comparison to NC, all RBMT scores (except 'recognizing objects' subtests) were significantly lower in MS patients, especially in those presenting a chronic-progressive form of the disease
Honan et al. (2015)	111 MS patients (2 groups : employed versus unemployed) 47.25y 33M/78F (RRMS: 74; SPMS: 23; PPMS: 8 other: 6)	*CAMPROMPT*: 3 TB/3 EB tasks	• Significantly lower total PM score observed in the unemployed MS patients • PM difficulties perceived at work related to reduced working hours and unemployment, independently from the score obtained on the CAMPROMPT
Miller et al. (2014)	96 MS 45.5y ±10.5y 21M/75F (RRMS; 62; SPMS: 2; PPMS: 2; PRMS: 2; uncertain: 20) 29 NC 38.9y ±12.2y 10M/19F matched for education	*MIST*: 8 PM tasks, varying in time interval between intention formation and action recall (2 or 15 min), type of task (TB and EB) and required action to perform (verbal or physical intention)	• MS patients performed significantly lower than NC (especially for the total score, the 15-min TB, the composite TB and items requiring a verbal response) • MS patients' performance on the MIST was highly correlated with physical pain severity suggesting that pain has a detrimental effect on PM in MS patients
Bruce et al. (2010)	55 MS 43.36y ±8.43y (6 M/49F)	*MIST*	• MS patients with adequate/good adherence performed significantly better than MS patients with variable/poor adherence
Bravin et al. (2000)	40 MS 45.75y (28–69y) 17M/23F 36 NC (14M/22F) matched for age and education	*Pulse task*: TB task (delay 60 min) *Clerical task*: TB task (delay 5 min) Separate analyses for RC and PC	• MS patients had more difficulty executing both tasks than NC • Pulse task RC was the only variable to reach significance between the groups (probably reflects the deleterious effect of the passage of time)
Rendell et al. (2007)	20 MS 42.9y ±8.87y (4M/16F) (RRMS: 18; PPMS: 2) 20 NC (5M/15F) matched for age and education	*Virtual Week*: board game in which participants perform various PM tasks (TB or EB)	• MS patient are significantly impaired in PM task irrespective of task demands (TB and EB, regular and irregular, focal and non-focal) • PM deficits cannot be attributed to retrospective memory problems • The PC is particularly affected in MS patients
Rendell et al. (2012)	30 MS 47y ±9.46y (6M/24F) 30 NC (6M/24F) matched for age and education	*Virtual Week* with the addition of an emotional content	• MS patients performed worse than the NC group across all three types of PM tasks but Group X Condition interaction was not significant. • MS patients' performance was better in EB tasks of positive valence than in EB tasks with negative valence. • No significant effect of valence was observed in TB tasks.
Kardiasmenos et al. (2008)	24 MS 42.8y ±9.3y (13M/11F) (RRMS: 18; SPMS: 6) 24 NC (12M/12F) matched for age and education	*Virtual Week*: adapted form to investigate PC and RC individually as well as the effect of *implementation intention* mnemonic strategy	• MS group performed worse on both PC and RC, especially when the task involved resource-demanding cognitive processes (weak cue–action association) than when automatic retrieval processes were solicited (strong cue–action association). • Only the PC deficit was shown to benefit from an *implementation intention* strategy.

Dagenais et al. (2016a)	39 MS patients 45y ±11.21y (8M/31F) (RRMS: 27; SPMS: 5; PPMS: 5; CIS: 2) 18 NC (6M/12F) matched for age and education	*Cue–action association*: word target cue detection during a lexical decision task and proper execution associated action for each word target cue (two related cue–action, two unrelated cue–action)	• Low-executive MS patients had more difficulty detecting and retrieving the PM action when cue and action were unrelated. • High-executive MS patients' performance was unaffected by cue–action association.
Dagenais et al. (2016b)	39 MS patients 45y ±11.21y (8M/31F) (RRMS: 27; SPMS: 5; PPMS: 5; CIS: 2) 18 NC (6M/12F) matched for age and education	*Cue salience*: low versus high salient PM cues embedded in a general knowledge trivia quiz	• MS patients performed worse that NC regardless of cue salience. • In low-executive patients, high cue salience improved PM performance.

Notes: MS: multiple sclerosis; NC: normal controls; RRMS: relapsing-remitting MS; SPMS: secondary-progressive MS; PRMS: progressive relapsing MS; PPMS: primary-progressive MS: CIS: clinically isolated syndrome. PM: prospective memory; TB: time-based; EB: event-based; PC: prospective component; RC: retrospective component. MIST: Memory for Intentions Test; CAMPROMPT: Cambridge Prospective Memory Test; RBMT: Rivermead Behavioral Memory Test.

interpretation of results. In that regard, it is important to mention that while the clinical significance of PM deficits is recognized, it is only in the last 10–15 years that systematic PM studies with various neurological pathologies have been published (Raskin, Buckheit, & Waxman, 2012), including traumatic brain injury (Henry et al., 2007; Potvin, Rouleau, Audy, Charbonneau, & Giguère, 2011), HIV (Doyle et al., 2015), Parkinson's disease (Durand et al., 2004, Fisk et al., 1994; Pirogovsky et al., 2012), Alzheimer's disease (Maylor, Smith, Sala, & Logie, 2002), as well as in individuals with mild cognitive impairment (Costa, Caltagirone, & Carlesimo, 2011; van den Berg, Kant, & Postma, 2012). Despite this growing interest, studies on PM in MS remain scarce.

Questionnaires

The first study on PM in MS was based on a self-administered questionnaire. In their large sample of MS patients (1180 patients aged 17–84 years, 11.3 years mean duration of illness), Sullivan, Edgley, and Dehoux (1990) reported that 18% of patients complained of PM difficulties in their daily lives compared to 23% who complained of RM difficulties. Most patients reported using external memory aids (i.e. agenda, notepad) to compensate for their forgetfulness. In a second study, Demers et al. (2011) administered the Prospective and Retrospective Memory Questionnaire (PRMQ) (Smith et al., 2000) and found that MS patients reported more PM errors than healthy controls; this was more evident in patients with mild cognitive impairment than in those with moderate to severe cognitive impairment. Moreover, the Beck Depression Inventory was significantly correlated to the PM index of the PRMQ, suggesting that depression can influence the subjective estimation of PM difficulties and/or contribute to their presence (Honan, Brown, & Batchelor, 2015). In a third most recent publication (Hughes et al., 2017), MS patients answered the Perceived Deficits Questionnaire (Marrie, Miller, Chelune, & Cohen, 2003), containing a few items on PM, in order to explore the speculated relation between sleep quality and cognitive impairment. Results indicated that a subjective poor rating of sleep quality was related to PM complaints, but not to objective cognitive deficits. While they do reveal interesting clinical information and are easy to administer, self-reported questionnaires remain of limited value when searching to identify the specific cognitive mechanisms underlying PM impairment in MS. In addition, while these questionnaires certainly reveal how the patient subjectively evaluates his cognition, they may not constitute a reliable measure of objective cognitive functioning. The same limitation applies to the Multiple Sclerosis Screening Questionnaire (MSNQ), a commonly used self-reported questionnaire. In a recent study, Dagenais et al. (2013) reported that MS patients (MSNQ-patient version) were less accurate than their informant (MSNQ-informant version) in estimating their objective cognitive functioning as assessed by a comprehensive neuropsychological test battery.

Clinical evaluation with standardized tests

Few studies on MS have assessed PM by means of standardized tasks in a clinical setting (Table 1). McIntosh-Michaelis et al. (1991) were the first to do so in comparing MS patients to rheumatoid arthritis patients (considered as a control group) on the 'belonging' PM items of the RBMT (Wilson & Baddeley, 1985). This task requires an action response from the participant who is asked to claim at the end of the evaluation session a personal object that has been temporarily given to the examiner at the beginning of the session. Results revealed that 44% of patients with rheumatoid arthritis and 57% of those with MS failed to execute the action response, a difference that was insignificant. However, it is worth mentioning that pain and fatigue, often associated to rheumatoid arthritis, might explain the high percentage of PM deficits in their 'control' group. Years later, (Haupts, Calabrese, Babinsky, Markowitsch, & Gehlen, 1994) replicated the previous study's procedure and reported that all RBMT scores (except 'recognizing objects' subtests) were significantly lower in MS patients in comparison to healthy controls, especially in those presenting a chronic-progressive form of the disease.

To our knowledge, only one study has been published on MS (Honan et al., 2015) using the CAMPROMPT (Wilson, 2005). In this test, the participant must perform a series of PM tasks, including three TB and three EB, while busy completing paper-and-pencil puzzles and quizzes. He is also allowed to take notes to help him remember the PM tasks. Honan et al. (2015) reported a significant difference in the total score between employed and unemployed MS patients. They also found that PM difficulties perceived at work were related to reduced working hours and unemployment, independent of the score obtained on the CAMPROMPT.

The MIST (Raskin, 2009) was used in two MS studies. This standardized test contains eight PM tasks, varying in time interval between intention formation and action recall (2 or 15 min), type of task (TB and EB), and required action to perform (verbal or physical intention). Miller, Basso, Candilis, Combs, and Woods (2014) compared MIST scores of 96 MS patients to 29 healthy controls and, as expected, found that the former performed significantly lower. Some subtests were more affected than others, particularly the total score, the 15-min TB, the composite TB, and items requiring a verbal response. The authors further observed that patients' performance on the MIST was highly correlated with the severity of physical pain reported in the Medical Outcomes Study Pain Effects Scale, suggesting that pain affects the ability to remember new intentions and has a detrimental effect on PM in MS patients. The MIST was also used in another study that examined treatment adherence in MS (Bruce, Hancock, Arnett, & Lynch, 2010). Significant differences were found between patients with adequate/good adherence versus patients with variable/poor adherence. The latter also performed worse on a delayed recall of a word list. Many factors may contribute to poor treatment adherence in MS (anxiety, depression, reduced consciousness, etc.); however, these results suggest that a careful evaluation of PM functioning in MS patients could help in understanding one aspect of treatment adherence and in selecting appropriate intervention.

To date, PM screening tools like the envelope test (Huppert, Johnson, & Nickson, 2000; Marcone et al., 2017) have not been administered to a large sample of MS patients. Due to its known low sensitivity to MCI, especially to non-amnestic MCI, the envelope test is probably not a useful tool to screen for PM deficits in MS. Further research is required to develop a PM screening tool that could be sensitive enough for MS patients.

Laboratory measures

Although standardized PM tests are now available and are expected to be increasingly used in clinical settings, laboratory measures are still needed to explore the various variables that influence PM performance, such as the characteristics of the cue, the intention, and the ongoing activity as well as to investigate the underlying mechanisms contribution to PM impairment in MS.

To our knowledge, Bravin, Kinsella, Ong, and Vowels (2000) were the first to report a laboratory study of PM in MS (Table 1). In an effort to examine the prospective (PC) and the retrospective (RC) components separately, they designed two TB naturalistic PM tasks, namely (1) the *Pulse Task* where the participant was asked to remind the examiner to re-measure his/her pulse one hour later (±5 min) and (2) the *Clerical Task* where the participant needed to interrupt oneself five minutes (±10 s) following the beginning of a clerical task in order to write his/her name anywhere on the bottom of the page. Overall, patients with MS had more difficulty executing both tasks than healthy controls. On the *Pulse Task*, however, groups differed only on the RC, not the PC. In other words, both MS patients and healthy control participants remembered they had something to do (PC) but only MS patients failed to remember what that was (RC). On the *Clerical Task*, the difference in the proportion of subjects who failed the task didn't reach significance, probably due to a lack of statistical power (MS: 57.9% vs. controls: 37.9%). Unexpectedly, participants were more likely to fail on the PC or the RC than to fail both components. The fact that the *Pulse Task* RC was the only score to reach statistical significance probably reflects the deleterious effect of the passage of time on the retention of the planned action, a finding consistent with the significant correlation that was reported in MS patients between success on the *Pulse Task* and delayed recall measure on the Rey Auditory Verbal Learning Test, a word list learning test.

To date, the task that has been most frequently used to assess PM in MS is the *Virtual Week*, a task initially developed by Rendell and Craik (2000) for an aging population. Since then, it has gained popularity in the research community and has been used in numerous neurological and psychiatric conditions, such as Parkinson's disease, traumatic brain injury, autism, and schizophrenia. *Virtual Week* is a board game where various prospective actions (TB, EB, regular and irregular), similar to everyday life demands, must be carried out. In a first study, Rendell, Jensen, and Henry (2007) compared the performance of 20 MS patients (relapsing-remitting or secondary progressive) to 20 healthy controls. An overall PM deficit was observed in MS, regardless of the type of prospective task (TB or EB). The observed deficit was not due to RM impairment since MS patients performed comparably to healthy controls (matched on age and education) on measures of word list learning and delayed recall. The PC (remembering that something had to be done in irregular conditions) was particularly affected in MS patients, a finding that was contrary to Bravin et al. (2000) who reported more difficulties with the RC in the *Pulse Task* in their MS sample. The difference between both studies might be due to the number of PM actions to perform (higher in the *Virtual Week*), and to the delay between intention formation and intention execution (longer in the *Pulse Task*).

In their second study, Rendell et al. (2012) once again assessed PM in MS with the *Virtual Week* and particularly examined the effect of emotional valence on PM performance based on the fact that a number of previous studies had shown that emotional valence modulated RM. Overall, MS patients performed worse than the healthy control group, irrespective of the type of PM tasks (regular or irregular, TB or EB). However, none of the group X condition interactions were significant, suggesting that the experimental manipulation equally affected participants. As observed in healthy controls, MS patients' performance was better in EB tasks of positive valence than on negative EB tasks. There was no effect of valence observed on TB tasks. According to Rendell et al. (2012), these results confirm the presence of PM deficits in MS, even in tasks that are not demanding on the strategic monitoring process, such as the regular EB tasks.

Through an adapted version of the *Virtual Week*, Kardiasmenos, Clawson, Wilken, and Wallin (2008) reported impairment on both PM components (PC and RC) in 24 MS patients (with relapsing-remitting and secondary progressive subtypes) and 24 healthy controls. They additionally observed that difficulties on both components were more pronounced when the task involved resource-demanding cognitive processes (in the case of a weak associative strength between the cue and action) than when automatic retrieval processes were solicited due to the strong associative link between cue and action. They also showed that the PC deficit could be reduced by using an *implementation intention*, which refers to a mnemonic strategy based on planning ahead, when, where, and how the action will be performed and visualizing oneself performing the prospective action in the specified context. However, this strategy had no significant effect on the RC, suggesting that this technique selectively improves the detection of the cue without having any substantial benefit in helping remember the content of the action to perform.

Effects of the associative cue–action strength on PM performance in MS were more thoroughly investigated by Dagenais et al. (2016b). A sample of 39 MS patients was compared to 18 healthy controls on a lexical decision task where participants responded to four different cues (each presented twice) by performing one of four previously learnt corresponding actions (2 cue–action related, 2 cue–action unrelated). Consistent with previous findings (Kardiasmenos et al., 2008), deficits in both PC and RC of PM were confirmed in MS patients. In addition, while highly associated cues and actions improved intention retrieval (RC), this had almost no impact on cue detection (PC). These results are in line with what was previously mentioned regarding the effect of *implementation intention* (Kardiasmenos et al., 2008). Another key finding supporting this argument comes from multiple regression analyses, which revealed executive functioning to significantly modulate PM impairment, whereas RM seemed to have little impact on PM performance. In other words, low-executive functioning MS patients had more difficulty detecting and, especially, retrieving the appropriate action when the cue and the action were unrelated, whereas high-executive functioning MS patients' performance seemed to be virtually unaffected by the strength of the cue–action association.

To further explore MS patients' PM deficits, Dagenais et al. (2016a) used a laboratory task that manipulated cue salience adapted from McDaniel, Glisky, Guynn, and Routhieaux (1999). The task consisted of a general knowledge questionnaire presented on a computer screen. Cues (the word 'premier') randomly embedded in the questionnaire were either presented in lowercase (low salience: premier) or uppercase letters (high salience: PREMIER). As expected, MS patients performed worse than healthy controls on the PM task, regardless of cue salience. There was however a differential effect of cue salience on PM performance between low and high executive functioning MS patients: low-executive functioning MS patients benefitted more from high salient cues than high-executive functioning patients. There was no effect of RM functioning on PM performance. Observations seem to suggest that high cue salience improves PM performance in low-executive functioning MS patients by reducing the detection threshold as well as the need for environmental monitoring.

PM intervention in MS

Despite the growing interest regarding PM intervention among various neurological and psychiatric populations and the recent recognition of PM deficits in MS, no study to date has directly addressed PM intervention in MS. In their recent review on cognitive intervention in people with MS, das Nair, Martin, and Lincoln (2016) identified a couple of studies that have used the RBMT (Wilson & Baddeley, 1985), containing a few PM items, but as their cognitive intervention programs were not specifically designed at improving PM, their results on these items were not presented separately (Chiaravalloti, Moore, Nikelshpur, & DeLuca, 2013; das Nair & Lincoln, 2012).

While not directly targeting PM, a number of recent exhaustive reviews on cognitive intervention in MS have been published (das Nair et al., 2016; Hämäläinen & Rosti-Otajärvi, 2016; Mitolo, Venneri, Wilkinson, & Sharrack, 2015), including studies using various neuroimaging techniques (fMRI and resting state functional connectivity) to explore the effect of cognitive remediation in MS patients (Chiaravalloti, Genova, & DeLuca, 2015). Since PM is a complex function involving attention, memory and executive functions, cognitive remediation programs targeting any of these domains could potentially improve PM functioning in MS patients. For instance, training divided attention abilities could improve the capacity to respond to a PM cue while performing a concurrent task. Similarly, PM could benefit from a program aimed at providing various strategies to strengthen encoding mechanisms that may in turn enhance PM cue detection and intention retrieval. However, as mentioned in these reviews, many studies (that were excluded from these reviews) contain a number of methodological flaws rendering their conclusions questionable. One of the main issues concerns the absence of an active control group (as opposed to a waiting list). This is obviously not specific to research on MS, but some researchers have made specific recommendations as to the basic criteria to be met in order to ensure the scientific validity of studies on cognitive remediation (Piras, Borella, Incoccia, & Carlesimo, 2011).

Even if the MS population has been neglected by the literature, PM rehabilitation has been the focus of many studies of other clinical populations, such as Alzheimer's disease (Kinsella, Ong, Storey, Wallace, & Hester, 2007), Parkinson's disease (Costa, Carlesimo, & Caltagirone, 2012), individuals with mild cognitive impairment (Costa et al., 2011), and traumatic brain injury (Raskin, Smith, Mills, Pedro, & Zamroziewicz, 2017; Raskin & Sohlberg, 2009). Drawing from the similarities observed in TBI and MS neuropsychological profiles (O'brien, Chiaravalloti, Carlos Arango-Lasprilla, Lengenfelder, & Deluca, 2007), cognitive rehabilitation programs developed for TBI patients appear particularly relevant to an MS population. For example, some programs use external aids, such as paper or electronic diaries and notepads (Fleming, Shum, Strong, & Lightbody, 2005; Sohlberg, 2005; Van den Broek, Downes, Johnson, Dayus, & Hilton, 2000); however, these techniques remain inflexible and are not always on-hand when an intention is formed and needs to be performed. Flexible methods, like the use of visual imagery to reinforce the link between the cue and the prospective action, have been previously proven as effective (Potvin et al., 2011; Raskin et al., 2017) and could certainly be appropriate for the PM rehabilitation in people with MS, given the nature of their cognitive deficits.

In conclusion, PM deficits are frequent in people living with MS and significantly interfere with professional, personal, and social functioning. An objective assessment, through the use of newly available standardized PM measures, is encouraged since subjective reports by means of self-administered questionnaires may be influenced by the patient's depression and cognitive status (Demers et al., 2011). This, however, isn't a reason to disregard subjective estimation of PM functioning. On the contrary, both should be administered to get a clear view of the nature of PM impairment and to decide whether cognitive rehabilitation is appropriate, if available. In most cases, psychoeducation is sufficient to help the patient understand PM functioning and the strategies that can be adopted to improve its efficiency in daily life. By helping the patient to better encode new information and to organize and plan his activities in advance, strategies may increase the control one has over his life, which in turn positively affects the subjective appraisal of difficulties. Duly note, however, that psychoeducation may not suffice for some patients. It is in these cases that cognitive rehabilitation is preferred. While the use of standardized PM tests is valuable for the latter, it is often necessary to perform a more extensive PM assessment in order to specifically identify the underlying mechanisms contributing to their PM deficit (e.g. impairment in intention formation? in intention retention over time? in the strategic monitoring necessary for cue detection? etc.) and the effect of various parameters (such as varying cue salience, or increasing the strength of the cue–action association by visual imagery, etc.) on PM task performances. Data obtained will be invaluable to help tailor the rehabilitation intervention to each patient and to maximize its long-term effect, which is essential given the time and energy invested for its implementation.

Acknowledgments

We would like to thank Sonia Marcone and Peter Scherzer for their linguistic revision of the manuscript.

Disclosure statement

The authors report no conflicts of interest.

References

Amato, M. P., Ponziani, G., Siracusa, G., & Sorbi, S. (2001). Cognitive dysfunction in early-onset multiple sclerosis: A reappraisal after 10 years. *Archives of Neurology, 58*, 1602–1606.

Amato, M. P., Zipoli, V., & Portaccio, E. (2006). Multiple sclerosis-related cognitive changes: A review of cross-sectional and longitudinal studies. *Journal of the Neurological Sciences, 245*, 41–46. doi:10.1016/j.jns.2005.08.019

Benedict, R. H., & Zivadinov, R. (2011). Risk factors for and management of cognitive dysfunction in multiple sclerosis. *Nature Reviews Neurology, 7*, 332–342.

Bobholz, J. A., & Rao, S. M. (2003). Cognitive dysfunction in multiple sclerosis: A review of recent developments. *Current Opinion in Neurology, 16*, 283–288.

Bravin, J. H., Kinsella, G. J., Ong, B., & Vowels, L. (2000). A study of performance of delayed intentions in multiple sclerosis. *Journal of Clinical and Experimental Neuropsychology, 22*, 418–429.

Brochet, B., Bonnet, M., Deloire, M., Hamel, D., & Salort-Campana, E. (2007). Les troubles cognitifs au cours de la sclérose en plaques [Cognitive disorders in multiple sclerosis]. *Revue Neurologique, 163*, 697–702.

Bruce, J. M., Hancock, L. M., Arnett, P., & Lynch, S. (2010). Treatment adherence in multiple sclerosis: Association with emotional status, personality, and cognition. *Journal of Behavioral Medicine, 33*, 219–227.

Calabrese, M., Magliozzi, R., Ciccarelli, O., Geurts, J. J., Reynolds, R., & Martin, R. (2015). Exploring the origins of grey matter damage in multiple sclerosis. *Nature Reviews Neuroscience, 16*, 147–158.

Chalah, M. A., & Ayache, S. S. (2017). Deficits in social cognition: An unveiled signature of multiple sclerosis. *Journal of the International Neuropsychological Society, 23*, 266–286.

Chiaravalloti, N. D., & DeLuca, J. (2008). Cognitive impairment in multiple sclerosis. *The Lancet Neurology, 7*, 1139–1151.

Chiaravalloti, N. D., Genova, H. M., & DeLuca, J. (2015). Cognitive rehabilitation in multiple sclerosis: The role of plasticity. *Frontiers in Neurology, 6*. Article 67. doi:10.3389/fneur.2015.00067.

Chiaravalloti, N. D., Moore, N. B., Nikelshpur, O. M., & DeLuca, J. (2013). An RCT to treat learning impairment in multiple sclerosis The MEMREHAB trial. *Neurology, 81*, 2066–2072.

Cona, G., Scarpazza, C., Sartori, G., Moscovitch, M., & Bisiacchi, P. S. (2015). Neural bases of prospective memory: A meta-analysis and the "Attention to Delayed Intention"(AtoDI) model. *Neuroscience & Biobehavioral Reviews, 52*, 21–37.

Costa, A., Caltagirone, C., & Carlesimo, G. A. (2011). Prospective memory impairment in mild cognitive impairment: An analytical review. *Neuropsychology Review, 21*, 390–404.

Costa, A., Carlesimo, G. A., & Caltagirone, C. (2012). Prospective memory functioning: a new area of investigation in the clinical neuropsychology and rehabilitation of Parkinson's disease and mild cognitive impairment. Review of evidence. *Neurological Sciences, 33*, 965–972.

Dagenais, E., Rouleau, I., Demers, M., Jobin, C., Roger, É., Chamelian, L., & Duquette, P. (2013). Value of the MoCA test as a screening instrument in multiple sclerosis. *The Canadian Journal of Neurological Sciences, 40*, 410–415.

Dagenais, E., Rouleau, I., Tremblay, A., Demers, M., Roger, É., Jobin, C., & Duquette, P. (2016a). Prospective memory in multiple sclerosis: The impact of cue distinctiveness and executive functioning. *Brain and Cognition, 109*, 66–74.

Dagenais, E., Rouleau, I., Tremblay, A., Demers, M., Roger, É., Jobin, C., & Duquette, P. (2016b). Role of executive functions in prospective memory in multiple sclerosis: Impact of the strength of cue–action association. *Journal of Clinical and Experimental Neuropsychology, 38*, 127–140.

das Nair, R., & Lincoln, N. B. (2012). Evaluation of rehabilitation of memory in neurological disabilities (ReMiND): a randomized controlled trial. *Clinical Rehabilitation, 26*, 894–903.

das Nair, R., Martin, K. J., & Lincoln, N. B. (2016). Memory rehabilitation for people with multiple sclerosis. *Cochrane Database of Systematic Reviews* 2016. Article no. CD008754. doi:10.1002/14651858.CD008754.pub3.

DeLuca, J., Barbieri-Berger, S., & Johnson, S. K. (1994). The nature of memory impairments in multiple sclerosis: Acquisition versus retrieval. *Journal of Clinical and Experimental Neuropsychology, 16*, 183–189.

DeLuca, J., Gaudino, E. A., Diamond, B. J., Christodoulou, C., & Engel, R. A. (1998). Acquisition and storage deficits in multiple sclerosis. *Journal of Clinical and Experimental Neuropsychology, 20*, 376–390.

Demers, M., Rouleau, I., Scherze, P., Ouellet, J., Jobin, C., & Duquette, P. (2011). Impact of the cognitive status on the memory complaints in MS patients. *Canadian Journal of Neurological Sciences/Journal Canadien des Sciences Neurologiques, 38*, 728–733.

DeSousa, E. A., Albert, R. H., & Kalman, B. (2002). Cognitive impairments in multiple sclerosis: A review. *American Journal of Alzheimer's Disease and Other Dementias, 17*, 23–29.

Doyle, K. L., Weber, E., Morgan, E. E., Loft, S., Cushman, C., Villalobos, J., … Woods, S. P. (2015). Habitual prospective memory in HIV disease. *Neuropsychology, 29*, 909–918.

Durand, M.-J., Vachon, B., Hong, Q. N., Imbeau, D., Amick, B. C., III, & Loisel, P. (2004). The cross-cultural adaptation of the work role functioning questionnaire in Canadian French. *International Journal of Rehabilitation Research, 27*, 261–268.

Edgar, C., Jongen, P. J., Sanders, E., Sindic, C., Goffette, S., Dupuis, M., … Wesnes, K. (2011). Cognitive performance in relapsing remitting multiple sclerosis: a longitudinal study in daily practice using a brief computerized cognitive battery. *BMC Neurology, 11*, 68.

Ferreira, M. L. B. (2010). Cognitive deficits in multiple sclerosis: A systematic review. *Arquivos de Neuro-Psiquiatria, 68*, 632–641.

Fisk, J. D., Ritvo, P. G., Ross, L., Haase, D. A., Marrie, T. J., & Schlech, W. F. (1994). Measuring the functional impact of fatigue: initial validation of the fatigue impact scale. *Clinical Infectious Diseases, 18*(Suppl. 1), S79–S83.

Fleming, J. M., Shum, D., Strong, J., & Lightbody, S. (2005). Prospective memory rehabilitation for adults with traumatic brain injury: A compensatory training programme. *Brain Injury, 19*(1), 1–10.

Gaudino, E. A., Chiaravalloti, N. D., DeLuca, J., & Diamond, B. J. (2001). A comparison of memory performance in relapsing–remitting, primary progressive and secondary progressive, multiple sclerosis. *Cognitive and Behavioral Neurology, 14*, 32–44.

Goverover, Y., Genova, H. M., Hillary, F. G., & DeLuca, J. (2007). The relationship between neuropsychological measures and the timed instrumental activities of daily living task in multiple sclerosis. *Multiple Sclerosis Journal, 13*, 636–644.

Goverover, Y., Johnston, M. V., Toglia, J., & DeLuca, J. (2007). Treatment to improve self-awareness in persons with acquired brain injury. *Brain Injury, 21*, 913–923.

Hämäläinen, P., & Rosti-Otajärvi, E. (2016). Cognitive impairment in MS: Rehabilitation approaches. *Acta Neurologica Scandinavica, 134*(S200), 8–13.

Haupts, M., Calabrese, P., Babinsky, R., Markowitsch, H., & Gehlen, W. (1994). Everyday memory impairment, neuroradiological findings and physical disability in multiple sclerosis. *European Journal of Neurology, 1*, 159–163.

Henry, J. D., Phillips, L. H., Crawford, J. R., Kliegel, M., Theodorou, G., & Summers, F. (2007). Traumatic brain injury and prospective memory: Influence of task complexity. *Journal of Clinical and Experimental Neuropsychology, 29*, 457–466.

Henry, A., Tourbah, A., Chaunu, M.-P., Rumbach, L., Montreuil, M., & Bakchine, S. (2011). Social cognition impairments in relapsing-remitting multiple sclerosis. *Journal of the International Neuropsychological Society, 17*, 1122–1131.

Honan, C. A., Brown, R. F., & Batchelor, J. (2015). Perceived cognitive difficulties and cognitive test performance as predictors of employment outcomes in people with multiple sclerosis. *Journal of the International Neuropsychological Society, 21*, 156–168.

Hughes, A. J., Parmenter, B. A., Haselkorn, J. K., Lovera, J. F., Bourdette, D., Boudreau, E., … Turner, A. P. (2017). Sleep and its associations with perceived and objective cognitive impairment in individuals with multiple sclerosis. *Journal of sleep research, 26*, 428–435.

Huijbregts, S. C., Kalkers, N. F., de Sonneville, L. M., de Groot, V., & Polman, C. H. (2006). Cognitive impairment and decline in different MS subtypes. *Journal of the Neurological Sciences, 245*, 187–194.

Huppert, F. A., Johnson, T., & Nickson, J. (2000). High prevalence of prospective memory impairment in the elderly and in early-stage dementia: Findings from a population-based study. *Applied cognitive psychology, 14*, S63–S81.

Jobin, C., Larochelle, C., Parpal, H., Coyle, P. K., & Duquette, P. (2010). Gender issues in multiple sclerosis: An update. *Women's Health, 6*, 797–820.

Kalmar, J. H., Gaudino, E. A., Moore, N. B., Halper, J., & DeLuca, J. (2008). The relationship between cognitive deficits and everyday functional activities in multiple sclerosis. *Neuropsychology, 22*, 442–449.

Kardiasmenos, K. S., Clawson, D. M., Wilken, J. A., & Wallin, M. T. (2008). Prospective memory and the efficacy of a memory strategy in multiple sclerosis. *Neuropsychology, 22*, 746–754.

Kinsella, G. J., Ong, B., Storey, E., Wallace, J., & Hester, R. (2007). Elaborated spaced-retrieval and prospective memory in mild Alzheimer's disease. *Neuropsychological Rehabilitation, 17*, 688–706.

Marcone, S., Gagnon, J.-F., Lecomte, S., Imbeault, H., Limoges, F., Postuma, R. B., … Rouleau, I. (2017). Clinical utility of the envelope task in mild cognitive impairment and dementia. *Canadian Journal of Neurological Sciences, 44*, 9–16.

Marrie, R. A., Miller, D. M., Chelune, G. J., & Cohen, J. A. (2003). Validity and reliability of the MSQ LI in cognitively impaired patients with multiple sclerosis. *Multiple Sclerosis Journal, 9*, 621–626.

Maylor, E. A., Smith, G., Sala, S. D., & Logie, R. H. (2002). Prospective and retrospective memory in normal aging and dementia: An experimental study. *Memory & Cognition, 30*, 871–884.

McDaniel, M. A., Bugg, J. M., Ramuschkat, G. M., Kliegel, M., & Einstein, G. O. (2009). Repetition errors in habitual prospective memory: Elimination of age differences via complex actions or appropriate resource allocation. *Aging, Neuropsychology, and Cognition, 16*, 563–588.

McDaniel, M. A., & Einstein, G. O. (2000). Strategic and automatic processes in prospective memory retrieval: A multiprocess framework. *Applied Cognitive Psychology, 14*, S127–S144.

McDaniel, M. A., Glisky, E. L., Guynn, M. J., & Routhieaux, B. C. (1999). Prospective memory: A neuropsychological study. *Neuropsychology, 13*, 103–110.

McIntosh-Michaelis, S., Roberts, M., Wilkinson, S., Diamond, I., McLellan, D., Martin, J., & Spackman, A. (1991). The prevalence of cognitive impairment in a community survey of multiple sclerosis. *British Journal of Clinical Psychology, 30*, 333–348.

Miller, A. K., Basso, M. R., Candilis, P. J., Combs, D. R., & Woods, S. P. (2014). Pain is associated with prospective memory dysfunction in multiple sclerosis. *Journal of Clinical and Experimental Neuropsychology, 36*, 887–896.

Mitolo, M., Venneri, A., Wilkinson, I. D., & Sharrack, B. (2015). Cognitive rehabilitation in multiple sclerosis: A systematic review. *Journal of the Neurological Sciences, 354*(1–2), 1–9.

Morrow, S. A., Drake, A., Zivadinov, R., Munschauer, F., Weinstock-Guttman, B., & Benedict, R. H. (2010). Predicting loss of employment over three years in multiple sclerosis: Clinically meaningful cognitive decline. *The Clinical Neuropsychologist, 24*, 1131–1145.

Muller S., Saur, R., Greve, B., Melms, A., Hautzinger, M., Fallgatter, A. J., & Leyhe, T. (2013). Recognition performance differentiates between elderly patients in the long term course of secondary progressive multiple sclerosis and amnestic mild cognitive impairment. *Multiple Sclerosis Journal, 19*, 799–805. doi:10.1177/1352458512461392

Multiple Sclerosis International Federation. (2016). *Who gets MS?* Retrieved from https://www.msif.org/research/epidemiology-of-ms/

O'brien, A., Chiaravalloti, N., Carlos Arango-Lasprilla, J., Lengenfelder, J., & Deluca, J. (2007). An investigation of the differential effect of self-generation to improve learning and memory in multiple sclerosis and traumatic brain injury. *Neuropsychological Rehabilitation, 17*, 273–292.

Ouellet, J., Scherzer, P. B., Rouleau, I., Metras, P., Bertrand-Gauvin, C., Djerroud, N., ... Duquette, P. (2010). Assessment of social cognition in patients with multiple sclerosis. *Journal of the International Neuropsychological Society, 16*, 287–296.

Piras, F., Borella, E., Incoccia, C., & Carlesimo, G. (2011). MINERVA MEDICA COPYRIGHT®. *European Journal of Physical and Rehabilitation Medicine, 47*, 149–175.

Pirogovsky, E., Woods, S. P., Filoteo, J. V., & Gilbert, P. E. (2012). Prospective memory deficits are associated with poorer everyday functioning in Parkinson's disease. *Journal of the International Neuropsychological Society, 18*, 986–995.

Potvin, M.-J., Rouleau, I., Audy, J., Charbonneau, S., & Giguère, J.-F. (2011). Ecological prospective memory assessment in patients with traumatic brain injury. *Brain Injury, 25*, 192–205.

Rao, S. M., Leo, G. J., Bernardin, L., & Unverzagt, F. (1991). Cognitive dysfunction in multiple sclerosis. I. Frequency, patterns, and prediction. *Neurology, 41*, 685–691.

Rao, S. M., Leo, G. J., Ellington, L., Nauertz, T., Bernardin, L., & Unverzagt, F. (1991). Cognitive dysfunction in multiple sclerosis. II. Impact on employment and social functioning. *Neurology, 41*, 692–696.

Raskin, S. A. (2009). Memory for intentions screening test: Psychometric properties and clinical evidence. *Brain Impairment, 10*, 23–33.

Raskin, S. A., Buckheit, C. A., & Waxman, A. (2012). Effect of type of cue, type of response, time delay and two different ongoing tasks on prospective memory functioning after acquired brain injury. *Neuropsychological Rehabilitation, 22*, 40–64.

Raskin, S. A., Smith, M. P., Mills, G., Pedro, C., & Zamroziewicz, M. (2017). Prospective memory intervention using visual imagery in individuals with brain injury. *Neuropsychological Rehabilitation,4*, 1–16.

Raskin, S. A., & Sohlberg, M. M. (2009). Prospective memory intervention: A review and evaluation of a pilot restorative intervention. *Brain Impairment, 10*, 76–86.

Rendell, P. G., & Craik, F. I. (2000). Virtual week and actual week: Age-related differences in prospective memory. *Applied Cognitive Psychology, 14*, S43–S62.

Rendell, P. G., Henry, J. D., Phillips, L. H., de la Piedad Garcia, X., Booth, P., Phillips, P., & Kliegel, M. (2012). Prospective memory, emotional valence, and multiple sclerosis. *Journal of Clinical and Experimental Neuropsychology, 34*, 738–749.

Rendell, P. G., Jensen, F., & Henry, J. D. (2007). Prospective memory in multiple sclerosis. *Journal of the International Neuropsychological Society, 13*, 410–416.

Sicotte, N., Kern, K., Giesser, B., Arshanapalli, A., Schultz, A., Montag, M., ... Bookheimer, S. (2008). Regional hippocampal atrophy in multiple sclerosis. *Brain, 131*, 1134–1141.

Smith, G., Del Sala, S., Logie, R. H., & Maylor, E. A. (2000). Prospective and retrospective memory in normal ageing and dementia: A questionnaire study. *Memory, 8*, 311–321.

Sohlberg, M. M. (2005). External aids for management of memory impairment. In Walter M. High Jr, Angelle M. Sander, Margaret A. Struchen, & Karen A. Hart (Eds.), *Rehabilitation for traumatic brain injury* (pp. 47–70). Oxford: Oxford University Press.

Sullivan, M. J., Edgley, K., & Dehoux, E. (1990). A survey of multiple sclerosis: I. Perceived cognitive problems and compensatory strategy use. *Canadian Journal of Rehabilitation, 4*, 99–105.

Thornton, A. E., & Raz, N. (1997). *Memory impairment in multiple sclerosis: A quantitative review.* Neuropsychology, *11*, 357–366.

van den Berg, E., Kant, N., & Postma, A. (2012). Remember to buy milk on the way home! A meta-analytic review of prospective memory in mild cognitive impairment and dementia. *Journal of the International Neuropsychological Society, 18*, 706–716.

Van den Broek, M., Downes, J., Johnson, Z., Dayus, B., & Hilton, N. (2000). Evaluation of an electronic memory aid in the neuropsychological rehabilitation of prospective memory deficits. *Brain Injury, 14*, 455–462.

West, R., McNerney, M. W., & Krauss, I. (2007). Impaired strategic monitoring as the locus of a focal prospective memory deficit. *Neurocase, 13*, 115–126.

Wilson, B. A. (2005). *The Cambridge Prospective Memory Test: CAMPROMPT*. London: Pearson Assessment.

Wilson, B. C. J., & Baddeley, A. (1985). *The Rivermead Behavioral Memory Test*. London: Pearson Assessment.

Winkelmann, A., Engel, C., Apel, A., & Zettl, U. K. (2007). Cognitive impairment in multiple sclerosis. *J Neurol, 254*, II35–II42.

Woods, S. P., Moran, L. M., Dawson, M. S., Carey, C. L., Grant, I., & The HIV Neurobehavioral Research Center (HNRC) Group (2008). Psychometric characteristics of the memory for intentions screening test. *The Clinical Neuropsychologist, 22*, 864–878.

Woods, S. P., Weinborn, M., Velnoweth, A., Rooney, A., & Bucks, R. S. (2012). Memory for intentions is uniquely associated with instrumental activities of daily living in healthy older adults. *Journal of the International Neuropsychological Society, 18*, 134–138.

Prospective memory functioning in individuals with Parkinson's disease: a systematic review

Alberto Costa, Carlo Caltagirone and Giovanni Augusto Carlesimo

ABSTRACT

Objective: There is growing interest in investigating prospective memory (PM) functioning in individuals with Parkinson's disease (PD) without dementia because evidence suggests that PM may be impaired in this clinical population. This paper reviews current literature on PM functioning in PD patients with the aim of discussing (i) the potential contribution of executive and episodic memory disorders to PM impairments, (ii) whether PM impairment is an independent disorder in PD or whether it is a sign of mild cognitive impairment (MCI) and (iii) the efficacy of cognitive interventions in treating PM disorders in these patients.

Method: A search of the relevant literature revealed 21 original research papers and five review/meta-analyses that directly investigated PM abilities in PD samples.

Results: Analysis of the reported data revealed that both executive functions and episodic memory are involved in the PM performance of patients with PD. Moreover, sparse evidence suggests that PM is not impaired in all PD patients but, rather, that PM deficits may be specifically associated with MCI. Finally, preliminary findings suggest that cognitive interventions may be effective in improving PM functioning in PD patients with MCI who present a well-established neuropsychological profile.

Conclusions: Although some shortcomings of the PM literature on PD patients prevent drawing firm conclusions, this review of current evidence highlights the importance of including PM assessment in the standard neuropsychological evaluation of patients with PD. Moreover, there are indications that ad hoc cognitive programs applied according to the qualitative cognitive profile of patients could improve their PM abilities.

Introduction

Parkinson's disease

Parkinson's disease (PD) is a neurodegenerative disease that primarily involves depletion of dopamine neurons of the substantia nigra with subsequent deafferentation of nigrostriatal pathways (Robbins & Cools, 2014). Thus, motor symptoms are the main clinical changes that lead to the medical diagnosis. However, in the last two decades data from both empirical research and clinical observations clearly indicate that individuals with PD suffer from subtle cognitive deficits (mainly concerning executive functions, episodic memory and visual-spatial domains) even in the early stages, and that they have a high risk of developing dementia (Aarsland et al., 2017; Dubois et al., 2007; Svenningsson, Westman, Ballard, & Aarsland, 2012). Recently, great attention has been given to the potential clinical usefulness of adopting the category of mild cognitive impairment (MCI) to frame the cognitive deficits that are observed in PD patients without dementia and, in fact, formal nosographic criteria have been proposed (Litvan et al., 2012). MCI refers to a condition characterized by the subjective decline of cognitive capacities (confirmed by poor performance on neuropsychological tests) that is not severe enough to interfere with daily living activities (see Table 1 for PD-MCI criteria of the Movement Disorders Society Task Force Guidelines; Litvan et al., 2012). Depending on the psychometric parameters used, MCI has been found to affect up to 42% of PD patients (Aarsland et al., 2010; Litvan et al., 2012; Yarnall et al., 2014). Moreover, some data indicate that MCI might represent the prodromal phase of dementia also in PD; indeed, PD patients with MCI have a greater risk of suffering from dementia than PD patients without MCI (Broeders et al., 2013; Janvin et al., 2006; Pedersen, Larsen, Tysnes, & Alves, 2013, 2017; Pigott et al., 2015; Santangelo et al., 2015).

Prospective memory

Prospective memory (PM) is the cognitive ability that enables individuals to form, maintain in memory and carry out delayed intentions at a certain time (*time-based PM*) or when a specific event occurs (*event-based PM*). In a prototypical PM experiment, participants are engaged in an attention-demanding ongoing activity; then, at the occurrence of the target event (event-based PM) or at the expiration of a predefined time (time-based PM) the subject has to perform one or more specified actions. According to Kliegel, Phillips, Lemke, and Kopp (2005), PM tasks are commonly articulated in four phases. In the first phase (i.e. *intention formation*), the subject has to form the intention, i.e. to plan which actions he has to perform in the future and then to encode the plan in memory. In the second phase (i.e. *intention retention*), he has to keep the intention in memory while working on other tasks (ongoing

Table 1. Inclusion and exclusion criteria for PD-MCI according to the Movement Disorder Society Task Force Guidelines (Modified from Litvan et al., 2012).

(I). Inclusion criteria

- Diagnosis of Parkinson's disease based on the U.K. PD Brain Bank Criteria.
- Gradual decline (in the context of established PD) in cognitive ability reported by either the patient or informant, or observed by the clinician.
- Cognitive deficits on either formal neuropsychological testing or a scale of global cognitive abilities.
- Cognitive deficits are not serious enough to interfere significantly with functional independence, but subtle difficulties on complex functional tasks may be observed.

(II). Exclusion criteria

- Diagnosis of PD dementia based on MDS Task Force proposed criteria.
- Other primary explanations for cognitive impairment (e.g. delirium, stroke, major depression, metabolic abnormalities, adverse effects of medication or head trauma).
- Other PD-associated comorbid conditions (e.g. motor impairment or severe anxiety, depression, excessive daytime sleepiness or psychosis) that, in the opinion of the clinician, significantly influence cognitive testing.

activity). The third phase (i.e. *intention re-instantiation*) begins when the event or the time cueing the intended action occurs. Here, the subject has to inhibit ongoing activities and re-instantiate the intended plan. Success in this phase depends greatly on how well the subject monitors the environment for the time- or event-related) signal to perform the delayed intention. In the last phase (i.e. *action initiation*), as previously planned the intended action has to be carried out on the subject's own initiative.

It is generally accepted that two cognitive components are critical for the correct delayed execution of planned actions: (i) a retrospective memory component, which allows effectively encoding and successively recalling the cued event or time and the particular actions to be performed; and (ii) a more typical prospective component, which allows reactivating the intention to perform the planned actions at the appropriate time or when the event occurs without any explicit external prompt (Kvavilashvili, 1987). It is generally acknowledged that executive and episodic memory abilities are differently implicated in the two PM components. Indeed, the encoding and long-term retention of the associative relationship between a specific event or time and the concrete actions to be performed requires the correct functioning of the same episodic memory system that is also implicated in the encoding and retrieval of previous events and information. Conversely, the executive system is mainly involved in controlling the mental operations needed to spontaneously activate the prospective intention at the appropriate time or at the occurrence of the target event. In fact, as performing a PM task is typically embedded in an ongoing, attention consuming activity, subjects have to divide their cognitive resources between performing the ongoing task and keeping track of the PM task (e.g. by periodically reminding themselves about the prospective intention, actively monitoring the external environment, checking the passing of time, etc.). Moreover, at the appropriate moment (i.e. at the occurrence of the critical event or time), they must stop performing the ongoing task and begin performing the intended action. Top-down attentional control, strategic monitoring of the external environment and/or of the time passing and shifting between concurring activities are all cognitive abilities that are under the control of the executive system (Burgess & Shallice, 1997; Carlesimo, Casadio, & Caltagirone, 2004; McDaniel, Glisky, Rubin, Guynn, & Routhieaux, 1999; McFarland & Glisky, 2009). However, the active role of the executive system in coordinating the multiple cognitive operations needed to perform the ongoing task and not to miss the target event that triggers recall of the prospective intention might not be equally critical for all PM tasks. In this regard, McDaniel, Guynn, Einstein, and Breneiser (2004) proposed the *multi-process framework*. According to these authors, retrieval of the prospective intention in an event-based PM task may be underpinned by different cognitive processes, which they term *reflexive-associative* (or *automatic*) and *cue-focused* (or *strategic-voluntary*), respectively, depending on the specific experimental conditions. The relative contribution of these two processes to performance on a PM paradigm can be manipulated by varying the association between the prospective cue and the actions to be performed, the emotional salience of the cue and the way in which the ongoing task promotes the elaboration of the characteristics of the target event (focal and non-focal PM paradigms). In fact, when the cue is highly associated with the action to be performed (e.g. the PM target is one word and the PM action requires copying that word on a sheet of paper) it is emotionally salient with respect to the other stimuli processed in the ongoing task (e.g. the PM target stimulus is represented by one word with emotional valence in the context of an ongoing task in which neutral words are presented) or it is the focus of the ongoing task (e.g. when the PM target stimulus is one word and in the ongoing activity the subject is required to execute a lexical-decision task) the subject might rely mainly on automatic processes to recall the prospective intention at the appearance of the prospective cue. In the opposite condition, i.e. low association between cue and action (e.g. the PM target is one word and the PM action requires pressing a key button on the keyboard), low cue salience (e.g. the PM target is represented by a syllable and in the ongoing task word sequences are presented) and non-focal cues (e.g. when the PM target is a syllable and in the ongoing activity the subject is required to perform a lexical decision task), strategically driven, cue-focused processes should be implemented to detect the target stimulus and to recall the associated prospective intention (McDaniel & Einstein, 2011; McDaniel et al., 2004).

A large number of paradigms have been used to assess PM. Those most frequently used in clinical populations are the Virtual Week (Rendell & Henry, 2009) and the Memory for Intentions Screening Test (MIST; Raskin, 2004). Table 2 provides a brief description of the two test paradigms.

Aims of this review

This review was aimed at examining current findings on PM functioning in PD patients in order to discuss three opens issues that appear to be relevant from both theoretical and clinical perspectives. The first point we wish to clarify is the role of executive and episodic memory processes in the PM functioning of PD patients. Indeed, frontal-related abilities, which are heavily involved in PM processes (Barban, Carlesimo, Macaluso, Caltagirone, & Costa, 2014; Burgess, Gonen-Yaacovi, & Volle, 2011), are frequently altered in PD patients from the early phases of the disease. However, there is also evidence that PD patients have an episodic memory impairment (Aarsland et al., 2010; Brønnick, Alves, Aarsland, Tysnes, & Larsen, 2011; Carlesimo et al., 2012; Chiaravalloti et al., 2014; Cohn, Giannoylis, De Belder, Saint-Cyr, & McAndrews, 2016) that could be responsible of a PM impairment for a deficit of the retrospective component. A second related issue that needs to be addressed here is whether in PD patients the PM deficit occurs early and is associated with MCI. The answer to this question is particularly important for making a neuropsychological diagnosis of these patients. Indeed, it would help clarify whether PM failure in this population is a specific sign of early cognitive decline and, if so, whether it is useful to introduce PM assessment in the standard neuropsychological examination of PD patients.

Table 2. Brief presentation of the Virtual week (Rendell & Henry, 2009) and the Memory for Intentions Screening (Raskin, 2004), two of the most used tests for assessing clinical populations.

The *Virtual week* test (Rendell & Henry, 2009) is a board game in which participants move a token around the board by rolling dice. The consecutive hours of the day when people are usually awake are marked on the board, and each circuit on the board represents a day. As participants move the token around the board, they are required to make choices about daily activities and remember to carry out lifelike activities (prospective memory tasks). The prospective tasks may be time-based (e.g. take asthma medication at 11 A.M. and 9 P.M., triggered by passing the 11 A.M. square and the 9 P.M. square), or event-based (e.g. take antibiotics at breakfast and dinner, triggered by event cards featuring breakfast and dinner). Moreover, the time-based and the event-based tasks may be regular (a routine task involving remembering to take medication) daily or irregular (a one-off, nonrecurring task that differs for each virtual day)
The *Memory for Intentions Screening Test* (MIST; Raskin, 2004) was expressly devised for the purpose of meeting the basic parameters of a PM task. Namely, the MIST requires the delayed execution of intended actions, in the context of an ongoing foreground (i.e. distractor) task and provides a constrained window of time in which the intention may be initiated and executed. Specifically, participants are asked to perform eight different PM tasks over a 30-min period, during which time they are engaged in a word-search puzzle that serves as the foreground (i.e. distractor) task. The tasks are balanced in terms of delay interval (i.e. either a 2-min or 15-min delay), cue (i.e. either a time-based or event-based cue), and response modality (i.e. either a verbal or a physical response)

Finally, we will discuss current evidence on the rehabilitation of PM disorders in PD. In particular, in view of the hypothesis that PM disorders in PD are mainly subsumed by executive dysfunction, we will analyze whether the training of executive deficits and/or the use of strategies aimed at reducing executive requests in PM tasks would lead to improved PM performance in PD patients.

Methods

Information sources and search

A comprehensive electronic literature research strategy was carried out by systematically searching the following international databases: PubMed/medline, Scopus and Web of Science from inception of each database to January 2017. We also performed a manual search by analyzing the reference lists and citations of all initially identified articles to look for other potentially relevant papers not previously identified by the systematic search. Concerning the search strategy we adopted to screen the research-literature for titles, abstracts and topics, the various combinations of terms used as keywords were the following: 'Parkinson's disease' and 'prospective memory' or 'Parkinson's disease' and 'prospective intentions' or 'Parkinson's disease' and 'future thinking'. Concerning our data extraction method, titles and abstracts were initially identified and screened by one of the authors (AC). Subsequently, papers that seemed potentially relevant were retrieved and two reviewers (AC and GAC) independently evaluated each of the full text reports and arrived at a consensus regarding eligibility. Finally, if information was missing in the selected articles, we contacted the corresponding author and asked for the missing details. This search disclosed 23 original research papers, eight review/meta-analyses, one book chapter, one editorial paper and five conference proceedings. As for original research papers, we excluded from this review three studies that did not directly investigate prospective memory functioning in individuals with Parkinson's disease and two non-english language studies. One original research paper published after the present review was performed was included during the first round of the review process of the paper. Therefore, 19 original research papers investigating prospective memory functioning in individuals with PD were eventually included in this review.

Analysis and data synthesis

With regard to statistics, when we took into account the significant heterogeneity of the experimental study designs (i.e. cross-sectional, observational, single case, or longitudinal/follow-up studies) as well as the different definitions and measurement methods used to evaluate PM in patients with PD, a meta-analysis did not seem completely appropriate. Therefore, we made a qualitative synthesis of relevant results by carrying out a systematic review of the literature.

Prospective memory in PD

General overview

Available data consistently show that PD patients perform worse than healthy controls (HCs) in both laboratory and ecological PM paradigms (Costa, Carlesimo, & Caltagirone, 2012;

Ramanan & Kumar, 2013). However, since the publication of Katai, Maruyama, Hashimoto, and Ikeda's (2003) pioneer study, which demonstrated that PD patients have difficulty in performing PM tasks, a number of studies have been carried out to investigate different aspects of PM functioning in individuals with PD; most of these studies included patients without dementia. Data from these investigations reliably document that PD patients obtain significantly lower accuracy scores than HCs (Costa, Peppe, Caltagirone, & Carlesimo, 2013; Foster, Rose, McDaniel, & Rendell, 2013; Kliegel et al., 2005; Mioni et al., 2015; Ramanan & Kumar, 2013; but see Altgassen, Zöllig, Kopp, Mackinlay, & Kliegel, 2007 for partially divergent results). Whittington, Podd, and Stewart-Williams (2006) also showed that PM deficits were associated with disease severity and recent reports document that poor PM performance in this population is significantly associated with reduced functional abilities in daily living activities, which could, for instance, affect the autonomous management of pharmacological treatment (Costa, Peppe, et al., 2015, Costa, Zabberoni, et al., 2015; Pirogovsky, Woods, Vincent Filoteo, & Gilbert, 2012). The above observations highlight the potential clinical relevance of PM disorders in PD patients and reinforce the need to better understand the characteristics and mechanisms underlying this deterioration.

The role of executive abilities and episodic memory in PM functioning in PD

Kliegel et al. (2005) first advanced the hypothesis that reduced PM accuracy, in particular the prospective component, in PD patients might depend on executive impairment (see also Kliegel, Altgassen, Hering, & Rose, 2011). In particular, these authors proposed that in PD patients PM deficits are mainly a consequence of impaired planning, monitoring and shifting processes which affect some specific phases of the PM process (e.g. intention formation and action initiation). This hypothesis is in line with the suggestion that mental disorders in the early stages of PD are mainly due to a dysregulation of the activity of the neural pathways that connect the anterior striatal structures (i.e. anterior caudate nucleus) with the mesial and dorsal prefrontal regions as a consequence of dopamine deafferentation (Cools & D'Esposito, 2011). In fact, in a previous paper we demonstrated that therapeutic withdrawal of dopamine compounds ('Off' state) leads to significant worsening of performance in patients with PD (Costa, Peppe, Brusa, et al., 2008; but see Foster, McDaniel, Repovs, & Hershey, 2009 for partially divergent results).

As noted above, however, there is evidence that PD patients also suffer from an episodic memory impairment. For example, Aarsland et al. (2010) reported that memory deficits were even more frequent than executive dysfunction. In particular, the authors found that of the 25% of PD patients with MCI, 50% had a memory impairment, and 39% an executive impairment. The episodic memory impairment, in turn, could be responsible for a PM deficit because of failure of the restrospective component. It is, however, unclear whether the involvement of episodic memory in PD depends on altered encoding/retrieval processes or storage failure. According to the encoding/retrieval deficit hypothesis, the memory impairment in PD is related to a deficit of elaborative encoding of the incoming information and/or to reduced strategic access to otherwise accurately stored information (Brønnick et al., 2011; Chiaravalloti et al., 2014; Costa et al., 2014; Emre et al., 2007; Weintraub, Moberg, Culbertson, Duda, & Stern, 2004). As the difficulty in implementing effective encoding or retrieval strategies is generally attributed to deficits in the executive/attention domain, the same neurobiological substrate, e.g. altered activity of the neural pathways that connect the anterior striatal structures to the mesial and dorsal prefrontal regions as a consequence of dopamine dysregulation, should underlie the memory impairment and executive deficits in PD patients without dementia (Yeterian & Pandya, 1991). The alternative hypothesis, i.e. that the retrospective memory disorders in these patients are due to altered consolidation mechanisms, has also been advanced. This hypothesis is based on some reports which demonstrated that PD patients' performance on episodic memory tests is associated with gray matter microstructural (i.e. increased mean diffusivity) (Carlesimo et al., 2012) and macrostructural (i.e. atrophy) (Beyer et al., 2013; Foo et al., 2016) changes in the hippocampal formation as well as reduced functional MRI activation during associative memory tasks in the same region (Cohn et al., 2016). A recent paper documenting a hippocampal-like, as opposed to a frontal-like, pattern of memory impairment in a group of PD patients without dementia is in line with this hypothesis (Edelstyn et al., 2015).

To examine the possible contribution of executive deficits to the reduced PM performance of PD patients we will review the extant data to answer the following questions: Do PD patients perform differently on time- vs. event-based tasks? Does event-based PM performance depend on altered executive control in PD patients? Moreover, to evaluate the possible contribution of altered episodic memory to PM performance, extant data will be reviewed to answer the question: Are the prospective and retrospective components of the PM task differentially impaired in this population?

Time-based vs. event-based task

The first way to investigate the contribution of executive functions to PM performance is to examine data from studies that directly investigated time- vs. event-based PM in the same PD sample. Typically, time-based procedures require participants to perform planned actions after a temporal delay (unscheduled tasks) or at a precise time (scheduled tasks), whereas event-based paradigms ask subjects to perform a delayed action at the occurrence of an environmental cue. During the delay between the moment when the prospective instructions are given and the moment in which the intention to perform the actions has to be carried out, subjects are engaged in intercurrent ongoing activities with variable attentional demand. Time-based paradigms are generally considered more demanding than event-based tasks in terms of the attention and executive resources they require. Indeed, in time-cued tasks the moment when the intention has to be retrieved is not prompted by the occurrence of any cue (target); thus, the activation of prospective intention is completely self-guided. Conversely, in the event-cued paradigms the occurrence of an environmental event marks the moment when the prospective intention has to be fulfilled, thus it represents a sort of facilitation for intention activation. Accordingly, findings that PD patients are significantly impaired in time-based but not in event-based tasks could support the hypothesis that attention and executive deficits significantly affect their performance.

In this vein, Raskin et al. (2011) administered the Memory for Intention Screening Test (Raskin, 2004), which includes time- and event-cued PM tasks, to a group of 54 PD patients without dementia and 34 HCs. Results showed significantly reduced time-based PM abilities in PD patients compared to HCs; however, the between group difference in the event-based condition only approached statistical significance. Moreover, by applying a linear regression model the authors demonstrated that the score on the 'Resistance to Interference' condition of the Stroop test was a specific independent predictor of PD patients' time-based PM performance. Furthermore, in a group of 16 patients with PD compared with 16 HCs Smith, Souchay, and Moulin (2011) reported reduced accuracy in a time-based PM procedure that required pressing a key at precise times, but spared capacity in performing event-based tasks in which a key had to be pressed at the occurrence of target words. These results are consistent with findings of Costa, Peppe, Caltagirone, and Carlesimo (2008) in a study in which 23 individuals with PD without dementia and 25 HCs were administered experimental time- and event-based procedures. In the time-based procedure, subjects were instructed to perform three unrelated actions after 20 min had elapsed. Instead, in the event-based procedure, participants had to carry out three unrelated actions when a timer rang. With respect to HCs the PD patients showed reduced ability to spontaneously activate the intention only in the time-based task and a trend towards a correlation with performance on executive/working memory standardized tests (i.e. Modified card sorting test and Digit Span).

These findings, which indicate a disproportionate impairment of PD patients in time- vs. event-based performance accuracy and a significant association with performance on executive tests, suggest that executive functions are involved in the PM processes of these patients. However, other studies have reported discordant results. Indeed, Katai et al. (2003) administered a time-based task to a group of 20 PD patients and 20 HCs. The subjects had to perform an action after a time interval and an event-based task in which they were required to perform an action at the occurrence of a target word. Results showed that the PD patients performed less accurately than the HCs on the event-based but not the time-based task. Moreover, no significant correlation was found between PM and executive test scores. Pirogovsky et al. (2012) administered the Memory for Intention Screening Test to a PD sample ($n = 33$) that included individuals with dementia ($n = 7$) and to HCs ($n = 26$). Results showed that PD patients obtained lower accuracy scores than HCs on both time- and event-based tasks but that the Cohen's d effect size was higher in the former ($d = 1.3$) than the latter ($d = 0.63$) task.

Impairment on an event-based PM task was also reported by Foster et al. (2013) and Costa et al. (2013, 2014, Costa, Peppe, et al., 2015) in samples of PD patients without dementia. However, as the time-based PM condition was not investigated in these studies a direct comparison cannot be made with event-based perfomance.

In summary, the data reported above do not provide convergent evidence of a differential impairment in time-based vs. event-based PM functioning in PD. This same observation was also made by Ramanan and Kumar (2013) in a recent meta-analysis in which they performed quantitative analyses on the effect size of nine studies that investigated PM in PD patients (four investigated both time- and event-based PM; five focused on only one of the two PM tasks). The authors did not find a significant difference between the effect size observed for time-based (Hedges' g effect size = 0.71) and event-based ($g = 0.55$) tasks ($p = 0.30$). As these authors note, the different cues used in the event-based paradigms, which appeared to be particularly salient in some cases (e.g. Costa, Peppe, Caltagirone, et al., 2008) or were embedded in the ongoing task in other cases (e.g. Costa et al., 2013, Costa, Peppe, et al., 2015; Katai et al., 2003), make it impossible to directly compare the results of the above studies. More generally, both clinical characteristics and the size of the samples recruited appear to be quite heterogeneous across studies.

Effects size for the comparison between PD patients and healthy subjects on those studies in which both time-based and event-based PM tasks were administered are reported in Table 3.

Table 3. Effects size for the comparison between PD patients and healthy subjects on those studies in which both time-based and event-based PM tasks were administered.

	Comparisons between PD patients and Healthy controls	
	Time-based Task	Event-based task
Study	Cohen's *d* effect size	
Katai et al. (2003)	0.14	1.27
Costa, Peppe, Caltagirone, et al. (2008)	0.92	0.54
Raskin et al. (2011)	1.07	0.48
Smith et al. (2011)	0.79	0.07
Pirogovsky et al. (2012)	1.30	0.63

Event-based PM performance and executive control in PD patients

As noted above, event-based PM performance may be significantly affected in PD patients. However, in view of the evidence that a high proportion of PD patients without dementia present executive dysfunction, the hypothesis can be advanced that altered executive control may also account for their performance on event-based tasks. Most of the studies that investigated the extent to which executive control mediates event-cued PM retrieval in PD patients followed the above-described multiprocess framework proposed by McDaniel et al. (2004). According to this framework, PD patients' disproportionate impairment in non-focal compared to focal event-based tasks could indicate significant involvement of altered executive control in their PM performance.

Data in line with this hypothesis were reported by Mioni et al. (2015) who manipulated the salience of the PM context using stimuli with emotional valence. Indeed, these authors showed that the emotional valence of target cues could modulate PD patients' event-based performance. In particular, in this study Mioni et al. (2015) gave 21 PD patients without dementia and 25 HCs a modified version of the Virtual Week task (Rendell & Henry, 2009) in which PM cues were represented by pictures with positive, negative and neutral emotional valence. Results showed that the PD patients were as sensitive as HCs to positive emotional cues and showed accuracy enhancement in these trials compared to neutral trials. Nevertheless, the effect seems quite specific for stimuli with positive emotional valence as performance improvement was not observed in negative trials. Foster et al. (2009) examined performance on focal and non-focal PM tasks in a group of 24 PD patients and in 30 HCs. PD patients were assessed in both the 'off' state (after 8 h of dopamine medication washout) and the 'on' state (after they took their usual dopamine medication). Results showed that PD patients' accuracy was significantly lower than that of HCs only on the non-focal task (independently of the 'off' and 'on' conditions). Similarly, in another study in which 24 PD patients without dementia were administered the Virtual Week paradigm, Foster et al. (2013) found that PD patients performed worse than HCs in non-focal compared to focal conditions. In this same study, PD patients' PM retrieval was significantly modulated by the degree of the cue-action association; that is, compared to HCs, PD patients showed a disproportionate PM impairment in those conditions in which the cue-action association was low with respect to the conditions in which the cue-action association was high.

Partially divergent data were obtained by Costa, Peppe, et al. (2015). In this study, a group of 30 PD patients with MCI and 27 HCs were administered an event-based PM procedure that included both focal and non-focal conditions. Results showed that PD patients with MCI performed worse than HCs independently of cue focality. However, these findings do not simply indicate that executive control is not involved in PM performance. Indeed, we found that low accuracy on PM tasks was significantly associated with two indices of shifting capacities (i.e. perseverative errors on the Modified Card Sorting Test and an increase in response time passing from performance of the Trail Making Test-Part A to the Trail Making Test-Part B). The difference between the results of this latter study and the results of Foster et al.'s (2009, 2013) studies might be primarily related to the characteristics of the samples recruited. Indeed, compared to the PD participants in the studies by Foster et al. (2009, 2013), the PD participants with MCI in the study by Costa, Peppe, et al. (2015) suffered from a more pronounced executive dysfunction that in the end might have caused reduced efficiency of the PM mechanisms.

This hypothesis is strengthened by the results of another study in which a different approach was used to investigate the potential association between executive control and event-based PM performance in PD patients (Costa et al., 2014). In this study, 17 PD patients with MCI who exhibited a dysexecutive profile underwent cognitive training focused on the potentiation of shifting abilities to verify their effects on PM efficiency. PD patients were randomly assigned to two treatment groups: a placebo group, which underwent 12 sessions of training focused on basic attentional capacities, and an experimental group, which was submitted to 12 sessions of shifting training. Before and immediately after the end of the treatments, the PD patients were assessed with both focal and non-focal event-based tasks. Before treatment, PD patients showed lower accuracy than HCs on all PM tasks administered. After treatment, PD patients in the experimental group, but not those in the placebo group, significantly improved their PM performance in both tasks. A significant correlation was also found between the increase in PM accuracy and the rate of improvement on the shifting tasks (i.e. alternating phonemic-semantic fluency). Therefore, these findings support the idea that the PM performance of PD patients with MCI depends on their executive dysfunction; however, this relationship is not supported by discrepant performance on focal and non-focal PM paradigms.

In summary, current evidence deriving from event-based PM paradigms shows that PD patients are particularly sensitive to task demands in terms of strategic-voluntary processes. Moreover, some preliminary findings also show that in PD patients with MCI who, compared to HCs, show impaired performance on event-based tasks which involve automatic and voluntary mechanisms (i.e. focal and non-focal tasks), performance on PM tasks might be improved by potentiating cognitive flexibility processes.

Effects size for the comparison between PD patients and healthy subjects on those studies in which both cue-focused and reflexive-associative PM tasks were administered are reported in Table 4.

Table 4. Effects size for the comparison between PD patients and healthy subjects on those studies in which both cue-focused and reflexive-associative PM tasks were administered.

	Comparisons between PD patients and Healthy controls	
	Cue-focused tasks	Reflexive-associative tasks
Study	Cohen's *d* effect size	
Foster et al. (2009)	0.81	0.24
Costa et al. (2014)	1.99	0.50
Costa, Peppe, et al. (2015)	0.93	1.02
Mioni et al. (2015)	0.81	0.54

Prospective vs. retrospective component functioning in PD patients

More evidence of a strict relationship between executive and PM disorders in PD patients might be found by examining the results of studies in which the prospective and retrospective components of PM (Einstein & McDaniel, 1990) were assessed separately. As previously noted, the prospective component of a PM task refers to the ability to spontaneously retrieve the intention to perform the planned action at the occurrence of the event or when the time has elapsed, without any explicit prompt to recall being given by the examiner. This implies that subjects have to actively monitor the external environment and/or the time passing to avoid missing the right moment to re-instantiate the intention while performing ongoing activities. Clearly, strategic attention allocation, planning and shifting abilities are highly involved in this component of a PM task (Burgess & Shallice, 1997; Carlesimo et al., 2004; Costa, Caltagirone, & Carlesimo, 2011; Costa et al., 2012; McDaniel & Einstein, 2011; McFarland & Glisky, 2009). The retrospective component, instead, refers to the 'content' of intention. It includes the initial encoding and long-term retention of the specific actions to be performed and of the associative link between the target event or time and the intention itself. It is generally agreed that episodic memory, which supports intention encoding and consolidation and recollection of the event/time target, is responsible for the correct functioning of the retrospective component. In line with the observations above, the finding of failure of the prospective component and parallel sparing of the retrospective component further supports the idea that executive dysfunction contributes to PM failure in individuals with PD. Vice versa, a concurrent impairment of the two components also suggests the involvement of episodic memory mechanisms.

In this regard, various authors have reported that PD patients show impaired ability to autonomously activate the intention to perform a planned action after the time has elapsed or when a target event occurs, with parallel normal ability to recollect target events and PM instructions (Katai et al., 2003; Kliegel et al., 2005; Pagni et al., 2011). Particularly interesting is the finding of Pagni et al. (2011) that even drug naïve PD patients (i.e. PD patients in the early stages of the disease who have never been treated with dopamine medications; $n = 41$) tended to perform worse than HCs ($n = 40$) on the prospective component of an event-based task. However, PD patients were as accurate as HCs on the retrospective component of the PM task.

A study by Costa et al. (2013) directly investigated the contribution of the retrospective component to PM performance. In this investigation, 20 PD patients without dementia and 20 HCs were administered an event-based procedure in which they were presented with sequences of words and were instructed to perform an ongoing short-term memory task. The PM instructions required subjects to press a button on the keyboard at the occurrence of a target word. To determine whether PM performance depended on retrospective memory mechanisms, we manipulated the memory load of the retrospective component so that in one condition the cue for the PM task consisted of four words and in another condition the cue consisted of only one word. Results showed that, compared to HCs, PD patients' ability to retrieve the prospective intentions was significantly reduced independently of the memory load of the retrospective component. Moreover, analysis of the item-by-item correspondence between prospective and retrospective component accuracy revealed that PD patients' accuracy in performing the intended action at the appearance of the target word was independent from accuracy in recollecting the target words in a final recall task. Indeed, PM accuracy in PD patients was lower than that exhibited by HCs for both recollected and non-recollected words (Costa et al., 2013).

Taken together, the above findings suggest that in PD patients PM impairment does not depend on reduced capacity to retain long-term PM instructions. Rather, it seems to depend on specific difficulty in self-initiating the intention (Kliegel et al., 2011), which supports the view of specific involvement of the executive processes.

However, results from other studies do not support this linear interpretation. In fact, both prospective and retrospective components were found to be impaired in several investigations (e.g. Foster et al., 2013; Mioni et al., 2015; Smith et al., 2011). In their study, Foster et al. (2013) administered the Virtual Week task to 24 PD patients and 28 HCs. They found that in the PM condition with a high retrospective memory demand, PD participants showed worse recognition of PM actions than HCs. Moreover, their poor episodic memory performance was significantly associated with the PM score. Indeed, when the authors included only those tasks with accurate retrospective memory in the analyses, the PD patients no longer showed reduced PM performance (Foster et al., 2013). These findings are congruent with results of the previously mentioned study by Raskin et al. (2011). Indeed, these authors found that PD patients performed worse than HCs in recognizing PM actions, which probably indicates retrospective memory failure. Interestingly, a significant positive correlation between PD patients' accuracy on both time- and event-based PM tasks and a classical test of episodic memory (i.e. the WMS-III Logical Memory subtest) was also reported.

Therefore, this second body of evidence implies that the retrospective component of the PM task may also be impaired in PD patients. This suggests that altered episodic memory functioning might contribute to PM failure in this population. As previously noted, however, it is unclear whether the involvement of episodic memory in PD depends on altered encoding, storage or retrieval processes. Studies aimed at disentangling, in PD patients, the different contribution of these mechanisms to retrospective deficits in PM tasks are sparse and contradictory. As Foster et al. (2013) argued, the poor retrospective memory performance exhibited by the PD patients in their study could have been related to initial encoding failure rather than to disrupted consolidation. Moreover, in a recent study (Costa, Zabberoni et al., 2015) the poor scores obtained by a group of PD patients with MCI on the retrospective PM component did not correlate with their scores on a classical episodic memory test in which there was no great requirement for encoding and retrieval strategies (i.e. the Short story recall).

In conclusion, current data are quite discordant and do not allow us to unequivocally disentangle the contribution of prospective and retrospective component failure in the PM performance of PD patients. On the other side, the neurobiological underpinning of the prospective and retrospective deficits in the PM performance of PD patients is still a matter of debate. The demonstration that retrospective component deficits actually depend on episodic memory dysfunction due to impaired encoding/retrieval processes would support a unitary hypothesis, whereas the frontal dysfunction resulting from dopamine depletion in the striatal circuits would be responsible for both the prospective and retrospective PM deficits in PD patients. On the other side, if the episodic memory deficit is primarily of hippocampal origin (i.e. it affects the consolidation of the memory traces supporting the retrospective component of the PM task), one should conclude that the presence of two independent cognitive deficits underlies the failure of the prospective and retrospective components, respectively. Further studies are obviously needed to gather new evidence on this issue.

Effects size for the comparison between PD patients and healthy subjects on those studies in which the prospective and retrospective components of PM tasks were separately assessed are reported in Table 5.

Is PM failure an early sign of cognitive decline in patients with PD?

The case of PD-MCI

The second main aim of this review was to explore the hypothesis that in PD patients without dementia PM failure might be specifically associated with MCI. Indeed, very few studies have investigated whether PM is early impaired in PD patients without dementia or whether its impairment can be inserted in a broader neuropsychological picture characterized by the presence of a significant decline in different cognitive domains.

Two of these studies were carried out by our group. In the first study (previously mentioned in the manuscript), we recruited two groups of PD patients with MCI (15 PD patients with single domain MCI and 15 with multiple domain MCI; patients in both groups had a higher prevalence of dysexecutive impairments), a group of PD patients without cognitive impairments ($n = 17$) and a group of HCs ($n = 25$) (Costa, Peppe, et al., 2015). The presence of cognitive impairment was determined by administering an extensive neuropsychological battery that consisted of standardized tests, according to Litvan et al.'s (2012) criteria. We administered all participants a PM procedure with verbal stimuli that included both focal (i.e. PM cue is processed in the ongoing task) and non-focal (i.e. PM cue is not processed in the ongoing task) conditions. Results showed that the two MCI subgroups performed worse in both PM conditions than the PD patients without MCI and the HCs. Instead, no significant difference in PM accuracy scores was found between the two latter groups. Low accuracy on PM tasks was associated with measures of executive functioning and with measures investigating patients' ability to self-manage medication (scores on the Pill Questionnaire).

In a second study (Costa, Zabberoni et al., 2015), we adopted a similar experimental design to investigate the relationship between MCI and, in this case, time-based PM functioning in PD patients. In particular, two PD samples of individuals with MCI (20 with single domain and 28 with multiple domain MCI, with a higher prevalence of executive deficits in both groups), a group of PD patients without MCI ($n = 33$) and a group of matched HCs ($n = 20$) were recruited. In the time-based procedure, subjects were required to perform a specified

Table 5. Effects size for the comparison between PD patients and healthy subjects on those studies in which the prospective and retrospective components of PM tasks were separately assessed.

	Comparisons between PD patients and Healthy controls	
	Prospective component	Retrospective component
Study	Cohen's *d* effect size	
Katai et al. (2003)	0.70	0.24
Pagni et al. (2011)	0.51	0.21
Smith et al. (2011)	0.44	0.43
Raskin et al. (2011)	0.73	0.44
Costa et al. (2013)	0.77	0.53
Costa, Zabberoni, et al. (2015)	0.62	0.48
Mioni et al. (2015)	0.63	0.60

action after ten minutes had elapsed (four consecutive trials were administered). The procedure allowed separating assessment of the prospective component (which referred to autonomous activation to perform the action) and the retrospective component (which referred to recalling the action to be performed in the PM task). For this purpose, the subjects' ability to remember the target actions was tested also if, at the expiration of the established time, they did not engage in any action by asking them: 'Do you remember that at this point you were supposed to do something'? Results are quite interesting because PD patients with both single and multiple-domain MCI performed significantly worse than HCs on both the prospective and retrospective components of the PM task. Moreover, individuals with MCI also tended to exhibit lower PM accuracy than PD patients without MCI, whose performance accuracy was comparable to that of HCs. Very interestingly, in this study, we also found that the prospective component score on the PM task significantly predicted the ability of PD participants with MCI to autonomously manage daily medication. We did not, however, find any significant correlation between PM scores (either prospective or retrospective component scores) and standardized neuropsychological tests investigating executive and episodic memory functioning.

In a more recent study, Marcone et al. (2017) investigated PM functioning in patients with Alzheimer's disease ($n = 41$) and in individuals with MCI ($n = 64$) that included a PD sample ($n = 27$). Subjects were administered the 'envelope task' (an event-based single trial PM task) (Huppert, Johnson, & Nickson, 2000), which showed relatively low sensitivity to the presence of MCI. Unfortunately, however, in this study PD patients' data were not evaluated separately from those of the whole MCI sample, which made it difficult to correctly interpret the reported findings.

To summarize, the results of the two studies by our group (Costa, Peppe, et al., 2015, Costa, Zabberoni, et al., 2015) suggest that PM is not impaired in all PD patients but, rather, that it is associated with the presence of MCI. If confirmed, this would be quite important from a clinical perspective. Indeed, as previously discussed in this manuscript, MCI is a sub-clinical condition associated with increased risk of dementia in PD patients (Janvin et al., 2006; Litvan et al., 2012; Pigott et al., 2015). Improving the diagnostic process would allow early detection and better management of the disease. In this vein, the above data preliminarily support the hypothesis that assessing PM abilities in PD patients might contribute to differentiating between individuals with and without MCI, thus encouraging the inclusion of PM evaluation in the neuropsychological assessment of these patients. However, due to the paucity of dedicated studies, this issue needs further investigation. A related issue also refers to whether PM assessment in PD adds valuable information for predicting dementia with respect to tests that investigate other cognitive functions. However, this issue has not as yet been explored.

Clues for PM assessment in patients with PD

As shown in Table 6, the methods used to assess PM in patients with PD in currently published studies are quite heterogeneous. Indeed, in most of the studies home-made experimental procedures were administered. Therefore, it is difficult to find reliable tools with well-defined psychometric properties that should be further explored in PD. Another point worth investigating is whether PM performance in administered tasks predicts patients' functional ability

Table 6. Summary of studies on prospective memory functioning in patients with PD.

Study (year)	PD sample	Pharmacological medication	Performance-based PM task	Relationship with daily living activities
Marcone et al. (2017)	27 PD patients with MCI	Not reported	Envelope task	Not investigated
Mioni et al. (2015)*	21 PD patients without dementia	Usual dopamine therapy (not specified)	Computerized version of the Virtual Week procedure	Not investigated
Costa, Zabberoni, et al. (2015)*	48 PD patients with MCI; 33 PD patients without cognitive disorders	Levodopa; dopamine agonists; monoamine oxidase inhibitor	Time-based experimental task	Significant association between PM accuracy and ability to self-manage pharmacological therapy
Costa, Peppe et al. (2015)*	30 PD patients with MCI; 17 PD patients without cognitive disorders	Levodopa; dopamine agonists; monoamine oxidase inhibitor	Event-based experimental task	Significant association between PM accuracy and ability to self-manage pharmacological therapy
Costa et al. (2014)*	17 PD patients with MCI	Levodopa; dopamine agonists	Event-based experimental task	Not investigated
Costa et al. (2013)	21 PD patients without dementia	Levodopa; dopamine agonists; monoamine oxidase inhibitor	Event-based experimental task	Not investigated
Foster et al. (2013)	24 PD patients without dementia	Levodopa; dopamine agonists; catechol-O-methyl transferase inhibitor	Computerized version of the Virtual Week procedure	Not investigated
Pirogovsky et al. (2012)	26 PD patients without dementia; 7 PD patients with dementia	Levodopa; dopamine agonists; amantadine; monoamine oxidase inhibitor	Memory for Intention Screening Test	Significant correlation between PM accuracy and the ability to manage medication
Pagni et al. (2011)*	41 PD patients without dementia	Drug-naïve PD patients	Event-based experimental task	Not investigated
Smith et al. (2011)	16 PD patients without dementia	Levodopa	Time- and event-based experimental tasks	Not investigated
Raskin et al. (2011)*	54 PD patients without dementia	Usual dopamine medication (not specified)	Memory for Intention Screening Test	Not investigated
Foster et al. (2009)*	24 PD patients without dementia	PD patients were assessed in "off" condition (after 8-h dopamine medication washout) and in "on" condition (after administration of their usual dopamine medication: levodopa; dopamine agonists; catechol-O-methyl transferase inhibitor)	Event-based experimental task	Not investigated
Costa, Peppe, Brusa, et al. (2008)	23 PD patients without dementia	Levodopa; dopamine agonists	Time- and event-based experimental tasks	Not investigated

(*Continued*)

Table 6. (*Continued*).

Study (year)	PD sample	Pharmacological medication	Performance-based PM task	Relationship with daily living activities
Costa, Peppe, Caltagirone, et al. (2008)*	20 PD patients without dementia	PD patients were assessed in "off" condition (12-h dopamine medication washout) and in "on" condition (after levodopa administration)	Time-based experimental task	Not investigated
Altgassen et al. (2007)*	13 PD patients without dementia	PD patients were assessed in "off" condition (after 12-h dopamine medication washout)	Event-based experimental task	Not investigated
Whittington et al. (2006)	41 PD patients without dementia	Levodopa; anticholinergic medication	Event-based task	Not investigated
Kliegel et al. (2005)*	16 PD patients without dementia	Levodopa; dopamine agonists	Event-based experimental task	Not investigated
Katai et al. (2003)*	PD patients without dementia	Levodopa; dopamine agonists; antimuscarinic	Time-and event-based experimental tasks	Not Investigated

Notes: *Indicates studies investigating the association between prospective memory scores and performance on cognitive tests sensitive to executive functioning and/or episodic memory.

in daily living. In fact, this is an important issue for clarifying the clinical relevance of reduced PM performance in these patients.

As previously noted, the MIST (Raskin, 2004) and the Virtual Week (Rendell & Henry, 2009) procedure are the tools most frequently used. Both allow examining the different components of PM and have good psychometric properties. In fact, these tests have also been used in patients with other neurological diseases that are associated with PM impairments (e.g. Mioni et al., 2017; Tay, Ang, Lau, Meyyappan, & Collinson, 2010). Moreover, Pirogovsky et al. (2012) showed that in patients with PD the accuracy score on the Memory for Intention Screening Test significantly correlated with patients ability to manage their medication.

However, in a clinical context, including a PM task in the standard neuropsychological exam could add a significant time cost. The attentional resources of the patient could also be excessively strained. In this regard, interesting data are provided in a previous study in which PD patients with MCI were administered a time-based PM task that was incorporated in the standard neuropsychological battery (Costa, Zabberoni, et al., 2015). In this task, participants were required to perform one simple action (e.g. remember to turn on the computer) after 10 minutes had elapsed (four trials were administered). During the delay interval, subjects were administered the neuropsychological tests of a standard screening battery currently used to assess cognitive disorders in PD patients. Results showed that PM score accuracy was sensitive to MCI and that it significantly predicted the ability of PD participants to autonomously manage daily medication (Costa, Zabberoni, et al., 2015). The time-based task administered in this study has the great advantage of not requiring much additional time to assess PM; thus, it is an interesting tool that should be further investigated in PD patients.

Rehabilitation of PM in patients with PD

It is still unclear whether interventions to rehabilitate cognitive functions in PD are effective. Indeed, few studies have been performed to explore this issue and very little attention has been dedicated to investigating the cognitive rehabilitation of PM disorders in PD. Nevertheless, research in this area is increasing as there is evidence that PD patients with cognitive difficulties are able to provide insights into the everyday cognitive difficulties that they experience, thus highlighting possible domains as targets for intervention and setting realistic goals for performance improvement (Vlagsma et al., 2016; Watermeyer et al., 2016).

Fish, Wilson, and Manly (2010) provided useful indications for rehabilitating PM disorders in PD patients without dementia in their review which focused on retraining PM disorders in people with brain diseases by means of retrospective memory strategies, problem-solving training and electronic memory aids. Indeed, as discussed above, there is evidence that in this clinical population executive and episodic memory dysfunctions account for altered self-initiation of the prospective intention as well as for the reduced elaborative encoding and strategic retrieval of the retrospective component of the PM task. In this vein, implementing strategies that lead these patients to overcome their executive and/or memory difficulties could be effective in remediating their PM deficits. In fact, Altgassen et al. (2007) demonstrated that PD patients performed as well as healthy controls when the focus was on the PM task but worse than controls when the ongoing activity was stressed.

Therefore, in line with the above observations, an accurate neuropsychological assessment should be carried out prior to planning cognitive interventions for PM disorders in PD patients without dementia. Neuropsychological examinations should allow making neuropsychological diagnosis and establishing qualitative cognitive profiles. This would permit planning tailored interventions based on whether the patients present, for example, executive or episodic memory disorders.

In this vein, encouraging data have been reported in a study in which PD patients with MCI who had a dysexecutive profile and showed PM impairments were submitted to cognitive training aimed at potentiating shifting capacities (Costa et al., 2014). Results of the study showed that the treated PD patients significantly improved their PM performance after a 12-session intervention.

Another interesting approach that has been used in PD consists of improving the encoding strategies of PM tasks through the formation of 'implementation intentions'. In this approach, subjects are encouraged to 'visualize' the scenario in which they will perform the prospective intention. This method (which has proved to be effective in improving PM performance in both healthy elderly subjects and patients with very mild Alzheimer's disease; Shelton et al., 2016) could be investigated in PD patients who have executive and episodic memory disorders as it is aimed at improving initial planning and establishing the association between PM cue, context and action. In fact, in a recent study by Foster, McDaniel, and Rendell (2017), PD patients without dementia were randomly chosen to perform a computerized Virtual Week task after receiving instructions to encode the prospective intention under 'implementation intentions' or 'rehearsal' strategies. The results showed that PM performance was better when either of these strategies were used compared to standard instructions. Moreover, the 'implementation intentions' strategy was better than the 'rehearsal' strategy for performance of the unrepeated tasks (e.g. tasks that occur only once in the game).

Although further research is needed to investigate and confirm the efficacy of cognitive interventions aimed at remediating the PM deficits in PD, the results of these studies suggest that in PD patients PM might be enhanced by retraining the cognitive sub-processes that underlie PM operations (Fish et al., 2010).

Conclusions

Unlike other available reviews, this one aimed to explore some open issues concerning PM functioning in PD patients by providing valuable clues about how to interpret PM performance in these patients and possible directions for further research in this field. First, we reviewed extant data to explore the hypothesis that altered executive processes might contribute to PM performance in PD patients without dementia. This hypothesis is grounded on evidence that executive functions are affected early in PD (Cools & D'Esposito, 2011) and on the observation that executive abilities are involved in PM tasks. We first examined studies that compared time- vs. event-based PM functioning. However, this literature does not allow reliably clarifying the relationship between executive and PM impairment in PD patients. More convincing evidence of the existence of such an association is provided by data from studies aimed at investigating whether executive control mediates event-cued PM retrieval in these patients. Results showed that PD patients are particularly sensitive to task demands in terms of strategic-voluntary processes.

In view of the clinical observation that many PD patients also have episodic memory impairments (Aarsland et al., 2010), we also explored the hypothesis of a relationship between altered episodic memory and reduced PM efficiency. With this in mind, we reviewed the data of studies that separately assessed the prospective and retrospective components of the PM task. Although results do not converge, some of them show that the retrospective component of the task is impaired in these patients. This suggests that altered episodic memory also contributes to the pattern of PM performance observed in PD patients. In any case, the potential (combined) implications of both self-guided strategies and consolidation/retrieval mechanisms in PM functioning should be further explored.

We also investigated whether PM is specifically associated with MCI in the PD population. Although results from the two studies that compared PM performance in PD patients without MCI and PD patients with MCI document that PM is specifically impaired in the latter group (Costa, Peppe, et al., 2015, Costa, Zabberoni, et al., 2015), it is premature to draw any definite conclusions from such a small sample of studies. For example, it may be that patients with MCI have more widespread deficits (e.g. more automatic and strategic ones) while those without MCI have only very subtle/specific deficits (e.g. highly strategic ones) that would be detected with more sensitive paradigms. Also, the neuropsychological criteria used to define the MCI diagnosis in PD patients might also be relevant for this purpose. It is possible, for example, that if a more conservative cut-off (e.g. 2 SD below the mean of normal controls; Goldman et al., 2013) were used more impaired group of PD-MCI patients would be included or, rather, that even more impaired non-MCI PD group could be selected and yield a different pattern of group-related PM findings. In conclusion, this specific issue warrants further explicit investigation before firm conclusions can be drawn.

Finally, we reviewed current evidence on the application of cognitive interventions to treat PM disorders in PD patients. Although very little is known about this issue, existing data suggest that training focused on specific abilities involved in PM operations might improve performance depending on patients' specific neuropsychological profiles. The evidence that PM failures are associated with a significant reduction of the autonomous management of daily living activities also in PD patients without dementia (Costa, Peppe, et al., 2015, Costa, Zabberoni, et al., 2015) makes this issue urgent.

Some methodological limitations of current PM studies should be highlighted. In most of the published studies, PD patients were assessed while undergoing their usual dopamine therapy, which seems to be quite heterogeneous as it typically, includes levodopa and/or dopamine agonists and/or monoamine oxidase inhibitor. With regard to this, it has been reported that the different molecules present in dopaminergic compounds have different effects on cognitive functions depending on their differential affinity with brain D_n receptors (Cools, 2006). Moreover, in some studies the delay between the time when the PD patients took their dopamine therapy and the moment when the PM assessment was made is not clearly reported, thus making it impossible to determine the potential contribution of dopamine stimulation to their performance.

Disclosure statement

The authors have no conflicts of interest to report.

References

Aarsland, D., Bronnick, K., Williams-Gray, C., Weintraub, D., Marder, K., Kulisevsky, J., … Emre, M. (2010). Mild cognitive impairment in Parkinson disease. A multicenter pooled analysis. *Neurology, 75*, 1062–1069.

Aarsland, D., Creese, B., Politis, M., Chaudhuri, K. R., Ffytche, D. H., Weintraub, D., & Ballard, C. (2017). Cognitive decline in Parkinson disease. *Nature Reviews Neurology, 13*, 217–231.

Altgassen, M., Zöllig, J., Kopp, U., Mackinlay, R., & Kliegel, M. (2007). Patients with Parkinson's disease can successfully remember to execute delayed intentions. *Journal of the International Neuropsychological Society, 13*, 888–892.

Barban, F., Carlesimo, G. A., Macaluso, E., Caltagirone, C., & Costa, A. (2014). Functional interplay between stimulus-oriented and stimulus-independent attending during a prospective memory task. *Neuropsychologia, 53*, 203–212. doi:10.1016/j.neuropsychologia.2013.12.001

Beyer, M. K., Bronnick, K. S., Hwang, K. S., Bergsland, N., Tysnes, O. B., Larsen, J. P., … Apostolova, L. G. (2013). Verbal memory is associated with structural hippocampal changes in newly diagnosed Parkinson's disease. *Journal of Neurology, Neurosurgery and Psychiatry, 84*, 23–28.

Broeders, M., de Bie, R. M., Velseboer, D. C., Speelman, J. D., Muslimovic, D., & Schmand, B. (2013). Evolution of mild cognitive impairment in Parkinson disease. *Neurology, 81*, 346–352. doi:10.1212/WNL.0b013e31829c5c86

Brønnick, K., Alves, G., Aarsland, D., Tysnes, O. B., & Larsen, J. P. (2011, January). Verbal memory in drug-naive, newly diagnosed Parkinson's disease. The retrieval deficit hypothesis revisited. *Neuropsychology, 25*(1), 114–124.

Burgess, P. W., Gonen-Yaacovi, G., & Volle, E. (2011). Functional neuroimaging studies of prospective memory: What have we learnt so far? *Neuropsychologia, 49*, 2246–2257. doi:10.1016/j.neuropsychologia.2011.02.014

Burgess, P. W., & Shallice, T. (1997). The relationship between prospective and retrospective memory: Neuropsychological evidence. In M. A. Conway (Ed.), *Cognitive models of memory* (pp. 242–272). Hove, England: Psychology Press.

Carlesimo, G. A., Casadio, P., & Caltagirone, C. (2004). Prospective and retrospective components in the memory for actions to be performed in patients with severe closed-head injury. *Journal of the International Neuropsychological Society, 10*, 679–688.

Carlesimo, G. A., Piras, F., Assogna, F., Pontieri, F. E., Caltagirone, C., & Spalletta, G. (2012). Hippocampal abnormalities and memory deficits in Parkinson disease: A multimodal imaging study. *Neurology, 78*, 1939–1945.

Chiaravalloti, N. D., Ibarretxe-Bilbao, N., DeLuca, J., Rusu, O., Pena, J., García-Gorostiaga, I., & Ojeda, N. (2014, May). The source of the memory impairment in Parkinson's disease: Acquisition versus retrieval. *Movement Disorder, 29*(6), 765–771.

Cohn, M., Giannoylis, I., De Belder, M., Saint-Cyr, J. A., & McAndrews, M. P. (2016, September). Associative reinstatement memory measures hippocampal function in Parkinson's Disease. *Neuropsychologia, 90*, 25–32.

Cools, R. (2006). Dopaminergic modulation of cognitive function-implications for L-DOPA treatment in Parkinson's disease. *Neuroscience and biobehavioral reviews, 30*, 1–23.

Cools, R., & D'Esposito, M. (2011). Inverted-U-shaped dopamine actions on human working memory and cognitive control. *Biological Psychiatry, 69*, e113–e125. doi:10.1016/j.biopsych.2011.03.028

Costa, A., Caltagirone, C., & Carlesimo, G. A. (2011). Prospective memory impairment in mild cognitive impairment: An analytical review. *Neuropsychology Review, 21*, 390–404. doi:10.1007/s11065-011-9172-z

Costa, A., Carlesimo, G. A., & Caltagirone, C. (2012). Prospective memory functioning: A new area of investigation in the clinical neuropsychology and rehabilitation of Parkinson's disease and mild cognitive impairment. Review of evidence. *Neurological Sciences, 33*, 965–972. doi:10.1007/s10072-012-0935-y

Costa, A., Peppe, A., Brusa, L., Caltagirone, C., Gatto, I., & Carlesimo, G. A. (2008). Levodopa improves prospective memory in Parkinson's disease. *Journal of the International Neuropsychological Society, 14*, 601–610.

Costa, A., Peppe, A., Caltagirone, C., & Carlesimo, G. A. (2008b). Prospective memory impairment in individuals with Parkinson's disease. *Neuropsychology, 22*, 283–292.

Costa, A., Peppe, A., Caltagirone, C., & Carlesimo, G. A. (2013). Decreased event-based prospective memory functioning in individuals with Parkinson's disease. *Journal of Neuropsychology, 7*, 153–163. doi:10.1111/jnp.12024

Costa, A., Peppe, A., Serafini, F., Zabberoni, S., Barban, F., Caltagirone, C., & Carlesimo, G. A. (2014). Prospective memory performance of patients with Parkinson's disease depends on shifting aptitude: Evidence from cognitive rehabilitation. *Journal of the Internationa Neuropsychological Society, 20*, 717–726. doi:10.1017/S1355617714000563

Costa, A., Peppe, A., Zabberoni, S., Serafini, F., Barban, F., Scalici, F., … Carlesimo, G. A. (2015). Prospective memory performance in individuals with Parkinson's disease who have mild cognitive impairment. *Neuropsychology, 29*, 782–791. doi:10.1037/neu0000184

Costa, A., Zabberoni, S., Peppe, A., Serafini, F., Scalici, F., Caltagirone, C., & Carlesimo, G. A. (2015). Time-based prospective memory functioning in mild cognitive impairment associated with Parkinson's disease: Relationship with autonomous management of daily living commitments. *Frontiers in Human Neuroscience, 10*(9), 333. doi:10.3389/fnhum.2015.00333

Dubois, B., Burn, D., Goetz, C., Aarsland, D., Brown, R. G., Broe, G. A., … Emre, M. (2007). Diagnostic procedures for Parkinson's disease dementia: Recommendations from the movement disorder society task force. *Movement Disorders, 22*, 2314–2324. doi:10.1002/mds.21844

Edelstyn, N. M., John, C. M., Shepherd, T. A., Drakeford, J. L., Clark-Carter, D., Ellis, S. J., & Mayes, A. R. (2015, October). Evidence of an amnesia-like cued-recall memory impairment in nondementing idiopathic Parkinson's disease. *Cortex, 71*, 85–101.

Einstein, G. O., & McDaniel, M. A. (1990). Normal aging and prospec- tive memory. *Journal of Experimental Psychology. Learning, Memory, and Cognition, 16*, 717–726.

Emre, M., Aarsland, D., Brown, R., Burn, D. J., Duyckaerts, C., Mizuno, Y., … Dubois, B. (2007). Clinical diagnostic criteria for dementia associated with Parkinson's disease. *Movement Disorders, 22*, 1689–1707.

Fish, J., Wilson, B. A., & Manly, T. (2010). The assessment and rehabilitation of prospective memory problems in people with neurological disorders: A review. *Neuropsychological Rehabilitation, 20*, 161–179. doi:10.1080/09602010903126029

Foo, H., Mak, E., Chander, R. J., Ng, A., Au, W. L., Sitoh, Y. Y., … Kandiah, N. (2016). Associations of hippocampal subfields in the progression of cognitive decline related to Parkinson's disease. *Neuroimage Clinical, 14*, 37–42. doi:10.1016/j.nicl.2016.12.008

Foster, E. R., McDaniel, M. A., & Rendell, P. G. (2017). Improving prospective memory in Persons with Parkinson disease: A randomized controlled trial. *Neurorehabilitation and Neural Repair, 31*, 451–461. doi:10.1177/1545968317690832

Foster, E. R., McDaniel, M. A., Repovs, G., & Hershey, T. (2009). Prospective memory in Parkinson's disease across laboratory and self- reported everyday performance. *Neuropsychology, 23*, 347–358.

Foster, E. R., Rose, N. S., McDaniel, M. A., & Rendell, P. G. (2013). Prospective memory in Parkinson disease during a virtual week: Effects of both prospective and retrospective demands. *Neuropsychology, 27*, 170–181. doi:10.1037/a0031946

Goldman, J. G., Holden, S., Bernard, B., Ouyang, B., Goetz, C. G., & Stebbins, G. T. (2013). Defining optimal cutoff scores for cognitive impairment using movement disorder society task force criteria for mild cognitive impairment in Parkinson's disease. *Movement Disorders, 28*, 1972–1979. doi:10.1002/mds.25655

Huppert, F. A., Johnson, T., & Nickson, J. (2000). High prevalence of prospective memory impairment in the elderly and in early-stage dementia: Findings from a population-based study. *Applied Cognitive Psychology, 14*, S63–S81.

Janvin, C. C., Larsen, J. P., Salmon, D. P., Galasko, D., Hugdahl, K., & Aarsland, D. (2006). Cognitive profiles of individual patients with Parkinson's disease and dementia: Comparison with dementia with lewy bodies and Alzheimer's disease. *Movement Disorders, 21*, 337–342.

Katai, S., Maruyama, T., Hashimoto, T., & Ikeda, S. (2003). Event based and time based prospective memory in Parkinson's disease. *Journal of Neurology, Neurosurgery and Psychiatry, 74*, 704–709.

Kliegel, M., Altgassen, M., Hering, A., & Rose, N. S. (2011). A process- model based approach to prospective memory impairment in Parkin- son's disease. *Neuropsychologia, 49*, 2166–2177. doi:10.1016/j.neuropsychologia.2011.01.024

Kliegel, M., Phillips, L. H., Lemke, U., & Kopp, U. A. (2005). Planning and realization of complex intentions in patients with Parkinson's disease. *Journal of Neurology, Neurosurgery and Psychiatry, 76*, 1501–1505.

Kvavilashvili, L. (1987). Remembering intention as a distinct form of memory. *British Journal of Psychology, 78*, 507–518.

Litvan, I., Goldman, J. G., Tröster, A. I., Schmand, B. A., Weintraub, D., Petersen, R. C., ... Emre, M. (2012). Diagnostic criteria for mild cognitive impairment in Parkinson's disease: Movement disorder society task force guidelines. *Movement Disorders, 27*, 349–356. doi:10.1002/mds.24893

Marcone, S., Gagnon, J. F., Lecomte, S., Imbeault, H., Limoges, F., Postuma, R. B., ... Rouleau, I. (2017). Clinical utility of the envelope task in mild cognitive impairment and dementia. *The Canadian Journal of Neurological Sciences, 44*, 9–16. doi:10.1017/cjn.2016.298

McDaniel, M. A., & Einstein, G. O. (2011). The neuropsychology of prospective memory in normal aging: A componential approach. *Neuropsychologia, 49*, 2147–2155.

McDaniel, M. A., Glisky, E. L., Rubin, S. R., Guynn, M. J., & Routhieaux, B. C. (1999). Prospective memory: A neuropsychological study. *Neuropsychology, 13*, 103–110.

McDaniel, M. A., Guynn, M. J., Einstein, G. O., & Breneiser, J. (2004). Cue-focused and reflexive-associative processes in prospective memory retrieval. *Journal of Experimental Psychology. Learning, Memory, and Cognition, 30*, 605–614.

McFarland, C. P., & Glisky, E. L. (2009). Frontal lobe involvement in a task of time-based prospective memory. *Neuropsychologia, 47*, 1660–1669. doi:10.1016/j.neuropsychologia.2009.02.023

Mioni, G., Bertucci, E., Rosato, A., Terrett, G., Rendell, P. G., Zamuner, M., & Stablum, F. (2017). Improving prospective memory performance with future event simulation in traumatic brain injury patients. *The British journal of clinical psychology, 56*, 130–148. doi:10.1111/bjc.12126

Mioni, G., Meligrana, L., Rendell, P. G., Bartolomei, L., Perini, F., & Stablum, F. (2015). Event-based prospective memory in patients with Parkinson's disease: The effect of emotional valence. *Frontiers in Human Neuroscience, 24*(9), 427. doi:10.3389/fnhum.2015.00427

Pagni, C., Frosini, D., Ceravolo, R., Giunti, G., Unti, E., Poletti, M., ... Tognoni, G. (2011). Event-based prospective memory in newly diagnosed, drug-naive Parkinson's disease patients. *Journal of the International Neuropsychological Society, 17*, 1158–1162. doi:10.1017/S1355617711001214

Pedersen, K. F., Larsen, J. P., Tysnes, O. B., & Alves, G. (2013). Prognosis of mild cognitive impairment in early Parkinson disease: The Norwegian ParkWest study. *JAMA Neurology, 70*, 580–586. doi:10.1001/jamaneurol.2013.2110

Pedersen, K. F., Larsen, J. P., Tysnes, O. B., & Alves, G. (2017). Natural course of mild cognitive impairment in Parkinson disease: A 5-year population-based study. *Neurology, 88*(8), 767–774. pii: 10.1212/WNL.0000000000003634. doi:10.1212/WNL.0000000000003634

Pigott, K., Rick, J., Xie, S. X., Hurtig, H., Chen-Plotkin, A., Duda, J. E., ... Weintraub, D. (2015). Longitudinal study of normal cognition in Parkinson disease. *Neurology, 85*, 1276–1282. doi:10.1212/WNL.0000000000002001

Pirogovsky, E., Woods, S. P., Vincent Filoteo, J., & Gilbert, P. E. (2012). Prospective memory deficits are associated with poorer everyday functioning in Parkinson's disease. *Journal of the International Neuropsychological Society, 18*, 986–995. doi:10.1017/S1355617712000781

Ramanan, S., & Kumar, D. (2013). Prospective memory in Parkinson's disease: A meta-analysis. *Journal of the International Neuropsychological Society, 19*, 1109–1118. doi:10.1017/S1355617713001045

Raskin, S. A. (2004). The Memory for Intentions Screening Test. *Journal of the International Neuropsychological Society, 10*(S1), 110.

Raskin, S. A., Woods, S. P., Poquette, A. J., McTaggart, A. B., Sethna, J., Williams, R. C., & Tröster, A. I. (2011). A differential deficit in time- versus event-based prospective memory in Parkinson's disease. *Neuropsychology, 25*, 201–209.

Rendell, P. G., & Henry, J. D. (2009). A review of virtual week for prospective memory assessment: Clinical implications. *Brain Impairment, 10*, 14–22. doi:10.1375/brim.10.1.14

Robbins, T. W., & Cools, R. (2014). Cognitive deficits in Parkinson's disease: A cognitive neuroscience perspective. *Movement Disorders, 29*, 597–607. doi:10.1002/mds.25853

Santangelo, G., Vitale, C., Picillo, M., Moccia, M., Cuoco, S., Longo, K., … Barone, P. (2015). Mild cognitive impairment in newly diagnosed Parkinson's disease: A longitudinal prospective study. *Parkinsonism and Related Disorders, 21*, 1219–1226.

Shelton, J. T., Lee, J. H., Scullin, M. K., Rose, N. S., Rendell, P. G., & McDaniel, M. A. (2016). Improving prospective memory in healthy older adults and individuals with very mild Alzheimer's disease. *Journal of the American Geriatrics Society, 64*, 1307–1312. doi:10.1111/jgs.14134

Smith, S. J., Souchay, C., & Moulin, C. J. (2011). Metamemory and prospective memory in Parkinson's disease. *Neuropsychology, 25*, 734–740. doi:10.1037/a0025475

Svenningsson, P., Westman, E., Ballard, C., & Aarsland, D. (2012). Cognitive impairment in patients with Parkinson's disease: Diagnosis, biomarkers, and treatment. *Lancet Neurology, 11*, 697–707.

Tay, S. Y., Ang, B. T., Lau, X. Y., Meyyappan, A., & Collinson, S. L. (2010). Chronic impairment of prospective memory after mild traumatic brain injury. *Journal of Neurotrauma, 27*, 77–83. doi:10.1089/neu.2009.1074

Vlagsma, T. T., Koerts, J., Fasotti, L., Tucha, O., van Laar, T., Dijkstra, H., & Spikman, J. M. (2016). Parkinson's patients' executive profile and goals they set for improvement: Why is cognitive rehabilitation not common practice? *Neuropsychological Rehabilitation, 26*, 216–235. doi:10.1080/09602011.2015.1013138

Watermeyer, T. J., Hindle, J. V., Roberts, J., Lawrence, C. L., Martyr, A., Lloyd-Williams, H., … Clare, L. (2016). Goal setting for cognitive rehabilitation in mild to moderate parkinson's disease dementia and dementia with lewy bodies. *Parkinson's Disease, 2016*, 8285041. doi:10.1155/2016/8285041

Weintraub, D., Moberg, P. J., Culbertson, W. C., Duda, J. E., & Stern, M. B. (2004). Evidence for impaired encoding and retrieval memory profiles in Parkinson disease. *Cognitive and Behavioral Neurology, 17*, 195–200.

Whittington, C. J., Podd, J., & Stewart-Williams, S. (2006). Memory deficits in Parkinson's disease. *Journal of Clinical and Experimental Neuropsychology, 28*, 738–754.

Yarnall, A. J., Breen, D. P., Duncan, G. W., Khoo, T. K., Coleman, S. Y., Firbank, M. J., … Burn, D. J. (2014). ICICLE-PD study group. Characterizing mild cognitive impairment in incident Parkinson disease: The ICICLE-PD study. *Neurology, 82*, 308–316. doi:10.1212/WNL.0000000000000066

Yeterian, E. H., & Pandya, D. N. (1991). Prefrontostriatal connections in relation to cortical architectonic organization in rhesus monkeys. *The Journal of Comparative Neurology, 312*, 43–67.

Mild cognitive impairment and prospective memory: translating the evidence into neuropsychological practice

Glynda J. Kinsella, Kerryn E. Pike, Marina G. Cavuoto and Stephen D. Lee

ABSTRACT

Objective: There has been a recent rapid development of research characterizing prospective memory performance in mild cognitive impairment (MCI) in older age. However, this body of literature remains largely separated from routine clinical practice in neuropsychology. Furthermore, there is emerging evidence of effective interventions to improve prospective memory performance. Therefore, our objective in this article was to offer a clinical neuropsychological perspective on the existing research in order to facilitate the translation of the evidence-base into clinical practice. **Method:** By conducting a critical review of the existing research related to prospective memory and MCI, we highlight how this data can be introduced into clinical practice, either within diagnostic assessment or clinical management. **Conclusions:** Prospective memory is impaired in older adults with MCI, with a pattern of performance that helps with differential diagnosis from healthy aging. Clinical neuropsychologists are encouraged to add prospective memory assessment to their toolbox for diagnostic evaluation of clients with MCI. Preliminary findings of prospective memory interventions in MCI are promising, but more work is required to determine how different approaches translate to increasing independence in everyday life.

Introduction

Many older people presenting at memory clinics report changes in ability to *remember to remember*, or prospective memory, which involves remembering to perform an intended action at an appropriate time or event in the future (Brandimonte, Einstein, & McDaniel, 2014). Prospective memory is important for the social and practical aspects of life, such as remembering to return a telephone call or attending an appointment; and, in older people, has been linked to everyday function (Beaver & Schmitter-Edgecombe, 2017; Schmitter-Edgecombe, Woo, & Greeley, 2009) and the capacity for maintaining independent living (Woods, Weinborn, Velnoweth, Rooney, & Bucks, 2012). Driven by both theoretical and clinical interest, prospective memory is increasingly investigated as a feature of *Mild Cognitive Impairment* (or MCI), which is a broad term that has been applied when (i) the client (or family member) presents with a concern about a recent decline in cognitive capacity; (ii) impairment in cognition is demonstrated on neuropsychological tests; (iii) independence in activities of daily living is present, although compromise can be observed in complex activities; and (iv) the client does not fulfill criteria for clinical dementia (Albert et al., 2011; Petersen et al., 2014). Multiple underlying disorders can contribute to MCI, but older people with MCI are frequently conceptualized as being at high risk of Alzheimer's disease and later development of dementia. In the recent practice guidelines for MCI (Petersen et al., 2018), a meta-analysis estimated that people with MCI vs. healthy older adults have triple the risk of being diagnosed with Alzheimer's dementia within 2–5 years (RR 3.0, 95% CI 2.1–4.8).

The purpose of this article is to provide a clinician's perspective on existing evidence-based literature in prospective memory as applied in MCI. We addressed this through identifying the current themes that have immediate relevance for neuropsychological practice. This is not an exhaustive systematic review but provides a critical analysis on issues that may influence how the clinician approaches assessing and managing prospective memory in the context of MCI. Necessarily, our interpretation of the literature may suffer from personal biases but we hope that the article provides useful information for translating research into practice. We have confined our commentary to the published prospective memory literature that concerns MCI, apart from instances where more general discussion of relevant research in prospective memory assists in suggesting future research and/or practice (for example, in describing theoretical models of prospective memory, or the use of external aids to manage impaired prospective remembering). We accessed articles from PsychINFO and Ovid MEDLINE (year 2000 onwards), using search terms of 'mild cognitive impairment' or 'MCI' AND 'prospective memory', or 'prospective remembering', or 'delayed intentions' in addition to MESH/indexed terms as appropriate to each database.

There are several challenges in evaluating the relationship between prospective memory and MCI. Firstly, MCI was initially conceptualized as applying to memory impairment (Petersen et al., 1999) but recent models have applied the term to other cognitive domains, with a broad distinction between amnestic MCI (aMCI) and nonamnestic MCI (naMCI) (Albert et al., 2011; Petersen et al., 2014; Scheltens et al., 2017). MCI is now used as a generic term to signal that some aspect of cognition is impaired relative to normative test standards. By implication, the term 'MCI' describes a very heterogeneous patient group in terms of cognition and neuropathology. Furthermore, although there is agreement that cognitive impairment in MCI has to be demonstrated on neuropsychological tests, it remains contended as to which individual tests and cut-off for impairment should be used for operationalization of MCI. This is important as identification of MCI can vary with the test used (e.g. Petersen et al., 2018; Pike et al., 2013), adding to the complexity of comparing prospective memory performance across studies. Consequently, these issues need consideration in translating the evidence-base about prospective memory and MCI into clinical practice.

Current knowledge of prospective memory deficits in MCI

There is strong evidence that prospective memory is significantly impaired in MCI compared with healthy older adults, as summarized in two critical analyses (Costa, Caltagirone, & Carlesimo, 2011; Spíndola & Brucki, 2011), and a meta-analysis (van den Berg, Kant, & Postma, 2012). van den Berg et al. (2012), in their meta-analysis, found no significant difference in size of effect for prospective memory impairment between MCI and dementia. This highlights the considerable utility of prospective memory as an early cognitive marker of evolving dementia.

The vulnerability of prospective memory in MCI reflects a model whereby successful performance requires not only retrieval of delayed intentions (episodic memory) through spontaneous processes dependent on an automatic-associative memory system (McDaniel & Einstein, 2011), but also a strategic monitoring system (Arnold, Bayen, & Smith, 2015; R. E. Smith & Bayen, 2004). This latter system is especially recruited when prospective memory tasks require attention allocation, or executive attention, for cues in the environment (internal or external) to activate delayed intentions; for example, *listening for the arrival of an ordered taxi whilst watching a favorite television program*. The neuropathology in aMCI involves mesial temporal lobe structures, particularly the entorhinal cortex and the hippocampus (Markesbery et al., 2006), which support the spontaneous retrieval of encoded information (episodic memory). Furthermore, neuropathology in the frontal system for attention allocation (executive attention) has also been implicated for both aMCI and naMCI (Haroutunian, Hoffman, & Beeri, 2009; Libon et al., 2010). Therefore, various underlying neural impairments exist that will challenge prospective memory in MCI (aMCI and naMCI sub-types; Hernandez Cardenache, Burguera, Acevedo, Curiel, & Loewenstein, 2014); either through impairment in the automatic-associative system (as required in encoding and timely retrieval of delayed intentions), or the strategic monitoring system (for flexibly switching attention between ongoing activities and the intended task), or most commonly an interaction of both systems (see Kliegel, McDaniel, & Einstein, 2000; and Kliegel et al., 2016 for discussion of multiphase models of prospective memory, and their application to older age).

Much of the literature on prospective memory in MCI has contrasted performance on event-based tasks (performing an intended action when an event occurs) to time-based tasks (remembering to perform an intended action at a specified time) (Troyer & Murphy, 2007; Costa et al., 2011; van den Berg et al., 2012). Time-based prospective memory tasks are inferred to be more reliant on effortful strategic monitoring than most event-based tasks, and therefore more cognitively demanding, as they are not automatically prompted by an external cue. Using only a time-based task, Costa et al. (2015) reported that the prospective memory task improved the accuracy in discrimination between MCI and healthy control participants. In their meta-analysis, however, van den Berg et al. (2012) reported that impairments in MCI were comparable in event-based and time-based tasks, converging with the expectation of a common (but not universal) interaction of cognitive impairments in MCI, which compromise both the automatic-associative and strategic monitoring systems of prospective memory (Costa et al., 2011).

An alternative approach to investigating prospective memory evaluates how the cue for remembering (focal or nonfocal) influences performance. In focal conditions, an ongoing activity encourages processing of the cue for prospective remembering. This limits the demand on strategic monitoring and encourages more spontaneous retrieval of delayed intentions (for example, *remembering to use a retail gift card instead of a credit card to pay for goods when next shopping at the supermarket*). In contrast, in nonfocal conditions, the cue is distinct or peripheral to the essential elements of the ongoing activity (for example, *while cooking dinner, remembering to give your spouse a retail gift card before he or she goes to the supermarket*). In situations like the latter, retrieval of intentions is more reliant on strategic monitoring resources (Scullin, Bugg, McDaniel, & Einstein, 2011).

Typically, age-related impairments are greater for nonfocal prospective memory tasks than for focal tasks due to declining cognitive resources for strategic monitoring (Kliegel, Jäger, & Phillips, 2008). In relation to MCI, however, the evidence is not so clear. Blanco-Campal, Coen, Lawlor, Walsh, and Burke (2009) used an event-based prospective memory task that was manipulated to have focal and nonfocal conditions. They reported that both conditions discriminated aMCI from healthy controls; but the nonfocal condition did so better. Similarly, in a study confined to investigating performance on a nonfocal event-based task, Tam and Schmitter-Edgecombe (2013) reported that participants with aMCI performed more poorly than age-matched controls. However, Chi et al. (2014) found that those with MCI (aMCI and naMCI) were more impaired in the focal condition of a task relative to healthy controls (also see Niedzwienska, Kvavilashvili, Ashaye, & Neckar, 2017). The reason for these discrepant findings is not easily interpreted and reflects the difficulty in comparing across samples of MCI due to known variability in cognitive impairment within diagnostic groups (Libon et al., 2010). Nevertheless, McDaniel, Shelton, Breneiser, Moynan, and Balota (2011) also found that participants with very mild Alzheimer's disease (arguably similar to aMCI) were most accurately discriminated from healthy controls by impaired focal prospective memory, with nonfocal performance close to floor for both groups. This suggests that although nonfocal prospective remembering will be challenging for people with aMCI and for healthy older adults, it is an impaired automatic-associative system that provides the characteristic hallmark of additionally impaired focal prospective memory performance, especially in aMCI. For the clinician, this performance pattern may be able to distinguish aMCI from healthy older adults who are expected to retain capacity on focal tasks as distinct from nonfocal tasks (a dissociation in performance as outlined above).

Interestingly in the Chi et al. (2014) study, secondary analysis suggested that the naMCI group also showed more impairment on the nonfocal task, which the researchers interpreted as reflective of additional deficits in executive attention and prefrontal systems. This suggests that the approach of manipulating the cue for prospective remembering could offer a sensitive approach to detect sub-type differences in MCI. However, the practical difficulty in demonstrating this dissociation in performance through clinical assessment is that the focal and nonfocal tasks need to be similar in task content before manipulating the prospective memory cue, and also that older clients with MCI can present with a mixed profile of memory impairment and impairments in other cognitive domains, including executive attention (mixed MCI; Libon et al., 2010). Therefore, although the distinction between focal and nonfocal tasks is important in the development of our theoretical understanding of prospective memory, reliably demonstrating this effect in a clinical context may be more difficult to achieve.

The types of errors most often seen in MCI in daily life

An early debate in prospective memory and healthy aging research relates to the observation that older adults are impaired on laboratory-based tasks but their performance can be equivalent, or even surpass, the performance of younger adults in naturalistic settings (Henry, MacLeod, Phillips, & Crawford, 2004; Rendell & Craik, 2000). This has been referred to as the *age-prospective memory paradox*; and, the continuing ability in older age to apply well-learnt memory strategies in naturalistic settings has been suggested as one reason for age differences in performances across settings (Maylor, 1996). Clearly, this issue needs careful consideration by the clinician to establish the extent to which the clinical assessment of prospective memory generalizes to daily activities.

Most studies of prospective memory in MCI have been conducted with experimental tasks in a laboratory setting. However, Karantzoulis, Troyer, and Rich (2009) used the *Memory For Intentions Screening Test* (Raskin, 2009) that includes a naturalistic task in which the participant is requested to telephone the clinician after a delay of 24 h. In addition to poorer performance on the overall battery of tests, the MCI sample was less likely to make the telephone call as compared to controls. This provided an early indication that people with MCI are more likely to experience prospective memory failures in everyday activities than healthy older adults (also see Rabin et al., 2014). Indeed, in a survey of a memory training group, 62% reported that prospective memory errors (such as forgetting to call someone) were one of the most important experienced (Kliegel & Martin, 2003).

Prospective memory in an everyday setting (turning on a handheld electronic organizer once per day for two days at a predetermined time) was further evaluated by Thompson, Henry, Withall, Rendell, and Brodaty (2011), who reported that in a mixed sample of participants with MCI (aMCI and naMCI) they did not show deficits compared to healthy controls. This may have related to participants being instructed not to use strategies (such as writing notes or creating conjunction cues) to act as reminders to perform the task. Therefore, the known advantage for healthy controls of strategy use in naturalistic prospective memory was absent, and it remained unclear whether group differences would emerge if strategies were permitted.

To further evaluate this issue, Delprado, Kinsella, Ong, and Pike (2013) used tasks that were either experimenter-introduced (telephoning the experimenter with a message at predetermined times across two weeks) or self-generated (the participant formed a list of their own tasks to be completed for the week, recording task success or otherwise at the end of the week). Importantly, participants were allowed to use strategies. Regardless of whether the tasks were experimenter- or self-generated, participants with aMCI displayed significant difficulty in carrying out the prospective memory tasks as compared to healthy older adults; for example, *remembering to take a bottle of wine for dinner with friends, buy a lottery ticket on Wednesday, or remembering to telephone overseas family at an appropriate time*. Notably, when questioned about strategies used, healthy older adults used more external strategies (e.g. written notes), whereas participants with aMCI relied more on another person to provide a reminder. In addition to being less reliable, relying on someone else is likely to increase burden of support on close family and also provides context for why prospective memory failures cause the greatest frustration in family supporters of people with impaired memory (Crawford, Smith, Maylor, Della Sala, & Logie, 2003).

Another approach to exploring how people with MCI are challenged by prospective memory tasks in everyday activities is to consider the distinction between habitual and episodic tasks. Habitual prospective memory involves performing a task which is regular or routine such as measuring blood glucose levels following a meal or taking the bins out for rubbish collection (Ellis, 1996; Meacham & Leiman, 1982). In contrast, episodic tasks refer to a one-off or irregular action (McDaniel & Einstein, 2011). A major difference between habitual and episodic prospective memory is that the intention for the episodic task must be encoded and retrieved prior to the execution of the task, whereas once a habitual task is established as a habit, the encoding of the intention (intention formation) does not need to occur prior to each execution (Dismukes, 2008). Unpublished data from our group (Cavuoto, Kinsella,

Ong, Pike, & Nicholas, 2017) demonstrated that participants with aMCI were significantly impaired compared to controls in performing a new habitual prospective memory task which simply involved pressing a button daily on a time-logged activity monitor over two weeks (for further task details see Cavuoto, Ong, Pike, Nicholas, & Kinsella, 2017). This indicates that for people with MCI not only will errors be noted for novel irregular tasks but significant support will be required to change or modify established routines, and to establish and maintain a new routine or habit.

In summary, the available research suggests that people with MCI, in comparison to healthy older adults, are at high risk of frequent prospective memory failures in everyday activities (e.g. *returning phone calls*). These failures are broad-based and are liable to occur for both time-based tasks (*attending a nephew's football game at 5 pm*) and event-based tasks (*taking medications with breakfast*). Failures are not confined to novel unfamiliar tasks but are also likely to occur for routine, habitual tasks (*remembering to feed pets or lock the back door when leaving the house*). These latter failures can be particularly frustrating for the client and for the family as they are often unexpected and can lead to discussions about capacity for ongoing independent living. For many older people who live alone, fear of being unable to maintain independent living is liable to provoke high anxiety. Anxiety per se is known to interfere directly with prospective memory (Harris & Cumming, 2003), or indirectly through working memory (Darke, 1988), a primary cognitive resource for prospective memory. Therefore, the clinician should carefully evaluate non-cognitive factors that additionally impact prospective memory in everyday life.

The research has also highlighted that people with MCI do not spontaneously use effective compensatory memory strategies, suggesting that targeted interventions to develop skills in compensatory strategy use are warranted. Reflecting the heterogeneity of cognitive deficit in clients with MCI, selection of approach to strategy training will be variable (see the following section on intervention).

Approaches to clinical assessment of prospective memory in MCI

A major issue for clinicians in the context of MCI is that the purpose of neuropsychological assessment is often to contribute to the diagnosis of an underlying degenerative disease. Necessarily, this demands careful evaluation of the patient's test performances against normative standards. To date, few prospective memory measures provide comprehensive norms, especially in advanced age groups, which may contribute to the relatively rare occurrence of prospective memory testing within a neuropsychological assessment for MCI. Other concerns relate to reliability and sensitivity, practice effects, and length of time for administration (see the next sub-sections for further discussion on these issues). Nevertheless, as the field develops the following approaches have demonstrated potential value for consideration in neuropsychological assessment.

Quasi-naturalistic single-event probes of prospective memory

Single-event and single-trial prospective memory tasks are simple tasks that require the client to complete an intended action when the appropriate time or event occurs; for example, asking the client to remind the clinician at the end of the assessment to provide an appointment card for the next appointment. These tasks are attractive for clinicians because they tend to be more naturalistic than other approaches and provide a perspective on how the client might behave in everyday life. This can enhance the ecological relevance of assessment and be useful in client and family feedback. They are also brief to administer, which is important in time-pressured diagnostic assessments that need to cover multiple domains of cognition.

Examples of this approach can be found in several test batteries for prospective memory assessments, which will be described in the next section. A further example is the *Envelope Task* (Huppert, Johnson, & Nickson, 2000) which is a single-event task used to discriminate older people with MCI from healthy older adults (see Table 1). The task instructs clients that later during assessment (the ongoing task) they will be presented with an envelope and asked to write a dictated name and address on the envelope (prospective memory cue). At that point, they need to remember, without prompting by the examiner, to turn over the envelope and write their name and initials on the back of the envelope (initiation and execution of the delayed intention). Huppert et al. (2000) demonstrated that in a mixed sample of older adults ($n = 11{,}956$) including people with probable dementia, only 54% were successful on the task; and, in the sub-group of older adults with probable dementia, only 8% of 388 participants were able to perform the task. These figures caused the researchers to recommend that assessment of prospective memory should be routinely incorporated into management plans for the ongoing safety and support of older people with very mild stage dementia. The task was later adapted by Kinsella et al. (2009) and found useful for describing prospective memory gains in response to a cognitive intervention program for people with aMCI. Additionally, Lee et al. (2016) reported good discrimination between aMCI ($n = 76$) and healthy older adults ($n = 77$) when using the *Envelope Task* (AUC .83, 95% CI .75, .90), suggesting its use in clinical practice as a screening measure of prospective memory.

Nevertheless, it should be noted that although the *Envelope Task* demonstrated excellent specificity (91.9%), its sensitivity was not as encouraging, potentially relating to its limited scale (possible range 0–4). These results, which are similar to those reported by Delprado, Kinsella, Ong, and Pike (2012) and Marcone et al. (2017), suggest that a normal performance on the *Envelope Task* cannot rule out the actual presence of MCI, and, therefore, the test will need to be contextualized within a more comprehensive neuropsychological assessment if to be used in clinical practice. This illustrates the complexity of assessing and interpreting prospective memory through quasi-naturalistic approaches, even though they offer an avenue for introducing more ecologically relevant data into the assessment.

Test batteries of prospective memory

These batteries provide opportunity for investigating prospective memory in MCI under controlled conditions (e.g. event- vs. time-based tasks) so that a more comprehensive profile of prospective memory can be identified. Examples of batteries (see Table 1) that have been used to distinguish MCI from healthy older adults include (i) the *Cambridge Assessment of Prospective Memory* (*CAMPROMPT*; Wilson, 2005); (ii) *the Memory for Intentions Screening Test* (MIST; Raskin, 2009; Raskin, Buckheit, & Sherrod, 2010); (iii) the *Royal Prince Alfred Prospective Memory Test* (RPA-ProMem; Radford, Lah, Say, & Miller, 2011); and, (iv) the *Virtual Week* (Rendell & Craik, 2000). The advantages of these batteries are: information about reliability and validity, inclusion of ecologically valid sub-tests, frequent availability of parallel test forms, and preliminary normative data. The main detraction of the battery approach for

Table 1. Measurement properties of clinical measures of prospective memory used in mild cognitive impairment.

Single event probes	Description	Psychometrics	Findings in MCI
Envelope Task (Huppert, et al., 2000)	Patient asked to remember (after 20 min) to seal and initial an envelope (unprompted) after a name and address is dictated.	Not available	Huppert et al. (2000): 92% PM failure for people with early dementia (similar to MCI) compared to 46% for controls. Delprado et al. (2012): sensitivity of 66% and specificity 81% to discriminate aMCI from controls. Lee et al. (2016): sensitivity of 64% and a specificity of 92% to discriminate aMCI from controls.
Questionnaires			
CAPM (Roche et al., 2002)	Self- and informant-reports of PM. 3 subscales: A) frequency of failure (39 items), B) amount of concern about failures (39 items), and C) reasons for PM success or failures (15 items)	Chau, Lee, Fleming, Roche, and Shum (2007): frequency of failure section (A) – test–retest reliability (.74–.77), internal consistency (.74–.94). No psychometric properties available for section B.	Rabin et al. (2014): section B – mixed sample (amnestic and nonamnestic MCI, subjective cognitive decline, and controls) informant reports ($r = -.23$) but not self-reports ($r = -.09$) correlated with a measure of PM performance (RPA-ProMem). Chi et al. (2014): section B – mixed sample (amnestic and nonamnestic MCI, subjective cognitive decline, and controls) informant-reports only negatively related to prospective memory under nonfocal ($r = -.22$) but not focal cue ($r = -.07$) conditions.
PRMQ (Smith et al., 2000)	16-item self-report scale with 8 items each for retrospective (RM) and prospective (PM) subscales, as well as a Total score.	Smith et al. (2000): Split-half reliability (.84).	Eschen et al. (2009): no differences in RM and PM between controls and MCI. Thompson et al. (2015): no differences in self-report PM between controls, MCI and dementia, but greater reports of PM problems by informants in dementia than controls and MCI, with latter two not different on informant reports
	Informant version also available (Crawford et al., 2006).	Crawford et al. (2003): scale reliability (.80–.89); confirmed tripartite factor structure (total, RM, PM).	Lee et al. (2016): PM and RM lower in aMCI than controls; but discrimination of aMCI from controls only 50% sensitivity and 75.7% specificity for total PRMQ.

Clinical Batteries	Administration	Norms	Alt form	Psychometrics	Findings in MCI
CAMPROMPT (Wilson et al., 2005)	Three time- and event-based PM tasks over 25 min while completing puzzle filler tasks.	Yes	Yes	Reliability: Wilson et al. (2005): Inter-rater (.998) Test–retest (.64) Inter-item (.475) Delprado et al. (2012): Inter-item (.75)	Delprado et al. (2012): aMCI performed below controls for total score, and more poorly on time- than event-based PM tasks. Discrimination between aMCI from controls: time-based 69% sensitivity and 69% and specificity; and event-based 73% sensitivity and 70% specificity.

MIST (Raskin, 2009); Raskin et al., 2010)	Eight PM tasks over 30 min while completing distractor word search puzzles.	Yes	Yes	Reliability: Raskin (2009): Inter-form (.89) Split-half (.70) Inter-item (.475) Reliability (.886)	Karantzoulis et al. (2009): aMCI performed below controls on MIST total score (Cohen's *d* 1.14). Rabin et al. (2014): aMCI and naMCI underperformed controls, although not after adjusting for education, race/ethnicity and mood.
RPA-ProMemRadford et al. (2011)	Four parts: one time- and one event-based task completed after 15 and 30 min, respectively, within assessment. Further time- and event-based tasks completed at home.	No	Yes	Reliability: Radford et al. (2011): Inter-rater (.90) Alternate form (.71) Inter-rater (.97) Rabin et al. (2014): Mixed sample including MCI inter-rater reliability (.97)	Rabin et al. (2014): Performance poorer for aMCI but not naMCI than controls on the total score ($p < .001$). RPA-ProMem performance related to MIST performance ($r = .35$). Aronov et al. (2015): both MCI and subjective cognitive decline groups had lower overall PM scores than controls
Virtual WeekRendell and Craik (2000)	Simulates daily living tasks using a board game (over 30 min) based on seven virtual days. As participants move around the board they are required to carry out lifelike activities PM tasks include regular and irregular time- and event-based tasks.	No	Yes	Reliability: Rose, Rendell, McDaniel, Aberle, and Kliegel (2010): Split-half (.86 - .94). Henry, Rendell, Kliegel, and Altgassen (2007): split-half (.66) Mioni, Rendell, Stablum, Gamberini, and Bisiacchi (2015): test–retest (.31 - .81) for older adults. Internal consistency (.86–.92)	Thompson et al. (2015): performance poorer in MCI than controls, and poorer in dementia than MCI.

Notes: CAPM: The Comprehensive Assessment of Prospective Memory, PRMQ: The Prospective and Retrospective Memory Questionnaire, CAMPROMT: The Cambridge Prospective Memory Test, MIST: Memory for Intentions Screening Test, RPA-ProMem: Royal Prince Alfred Prospective Memory Test, RM: retrospective memory, PM: prospective memory, RM, retrospective memory, MCI: mild cognitive impairment aMCI: amnestic mild cognitive impairment, Alt form: alternate form.

clinicians is the time required for completion; usually at least 10–30 min. This is relevant where there may not be opportunity to assess the client on more than a single session. If the purpose is to provide a comprehensive baseline to assess gains made from an intervention, however, these approaches may be useful.

Self- and informant-report questionnaires

Healthy older adults' subjective ratings of memory performance in everyday life have been questioned with regard to their relationship to observable memory performance (Crumley, Stetler, & Horhota, 2014). However, they do represent the perspective of the individual, which is important in client-centered service delivery. Given that self- or informant-report of cognitive decline is a core criterion of MCI (Petersen et al., 2018), examining the prognostic utility of these measures will be important to further evaluate (see Table 1).

The Comprehensive Assessment of Prospective Memory, Section B (*CAPM*; Roche, Fleming, & Shum, 2002) is a 39-item self- and informant-report questionnaire that has been used to explore the association between self-and informant-reports and prospective memory performance in clinical groups, including people with MCI (Chi et al., 2014; Rabin et al., 2014). For each item the respondent is requested to rate how much of a problem is a common everyday memory failure (e.g. forgetting to take tablets at the prescribed time). In a combined sample ($n = 257$, including healthy older adults, aMCI, naMCI, and subjective cognitive decline), Rabin et al. (2014) found that informant ratings (but not self-ratings) of everyday memory difficulties were related to poorer performance on a prospective memory test battery ($r = -.23$), and Chi et al. (2014) reported that informant-reports only were significantly related, albeit weakly, to prospective memory under nonfocal ($r = -.22$) but not focal cue ($r = -.07$) conditions. These studies indicate small but significant associations between a family or friend's perspective and actual prospective memory performance in a mixed ability sample of older people, although self-reports do not show strong association with actual performance and the specific results for the MCI participants and their informants were not provided.

The Prospective and Retrospective Memory Questionnaire (*PRMQ*; G. Smith, Del Sala, Logie, & Maylor, 2000) is a 16-item self-report scale relating to prospective and retrospective memory failures in everyday activities and was developed to evaluate memory difficulties in older people and in dementia. Each prospective ($n = 8$ items) and retrospective ($n = 8$ items) subscale is further subdivided into short/long term-items and self-cued/environmentally cued items to provide a profile of the type of everyday task that respondents experience as especially challenging. The questionnaire has a large normative base and has undergone extensive psychometric evaluation (Crawford et al., 2003). An informant (Proxy) version is also available (Crawford, Henry, Ward, & Blake, 2006). Although self-ratings on the PRMQ (prospective and retrospective sub-scales) have been noted to be poorer in aMCI than in healthy adults (Lee et al., 2016), they have not been consistently found to discriminate between MCI and healthy older people (Eschen, Martin, Gasser, & Kliegel, 2009; Lee et al., 2016; Ryu, Lee, Kim, & Lee, 2016; Thompson, Henry, Rendell, Withall, & Brodaty, 2015). This may reflect varying levels of self-awareness of memory difficulties in people with MCI (Roberts, Clare, & Woods, 2009; Wolfsgruber et al., 2014), which can vary according to the cognitive status of the person with MCI (Piras, Piras, Orfei, Caltagirone, & Spalletta, 2016). Therefore, while incorporating self-report measures of memory into neuropsychological assessment of MCI is best-practice in a clinical context, the above studies highlight that it cannot stand in place of objective memory testing (Thompson et al., 2015) and reiterates the need for ecologically valid measures of prospective memory that can be easily incorporated into clinical practice.

Challenges and opportunities in assessment of prospective memory in MCI

The optimal methods for assessing prospective memory in people with MCI continue to be evaluated by various research groups. Although, prospective memory batteries tend to have higher reliability and sensitivity than single-event probes, their lengthy administration times are a major drawback in a time-pressured diagnostic setting. Nevertheless, single-event probes may be a quick and useful way to demonstrate to clients and families the impact that cognitive impairment may have on everyday tasks and behavior. In this regard, rather than conceiving prospective memory as a discrete cognitive function to be measured in the diagnostic assessment, it may be more useful to conceptualize poor prospective memory as a behavioral expression of the profile of impairment in associative memory and/or executive attention in the person with MCI; domains of cognition which are traditionally already part of a neuropsychological assessment.

Similarly, the utility of self-report measures for diagnosis of MCI can be confounded by the impact of limited awareness of some people with MCI. Nevertheless, they do offer a means to capture the subjective experience of prospective memory failure in everyday life, and, again, can be employed as a useful tool when providing neuropsychological feedback to the client and/or family.

In relation to the longer prospective memory batteries, there may be more scope for their inclusion in neuropsychological assessments where the aim is to plan management strategies and responsiveness to cognitive intervention, or to evaluate cognitive change over time. However, further research will be needed in this area because tracking change in performance may be confounded by the broader issue of potential practice effects when the novel and unusual elements of prospective memory tasks are diminished by repeated presentation, as is the case with repeated executive function assessment (Lemay, Bedard, Rouleau, & Tremblay, 2004). An alternative approach to using tests to assess responsiveness to prospective memory intervention could be to improve prospective memory function in the context of an actual task or real-life function, rather than test performance alone. This demonstration of 'real' benefit is crucial in the current context where governments are seeking evidence of impact of public research funds on the benefit to the broader community, which may determine future allocation of research funding (Penfield, Baker, Scoble, & Wykes, 2014).

Evidence-based approaches to treatment

MCI is common within older adults living in the community, with a prevalence of approximately 17% (Petersen et al., 2018; supplementary guidelines). Therefore, interventions that moderate memory difficulties would impact a large number of older people, especially if maintaining independent living. Although, there is a growing literature on interventions for MCI, the field is yet to reach a clear consensus about intervention gains. Some meta-analyses report positive gains (Chandler, Parks, Marsiske, Rotblatt, & Smith, 2016; Li et al., 2011), and other reviews report none, or only limited gains (Martin, Clare, Altgassen, Cameron, &

Zehnder, 2011; Reijnders, van Heugten, & van Boxtel, 2013). Furthermore, very few studies have focused on prospective memory, whether through specific interventions or through outcome assessment. Thus, there is little direct evidence for the efficacy of specific techniques to improve prospective memory in MCI. In this section we will describe the main approaches for improving prospective memory generally, and then describe those recent studies that have aimed to improve prospective memory in MCI (or an MCI-like group). Areas for further research will be highlighted.

Hering, Rendell, Rose, Schnitzspahn, and Kliegel (2014) outline a model for approaching prospective memory intervention that can be adapted to working with MCI. They propose two broad approaches to training prospective memory. Firstly, process training is based on restoring or improving discrete cognitive processes, whereas strategy-based training focuses on compensating for limitations in cognitive processes. Process training usually involves controlled practice on memory tasks, typically computer-based. Using this approach, there have been some impressive results demonstrating the potential for neuronal plasticity in healthy older brains (Anguera et al., 2013). Nevertheless, lack of transfer and generalization to everyday tasks remains a criticism, and this is particularly relevant when considering the purpose of intervention for MCI.

The alternative approach of strategy training has received more attention in MCI, although there are only a handful of studies examining prospective memory strategies. Hutchens et al. (2012) reported that, in comparison to healthy controls, people with aMCI demonstrate less accessible knowledge of strategies (both for prospective and retrospective memory tasks). Moreover, although no difference was found in observed level of external strategy use (note taking) between aMCI and controls, for the aMCI group, greater use of strategies was associated with better prospective memory performance. Similarly, Aronov et al. (2015) reported no difference between participants with aMCI and healthy controls in their observed use of external strategies, but that increased use of external strategies was associated with better prospective memory. These findings provide support for including strategy training as an approach to prospective memory intervention.

In considering which component of prospective memory to focus intervention efforts, Kliegel et al.'s (2000) four-phase model of prospective memory provides a framework for approaching intervention. Briefly, the model suggests that: (i) the *intention formation* phase involves planning the intention, relying on encoding and planning cognitive resources; (ii) the *intention retention* phase, or maintenance over time of the intention, depends on an elaborated representation of the intention for assisting later retrieval, and working memory for periodic renewal of the intended action; (iii) *intention initiation*, involves executive attention processes of environmental monitoring, attention switching and inhibition to move attention between an ongoing task and the intended action; and, (iv) *intention execution*, requires attention switching. In addition to this basic model, metacognitive processes have been identified for successful prospective remembering, including self-efficacy, cognitive beliefs, motivation, and emotional status. All these variables are viable candidates for intervention in MCI with known neuropathology impacting on a broad range of cognitions and behaviors, including neuropsychiatric symptoms such as apathy, depression, and anxiety (Gallagher, Fischer, & Iaboni, 2017).

Considering the hallmark of impaired episodic memory in MCI, it is not surprising to see the recent exploration of elaborated encoding strategies to improve the likelihood of maintenance and delayed retrieval of an intention. Pereira et al. (2015) found that physical enactment at encoding, as well as increased relatedness of target–action pairs, improved prospective memory on a laboratory-based task in people with aMCI. Three further studies in samples including people with MCI (along with people with subjective memory complaints only as well as people with dementia) have investigated the use of *implementation intentions,* a memory-encoding technique that strengthens intention formation, retention, and initiation, and has been used successfully with healthy adults to improve prospective memory (Liu & Park, 2004). *Implementation intentions* requires an individual to verbalize and visualize a retrieval cue and link the cue to a delayed intention; for example, *When I go into my kitchen after tennis this afternoon, I will ring my daughter.* Shelton et al. (2016) found that implementation intentions improved prospective memory performance on a laboratory-based task in very mild Alzheimer's disease (CDR = .5; similar to a diagnosis of MCI).

The impact of implementation intentions on more naturalistic prospective memory tasks (single probes embedded within the clinical neuropsychology assessment) was examined by Burkard, Rochat, Van der Linden, Gold, and Van der Linden (2014) in a mixed sample of memory clinic attendees (older people with subjective memory complaints, mild cognitive impairment, or dementia). In this study, working memory capacity moderated the effect of the intervention on prospective memory; such that only those with good working memory benefitted. The researchers suggested that for clients with significant working memory impairment, alternative strategies should be examined to support prospective memory; for example, external aids such as diaries and planners (electronic or paper). Both of these studies used explicit experimenter instruction on creating implementation intentions for the prospective memory outcome measures. Training individuals to use implementation intentions independently to improve prospective memory in daily life might be a different matter and was examined in a pilot study by Burkard et al. (2014). The program was feasible and the mixed sample memory clinic participants improved in their self-reported goal-directed behaviors in everyday life (i.e. everyday prospective memory tasks), but it did involve a five-week program (10 h per week) focused solely on using implementation intentions, suggesting translation of strategy use to everyday life may require substantial training time.

Although external aids such as diaries and planners are well-known to be useful for supporting prospective memory, there have been few formal studies examining their use to improve prospective memory in MCI. Work by Smith's research team (Greenaway, Hanna, Lepore, & Smith, 2008; Greenaway, Duncan, & Smith, 2013; Chandler et al., 2017) has examined the training of people with aMCI and their caregivers to use a paper notebook/ calendar system, the *Memory Support System,* with an appointment, to-do, and journaling section. Across studies they consistently found that people with aMCI allocated to the training condition had higher adherence in using the system, improved functional ability (including informant report of everyday memory), and self-efficacy; and their caregivers reported improved mood. Note that prospective memory itself was not examined, other than 2/8 items collapsed within an overall measure of everyday memory. Similarly, Schmitter-Edgecombe and Dyck (2014) also reported improved everyday functioning and memory following training of people with MCI and their caregiver to use a memory notebook, although again, prospective memory was not examined as a separate outcome measure.

Electronic aids are proposed to be useful for prospective memory tasks such as keeping appointments and attending social activities (Arntzen, Holthe, & Jentoft, 2016); and, have the advantage over other memory aids in that they can be programmed to provide reminders. A pilot study by Oriani et al. (2003) reported on the use of an electronic memory aid for patients in the early stages of Alzheimer disease. The ability to remember to carry out several tasks at a particular time (prospective memory) significantly improved with an electronic memory aid, whilst provision of a written list or simply attempting free recall were not useful strategies. Nevertheless, in a review of electronic aids for prospective memory loss in dementia, King and Dwan (2017) caution that although the available literature is positive about potential benefits, the evidence is limited. The literature is even more limited regarding the use of electronic aids for people with MCI, and further studies conducted within the home and with everyday tasks will provide a better understanding of their specific benefits.

As evidenced in Burkard et al.'s (2014) work on training independent use of implementation intentions for everyday prospective memory, translating promising memory strategies from the laboratory to everyday life is not always straightforward. It is recognized that translating memory strategies to everyday situations requires behavior change, and interventions that focus on personal goals and build self-confidence in applying new skills are more likely to encourage older adults to actually use strategies in daily activities (Stine-Morrow & Basak, 2011; Troyer, Murphy, Anderson, Moscovitch, & Craik, 2008; West, Bagwell, & Dark-Freudeman, 2008). Furthermore, group-based interventions (memory groups) that offer opportunities for peer-learning and practice in skill application have been reported to produce better results in healthy older people than individualized training (Kelly et al., 2014). On this basis, in a preliminary study of older people with aMCI, Kinsella et al. (2009) investigated the benefit from a memory group to prospective memory performance. The group-based intervention used an evidence-based multi-strategy approach (including external aids and implementation intentions for prospective memory) and also included education and training about health behaviors that assist memory performance through managing non-cognitive factors known to impact memory performance (knowledge about memory strategies, memory self-efficacy, and anxiety). The trial demonstrated that older people with aMCI could benefit from a group-based cognitive-behavioral intervention by improving performance on naturalistic prospective memory tasks. In a subsequent larger randomized-controlled trial of the memory group intervention, Kinsella et al. (2016) found that healthy older adults displayed gains in prospective memory performance immediately following intervention and at six-month follow-up, whereas participants with aMCI only showed improvement in prospective memory performance at six-month follow-up. These findings suggest that change in actual everyday behaviors (prospective memory) may take longer to effect in MCI than observed with healthy older people. This has implications for the approach to clinical management of people with MCI. Furthermore, the involvement of a supportive family member, where possible, is likely to enhance behavior change in everyday life (Schmitter-Edgecombe & Dyck, 2014).

Overall, the evidence on specific interventions to improve prospective memory performance in MCI is still developing, with only a handful of published studies. Positive findings in response to specific elaborated encoding techniques, particularly implementation intentions, have been reported. However, studies are limited by the use of primarily laboratory-based prospective memory tasks as well as inclusion of mixed samples, combining MCI participants (aMCI and naMCI) along with those with subjective memory complaints only, as well as those with dementia. External aids to support everyday prospective memory function are also likely to be worthwhile but research specifically using prospective memory as an outcome measure in MCI is not yet available. Future research directions should continue to consider the relevance of interventions for improving prospective memory in everyday life, as well as including direct comparison of the efficacy of different techniques (elaborated encoding, external aids), which is likely to depend on task characteristics as well as individual differences (Burkard et al., 2014). Finally, there is support for prospective memory gains following group-based multi-strategy interventions, which include building self-confidence in applying strategies and optimizing behavior change in everyday activities.

Suggestions for management of prospective memory deficits for individuals with MCI

As the field continues to evaluate the utility of specific techniques for managing prospective memory errors, the clinician will have a larger toolbox for responding to the needs of the client with MCI. At the same time, there are some key issues that need to be considered when tailoring management plans to an individual client rather than a clinical population in general. Firstly, as discussed, there is considerable variation in the profile of cognitive impairments in MCI and this will influence the choice of intervention strategy. Furthermore, different people naturally use different strategies to perform everyday tasks (Dunlosky & Metcalfe, 2008); for example, use of a written shopping list (external aid) vs. mental semantic grouping of to-be-remembered items (semantic association) when shopping for dinner at a supermarket. This suggests that a multi-strategy approach to intervention (Kinsella et al., 2016, 2009), will likely result in more success for the MCI client when responding to the complexities of prospective remembering in everyday life.

A further issue is that the client with MCI is likely to need strong support to translate strategy knowledge to actual use of the strategy in daily activities. There are multiple reasons why knowledge per se does not guarantee application, including lack of confidence and memory self-efficacy. These co-existing factors can sometimes be optimally addressed within a group context, building memory self-efficacy through peer support (*if she can do it, I can do it*) and sharing of experience (West et al., 2008). Although the group format may be a useful method for the client to begin the journey of behavior change, it can also be strengthened by combining with individualized goal-oriented sessions (Clare et al., 2013). Such sessions focus on practice in the application of specific techniques for attaining personalized goals; for example, practice in elaborated encoding techniques, for remembering a new regime of medications (Liu & Park, 2004), or individualized training in using the range of functions of a mobile phone (external aid).

A final issue that will be of concern to the clinician is how to sustain training effects over extended periods of time. There is some limited evidence from the healthy aging literature that booster sessions to consolidate new skills may be helpful (Rebok et al., 2014). This also provides opportunity to review and adjust strategies. This is important for the clinician, as MCI is typically a progressive disorder and intervention is not so much about altering the underlying neuropsychological impairment but reducing the disability arriving from the impairment, i.e. minimizing prospective memory errors in daily life, improving quality of life, and sustaining independent living as long as possible.

Conclusions

Effective prospective memory performance is heavily challenged in people with MCI, resulting in a broad range of everyday difficulties. Further development in ecologically valid prospective memory tests, suitable for use in a clinical neuropsychological assessment for MCI, will enable the clinician to assess competency in this important area of applied cognition. Findings from MCI studies investigating response to intervention for prospective memory impairment have been promising, but translational work is still needed to evaluate how different approaches improve independence in real-time everyday activities.

Disclosure statement

No potential conflict of interest was reported by the authors.

ORCID

Glynda J. Kinsella http://orcid.org/0000-0002-5859-0934

References

References marked with an asterisk were included in the preliminary database search

Albert, M., DeKosky, S., Dickson, D., Dubois, B., Feldman, H., & Fox, N. (2011). The diagnosis of mild cognitive impairment due to Alzheimer's disease: Recommendations from the National Institute on Aging – Alzheimer's Association workgroups on diagnostic guidelines for Alzheimer's disease. *Alzheimer's & Dementia, 7*(3), 270–279. doi:10.1016/j.jalz.2011.03.008

Anguera, J. A., Boccanfuso, J., Rintoul, J. L., Al-Hashimi, O., Faraji, F., Janowich, J., ... Gazzaley, A. (2013). Video game training enhances cognitive control in older adults. *Nature, 501*(7465), 97–101. doi:10.1038/nature12486

Arnold, N. R., Bayen, U. J., & Smith, R. E. (2015). Hierarchical multinomial modeling approaches: An application to prospective memory and working memory. *Experimental Psychology, 32*(3), 143–152. doi:10.1027/1618-3169/a000287

Arntzen, C., Holthe, T., & Jentoft, R. (2016). Tracing the successful incorporation of assistive technology into everyday life for younger people with dementia and family carers. *Dementia, 15*(4), 646–662. doi:10.1177/1471301214532263

Aronov, A., Rabin, L. A., Fogel, J., Chi, S. Y., Kann, S. J., Abdelhak, N., & Zimmerman, M. E. (2015). Relationship of cognitive strategy use to prospective memory performance in a diverse sample of nondemented older adults with varying degrees of cognitive complaints and impairment. *Aging, Neuropsychology, and Cognition, 22*(4), 486–501. doi:10.1080/13825585.2014.984653*

Beaver, J. K., & Schmitter-Edgecombe, M. (2017). Multiple memory processes and everyday functional assessment in community-dwelling older adults. *Archives of Clinical Neuropsychology, 32*, 413–426.*

van den Berg, E., Kant, N., & Postma, A. (2012). Remember to buy milk on the way home! A meta-analytic review of prospective memory in mild cognitive impairment and dementia. *Journal of the International Neuropsychological Society, 18*(4), 706–716. doi:10.1017/S1355617712000331.*

Blanco-Campal, A., Coen, R. F., Lawlor, B. A., Walsh, J. B., & Burke, T. E. (2009). Detection of prospective memory deficits in mild cognitive impairment of suspected Alzheimer's disease etiology using a novel event-based prospective memory task. *Journal of the International Neuropsychological Society, 15*(1), 154–159. doi:10.1017/S1355617708090127*

Brandimonte, M. A., Einstein, G. O., & McDaniel, M. A. (2014). *Prospective memory: Theory and applications*. New York, NY: Psychology Press.

Burkard, C., Rochat, L., Van der Linden, A.-C. J., Gold, G., & Van der Linden, M. (2014). Is working memory necessary for implementation intentions to enhance prospective memory in older adults with cognitive problems? *Journal of Applied Research in Memory and Cognition, 3*(1), 37–43. doi:10.1016/j.jarmac.2014.01.004

Cavuoto, M. G., Kinsella, G. J., Ong, B., Pike, K. E., & Nicholas, C. L. (2017). *Sleep and memory in older adults with amnestic mild cognitive impairment [unpublished raw data]*. Melbourne: La Trobe University, School of Psychology & Public Health.

Cavuoto, M. G., Ong, B., Pike, K. E., Nicholas, C. L., & Kinsella, G. J. (2017). Naturalistic prospective memory in older adults: Predictors of performance on a habitual task. *Neuropsychological Rehabilitation, 27*(5), 744–758. doi:10.1080/09602011.2015.1074590

Chandler, M. J., Parks, A. C., Marsiske, M., Rotblatt, L. J., & Smith, G. E. (2016). Everyday impact of cognitive interventions in mild cognitive impairment: A systematic review and meta-analysis. *Neuropsychology Review, 26*(3), 225–251. doi:10.1007/s11065-016-9330-4

Chandler, M. J., Locke, D. E. C., Duncan, N. L., Hanna, S. M., Cuc, A. V., Fields, J. A., ... Smith, G. E. (2017). Computer versus compensatory calendar training in individuals with mild cognitive impairment: Functional impact in a pilot study. *Brain Sciences,7*(9), 112. doi:10.3390/brainsci7090112

Chau, L. T., Lee, J. B., Fleming, J., Roche, N., & Shum, D. (2007). Reliability and normative data for the Comprehensive Assessment of Prospective Memory (CAPM). *Neuropsychological Rehabilitation, 17*(6), 707–722. doi:10.1080/09602010600923926

Chi, S. Y., Rabin, L. A., Aronov, A., Fogel, J., Kapoor, A., & Wang, C. (2014). Differential focal and nonfocal prospective memory accuracy in a demographically diverse group of nondemented community-dwelling older adults. *Journal of the International Neuropsychological Society, 20*(10), 1015–1027. doi:10.1017/S1355617714000964*

Clare, L., Bayer, A., Burns, A., Corbett, A., Jones, R., Knapp, M., ... Whitaker, R. (2013). Goal-oriented cognitive rehabilitation in early-stage dementia: Study protocol for a multi-centre single-blind randomised controlled trial (GREAT). *Trials, 14*(1), 152. doi:10.1186/1745-6215-14-152

Costa, A., Caltagirone, C., & Carlesimo, G. A. (2011). Prospective memory impairment in mild cognitive impairment: An analytical review. *Neuropsychology Review, 21*(4), 390–404. doi:10.1007/s11065-011-9172-z*

Costa, A., Fadda, L., Perri, R., Brisindi, M., Lombardi, M. G., Caltagirone, C., & Carlesimo, G. A. (2015). Sensitivity of a time-based prospective memory procedure in the assessment of amnestic mild cognitive impairment. *Journal of Alzheimer's Disease, 44*(1), 63–67. doi:10.3233/JAD-142070*

Crawford, J., Smith, G., Maylor, E., Della Sala, S., & Logie, R. (2003). The prospective and retrospective memory questionnaire (PRMQ): Normative data and latent structure in a large non-clinical sample. *Memory, 11*(3), 261–275.

Crawford, J. R., Henry, J. D., Ward, A. L., & Blake, J. (2006). The prospective and retrospective memory questionnaire (PRMQ): Latent structure, normative data and discrepancy analysis for proxy-ratings. *British Journal of Clinical Psychology, 45*(1), 83–104. doi:10.1348/014466505X28748

Crumley, J. J., Stetler, C. A., & Horhota, M. (2014). Examining the relationship between subjective and objective memory performance in older adults: A meta-analysis. *Psychology and Aging, 29*(2), 250–263. doi:10.1037/a0035908

Darke, S. (1988). Anxiety and working memory capacity. *Cognition and Emotion, 2*(2), 145–154. doi:10.1080/02699938808408071

Delprado, J., Kinsella, G., Ong, B., & Pike, K. (2012). Clinical measures of prospective memory in amnestic mild cognitive impairment. *Journal of the International Neuropsychological Society, 18*(2), 295–304. doi:10.1017/S135561771100172X*

Delprado, J., Kinsella, G., Ong, B., & Pike, K. (2013). Naturalistic measures of prospective memory in amnestic mild cognitive impairment. *Psychology and Aging, 28*(2), 322–332. doi:10.1037/a0029785.*

Dismukes, R. (2008). Prospective memory in aviation and everyday settings. In M. Kliegel, M. A. McDaniel, & G. O. Einstein (Eds.), *Prospective memory: Cognitive, neuroscience, developmental, and applied perspectives* (pp. 411–428). New York, NY: Lawrence Erlbaum.

Dunlosky, J., & Metcalfe, J. (2008). *Metacognition*. Thousand Oaks, CA: Sage.

Ellis, J. (1996). Prospective memory or the realization of delayed intentions: A conceptual framework for research. In M. Brandimonte, G. O. Einstein, & M. A. McDaniel (Eds.), *Prospective memory: Theory and applications* (pp. 1–22). New York, NY: Lawrence Erlbaum.

Eschen, A., Martin, M., Gasser, U. S., & Kliegel, M. (2009). Prospective and retrospective memory complaints in mild cognitive impairment and mild Alzheimer's disease. *Brain Impairment, 10*(1), 59–75. doi:10.1375/brim.10.1.59*

Gallagher, D., Fischer, C. E., & Iaboni, A. (2017). Neuropsychiatric symptoms in mild cognitive impairment: An update on prevalenece, mechanisms, and clinical significance. *The Canadian Journal of Psychiatry, 62*(3), 161–169. doi:10.1177/0706743716648296

Greenaway, M. C., Hanna, S. M., Lepore, S. W., & Smith, G. E. (2008). A behavioral rehabilitation intervention for amnestic mild cognitive impairment. *American Journal of Alzheimer's Disease and Other Dementias, 23*(5), 451–461.

Greenaway, M. C., Duncan, N. L., & Smith, G. E. (2013). The memory support system for mild cognitive impairment: Randomized trial of a cognitive rehabilitation intervention. *International Journal of Geriatric Psychiatry, 28*(4), 402–409.

Haroutunian, V., Hoffman, L. B., & Beeri, M. S. (2009). Is there a neuropathology difference between mild cognitive impairment and dementia? *Dialogues in Clinical Neuroscience, 11*(2), 171–179.

Harris, L. M., & Cumming, S. R. (2003). An examination of the relationship between anxiety and performance on prospective and retrospective memory tasks. *Australian Journal of Psychology, 55*(1), 51–55. doi:10.1080/00049530412331312874

Henry, J. D., MacLeod, M. S., Phillips, L. H., & Crawford, J. R. (2004). A meta-analytic review of prospective memory and aging. *Psychology and Aging, 19*(1), 27–39. doi:10.1037/0882-7974.19.1.27

Henry, J. D., Rendell, P. G., Kliegel, M., & Altgassen, M. (2007). Prospective memory in schizophrenia: Primary or secondary impairment? *Schizophrenia Research, 95*(1–3), 179–185. doi:10.1016/j.schres.2007.06.003*

Hering, A., Rendell, P. G., Rose, N. S., Schnitzspahn, K. M., & Kliegel, M. (2014). Prospective memory training in older adults and its relevance for successful aging. *Psychological Research, 78*(6), 892–904. doi:10.1007/s00426-014-0566-4

Hernandez Cardenache, R., Burguera, L., Acevedo, A., Curiel, R., & Loewenstein, D. A. (2014). Evaluating different aspects of prospective memory in amnestic and nonamnestic mild cognitive impairment. *ISRN Neurology, vol 2014, Article ID 805929*, 7 pages. doi:10.1155/2014/805929*

Huppert, F. A., Johnson, T., & Nickson, J. (2000). High prevalence of prospective memory impairment in the elderly and in early-stage dementia: Findings from a population-based study. *Applied Cognitive Psychology, 14*(7), S63–S81. doi:10.1002/acp.771

Hutchens, R. L., Kinsella, G. J., Ong, B., Pike, K. E., Parsons, S., Storey, E., … Clare, L. (2012). Knowledge and use of memory strategies in amnestic mild cognitive impairment. *Psychology and Aging, 27*(3), 768–777.*

Karantzoulis, S., Troyer, A. K., & Rich, J. B. (2009). Prospective memory in amnestic mild cognitive impairment. *Journal of the International Neuropsychological Society, 15*(3), 407–415. doi:10.1017/S1355617709090596*

Kelly, M. E., Loughrey, D., Lawlor, B. A., Robertson, I. H., Walsh, C., & Brennan, S. (2014). The impact of cognitive training and mental stimulation on cognitive and everyday functioning of healthy older adults: A systematic review and meta-analysis. *Ageing Research Reviews, 15*, 28–43. doi:10.1016/j.arr.2014.02.004

King, A. C., & Dwan, C. (2017). Electronic memory aids for people with dementia experiencing prospective memory loss: A review of empirical studies. *Dementia, Jan 1: 1471301217735180.* doi:10.1177/1471301217735180 [Epub ahead of print]

Kinsella, G. J., Mullaly, E., Rand, E., Ong, B., Burton, C., Price, S., … Storey, E. (2009). Early intervention for mild cognitive impairment: A randomised controlled trial. *Journal of Neurology, Neurosurgery & Psychiatry, 80*(7), 730–736. doi:10.1136/jnnp.2008.148346*

Kinsella, G. J., Ames, D., Storey, E., Ong, B., Pike, K. E., Saling, M. M., & Rand, E. (2016). Strategies for improving memory: A randomized trial of memory groups for older people, including those with mild cognitive impairment. *Journal of Alzheimer's Disease, 49*(1), 31–43. doi:10.3233/JAD-150378*

Kliegel, M., & Martin, M. (2003). Prospective memory research: Why is it relevant? *International Journal of Psychology, 38*(4), 193–194. doi:10.1080/00207590344000114

Kliegel, M., McDaniel, M. A., & Einstein, G. O. (2000). Plan formation, retention, and execution in prospective memory: A new approach and age-related effects. *Memory & Cognition, 28*(6), 1041–1049. doi:10.3758/BF03209352

Kliegel, M., Jäger, T., & Phillips, L. H. (2008). Adult age differences in event-based prospective memory: A meta-analysis on the role of focal versus nonfocal cues. *Psychology and Aging, 23*(1), 203–208. doi:10.1037/0882-7974.23.1.203

Kliegel, M., Ballhausen, N., Hering, A., Ihle, A., Schnitzspahn, K. M., & Zuber, S. (2016). Prospective memory in older adults: Where we are now and what is next. *Gerontology, 62*(4), 459–466. doi:10.1159/000443698

Lee, S., Ong, B., Pike, K. E., Mullaly, E., Rand, E., Storey, E., … Kinsella, G. J. (2016). The contribution of prospective memory performance to the neuropsychological assessment of mild cognitive impairment. *The Clinical Neuropsychologist, 30*(1), 131–149. doi:10.1080/13854046.2015.1135983*

Lemay, S., Bedard, M., Rouleau, I., & Tremblay, P. L. (2004). Practice effect and test-retest reliability of attentional and executive tests in middle-aged to elderly subjects. *The Clinical Neuropsychologist, 18*(2), 284–302. doi:10.1080/13854040490501718

Li, H., Li, J., Li, N., Li, B., Wang, P., & Zhou, T. (2011). Cognitive intervention for persons with mild cognitive impairment: A meta-analysis. *Ageing Research Reviews, 10*(2), 285–296. doi:10.1016/j.arr.2010.11.003

Libon, D. J., Xie, S. X., Eppig, J., Wicas, G., Lamar, M., Lippa, C., … Wambach, D. M. (2010). The heterogeneity of mild cognitive impairment: A neuropsychological analysis. *Journal of the International Neuropsychological Society, 16*(1), 84–93.

Liu, L. L., & Park, D. C. (2004). Aging and medical adherence: The use of automatic processes to achieve effortful things. *Psychology and Aging, 19*(2), 318–325. doi:10.1037/0882-7974.19.2.318

Marcone, S., Gagnon, J.-F., Lecomte, S., Imbeault, H., Limoges, F., Postuma, R. B., … Rouleau, I. (2017). Clinical utility of the envelope task in mild cognitive impairment and dementia. *The Canadian Journal of Neurological Sciences, 44*(1), 9–16. doi:10.1017/cjn.2016.298*

Markesbery, W. R., Schmitt, F. A., Kryscio, R. J., Davis, D. G., Smith, C. D., & Wekstein, D. R. (2006). Neuropathologic substrate of mild cognitive impairment. *Archives of Neurology, 63*(1), 38–46. doi:10.1001/archneur.63.1.38

Martin, M., Clare, L., Altgassen, A. M., Cameron, M. H., & Zehnder, F. (2011). Cognition-based interventions for healthy older people and people with mild cognitive impairment. *Cochrane Database of Systematic Reviews* (1), CD006220. doi:10.1002/14651858.CD006220.pub2

Maylor, E. A. (1996). Does prospective memory decline with age? In M. Brandimonte, G. O. Einstein, & M. A. McDaniel (Eds.), *Prospective memory: Theory and applications* (pp. 173–197). Mahwah, NJ: Lawrence Erlbaum.

McDaniel, M. A., & Einstein, G. O. (2011). The neuropsychology of prospective memory in normal aging: A componential approach. *Neuropsychologia, 49*(8), 2147–2155. doi:10.1016/j.neuropsychologia.2010.12.029

McDaniel, M. A., Shelton, J. T., Breneiser, J. E., Moynan, S., & Balota, D. A. (2011). Focal and nonfocal prospective memory performance in very mild dementia: A signature decline. *Neuropsychology, 25*(3), 387–396. doi:10.1037/a0021682

Meacham, J. A., & Leiman, B. (1982). Remembering to perform future actions. In R. C. Atckinson, J. Freedman, G. Lindzey, & R. F. Thomspson (Eds.), *Memory observed: Remembering in Natural Contexts* (pp. 327–336). San Francisco, CA: Freeman.

Mioni, G., Rendell, P. G., Stablum, F., Gamberini, L., & Bisiacchi, P. S. (2015). Test-retest consistency of Virtual Week: A task to investigate prospective memory. *Neuropsychological Rehabilitation, 25*(3), 419–447. doi:10.1080/09602011.2014.941295*

Niedzwienska, A., Kvavilashvili, L., Ashaye, K., & Neckar, J. (2017). Spontaneous retrieval deficits in amnestic mild cognitive impairment: A case of focal event-based prospective memory. *Neuropsychology, 31*(7), 735–749. doi:10.1037/neu0000378*

Oriani, M., Moniz-Cook, E., Binetti, G., Zanieri, G., Frisoni, G., Geroldi, C., … Zanetti, O. (2003). An electronic memory aid to support prospective memory in patients in the early stages of Alzheimer's disease: A pilot study. *Aging & Mental Health, 7*(1), 22–27. doi:10.1080/1360786021000045863

Penfield, T., Baker, M. J., Scoble, R., & Wykes, M. C. (2014). Assessment, evaluations, and definitions of research impact: A review. *Research Evaluation, 23*(1), 21–32. doi:10.1093/reseval/rvt021

Pereira, A., de Mendonça, A., Silva, D., Guerreiro, M., Freeman, J., & Ellis, J. (2015). Enhancing prospective memory in mild cognitive impairment: The role of enactment. *Journal of Clinical and Experimental Neuropsychology, 37*(8), 863–877. doi:10.1080/13803395.2015.1072499*

Petersen, R. C., Smith, G. E., Waring, S. C., Ivnik, R. J., Tangalos, E. G., & Kokmen, E. (1999). Mild cognitive impairment: Clinical characterization and outcome. *Archives of Neurology, 56*(3), 303–308. doi:10.1001/archneur.56.3.303

Petersen, R. C., Caracciolo, B., Brayne, C., Gauthier, S., Jelic, V., & Fratiglioni, L. (2014). Mild cognitive impairment: A concept in evolution. *Journal of Internal Medicine, 275*(3), 214–228. doi:10.1111/joim.12190

Petersen, R. C., Lopez, O., Armstrong, M. J., Getchius, T. S. D., Ganguli, M., & Gloss, D., Rae-Grant, A. (2018). Practice guideline update summary: Mild cognitive impairment: Report of the guideline development, dissemination, and implementation subcommittee of the American Academy of Neurology. *Neurology, 90*(3), 1–10. doi:10.1212/WNL.0000000000004826

Pike, K. E., Kinsella, G. J., Ong, B., Mullaly, E., Rand, E., Storey, E., & Parsons, S. (2013). Is the WMS-IV verbal paired associates as effective as other memory tasks in discriminating amnestic mild cognitive impairment from normal aging? *The Clinical Neuropsychologist, 27*(6), 908–923. doi:10.1080/13854046.2013.809149*

Piras, F., Piras, F., Orfei, M. D., Caltagirone, C., & Spalletta, G. (2016). Self-awareness in mild cognitive impairment: Quantitative evidence from systematic review and meta-analysis. *Neuroscience & Biobehavioral Reviews, 61*, 90–107. doi:10.1016/j.neubiorev.2015.10.002

Rabin, L. A., Chi, S. Y., Wang, C., Fogel, J., Kann, S. J., & Aronov, A. (2014). Prospective memory on a novel clinical task in older adults with mild cognitive impairment and subjective cognitive decline. *Neuropsychological Rehabilitation, 24*(6), 868–893. doi:10.1080/09602011.2014.915855*

Radford, K. A., Lah, S., Say, M. J., & Miller, L. A. (2011). Validation of a new measure of prospective memory: The Royal Prince Alfred prospective memory test. *The Clinical Neuropsychologist, 25*(1), 127–140. doi:10.1080/13854046.2010.529463

Raskin, S. A. (2009). Memory for intentions screening test: Psychometric properties and clinical evidence. *Brain Impairment, 10*(1), 23–33. doi:10.1375/brim.10.1.23

Raskin, S. A., Buckheit, C., & Sherrod, C. (2010). *Memory for intentions test.* Lutz, FL: Psychological Assessment Resources.

Rebok, G. W., Ball, K., Guey, L. T., Jones, R. N., Kim, H. Y., King, J. W. … ACTIVE Study Group (2014). Ten-year effects of the advanced cognitive training for independent and vital elderly cognitive training trial on cognition and everyday functioning in older adults. *Journal of the American Geriatrics Society, 62*(1), 16–24. doi:10.1111/jgs.12607

Reijnders, J., van Heugten, C., & van Boxtel, M. (2013). Cognitive interventions in healthy older adults and people with mild cognitive impairment: A systematic review. *Ageing Research Reviews, 12*(1), 263–275. doi:10.1016/j.arr.2012.07.003

Rendell, P. G., & Craik, F. I. (2000). Virtual week and actual week: Age-related differences in prospective memory. *Applied Cognitive Psychology, 14*(7), S43–S62. doi:10.1002/acp.770

Roberts, J. L., Clare, L., & Woods, R. T. (2009). Subjective memory complaints and awareness of memory functioning in mild cognitive impairment: A systematic review. *Dementia and Geriatric Cognitive Disorders, 28*(2), 95–109. doi:10.1159/000234911

Roche, N. L., Fleming, J. M., & Shum, D. H. K. (2002). Self-awareness of prospective memory failure in adults with traumatic brain injury. *Brain Injury, 16*(11), 931–945. doi:10.1080/02699050210138581

Rose, N. S., Rendell, P. G., McDaniel, M. A., Aberle, I., & Kliegel, M. (2010). Age and individual differences in prospective memory during a 'Virtual Week': The role of working memory, task regularity and cue focality. *Psychology and Aging, 25*(3), 595–605. doi:10.1037/a0019771

Ryu, S. Y., Lee, S. B., Kim, T. W., & Lee, T. J. (2016). Memory complaints in subjective cognitive impairment, amnestic mild cognitive impairment and mild Alzheimer's disease. *Acta Neurologica Belgica, 116*(4), 535–541.*

Scheltens, N. M., Tijms, B. M., Koene, T., Barkhof, F., Teunissen, C. E., Wolfsgruber, S., … Amsterdam Dementia Cohort. (2017). Cognitive subtypes of probable Alzheimer's disease robustly identified in four cohorts. *Alzheimer's & Dementia, 13*(11), 1226–1236. doi:10.1016/j.jalz.2017.03.002

Schmitter-Edgecombe, M., & Dyck, D. (2014). A cognitive rehabilitation multi-family group intervention for individuals with mild cognitive impairment and their care-partners. *Journal of the International Neuropsychological Society, 20*(9), 897–908. doi:10.1017/S1355617714000782

Schmitter-Edgecombe, M., Woo, E., & Greeley, D. R. (2009). Characterizing multiple memory deficits and their relation to everyday functioning in individuals with mild cognitive impairment. *Neuropsychology, 23*(2), 168–177. doi:10.1037/a0014186*

Scullin, M. K., Bugg, J. M., McDaniel, M. A., & Einstein, G. O. (2011). Prospective memory and aging: Preserved spontaneous retrieval, but impaired deactivation, in older adults. *Memory & Cognition, 39*(7), 1232–1240. doi:10.3758/s13421-011-0106-z

Shelton, J. T., Lee, J. H., Scullin, M. K., Rose, N. S., Rendell, P. G., & McDaniel, M. A. (2016). Improving prospective memory in healthy older adults and individuals with very mild Alzheimer's disease. *Journal of the American Geriatrics Society, 64*(6), 1307–1312. doi:10.1111/jgs.14134

Smith, R. E., & Bayen, U. J. (2004). A multinomial model of event-based prospective memory. *Journal of Experimental Psychology: Learning, Memory, and Cognition, 30*(4), 756–777. doi:10.1037/0278-7393.30.4.756

Smith, G., Del Sala, S., Logie, R. H., & Maylor, E. A. (2000). Prospective and retrospective memory in normal ageing and dementia: A questionnaire study. *Memory, 8*(5), 311–321. doi:10.1080/09658210050117735

Spíndola, L., & Brucki, S. M. D. (2011). Prospective memory in Alzheimer's disease and mild cognitive impairment. *Dementia & Neuropsychologia, 5*(2), 64–68. doi:10.1590/S1980-57642011DN05020002*

Stine-Morrow, E. A., & Basak, C. (2011). Cognitive interventions. In K. Schaie & S. Willis (Eds.), *Handbook of the psychology of aging* (pp. 153–171). San Diego, CA: Academic Press.

Tam, J. W., & Schmitter-Edgecombe, M. (2013). Event-based prospective memory and everyday forgetting in healthy older adults and individuals with mild cognitive impairment. *Journal of Clinical and Experimental Neuropsychology, 35*(3), 279–290. doi:10.1080/13803395.2013.770823*

Thompson, C., Henry, J. D., Withall, A., Rendell, P. G., & Brodaty, H. (2011). A naturalistic study of prospective memory function in MCI and dementia. *British Journal of Clinical Psychology, 50*(4), 425–434. doi:10.1111/j.2044-8260.2010.02004.x*

Thompson, C. L., Henry, J. D., Rendell, P. G., Withall, A., & Brodaty, H. (2015). How valid are subjective ratings of prospective memory in mild cognitive impairment and early dementia? *Gerontology, 61*(3), 251–257. doi:10.1159/000371347*

Troyer, A. K., & Murphy, K. J. (2007). Memory for intentions in amnestic mild cognitive impairment: Time- and event-based prospective memory. *Journal of the International Neuropsychological Society, 13*(2), 365–369.*

Troyer, A. K., Murphy, K. J., Anderson, N. D., Moscovitch, M., & Craik, F. I. M. (2008). Changing everyday memory behavior in amnestic mild cognitive impairment: A randomized controlled trial. *Neuropsychological Rehabilitation, 18*(1), 65–88. doi:10.1080/09602010701409684

West, R. L., Bagwell, D. K., & Dark-Freudeman, A. (2008). Self-efficacy and memory aging: The impact of a memory intervention based on self-efficacy. *Aging, Neuropsychology, and Cognition, 15*(3), 302–329. doi:10.1080/13825580701440510

Wilson, B. A., Evans, J. J., Emslie, H., Foley, J., Shiel, A., Watson, P., & Groot, Y. (2005). *The Cambridge Prospective Memory Test*. London: Harcourt Assessment.

Wolfsgruber, S., Wagner, M., Schmidtke, K., Frölich, L., Kurz, A., Schulz, S., … Jessen, F. (2014). Memory concerns, memory performance and risk of dementia in patients with mild cognitive impairment. *PLoS ONE, 9*(7), e100812. doi:10.1371/journal.pone.0100812

Woods, S. P., Weinborn, M., Velnoweth, A., Rooney, A., & Bucks, R. S. (2012). Memory for intentions is uniquely associated with instrumental activities of daily living in healthy older adults. *Journal of the International Neuropsychological Society, 18*(1), 134–138. doi:10.1017/S1355617711001263

Time-based prospective memory in children and adolescents with 22q11.2 deletion syndrome

Céline Souchay, Lydia Dubourg, Nicola Ballhausen, Maude Schneider, Charline Cerf, Katharina Schnitzspahn, Laurence Faivre, Matthias Kliegel and Stephan Eliez

ABSTRACT

Objective: 22q11.2 deletion syndrome, also known as velo-cardio-facial syndrome (VCFS) is a genetic disorder caused by a microdeletion on chromosome 22q11.2 and characterized by marked impairment in visual attention and executive function. The present study examined if this cognitive deficit extends to prospective memory (the type of memory involved in remembering to perform actions in the future). **Method:** 20 participants with 22q11.2DS aged between 6 and 14 were included in the study as well as 22 typically developing individuals (TDC) aged 6–12. To measure prospective memory, participants were asked to play a driving game (the *Dresden Cruiser*). This time-based prospective memory task required children to remember to refuel their car when the fuel level was low by pressing a refuel button while driving. **Results and discussion:** Participants with 22q11.2DS remembered less often to refuel the car. Furthermore, participants with 22q11.2DS checked the fuel gage significantly less often than the controls. **Conclusions:** Participants with 22q11.2DS therefore demonstrate difficulties completing a time-based prospective memory task. This can be explained by a generally less frequent time checking behavior in comparison to TDC.

Introduction

22q11.2 deletion syndrome (22q11.2DS), also known as velo-cardio-facial syndrome (VCFS), is a genetic disorder caused by a microdeletion on chromosome 22q11.2, estimated to occur in one of every 6000 live births (e.g. Botto et al., 2003). Most school-aged children with 22q11.2DS have lower than typical full scale IQ with borderline intellectual function (FSIQ 70–75) (Karayiorgou, Simon, & Gogos, 2010). In late adolescence and early adulthood, up to one-third of people with 22q11.2DS develop schizophrenia or schizoaffective disorder (see Schneider et al., 2014, for a review including over 1400 patients).

A number of studies have explored structural brain differences in 22q11.2DS, typically reporting reduced brain volume (between 8 and 11% smaller than typically developing controls). Most neuroimaging studies report a reduction in total hippocampal volume (Debbané, Glaser, David, Feinstein, & Eliez, 2006; Deboer, Wu, Lee, & Simon, 2007; Flahault, Schaer, Ottet, Debbané, & Eliez, 2012; Kates et al., 2006). According to Flahault et al. (2012) this reduction in volume could be due to a reduction in the amount of input received from connected cortical regions such as the parieto-lateral cortex, the posterior cingulate and the temporal cortical structures, known also to be reduced in 22q11.2DS. Brain function in 22q11.2DS is affected by reduced gene-dosage of more than one gene. For example, DGCR8 (DiGeorge syndrome critical region 8), PRODH (proline dehydrogenase) or COMT (catechol-O-methyltransferase) have been linked to neural changes and cognitive deficits (see Karayiorgou et al., 2010, for a review).

Besides these structural brain abnormalities, many studies have also attempted to better define cognitive functioning in 22q11.2DS (for a review, see Biswas & Furniss, 2016). The main findings so far suggest a specific cognitive phenotype and not merely a lower IQ more generally. For example, performance in reading is better than in mathematics, with specific difficulties in resolution of problems including spatial, temporal or numerical information (Sobin et al., 2004). Studies have also assessed executive functioning and report that people with the 22q11.2 deletion syndrome have marked impairment in visual attention and executive function (Maeder et al., 2016; Sobin, Kiley-Brabeck, & Karayiorgou, 2005; Sobin et al., 2004). Shapiro, Tassone, Choudhary, and Simon (2014) point to deficits in response inhibition, cognitive flexibility, and working memory. Several studies report working memory impairments in children and adolescents with 22q11.2DS (Bearden et al., 2001; Kates et al., 2007; Lajiness-O'Neill et al., 2005; Montojo et al., 2014; Sanders, Hobbs, Stephenson, Laird, & Beaton, 2017; Simon, Bearden, Mc-Ginn, & Zackai, 2005). Maeder et al. (2016) showed atypical developmental trajectories for working memory and verbal fluency, suggesting different developmental patterns of these executive functions in 22q11.2DS. Azuma et al. (2009) also showed that differences in brain activation (parietal and occipital regions) explained deficits on a visuospatial working memory task, thus suggesting that differences in the development of specific brain structures might underpin the cognitive deficits in this population.

This study focuses on memory. To the best of our knowledge, studies so far have only explored retrospective memory in 22q11.2DS, which is the ability to remember something from the past (words, people, events, etc.). First of all, the existing literature suggests better performance on verbal than on visuospatial memory tasks (Wong, Riggins, Harvey, Cabaral, & Simon, 2014; Woodin et al., 2001). People with 22q11.2DS have difficulties in memorizing faces, shapes, line orientation or spatial localizations (Gur et al., 2014; Woodin et al., 2001), with greater difficulties in remembering faces or objects than localizations (Bostelmann et al., 2016; Campbell et al., 2010; Vicari et al., 2012). Studies exploring episodic memory (i.e. the ability to retrieve recently learned episodes such as a list of words) report relatively spared performance in 22q11.2DS. For example, some studies suggest that people with 22q11.2DS (adolescents and adults) demonstrate similar levels of recognition performance to healthy controls for materials such as words, pictures or even action statements (Debbané, Glaser, & Eliez, 2008; Debbané, Van der Linden, Glaser, & Eliez, 2008). Two studies also reported intact rote verbal recall (Woodin et al., 2001), and story and word recall (Lajiness-O'Neill et al., 2005). However, other studies showed deficits in contextual information leading to source confusion errors suggesting that memory deficits in this population are possibly due to difficulties in binding contextual information to gist information. In other words, episodic memory in 22q11.2DS could be characterized by a deficit in retrieval of contextual information associated with memory content.

The novelty of this study is to explore prospective memory in 22q11.2DS. Prospective memory (PM) refers to the type of memory involved in remembering to perform actions in the future (Einstein & McDaniel, 1990). It combines executive processes (executing the action at the appropriate time) with memory processes (remembering the content of an intention) (Mahy, Moses, & Kliegel, 2014). Typical examples (in children) are remembering to return homework or remembering to reply to a birthday invitation and (in adults) to take the right medication at the right time. PM therefore plays a key role in everyday life and has been shown to be related to activities of daily living in adults (Woods, Weinborn, Velnoweth, Rooney, & Bucks, 2012). Typically, PM is investigated by giving participants PM instructions to complete while working on an ongoing task (Einstein & McDaniel, 1990). It comprises two components; a retrospective component (ability to recall the PM instructions) and a prospective component (performing an action in response to a cue) (Einstein & McDaniel, 1990). Einstein and McDaniel (1990) also distinguish between event-based and time-based PM. Time-based PM involves initiation of an activity at a given time or after a certain time has elapsed, whereas event-based PM involves initiating an action in response to an external target cue. In contrast to event-based PM where an external target event prompts the intention, time-based PM relies on self-initiation of the intended action (Mäntylä, Carelli, & Forman, 2007). Hence, it is crucial that the passage of time is strategically monitored (e.g. Mackinlay, Kliegel, & Mäntylä, 2009), which implies executively demanding processes.

PM is an ability that is detectable as early as 3 years of age (Kliegel & Jäger, 2007). Both event-and time-based PM performance improve across childhood, and even into adolescence (Kliegel & Jäger, 2007; Kvavilashvili, Messer, & Ebdon, 2001). This developmental trend is interesting given that PM plays a key role in independent living (Kliegel & Martin, 2003). The most noticeable memory errors in our everyday lives, or at least the ones with the most direct impact in everyday life would probably be PM errors and not retrospective memory errors. As a result, because PM failure could be a threat to an individual's independence, safety or even health, several studies have begun to look at PM performance in clinical populations. Of particular interest to the present study, PM has been found to be impaired in autism (Henry et al., 2014), ADHD (Altgassen, Kretschmer, & Kliegel, 2014), and schizophrenia (Ordemann, Opper, & Davalos, 2014), which are all commonly found in 22q11.2DS (Biswas & Furniss, 2016). However, to the best of our knowledge, PM has not been explored in 22q11.2DS.

The present study had the main goal of determining whether or not PM impairments are part of the cognitive phenotype that can be found in 22q11.2DS. On a clinical level, such an investigation might help carers and patients to have more realistic expectations in terms of how well these patients can remember future events, such as taking their medication. The cognitive phenotype observed in 22q11.2DS would lead us to predict PM failures. Successful PM combines retrospective memory processes and a prospective component related to executive function and working memory (executing the action at the appropriate time). Whilst previous findings in schizophrenia (Ordemann et al., 2014), autism (Henry et al., 2014), or ADHD (Altgassen et al., 2014) lead us to predict that PM will be impaired in people with 22q11.2.DS, the memory phenotype found in 22q11.2DS suggests that this PM impairment will not be due to retrospective memory difficulties. Several studies have shown that verbal memory, recall or recognition of words or stories, is mostly preserved in 22q11.2DS (Debbané, Glaser, et al., 2008; Debbané, Van der Linden, et al., 2008; Lajiness-O'Neill et al., 2005; Woodin et al., 2001). In other words, any PM deficit in 22q11.2DS is unlikely to be due to participants forgetting the instructions. Rather we suggest that people with 22q11.2DS might show PM deficits due to difficulties managing the prospective component of the task, which requires time managing or time monitoring. In a paper on multitasking, Schneider et al. (2016) found that people with 22q11.2DS checked the time less frequently than controls during the tasks. For this reason, time-based PM might be more sensitive than event-based PM to detect PM impairments in 22q11.2DS as it requires controlled checking behaviors. Time-based PM was therefore the central measure used in the current study.

Method

Participants

Twenty participants with 22q11.2DS aged between 6 and 14 were included in the current study (mean age = 10.70 ± 2.31). Individuals with 22q11.2DS were recruited through the Dijon Hospital genetic center and French-speaking parent associations in Geneva. The presence of a 22q11.2 was confirmed using Fluorescent in Situ Hybridization (FISH) or Quantitative Fluorescence Polymerase Chain reaction (QF-PCR). Some patients met diagnostic criteria for psychiatric conditions (1 major depression, 5 simple phobia, 7 generalized anxiety disorder, 6 ADHD) and 6 participants were under medication at the time of testing (2 taking antipsychotics, 4 taking Methylphenidate).

Twenty-two typically developing individuals (TDC) aged 6–12 (mean age = 10.63 ± 2.01) also participated in the study. The exclusion criterion for TD participants was the presence of any learning or behavioral/psychiatric disorder. Typically developing individuals were recruited via local kindergartens, primary and secondary schools.

Both groups were matched for age ($F(1, 40) = .009, p = .925$) and gender distribution ($F(1, 40) = .644, p = .427$) – one way ANOVAS on these measures did not reveal any group differences. Mean full-scale IQ was 71.6 ($SD = 10.8$) in patients with 22q11.2DS, but was not measured in control participants.

All participants were tested in a quiet room at the hospital and all mandatory laboratory health and safety procedures were adhered to within the course of conducting the experimental work reported here. Written informed consent was obtained from participants and their parents according to protocols approved by the Central Research Ethics Committee of Geneva (IRB number: PB-2016-01470) and by the local ethics committee for Dijon University.

Prospective memory task

Ongoing task component

The *PM task* was the *Dresden Cruiser* (Voigt et al., 2014), a driving simulation game originally developed by Kerns (2000) that requires children to drive a target vehicle on a road without crashing into other cars. The car drove on a two-dimensional road displayed vertically on a computer monitor, consisting of three parallel lanes, with other vehicles driving in the same direction on the road. The ongoing task required participants to pass the other cars without hitting them in order to earn points. A score was permanently displayed in the lower right corner of the screen during the game to increase children's motivation. To account for differences in ongoing task performance, the difficulty of the driving game was adapted to each participant's individual performance level (number of car crashes) on a baseline block (Kvavilashvili, Kyle, & Messer, 2008). There were five difficulty levels of the *Dresden Cruiser* that varied the number of other cars presented on the road per minute (ranging from 25 to 65 cars per minute). Before starting the baseline task, participants underwent a practice trial to ensure understanding of the task. The instructions were simple to understand: children were asked to play a car game and pass other cars to earn points. They were also informed that they would lose 100 points if they crashed into another car. Children were therefore told to avoid crashes to earn as many points as possible. Points already achieved appeared in the right corner of the screen. Children were given a practice trial and shown that the car was maneuvered with two arrows, the arrow on the left to go left and the arrow on the right to go right.

Prospective memory task component

The time-based PM task required children to remember to refuel their car when the fuel level was low by pressing a refuel button while driving. The fuel level was displayed on a fuel gage that children could check by pressing a button (which would reveal the fuel gage for 3 s in the left corner of the screen). By pressing a second button on the gamepad, participants could refuel the car whenever the fuel gage dropped into the red area (indicating that the tank was less than 1/6 full). To increase task motivation, children received 100 additional points each time they refueled the car within the appropriate timeframe (in comparison, participants only received 33 points for passing a car). If the car ran out of fuel, the tank was refilled automatically without any signal to indicate that there was a failure to refuel. A test block consisted of four one-minute trials and thus four opportunities to complete the PM task. There were two test blocks. In each trial, the car had to be refilled after 50 s of driving (when the fuel gage indicated the tank was only 1/6th full) and within 10 s (before the tank was refilled automatically). Participants were not given any information about the temporal characteristics of the task. Participants were given a practice trial before the actual task and were told that they would play the car game several times. In this, they were reminded of the fact that they were not supposed to crash into other cars, and to check the amount of points in the right corner of the screen. After the practice trial, they were also told that from now on they would have to not hit other cars *and* make sure that their car always had enough fuel. To check how much fuel they had left, children had to press a yellow key on the keyboard. If the needle was in the red area of the fuel gage, it meant that the car needed more fuel. Children were told that they would earn 100 points for refueling the car at the right time. Children were also explained that if they forgot to refuel and the tank was completely empty, it will be refueled automatically, but they will not gain any additional points.

Procedure

Children were tested individually in a single 15–30-min testing session. Figure 1 shows a diagram of the order in which tasks were carried out. First, children were given the instructions explaining the task and then practiced the ongoing task (1 min) to familiarize themselves with the driving component of the game. Then, children were asked to 'play again' for 4 min (baseline block). On the basis of the children's baseline performance, a difficulty

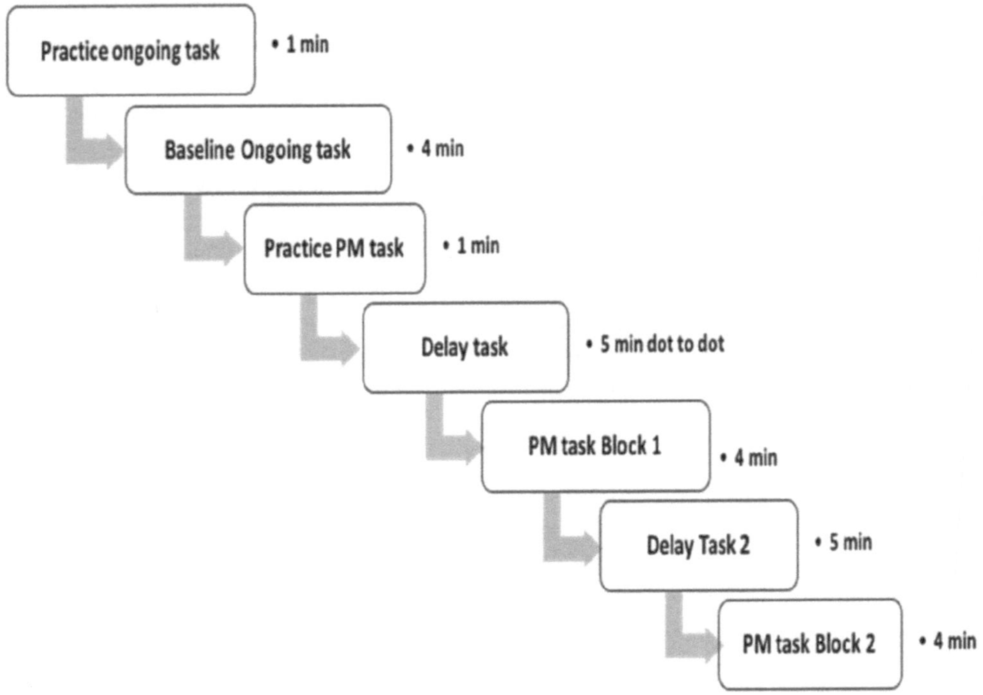

Figure 1. Prospective memory task procedure.

level for the ongoing task was chosen for the two following PM tasks. The cruiser had five difficulty levels ranging from 1 (95 cars) to 5 (271 cars). On the basis of their baseline performance, the average level chosen for the children with 22q11.2DS was 2.4 (150 cars) ranging from 2 to 3 whilst the average level for the controls was 4.5 (250 cars) ranging from 3 to 5. The children were then given the PM instructions and were also asked to recall the instructions to ensure accurate understanding.

As suggested by Ellis and Kvavilashvili (2000), a delay between task instructions and subsequent execution of the PM task was implemented. Children were asked to complete dot-to-dot puzzles (connecting dots to make a shape appear) for 5 min. Then children were asked to complete the first PM test block without any reminding of the need to refuel. Afterward, children were reminded of the instructions for the PM task and asked to play dot-to-dot again for 5 min before performing the second PM block. After children had completed the *Dresden Cruiser*, they were asked to recall the instructions and only children who could recall the PM task instructions were included in the data analysis. In this study, all tested children were able to recall the PM instructions and were all therefore included.

Results

Ongoing task performance in the PM task was measured by the number of crashes (Hit count). A one-way ANOVA revealed no group difference on this measure ($F(1, 40) = .003$, $p = .954$, $\eta^2 = .000$) therefore showing that ongoing task difficulty was comparable for both groups ($M = 39.58$, $SD = 14.02$ for 22q11.2, $M = 39.84$, $SD = 14.20$ for TDC).

PM performance was analyzed using the number of correct on-time refuels across the two blocks (maximum score of 8). A one-way ANOVA showed a significant group effect, with control participants ($M = 3.13$, $SD = 1.03$) remembering to refuel the car more often than the participants with 22q11.2DS ($M = 2.01$, $SD = 1.35$), $F(1, 40) = 9.145$, $p = .004$, $\eta^2 = .186$. To determine whether PM deficits could be considered as a specific cognitive trait beyond the global effect of intellectual disability, correlations between PM performance and IQ were carried out in the group of participants with 22q11.2DS. The correlation between IQ and the PM measure (number of correct on-time refuels) was found to be non-significant in the group of participants with 22q11.2DS ($r = .092$, $p = .736$).

Time monitoring

Furthermore, to gain insight into the processes underlying the observed PM deficit, time monitoring was analyzed in two different ways. First, as in previous studies (Mäntylä et al., 2007) analyses focused on the total number of fuel gage checks across the two blocks. The one-way ANOVA here revealed a significant group effect ($F(1, 40) = 10.77$, $p = .002$, $\eta^2 = .212$), showing that participants with 22q11.2DS checked the fuel gage significantly less often than the controls, with an average of 11.9 checks for the controls compared to 7.9 for the participants with 22q11.2DS.

Second, following the standard procedure in analyzing time monitoring patterns (e.g. Kerns, 2000; Kliegel et al., 2005), the number of gage checks across the length of one trial was analyzed by dividing it into four intervals (see Figure 2). Following Mahy et al. (2015), the average number of gage checks within the first three intervals was compared with the average number of gage checks in the fourth interval directly preceding the PM target time. Strategic monitoring would be reflected by a higher number of gage checks in the fourth interval compared to earlier gage checks. A 2 (Time interval: first three vs. fourth interval) x 2 (Group) ANOVA first confirmed a significant group effect ($F(1, 40) = 8{,}18$, $p = .007$, $\eta^2 = .170$) showing that overall participants with 22q11.2DS monitored the time less often than typically

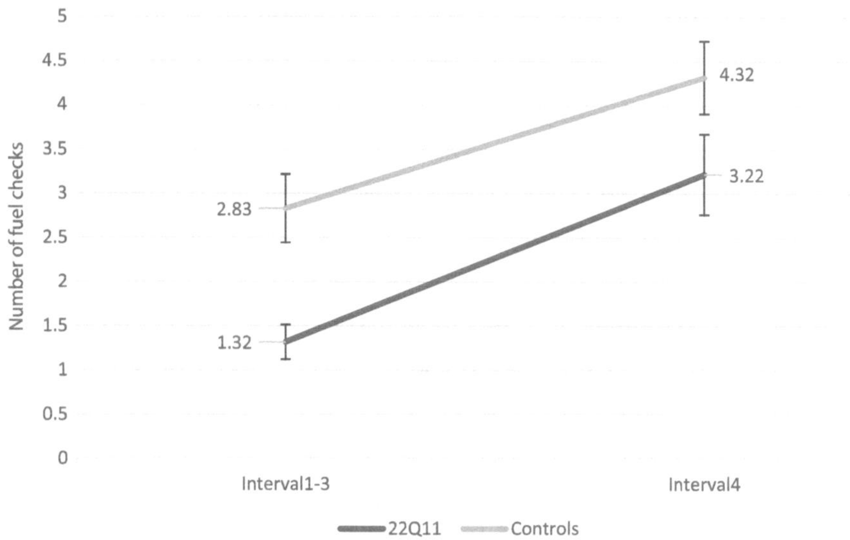

Figure 2. Average fuel gage checks per interval over the two trials.

developing children. On average, in the first interval, control participants checked the gage 1.9 times against 1.17 for the 22q11.2.DS participants. In the second interval, controls checked the gage on average 2.5 times against 1.3 for the 22q11.2DS participants. In the third interval, the control participants checked the gage on average 4.04 times and the 22q11.2DS 1.4 times. For the fourth interval, control participants checked the gage 4.3 times and the 22q11.2DS 3.22 times. Furthermore, on average, control participants checked the time every 21.8 s ($SD = 12,61$) against 29.87 s for the 22q11.2DS group (DS = 19,95). The two-way ANOVA also revealed a significant effect of time interval ($F(1, 40) = 34.14$, $p < .001$, $\eta^2 = .460$), with more checks in the final interval compared to the first three intervals in both groups. No significant interaction between Group and Time interval was found.

Prospective memory and time monitoring

To further explore the relation between monitoring and PM performance, correlations were carried out between the PM measure (number of correct on-time refuels) and the total number of fuel gage checks. The results showed that for both groups, monitoring the gage was clearly linked to PM performance ($r = .568$, $p = .006$ for controls; $r = .643$, $p = .002$ for participants with 22q11.2DS). This is in line with other studies on time-based PM in children (e.g. Mackinlay et al., 2009).

Discussion

The current study revealed time-based PM deficits in 22q11.2DS. First, results showed that participants with 22q11.2DS remembered less often to refuel the car, therefore failing to execute the PM action. It is important to note here that all participants were able to recall the instructions, insuring that the PM failure could not be due to forgetting what the action to perform was, and therefore we can rule out that this was due to a retrospective memory failure. That is, all participants including participants with 22q11.2DS correctly recalled the instructions. Furthermore, the PM failure found in this study cannot be explained by differences in difficulty levels of the ongoing task, as the PM task level was chosen on the participants' baseline performance on the ongoing task and the results showed no group differences on the ongoing task.

Second, participants with 22q11.2DS were found to check the fuel gage significantly less often than the controls. This deficient checking behavior is in agreement with what Schneider et al. (2016) observed in a study on multitasking in which adolescents with 22q11.2DS were found to check the time less often (note, however, that PM needs to be differentiated from multitasking, see McDaniel & Einstein, 2007, for more details). Furthermore, the results showed that PM performance was clearly correlated with the number of fuel gage checks, suggesting that low PM performance is directly linked to a failure to check the gage. This deficient checking behavior could somehow be due to group differences in motivation. Control participants, in comparison to children with 22q11.2DS, might be more sensitive to, and therefore more motivated by, a reward system based on points. That is, failure to check the gage in children with 22q11.2DS might reflect more a lack of initiation due to motivational problems than a real difficulty in PM. This is in accordance with the literature showing negative symptoms including a lack of motivation in people with 22q11.2DS (Schneider et al., 2014). According to this reasoning, one possible limitation of the current study is that the failure to refuel did not result in any penalty in this task. The car continues to run without fuel and the tank is refueled automatically (this was done in order to not provide an additional reminder of the PM task). Therefore, children with 22q11.2DS might have focused on the ongoing task to try and reduce the number of car crashes which, as opposed to forgetting to refuel, could have resulted in major loss of points. This means a priority is to test for potential group differences in motivation. Future studies should also explore the link with general intelligence, by for example comparing groups with different IQ levels, although it should be pointed out that in the current study no correlations were found between IQ and PM performance in the group of 22q11.2DS participants. Furthermore, the marked increase in monitoring (number of gage checks) in the final interval, for both groups, suggests that all participants, including participants with 22q11.2DS, were able to anticipate the target time correctly and use a strategic monitoring behavior in response. According to Mahy et al. (2015), this increase in monitoring reflects a proactive time monitoring strategy. Therefore, this study suggests that people with 22q11.2DS are able to monitor the passage of time to some extent and to proactively regulate their monitoring behavior, as found in studies on TDC (Kerns, 2000; Voigt et al., 2014). This is interesting considering that Debbané, Glaser, Gex-Fabry, and Eliez (2005), with a larger sample and therefore more statistical power, showed that time perception was impaired in 22q11.2DS. However, it could be argued here that the more naturalistic PM task used in this experiment facilitated time perception.

To conclude, this study shows that children and adolescents with 22q11.2DS have difficulties completing a time-based PM task. This can be explained by the patient group less frequently checking time in comparison to controls. However, it is important to note that children and adolescents with 22q11.2DS both demonstrated an increase in gage checks closer to the target time reflecting, some preservation of strategic time monitoring. Thus, PM deficits were not caused by proactive control impairments.

According to Mahy et al. (2014), PM performance is modulated by different factors such as the nature of the intention, the length and nature of the delay before the PM task, the nature of the ongoing task, and the nature of the prospective cues. These factors would impact on PM performance via their effect on executive function. In line with this theoretical framework, the observed PM deficits might be explained by group differences in working memory performance. For example, one could suggest that children and adolescents with 22q11.2DS remember the task and check the gage but then the intention to press the right key to refuel would slip out of their working memory. To explore this question, in a further study, working memory load could be manipulated (see Voigt et al., 2014). They could also struggle to inhibit the ongoing task response or fail to shift between two tasks, (see Schnitzspahn, Stahl, Zeintl, Kaller, & Kliegel, 2013 for an example of a relation between these two facets of executive function and PM in aging). From our point of view, future studies should consider all three executive function facets, as well as potential motivation differences. Finally, having found evidence of impaired PM, and PM being highly important in everyday life, future studies should explore the potential relationship between PM deficits, behavioral problems in 22q11.2DS and psychiatric diagnosis.

Acknowledgments

The authors thank the Swiss National Science Foundation (SNSF, Switzerland) and the Agence Nationale de la Recherche (ANR, France) for their support.

Disclosure statement

The authors report no conflict of interest.

Funding

This work was supported by the Swiss National Science Foundation (SNSF, Switzerland) and the Agence Nationale de la Recherche (ANR, France).

References

Altgassen, M., Kretschmer, A., & Kliegel, M. (2014). Task dissociation in prospective memory performance in individuals with ADHD. *Journal of Attention Disorders, 18*(7), 617–624. doi:10.1177/1087054712445484

Azuma, R., Daly, E. M., Campbell, L. E., Stevens, A. F., Deeley, Q., Giampietro, V., ... Murphy, K. C. (2009). Visuospatial working memory in children and adolescents with 22q11.2 deletion syndrome; an fMRI study. *Journal of Neurodevelopmental Disorders, 1*(1), 46–60. doi:10.1007/s11689-009-9008-9

Bearden, C. E., Woodin, M. F., Wang, P. P., Moss, E., McDonald-McGinn, D., Zackai, E., ... Cannon, T. D. (2001). The neurocognitive phenotype of the 22q11.2 deletion syndrome: Selective deficit in visual-spatial memory. *Journal of Clinical and Experimental Neuropsychology, 23*(4), 447–464. doi:10.1076/jcen.23.4.447.1228

Biswas, A. B., & Furniss, F. (2016). Cognitive phenotype and psychiatric disorder in 22q11.2 deletion syndrome: A review. *Research in Developmental Disabilities, 53–54*, 242–257. doi:10.1016/j.ridd.2016.02.010

Bostelmann, M., Schneider, M., Padula, M. C., Maeder, J., Schaer, M., Scariati, E., ... Eliez, S. (2016). Visual memory profile in 22q11.2 microdeletion syndrome: Are there differences in performance and neurobiological substrates between tasks linked to ventral and dorsal visual brain structures? A cross-sectional and longitudinal study. *Journal of Neurodevelopmental Disorders, 8*, 41. doi:10.1186/s11689-016-9174-5

Botto, L. D., May, K., Fernhoff, P. M., Correa, A., Coleman, K., Rasmussen, S. A., ... Campbell, R. M. (2003). A population-based study of the 22q11.2 deletion: Phenotype, incidence, and contribution to major birth defects in the population. *Pediatrics, 112*(1 Pt 1), 101–107.

Campbell, L. E., Azuma, R., Ambery, F., Stevens, A., Smith, A., Morris, R. G., ... Murphy, K. C. (2010). Executive functions and memory abilities in children with 22q11.2 deletion syndrome. *Australian & New Zealand Journal of Psychiatry, 44*(4), 364–371. doi:10.3109/00048670903489882

Debbané, M., Glaser, B., David, M. K., Feinstein, C., & Eliez, S. (2006). Psychotic symptoms in children and adolescents with 22q11.2 deletion syndrome: Neuropsychological and behavioral implications. *Schizophrenia Research, 84*(2–3), 187–193. doi:10.1016/j.schres.2006.01.019

Debbané, M., Glaser, B., & Eliez, S. (2008). Encoding and retrieval processes in velo-cardio-facial syndrome (VCFS). *Neuropsychology, 22*(2), 226–234. doi:10.1037/0894-4105.22.2.226

Debbané, M., Glaser, B., Gex-Fabry, M., & Eliez, S. (2005). Temporal perception in velo-cardio-facial syndrome. *Neuropsychologia, 43*(12), 1754–1762. doi:10.1016/j.neuropsychologia.2005.02.006

Debbané, M., Van der Linden, M., Glaser, B., & Eliez, S. (2008). Source monitoring for actions in adolescents with 22q11.2 deletion syndrome (22q11DS). *Psychological Medicine, 38*(6), 811–820. doi:10.1017/S003329170700222X

Deboer, T., Wu, Z., Lee, A., & Simon, T. J. (2007). Hippocampal volume reduction in children with chromosome 22q11.2 deletion syndrome is associated with cognitive impairment. *Behavioral and Brain Functions, 3*, 54. doi:10.1186/1744-9081-3-54

Einstein, G. O., & McDaniel, M. A. (1990). Normal aging and prospective memory. *Journal of Experimental Psychology: Learning, Memory, and Cognition, 16*(4), 717–726.

Ellis, J., & Kvavilashvili, L. (2000). Prospective memory in 2000: Past, present, and future directions. *Applied Cognitive Psychology, 14*, S1–S9. doi:10.1002/acp.767.abs

Flahault, A., Schaer, M., Ottet, M. C., Debbané, M., & Eliez, S. (2012). Hippocampal volume reduction in chromosome 22q11.2 deletion syndrome (22q11.2DS): A longitudinal study of morphometry and symptomatology. *Psychiatry Research, 203*(1), 1–5. doi:10.1016/j.pscychresns.2011.09.003

Gur, R. E., Yi, J. J., McDonald-McGinn, D. M., Tang, S. X., Calkins, M. E., Whinna, D., … Gur, R. C. (2014). Neurocognitive development in 22q11.2 deletion syndrome: Comparison with youth having developmental delay and medical comorbidities. *Molecular Psychiatry, 19*(11), 1205–1211. doi:10.1038/mp.2013.189

Henry, J. D., Terrett, G., Altgassen, M., Raponi-Saunders, S., Ballhausen, N., Schnitzspahn, K. M., & Rendell, P. G. (2014). A Virtual Week study of prospective memory function in autism spectrum disorders. *Journal of Experimental Child Psychology, 127*, 110–125. doi:10.1016/j.jecp.2014.01.011

Karayiorgou, M., Simon, T. J., & Gogos, J. A. (2010). 22q11.2 microdeletions: Linking DNA structural variation to brain dysfunction and schizophrenia. *Nature Reviews Neuroscience, 11*(6), 402–416. doi:10.1038/nrn2841

Kates, W. R., Krauss, B. R., Abdulsabur, N., Colgan, D., Antshel, K. M., Higgins, A. M., & Shprintzen, R. J. (2007). The neural correlates of non-spatial working memory in velocardiofacial syndrome (22q11.2 deletion syndrome). *Neuropsychologia, 45*(12), 2863–2873. doi:10.1016/j.neuropsychologia.2007.05.007

Kates, W. R., Miller, A. M., Abdulsabur, N., Antshel, K. M., Conchelos, J., Fremont, W., & Roizen, N. (2006). Temporal lobe anatomy and psychiatric symptoms in velocardiofacial syndrome (22q11.2 deletion syndrome). *Journal of the American Academy of Child and Adolescent Psychiatry, 45*(5), 587–595. doi:10.1097/01.chi.0000205704.33077.4a

Kerns, K. A. (2000). The CyberCruiser: An investigation of development of prospective memory in children. *Journal of the International Neuropsychological Society, 6*(1), 62–70.

Kliegel, M., & Jäger, T. (2007). The effects of age and cue-action reminders on event-based prospective memory performance in preschoolers. *Cognitive Development, 22*(1), 33–46. doi:10.1016/j.cogdev.2006.08.003

Kliegel, M., Jäger, T., Phillips, L. H., Federspiel, E., Imfeld, A., Keller, M., & Zimprich, D. (2005). Effects of sad mood on time-based prospective memory. *Cognition & Emotion, 19*(8), 1199–1213. doi:10.1080/02699930500233820

Kliegel, M., & Martin, M. (2003). Prospective memory research: Why is it relevant? *International Journal of Psychology, 38*(4), 193–194. doi:10.1080/00207590344000114

Kvavilashvili, L., Kyle, F., & Messer, D. J. (2008). The development of prospective memory in children: Methodological issues, empirical findings, and future directions. In M. Kliegel, M. A. McDaniel, & G. O. Einstein (Eds.), *Prospective memory: Cognitive, neuroscience, developmental, and applied perspectives* (pp. 115–140). Mahweh, NJ: Lawrence Erlbaum Associates.

Kvavilashvili, L., Messer, D. J., & Ebdon, P. (2001). Prospective memory in children: The effects of age and task interruption. *Developmental Psychology, 37*(3), 418–430. doi:10.1037/0012-1649.37.3.418

Lajiness-O'Neill, R. R., Beaulieu, I., Titus, J. B., Asamoah, A., Bigler, E. D., Bawle, E. V., & Pollack, R. (2005). Memory and learning in children with 22q11.2 deletion syndrome: Evidence for ventral and dorsal stream disruption? *Child Neuropsychology, 11*(1), 55–71. doi:10.1080/09297040590911202

Mackinlay, R. J., Kliegel, M., & Mäntylä, T. (2009). Predictors of time-based prospective memory in children. *Journal of Experimental Child Psychology, 102*(3), 251–264. doi:10.1016/j.jecp.2008.08.006

Maeder, J., Schneider, M., Bostelmann, M., Debbané, M., Glaser, B., Menghetti, S., … Eliez, S. (2016). Developmental trajectories of executive functions in 22q11.2 deletion syndrome. *Journal of Neurodevelopmental Disorders, 8*, 10. doi:10.1186/s11689-016-9141-1

Mahy, C. E. V., Moses, L. J., & Kliegel, M. (2014). The development of prospective memory in children: An executive framework. *Developmental Review, 34*(4), 305–326. doi:10.1016/J.Dr.2014.08.001

Mahy, C. E. V., Voigt, B., Ballhausen, N., Schnitzspahn, K., Ellis, J., & Kliegel, M. (2015). The impact of cognitive control on children's goal monitoring in a time-based prospective memory task. *Child Neuropsychology, 21*(6), 823–839. doi:10.1080/09297049.2014.967202

Mäntylä, T., Carelli, M. G., & Forman, H. (2007). Time monitoring and executive functioning in children and adults. *Journal of Experimental Child Psychology, 96*(1), 1–19. doi:10.1016/j.jecp.2006.08.003

McDaniel, M. A., & Einstein, G. O. (2007). *Prospective memory: An overview and synthesis of an emerging field*. Thousand Oaks, CA: Sage.

Montojo, C. A., Ibrahim, A., Karlsgodt, K. H., Chow, C., Hilton, A. E., Jonas, R. K., … Bearden, C. E. (2014). Disrupted working memory circuitry and psychotic symptoms in 22q11.2 deletion syndrome. *NeuroImage: Clinical, 4*, 392–402. doi:10.1016/j.nicl.2014.01.010

Ordemann, G. J., Opper, J., & Davalos, D. (2014). Prospective memory in schizophrenia: A review. *Schizophrenia Research, 155*(1–3), 77–89. doi:10.1016/j.schres.2014.03.008

Sanders, A. F., Hobbs, D. A., Stephenson, D. D., Jr, Laird, R. D., & Beaton, E. A. (2017). Working memory impairments in chromosome 22q11.2 deletion syndrome: The roles of anxiety and stress physiology. *Journal of Autism and Developmental Disorders, 47*(4), 992–1005. doi:10.1007/s10803-016-3011-2

Schneider, M., Debbane, M., Bassett, A. S., Chow, E. W., Fung, W. L., van den Bree, M., … Behavior in 22q11.2 Deletion, S. (2014). Psychiatric disorders from childhood to adulthood in 22q11.2 deletion syndrome: Results from the international consortium on brain and behavior in 22q11.2 deletion syndrome. *The American Journal of Psychiatry, 171*(6), 627–639. doi:10.1176/appi.ajp.2013.13070864

Schneider, M., Eliez, S., Birr, J., Menghetti, S., Debbané, M., & Van der Linden, M. (2016). Multitasking abilities in adolescents with 22q11.2 deletion syndrome: Results from an experimental ecological paradigm. *American Journal on Intellectual and Developmental Disabilities, 121*(2), 151–164. doi:10.1352/1944-7558-121.2.151

Schnitzspahn, K., Stahl, C., Zeintl, M., Kaller, C., & Kliegel, M. (2013). The role of shifting updating and inhibition in prospective memory performance in young and older adults. *Developmental Psychology, 49*(8), 1544–1553.

Shapiro, H. M., Tassone, F., Choudhary, N. S., & Simon, T. J. (2014). The development of cognitive control in children with chromosome 22q11.2 deletion syndrome. *Frontiers in Psychology, 5*, 566. doi:10.3389/fpsyg.2014.00566

Simon, T. J., Bearden, C. E., Mc-Ginn, D. M., & Zackai, E. (2005). Visuospatial and numerical cognitive deficits in children with chromosome 22q11.2 deletion syndrome. *Cortex, 41*(2), 145–155.

Sobin, C., Kiley-Brabeck, K., Daniels, S., Blundell, M., Anyane-Yeboa, K., & Karayiorgou, M. (2004). Networks of attention in children with the 22q11 deletion syndrome. *Developmental Neuropsychology, 26*(2), 611–626. doi:10.1207/s15326942dn2602_5

Sobin, C., Kiley-Brabeck, K., & Karayiorgou, M. (2005). Associations between prepulse inhibition and executive visual attention in children with the 22q11 deletion syndrome. *Molecular Psychiatry, 10*(6), 553–562. doi:10.1038/sj.mp.4001609

Vicari, S., Mantovan, M., Addona, F., Costanzo, F., Verucci, L., & Menghini, D. (2012). Neuropsychological profile of Italian children and adolescents with 22q11.2 deletion syndrome with and without intellectual disability. *Behavior Genetics, 42*(2), 287–298. doi:10.1007/s10519-011-9499-5

Voigt, B., Mahy, C. E. V., Ellis, J., Schnitzspahn, K., Krause, I., Altgassen, M., & Kliegel, M. (2014). The development of time-based prospective memory in childhood: The role of working memory updating. *Developmental Psychology, 50*(10), 2393–2404. doi:10.1037/A0037491

Wong, L. M., Riggins, T., Harvey, D., Cabaral, M., & Simon, T. J. (2014). Children with chromosome 22q11.2 deletion syndrome exhibit impaired spatial working memory. *American Journal on Intellectual and Developmental Disabilities, 119*(2), 115–132. doi:10.1352/1944-7558-119.2.115

Woodin, M., Wang, P. P., Aleman, D., McDonald-McGinn, D., Zackai, E., & Moss, E. (2001). Neuropsychological profile of children and adolescents with the 22q11.2 microdeletion. *Genetics in Medicine, 3*(1), 34–39. doi:10.109700125817-200101000-00008

Woods, S. P., Weinborn, M., Velnoweth, A., Rooney, A., & Bucks, R. S. (2012). Memory for intentions is uniquely associated with instrumental activities of daily living in healthy older adults. *Journal of the International Neuropsychological Society, 18*(1), 134–138. doi:10.1017/S1355617711001263

Prospective memory in first-degree relatives of patients with schizophrenia

Saima Saleem, Devvarta Kumar and Ganesan Venkatasubramanian

ABSTRACT

Objectives: Among various cognitive impairments in schizophrenia, prospective memory (ProM) deficit is unequivocally established. However, there is a paucity of research examining whether ProM impairment can be considered a cognitive endophenotypic marker in schizophrenia. An important step toward this is to assess the status of ProM in first-degree relatives (FDRs) of patients with schizophrenia. Keeping this in view, present study has been conducted to assess event- and time-based ProM in FDRs of patients with schizophrenia. **Methods:** Twenty patients with schizophrenia, 20 FDRs of these patients, and 20 nonpsychiatric (healthy) controls were administered event- and time-based ProM tasks. **Results:** Findings show that the FDRs had poorer performance on event-based ProM task in comparison to healthy controls. On time-based task, though the FDRs performed poorly in comparison to healthy controls the difference was statistically non-significant. The patient group performed poorer than healthy controls on both event- and time-based tasks. **Conclusions:** Findings of the present study indicate that the FDRs of patients with schizophrenia exhibit ProM impairment, though to a lesser degree than the patients with schizophrenia.

Introduction

Prospective memory (ProM) impairment in schizophrenia is established (Kumar, Nizamie, & Jahan, 2005, 2008; Ordemann, Opper, & Davalos, 2014; Wang et al., 2009). ProM impairment has direct clinical implications such as forgetting to take medication on scheduled time and missing appointments with the doctor. Though ProM in schizophrenia has been assessed form various perspectives such as the impact of varying retrospective memory load (Altgassen, Kliegel, Rendell, Henry, & Zöllig, 2008), effect on activities of daily living (Ungvari, Xiang, Tang, & Shum, 2008), relationship with other cognitive functions (Raskin et al., 2014; Xiang, Shum, Chiu, Tang, & Ungvari, 2010) and its neural correlates (Cheng, Wang, Xi, Niu, & Fu, 2008); the endophenotypic value of this cognitive construct is less researched. Of late, there is growing interest in studying the potential endophenotypes of schizophrenia (e.g.

Seidman et al., 2015) as endophenotypes are seen closely linked to the heritable risk factors (Braff, Freedman, Schork, & Gottesman, 2007). Research has shown that various cognitive functions such as episodic memory, working memory, perceptual vigilance, visual abstraction, and inhibitory processing can be considered endophenotypes in schizophrenia (Gur et al., 2007; Seidman et al., 2015).

There are convincing reasons to assess the possibility of ProM as a candidate endophenotype in schizophrenia. Cognitive functions have been included in the Consortium on the Genetics of Endophenotypes in Schizophrenia (COGS) for consideration as candidate endophenotypes on following criteria (Gur et al., 2007): (1) there should be association with illness (manifested by differences of moderate to large effect sizes between patients and healthy controls in performance on assessment tools measuring a given cognitive function), (2) the impairments should be state independent, (3) there should be heritability, and (4) impairments should be found in unaffected relatives at a higher rate than in the general population. Various studies indicate that ProM in schizophrenia fulfills first two criteria (Kumar et al., 2005; Ungvari et al., 2008). To establish the next two criteria, there should be studies on status of ProM in unaffected relatives of patients with schizophrenia. To date there are two published studies in this area. Wang et al. (2010) reported that event- and time-based ProM is impaired in unaffected first-degree relatives (FDRs) of patients with schizophrenia. However, the limitation of the study is that it did not include patients with schizophrenia as a comparison group. Though it can be argued that ProM impairment in schizophrenia is established and, therefore, there is no need for inclusion of this group but we know that methodological differences among studies (such as the tasks used to assess ProM and socio-demographics of sample) can have their own effects and, therefore, generalizations of findings can be questionable. In another study, Lui et al. (2011) studied ProM performance of recent onset patients with schizophrenia, their FDRs and healthy controls. The findings indicate that the FDRs of patients with schizophrenia do not exhibit impairment in ProM. Thus, two studies that have been done in this area report opposite findings. Though, both Wang et al. (2010) and Lui et al. (2011) used same task for event- and time-based ProM assessment, the sample of FDRs of the former consisted of both siblings and parents of patients with schizophrenia whereas the later had only siblings. With similar tasks, the differences in findings of two studies can be attributed to the differences in the type of FDRs as there was substantial age difference in the FDR samples of these studies.

Present study was conducted to examine how FDRs of patients with schizophrenia perform on event- and time-based ProM tasks in comparison to patients with schizophrenia and healthy community dwellers. We recruited FDRs of the patients who participated in the study and also included patients with varying duration of illness.

Method

Participants

Twenty patients with schizophrenia; diagnosed as per the International Classification of Diseases-10 criteria (World Health Organization, 1992), 20 FDRs of these patients and 20 nonpsychiatric comparison participants (healthy controls) were recruited for the study. Patients with schizophrenia were recruited from the National Institute of Mental Health and Neurosciences, Bangalore, India through purposive sampling method (only those patients were included who were cooperative for a detailed assessment). All the patients were on antipsychotic medications. Any co-morbid psychiatric or neurologic diagnosis and electroconvulsive treatment in past six months were exclusion criteria for patients. FDRs and healthy controls were recruited after a detailed interview by the first author to rule out presence of/ history of any psychiatric or neurological illness, or substance dependence. Additionally, the interviewer ensured that any FDR of healthy controls did not have significant history of any psychiatric illness. Informed consent was obtained from all the participants. Majority of FDRs were either parents (10, 50%) or siblings (9, 45%). Only one (5%) FDR was offspring. All the participants were between the ages of 18 and 54 and had, at least, 10 years of education. Participants (in any group) were not recruited if there was an indication of intellectual disability (please see Table 1 for further socio-demographic and clinical details of the participants).

Procedure

The participants were assessed individually and the assessment was done at a place where extraneous disturbances were minimal. The tasks for event- and time-based ProM were designed on the basis of Einstein and McDaniel's dual task paradigm for assessment of ProM (1990). This paradigm in which amid a continuous activity, intermittently ProM targets occur (either in terms of occurrence of an event; for example, a specific word, or in terms of lapse of a specific period; for example, two minutes from the onset of a task), has been used frequently in last two decades. The corresponding author of the paper has used same event-based task (the task that has been used in the present study) in one of his previously published work (Kumar et al., 2005). Dalla Barba (1991) has proposed that any valid ProM task should have three components – formation of an intention to execute an action in future, a temporal gap between formation of intention and action (the gap should be so much that it exceeds the short-term memory capacity) and execution of action at the right juncture. Einstein and McDaniel's dual task paradigm fulfills all these criteria, provided a precaution is taken while designing a task based on this paradigm, that is, the temporal gap between the occurrences of two ProM targets should not be too short to enable the individual to keep the intention actively in conscious awareness. If the temporal gap between two ProM targets is too short it becomes a vigilance task rather than a ProM task. The paradigm that we have used (both for event- and time-based ProM) required the participants to form an intention to be executed at specified juncture (on occurrence of the word "state" in case of event-based task

Table 1. Socio-demographic and clinical details of patient, FDR and healthy control groups.

		Patient (n = 20)	FDR (n = 20)	Healthy controls (n = 20)	
		Mean(*SD*)	Mean(*SD*)	Mean(*SD*)	*F*
Age (in years)		28.80 (7.78)	39.00 (12.03)	34.40 (9.20)	5.34* (FDR > Pt*)
Education (in years)		14.95 (1.61)	15.50 (2.40)	15.05 (2.14)	.4
Duration of illness (in months)		77.10 (40.89)			
SAPS total score		7 (3.46)			
		n (%)	*n* (%)	*n* (%)	X^2
Gender	Male	13 (65)	10 (50)	04 (20)	8.48*
	Female	07 (35)	10 (50)	16 (80)	

Notes: FDR = First-degree relatives, SAPS = Scale for the Assessment of Positive Symptoms.
*$p \leq .01$.

and lapse of 5 min in case of time-based task) and there was sufficient temporal gap between formation of intention and action (every 15th item in case of the event-based task and 5 min in case of the time-based task). For both the event- and time-based tasks, it was difficult for the participants to actively keep thinking about execution of formed intention as in case of the time-based task they had to keep it in working memory for 5 min and in case of the event-based tasks also it was roughly 5 min or more as reading a general knowledge item and deciding its correct answer would take approximately 15–20 s and between the occurrence of two ProM targets there were 14 such general knowledge items. Details of the tasks have been given below.

Event-based ProM task

For the assessment of event-based ProM, a list of 75 general knowledge items were prepared having 5 items with embedded ProM target (general knowledge items with the term "state" as ProM target). For each item, the participants had to choose one answer from four possible answers. ProM targets were embedded in every 15th item. However, in order to prevent the participants inferring the sequence of ProM target presentation (i.e. he/she has to execute the intended ProM activity on every 15th item), the items were not numbered. To reduce their anxiety, participants were told that the general knowledge items were not meant for assessment of their intelligence and that the experimenter was interested in just knowing their level of general awareness. Moreover, in order to keep the filler task less cognitively demanding, very simple general knowledge items were included (e.g. "Which state in India has the largest area?"). Participants were told that while working on the general knowledge items, from time to time they would see questions that would have the word "state" and at that time, apart from answering the question, they had to tap the table too.

Time-based ProM task

For assessing time-based ProM, the participants were presented with a set of simple reasoning tasks on a computer. Each task had four alternatives and the participants were required to choose one alternative from them. Similar to event-based ProM, the items in this task were also kept very simple (e.g. finding odd one out from four simple alternatives). While doing this task, the participants were instructed to tap the table with one hand at the interval of every fifth minute, apart from solving the reasoning task. The task ran for 26 min. The task was shown on a computer as a power point and in the upper left corner of the screen a clock was on when the task was running.

Patients with schizophrenia were additionally administered the Scale for the Assessment of Positive Symptoms (SAPS) (Andreasen, 1984). The SAPS rating was done by the first author. As part of her training course in Clinical Psychology, she was trained in administration and interpretation of various tests and scales including SAPS. Also, one patient was separately rated by her and the second author, who is a trained Clinical Psychologist, and there was consonance in their ratings.

Statistical analysis

On both event- and time-based ProM, a score of 1 was given for each correct answer and 0 was given for failure (thus, in the event-based task if the participant tapped the table when an item with the word "state" appeared s/he got a score of 1. Likewise, in the time-based task when the participant tapped the table at the lapse of fifth minute while solving the reasoning task, s/he got a score of 1).

We conducted univariate analysis of covariance (ANCOVA) to assess group differences in event- and time-based ProM performance with age as a covariate. It was followed by post-hoc comparisons between patients and FDRs, patients and healthy controls and FDRs and healthy controls. Age was taken as a covariate as the three groups differed in terms of age [$F(2, 57) = 5.34$, $p < .01$]. Further, between group effect sizes were calculated using Cohen's *d* (Cohen, 1988) while partial eta-squared (η_p^2) was calculated to see the overall effect-size of the ANCOVA. Pearson correlation was calculated to see if event- and time-based ProM scores correlated with clinical variables such as the duration of illness and psychopathology scores.

Results

Mean successful executions of event- and time-based ProM have been shown in Figure 1. Univariate ANCOVA (with age as a covariate) showed that the groups differed on both event-based [$F(2, 56) = 15.85$, $p < .001$, $\eta_p^2 = .36$] and time-based [$F(2, 56) = 7.92$, $p < .01$, $\eta_p^2 = .22$] ProM tasks and the effect sizes for both the group effects were large. The post-hoc test revealed that on the event-based task the FDRs had poorer performance than the healthy controls ($p < .05$, $d = .84$) and better performance than the patient group ($p < .01$, $d = .52$). On the time-based task, the difference between the level of performance of FDRs and healthy controls did not attain statistical significance, though the effect-size of the difference was medium ($p > .05$, $d = .52$). Further, the FDRs had better performance than the patient group ($p < .01$, $d = .64$) on time-based task. The patient group performed poorly than the healthy controls on both event- and time-based tasks ($p < .001$, $d = 1.80$ and $p < .001$, $d = 1.17$ respectively).

In the correlation analysis, neither the duration of illness nor SAPS total score correlated with event- and time-based ProM performance (duration of illness and event-based ProM

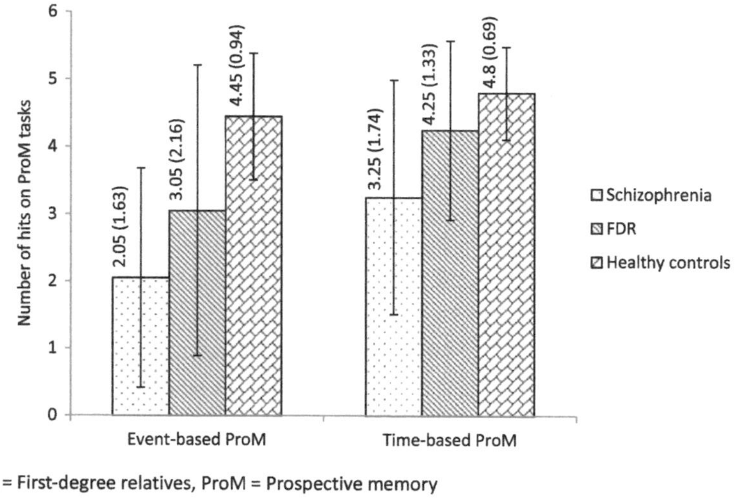

Figure 1. Performance (mean ± *SD*) of patients with schizophrenia ($n = 20$), FDR ($n = 20$) and healthy adults ($n = 20$) on the ProM measures. FDR = First-degree relatives, ProM = Prospective memory.

$r = .03, p > .05$; duration of illness and time-based ProM $r = .12, p > .05$) (SAPS total score and event-based ProM $r = -.27, p > .05$; SAPS total score and time-based ProM $r = .09, p > .05$).

Discussion

Present study was conducted to see the status of event- and time-based ProM in the FDRs of patients with schizophrenia. Performances of FDRs on event- and time-based ProM tasks were compared with performances of nonpsychiatric (healthy) controls and patients with schizophrenia on these tasks. The findings show that the FDRs performed poorly on the event-based task in comparison to the nonpsychiatric controls. Likewise, on the time-based task the FDRs performed poorly than the nonpsychiatric controls ($d = .52$), however, the difference did not attain statistical significance. Further, the FDRs had better performance than the patient group on both event- and time-based tasks. The patients with schizophrenia performed poorly on event- and time-based tasks in comparison to healthy controls as well as FDRs. Thus, the findings of the present study indicate that ProM is impaired in FDRs of patients with schizophrenia and between event- and time-based ProM, they show more impairment in event-based ProM.

Findings of the present study partly support and partly refute the findings of previous two studies in this area. Wang et al. (2010) found FDRs performing poorer than healthy controls on both event- and time-based tasks whereas Lui et al. (2011) did not find impairment in performance of FDRs (in comparison to healthy controls) on any type of ProM task. The reason for similarities and discrepancies in the findings of the present study and the previous two studies (Wang et al., 2010; Lui et al., 2011) can lie in the nature of sample as well as the type of tasks used for the assessment of ProM in these studies. Similar to Wang et al., we recruited various FDRs (such as parents and siblings) whereas Lui et al. recruited only siblings. As the type of FDRs can have effect on the average age of sample it can have bearing on the discrepancy between the findings of Lui et al., present study and that of Wang et al. However, only age cannot be considered responsible for similarities and discrepancies in the findings of the three studies as in that case the findings of the present study should have completely matched with the findings of Wang et al., which is not the case. Another important reason for the difference can be the nature of the tasks used in the present study and other two studies. Though all the three studies have used the dual tasks paradigm (Einstein & McDaniel, 1990) for assessing ProM, there are some inherent differences in the tasks of these studies. First, the temporal gap between the occurrences of ProM targets in Lui et al. and Wang et al. was one minute whereas in the present study it was around 5 min. If the temporal gap between the occurrences of ProM targets is too short, as stated earlier, more than a ProM task it may become a vigilance task as the individual can keep the intention into active conscious awareness. Second, both in Lui et al. and Wang et al. studies, the participants had to do the same tasks for both event- and time-based ProM (semantic tasks twice and perceptual tasks twice). On the one hand, it may lead to repetition effect and may enhance the performance; on the other hand, it may also have inhibitory effect as on the same task the subject has to press a designated key on the computer key-board on seeing a particular word in event-based condition and after elapse of a particular duration in time-based condition. Thus, it is likely that if the time-based ProM assessment is preceded by the event-based ProM assessment, the participants keep hitting the specified key on occurrence of a given word and not on elapse of time and vice versa. In the present study, different stimuli (general knowledge items for event-based ProM and reasoning task for time-based ProM) were used.

Now the question arises why the FDRs performed differently on event-and time-based tasks in the present study. The reason for difference could lie in the difference of cue prominence between the event- and time-based ProM tasks. In the time-based task, a clock was visible in the upper left corner of the computer screen. This could have worked as a constant reminder for the participants and, thus, the time-based task became easier for all the participants. Perhaps, this is why participants of all the three groups performed better on the time-based task as compared to the event-based task (see Figure 1). In some of the previous studies, the participants had to press the spacebar on the computer key-pad to bring the clock on the screen and then, if the desired amount of time had elapsed, they could execute the intended action. We did not include the pressing the space bar component as it involves another task of continuous anticipation of time and it can affect the performance on ProM task as it would be an additional burden on working memory.

The severity of psychopathology and the duration of illness did not correlate with either event- or time-based ProM scores. No correlation between psychopathology score and the ProM scores could be indicative of ProM as a trait marker in schizophrenia (as we have proposed in our another study; Kumar et al., 2005); however, this finding should be taken cautiously as the SAPS total score of the patient group in the present study was very low indicating that most of the patients were minimally symptomatic and, hence, the correlation scores may not be valid. On the other hand, lack of correlation between the duration of illness and ProM scores cannot be attributed to such confound and should be considered indicative that patients with schizophrenia invariably have ProM impairments irrespective of duration of their illness.

There are several limitations in the present study and the most important among them is the lack of assessment of other cognitive functions. Without this, it is difficult to comment on the specificity of ProM impairments in patients with schizophrenia and their FDRs as we are not able to assess whether or not (a) impairments in other cognitive domains correlate with ProM impairment and (b) one or more cognitive variables play mediating role in ProM impairment in patients with schizophrenia and their FDRs. Most importantly, it refrains us from reaching to a definite conclusion that ProM impairment could be a putative endophenotype of schizophrenia as the ProM performance can be differentially affected by different cognitive functions in the three groups (especially, the schizophrenia group in comparison to the FDR and healthy control groups). For example, attentional impairment in patients with schizophrenia is unequivocally established (Liu et al., 2002; Nuechterlein et al., 2015) and this can affect the performance on any test assessing a higher order cognitive function, including ProM. Small sample size is another limitation of the study and limits the generalizability of the findings. Further, now that there is availability of ecologically valid and standardized tools for ProM assessment (such as the Memory for Intention Screening Test; Raskin, 2009), it would have been better to use such tools instead of specifically designed experimental tool. Also, all the patients were on antipsychotic medications which could affect their performance on a cognitive task. However, it is important to note that controlling this variable was difficult as we were not supposed to make any changes in ongoing treatment. As our institute is a tertiary referral center, most of the patients visit while on medication and thus even drug naïve patients could not be recruited.

To summarize, our preliminary observations from this sample suggest impairment of ProM in FDRs of schizophrenia. These observations need replication and further systematic exploration in future research.

Acknowledgment

We are grateful to the editor and the two anonymous reviewers for their constructive inputs.

Disclosure statement

No potential conflict of interest was reported by the authors.

References

Altgassen, M., Kliegel, M., Rendell, P., Henry, J. D., & Zöllig, J. (2008). Prospective memory in schizophrenia: The impact of varying retrospective-memory load. *Journal of Clinical and Experimental Neuropsychology, 30*(7), 777–788.

Andreasen, N. C. (1984). *The scale for the assessment of positive symptoms*. Iowa, IA: The University of Iowa.

Braff, D. L., Freedman, R., Schork, N. J., & Gottesman, I. I. (2007). Deconstructing schizophrenia: An overview of the use of endophenotypes in order to understand a complex disorder. *Schizophrenia bulletin, 33*(1), 21–32.

Cheng, H. D., Wang, K., Xi, C. H., Niu, C. S., & Fu, X. M. (2008). Prefrontal cortex involvement in the event-based prospective memory: Evidence from patients with lesions in the prefrontal cortex. *Brain Injury, 22*(9), 697–704.

Cohen, J. (1988). *Statistical power analysis for the behavioural sciences*. New York, NY: Academic Press.

Dalla Barba, G. (1991). Prospective memory: A new memory system?. In F., Boller & J., Cyrafman (Eds.), Handbook of neuropsychology, Vol. 8 (pp. 239–251). New York, NY: Elsevier Science Publishers.

Einstein, G. O., & McDaniel, M. A. (1990). Normal aging and prospective memory. *Journal of Experimental Psychology: Learning Memory and Cognition, 16*, 717–726.

Gur, R. E., Calkins, M. E., Gur, R. C., Horan, W. P., Nuechterlein, K. H., Seidman, L. J., & Stone, W. S. (2007). The consortium on the genetics of schizophrenia: Neurocognitive endophenotypes. *Schizophrenia Bulletin, 33*(1), 49–68.

Kumar, D., Nizamie, S. H., & Jahan, M. (2005). Event-based Prospective memory in Schizophrenia. *Journal of Clinical and Experimental Neuropsychology, 27*(7), 867–872.

Kumar, D., Nizamie, S. H., & Jahan, M. (2008). Activity-based prospective memory in Schizophrenia. *The Clinical Neuropsychologist, 22*(3), 497–506.

Liu, S. K., Chiu, C. H., Chang, C. J., Hwang, T. J., Hwu, H. G., & Chen, W. J. (2002). Deficits in sustained attention in Schizophrenia and affective disorders: Stable versus state-dependent markers. *American Journal of Psychiatry, 159*(6), 975–982.

Lui, S. S., Wang, Y., Liu, A. C., Chui, W. W., Gong, Q. Y., Shum, D., … Chan, R. C. (2011). Prospective memory in patients with first-onset schizophrenia and their non-psychotic siblings. *Neuropsychologia, 49*(8), 2217–2224.

Nuechterlein, K. H., Green, M. F., Calkins, M. E., Greenwood, T. A., Gur, R. E., Gur, R. C., … Siever, L. J. (2015). Attention/vigilance in schizophrenia: Performance results from a large multi-site study of the consortium on the genetics of Schizophrenia (COGS). *Schizophrenia Research, 163*(1), 38–46.

Ordemann, G. J., Opper, J., & Davalos, D. (2014). Prospective memory in schizophrenia: A review. *Schizophrenia Research, 155*(1), 77–89.

Raskin, S. A. (2009). Memory for intentions screening test: Psychometric properties and clinical evidence. *Brain Impairment, 10*(01), 23–33.

Raskin, S. A., Maye, J., Rogers, A., Correll, D., Zamroziewicz, M., & Kurtz, M. (2014). Prospective memory in schizophrenia: Relationship to medication management skills, neurocognition, and symptoms in individuals with schizophrenia. *Neuropsychology, 28*(3), 359.

Seidman, L. J., Hellemann, G., Nuechterlein, K. H., Greenwood, T. A., Braff, D. L., Cadenhead, K. S., … Lazzeroni, L. C. (2015). Factor structure and heritability of endophenotypes in schizophrenia: Findings from the Consortium on the Genetics of Schizophrenia (COGS-1). *Schizophrenia Research, 163*(1), 73–79.

Ungvari, G. S., Xiang, Y. T., Tang, W. K., & Shum, D. (2008). Prospective memory and its correlates and predictors in schizophrenia: An extension of previous findings. *Archives of Clinical Neuropsychology, 23*(5), 613–622.

Wang, Y., Chan, R. C., Cui, J., Deng, Y., Huang, J., Li, H., … Li, Z. (2010). Prospective memory in non-psychotic first-degree relatives of patients with schizophrenia. *Psychiatry Research, 179*(3), 285–290.

Wang, Y., Cui, J., Chan, R. C., Deng, Y., Shi, H., Hong, X., … Shum, D. (2009). Meta-analysis of prospective memory in schizophrenia: Nature, extent, and correlates. *Schizophrenia Research, 114*(1), 64–70.

World Health Organization. (1992). *The ICD-10 classification of mental and behavioural disorders: Clinical description and diagnostic guidelines*. Geneva: Author.

Xiang, Y. T., Shum, D., Chiu, H. F., Tang, W. K., & Ungvari, G. S. (2010). Association of demographic characteristics, symptomatology, retrospective and prospective memory, executive functioning and intelligence with social functioning in Schizophrenia. *Australian and New Zealand Journal of Psychiatry, 44*(12), 1112–1117.

Long-term prospective memory impairment following mild traumatic brain injury with loss of consciousness: findings from the Canadian Longitudinal Study on Aging

Marc Bedard, Vanessa Taler and Jason Steffener

ABSTRACT

Objective: We aimed to examine the extent to which loss of consciousness (LOC) following mild traumatic brain injury (mTBI) may be associated with impairments in time- and event-based prospective memory (PM). PM is thought to involve executive processes and be subserved by prefrontal regions. Neuroimaging research suggests alterations to these areas of the brain several years after mTBI, particularly if LOC was experienced. However, it remains unclear whether impairments in time- or event-based functioning may persist more than a year after mTBI, and what the link with duration of LOC may be. **Method:** Analyses were run on data from the Canadian Longitudinal Study on Aging, a nationwide study on health and aging involving individuals between the ages of 45–85. The present study consisted of 1937 participants who experienced mTBI more than 12 months prior, of whom 1146 reported spending less than 1 min unconscious, and 791 had LOC between 1 and 20 min, and 13,525 cognitively healthy adults. Participants were administered the Miami Prospective Memory Test, and tests of retrospective memory and executive functioning. **Results:** Both mTBI groups were impaired in time-based PM relative to people with no history of TBI. Time- and event-based impairments were predicted by older age, and executive dysfunction among those who spent more time unconscious. **Conclusions:** Those with mTBI with LOC may experience impairments in PM, particularly in conditions of high demand on executive processes (time-based PM). Implications for interventions aimed at ameliorating PM among those who have experienced mTBI are discussed.

Introduction

Traumatic brain injuries (TBI) are a common source of neurological disability, estimated to have an annual incidence of 400 per 100,000 individuals (Bruns, Jr. & Hauser, 2003; Voss, Connolly, Schwab, & Scher, 2015), although this figure is thought to be an underestimate, because many brain injuries go unreported (Voss et al., 2015). Most reported cases would be classified as mild traumatic brain injury (mTBI), which is thought to comprise around 70%

of all TBI (Cassidy et al., 2004; Voss et al., 2015). Although there is a great deal of heterogeneity in definitions of TBI severity (Saatman et al., 2008), mTBIs are commonly defined based on the presence of any one of the following: loss of consciousness (LOC), amnesia surrounding the incident, altered mental state following the incident, or focal neurological deficits (American Congress of Rehabilitation Medicine, 1993). In addition, any LOC must not exceed 30 min, posttraumatic amnesia should not have persisted for more than 24 h, and Glasgow Coma Scale scores should be 13 or higher 30 min following the incident.

Despite the fact that 70% of TBIs are classified as mild, much of the research literature has focused on those who have sustained moderate-to-severe TBIs (those exceeding the previous criteria; American Congress of Rehabilitation Medicine, 1993). There is, however, burgeoning concern surrounding the nature of post-concussive symptoms following mTBI, most notably cognitive problems. Studies suggest that deficits in executive functioning and episodic memory may be most evident immediately after the brain injury and for up to two months afterwards (Karr, Areshenkoff, & Garcia-Barrera, 2014), and are thought to remit in a majority of individuals with mTBI by 3 months post-injury (Karr et al., 2014; Mayer, Quinn, & Master, 2017). However, neuropsychological deficits may persist in a minority of patients several months or even years after the mTBI (Karr et al., 2014; Mayer et al., 2017). For those that do exhibit ongoing cognitive dysfunction following brain injury, studies have found that a variety of variables, including individual factors (although not exhaustive), such as: increased age, lower levels of education, emotional distress prior to and after injury, and sleep difficulties may be implicated (Segev et al., 2016; van der Naalt et al., 2017).

Common among those that have experienced moderate or severe TBI are prospective memory (PM) deficits (Shum, Fleming, & Neulinger, 2002). PM is an aspect of episodic memory, but unlike conventional episodic memory, which involves retrospective memory – the ability to recall past facts and events – PM comprises our ability to 'remember to remember' to do something at a future time (Ellis & Kvavilashvili, 2000). For example, PM tasks may include remembering to take medication at specific times, or to attend medical appointments in the future. As such, PM is a crucial aspect of cognition and a necessity for independent daily functioning (Smith, Della Sala, Logie, & Maylor, 2000).

Neural correlates of PM

Mounting evidence from neuroimaging studies and electrophysiological recordings indicates that frontal lobe regions, particularly the rostral prefrontal cortex (i.e. Brodmann's area 10) subserve PM (Burgess, Gonen-Yaacovi, & Volle, 2011; Burgess, Quayle, & Frith, 2001; Burgess, Scott, & Frith, 2003; McFarland & Glisky, 2009). In addition, co-activations within parietal (Burgess et al., 2001, 2011; Gilbert, Gollwitzer, Cohen, Burgess, & Oettingen, 2009) and medial temporal lobes (Gordon, Shelton, Bugg, McDaniel, & Head, 2011; Moscovitch, 1994) are commonly found to support encoding, maintenance, and processes associated with spontaneous retrieval. There is also evidence for a role of the anterior cingulate cortex in processes implicated in preparatory attention toward fulfilling a prospective intention (Hashimoto, Umeda, & Kojima, 2011). Notwithstanding those associations, PM is mostly reliant on the executive processes underlying PM, including the following list of: planning, self-initiated retrieval, and strategic monitoring, which are subserved by frontal systems (Gilbert et al., 2009; McDaniel & Einstein, 2011).

Neuroimaging in mTBI

Neuroimaging studies have revealed structural and functional alterations to frontal areas of the brain following mTBI (Abdel-Dayem et al., 1998; Mayer, Mannell, Ling, Gasparovic, & Yeo, 2011; McDonald, Saykin, & McAllister, 2012; Sorg et al., 2014; Strangman et al., 2010), found also in those with persistent cognitive dysfunction (Hartikainen et al., 2010; Mac Donald et al., 2017). Moreover, these alterations may be more pronounced when LOC is experienced (Kraus et al., 2007; Sorg et al., 2014; Strangman et al., 2010). Despite these associations, only two studies have investigated PM function in those with mTBI. Of these, it has been reported that compared to controls, adults with mTBI may exhibit deficits on PM within a month of the incident, which may persist three months following the mTBI (Tay, Ang, Lau, Meyyappan, & Collinson, 2010). In addition, those over the age of 65 may exhibit deficits relative to controls on PM three months following the mTBI (Kinsella, Olver, Ong, Gruen, & Hammersley, 2014). Given the paucity of research in these areas, there is clearly a need for more extensive research into the impact on PM of mild forms of TBI, particularly in the long term (beyond 3 months post-injury), but also with older samples generally (Thompson, McCormick, & Kagan, 2006; although see Kinsella et al., 2014). Moreover, although LOC has been found to exacerbate the effects of mTBI on the frontal lobe, little is known about the effects of LOC on PM function.

It has been suggested that the relative requirements for strategic monitoring and self-initiated retrieval during the execution of PM may vary depending on whether the PM cue is event-based or time-based (McDaniel & Einstein, 2000). Whereas an event-based PM task is completed based on the presence of an external cue (e.g. remembering to refill a prescription at a medical appointment), a time-based PM task involves the execution of a planned intention following a certain amount of time or at a given time (e.g. remembering to take medication at a certain time). Due to increased demands for self-initiated retrieval and monitoring (Einstein, McDaniel, Richardson, Guynn, & Cunfer, 1995), time-based tasks have been posited to place more demands on the frontal lobe (Burgess et al., 2001, 2003; Oksanen, Waldum, McDaniel, & Braver, 2014; Okuda et al., 2007). Thus, given that frontal lobe dysfunction has been found in long-term survivors of mTBI (Hartikainen et al., 2010; Mac Donald et al., 2017; Matsushita, Hosoda, Naitoh, Yamashita, & Kohmura, 2011), we hypothesize that, compared to controls, those who experienced mTBI with LOC will exhibit greater deficits in time-based than event-based PM tasks. We also hypothesize that greater time spent unconscious will be associated with lower PM performance.

The present study reports data from a large population-based study of aging, the Canadian Longitudinal Study on Aging (CLSA), which evaluated PM using the Miami Prospective Memory Test (MPMT; Lowenstein & Acevedo, 2004). The MPMT consists of one event-based and two time-based tasks (only one is administered in the CLSA protocol), which are scored to allow for the assessment of the relative contribution of the memory intention (i.e., the extent to which the participant remembers that they are supposed to do something), accuracy (i.e., their ability to remember what it is that they are to do), and the need for reminders or prompting, with regard to PM performance. This coding system may allow for an evaluation of whether PM deficits may be due to a retrospective memory failure, as indicated by lower accuracy scores, or whether PM dysfunction may be driven by deficits in executive processes (Hernandez Cardenache, Burguera, Acevedo, Curiel, & Loewenstein, 2014). Finally, as mentioned above, PM may be associated with executive functioning (e.g., planning, strategic monitoring, or even impulsivity) and retrospective memory abilities (to remember the content of the intention); we thus examined these associations among CLSA participants with mTBI.

Materials and procedures

We used data from the CLSA, an ongoing long-term study consisting of a national stratified random sample of over 50,000 male and female Canadians aged 45–85 (Raina et al., 2009). Ethical review of the CLSA protocol was conducted by the Ethical, Legal, and Social Issues Committee, which falls under the jurisdiction of the Canadian Institutes of Health Research (CIHR). Further institutional research ethics board approval was acquired from each individual research site prior to data collection. Participant data will be collected at 3-year intervals for a span of at least 20 years to examine health transitions and trajectories. Baseline information, including demographic and clinical information has been collected for all participants, with approximately 30,000 (Comprehensive Cohort) evaluated through 90-min in-home interviews, in addition to more in-depth physical and cognitive assessments conducted at one of 11 data collection sites across Canada. Participants in the Comprehensive Cohort were recruited from within a 25-km radius of the data collection sites, and were assessed within 2–3 weeks of the in-home interview (see Raina et al., 2009 for more detailed sampling frame information). The present study uses baseline data from participants in the Comprehensive Cohort. The other 20,000 participants in the Tracking cohort participants did not complete PM testing. The present study was approved by the research ethics boards at our institutions, responsible for reviewing studies including human participants.

Participants

Although detailed information on the sampling frame is provided in Raina et al. (2009), briefly, CLSA participants include adults between the ages of 45–85 years who are fluent in English and/or French. For the present investigation, individuals were excluded from the current analyses if they were ever diagnosed with a neurological disorder (e.g. Alzheimer's or Parkinson's diseases, multiple sclerosis), had ever had a cerebral vascular accident or transient ischemic attack, or those that experienced a brain injury or received multiple injuries (which may include brain injury) in the past 12 months. Thus, those that had self-reported having lost consciousness as a result of a head injury that occurred more than 12 months prior to study recruitment were included for our mTBI sample. They were further divided based on length of LOC, as captured in the CLSA protocol, for which we have data on those who experienced LOC for less than 1 min, and those who experienced LOC for between 1 and 20 min. Although the CLSA also includes those who lost consciousness for more than 20 min, as the present study sought to examine PM functioning in those with mTBI, those with LOC greater than 20 min were excluded, as it is not possible to ascertain whether they are all mild cases, or include moderate-to-severe TBI based on established conventions (i.e. LOC greater than 30 min; American Congress of Rehabilitation Medicine, 1993). However, it should be noted that the CLSA does not include data on posttraumatic amnesia, information for the calculation of a Glasgow Coma Scale score, nor date of brain injury. Finally, in addition to the mTBI groups, we included those that had never experienced a brain injury as our control group. We further only included participants for which we had data on all the variables detailed below.

Measures

Demographic and clinical information, including age, education level, sex, marital status, and previous injury within the past 12 months were self-reported by participants using questionnaires that were administered through structured in-person interviews. All participants provided informed consent prior to completing the questionnaires and the neuropsychological assessments described below.

Traumatic brain injury

Data pertaining to participant TBI(s) were recorded with the use of the Brief Traumatic Brain Injury Screen (BTBIS; Schwab et al., 2007), which was designed as a quick self-report screening tool of TBI for use with large numbers of individuals. This measure collects data on the number of lifetime TBIs, and length of unconsciousness following TBI (longest duration in the case of multiple TBIs), measured on a three-point Likert scale, with LOC reported as having been less than 1 min, between 1 and 20 min, or greater than 20 min.

Depression

Depressive symptoms were assessed with the Center for Epidemiologic Studies Short Depression Scale (CES-D10; Andresen, Malmgren, Carter, & Patrick, 1994), which comprises 10 questions rated on a four-point Likert scale. Total scores range from 0 to 30, with higher scores indicating greater depressive symptomatology (Cronbach's $\alpha = 0.79$). A score of 10 or more is indicative of clinically significant depressive symptomatology.

Prospective memory

PM was evaluated with the Miami Prospective Memory Test (MPMT; Hernandez Cardenache et al., 2014; Lowenstein & Acevedo, 2004), a 30-min test. See Hernandez Cardenache et al. (2014) for a complete description of the administration and scoring procedures. The MPMT is composed of 1 event-based trial, in which the participant is asked to select (from a number of different denominations of bills and change) a \$5 bill, to be handed to the examiner, and a \$10 bill that is to be taken and kept by the participant, after hearing a loud timer that is set for 30 min. For the time-based task, a clock placed on the wall behind the examiner and in view of the participant is initially set to 08:00. At 08:15 (and 08:30 for Trial 2), the participant is to request from the examiner an envelope, which has five numbered cards (28, 14, 17, 13, and 11), and to give card number 17 to the examiner. There is another similar time-based task at 30 min, but this second trial was not administered in the CLSA protocol.

Each of the MPMT trials are scored based on intention to perform (i.e. whether the participant performed the action, or their relative degree of failure to acknowledge the cue) scored from 0 to 3; accuracy (i.e. degree to which the participant correctly recalls the content, or substitutes the content of the response) scored from 0 to 3; and need for reminders, scored from 0 to 3. Reminders are provided in a hierarchical order after 4 min without response during the time-based trials, or if the participant has not initiated a response within 60 s of the timer going off in the event-based trial. Scores for intention to perform, accuracy, and need for reminders are summed for each trial, with trial scores ranging from 0 to 9, with higher scores indicating fewer errors.

Neuropsychological assessment

Additional measures of episodic memory and executive functions were completed by participants, including the Rey Auditory Verbal Learning Test (RAVLT; Rey, 1964) immediate and delayed recall, the F-A-S Controlled Oral Word Association Test (COWAT; Spreen & Benton, 1977), the Mental Alternation Test (MAT; Teng, 1994), and the Victoria Stroop Test (VST; Regard, 1981; although for a description see Strauss, Sherman, & Spreen, 2006), which was used to generate an interference score, calculated by dividing the completion time of the Color-Word trial by the Dot trial, to correct for the influence of cognitive slowing (Strauss et al., 2006).

Statistical analyses

Statistical analyses were performed using SPSS version 24 (Armonk, NY, USA: IBM Corp.). All continuous variables were checked for normality with the use of Q-Q plots, and through determining whether skew statistics remained between −2 and 2 (Curran, West, & Finch, 1996). Most variables were normally distributed, with the exception of all MPMT variables, which were negatively skewed, and the VST interference scores, which were positively skewed. Following recommended procedures (Tabachnick & Fidell, 2013), normality was achieved using inverse transformations on the MPMT variables and the VST interference scores were normalized with the use of logarithmic transformations; subsequent parametric analyses used these transformed variables.

Group differences on continuous demographic and clinical data, including age and depression were analyzed with univariate analysis of variance (ANOVA), with Bonferroni-corrected pairwise comparisons. Kruskal-Wallis tests were done to examine between-group differences on the categorical demographic data of education and marital status. Mann-Whitney U tests with Bonferroni corrections were used for pairwise comparisons on the categorical demographic data, and to examine for group sex differences.

To investigate for a differential deficit in time-based or event-based PM among those that sustained a mTBI with LOC relative to those who have not had a brain injury, a parametric repeated-measures analysis of covariance (ANCOVA) using group as the between-subjects factor (control and each of the TBI groups) and PM cue type (time- vs. event-based) as the within-subjects factor was conducted, which included testing language (French or English), age, education, sex, depressive symptomatology, and number of lifetime TBIs as covariates. Pairwise comparisons were conducted with Bonferroni correction.

Following this, impairment on time- and event-based functioning were defined as scoring below the 5th percentile of control group time- and event-based performance, respectively. Kruskal-Wallis tests were used to compare between-group rates of impairment in time- and event-based conditions; pairwise comparisons were completed with Mann-Whitney U tests with Bonferroni corrections, to adjust for the number of comparisons made within each impairment cue type (i.e., time- and event-based).

An additional aim of the present study was to determine whether differential functioning was observed on intention to perform, accuracy, and the need for reminders. This analysis was performed by first combining each domain score across the event- and time-based tasks to get composite error scores. We conducted a 3 x 3 parametric repeated-measures ANCOVA in which the between-subjects factor was group and the within-subjects factor was domain type (i.e. inverse transformed intention to perform, accuracy, and need for reminders); the same covariates were entered as in the ANCOVA described above.

Finally, logistic regression analyses were conducted to examine the distinctive contributions of a priori selected measures of executive functioning and retrospective memory on PM impairment, conducted separately for each TBI group. Raw scores of these neuropsychological measures were examined in the logistic regression, and the same covariates that were entered in the previous ANCOVAs were also included. A significance level of $p < .05$ was used for all analyses.

Results

Demographic characteristics

Table 1 details demographic and clinical characteristics. There were a total of 15,462 participants included in the study for which data were available on all variables of interest. 13,525 were controls, and the remaining 1937 belonged to the mTBI groups, consisting of those who experienced LOC for less than 1 min ($n = 1146$), and those between 1 and 20 min ($n = 791$). The three groups were comparable in terms of education ($p = .936$) and marital status ($p = .162$), but differed with respect to age ($p < .001$), and sex ($p < .001$). Specifically, control participants were older than the two mTBI groups (*p*s < .05), which did not differ ($p = .130$). The control group contained a higher proportion of women compared to the mTBI groups ($p < .001$), which did not differ ($p = .352$).

Clinical characteristics

Levels of depressive symptoms were found to differ between the groups ($p < .001$). Bonferroni-corrected pairwise comparisons indicated that the control group had lower

Table 1. Demographic and clinical characteristics of the mild traumatic brain injury groups and controls.

		Mild traumatic brain injury	
	Controls ($n = 13{,}525$)	LOC < 1 min ($n = 1146$)	LOC 1–20 min ($n = 791$)
Age, mean (SD)	61.76 (9.90)	60.03 (9.10)	60.88 (9.78)
Sex			
Female (%)	54.3	38.7	40.3
Male (%)	45.7	61.3	59.7
Education			
< High school (%)	2.5	2.6	2.9
High school (%)	7.5	8.1	7.5
College (%)	34.5	34.0	36.0
University degree (%)	29.0	28.1	25.4
Graduate degree (%)	26.6	27.1	28.2
Marital status			
Married (%)	71.6	75.5	72.6
Widowed (%)	7.5	4.6	6.8
Divorced (%)	9.7	9.3	9.1
Separated (%)	2.6	3.1	2.0
Single (%)	8.5	7.5	9.5
Depression, mean (SD)	4.73 (4.30)	5.46 (4.62)	5.56 (4.78)
Number of TBIs, mean (SD)	0	2.36 (2.29)	2.03 (2.01)

Note: TBI = traumatic brain injury; LOC = loss of consciousness. In individuals that experienced more than one TBI, LOC refers to the longest period of unconsciousness experienced.

depression scores than either of the mTBI groups (*ps* < .001), while no differences were observed between the mTBI groups (*p* = 1.0). Moreover, participants with LOC < 1 min were found to have experienced more TBIs in their lifetime compared to those with LOC of 1–20 min (*p* < .001).

Prospective memory functioning

Means and standard deviations by group on the MPMT are presented in Table 2. A repeated measures ANCOVA revealed a significant main effect of group $F(2, 15454) = 4.18$, $p = .015$, $\eta^2 = 0.001$), a significant main effect of cue type, $F(1, 15454) = 71.71$, $p < .001$, $\eta^2 = 0.005$) with lower event- vs. time-based performance, and a significant interaction between group and cue type, $F(3, 15454) = 18.60$, $p < .031$, $\eta^2 = 0.002$. Pairwise comparisons revealed that in time-based PM, both mTBI groups performed more poorly than the controls (*ps* < .001), and that those with LOC < 1 min did not differ from those with LOC 1–20 min (*p* = 1.0). In event-based PM, those with LOC < 1 min were found to perform better than controls (*p* = .005) and those with LOC 1–20 min (*p* = .044), and controls did not differ from those with LOC 1-20 min (*p* = 1.0).

Comparisons of error types

To investigate between-group differences on intention to perform, accuracy, and need for prompts, an additional repeated measures ANCOVA was conducted. It revealed a marginally significant main effect of group $F(2, 15454) = 2.947$, $p = .053$, $\eta^2 = 0.000$, a main effect of measurement type (intention, accuracy, and reminder), $F(2, 15454) = 9.46$, $p = .002$, $\eta^2 = 0.001$, and a significant interaction between group and measurement type, $F(2, 15454) = 8.99$, $p < .001$, $\eta^2 = 0.001$. Pairwise comparisons indicated that none of the groups differed on

Table 2. Prospective memory and cognitive test performance in the study samples.

			Mild traumatic brain injury			
	Control (*n* = 13,525)		LOC < 1 min (*n* = 1146)		LOC 1-20 min (*n* = 791)	
Test	*M*	*SD*	*M*	*SD*	*M*	*SD*
Prospective memory						
Time-based (0–9)	8.76	0.78	8.66	0.92	8.65	0.97
Event-based (0–9)	8.53	1.27	8.71	0.977	8.56	1.20
Impairment rates						
Time-based (%)	4.6		7.2		6.9	
Event-based (%)	1.6		0.4		1.3	
MPMT Errors						
Intention to perform (0–6)	5.55	1.03	5.57	0.97	5.49	1.10
Reminder (0–6)	5.83	0.49	5.87	0.37	5.82	0.47
Accuracy (0–6)	5.91	0.41	5.93	0.30	5.90	0.40
Executive functioning						
COWAT	40.73	12.43	41.67	12.12	41.11	12.79
VST Interference	2.11	0.73	2.08	0.54	2.11	0.74
MAT	27.49	8.30	28.24	8.31	27.77	8.50
Declarative Memory						
RAVLT immediate	6.10	1.86	6.14	1.81	6.07	1.92
RAVLT delayed	4.29	2.15	4.36	2.10	4.20	2.15

Note: LOC = loss of consciousness; MPMT = Miami Prospective Memory Test; COWAT = Controlled Oral Word Association Test; VST = Victoria Stroop Test; MAT = Mental Alternation Test; RAVLT = Rey Auditory Verbal Learning Test.

accuracy or need for reminders (*ps* > .05). For intention to perform, those with LOC 1–20 min were found to score lower than controls ($p = .023$), while those with LOC < 1 min did not differ from the LOC 1–20 min group ($p = .969$), nor from the control group ($p = .274$).

Time- and event-based impairment

After applying the impairment criteria (i.e. scoring below the 5th percentile cut-off of the control group), 4.6% of controls, 7.2% for those with LOC < 1 min, and 6.9%, of those with LOC 1–20 min were impaired on time-based PM, χ^2 (2) = 22.39, $p < .001$. Pairwise comparisons revealed that both mTBI groups had a higher rate of time-based PM impairment than controls (*ps* < 0.01), and those with LOC < 1 min were not found to differ from those with LOC 1–20 min ($p = 1.0$). In event-based functioning, impairment rates were 1.6% for controls and 0.4% for those with LOC < 1 min, and 1.3%, for those with LOC 1–20 min, χ^2 (2) = 19.55, $p = .006$. Pairwise comparisons indicated that those with LOC < 1 min were less likely to be classified as impaired on event-based performance than the other groups (*ps* < .05), which did not differ ($p = 1.0$).

Predictors of PM impairment

Time-based impairment

Descriptive data on the other neuropsychological tasks are provided in Table 2. To identify the unique contributions of retrospective memory (RAVLT immediate and delayed) and executive functioning (COWAT and MAT) to time-based PM impairments for each of the mTBI groups, logistic regressions were run, separately for each group, including the raw retrospective memory and executive function scores entered as predictors in addition to the demographic and clinical characteristics from the ANCOVA. For those with LOC of < 1 min, a test of the full model against a constant-only model was statistically significant, χ^2 (14) = 55.38, $p < .001$, Nagelkerke $R^2 = 0.12$. As shown in Table 3, an increase of one year of age (OR = 1.050, 95% CI = 1.022–1.080) was associated with a 5% increase in the odds of being classified as impaired, while a single-point increase in the RAVLT delayed score (OR = 0.815, 95% CI = 0.700–0.948) was associated with a 19% decrease in the odds of being classified as impaired. Among those with LOC of 1–20 min, χ^2 (14) = 37.84, $p < .001$, Nagelkerke $R^2 = 0.12$, an increase of one year of age (OR = 1.063, 95% CI = 1.029–1.099) was associated with a 6.3% increase in odds, and an increase in one lifetime mTBI experienced (OR = 1.183, 95% CI = 1.058–1.322) was associated with an 18.3% increase in odds of being classified as impaired. In addition, of the variables entered into the analyses, it was found that a single point increase on the CES-D10 was associated with a 6% increase (OR = 1.062, 95% CI = 1.013–1.113) in the odds of being classified as impaired among those with LOC < 1 min. Among those with LOC 1–20 min, χ^2 (14) = 37.93, $p < .001$, Nagelkerke $R^2 = 0.12$, a single point increase in MAT scores was associated with a 3.1% decrease in odds of being impaired in time-based functioning (OR = 0.969, 95% CI = 0.948–0.991).

Event-based impairment

As was done previously, logistic regressions were run, separately for each group, to investigate the unique predictors of event-based impairment, by including the raw retrospective memory and executive function scores and the demographic and clinical characteristics as

Table 3. Logistic regression model for predictors of time-based prospective memory impairment among the mild traumatic brain injury participants.

	LOC < 1 min		LOC 1–20 min	
	OR	95% C.I.	OR	95% C.I.
Executive functioning				
COWAT	0.996	0.976, 1.018	1.009	0.983, 1.035
VST Interference	1.071	0.715, 1.604	1.121	0.845, 1.487
MAT	0.975	0.947, 1.005	**0.969**	**0.948, 0.991**
Declarative memory				
RAVLT immediate	1.128	0.943, 1.348	0.906	0.725, 1.134
RAVLT delayed	**0.815**	**0.700, 0.948**	1.051	0.858, 1.286
Testing language				
English (reference)	1.00		1.00	
French	0.527	0.203, 1.367	0.422	0.145, 1.226
Number of TBIs	1.035	0.940, 1.139	**1.183**	**1.058, 1.322**
Depression scores	**1.062**	**1.013, 1.113**	1.039	0.981, 1.099
Age	**1.050**	**1.022, 1.080**	**1.063**	**1.029, 1.099**
Sex				
Male (reference)	1.00		1.00	
Female	0.674	0.393, 1.157	1.692	0.898, 3.187
Education				
< High school (reference)	1.00		1.00	
High school	2.386	0.442, 12.871	0.153	0.019, 1.202
College	2.518	0.529, 11.978	0.689	0.175, 2.717
University degree	1.198	0.234, 6.122	0.504	0.120, 2.116
Graduate degree	1.656	0.330, 8.309	0.647	0.153, 2.729

Note: LOC = loss of consciousness; COWAT = Controlled Oral Word Association Test; VST = Victoria Stroop Test; MAT = Mental Alternation Test; RAVLT = Rey Auditory Verbal Learning Test; TBI = traumatic brain injury; OR = Odds Ratio. Odds ratios that are significant ($p < .05$) have been bolded. Odds ratios greater than 1 indicate increased odds of being classified as impaired on time-based functioning, whereas odds ratios of less than 1 indicate decreased odds of impairment. For those with LOC < 1 min, $n = 1146$, and those with LOC 1–20 min, $n = 791$.

predictors. However, given the low number of individuals with mTBI that were classified as impaired, the education variable was excluded as a predictor in these analyses. As displayed in Table 4, results from logistic regressions to investigate the predictors of event-based impairment indicated that none of the variables entered into the model significantly predicted impairment status for either those with LOC < 1 min or those with LOC 1–20 min (*ps* > .05). However, marginal significance was found for an increase of one year of age being associated with a 7.6% (OR = 1.076, 95% CI = 0.999–1.159) increase in odds of impairment among those with LOC 1–20 min.

Unplanned post hoc analyses were conducted to investigate possible contributions to the counterintuitive finding of lower event-based impairment among those unconscious for less than one minute compared to controls. A binary logistic regression was run, collapsing the two groups, and by including the demographic and clinical characteristics (those covariates included in the earlier ANCOVA) as predictors of event-based impairment, χ^2 (9) = 260.48, $p < .001$, Nagelkerke $R^2 = 0.099$. This analysis indicated that age (OR = 1.100, 95% CI = 1.086–1.115) and depression scores (OR = 1.05, 95% CI = 1.024–1.078) were significant predictors of event-based impairment.

Table 4. Logistic regression model for predictors of event-based prospective memory impairment among the mild traumatic brain injury participants.

	LOC < 1 min		LOC 1-20 min	
	OR	95% C.I.	OR	95% C.I.
Executive functioning				
COWAT	1.001	0.907 1.105	0.945	0.891 1.003
VST Interference	1.609	0.562, 4.606	0.881	0.302, 2.574
MAT	0.915	0.824, 1.017	0.967	0.884, 1.058
Declarative memory				
RAVLT immediate	0.592	0.235, 1.491	0.796	0.493, 1.286
RAVLT delayed	1.371	0.587, 3.204	0.845	0.523, 1.364
Testing language				
English (reference)	1.00		1.00	
French	1.670	0.132, 21.184	0.454	0.053, 3.896
Number of TBIs	0.556	0.160, 1.926	1.042	0.826, 1.313
Depression scores	1.060	0.892, 1.260	0.979	0.857, 1.119
Age	0.949	0.837, 1.077	1.076	0.999, 1.159
Sex				
Male (reference)	1.00		1.00	
Female	0.656	0.076, 5.683	0.324	0.083, 1.260

Note: LOC = loss of consciousness; COWAT = Controlled Oral Word Association Test; VST = Victoria Stroop Test; MAT = Mental Alternation Test; RAVLT = Rey Auditory Verbal Learning Test; TBI = traumatic brain injury; OR = Odds Ratio. Odds ratios that are significant ($p < .05$) have been bolded. Odds ratios greater than 1 indicate increased odds of being classified as impaired on time-based functioning, whereas odds ratios of less than 1 indicate decreased odds of impairment. For those with LOC < 1 min, $n = 1146$, and those with LOC 1–20 min, $n = 791$.

Discussion

Prior research has indicated that frontal areas of the brain may be compromised in people who have experienced even mild TBI (Abdel-Dayem et al., 1998; Mayer et al., 2011; McDonald et al., 2012; Sorg et al., 2014; Strangman et al., 2010), particularly in those who have experienced LOC (Kraus et al., 2007; Sorg et al., 2014; Strangman et al., 2010). Moreover, there is growing concern that, at least in a subset of those who have experienced a mTBI, alterations to frontal regions may persist many years after the brain injury (Hartikainen et al., 2010; Mac Donald et al., 2017; Matsushita et al., 2011). In addition, it has been recognized that time-based tasks may place more demands on executive processes than event-based tasks (McDaniel & Einstein, 2000), which are subserved by the frontal lobe (Burgess et al., 2001, 2003, 2011; Oksanen et al., 2014; Okuda et al., 2007). However, to the best of our knowledge, no studies have investigated whether PM deficits may persist into the long-term (i.e. beyond 3-months post-injury), and if length of LOC may influence PM functioning in mTBI. The present study thus had two goals: first, to evaluate performance of time- and event-based PM tasks among those who have experienced mTBI with LOC, more than 12 months ago, and second, to assess the relative contributions of executive function, and retrospective memory performance in predicting PM impairments among people with a longstanding history of mTBI.

Initial findings from the present study of a nationally representative sample of adults aged 45–85 provides evidence for a disproportionate deficit on time-based PM performance for those that experienced a mTBI with LOC less than 1 min and for those with LOC between 1 and 20 min. At first blush, the present data indicate subtle time-based PM deficits among those who experienced mTBI with LOC, similar in magnitude to those observed in meta-nalyses of neuropsychological deficits 3 or more months post-TBI (Binder, Rohling, & Larrabee, 1997; Frencham, Fox, & Maybery, 2005; Schretlen & Shapiro, 2003). However, after applying impairment criteria, a higher proportion of people in the mTBI groups exhibited time-based PM impairments (7.2 and 6.9%) than in the control group (4.6%). Our results, therefore, seem to align with the perspective that although a large proportion of those who experience mTBI may not develop persistent dysfunction, a small subset may continue to exhibit cognitive impairment (Bigler et al., 2013; Iverson, 2010; Karr et al., 2014; Mayer et al., 2017; Pertab, James, & Bigler, 2009; Rohling, Larrabee, & Millis, 2012).

Performance on the event-based task was found to be more nuanced, with controls not differing from those with LOC between 1 and 20 min, while those with LOC < 1 min were actually found to outperform the former groups. This was an unexpected finding because previous studies have observed deficits in event-based functioning following mTBI, relative to controls (Kinsella et al., 2014; Tay et al., 2010). Thus, this counterintuitive finding in the present study was explored through post hoc logistic regression analyses, which found age and depressive symptomatology to be significant predictors of event-based impairment among those who were unconscious for less than a minute as well as controls. This, therefore, suggests that these discrepant results may have been a function of the lower age found among those unconscious for less than a minute, which is consistent with the notion that performance on event-based PM tasks may decrease with advancing age (Kleigel, Jäger, & Phillips, 2008; Maylor, 1996; Smith & Bayen, 2006).

Importantly, we found evidence for a differential pattern of time- and event-based impairment in individuals 12 months after they had lost consciousness following mTBI. While performance on the event-based task was not sensitive to mTBI, people who experienced mTBI with LOC of any length were more likely to exhibit time-based impairment than those with no history of mTBI. This finding, therefore, suggests that spending any amount of time unconscious may be a useful indicator of the likelihood of exhibiting PM impairments in time-based tasks, which are thought to be more reliant on the frontal lobe (Burgess et al., 2001, 2003, 2011; Oksanen et al., 2014; Okuda et al., 2007).

An additional aim of the present study was to evaluate the cognitive functions associated with PM impairments in people with mTBI with LOC. Given that the data reported here show similar rates of PM impairments in people with LOC < 1 min and those with LOC of 1–20 min, it may be argued that those groups should be considered together. However, error analysis suggested that PM deficits were associated with executive dysfunction (e.g., self-initiated retrieval or strategic monitoring), rather than a failure to recall the content of the PM task (i.e., retrospective component), only among those who reported LOC between 1 and 20 min. Logistic regression analyses supported this finding of executive dysfunction: a single-point increase on the Mental Alternation Test was associated with decreased odds of time-based impairment for those who reported unconsciousness between 1 and 20 min. Among those with LOC of less than 1 min, PM impairments generally seemed to emerge with lower retrospective memory ability, which appears to be consistent with imaging data indicating smaller medial temporal lobe volumes in those who had a mTBI decades prior to evaluation (Monti et al., 2013). These findings, therefore, seems to parallel previous work indicating that more time spent unconscious may be associated with greater frontal lobe and executive dysfunction (Kraus et al., 2007; Sorg et al., 2014; Strangman et al., 2010), and thus LOC may serve as an important variable to consider in outcomes from mTBI.

A number of limitations to the present study must be noted. First, the data on mTBI were self-reported and are, therefore, biased by retrospective recall, which may have limited our ability to distinguish individuals that may have experienced LOC between 1 and 20 min from those who lost consciousness for less than 1 min. In addition, it is acknowledged that data were not available for post-traumatic amnesia, nor were Glasgow Coma Scale scores. Similarly, an acknowledged limitation is a lack of data on the exact time since injury. Given the prevalence of mTBI in younger adults, and that this study included individuals between the ages of 45–85, it is not exactly clear what the contribution of time since injury is, nor the impact of temporal span between brain injuries among those who experienced multiple brain injuries. Moreover, these findings are based on cross-sectional data and information about premorbid function is not available. Pre-mTBI cognitive assessments would be useful for identifying the factors (e.g., pre-mTBI executive dysfunction, emotional distress, or old age) that predispose someone to long-term PM impairments resulting from a mTBI. For instance, the present study suggests that age may be an important factor: age was a predictor of time-based PM impairment in all groups. Future CLSA data will allow us to address some of these questions.

Clinical implications

As mentioned, future research should evaluate who may be particularly predisposed to PM impairments following mTBI, and investigate the utility of early interventions in these individuals. For instance, as the present study found evidence of executive dysfunction underlying time-based impairments, there has been work to suggest that implementation intentions, which are if-then conditions between an event and an intended action, may provide improvements in intention retrieval (Smith, McConnell Rogers, McVay, Lopez, & Loft, 2014). Moreover, visual imagery, an internal memory strategy, has been shown to strengthen retrieval by increasing the automaticity of recall (Thöne-Otto & Walther, 2008), and may be of benefit to increase time- and event-based memory functioning in patients with traumatic brain injury (Potvin, Rouleau, Sénéchal, & Giguère, 2011). In addition, future research may wish to examine external compensatory approaches (Fleming, Shum, Strong, & Lightbody, 2005) (e.g., Google calendar on mobile phones; Baldwin & Powell, 2015; McDonald et al., 2011) to bypass the impaired self-initiated retrieval processes could prove beneficial for both time- and event-based tasks encountered in daily life.

Conclusions

The present investigation provides evidence that those who have experienced mTBI with LOC more than 12 months ago are more likely to exhibit deficits in time-based than event-based PM tasks, and that these impairments appear to be associated with executive dysfunction in those with more time spent unconscious. As PM is essential to everyday functioning, the findings from this study are relevant in terms of developing cognitive rehabilitation strategies aimed at ameliorating PM among long-term survivors of mTBI.

Acknowledgements

This research was made possible using the data collected by the Canadian Longitudinal Study on Aging (CLSA). This research has been conducted using the CLSA Baseline Comprehensive dataset version 3.0 under Application Number 161009. Funding for the Canadian Longitudinal Study on Aging (CLSA) is provided by the Government of Canada through the Canadian Institutes of Health Research (CIHR) under grant reference: LSA 94473 and the Canada Foundation for Innovation. The CLSA is led by Drs. Parminder Raina, Christina Wolfson and Susan Kirkland.

Disclosure statement

No potential conflict of interest was reported by the authors.

Funding

This work was supported by the Canada Foundation for Innovation; Canadian Institutes of Health Research (CIHR).

References

Abdel-Dayem, H. M., Abu-Judeh, H., Kumar, M., Atay, S., Naddaf, S., El-Zeftawy, H., & Luo, J. Q. (1998). SPECT brain perfusion abnormalities in mild or moderate traumatic brain injury. *Clinical Nuclear Medicine, 23*(5), 309–317.

American Congress of Rehabilitation Medicine, Mild Traumatic Brain Injury Committee of the Interdisciplinary Special Interest Group. (1993). Definition of mild traumatic brain injury. *Journal of Head Trauma and Rehabilitation, 8*(3), 86–87.

Andresen, E. M., Malmgren, J. A., Carter, W. B., & Patrick, D. L. (1994). Screening for depression in well older adults: Evluation of a short form of the CES-D (center for epidemiologic studies depression scale). *American Journal of Preventative Medicine, 10*(2), 77–84.

Baldwin, V. N., & Powell, T. (2015). Google calendar: A single case experimental design study of a man with severe memory problems. *Neuropsychological Rehabilitation, 25*(4), 617–636.

Bigler, E. D., Farrer, T. J., Pertab, J. L., James, K., Petrie, J. A., & Hedges, D. W. (2013). Reaffirmed limitations of meta-analytic methods in the study of mild traumatic brain injury: A response to Rohling et al. *The Clinical Neuropsychologist, 27*, 176–214.

Binder, L. M., Rohling, M. L., & Larrabee, G. J. (1997). A review of mild head trauma. Part I: Meta-analytic review of neuropsychological studies. *Journal of Clinical and Experimental Neuropsychology, 19*(3), 421–431.

Bruns, Jr., J., & Hauser, W. A. (2003). The epidemiology of traumatic brain injury: A review. *Epilepsia, 44*(10), 2–10.

Burgess, P. W., Gonen-Yaacovi, G., & Volle, E. (2011). Functional neuroimaging studies of prospective memory: What have we learnt so far? *Neuropsychologia, 49*, 2246–2257.

Burgess, P. W., Quayle, A., & Frith, C. D. (2001). Brain regions involved in prospective memory as determined by positron emission tomography. *Neuropsychologia, 39*, 545–555.

Burgess, P. W., Scott, S. K., & Frith, C. D. (2003). The role of the rostral frontal cortex (area 10) in prospective memory: A lateral versus medial dissociation. *Neuropsychologia, 41*, 906–918.

Cassidy, J. D., Carroll, L. J., Peloso, P. M., Borg, J., von Holst, H., Holm, L., … WHO Collaborating Centre Task Force on Mild Traumatic Brain Injury. (2004). Incidence, risk factors and prevention of mild traumatic brain injury: Results of the WHO collaborating centre task force on mild traumatic brain injury. *Journal of Rehabilitation Medicine, 36*, 28–60.

Curran, P. J., West, S. G., & Finch, J. F. (1996). The robustness of test statistics to nonnormality and specification error in confirmatory factor analysis. *Psychological Methods, 1*(1), 16–29.

Einstein, G. O., McDaniel, M. A., Richardson, S. L., Guynn, M. J., & Cunfer, A. R. (1995). Aging and prospective memory: Examining the influences of self-initiated retrieval processes. *Journal of Experimental Psychology: Learning, Memory, and Cognition, 2*, 996–1007.

Ellis, J., & Kvavilashvili, L. (2000). Prospective memory in 2000: Past, present, and future directions. *Applied Cognitive Psychology, 14*(7), S1–S9.

Fleming, J. M., Shum, D., Strong, J., & Lightbody, S. (2005). Prospective memory rehabilitation for adults with traumatic brain injury: A compensatory training programme. *Brain Injury, 19*(1), 1–10.

Frencham, K. A., Fox, A. M., & Maybery, M. T. (2005). Neuropsychological studies of mild traumatic brain injury: A meta-analytic review of research since 1995. *Journal of Clinical and Experimental Neuropsychology, 27*(3), 334–351.

Gilbert, S. J., Gollwitzer, P. M., Cohen, A.-L., Burgess, P. W., & Oettingen, G. (2009). Separable brain systems supporting cued versus self-initiated realization of delayed intentions. *Journal of Experimental Psychology: Learning, Memory, and Cognition, 35*, 905–915.

Gordon, B. A., Shelton, J. T., Bugg, J., McDaniel, M. A., & Head, D. (2011). Structural correlates of prospective memory. *Neuropsychologia, 49*(14), 3795–3800.

Hartikainen, K. M., Wäljas, M., Isoviita, T., Dastidar, P., Liimatainen, S., Solbakk, A.-K., ... Öhman, J. (2010). Persistent symptoms in mild to moderate traumatic brain injury associated with executive dysfunction. *Journal of Clinical and Experimental Neuropsychology, 32*(7), 767–774.

Hashimoto, T., Umeda, S., & Kojima, S. (2011). Neural substrates of implicit cueing effect on prospective memory. *NeuroImage, 54*(1), 645–652.

Hernandez Cardenache, R., Burguera, L., Acevedo, A., Curiel, R., & Loewenstein, D. A. (2014). Evaluating different aspects of prospective memory in amnestic and nonamnestic mild cognitive impairment. *International Scholarly Research Notices: Neurology, 2014*, 1–7. Article ID 805929.

Iverson, G. L. (2010). Mild traumatic brain injury meta-analyses can obscure individual differences. *Brain Injury, 24*, 1246–1255.

Karr, J. E., Areshenkoff, C. N., & Garcia-Barrera, M. A. (2014). The neuropsychological outcomes of concussion: A systematic review of meta-analyses on the cognitive sequelae of mild traumatic brain injury. *Neuropsychology, 28*(3), 321–336.

Kinsella, G. J., Olver, J., Ong, B., Gruen, R., & Hammersley, E. (2014). Mild traumatic brain injury in older adults: Early cognitive outcome. *Journal of the International Neuropsychological Society, 20*, 663–671.

Kleigel, M., Jäger, T., & Phillips, L. H. (2008). Adult age differences in event-based prospective memory: A meta-analysis on the role of focal versus nonfocal cues. *Psychology and Aging, 23*(1), 203–208.

Kraus, M. F., Susmaras, T., Coughlin, B. P., Walker, C. J., Sweeney, J. A., & Little, D. M. (2007). White matter integrity and cognition in chronic traumatic brain injury: A diffusion tensor imaging study. *Brain, 130*(10), 2508–2519.

Lowenstein, D., & Acevedo, A. (2004). *The prospective memory test: Administration and scoring manual*. Miami, FL: University of Miami School of Medicine.

Mac Donald, C. L., Barber, J., Andre, J., Evans, N., Panks, C., Sun, S., ... Temkin, N. (2017). 5-Year imaging sequelae of concussive blast injury and relation to early clinical outcome. *NeuroImage: Clinical, 14*, 371–378.

Matsushita, M., Hosoda, K., Naitoh, Y., Yamashita, H., & Kohmura, E. (2011). Utility of diffusion tensor imaging in the acute stage of mild to moderate traumatic brain injury for detecting white matter lesions and predicting long-term cognitive function in adults. *Journal of Neurosurgery, 115*(1), 130–139.

Mayer, A. R., Mannell, M. V., Ling, J., Gasparovic, C., & Yeo, R. A. (2011). Functional connectivity in mild traumatic brain injury. *Human Brain Mapping, 32*(11), 1825–1835.

Mayer, A. R., Quinn, D. K., & Master, C. L. (2017). The spectrum of mild traumatic brain injury. *Neurology, 89*(6), 623–632.

Maylor, E. A. (1996). Age-related impairment in an event-based prospective-memory task. *Psychology and Aging, 11*(1), 74–78.

McDaniel, M. A., & Einstein, G. O. (2000). Strategic and automatic processes in prospective memory retrieval: A multiprocess framework. *Applied Cognitive Psychology, 14*, S127–S144.

McDaniel, M. A., & Einstein, G. O. (2011). The neuropsychology of prospective memory in normal aging: A componential approach. *Neuropsychologia, 49*(8), 2147–2155.

McDonald, A., Haslam, C., Yates, P., Gurr, B., Leeder, G., & Sayers, A. (2011). Google calendar: A new memory aid to compensate for prospective memory deficits following acquired brain injury. *Neuropsychological Rehabilitation, 21*(6), 784–807.

McDonald, B. C., Saykin, A. J., & McAllister, T. W. (2012). Functional MRI of mild traumatic brain injury (mTBI): Progress and perspectives from the first decade of studies. *Brain Imaging and Behavior, 6*(2), 193–207.

McFarland, C. P., & Glisky, E. L. (2009). Frontal lobe involvement in a task of time-based prospective memory. *Neuropsychologia, 47*, 1660–1669.

Monti, J. M., Voss, M. W., Pence, A., McAuley, E., Kramer, A. F., & Cohen, N. J. (2013). History of mild traumatic brain injury is associated with deficits in relational memory, reduced hippocampal volume, and less neural activity later in life. *Frontiers in Aging Neuroscience, 5*(41), 1–9.

Moscovitch, M. (1994). Memory and working with memory: Evaluation of a component process model and comparisons with other models. In D. L. Schacter & E. Tulving (Eds.), *Memory systems* (pp. 269–310). Cambridge, MA: The MIT Press.

Oksanen, K. M., Waldum, E. R., McDaniel, M. A., & Braver, T. S. (2014). Neural mechanisms of time-based prospective memory: Evidence for transient monitoring. *PLoS ONE, 9*(3), e92123.

Okuda, J., Fujii, T., Ohtake, H., Tsukiura, T., Yamadori, A., Frith, C. D., & Burgess, P. W. (2007). Differential involvement of regions of rostral prefrontal cortex (Brodmann area 10) in time- and event-based prospective memory. *International Journal of Psychophysiology, 64*, 233–246.

Pertab, J. L., James, K. M., & Bigler, E. D. (2009). Limitations of mild traumatic brain injury meta-analyses. *Brain Injury, 23*, 498–508.

Potvin, M. J., Rouleau, I., Sénéchal, G., & Giguère, J. F. (2011). Prospective memory rehabilitation based on visual imagery techniques. *Neuropsychological Rehabilitation, 21*(6), 899–924.

Raina, P. S., Wolfson, C., Kirkland, S. A., Griffith, L. E., Oremus, M., Patterson, C., … Brazil, K. (2009). The Canadian longitudinal study on aging (CLSA). *Canadian Journal on Aging / La Revue canadienne du vieillissement, 28*(03), 221–229.

Regard, M. (1981). *Cognitive rigidity and flexibility: A neuropsychological study* (Unpublished Ph.D. dissertation), University of Victoria, Victoria.

Rey, A. (1964). *L'examen Clinique en psychologie* [Clinical examination in psychology]. Paris: Presses universitaire de France.

Rohling, M. L., Larrabee, G. J., & Millis, S. R. (2012). The "miserable minority" following mild traumatic brain injury: Who are they and do meta-analyses hide them? *The Clinical Neuropsychologist, 26*, 197–213.

Saatman, K. E., Duhaime, A. C., Bullock, R., Maas, A. I., Valadka, A., Manley, G. T., & Workshop Scientific Team and Advisory Panel Members. (2008). Classification of traumatic brain injury for targeted therapies. *Journal of Neurotrauma, 25*(7), 719–738.

Schretlen, D. J., & Shapiro, A. M. (2003). A quantitative review of the effects of traumatic brain injury on cognitive functioning. *International Review of Psychiatry, 15*(4), 341–349.

Schwab, K. A., Ivins, B., Cramer, G., Johnson, W., Sluss-Tiller, M., Kiley, K., … Warden, D. (2007). Screening for traumatic brain injury in troops returning from deployment in Afghanistan and Iraq. *Journal of Head Trauma Rehabilitation, 22*(6), 377–389.

Segev, S., Shorer, M., Rassovsky, Y., Pilowsky Peleg, T., Apter, A., & Fenning, S. (2016). The contribution of posttraumatic stress disorder and mild traumatic brain injury to persistent post concussive symptoms following motor vehicle accidents. *Neuropsychology, 30*(7), 800–810.

Shum, D., Fleming, J., & Neulinger, K. (2002). Prospective memory and traumatic brain injury: A review. *Brain Impairment, 3*(01), 1–16.

Smith, G., Della Sala, S., Logie, R. H., & Maylor, E. A. (2000). Prospective and retrospective memory in normal ageing and dementia: A questionnaire study. *Memory, 8*(5), 321–411.

Smith, R. E., & Bayen, U. J. (2006). The source of adult age differences in event-based prospective memory: A multinomial modeling approach. *Journal of Experimental Psychology: Learning, Memory, and Cognition, 32*(3), 623–635.

Smith, R. E., McConnell Rogers, M. D., McVay, J. C., Lopez, J. A., & Loft, S. (2014). Investigating how implementation intentions improve non-focal prospective memory tasks. *Consciousness and Cognition, 27*, 213–230.

Sorg, S. F., Delano-Wood, L., Luc, N., Schiehser, D. M., Hanson, K. L., Nation, D. A., … Bondi, M. W. (2014). White matter integrity in veterans with mild traumatic brain injury. *Journal of Head Trauma Rehabilitation, 29*(1), 21–32.

Spreen, O., & Benton, A. L. (1977). *Neurosensory center comprehensive examination for Aphasia: Manual of instructions (NCCEA)* (Rev ed.). Victoria: University of Victoria.

Strangman, G. E., O'Neil-Pirozzi, T. M., Supelana, C., Goldstein, R., Katz, D. I., & Glenn, M. B. (2010). Regional brain morphometry predicts memory rehabilitation outcome after traumatic brain injury. *Frontiers in Human Neuroscience, 4*(182), 1–11.

Strauss, E., Sherman, E. M. S., & Spreen, O. (2006). *A compendium of neuropsychological tests: Administration, norms, and commentary* (3rd ed.). New York, NY: Oxford University Press.

Tabachnick, B. G., & Fidell, L. S. (2013). *Using multivariate statistics* (6th ed.). New York, NY: Pearson.

Tay, S. Y., Ang, B. T., Lau, X. Y., Meyyappan, A., & Collinson, S. L. (2010). Chronic impairment of prospective memory after mild traumatic brain injury. *Journal of Neurotrauma, 27*(1), 77–83.

Teng, E. L. (1994). *The mental alternation test (MAT)*. Los Angeles, CA: Department of Neurology, University of Southern California School of Medicine.

Thompson, H. J., McCormick, W. C., & Kagan, S. H. (2006). Traumatic brain injury in older adults: Epidemiology, outcomes, and future implications. *Journal of the American Geriatrics Society, 54*(10), 1590–1595.

Thöne-Otto, A. I. T., & Walther, K. (2008). Assessment and treatment of prospective memory disorders in clinical practice. In M. Kliegel, M. A. McDaniel, & G. O. Einstein (Eds.), *Prospective memory: Cognitive, neuroscience, developmental, and applied perspectives* (pp. 321-345). New York, NY: Taylor & Francis Group.

van der Naalt, J., Timmerman, M. E., de Koning, M. E., van der Horn, H. J., Scheenen, M. E., Jacobs, B., … Spikman, J. M. (2017). Early predictors of outcome after mild traumatic brain injury (UPFRONT): An observational cohort study. *The Lancet Neurology, 16*, 532–540.

Voss, J. D., Connolly, J., Schwab, K. A., & Scher, A. I. (2015). Update on the epidemiology of concussion/mild traumatic brain injury. *Current Pain and Headache Reports, 19*(32), 1–8.

Prospective memory impairment in idiopathic REM sleep behavior disorder

Ondrej Bezdicek, Tomáš Nikolai, Jiří Nepožitek, Pavla Peřinová, David Kemlink, Pavel Dušek, Iva Příhodová, Simona Dostálová, Veronika Ibarburu, Jiří Trnka, Karel Kupka, Zuzana Mecková, Jiří Keller, Josef Vymazal, Evžen Růžička, Karel Šonka and Petr Dušek

ABSTRACT

Objective: The aim of the present study was to investigate if prospective memory (PM) is impaired in idiopathic rapid eye movement (REM) sleep behavior disorder (iRBD). RBD is a parasomnia characterized by dream enactment and by REM sleep without muscle atonia. iRBD is considered as the initial stage of neurodegeneration with pathological storage of alpha-synuclein. **Method**: Sixty iRBD patients with polysomnography-confirmed RBD without parkinsonism and dementia and 30 demographically matched normal controls (NC) were enrolled in the present study. Clinical assessment included Movement Disorders Society-Unified Parkinson's Disease Rating Scale (MDS-UPDRS), dopamine transporter single-photon emission computed tomography (DaT-SPECT) for imaging synapses of dopaminergic neurons in the striatum and a neuropsychological battery with embedded time-based and event-based PM measures. **Results**: iRBD differed significantly from NC in event-based PM, a number of event-based failures to recall intention and total PM performance (all $p < .001$) but did not differ in time-based PM and recognition. PM did not contribute to impairment of instrumental activities of daily living in iRBD. Despite being preserved in iRBD in comparison to NC, time-based PM correlated significantly with dopaminergic neuronal loss measured by DaT-SPECT. **Conclusions**: We show evidence for a differential pattern of PM impairment in iRBD with severe impairment of event-based and concurrent preservation of time-based PM. We theorize that event-based PM impairment in iRBD is caused by severe impairment of retention and recognition mechanisms in episodic memory whereas time-based PM seems to be affected by reduced striatal dopaminergic synapses.

Introduction

Rapid eye movement (REM) sleep behavior disorder (RBD) is a parasomnia characterized by dream enactment and by REM sleep without muscle atonia (Boeve, 2010; Ferini-Strambi, Rinaldi, Giora, Marelli, & Galbiati, 2016; Schenck, Bundlie, Ettinger, & Mahowald, 1986). In the absence of significant neurological signs or lesion in the central nervous system, RBD is defined as idiopathic. RBD is labeled as symptomatic when it occurs with neurodegenerative disorders such as Parkinson's disease (PD), Lewy body dementia (LBD), multiple system atrophy (MSA), focal brainstem lesions, narcolepsy, and more rarely with other neurological conditions. Idiopathic REM sleep behavior disorder (iRBD) is considered as the initial stage of neurodegeneration with pathological storage of alpha-synuclein in the brain (Boeve et al., 1998, 2013; Gagnon et al., 2002; Hu et al., 2015; Iranzo et al., 2005, 2006; Mahowald & Schenck, 2013; Postuma, Gagnon, & Montplaisir, 2013). Dopaminergic transporter single-photon emission computed tomography (DaT-SPECT) in iRBD shows that there is a continuum from normal finding to definitely reduced striatal uptake suggesting subclinical degeneration of dopaminergic neurons (Iranzo et al., 2010). Striatal uptake reduction was associated with increased muscle activity during REM sleep (Eisensehr et al., 2000, 2003). The prevalence of RBD is about 2% of people aged 60 and over and approximately from .5 to 1.6% in the general population with a strong disproportion regarding men (85%) vs. women (15%) (Bodkin & Schenck, 2009; Kang et al., 2013; Ohayon, Caulet, & Priest, 1997; Ohayon & Schenck, 2010). The risk estimates of iRBD conversion to diseases with dementia and parkinsonism increase each year from approximately 18–33% at 5 years to 75% at 10 years, and 90% at 14 years after onset (Iranzo et al., 2014; Youn et al., 2016).

The frequency of mild cognitive impairment (MCI) was estimated to be 33–50% in iRBD patients seen in sleep clinics and 63–73% in PD patients with RBD, respectively (Gagnon et al., 2009; Zhang et al., 2016). The high conversion rate of iRBD is interconnected with a 2.2-fold increased risk of developing MCI in a population-based sample (Boot et al., 2012; Gagnon, Bertrand, & Genier Marchand, 2012; Manni et al., 2013). Subsequently, MCI status in subjects with RBD strongly predicts conversion to dementia (Marchand, Montplaisir, Postuma, Rahayel, & Gagnon, 2017; Terzaghi, Zucchella, Rustioni, Sinforiani, & Manni, 2013). Cross-sectional studies indicate that a proportion of iRBD patients show a pattern of cognitive deficits similar to those typically found in patients with synucleinopathies, especially in LBD or PD with MCI or PD with dementia (Boeve et al., 1998; Manni et al., 2013; Marchand et al., 2017; Terzaghi et al., 2013). In addition to structural changes in cortical and subcortical brain areas (Rahayel et al., 2015), dysfunction of cholinergic, noradrenergic, and dopaminergic neurotransmitter networks can potentially play a role in the genesis of MCI in iRBD patients (Arnaldi et al., 2015; Brunetti et al., 2014). In iRBD selective attention, executive functions and episodic verbal and non-verbal memory are the most affected memory domains (Fantini et al., 2011; Ferini-Strambi et al., 2004; Massicotte-Marquez et al., 2008; Terzaghi et al., 2008). However, the presence of visuospatial and visuoconstructional deficits has also been reported by some studies (Fantini et al., 2011; Iranzo et al., 2006; Molano et al., 2010), especially in those iRBD subgroups who later convert to PD with dementia or DLB. On the other hand, according to Gagnon et al. (2009), praxis and language seem to be relatively spared in RBD. Recently, new studies have emerged, e.g. Rusz et al. (2016) found detectable speech impairment based on acoustic analysis in 88% of RBD subjects.

The identification of cognitive markers at initial stages of brain degeneration with pathological storage of synuclein is essential, as they could provide predictive information and outcome measures for future trials with disease-modifying therapies (Boeve, 2010; Marchand et al., 2017; Postuma, Gagnon, Bertrand, Genier Marchand, & Montplaisir, 2015; Schenck et al., 2013). Episodic memory seems to play a significant role in the functional independence in instrumental activities of daily living (IADL) of iRBD patients. However, previous studies focused only on its retrospective component (Ferini-Strambi et al., 2016; Massicotte-Marquez et al., 2008; Terzaghi et al., 2008). We argue that prospective memory (PM) functioning is also essential for independence of iRBD patients as is the case within the framework of PD (Costa et al., 2015; Di Fabio, Poryazova, Oberholzer, Baumann, & Bassetti, 2013; Einstein & McDaniel, 1996; Foster, McDaniel, Repovs, & Hershey, 2009; Marcone et al., 2017). PM refers to the ability to carry out intentions after a delay; for instance, to phone someone at a particular time in the future (Kliegel, McDaniel, & Einstein, 2008). PM is a subsystem of declarative, and in particular, episodic memory (Kliegel, Altgassen, Hering, & Rose, 2011; Squire, 2004; Tulving, 2002). It is comprised of several cognitive processes, namely intention formation, intention retention, intention initiation, and intention execution (Kliegel et al., 2011; McDaniel & Einstein, 2007). To the best of our knowledge, studies investigating episodic memory in more depth and more specifically PM impairments in iRBD have not been performed up until now.

The aim of the present study was, therefore, to better characterize PM functioning in a large cohort of iRBD patients by comparing them with a demographically matched normal control sample. Second, we aimed at investigating if PM performance in iRBD is related to MCI and IADL or can be predicted by cognitive or clinical variables. Third, we were looking for a possible association between PM functioning and markers of reduced striatal dopamine transporters using DaT-SPECT. More broadly, our goal was to contribute to the literature regarding the structure of memory impairment in iRBD patients.

Method

Study participants

The patients were recruited by a stepwise media and internet survey in 2014 and 2015 (Buskova, Ibarburu, Sonka, & Ruzicka, 2016). The clinical sample consisted of a total of 60 iRBD patients and 30 healthy controls (Table 1). All patients were diagnosed with RBD according to the International classification of sleep disorders, third edition (*American academy of sleep medicine. International classification of sleep disorders*, 2014) including videopolysomnography with the recording of superficial electromyography of flexor digitorum superficialis muscles of both sides by a trained sleep specialist (KŠ, SD, IP and VI). All patients fulfilled the following inclusion criteria: age >40 years; >8 years of education. Exclusion criteria were as follows: clinical signs of neurodegenerative disease, i.e. overt dementia or parkinsonism, RBD associated with narcolepsy, untreated major depression, encephalitis, EEG abnormalities suggesting epilepsy, severe sleep apnea (defined as apnea–hypopnoea index (AHI) ≥30), drug-induced RBD, head injury, or focal brain lesion indicative of secondary RBD. Dementia was defined according to the DSM-V criteria for major neurocognitive disorder. Parkinsonism was defined according to the MDS clinical diagnostic criteria as clearly present bradykinesia, in combination with either rest tremor, rigidity, or both (Postuma, Berg et al., 2015). RBD patients underwent a comprehensive clinical evaluation that included medical history, evaluation of functional abilities using the Movement Disorders Society-Unified Parkinson's Disease Rating Scale (MDS-UPDRS) part II, and motor status using the MDS-UPDRS part III by a neurologist experienced in movement disorders (VI, PD, ER). We have classified iRBD patients into iRBD-MCI and

Table 1. Socio-demographic and clinical characteristics of iRBD patients and controls.

	NC (*N* = 30)	iRBD (*N* = 60)	*p* value (NC vs. iRBD)
Age (years)	66.63 (69; 7.43)	68.08 (69; 7.91)	.53
Education (years)	13.57 (12; 2.91)	12.88 (12; 3.26)	.41
Gender (men %)	87	92	.51
Caucasian (%)	100	100	–
iRBD duration (years)	–	4.49 (6; 5.33)	–
Depression level (BDI-II)	5.60 (5; 3.58)	8.12 (7; 5.65)	.12
State anxiety (STAI-X1)	32.67 (32; 6.14)	36.26 (34.5; 7.71)	.06
Trait anxiety (STAI-X2)	36.95(35; 6.92)	39.02 (37; 8.35)	.30
ESS	–	7.60 (8; 3.94)	–
AHI	–	11.50 (5.5; 13.06)	–
MDS-UPDRS-III	–	5.58 (4; 5.32)	–
MDS-UPDRS-II	–	1.91 (1; 2.05)	–
DaTscan (n/ua/ba/nd)	–	32/5/17/6	–
Antidepressants only (%)	0	10 (17)	–
Anxiolytics only (%)	0	2 (3)	–
Combined (Ad+Ax; %)	0	3 (5)	–

Notes: Data presented as mean (median and SD) unless otherwise noted. NC = normal controls, iRBD = idiopathic rapid eye movement sleep behavior disorder; MoCA = Montreal Cognitive Assessment Czech version; BDI-II = the Beck Depression Inventory, Second Edition; STAI = the State-Trait Anxiety Inventory (state anxiety, X1) and (trait anxiety, X2); ESS = Epworth Sleepiness Scale; AHI, apnea–hypopnoea index; UPDRS-II and III, Unified Parkinson's Disease Rating Scale, Part II and III. DaTscan = dopamine transporter imaging using single-photon emission computed tomography; n = normal; ua = unilaterally abnormal; ba = bilaterally abnormal; nd = not done; Ad = antidepressants; Ax = anxiolytics. All between-groups comparisons are based on Mann–Whitney *U* Test except for gender which was based on a Chi-square test for independence (with Yates continuity correction).

iRBD-normal cognition (NC) groups using the MoCA total score (Kopecek et al., 2017) and a cutoff of 2.0 SD below the normative mean as suggested by Goldman (Goldman et al., 2013; Petersen, 2004; Petersen et al., 1999). All clinical participants also completed questionnaires to assess depression (Beck Depression Inventory, Second Edition (BDI-II), anxiety (the State-Trait Anxiety Inventory (STAI); Spielberger, Gorsuch, & Lushene, 1970) and daytime sleepiness (Epworth Sleepiness Scale) (Beck, Steer, & Brown, 1999; Johns, 1991), see Table 1.

The clinical sample (*N* = 60) was matched for age, gender, and education with normal controls (NC; *N* = 30; Table 1). Controls were recruited from the general community through advertisements and a brief medical history for each subject was obtained via telephone. Afterward, a detailed interview excluded all participants with a history of major head trauma, stroke, abuse of alcohol or other psychoactive substances, and individuals with a history of neurological or psychiatric disease (e.g. epilepsy, multiple sclerosis, schizophrenia, or delirium), individuals currently undergoing radio- or chemotherapy, with a major somatic illness (myocardial infarction, diabetes mellitus, etc.), or with uncompensated sensory deficits. Moreover, to exclude control subjects with cognitive impairment, limits for enrollment were set on the MoCA below 1.5 SD in comparison to Czech normative data (Kopecek et al., 2017). To exclude subjects with a higher level of depression, the BDI-II score was limited to <13 (Beck, Steer, & Brown, 1999). Demographic and clinical cohort characteristics are presented in Table 1. All tests were administered under standard neuropsychological laboratory conditions and were conducted by trained psychologists (OB, TN).

The hospital's IRB approved the study, and all subjects signed a written consent before their inclusion in the study.

Materials

Both participants (NC and iRBD) underwent a flexible neuropsychological battery (Kane, 1991). The battery consisted of one global screening measure and six tests in four cognitive domains:

the Montreal Cognitive Assessment (MoCA) (Kopecek et al., 2017; Nasreddine et al., 2005), (1) attention and working memory (Trail Making Test, Part A and Letter-Number Sequencing from Wechsler Adult Intelligence Scale, Third Revision) (Bezdicek et al., 2012; Reitan & Wolfson, 1985; Wechsler, 2010), (2) executive function (Trail Making Test, Part B and Prague Stroop Test interference condition) (Bezdicek et al., 2012, 2015; Reitan & Wolfson, 1985) (3) episodic memory (Rey Auditory Verbal Learning Test total immediate recall, delayed recall and total recognition) (Bezdicek, Stepankova et al., 2014; Schmidt, 1996), and (4) psychomotor and motor speed of upper limbs (Symbol Digit Modalities Test and Grooved Pegboard Test) (Bezdicek, Nikolai et al., 2014; Kløve, 1963; Smith, 1982). Both samples were assessed with a brief measure of PM functioning differentiating time-based and event-based PM (each on a six-point scale with a total of twelve points indicating perfect PM functioning). The brief PM measure was derived from the Memory for Intentions Screening Test (MIST). MIST was previously validated in the Czech version (Bezdicek, Raskin, Altgassen, & Ruzicka, 2014). Our validation study indicated very similar psychometric properties in comparison to other studies (Kamat et al., 2014; Raskin, 2009; Raskin, Buckheit, & Sherrod, 2010; Woods, Moran, Dawson, Carey, & Grant, 2008). The PM measure in the present study consists of three consecutive tasks for time-based PM (in 15 min, tell me that it is time to take a break; ask me what time this session ends today; use that paper to write the number of medications you are currently taking) and another consecutive three tasks for event-based PM (when I hand you a red pen, sign your name on your paper; when I hand you a post-card, self-address it; when I hand you a Request for Records Form, write your Doctors' names on it), all tasks were intersected with 1 min latency during encoding. As for the ongoing task, we administered other tests in the battery in a fixed order (Trails, Stroop, Symbol Digit and Grooved Pegboard). However, for brevity of the PM functioning tool in clinical settings, we aimed at increasing the level of interference in memory by ordering time-based and event-based tasks in a row during encoding and recall (Lewandowsky, Duncan, & Brown, 2004; Underwood, 1957). We scored several types of errors during the PM reproduction phase (loss of time, loss of content and task substitution). The measure also contained six forced-choice recognition questions (PM recognition).

Neuroimaging

Patients were examined on a 3T whole-body MRI system (Skyra, Siemens Healthcare, Erlangen, Germany) using a standard clinical T1-weighted and T2-weighted MRI protocol. Images were reviewed by experienced neuro-radiologists (JK, PeD) and focal lesions that may cause secondary RBD were excluded. Additionally, iRBD patients underwent dopamine transporter imaging using the ^{123}I-FP-CIT/Ioflupane (DaTscan™) SPECT in order to assess the degree of nigrostriatal degeneration. The scanning followed three hours after the application of 185 MBq (5 mCi) ^{123}I-FP-CIT and the 'uptake index' was calculated for putamen and the whole striatum bilaterally using occipital reference area based on the formula: (AROI-AOCC)/(AOCC). Three DaTscan markers were used for analyses: sum of striatal uptake indexes from both sides (DaTscan total), the lower striatal and putaminal uptake index (DaTscan striatum and DaTscan putamen respectively).

Statistical analysis

Statistical analyses were performed using IBM SPSS 22.0. To assess the normality of socio-demographic, clinical and cognitive variables, we examined Q-Q plots and performed the

Kolmogorov–Smirnov test, and in the case of two groups, we used Levene's test to assess the equality of variances. Given the non-parametric nature of the data, we used the Spearman Rank Correlation Coefficient (rho) to evaluate correlations between variables and point-biserial correlation coefficient for dichotomous variables (gender). The chi-square (χ^2) test was used to compare proportions by gender. The Mann–Whitney *U* test was applied to evaluate between-group differences. A one-way between-group ANCOVA was conducted to compare group differences without the influence of demographic (age and education), and general cognitive performance measure (MoCA) and retrospective episodic memory measures (RAVLT immediate, retention and recognition). These were taken as covariates in the model (Tabachnick & Fidell, 2012). Preliminary checks were conducted to ensure that there was no violation of the assumptions of normality, linearity, homogeneity of regression slopes, and reliable measurement of covariates (Pituch & Stevens, 2015). To show if any of demographic and clinical variables can predict PM measures or if PM measures can predict the impairment in IADL, we used standard and hierarchical multiple regression analysis. Statistical significance was set at $\alpha = .05$. The Bonferroni correction for multiple comparisons was applied in PM analyses. The magnitude of effect size in non-parametric tests (*r*) was estimated according to Cohen's effect sizes (Cohen, 1988) as small (>.1), medium (>.3), or large (>.5) and as partial eta squared in parametric analyses.

Results

Descriptive and neuropsychological analyses

Sociodemographic and clinical characteristics of iRBD and NC can be seen in Table 1. A comparison of both samples (iRBD vs. NC) has shown a statistical difference and medium effect size in the MoCA, Stroop interference and all RAVLT measures (Table 2). Furthermore, there was a significant difference in event-based PM and the number of PM event-based failures between iRBD and NC (forgetting to perform the intended action; Table 3 and Figure 1). It is noteworthy that a comparison between time-based and event-based PM performance within iRBD subjects provided a non-significant result. Furthermore, we see several highly significant medium associations between PM measures and demographic variables (the highest between PM recognition and age); medium associations between motor and PM performance (the highest between MDS-UPDRS III and PM total) and between PM and IADL (the highest between event-based PM and MDS-UPDRS II) and between daytime sleepiness and PM. The relation of depression level and PM was not significant in any of the PM measures, however, there were significant association between PM measures and state as well as trait anxiety (Table 4). There were significant correlations between prospective and retrospective episodic memory measures; the highest correlation was between RAVLT recognition and time-based PM (Table 4). No significant correlation was observed between AHI and any PM measure or between AHI and the MoCA.

Parametric analyses as a corollary of non-parametric neuropsychological analyses (iRBD vs. NC)

In the case of time-based PM, PM total and PM recognition Levene's Tests of Equality of Error Variances have not violated the assumption of equality of variance (for time-based PM $p = .55$, for PM total $p = .56$ and PM recognition $p = .54$), however, not in the case of event-based PM

Table 2. Cognitive performance on neuropsychological tests of all iRBD patients and NC.

	NC ($N = 30$)	iRBD ($N = 60$)	p value (effect size) in NC vs. iRBD
MoCA (screening)	25.53 (26; 1.64)	23.98 (24; 2.77)	<.01 (<.0005)* (.40)
1. *Attention and WM*			
TMT-A	39.40 (39; 9.66)	43.72 (38; 19.57)	.76
LNS (WAIS-III)	8.07 (7; 2.55)	7.50 (7; 2.59)	.06
2. *Executive functions*			
TMT-B	98.00 (94; 29.31)	113.86 (96; 69.14)	.61
PST interference	32.00 (33; (6.54)	38.60 (36; 11.56)	<.01 (<.001)* (.34)
3. *Episodic memory*			
RAVLT immediate recall	43.93 (43; 5.97)	37.41 (38; 8.24)	<.01 (<.0005)* (.39)
RAVLT retention	7.93 (7; 2.28)	6.19 (6; 2.78)	<.01 (<.0005)* (.37)
RAVLT recognition	44.67 (45; 2.72)	41.91 (43; 5.23)	<.01 (.003)* (.31)
4. *Psychomotor speed*			
SDMT	46.20 (44; 4.91)	39.60 (38; 10.30)	.10
GPT upper limbs	174.1 (167; 30.45)	178.84 (165; 44.67)	.75

Notes: Data presented as mean (median and SD) unless otherwise noted. MoCA = Montreal Cognitive Assessment; (1) attention and WM = working memory (TMT-A = Trail Making Test, Part A and LNS = Letter-Number Sequencing from Wechsler Adult Intelligence Scale, Third Revision); (2) executive function (TMT-B = Trail Making Test, Part B and PST = Prague Stroop test interference condition); (3) episodic memory (RAVLT = Rey Auditory Verbal Learning Test total immediate recall (the sum of all correct responses given over the five consecutive trials (T1 + T2 + T3 + T4 + T5), retention (delayed recall after 30 min) and total recognition), and (4) psychomotor and motor speed of upper limbs (SDMT = Symbol Digit Modalities Test and GPT = Grooved Pegboard Test). All between-groups comparisons are based on Mann–Whitney *U* Test. By *p* levels in parentheses we aimed at showing that the comparisons would still survive Bonferroni correction for ten comparisons ($\alpha < .005$).

*Still significant after Bonferroni correction.

Table 3. Prospective memory performance of iRBD patients and controls.

	NC ($N = 30$)	iRBD ($N = 60$)	p value (effect size) in NC vs. iRBD
PM time-based	4.17 (4; 1.46)	3.77 (4; 1.71)	.32
PM event-based	5.37 (6; 1.19)	3.76 (4; 1.73)	<.01 (<.0005)* (.46)
PM total	9.53 (10; 2.16)	7.53 (8; 2.24)	<.01 (<.0005)* (.43)
PM recognition	5.86 (6; .14)	5.63 (6; .71)	.29
PM time-based failures	.43 (0; .73)	.62 (0; .87)	.33
PM event-based failures	.10 (0; .40)	.73 (1; .82)	<.01 (<.0005)* (.43)
Loss of time errors	.23 (0; .57)	.50 (0; .98)	.30
Loss of content errors	.67 (1; .66)	.75 (1; .84)	.88
Task substitution errors	.33 (0; .71)	.27 (0; .55)	.82

Notes: Data presented as mean (median and SD) unless otherwise noted. PM = prospective memory. PM total = (time-based PM + event-based PM). All between-groups comparisons are based on Mann–Whitney *U* Test. Bonferroni correction for nine PM comparisons was applied ($\alpha < .0055$).

*Still significant after Bonferroni correction.

($p = .02$). After adjusting for covariates (age, education, MoCA, RAVLT immediate, retention and recognition), we have found a significant difference between iRBD vs. NC only in event-based PM $F(1, 77) = 10.84$, $p < .01$ (.002), partial eta squared = .13; other comparisons of PM scores were not significant: PM time-based $F(1, 77) = 2.51$, $p = .12$, partial eta squared = .04, PM total $F(1, 77) = 2.21$, $p = .14$, partial eta squared = .03, however, there was a trend in PM recognition $F(1, 77) = 3.87$, $p > .05$ (.053), partial eta squared = .05 (Appendix 1).

Standard multiple regression analysis (iRBD only)

Regarding the results of correlational analyses (Table 4), we aimed at addressing the question of how well demographic: age, education; clinical: iRBD duration, AHI, UPDRS-II and III; cognitive: MoCA, RAVLT immediate, retention, recognition, and affective variables: STAI (X1, X2)

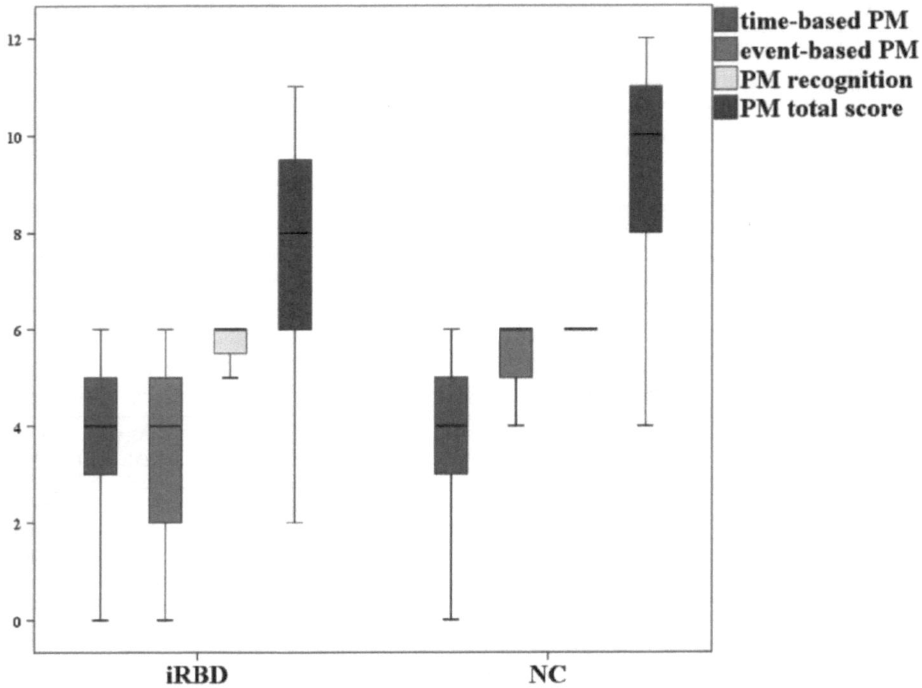

Figure 1. Boxplots showing prospective memory performance of iRBD patients and controls.
Notes: The length of the box is interquartile range and contains 50% of cases, the line inside of the box represents median and the whiskers represent the smallest and largest values. PM = prospective memory. PM total score = (time-based PM + event-based PM; min—max. 0–12 points). Time-based and event-based PM and PM recognition are sub-scores with min—max. 0–6 points. NC = normal controls, iRBD = idiopathic rapid eye movement sleep behavior disorder.

predict PM and which is the best predictor of PM performance in iRBD. The total variance explained by the model as a whole was 51.0% in PM total $F(13, 38) = 3.04$, $p < .01$ (.004) with the largest beta coefficient −.41 for STAI X1 and −.37 for age and .37 for RAVLT retention; the total variance explained was 42.7% in PM time-based $F(13, 38) = 2.18$, $p = .03$ with the largest beta coefficient .28 for RAVLT immediate; MoCA .23 and RAVLT recognition .21; the total variance explained was 58.7% in PM recognition $F(13, 38) = 4.16$, $p < .01$ (<.0005) with the largest beta coefficient −.36 for UPDRS-III, education .35 and STAI X1 −.26; however, non-significant in PM event-based $F(13, 38) = 1.44$, $p = .19$.

iRBD and MCI

The prevalence of MCI in our sample of iRBD was 15% (i.e. 9 out of 60 patients). There were significant trends for between-group differences in PM Total, PM Recognition, and a number of PM event-based failures that, however, did not survive Bonferroni correction (Table 5). Besides PM measures, the most discriminative tests were MoCA score (of note is that MoCA was used as an MCI status criterion) and TMT-B (Table 6).

iRBD and IADL

In addition, we used hierarchical multiple regression to assess the ability of event-based PM to predict levels of IADL (MDS-UPDRS II) in iRBD after controlling for the influence of age

Table 4. Correlations between demographic, clinical and prospective and retrospective memory measures.

	PM time-based	PM event-based	PM total	PM recognition
Age (years)	−.27**	−.13	−.28***	−.38****
Education (years)	.15	.23**	.30***	.32***
Gender	−.19	−.17	.04	−.25**
iRBD duration (years)	−.13	−.40****	−.38****	−.03
MoCA	.38****	.28***	.45****	.41****
BDI-II	−.07	−.13	−.17	−.14
ESS	−.02	−.43****	−.33***	−.03
State anxiety (STAI-X1)	.07	−.35****	−.21*	−.25**
Trait anxiety (STAI X2)	.07	−.14	−.08	−.25**
AHI	−.24*	.10	.05	−.08
UPDRS-II	−.04	−.36***	−.31***	−.18
UPDRS-III	−.19	−.40****	−.44****	−.20****
DaTscan total	.30**	.12	.09	.03
DaTscan striatum	.33**	−.06	.14	−.03
DaTscan putamen	.26*	−.08	.10	−.02
RAVLT immediate	.36****	.27**	.44****	.22**
RAVLT retention	.37****	.35***	.49****	.21*
RAVLT recognition	.45****	.25**	.46****	.19*

Notes: All correlations are based on Spearman rank order correlation except for gender (based on point-biserial correlation) and all correlations are based on both samples except for iRBD duration, ESS, UPDRS-II and III, and DaTscan which are based only on iRBD sample; PM = prospective memory; MoCA = Montreal Cognitive Assessment Czech version; BDI-II = the Beck Depression Inventory, Second Edition; STAI = the State-Trait Anxiety Inventory (state anxiety, X1) and (trait anxiety, X2); ESS = Epworth Sleepiness Scale; AHI, apnea–hypopnoea index; UPDRS-II and III, Unified Parkinson's Disease Rating Scale, Part II and III; DaTscan total = sum of striatal indexes from both sides; DaTscan striatum, DaTscan putamen = lower value of striatal and putaminal index respectively . RAVLT = Rey Auditory Verbal Learning Test.
*$p < .10$; **$p < .05$; ***$p < .01$; ****$p < .001$.

Table 5. Prospective memory performance of iRBD with MCI (iRBD-MCI) and iRBD without MCI (iRBD-NC).

	iRBD-NC (*N* = 51)	iRBD-MCI (*N* = 9)	*p* value
PM time-based	2.67 (4; 1.57)	3.96 (3; 2.12)	.09
PM event-based	3.84 (4; 1.74)	3.33 (2; 1.73)	.30
PM total	7.80 (8; 2.15)	6.00 (6; 2.24)	.03 (.026)
PM recognition	5.71 (6; .67)	5.22 (5; .83)	.03 (.032)
PM time-based failures	.55 (0; .76)	1.00 (0; 1.32)	.49
PM event-based failures	.65 (0; .80)	1.22 (1; .83)	.04 (.041)
Loss of time errors	.39 (0; .85)	1.11 (0; 1.45)	.09
Loss of content errors	.82 (1; .87)	.33 (0; .80)	.11
Task substitution errors	.27 (0; .57)	.22 (0; .44)	.97

Notes: Data presented as mean (median and SD) unless otherwise noted. iRBD-MCI = iRBD with mild cognitive impairment; iRBD-NC = iRBD without mild cognitive impairment; PM = prospective memory. PM total = (time-based PM + event-based PM). All between-group comparisons are based on Mann–Whitney *U* Test. Bonferroni correction for nine PM comparisons was applied ($\alpha < .0055$).

and motor performance (MDS-UPDRS III). Preliminary analyses were conducted to assess possible violations of the assumptions of linearity, multicollinearity, and homoscedasticity. However, the data violated the assumption of normality. Age (beta value non-significant) and MDS-UPDRS III (beta value .55) were entered in Step 1 explaining 29.5% of the variance in MDS-UPDRS II. After entry of event-based PM at Step 2, the total variance explained by the model as a whole was 29.9%, $F(3, 83) < 11.80$, $p < .01$. Event-based PM explained only an additional .4% of the variance in IADL, after controlling for age and MDS-UPDRS III. The association between UPDRS-III and UPDRS-II total scores in iRBD was significant ($r = .542$ $p < .001$).

Table 6. Cognitive performance on neuropsychological tests of iRBD-NC vs. iRBD-MCI.

	iRBD-NC ($N = 51$)	iRBD-MCI ($N = 9$)	p value (effect size) iRBD-NC vs iRBD-MCI
MoCA (screening)	24.74 (24.50; 1.89)	19.25 (19.50; 2.77)	<.01 (<.0005)* (0.61)
1. *Attention and WM*			
TMT-A	42.54 (37; 20.17)	51.13 (50; 14.05)	.10
LNS (WAIS-III)	7.58 (7; 2.56)	7.00 (7; 2.88)	.85
2. *Executive functions*			
TMT-B	99.68 (87.50; 52.18)	202.50 (160; 97.24)	<.01 (<.0005)* (0.48)
PST interference	37.20 (35.50; 8.23)	47.38 (40.50; 22.65)	.15
3. *Episodic memory*			
RAVLT immediate recall	38.56 (39; 7.89)	30.25 (30; 7.03)	.03 (.032)
RAVLT retention	6.38 (6.50; 2.86)	5.00 (5; 2.00)	.14
RAVLT recognition	42.06 (43; 5.16)	41.00 (41.50; 5.93)	.89
4. *Psychomotor speed*			
SDMT	39.35 (38; 6.85)	34.12 (35; 14.16)	.05 (.045)
GPT upper limbs	177.34 (164.50; 46.66)	188.25 (198.50; 29.81)	.28

Notes: Data presented as mean (median and SD) unless otherwise noted. MoCA = Montreal Cognitive Assessment; (1) attention and WM = working memory (TMT-A = Trail Making Test, Part A and LNS = Letter-Number Sequencing from Wechsler Adult Intelligence Scale, Third Revision); (2) executive function (TMT-B = Trail Making Test, Part B and PST = Prague Stroop test interference condition); (3) episodic memory (RAVLT = Rey Auditory Verbal Learning Test total immediate recall (the sum of all correct responses given over the five consecutive trials (T1 + T2 + T3 + T4 + T5), retention (delayed recall after 30 min) and total recognition), and (4) psychomotor and motor speed of upper limbs (SDMT = Symbol Digit Modalities Test and GPT = Grooved Pegboard Test). All between-group comparisons are based on Mann–Whitney *U* Test. By *p* levels in parentheses we aimed at showing that the comparisons would still survive Bonferroni correction for ten comparisons ($\alpha < .005$).

*Still significant after Bonferroni correction.

Imaging analyses

After showing a significant correlation between reduction in striatal and putaminal ^{123}I-FP-CIT uptake indices and time-based PM (Table 4), we investigated whether there are between-group differences in time-based PM in iRBD divided into a group in the first quartile (Q_1) with the lowest DaTscan sum striatal (DaTscan total) indices (i.e. patients with highest dopaminergic cell loss) and the rest ($Q_2 + Q_3 + Q_4$). This analysis did not show a significant difference in time-based PM in iRBD based on the Mann-Whitney *U* Test ($p = .29$).

Discussion

The present study aimed at investigating the relationship between explicit memory functioning and demographic, clinical, and imaging findings in iRBD. In general, we showed significant differences in cognitive functioning (memory, executive functions) between iRBD and NC which is in accordance with previous studies (Ferini-Strambi et al., 2004; Massicotte-Marquez et al., 2008; Terzaghi et al., 2008). Furthermore, our results indicate that MCI status in iRBD is not significantly related to PM performance despite a trend towards significance.

More specifically, we focused on the relationship between retrospective and prospective components of explicit memory and especially whether there is a differential impairment of time-based versus event-based PM. Regarding the retrospective component of explicit memory we found a significant impairment of each of basic explicit memory mechanisms in iRBD in comparison to controls in verbal learning (immediate recall), retention and recognition in RAVLT, which is in accordance with previous studies (Ferini-Strambi et al., 2004; Gagnon et al., 2009; Massicotte-Marquez et al., 2008; Terzaghi et al., 2008); only Massicotte-Marquez et al. (2008) have not found a deficit in retention in iRBD patients.

A novel piece of information in this respect is a differential impairment of event-based but not time-based PM in iRBD in the present study. Furthermore, iRBD patients showed significantly more event-based PM failures (true prospective component deficits) in comparison to controls. We surmise that a selective event-based PM impairment is interconnected with frank retrospective component deficits in retention and especially in recognition. This is because the stimulus presented during intention formation and retention that triggers the action to be performed in future in the event-based PM paradigm is presented again before intention initiation and execution. Consequently, when retrospective retention and recognition are impaired as indicated by more event-based PM failures, the same processes are recruited during event-based PM intention execution. We assume in accordance with dual-store models of memory that rehearsal is critical for encoding and retention of information in PM (Atkinson & Shiffrin, 1968; Raaijmakers & Shiffrin, 1980). However, the reason for selective event-based PM impairment that does not extend to time-based PM impairment as is the case in PD (Ramanan & Kumar, 2013) is not clear. We present two convergent explanations. We suppose that the first possible mechanism appeals to external cues. Cues encountered in the environment during the retention interval (a watch on the table in the time-based condition) prompted retrieval of the intended action creating Intention Superiority Effect, in which reaction times were more efficient to intention in a subsequent time-based rather than event-based task (Goschke & Kuhl, 1993; Kvavilashvili & Fisher, 2007; Sellen, Louie, Harris, & Wilkins, 1997). The second mechanism appears to converge nicely with findings that PM performance significantly improves when the retention interval contains breaks, particularly when the breaks are unfilled (Hicks, Marsh, & Russell, 2000). The time-based condition was in our design always presented first, so it did not suffer from proactive interference as did event-based from time-based condition and event-based condition was always presented directly after time-based condition, so there was no preceding break; time-based condition was therefore boosted by the primacy effect (Hicks et al., 2000; Murdock, 1962; Postman & Keppel, 1977; Underwood, 1957).

Furthermore, our results remained stable even after we considered important variables (covariates) that could influence the results of our non-parametric analyses, such as age, education, global cognitive performance (MoCA), and retrospective episodic memory measures (RAVLT). However, the results of this parametric analysis based on ANCOVA should be taken with caution and were done only for justification of the results of non-parametric analyses; the distribution of some variables is not normal and e.g. event-based PM does not fulfill the homogeneity of variance requirement. In the case of the standard regression, cognitive and clinical variables explained a large proportion (43–59%) of the variance in PM total, time-based and recognition. However, in PM event-based, the model was non-significant which is indicative that the difference in event-based PM in NC vs. iRBD was not influenced by those variables.

Hierarchical multiple regression provided negative results regarding the question of whether PM explains the variability in IADL in iRBD. It is MDS-UPDRS, Part III (beta value .55) but not age (beta value non-significant) that explained about one-third of the variability in IADL as measured by MDS-UPDRS, Part II. Hence, we conclude that the severity of motor impairment, although very mild, is related to IADL impairment in iRBD whereas cognitive factors such as PM functioning do not affect IADL. It remains an open question whether MDS-UPDRS, Part II can be taken as a representative measure of IADL in iRBD which leads several authors in PD research to the development of more sensitive and comprehensive measures for IADL measurement (Brennan et al., 2016; Shulman et al., 2016).

In the imaging part of the study, we have found a positive correlation between time-based PM performance and reduced striatal dopamine uptake on the more affected side. However, a between-group comparison in PM functioning of iRBD patients with more severe and less severe dopaminergic cell loss was not significant. This finding could be related to the idea that there is a direct connection between the dopaminergic system and the speed of an internal clock in early PD patients and that RBD associated with PD is a marker of worse cognitive functioning (Chahine et al., 2016; Malapani et al., 1998). Time-based PM is dependent on the integrity of the internal clock for interval timing estimates and may underlie the association observed in the present data (Buhusi & Meck, 2005; Costa et al., 2008; Labelle, Graf, Grondin, & Gagne-Roy, 2009; Smith, Harper, Gittings, & Abernethy, 2007). We believe, therefore that this association reflects an early internal clock impairment related to a dopaminergic deficit in iRBD patients and this interval timing deficit causes a selective dissociation between time-based and event-based PM and DaTscan results.

In general, the analysis of iRBD-NC vs. iRBD-MCI showed significant differences in the neuropsychological battery in set shifting (TMT-B) with medium effect size, and a trend for differences in learning (RAVLT immediate recall) and psychomotor speed (SDMT). These results are consistent with previous findings in which iRBD performed worse than controls and even than PD without RBD in these measures (Gagnon et al., 2009). Regarding PM performance iRBD-MCI were worse than iRBD-NC on PM measures assessing total PM delayed recall performance (with a non-significant trend favoring time-based rather than event-based PM impairment), PM recognition, and event-based PM failures. The results are in accordance with previous studies showing that iRBD-MCI has delayed memory as well as prospective and retrospective memory deficits (Gagnon et al., 2009; Marcone et al., 2017; Zhang et al., 2016). A recent study showed that cognitive tests assessing attention and executive functions predicted early conversion to dementia in RBD patients (Marchand et al., 2017). It would be intriguing to study whether prospective memory deficit is a risk factor for conversion into a specific subtype of synucleinopathy (Iranzo et al., 2010).

The present study has several limitations. First, DaTscan, MRI, and polysomnography were not performed in NC. However, none of NC indicated sleep problems, psychiatric, or neurological disease. Second, patients with periodic leg movements in REM sleep (PLMS) were not excluded because OSA and PLMS exclusion would lead to a significant reduction of the sample size (e.g. 46% of our iRBD patients had PLMS). However, PLMS frequency was associated with greater decline in cognition and neurocognitive dysfunction is commonly observed in patients with OSA (Leng et al., 2016; Zhou, Camacho, Tang, & Kushida, 2016). Third, our PM examination was performed in clinical settings and is an abbreviated version of a standard clinimetric tool for PM measurement (Bezdicek, Raskin et al., 2014; Raskin, 2009; Raskin et al., 2010). We could not estimate important variables in PM performance, such as exact time response accuracy, whether PM performance declines with higher cognitive load (interference effects), and whether a longer retention interval or distinctiveness of stimuli or focal or non-focal conditions play an important role in intention execution (Kliegel et al., 2011; Kvavilashvili & Fisher, 2007). Fourth, our parametric analyses should be taken just as support of non-parametric findings because the data violated some of the assumptions for ANCOVA or multiple regression (Tabachnick & Fidell, 2012).

In conclusion, the current study provides new clinical insights into the impaired mechanisms involved in PM functioning of iRBD patients. We argue for differential impairment of event-based PM functioning in iRBD which may be related to severely impaired retention and recognition mechanisms that were observed also in early PD patients (Bronnick, Alves, Aarsland, Tysnes, & Larsen, 2011; Chahine et al., 2016; Chiaravalloti et al., 2014; Cohn, Giannoylis, De Belder, Saint-Cyr, & McAndrews, 2016). On the other hand, we have shown a medium association between time-based PM and dopaminergic depletion in iRBD which may reflect early signs of internal clock dysregulation (Malapani et al., 1998). Most importantly, the study has generated several interesting avenues for future clinical research of cognitive impairment in iRBD.

Financial disclosure

The authors have no financial interests in the present research and have nothing to disclose. A proprietary test (Memory for Intentions Screening Test; MIST) was legally purchased by Psychological Assessment Resources (PAR) and an official Czech translation and back-translation of the MIST authorized by PAR and Professor S Raskin, PhD. MIST Czech version is the property of PAR, and the authors of the study have no financial interest in the test.

Authorship statement

Drs Ondřej Bezdíček, Petr Dušek, Evžen Růžička and Karel Šonka designed the study. Dr. Ondřej Bezdíček conducted the statistical analyses. Drs Tomáš Nikolai, Jiří Nepožitek, Pavla Peřinová, David Kemlink, Pavel Dušek, Iva Příhodová, Simona Dostálová, Veronika Ibarburu Lorenzo y Losada, and Bezdíček conducted the study recruitment, data collection, and clinical intervention. Drs Jiří Trnka, Karel Kupka, Zuzana Mecková, Jiří Keller, and Josef Vymazal, provided the expertise and data collection and interpretation of DaTscan and MRI. Dr Ondřej Bezdíček drafted the manuscript while all co-authors provided feedback and approved the final version.

Acknowledgment

We would like to thank Lívia Mayerová, MA, for help with the data collection. Study data were collected and managed using REDCap electronic data capture tools hosted at the Department of Neurology and Center of Clinical Neuroscience, First Faculty of Medicine, Charles University.

Disclosure statement

No potential conflict of interest was reported by the authors.

Funding

This study was supported by Czech Science Foundation [grant number (GAČR) 16-07879S]; The Ministry of Health of the Czech Republic [grant number GIGH-16-28914A]; and by Charles University [grant number GA UK 64216].

References

American academy of sleep medicine. International classification of sleep disorders. (2014). (3rd ed.). Darien, IL: American Academy of Sleep Medicine.

Arnaldi, D., De Carli, F., Picco, A., Ferrara, M., Accardo, J., Bossert, I., … Nobili, F. (2015). Nigro-caudate dopaminergic deafferentation: A marker of REM sleep behavior disorder? *Neurobiology of Aging, 36*(12), 3300–3305. doi:10.1016/j.neurobiolaging.2015.08.025

Atkinson, R. C., & Shiffrin, R. M. (1968). Human memory: A proposed system and its control processes1. In W. S. Kenneth & S. Janet Taylor (Eds.), *Psychology of Learning and Motivation* (Vol. 2, pp. 89–195). Cambridge, MA: Academic Press.

Beck, A. T., Steer, R. A., & Brown, G. K. (1999). *Beckova sebeposuzovací škála depresivity pro dospělé BDI-II: Příručka* [Beck depression inventory–second edition. Manual]. Brno: Psychodiagnostika.

Bezdicek, O., Moták, L., Axelrod, B. N., Preiss, M., Nikolai, T., Vyhnálek, M., … Růžička, E. (2012). Czech version of the trail making test: Normative data and clinical utility. *Archives of Clinical Neuropsychology, 27*(8), 906–914.

Bezdicek, O., Nikolai, T., Hoskovcova, M., Stochl, J., Brozova, H., Dusek, P., … Ruzicka, E. (2014). Grooved pegboard predicates more of cognitive than motor involvement in Parkinson's disease. *Assessment, 21*(6), 723–730. doi:10.1177/1073191114524271

Bezdicek, O., Raskin, S. A., Altgassen, M., & Ruzicka, E. (2014). Assessment of prospective memory – A validity study of memory for intentions screening test. *Ceska a Slovenska Neurologie a Neurochirurgie, 77*(4), 435–443.

Bezdicek, O., Stepankova, H., Motak, L., Axelrod, B. N., Woodard, J. L., Preiss, M., … Poreh, A. (2014). Czech version of Rey auditory verbal learning test: Normative data. *Aging Neuropsychology and Cognition, 21*(6), 693–721. doi:10.1080/13825585.2013.865699

Bezdicek, O., Lukavsky, J., Stepankova, H., Nikolai, T., Axelrod, B. N., Michalec, J., … Kopecek, M. (2015). The Prague Stroop Test: Normative standards in older Czech adults and discriminative validity for mild cognitive impairment in Parkinson's disease. *Journal of Clinical and Experimental Neuropsychology, 37*(8), 794–807. doi:10.1080/13803395.2015.1057106

Bodkin, C. L., & Schenck, C. H. (2009). Rapid eye movement sleep behavior disorder in women: Relevance to general and specialty medical practice. *Journal of Womens Health (Larchmt), 18*(12), 1955–1963. doi:10.1089/jwh.2008.1348

Boeve, B. F. (2010). REM sleep behavior disorder: Updated review of the core features, the REM sleep behavior disorder-neurodegenerative disease association, evolving concepts, controversies, and future directions. *Annals of New York Academy of Sciences, 1184*, 15–54. doi:10.1111/j.1749-6632.2009.05115.x

Boeve, B. F., Silber, M. H., Ferman, T. J., Kokmen, E., Smith, G. E., Ivnik, R. J., … Petersen, R. C. (1998). REM sleep behavior disorder and degenerative dementia: An association likely reflecting Lewy body disease. *Neurology, 51*(2), 363–370.

Boeve, B. F., Silber, M. H., Ferman, T. J., Lin, S. C., Benarroch, E. E., Schmeichel, A. M., … Dickson, D. W. (2013). Clinicopathologic correlations in 172 cases of rapid eye movement sleep behavior disorder with or without a coexisting neurologic disorder. *Sleep Medicine, 14*(8), 754–762. doi:10.1016/j.sleep.2012.10.015

Boot, B. P., Boeve, B. F., Roberts, R. O., Ferman, T. J., Geda, Y. E., Pankratz, V. S., … Petersen, R. C. (2012). Probable rapid eye movement sleep behavior disorder increases risk for mild cognitive impairment and Parkinson disease: A population-based study. *Annals of Neurology, 71*(1), 49–56. doi:10.1002/ana.22655

Brennan, L., Siderowf, A., Rubright, J. D., Rick, J., Dahodwala, N., Duda, J. E., … Weintraub, D. (2016). The Penn Parkinson's daily activities questionnaire-15: Psychometric properties of a brief assessment of cognitive instrumental activities of daily living in Parkinson's disease. *Parkinsonism and Related Disorders, 25*, 21–26. doi:10.1016/j.parkreldis.2016.02.020

Bronnick, K., Alves, G., Aarsland, D., Tysnes, O. B., & Larsen, J. P. (2011). Verbal memory in drug-naive, newly diagnosed Parkinson's disease. The retrieval deficit hypothesis revisited. *Neuropsychology, 25*(1), 114–124. doi:10.1037/a0020857

Brunetti, V., Losurdo, A., Testani, E., Lapenta, L., Mariotti, P., Marra, C., … Della Marca, G. (2014). Rivastigmine for refractory REM behavior disorder in mild cognitive impairment. *Current Alzheimer Research, 11*(3), 267–273.

Buhusi, C. V., & Meck, W. H. (2005). What makes us tick? Functional and neural mechanisms of interval timing. *Nature Review Neuroscience, 6*(10), 755–765. doi:10.1038/nrn1764

Buskova, J., Ibarburu, V., Sonka, K., & Ruzicka, E. (2016). Screening for REM sleep behavior disorder in the general population. *Sleep Medicine, 24*, 147. doi:10.1016/j.sleep.2016.07.003

Chahine, L. M., Xie, S. X., Simuni, T., Tran, B., Postuma, R., Amara, A., ... Weintraub, D. (2016). Longitudinal changes in cognition in early Parkinson's disease patients with REM sleep behavior disorder. *Parkinsonism and Related Disorders, 27*, 102–106. doi:10.1016/j.parkreldis.2016.03.006

Chiaravalloti, N. D., Ibarretxe-Bilbao, N., DeLuca, J., Rusu, O., Pena, J., Garcia-Gorostiaga, I., & Ojeda, N. (2014). The source of the memory impairment in Parkinson's disease: Acquisition versus retrieval. *Movement Disorders, 29*(6), 765–771. doi:10.1002/mds.25842

Cohen, J. (1988). *Statistical power analysis for the behavioral sciences* (2nd ed.). Hillsdale, NJ: Lawrence Erlbaum Associates.

Cohn, M., Giannoylis, I., De Belder, M., Saint-Cyr, J. A., & McAndrews, M. P. (2016). Associative reinstatement memory measures hippocampal function in Parkinson's Disease. *Neuropsychologia, 90*, 25–32. doi:10.1016/j.neuropsychologia.2016.04.026

Costa, A., Peppe, A., Brusa, L., Caltagirone, C., Gatto, I., & Carlesimo, G. A. (2008). Levodopa improves time-based prospective memory in Parkinson's disease. *Journal of the International Neuropsychological Society, 14*(4), 601–610. doi:10.1017/s135561770808082x

Costa, A., Zabberoni, S., Peppe, A., Serafini, F., Scalici, F., Caltagirone, C., & Carlesimo, G. A. (2015). Time-based prospective memory functioning in mild cognitive impairment associated with Parkinson's disease: Relationship with autonomous management of daily living commitments. *Frontiers in Human Neuroscience, 9*, 333. doi:10.3389/fnhum.2015.00333

Di Fabio, N., Poryazova, R., Oberholzer, M., Baumann, C. R., & Bassetti, C. L. (2013). Sleepwalking, REM sleep behaviour disorder and overlap parasomnia in patients with Parkinson's Disease. *European Neurology, 70*(5–6), 297–303. doi:10.1159/000353378

Einstein, G. O., & McDaniel, M. A. (1996). Retrieval processes in prospective memory: Theoretical approaches and some new findings. In M. Brandimonte, G. O. Einstein, & M. A. McDaniel (Eds.), *Prospective memory: Theory and applications* (pp. 115–143). London: Erlbaum.

Eisensehr, I., Linke, R., Noachtar, S., Schwarz, J., Gildehaus, F. J., & Tatsch, K. (2000). Reduced striatal dopamine transporters in idiopathic rapid eye movement sleep behaviour disorder. Comparison with Parkinson's disease and controls. *Brain, 123*(Pt 6), 1155–1160.

Eisensehr, I., Linke, R., Tatsch, K., Kharraz, B., Gildehaus, J. F., Wetter, C. T., ... Noachtar, S. (2003). Increased muscle activity during rapid eye movement sleep correlates with decrease of striatal presynaptic dopamine transporters. IPT and IBZM SPECT imaging in subclinical and clinically manifest idiopathic REM sleep behavior disorder, Parkinson's Disease, and controls. *Sleep, 26*(5), 507–512.

Fantini, M. L., Farini, E., Ortelli, P., Zucconi, M., Manconi, M., Cappa, S., & Ferini-Strambi, L. (2011). Longitudinal study of cognitive function in idiopathic REM sleep behavior disorder. *Sleep, 34*(5), 619–625.

Ferini-Strambi, L., Di Gioia, M. R., Castronovo, V., Oldani, A., Zucconi, M., & Cappa, S. F. (2004). Neuropsychological assessment in idiopathic REM sleep behavior disorder (RBD): Does the idiopathic form of RBD really exist? *Neurology, 62*(1), 41–45.

Ferini-Strambi, L., Rinaldi, F., Giora, E., Marelli, S., & Galbiati, A. (2016). REM sleep behaviour disorder. *Parkinsonism and Related Disorders, 22*(Suppl 1), S69–S72. doi:10.1016/j.parkreldis.2015.09.002

Foster, E. R., McDaniel, M. A., Repovs, G., & Hershey, T. (2009). Prospective memory in Parkinson disease across laboratory and self-reported everyday performance. *Neuropsychology, 23*(3), 347–358. doi:10.1037/a0014692

Gagnon, J. F., Bedard, M. A., Fantini, M. L., Petit, D., Panisset, M., Rompre, S., ... Montplaisir, J. (2002). REM sleep behavior disorder and REM sleep without atonia in Parkinson's disease. *Neurology, 59*(4), 585–589.

Gagnon, J. F., Vendette, M., Postuma, R. B., Desjardins, C., Massicotte-Marquez, J., Panisset, M., & Montplaisir, J. (2009). Mild cognitive impairment in rapid eye movement sleep behavior disorder and Parkinson's disease. *Annals of Neurology, 66*(1), 39–47. doi:10.1002/ana.21680

Gagnon, J. F., Bertrand, J. A., & Genier Marchand, D. (2012). Cognition in rapid eye movement sleep behavior disorder. *Frontiers in Neurology, 3*, 82. doi:10.3389/fneur.2012.00082

Goldman, J. G., Holden, S., Bernard, B., Ouyang, B., Goetz, C. G., & Stebbins, G. T. (2013). Defining optimal cutoff scores for cognitive impairment using Movement Disorder Society Task Force criteria for mild cognitive impairment in Parkinson's disease. *Movement Disorders, 28*(14), 1972–1979. doi:10.1002/mds.25655

Goschke, T., & Kuhl, J. (1993). Representation of intentions: Persisting activation in memory. *Journal of Experimental Psychology-Learning Memory and Cognition, 19*(5), 1211–1226. doi:10.1037/0278-7393.19.5.1211

Hicks, J. L., Marsh, R. L., & Russell, E. J. (2000). The properties of retention intervals and their affect on retaining prospective memories. *Journal of Experimental Psychology-Learning Memory and Cognition, 26*(5), 1160–1169. doi:10.1037/0278-7393.26.5.1160

Hu, Y., Yu, S. Y., Zuo, L. J., Cao, C. J., Wang, F., Chen, Z. J., … Zhang, W. (2015). Parkinson disease with REM sleep behavior disorder: Features, alpha-synuclein, and inflammation. *Neurology, 84*(9), 888–894. doi:10.1212/wnl.0000000000001308

Iranzo, A., Santamaria, J., Rye, D. B., Valldeoriola, F., Marti, M. J., Munoz, E., … Tolosa, E. (2005). Characteristics of idiopathic REM sleep behavior disorder and that associated with MSA and PD. *Neurology, 65*(2), 247–252. doi:10.1212/01.wnl.0000168864.97813.e0

Iranzo, A., Molinuevo, J. L., Santamaria, J., Serradell, M., Marti, M. J., Valldeoriola, F., & Tolosa, E. (2006). Rapid-eye-movement sleep behaviour disorder as an early marker for a neurodegenerative disorder: A descriptive study. *Lancet Neurology, 5*(7), 572–577. doi:10.1016/s1474-4422(06)70476-8

Iranzo, A., Lomena, F., Stockner, H., Valldeoriola, F., Vilaseca, I., Salamero, M., … Santamaria, J. (2010). Decreased striatal dopamine transporter uptake and substantia nigra hyperechogenicity as risk markers of synucleinopathy in patients with idiopathic rapid-eye-movement sleep behaviour disorder: A prospective study [corrected]. *Lancet Neurology, 9*(11), 1070–1077. doi:10.1016/s1474-4422(10)70216-7

Iranzo, A., Fernandez-Arcos, A., Tolosa, E., Serradell, M., Molinuevo, J. L., Valldeoriola, F., … Santamaria, J. (2014). Neurodegenerative disorder risk in idiopathic REM sleep behavior disorder: Study in 174 patients. *PLoS One, 9*(2), e89741. doi:10.1371/journal.pone.0089741

Johns, M. W. (1991). A new method for measuring daytime sleepiness: The epworth sleepiness scale. *Sleep, 14*(6), 540–545.

Kamat, R., Weinborn, M., Kellogg, E. J., Bucks, R. S., Velnoweth, A., & Woods, S. P. (2014). Construct validity of the memory for intentions screening test (MIST) in healthy older adults. *Assessment, 21*(6), 742–753. doi:10.1177/1073191114530774

Kane, R. L. (1991). Standardized and flexible batteries in neuropsychology: An assessment update. *Neuropsychology Review, 2*(4), 281–339.

Kang, S. H., Yoon, I. Y., Lee, S. D., Han, J. W., Kim, T. H., & Kim, K. W. (2013). REM sleep behavior disorder in the korean elderly population: Prevalence and clinical characteristics. *Sleep, 36*(8), 1147–1152. doi:10.5665/sleep.2874

Kliegel, M., McDaniel, M. A., & Einstein, G. O. (2008). *Prospective memory: Cognitive, neuroscience, developmental, and applied perspectives*. Mahwah, NJ: Erlbaum.

Kliegel, M., Altgassen, M., Hering, A., & Rose, N. S. (2011). A process-model based approach to prospective memory impairment in Parkinson's disease. *Neuropsychologia, 49*(8), 2166–2177. doi:10.1016/j.neuropsychologia.2011.01.024

Kløve, H. (1963). Clinical neuropsychology. In F. M. Forster (Ed.), *The medical clinics of North America* (pp. 1647–1658). New York, NY: Saunders.

Kopecek, M., Stepankova, H., Lukavsky, J., Ripova, D., Nikolai, T., & Bezdicek, O. (2017). Montreal cognitive assessment (MoCA): Normative data for old and very old Czech adults. *Applied Neuropsychology Adult, 24*(1), 23–29. doi:10.1080/23279095.2015.1065261

Kvavilashvili, L., & Fisher, L. (2007). Is time-based prospective remembering mediated by self-initiated rehearsals? Role of incidental cues, ongoing activity, age, and motivation. *Journal of Experimental Psychology-General, 136*(1), 112–132. doi:10.1037/0096-3445.136.1.112

Labelle, M. A., Graf, P., Grondin, S., & Gagne-Roy, L. (2009). Time-related processes in time-based prospective memory and in time-interval production. *European Journal of Cognitive Psychology, 21*(4), 501–521. doi:10.1080/09541440802031000

Leng, Y., Blackwell, T., Stone, K. L., Hoang, T. D., Redline, S., & Yaffe, K. (2016). Periodic limb movements in sleep are associated with greater cognitive decline in older men without dementia. *Sleep, 39*(10), 1807–1810. doi:10.5665/sleep.6158

Lewandowsky, S., Duncan, M., & Brown, G. D. (2004). Time does not cause forgetting in short-term serial recall. *Psychonomic Bulletin and Review, 11*(5), 771–790.

Mahowald, M.W., & Schenck, C. H. (2013). REM sleep behaviour disorder: A marker of synucleinopathy. *The Lancet Neurology, 12*(5), 417–419. doi:10.1016/S1474-4422(13)70078-4

Malapani, C., Rakitin, B., Levy, R., Meck, W. H., Deweer, B., Dubois, B., & Gibbon, J. (1998). Coupled temporal memories in Parkinson's Disease: A dopamine-related dysfunction. *Journal of Cognitive Neuroscience, 10*(3), 316–331.

Manni, R., Sinforiani, E., Pacchetti, C., Zucchella, C., Cremascoli, R., & Terzaghi, M. (2013). Cognitive dysfunction and REM sleep behavior disorder: Key findings in the literature and preliminary longitudinal findings. *International Journal of Psychophysiology, 89*(2), 213–217. doi:10.1016/j.ijpsycho.2013.04.003

Marchand, D. G., Montplaisir, J., Postuma, R. B., Rahayel, S., & Gagnon, J. F. (2017). Detecting the cognitive prodrome of dementia with lewy bodies: A prospective study of REM sleep behavior disorder. *Sleep, 40*(1), doi:10.1093/sleep/zsw014

Marcone, S., Gagnon, J. F., Lecomte, S., Imbeault, H., Limoges, F., Postuma, R. B., … Rouleau, I. (2017). Clinical utility of the envelope task in mild cognitive impairment and dementia. *Canadien Journal of Neurological Sciences, 44*(1), 9–16. doi:10.1017/cjn.2016.298

Massicotte-Marquez, J., Decary, A., Gagnon, J. F., Vendette, M., Mathieu, A., Postuma, R. B., … Montplaisir, J. (2008). Executive dysfunction and memory impairment in idiopathic REM sleep behavior disorder. *Neurology, 70*(15), 1250–1257. doi:10.1212/01.wnl.0000286943.79593.a6

McDaniel, M. A., & Einstein, G. O. (2007). *Prospective memory: An overview and synthesis of an emerging field*. Los Angeles, CA: Sage.

Molano, J., Boeve, B., Ferman, T., Smith, G., Parisi, J., Dickson, D., … Petersen, R. (2010). Mild cognitive impairment associated with limbic and neocortical lewy body disease: A clinicopathological study. *Brain, 133*(Pt 2), 540–556. doi:10.1093/brain/awp280

Murdock, B. B. (1962). Serial position effect of free-recall. *Journal of Experimental Psychology, 64*(5), 482–488. doi:10.1037/h0045106

Nasreddine, Z. S., Phillips, N. A., Bedirian, V., Charbonneau, S., Whitehead, V., Collin, I., … Chertkow, H. (2005). The montreal cognitive assessment, MoCA: A brief screening tool for mild cognitive impairment. *Journal of American Geriatric Society, 53*(4), 695–699. doi:10.1111/j.1532-5415.2005.53221.x

Ohayon, M. M., & Schenck, C. H. (2010). Violent behavior during sleep: Prevalence, comorbidity and consequences. *Sleep Medicine, 11*(9), 941–946. doi:10.1016/j.sleep.2010.02.016

Ohayon, M. M., Caulet, M., & Priest, R. G. (1997). Violent behavior during sleep. *Journal of Clinical Psychiatry, 58*(8), 369–376; quiz 377.

Petersen, R. C. (2004). Mild cognitive impairment as a diagnostic entity. *Journal of Internal Medicine, 256*(3), 183–194. doi:10.1111/j.1365-2796.2004.01388.x

Petersen, R. C., Smith, G. E., Waring, S. C., Ivnik, R. J., Tangalos, E. G., & Kokmen, E. (1999). Mild cognitive impairment: Clinical characterization and outcome. *Archives of Neurology, 56*(3), 303–308.

Pituch, K. E., & Stevens, J. (2015). *Applied multivariate statistics for the social sciences: Analyses with SAS and IBM's SPSS*. New York, NY: Routledge.

Postman, L., & Keppel, G. (1977). Condition of cumulative proactive-inhibition. *Journal of Experimental Psychology-General, 106*(4), 376–403.

Postuma, R. B., Gagnon, J.-F., & Montplaisir, J. (2013). Rapid eye movement sleep behavior disorder as a biomarker for neurodegeneration: The past 10 years. *Sleep Medicine, 14*(8), 763–767. doi:10.1016/j.sleep.2012.09.001

Postuma, R. B., Berg, D., Stern, M., Poewe, W., Olanow, C. W., Oertel, W., … Deuschl, G. (2015). MDS clinical diagnostic criteria for Parkinson's disease. *Movement Disorders, 30*(12), 1591–1601. doi:10.1002/mds.26424

Postuma, R. B., Gagnon, J. F., Bertrand, J. A., Genier Marchand, D., & Montplaisir, J. Y. (2015). Parkinson risk in idiopathic REM sleep behavior disorder: Preparing for neuroprotective trials. *Neurology, 84*(11), 1104–1113. doi:10.1212/wnl.0000000000001364

Raaijmakers, J. G. W., & Shiffrin, R. M. (1980). SAM: A theory of probabilistic search of associative memory. In H. B. Gordon (Ed.), *Psychology of learning and motivation* (Vol. 14, pp. 207–262). Cambridge, MA: Academic Press.

Rahayel, S., Montplaisir, J., Monchi, O., Bedetti, C., Postuma, R. B., Brambati, S., ... Gagnon, J. F. (2015). Patterns of cortical thinning in idiopathic rapid eye movement sleep behavior disorder. *Movement Disorders, 30*(5), 680–687. doi:10.1002/mds.25820

Ramanan, S., & Kumar, D. (2013). Prospective memory in Parkinson's disease: A meta-analysis. *Journal of the International Neuropsychological Society, 19*(10), 1109–1118. doi:10.1017/s1355617713001045

Raskin, S. A. (2009). Memory for intentions screening test: Psychometric properties and clinical evidence. *Brain Impairment, 10*(1), 23–33.

Raskin, S., Buckheit, C., & Sherrod, C. (2010). *Memory for Intentions test. Professional manual.* Lutz: Psychological Assessment Resources.

Reitan, R. M., & Wolfson, D. (1985). *The halstead-reitan neuropsychological test battery: Theory and interpretation*. Tucson, AZ: Neuropsychology Press.

Rusz, J., Hlavnicka, J., Tykalova, T., Buskova, J., Ulmanova, O., Ruzicka, E., & Sonka, K. (2016). Quantitative assessment of motor speech abnormalities in idiopathic rapid eye movement sleep behaviour disorder. *Sleep Medicine, 19*, 141–147. doi:10.1016/j.sleep.2015.07.030

Schenck, C. H., Bundlie, S. R., Ettinger, M. G., & Mahowald, M. W. (1986). Chronic behavioral disorders of human REM sleep: A new category of parasomnia. *Sleep, 9*(2), 293–308.

Schenck, C. H., Montplaisir, J. Y., Frauscher, B., Hogl, B., Gagnon, J. F., Postuma, R., ... Oertel, W. (2013). Rapid eye movement sleep behavior disorder: Devising controlled active treatment studies for symptomatic and neuroprotective therapy – A consensus statement from the International Rapid Eye Movement Sleep Behavior Disorder Study Group. *Sleep Medicine, 14*(8), 795–806. doi:10.1016/j.sleep.2013.02.016

Schmidt, M. (1996). *Rey Auditory Verbal Learning Test™ (RAVLT™)*. Torrance, CA: Western Psychological Services.

Sellen, A. J., Louie, G., Harris, J. E., & Wilkins, A. J. (1997). What brings intentions to mind? An in situ study of prospective memory. *Memory, 5*(4), 483–507. doi:10.1080/741941433

Shulman, L. M., Armstrong, M., Ellis, T., Gruber-Baldini, A., Horak, F., Nieuwboer, A., ... Martinez-Martin, P. (2016). Disability rating scales in Parkinson's disease: Critique and recommendations. *Movement Disorders, 31*(10), 1455–1465. doi:10.1002/mds.26649

Smith, A. (1982). *Symbol digits modalities test*. Los Angeles, CA: Western Psychological Services.

Smith, J. G., Harper, D. N., Gittings, D., & Abernethy, D. (2007). The effect of Parkinson's disease on time estimation as a function of stimulus duration range and modality. *Brain and Cognition, 64*(2), 130–143. doi:10.1016/j.bandc.2007.01.005

Spielberger, C. D., Gorsuch, R. L., & Lushene, R. D. (1970). *STAI: Manual for the state-trait anxiety inventory*. Palo Alto, CA: Consulting Psychologists Press.

Squire, L. R. (2004). Memory systems of the brain: A brief history and current perspective. *Neurobiology of Learning and Memory, 82*(3), 171–177. doi:10.1016/j.nlm.2004.06.005

Tabachnick, B. G., & Fidell, L. S. (2012). *Using multivariate statistics* (6th ed.). Boston, MA: Pearson.

Terzaghi, M., Sinforiani, E., Zucchella, C., Zambrelli, E., Pasotti, C., Rustioni, V., & Manni, R. (2008). Cognitive performance in REM sleep behaviour disorder: A possible early marker of neurodegenerative disease? *Sleep Medicine, 9*(4), 343–351. doi:10.1016/j.sleep.2007.06.013

Terzaghi, M., Zucchella, C., Rustioni, V., Sinforiani, E., & Manni, R. (2013). Cognitive performances and mild cognitive impairment in idiopathic rapid eye movement sleep behavior disorder: Results of a longitudinal follow-up study. *Sleep, 36*(10), 1527–1532. doi:10.5665/sleep.3050

Tulving, E. (2002). Episodic memory: From mind to brain. *Annual Review of Psychology, 53*, 1–25. doi:10.1146/annurev.psych.53.100901.135114

Underwood, B. J. (1957). Interference and forgetting. *Psychological Review, 64*(1), 49–60.

Wechsler, D. (2010). *Wechslerova inteligenční škála pro dospělé* [Wechsler adult intelligence scale–third revision]. Praha: Hogrefe - Testcentrum.

Woods, S. P., Moran, L. M., Dawson, M. S., Carey, C. L., & Grant, I. (2008). Psychometric characteristics of the memory for intentions screening test. *The Clinical Neuropsychologist, 22*(5), 864–878. doi:10.1080/13854040701595999

Youn, S., Kim, T., Yoon, I. Y., Jeong, J., Kim, H. Y., Han, J. W., ... Kim, K. W. (2016). Progression of cognitive impairments in idiopathic REM sleep behaviour disorder. *Journal of Neurology Neurosurgery and Psychiatry, 87*(8), 890–896. doi:10.1136/jnnp-2015-311437

Zhang, J. R., Chen, J., Yang, Z. J., Zhang, H. J., Fu, Y. T., Shen, Y., … Liu, C. F. (2016). Rapid eye movement sleep behavior disorder symptoms correlate with domains of cognitive impairment in Parkinson's disease. *Chinese Medical Journal (Engl), 129*(4), 379–385. doi:10.4103/0366-6999.176077

Zhou, J., Camacho, M., Tang, X., & Kushida, C. A. (2016). A review of neurocognitive function and obstructive sleep apnea with or without daytime sleepiness. *Sleep Medicine, 23*, 99–108. doi:10.1016/j.sleep.2016.02.008

Appendix 1

Table A1. Correlations between demographic, clinical and prospective and retrospective memory measures for NC (N = 30) and iRBD (N = 60) separately.

	PM time-based (NC vs iRBD)	PM event-based (NC vs iRBD)	PM total (NC vs iRBD)	PM recognition (NC vs iRBD)
Age (years)	**–.24 vs –.25**	**–.16 vs –.12**	**–.19 vs –.29***	**–.49† vs –.34†**
Education (years)	**.27 vs .11**	**.48† vs .10**	**.51† vs .20**	**–.01 vs .43‡**
Gender	**–.23 vs –.15**	**–.22 vs –.11**	**–.27 vs –.20**	**.08 vs .05**
iRBD duration (years)	–.13	–.40‡	–.38‡	–.03
MoCA	**.30 vs .46‡**	**.27 vs .01**	**.37* vs .36†**	**.01 vs .46‡**
BDI-II	**.29 vs –.12**	**.07 vs –.08**	**.25 vs –.18**	**–.08 vs –.15**
State anxiety (STAI-X1)	**.06 vs .09**	**.05 vs –34†**	**.12 vs –12**	**–.20 vs –.28***
Trait anxiety (STAI-X2)	**.39↑ vs –.01**	**.02 vs –.15**	**.38↑ vs –12**	**–.09 vs –.29***
ESS	–.02	–.43‡	–.33†	–.03
AHI	–.24↑	.10	.05	–.08
UPDRS-II	–.04	–.36†	–.31†	–.18
UPDRS-III	–.19	–.40‡	–.44‡	–.20‡
DaTscan total	.30*	.12	.09	.03
DaTscan striatum	.33*	–.06	.14	–.03
DaTscan putamen	.26↑	–.08	.10	–.02
RAVLT immediate	**.02 vs .49‡**	**.37* vs .03**	**.21 vs .38***	**.04 vs .30†**
RAVLT retention	**.19 vs .44‡**	**.34 vs .17**	**.32 vs .43***	**–.09 vs .27‡**
RAVLT recognition	**.21 vs .51‡**	**.25 vs .06**	**.26 vs .40†**	**–.05 vs .23**

Note. All correlations are based on Spearman rank order correlation except for gender (based on point-biserial correlation) and all correlations are based on both samples except for iRBD duration, ESS, UPDRS-II and III and DatScan which are based only on iRBD sample; PM = prospective memory; MoCA = Montreal Cognitive Assessment Czech version; BDI-II = the Beck Depression Inventory, Second Edition; STAI = the State-Trait Anxiety Inventory (state anxiety, X1) and (trait anxiety, X2); ESS = Epworth Sleepiness Scale; AHI, apnea–hypopnoea index; UPDRS-II and III, Unified Parkinson's Disease Rating Scale, Part II and III; DaTscan total = sum of striatal indexes from both sides; DaTscan striatum, DaTscan putamen = lower value of striatal and putaminal index, respectively. RAVLT = Rey Auditory Verbal Learning Test. Separate correlations in bold.

↑ $p < .10$; * $p < .05$; † $p < .01$; ‡ $p < .001$

Index